4-20-70

PEREGRINE FALCON POPULATIONS

PROCEEDINGS OF

AN INTERNATIONAL CONFERENCE

SPONSORED BY THE

UNIVERSITY OF WISCONSIN

1965

With the Support of

The National Institutes of Health,
Public Health Service
US Department of Health, Education and Welfare

The Rachel Carson Fund
of The National Audubon Society

The Frank M. Chapman Fund
of The American Museum of Natural History

The Harry Steenbock Fund
of The Wisconsin Society for Ornithology

The Peregrine Falcon in Adult Plumage. Photographed in Utah by R. J. Erwin and R. D. Porter

PEREGRINE FALCON POPULATIONS

THEIR BIOLOGY AND DECLINE

Edited by Joseph J. Hickey

The University of Wisconsin Press 1969
Madison, Milwaukee, and London

Published by the University of Wisconsin Press
Box 1379, Madison, Wisconsin 53701
The University of Wisconsin Press, Ltd.
27–29 Whitfield Street, London, W. 1

Printed in the United States of America by
Wisconsin Cuneo Press, Inc.
Milwaukee, Wisconsin
Standard Book Number 299–05050–5
Library of Congress Catalog Card
Number 68–9018

CONTRIBUTORS AND CONFEREES

CONFERENCE SESSION CHAIRMEN

Dean Amadon, American Museum of Natural History, Central Park West at 79th Street, New York, New York 10024

John L. Buckley, Fish and Wildlife Service, US Department of the Interior, Washington, DC 20240

Roland C. Clement, National Audubon Society, 1130 Fifth Avenue, New York, New York 10028

H. G. Geyer, Federal Extension Service, US Department of Agriculture, Washington, DC 20250

Frederick N. Hamerstrom, Jr., Conservation Division, Wisconsin Department of Natural Resources, RFD, Plainfield, Wisconsin 54966

Joseph J. Hickey, Department of Wildlife Ecology, University of Wisconsin, Madison, Wisconsin 53706

Robert A. McCabe, Department of Wildlife Ecology, University of Wisconsin, Madison, Wisconsin 53706

Roger Tory Peterson, Neck Road, Old Lyme, Connecticut 06371

Gustav A. Swanson, Department of Conservation, Cornell University, Ithaca, New York (now at Department of Fishery and Wildlife Biology, Colorado State University, Fort Collins, Colorado 80521)

PARTICIPANTS

*Daniel W. Anderson, Department of Wildlife Ecology, University of Wisconsin, Madison, Wisconsin 53706.

Richard C. Banks, Natural History Museum, San Diego, California (now at Bureau of Sport Fisheries and Wildlife, US National Museum, Washington, DC 20560)

*Denotes paper presented in his absence.

Frank L. Beebe, Provincial Museum, Victoria, British Columbia, Canada
Daniel D. Berger, 510 East MacArthur Road, Milwaukee, Wisconsin 53217
Tom J. Cade, Department of Zoology, Syracuse University, Syracuse, New York (now at Laboratory of Ornithology, Cornell University, Ithaca, New York 14850)
James H. Enderson, Department of Zoology, Colorado College, Colorado Springs, Colorado 80903
Richard Fyfe, Canadian Wildlife Service, 10015 103 Avenue, Edmonton, Alberta, Canada
Kenneth E. Gamble, Department of Wildlife Ecology, University of Wisconsin, Madison, Wisconsin 53706
Joseph A. Hagar, Marshfield Hills, Massachusetts 02051
Frances Hamerstrom, RFD, Plainfield, Wisconsin 54966
Robert P. Hanson, Department of Veterinary Science, University of Wisconsin, Madison, Wisconsin 53706
Mrs. Richard A. Herbert, RD 2, Middletown, Delaware 19709
Hans Herren, Winterfeldweg 41, 3018 Bern-Bümpliz, Switzerland
*Eldridge G. Hunt, California Department of Fish and Game, 987 Jedsmith Drive, Sacramento, California 95819
*Kurt Kleinstäuber, Christophstrasse 5, 9102 Limbach-Oberfrohna, DDR (German Democratic Republic)
Pentti Linkola, Kuhmoinen Poikkijärvi, Finland
*C. J. Mead, British Trust for Ornithology, Tring, Hertfordshire, Great Britain
Theodor Mebs, 2441 Weissenhaus/Ostee über Oldenburg/Holstein, West Germany
*Karl Heinz Moll, Falkenhäger Weg 35, Waren (Müritz), DDR (German Democratic Republic)
Helmut C. Mueller, Department of Zoology, University of North Carolina, Chapel Hill, North Carolina 27514
Morlan W. Nelson, Soil Conservation Service, US Department of Agriculture, Boise, Idaho 83707
*Günter Oehme, PI Lehrstuhl Biologie, Kröllwitzer Strasse 44, 402 Halle/S., DDR (German Democratic Republic)
Ian Prestt, The Nature Conservancy, Abbots Ripton, Huntingdon, England
Sergej Postupalsky, University of Michigan Biological Station (now 2926 W. 13 Mile Road, Royal Oak, Michigan 48073)
Derek A. Ratcliffe, The Nature Conservancy, Abbots Ripton, Huntingdon, England
James N. Rice, Contention Lane, Berwyn, Pennsylvania 19312
*James E. Roelle, Department of Wildlife Ecology, University of Wisconsin, Madison, Wisconsin 53706.

*Earl C. Schriver, Jr., 153 Parkhill Road, Baden, Pennsylvania 15005

*Horst Schröder, Müritz-Museum Waren, Friedenstrasse 5, 206 Waren (Müritz), DDR (German Democratic Republic)

Charles R. Sindelar, Jr., Wisconsin State University, Stevens Point, Wisconsin (now 1865 S. West Avenue, Waukesha, Wisconsin 53186)

Walter R. Spofford, II, Department of Anatomy, State University of New York Medical Center, Syracuse, New York 13062

Alexander Sprunt IV, National Audubon Society, Box 231, Tavernier, Florida 33070

*Robert M. Stabler, Department of Zoology, Colorado College, Colorado Springs, Colorado 80903

Lucille F. Stickel, Patuxent Wildlife Research Center, Fish and Wildlife Service, US Department of the Interior, Laurel, Maryland 20810

William H. Stickel, Patuxent Wildlife Research Center, Fish and Wildlife Service, US Department of the Interior, Laurel, Maryland 20810

Teuvo Suominen, Huopalahdentie 13 A 7, Helsinki 33, Finland

Jean-François Terrasse, 60, Rue Satoris, La Garenne (Seine), France

*Michel Y. Terrasse, 60, Rue Satoris, La Garenne (Seine), France

Daniel O. Trainer, Department of Veterinary Science, University of Wisconsin, Madison, Wisconsin 53706

Clayton M. White, Department of Zoology, University of Utah, Salt Lake City, Utah 84112

Howard F. Young, Department of Biology, Wisconsin State University, La Crosse, Wisconsin 54601

DISCUSSANTS AND OFFICIAL OBSERVERS

John W. Aldrich, Fish and Wildlife Service, US Department of the Interior, Washington, DC 20240

J. Dan Cover, North American Falconers' Association, Thayer, Missouri 65574

Ben Glading, California Department of Fish and Game, 1416 9th Street, Sacramento, California 95814

James B. Hale, Conservation Division, Wisconsin Department of Natural Resources, Nevin State Fish Hatchery, Route 2, Madison, Wisconsin 53711

David A. Hancock, Zoology Department, University of British Columbia, Vancouver, British Columbia

Steven G. Herman, North American Falconers' Association, c/o Department of Zoology, University of California, Davis, California 95616

W. Grainger Hunt, Alpine, Texas 79830

D. R. King, Cooperative State Research Service, US Department of Agriculture, Washington, D.C. 20250

Thomas H. Ripley, Forest Service, US Department of Agriculture, Ashville, North Carolina 28801
Joseph S. Simonyi, Hornby, Ontario, Canada
Walter E. Scott, Conservation Division, Wisconsin Department of Natural Resources, Madison, Wisconsin 53702
Jay H. Schenll, 1696 Papermill Road, Meadowbrook, Pennsylvania 19046
Donald G. Spencer, Agricultural Research Service, US Department of Agriculture, Washington, DC (now 13508 Sherwood Forest Terrace, Silver Spring, Maryland 20904)

PREFACE

During the years 1950 to 1965, a population crash of nesting peregrine falcons (*Falco peregrinus*) occurred in parts of Europe and North America on a scale that made it one of the most remarkable recent events in environmental biology. This book, in part an eyewitness account, presents the papers and discussions of a conference held by the University of Wisconsin from 29 August to 1 September 1965 to crystallize and evaluate some practical hypotheses to account for this extraordinary phenomenon. The conference had four specific aims:

1. To bring together Europeans and North Americans engaged in the study of nesting peregrines and to compare their data on the status of regional populations and the timing of declines where these occurred.
2. To contrast these events with significant population trends in certain other raptorial birds that, on a somewhat smaller scale, are regionally declining in the same mysterious fashion.
3. To review the implications (real or suspected) that these phenomena are associated with meteorological, pesticidal, epizootic, or other ecological factors.
4. To discuss the possibilities of coordinating research to further clarify the relative importance of the environmental factors now affecting the peregrine falcon.

Four of the main parts of the present volume are given over to these objectives. A fifth, the introduction, was prepared—after the conference—for readers unfamiliar with the ecology of this species. A sixth, on general behavior and ecology, represents some by-products of the conference which are primarily of interest to those more broadly concerned with the natural history of the peregrine.

The conference discussions have here been condensed, changed from spoken to written English, and regrouped for clarity and retrieval. The effect entails a discontinuity of ideas which, however uneven, follows the familiar pattern of the General Notes sections of journals reporting ornithological research. I must apologize to the discussants for my failure to submit these sections of the report to them for their approval before the publication of their remarks, and to the conferees in general for the long delays that have marked the editing and appearance of this report. Brief addenda to many of the papers were added just before these pages went to the printer in April 1968.

The photographs included in this volume were selected to illustrate something of the recent history and ecology of the peregrine falcon. Some come from regions where nesting peregrines have completely disappeared. I am much indebted to the many photographers who submitted over 800 pictures for this collection.

My own acknowledgments must be extended to the four agencies that financially supported this conference and made this publication possible: the National Institutes of Health, the Rachel Carson Fund of The National Audubon Society, the Frank M. Chapman Fund of the American Museum of Natural History, and the Harry Steenbock Fund of the Wisconsin Society for Ornithology. I also owe much to E. D. Ables, D. W. Anderson, R. K. Anderson, J. C. Bartonek, K. E. Gamble, and J. A. Keith, all of the University of Wisconsin, for their many services during the meeting itself. Mrs. Walter R. Spofford recorded the discussions, and Mrs. Robert S. Ellarson typed them. Thomas J. Dwyer and James E. Roelle gave bibliographic assistance during the final editing. All maps and charts are by the University of Wisconsin Cartographic Laboratory.

The peregrine falcon has evolved by natural selection to live near the top of a wide variety of ecosystems. It is a component of marine food webs in some parts of the world, aquatic food webs in others, terrestrial food webs in still others. It is hardly likely that the population dynamics of this scattered and once-successful species can everywhere be described in the terms of simple cause-and-effect systems. Not all the facts presented at the conference could be absorbed by the conferees in the time available to them at Madison. Their publication here within a single volume will, I hope, enable the reader to study the data at his leisure and comprehend the complex interactions that are now affecting this spectacular species.

JOSEPH J. HICKEY

Madison, Wisconsin
April 1968

TABLE OF CONTENTS

PART IV. POPULATION FACTORS

PATHOGENS, PARASITES AND PEREGRINE FALCONS

PESTICIDES AS POSSIBLE FACTORS AFFECTING BIRD POPULATIONS

PREDATION, SHOOTING, AND OTHER FACTORS

PART V. POPULATION DYNAMICS AND SIGNIFICANCE OF TRENDS

CONCLUSION

Erratum

The first five lines of the last paragraph on page 564 should read:

Elucidation of the mechanism producing these extraordinary changes in the calcium metabolism of bird- and fish-eating birds on two continents appeared in the scientific literature in 1967, the connection between the field evidence and laboratory findings being first suggested by Peakall (1967*a*). By a curious accident (chlordane had been used to eliminate

LIST OF ILLUSTRATIONS

following p. 200

PORTRAITS OF THE PEREGRINE

PEREGRINE ECOLOGY: TYPES OF NESTING SITES

PEREGRINE ECOLOGY: NESTING SUBSTRATES

LIST OF FIGURES

INTRODUCTION AND HISTORICAL PERSPECTIVE

Nowe do I holde it high time, and the place very convenient to write of such kinds of wormes, as do trouble and vexe ye poore hawke, as hir mortall enimies.

George Turbervile
The Booke of Faulconrie or Hawnting
1575

Of hawks there may be many and severall kindes; as the *Falcon, Merlin, Lanner, Tassell,* and sundrie others.

John Swan
Speculum Mundi
1635

It is, however, a remarkable fact in the history of this tribe of birds, that their nests are not more numerous than they were many centuries ago; and although they have broods every year, their numbers do not increase.

Giraldus Cambrensis
Topographia Hiberniae
1183–86
(translated by Thomas Forester)

. . . I confesse them somewhat out of my Road, but I assure you to pleasure you and satisfie myself, I have consulted the most approved Authors and given you here the creame and marrow of their severall experiences in their own expresse characters.

Matthew Stevenson
The Twelve Moneths
1661

CHAPTER 1

THE PEREGRINE FALCON: LIFE HISTORY AND POPULATION LITERATURE

Joseph J. Hickey
and Daniel W. Anderson

This paper is intended to summarize some pertinent literature on the biology of the peregrine falcon for readers who are generally unfamiliar with the ecology of this species. This literature is scattered not only among the world's major languages but among its libraries as well. Within the time and spatial limits available to us, our review of so many publications has had to be incomplete, and a scholarly book on this nearly worldwide species impresses us as a much needed and valuable undertaking. It would, we think, tax the talents of even the most accomplished linguist, and its compilation would be the despair of our unsung librarians who struggle with that invaluable but somewhat creaky system known as interlibrary loans. Yet the biology of a cosmopolitan species of bird is of particular interest to behaviorists, ecologists, morphologists, and physiologists—as well as to the laymen who so often see in the peregrine the simple fact that it is an extraordinarily interesting bird.

ZOOGEOGRAPHY AND TAXONOMY

Peregrines nest in the Arctic of both North America and Eurasia, and as far south as Tasmania, South Africa, and the region of Cape Horn. Their great powers of flight have enabled them to establish nesting populations on the Cape Verde and Falkland islands in the Atlantic and on the Volcano and the Solomon islands in the Pacific. As breeding birds, they are curiously absent from most of Central and South America, as well as from drier regions like the Sahara, Saudi Arabia, and central Asia. They have failed to colonize New Zealand and Iceland; and despite the presence of extensive cliff formations and large colonies of nesting seabirds, they do not breed on islands north of the Aleutian chain (Cade, 1960:159) nor in the Faroes (Voous, 1960).

It is probably safe to say, however, that as migrants peregrines have been recorded from every major region of the earth except Antarctica. There are many records of peregrines boarding ships at sea; two of these even involve type specimens of subspecies, *Falco peregrinus peregrinator* and *F. p. japonensis*. One of the more interesting reports that is apparently referable to this species involved a bird that boarded a Dutch factory ship at about 25°N, 34°W (more than 800 miles, or 1,300 km, off Africa), remained for most of 2 days, and departed when the ship was still more than 600 nautical miles (1,100 km) from South America (Voous, 1961). The best recent map of the birds' geographic range is given by Voous (1960) in his *Atlas of European Birds*. Only a handful of other avian species have so successfully penetrated to the ends of the earth, the raven and the osprey being the peregrine's chief rivals in this respect.

Throughout the world, peregrine populations vary enough in body size and color so that races or subspecies can be recognized by museum specialists. Peters (1931) regarded 15 races as valid; Swann and Wetmore (1936), 13; Wolfe (1938), 12; Dementiev (1951), 22; Vaurie (1965), 12–13. The total number is still not final. More recently, *F. peregrinus pelegrinoides* and *F. p. babylonicus* have together been considered to be a distinct species (Vaurie, 1961; Dementiev and Iljitschew, 1961), and a new subspecies has been described (*F. p. madens*) by Ripley and Watson (1963) from the Cape Verde Islands. The little-known falcon from the Tierra del Fuego region, *Falco kreyenborgi*, which is presently known only on the basis of three to five specimens in museum collections, now seems to be a distinct species and not a race of the peregrine (Stresemann and Amadon, 1963). The distribution of these subspecies has been mapped (Fig. 1.1) by Dementiev (1951). While additional museum specimens will inevitably lead to a better understanding of this Soviet list of races, its high breeding densities in western Europe suggest that *Falco peregrinus* originated in the Old World.

Migratory behavior in the peregrine is importantly restricted to the five more northern races. Within at least four of these subspecies, there presumably exists a continuum of behavior, individuals in the more southerly latitudes being nonmigratory, those in the north moving considerable distances. These latitudinal gradients are in turn strongly modified by the climatic amelioration produced by the oceans on the northwest sides of North America and Eurasia. As a result, migratory behavior in the peregrine also tends to increase as one goes east on each of these two continents.

The two western continental races, *F. p. peregrinus* and *F. p. pealei,* are dissimilar in that the range of the former extends deep into the Eurasian continent, while that of the latter is markedly restricted to a coastal environment (Fig. 1.1). Both are moderately migratory, with relatively sedentary populations in some parts of their range. British peregrines tend to remain in Britain (Thomson, 1958); and some peregrines are reported in winter in the Aleutians (O. J. Murie, *in* Gabrielson and Lincoln, 1959). Ringed Finnish peregrines are now known to winter importantly in France (Schüz and Weigold, 1931; Nordström, 1963). Migration, when it occurs in each of these races, seems to be to the southern breeding range or a little farther south (Vaurie, 1965), but *pealei* has been exceptionally recorded as far south as northern Baja California (Bent, 1938).

Three more eastern continental races of the peregrine are highly migratory, although the southern elements of two of these are not. *F. p. anatum* has wintered in the past as far north as southeastern British Columbia and Boston (Bent, 1938). Its more southern breeders remained at their eyries in winter, those nesting slightly to the north of them migrated as far south as Georgia (Herbert and Herbert, 1965). Birds of this race wintering in South America are now known or suspected to be peregrines that are raised in the Arctic (Cooke, 1943; Mueller and Berger, 1959; Enderson, 1965). *F. p. calidus* and *F. p. japonensis* [=*F. p. harterti*] mainly nest on the Eurasian tundra and, for the most part, migrate considerable distances south—as far as southern Africa and southern Asia (Vaurie, 1965).

It is clear that the peregrine tends to be sedentary in those districts where good supplies of winter food are available to it. Altitudinal movement of some sort almost certainly occurs among many mountain-nesting portions of the population but has not yet been verified by banding. Some unorientated wandering by young birds in their first fall has been indicated by banding recoveries: a nestling banded in New York State on 18 June 1929 was shot on 26 September 1929 in Nebraska about 1200 miles (19,200 km) WSW (Smiley and Smiley, 1930).

Many of these subspecies have in the past borne English vernacular names that are now going out of use: Peale's falcon for the peregrines in northwest North America, black-cheeked falcon for those in Australia and Tasmania, Hose's falcon for those in the southwest Pacific, shaheen falcon in India, and Cassin's falcon in southern South America. After some initial fumbling with its identity, the race most widely distributed in North America entered our literature as the great-footed hawk (Au-

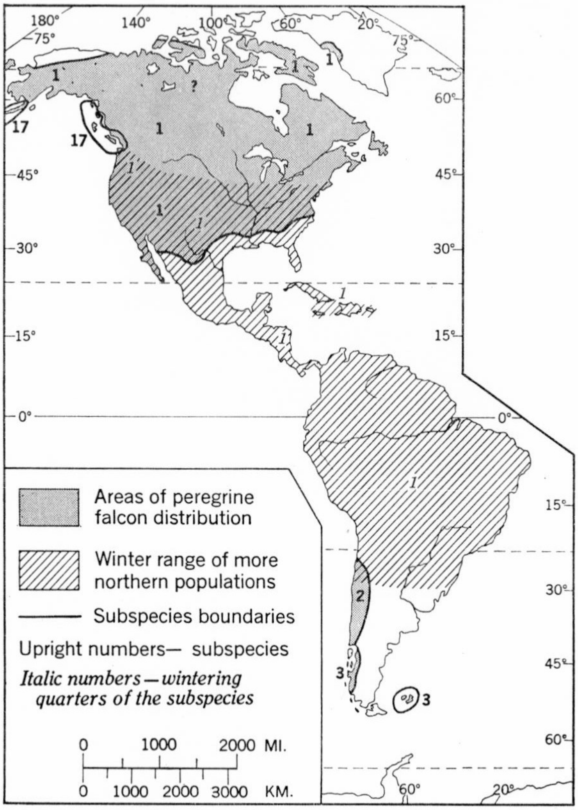

Fig. 1.1. Distribution of the subspecies of *Falco peregrinus* according to Dementiev (1951).
1. *anatum* 2. *cassini* 3. *kreyenborgi* 4. *perconfusus* 5. *radama* 6. *arabicus* 7. *pelegrinoides* 8. *brookei* 9. *caucasicus* 10. *macropus* 11. *peregrinator* 12. *ernesti* 13. *peregrinus* 14. *germanicus* 15. *brevirostris* 16. *kleinschmidti* 17. *pealei* 18. *pleskei* 19. *leucogenys* 20. *babylonicus* 21. *fruitii* 22. *nesiotes*

dubon, 1831; Wilson and Ord, 1808–14) and then for a century was known in the United States as the duck hawk. The Canadians were not, however, so easily fooled; amateur ornithologists have become less interested in subspecies; and within the past decades the term duck hawk has given way to the British name, peregrine falcon.

GENERAL ECOLOGY

CLIMATE AND ALTITUDE

It is obvious that the various subspecies of the peregrine must to some extent represent different (as yet unmeasured) physiological adjust-

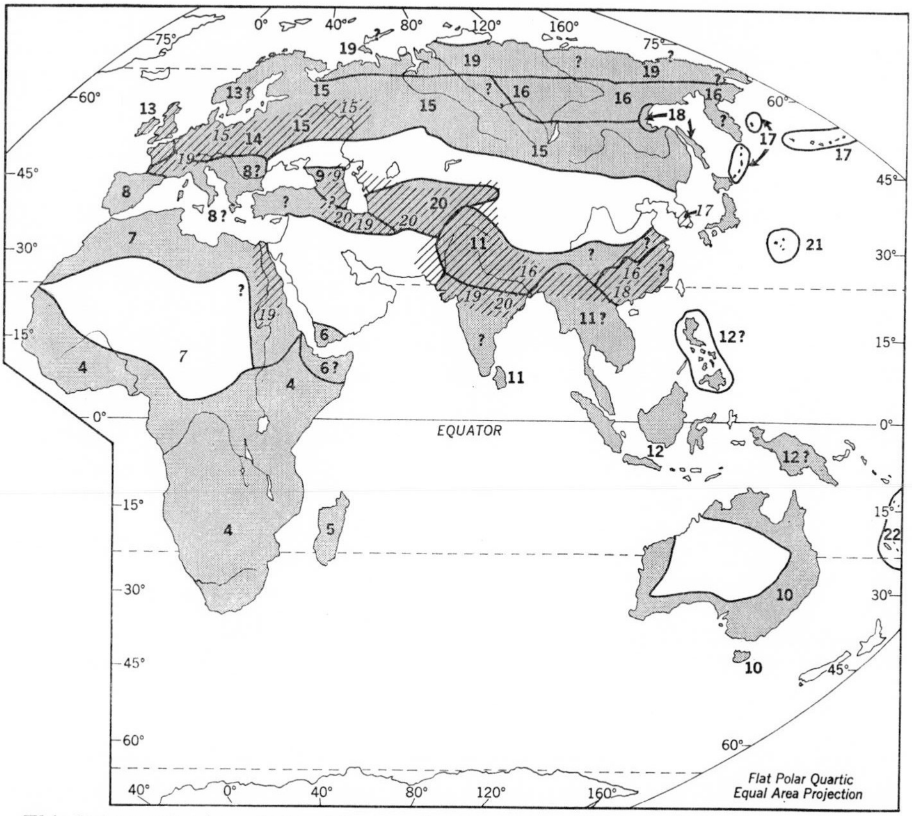

This list remains in a state of flux, and some taxonomists would limit it to 12 or 13 races. No. 3 has been proposed as a separate species, as have Nos. 7 and 20 (together). No. 1 is now known to winter as far south as central Argentina and to breed north to Thule. The exact distribution in the Southern Hemisphere remains to be worked out. After Dementiev (1951). UW Cartographic Lab.

ments to a fairly wide range of climates. Even within a single widespread race like *F. p. anatum* or *F. p. brevirostris* some extraordinary climatic extremes have been successfully encountered. Thus *anatum* breeds as far north as Thule Settlement in Greenland (Salomonsen, 1950) at 76°33′N latitude and as far south as Baja California and the Tropic of Cancer (Bond, 1946). According to Voous (1960), the distributional limits of the peregrine falcon lie between isotherms that are slightly under 41°F (5°C) and 90°F (32°C) or higher in the warmest month. At Khartoum, the Barbary peregrine (*F. p. pelegrinoides*), the small desert edition of the European peregrine falcon and perhaps a different species, rests in the shade of buildings at midday (Meinertzhagen, 1954). In Ceylon, the resident race is said to hunt chiefly early in the morning and in the evening (Wait, 1925). Climographic studies (Twomey, 1936) of the peregrine on a worldwide basis remain to be carried out.

The altitudinal distribution of peregrine nesting sites has been reported for only a few regions. Ratcliffe (1962) has given the altitude of 170 inland eyries in Britain. Greatest usage was at 1,250 to 1,500 ft (380–460 m), the maximum being 3,000 ft (914 m) due to climatic severity and the minimum governed by accessibility and human interference. Cade (1960:160–161) found the highest Alaskan eyrie at 2,200 ft (671 m) and thought food supplies for the peregrine ample there up to 3,000 ft (914 m). In western North America, Bond (1946) reported peregrines rarely nesting above 5,000 ft (1,524 m) with a few exceptional pairs up to 10,000 ft (3,048 m). In India, the peregrine nests up to 8,000 ft (2,438 m) (Ripley, 1961), and specimens have been taken in the Himalayas at 11,000 ft (3,353 m) (Whistler, 1926) and seemingly at over 13,000 ft (3,962 m) (Vaurie, 1965). Peregrine responses to altitude receive attention from Nelson (Chapter 4) and Herren (Chapter 20) in the present volume. On an intercontinental basis, this aspect of peregrine ecology deserves a much broader study.

HUNTING AND FOOD HABITS

The long-winged peregrine is specialized for one type of hunting. While some genera of raptorial birds soar or hover in the sky and others have evolved short wings and long tails for quick darting and short sprints in wooded terrain, the peregrine depends upon direct pursuit in the open. Although its level speed surpasses that of nearly all species of birds, it is skillful—at least as an adult—in seeking the advantage of height from which to launch its attack, and the impressive speed of its diving at prey remains to be accurately measured.

There are, of course, innumerable variations in the skill of individual peregrines and in the reactions of their intended victims; accounts of these have been collected or summarized by Bent (1938), Uttendörfer, Bodenstein, and Kuhk (1952), and Meinertzhagen (1959). Impressions of the birds' hunting prowess are perhaps exaggerated. Herbert and Hickey watched a pair fail in seven successive attempts to take racing pigeons (Hickey, 1942), and Rudebeck (1950–51) saw successful kills in only 7% of 260 hunts that he observed. Ratcliffe (1962) firmly believes that many "unsuccessful hunts" were never made in earnest. Variables here not only involve differences in the agility of the prey and the amount of cover immediately available to it, as Herbert and Herbert (1965) point out, but also the age of the peregrines themselves. It is generally recognized that young falcons are often quite unskillful when the bond with their parents is broken and the young must then depend on their own hunting efforts.

For such a worldwide predator, prey species are bound to vary from region to region. They may even vary from one nesting site to the next.

In Finland, Sulkava (1960) found that cliff-nesting pairs took more gulls and small birds; bog-nesting birds took more waterfowl, crows, and grouse. Uttendörfer *et al.* (1952) summarized the literature on the prey known to have been taken by 221 breeding pairs mostly at or near German inland sites. Up to the end of 1944, 123 species of prey had been recorded; by 1949, the list had grown to 145. Among 6,410 occurrences, 2,039 involved common pigeons, 1,209 starlings, 484 lapwings, 298 skylarks, 181 chaffinches, and 170 jays. Five species represented 66% of the preys reported. Lists of this type are biased toward the larger specimens of prey wherever the original investigator counts old remains found at feeding sites (Sulkava, 1960).

There seems to be little doubt that, where it is found, the domestic pigeon is the favorite prey of the peregrine. Audubon (1831) and Boudwin (1877) observed this in Philadelphia, and Errington (1933) noted it in rural Wisconsin. North (1912) describes dramatic captures of pigeons in Australia. Salomonsen (1950) mentions that Greenlanders and the Danish inhabitants of Greenland to some extent pursue the peregrine because of the damage that it does to domestic pigeons. In Britain, where at least 117 species of peregrine prey have been recorded, Ratcliffe (1963) has calculated that domestic pigeons constitute—by weight—about 29% of the peregrine's diet. Rodriguez de la Fuente (1964), after a 5-year study of 20 pairs spread over a wide plateau, concluded that pigeons, particularly domestic and feral, constitute about 75% of the diet of the Spanish peregrine.

The peregrine has to some extent followed the pigeon into all the great cities of the world, usually in the nonbreeding season. Certainly in earlier times the peregrine must have used castle towers and church spires as its favorite perching and feeding places in this restricted habitat. Within the present century, it has taken advantage of our larger public buildings and finally our skyscrapers. It has been recorded wintering on the towers of the City Hall in Philadelphia (Culver, 1919), the Customs House in Boston (Forbush, 1927), the Post Office in Washington (Bent, 1938), and the City Hall in Frankfurt (Klaas, 1941). At Aden it has been seen to knock down tame pigeons (Meinertzhagen, 1954), and in Japan it is occasionally reported on towers and chimneys eating pigeons (Nagahisa Kuroda, *in litt.*).

Its fondness for pigeons has placed the peregrine on the black lists of those keenly interested in racing pigeons as a sport. Kesteloot (1964) estimates that one-third of the world's pigeon fanciers are Belgian, 20% British, 18% German, 9% French, and another 9% Dutch. The hatred of these people for the peregrine is at times fanatical, and their repeated destruction of peregrine nestings has been regarded as one of the chief factors in the reproductive failure of this species in Germany in the 1950's (Mebs, 1960). In Belgium, where about 8% of the men are pigeon fanciers, 165,000 persons are members of the Belgium federation of pigeon fanciers, and a reward of 40 francs is offered for two complete legs of the peregrine—as well as those of the red kite, sparrow-hawk, and goshawk (Kesteloot, 1964). This reward system persists in violation of Belgium's ratification of the International Convention for the Protection of Birds. In Sweden, this controversy seems to have been settled by research: Breeding peregrines, consisting of at least 120 pairs in 1945, were estimated to take about 3% of the country's pigeon population (Lindquist, 1963).

It is, however, at the great nesting colonies of medium-sized seabirds that the peregrine has found a superabundance of food in the nesting season. Turner noted that there was scarcely an island near the seabird colonies in the Fort Chimo region in northeastern Canada without one or more pairs of peregrines nesting on or near it (Bent, 1938). On the Queen Charlotte Islands in British Columbia, one of the densest nesting populations in North America (Brooks, 1926) feeds on ancient murrelets, Cassin's auklets, Leach's petrels, and fork-tailed petrels (Green, 1916; Beebe, 1960). In the Volcano Islands, a volcanic chain about 660 miles (1,060 km) south of Tokyo, peregrines also subsist on petrels. Here, Momiyama (1930:118) reports [translation by Nagahisa Kuroda, *in litt.*], "Horst (1889) observed 4–5 pairs of peregrines and collected 2 birds on Iwô-to [=Iwo Jima or Sulphur Island]. They were said to be living on Bulwer's petrels, which were abundant on the island. After that, the breeding places of the petrels were destroyed by sugar-cane cultivation, and nowadays [these small birds] have entirely disappeared [from the area]. However, there is quite a number of this falcon found on Kita-Iwô-to [= Kita Iwo Jima or San Alessandro Island], and they are preying chiefly on abundant wedge-tailed . . . and gadfly petrels [=Bonin petrels]. . . ." In this familiar pattern of feeding habits during the nesting season, there remains an interesting question concerning the food resources available to these insular populations of predators each year after the seabirds have departed.

The occurrence of mammals in the peregrine's diet is infrequently reported and generally is insignificant. Rabbits are said to be taken in Western Australia (Serventy and Whittell, 1951) and Britain (Jourdain, *in* Witherby, Jourdain, Ticehurst, and Tucker, 1939). Lemmings are sometimes taken in numbers, but their population cycles have no known effect on peregrine densities (Cade, 1960:223–224).

Under certain conditions, peregrines inadvertently tend to concentrate their feeding upon male birds that are more conspicuous than females during part of the breeding cycle. The preys thus taken include ducks (Porsild. 1951; Cade, 1960:216–217), doves, and larks (Rodriguez de la Fuente, 1964), the latter being vulnerable during their nuptial flights. There is also increasing evidence that predators tend to cull out the weaker members of their prey populations (Borg, 1962; Allen and Mech, 1963; Mech, 1966). Ratcliffe (1963) has collected some statistics to show that this principle holds for the peregrine. The evidence includes unhealthy rooks constituting 40% of a sample killed by a trained falcon and 26% of a parallel sample that was shot (Eutermoser, 1961). The effect of this principle upon prey populations remains to be assessed, but its significance to the peregrine is stressed by Peterson in his discussion of pesticide phenomena later in this volume (Chapter 46).

BIOTOPES AND NESTING SITES

Having successfully evolved into an extremely efficient machine for capturing a wide variety of birds, the peregrine has been curiously restricted during its breeding season by its failure (except perhaps in southern Asia) to retain the nest-constructing habit characteristic of so many other birds. Throughout the world, it depends (1) mostly on cliffs for its nesting sites, but these intergrade with (2) slopes and river cutbanks in parts of the Far North, the continuum extending through (3) mounds, an occasional sand dune, and flat bogs and plains. Other nesting sites include (4) tree nests that (a) are dubiously said to be at least occasionally constructed by the peregrines themselves but (b) more often are the old stick nests of other large birds and (c) sometimes include hollows in old and very large trees. A final type (5) includes occasional attempts to convert man-made structures into eyries, the sites varying from a skyscraper to a barrel in a continuum that is obviously parallel to that found in numbers (1) to (3). For the most part, the attempts to break away from the traditional use of cliffs are geographically restricted, and each forms an absorbing study in animal behavior and ecology.

1. Cliffs are by far the peregrine's favorite type of nesting site, and its often-complete dependence on them seems to have prevented breeding of the peregrine in some regions. Nesting peregrines have, for instance, never been recorded from the flat plains of alluvial Bengal (Baker, 1917) nor from Florida and Ohio (Hickey, 1942), and they are quite rare or absent in low, marshy regions like the Yukon-Kuskokwim delta (Cade, 1960:158–159) and the mouth of the Rhone.

The birds readily accept both igneous and sedimentary rocks and are particularly fond of limestone cliffs, since these often abound in small caves which can be used as nest sites and as night roosts. The failure of slate formations to make for sharp cliffs probably underlies the peregrine's failure to nest in western Pennsylvania. It does, however, use slate in other regions.

Unlike the cliff-nesting auks (Johnson, 1941), peregrines have eggs that can easily roll away on hard surfaces, and these falcons probably lack the ability of the auks to recognize and retrieve their eggs. In compensation for these evolutionary failures, peregrines scrape shallow hollows in soil, decomposed rock, gravel, mats of vegetation, and the remains of prey in which they lay their eggs. This scrape appeared to Hickey (1942) to be an absolute requirement of the species and to Ferguson-Lees (1951) a psychological necessity, the latter a point which Cade (1960:164) has felt to be overstressed, if not altogether incorrect, in limiting the distribution of this species.

There has been some discussion about the basis of the traditional selection of specific sites by this species, Hickey (1942) regarding extremely high cliffs in the eastern United States as attractive to peregrines regardless of nesting success and Cade (1960:241) arguing that tradition largely consists of periods in which older birds die off and new partners are acquired by their surviving mates. We agree with Cade that population pressure and changing environmental conditions will influence the rapidity with which a missing pair is replaced at a given site, but we still remain impressed with the fact that, in the past and despite repeated nesting failures, large cliffs in the eastern United States could remain consistently tenanted and small cliffs could not. A psychological basis for tradition in northern regions made for an interesting discussion that is set forth later in this volume (Chapter 36).

In Tennessee, Spofford (1942) has classified local peregrine cliffs as mountain eyries, canyon eyries, and river bluff sites. The erosional importance of rivers in creating Alaskan nesting sites for the peregrine has been pointed out by Cade (1960:165–166) who mentions bluffs, talus slopes, and pinnacles as types of eyries in that region where the wide swaths cut by rivers in otherwise heavily forested country give peregrines open expanses over which they can readily hunt. This effect on the birds' hunting efficiency not only holds in the boreal forests, in which Cade worked, but in other forested regions as well.

In Britain, Ratcliffe (1962) found 16 "stream-ravines" represented among 170 inland eyries, only 9 of these being regularly occupied. These are probably similar to Spofford's canyon type and are apparently used by peregrines in many regions. It is Ratcliffe's experience, as well as ours, that this type is not held tenaciously. A world-wide geological classification of peregrine cliffs would be a particularly interesting undertaking.

The precise type of location on a cliff chosen by the falcon for her "nest" varies somewhat with the geological character of the cliff. After examining over 70 (mainly sea-cliff) sites in Britain, Walpole-Bond (1914) found about 60% to involve a big hole, wide slit, or recess, about 36% a broad ledge, buttress, or shelf, and about 4% a basin-like formation lying between some pillar or pinnacle and the main cliff. While open exposed ledges are used, the birds often seek the shelter of small shrubs or trees. One pair even used a man-made cave with an opening 30 ft above the sea (Nethersole-Thompson, 1931). Ratcliffe (1962) has characterized the favorite inland nest site in Britain as a flat grassy ledge or shelf 18 inches (46 cm) or more wide, of varying length, with a sheer fall of rock above and below.

The peregrine's habit of laying its eggs in the abandoned cliff nests of other large birds seems to vary widely between regions, perhaps as a result of availability. Only three instances of this behavior in the United States east of the Rocky Mountains have come to our attention. Allen (1872) found peregrine young in an old red-tailed hawk nest on a Kansas cliff in 1871; Gale found peregrine eggs in an old [golden?] eagle nest in Colorado in 1889 (Bendire, 1892), and Ganier saw eggs in a red-tail's nest in Tennessee in 1930 (Bent, 1938). The more frequent use of raven and red-tail nests in western North America is reported by Bond (1946). In Britain, peregrines resort to old cliff nests of other species more often. Nethersole-Thompson (1931) reports their eggs in ravens' and jackdaws' nests and once each in an old nest of the buzzard and the herring gull. Of 155 British eyries with eggs or young, Ratcliffe (1962) reported that 94 were ordinary ledges, 58 ravens' nests, 2 buzzard nests, and 1 was the rock nest of a carrion crow. Peregrines also occasionally use old eyries of the golden eagle in Scotland (Ratcliffe, *in litt.*). Stick nests of rough-legged hawks on cliffs are also used in Alaska (Cade, 1960:162) and in Canada's Northwest Territories (Richard Fyfe, *in litt.*).

In India, where peregrines typically nest on the bare ledges of cliffs, their nests are sometimes described as structures of sticks and branches to which the peregrines bring additions each year (Baker, 1917). Others in long use are said to be fairly substantial platforms or pads of twigs, sometimes lined with wool or grass (Sálim Ali, *in litt.*). Direct observations of peregrines carrying nesting materials are still lacking. Such a behavioral pattern is generally lacking in the genus *Falco*, and it should not be credited, we think, without a reliable eye-witness account.

The number of different nesting ledges used by a single pair of peregrines (or its successors) over a long period of years is known to vary from one or two (Herbert and Herbert, 1965) to seven in a 16-year period (Ratcliffe, 1962) and is to some extent a function of the number of ledges available. At a quarry site with only one nesting ledge, the birds once renested on top of the cliff (Herbert and Herbert, 1965), a most unusual procedure for that region. This use of alternative nesting sites by a pair of peregrines extends to different cliffs and complicates the work of observers intent on censusing the number of breeding pairs.

The maximum distance between alternate cliffs in different years for a British pair is reported by Ratcliffe (1962) to exceed 4 miles (6.4 km). Renesting in the same year usually involves a shift by the birds, but one British egg collector is said to have taken two fresh clutches of four eggs on the same ledge in less than 1 month (Walpole-Bond, 1914), and this may occur where alternate sites in the district are abundant (Nethersole-Thompson, 1931).

Linkola (1959) lists small low-lying islands as a special type of nesting site for the peregrine. These appear to be rarely used in Finland. Their presumed equivalent in Britain, "among heather on small islets off [the] coast," is mentioned by Jourdain (*in* Witherby *et al.*, 1939), and these perhaps should be classed as ground nests (No. 3 below). On islands off the coasts of California and Baja California, peregrines nest on cliffs that sometimes are only 10–20 ft high (Bent, 1938; Bond, 1946).

2. Nesting sites on slopes appear to be part of a continuum between cliff eyries and nesting sites on relatively flat plains. At the present time, these seem to be reported only for peregrines in the northern parts of the Northern Hemisphere. Coues (1874) found two such cutbank nests along the northern tributaries of the Milk River in Montana, where the birds were in effect nesting on the ground. Cutbank nests have frequently been found in western Canada (Preble, 1908), and we assume that this type is also used in the USSR. Of six such sites inspected by Enderson (1965) in Alberta, two had nesting ledges less than 4 m high, and four others were less than 13 m high. Of 57 eyries on the Colville River in Alaska, Cade (1960:102) classified 27 as on earthen or talus river banks. Staebler found two eggs in a ground nest on the steep side of a brush- and tree-covered sand dune on a Lake Michigan island in 1939 (Van Tyne, *in* Hatt *et al.*, 1948); the height and outlook of this eyrie were somewhat similar to that of an Arctic cutbank. On the Queen Charlotte Islands, where peregrines are attracted by the huge numbers of nesting seabirds in British Columbia, peregrines often nest near the top of very steep, grass-covered slopes that are nearly vertical (Beebe, 1960). They also do this on cutbanks in Alaska (Cade, 1960:163).

Cutbank eyries often involve the peregrine's use of old stick nests constructed by other species. On the Colville River, where 11 out of 57 eyries of the peregrine were in old rough-legged hawk nests (not all of which were on slopes), it seems likely that the highly active movement of the bluff surfaces increased the peregrines' tendencies toward this relatively unusual behavior (Cade, 1960:163).

3. Ground nests of the peregrine, defined here as those on generally flat plains, are not as geographically restricted, and a number of subtypes are discernible.

On the Eurasian tundra, small grassy mounds were found by Seebohm (1901) to serve as eyries, the grass on these being noticeably greener than that of the surrounding vegetation. Tundra ground nests are fairly frequent in the USSR (Dementiev, 1951). They are unrecorded in the Canadian Arctic where, however, the use of low sandy mounds has twice been reported (J. P. Kelsall, *in* Cade, 1960:162; Kuyt, 1966).

A second subtype, a forest bog or heath, is occupied by peregrines in the Baltic region where these sites are geographically interspersed with peregrine cliff and tree nests (Thomasson, 1947; see also Fig. 1.2). In a Finnish survey in 1958, 145 cliff nests were reported as well as 125

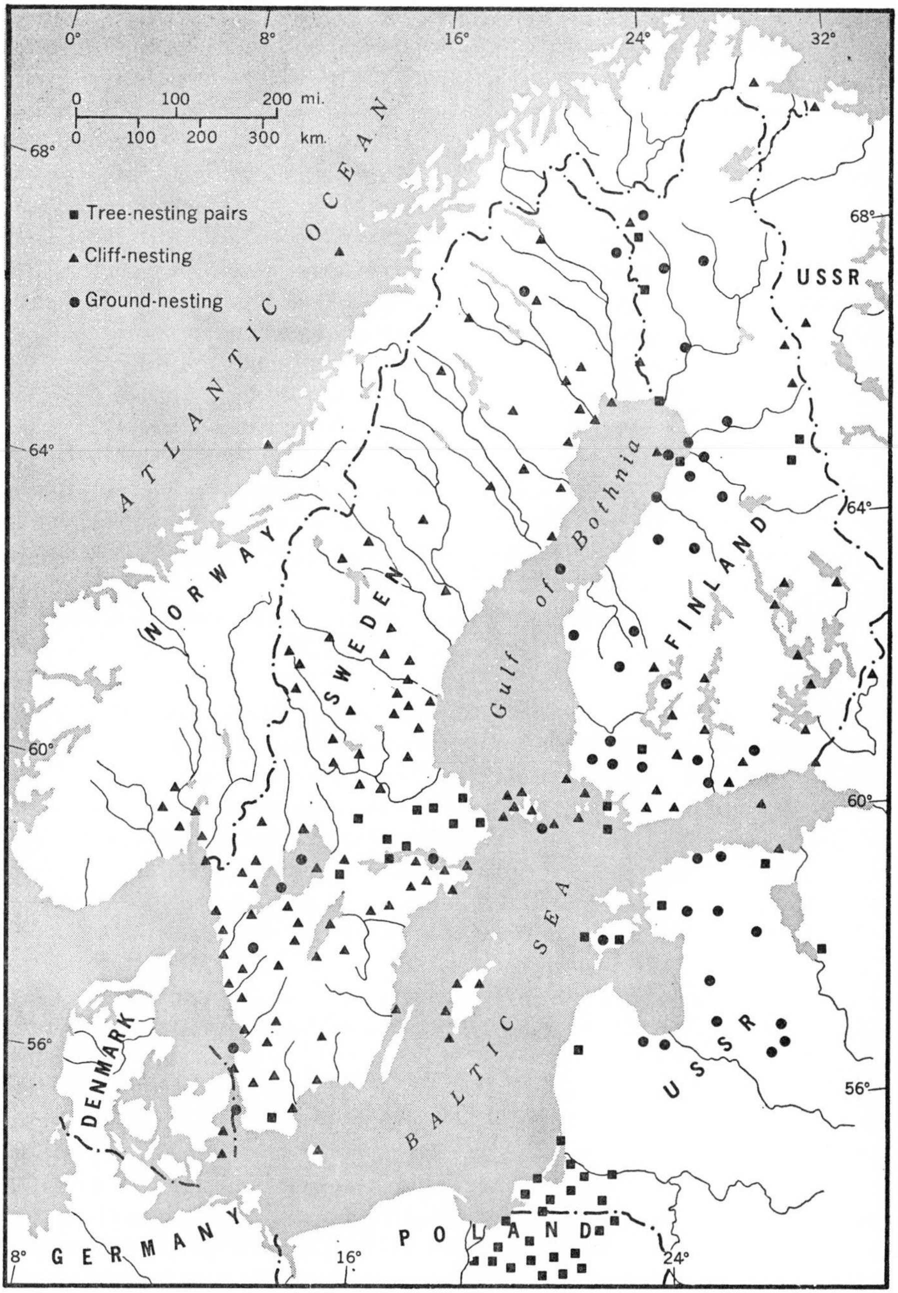

Fig. 1.2. Distribution of nesting peregrines in the Baltic region. German data omitted; after Thomasson (1947). UW Cartographic Lab.

open-bog nests; the ratio is not a true picture of peregrine usage, because cliffs are much easier to identify as eyries (Linkola, 1959). Some bog-nesting pairs have cliffs as alternative sites, others have tree nests of ospreys or rough-legged hawks (*ibid.*). In southern England, peregrines attempted to breed for two successive years on an open heath in Hampshire (Ashford, 1929; Jourdain, *in* Witherby *et al.*, 1939). Ratcliffe (*in litt.*) points out to us that this site is ecologically similar not only to those used by the peregrine in the Baltic but also to the innumerable forest bogs of Canada where nesting peregrines have yet to be recorded. There is also an isolated case of a peregrine pair nesting in 1949 on inland sand dunes in the Veluwe region of the Netherlands (van Ijzendoorn, 1950); the dunes contained a scattered growth of pines and, in this respect, the site was similar to some of the bogs used by peregrines in the Baltic region.

The use of bare sand dunes by nesting peregrines occurred in the Netherlands in 1926 (one young raised) and 1930 (three eggs seen); both sites were close to the sea (Brouwer, 1927; van Ijzendoorn, 1950). In China peregrines are also said to nest sometimes on the ground (Cheng Tso-hsin, 1963) and in Australia under grass tussocks on a plain (Campbell, 1901).

In resorting to cutbank and ground nests, the peregrine appears to have done so in regions where human populations are relatively low. Cliffs thus tend to represent the equivalent of escape cover to the peregrine (Hickey, 1942; Ratcliffe, 1962). In the eastern United States, this species can apparently tolerate a good deal of human activity below its high nesting ledges, but very little on top of its cliffs (Hickey, 1942). In British Columbia, Beebe (1960) has reported diametrically opposite reactions. In Britain, Ratcliffe (1962) concluded that an eyrie must be at least a half mile (0.8 km) from the nearest human habitation, unless the cliff is particularly high and precipitous.

4. The use of tree nests built by other large birds represents the peregrine's most successful attempt to break away from the limitations imposed by the scarcity of cliffs. The practice, at least in the recent past, was especially prevalent in the Baltic region (Thomasson, 1947) and importantly enabled the peregrine to invade the north German plain (Kuhk, 1939). It is also reported in middle Russia and Siberia (Dementiev, 1951). In one Australian region, Dudley Dickinson (*in litt.*) has found approximately two tree nests to each cliff nest, the former including deserted ravens' nests and sometimes hollows in trees. Among the nests involved in this breakthrough in Europe are those of raven, heron, rook, and large raptors (Niethammer, 1938; Jourdain, *in* Witherby *et al.*, 1939). The buzzard, goshawk, gray sea eagle, and osprey all appear to have helped the peregrine in this fashion.

North American records of this tree-nesting behavior are rare and ambiguous. Peck (1924) said he took a peregrine egg from a bald eagle nest "many years ago," and Jones (1946) reported young in two tree nests in eastern Virginia. The type of nest involved in this latter record is explained later in this volume (Chapter 14) by W. R. Spofford. Another equally cryptic report concerns two birds which are said to have had a nest "in a dead spruce" near Nuk'Koh, Alaska; these birds were collected on 1 June 1867 when they had young nearly ready to fly (Dall and Bannister, 1867–69). This record was recently verified by Cade (1960:161), who suggests that a small tree-nesting population may yet be found in the Yukon Flats. Tree nesting by the peregrine has been reported in Ceylon by Legge (1878–80) but never substantiated. In southern Asia it seems to be rare, and the possibility that the nests there were constructed by the birds themselves is not yet to be taken seriously.

If the great, bulky nesting platforms of eagles and ospreys attract peregrines much as the open ledges of cliffs, large holes in great trees may, to a limited extent, represent the physical equivalent of small caves in cliffs. Peregrines, however, will not nest in dense forests, and their ventures in tree-hole nesting have been rather limited. Tree holes are used by peregrines in Australia (McGilp, 1934; Serventy and Whittell, 1951) but not in Europe.

There are 10 definite records of pairs displaying this interesting behavior in North America. Three such pairs were found in Kansas in 1875–77 by Goss (1878), and three more in the vicinity of Mt. Carmel, Illinois, in 1878 by Ridgway (1895). These latter birds evidently were part of a population that extended into nearby Indiana (Butler, 1898). Five of these nests were in sycamores (*Platanus occidentalis*); the sixth, in a cottonwood (*Populus deltoides*); a height of "50 ft" (15 m) was estimated in one case and 89 ft (27.1 m) measured in a second. One nesting hole had an entrance with a diameter not over 5–6 inches (12.7–15.2 cm).

This hole-nesting population in the bottomland forests of the United States interior all but disappeared with the felling of the great trees on which it depended. Four more pairs were ultimately discovered in 1932–42 in northwestern Tennessee (Ganier, 1932; Bellrose, 1938; Spofford, 1942, 1943, 1945, 1947) and northeast Louisiana (Peterson, 1948:137), this time mostly in bald cypress (*Taxodium distichum*). The peregrines in general seem to have used holes created when great limbs were blown down or the tops of the trees broken off. Audubon (1831) observed a peregrine roosting every night in a hole in a dead sycamore in Kentucky; this bird could easily have been from the small Illinois-Indiana population which at that time may have inhabited a larger region.

Generally, this behavioral trait in North America has been an ecological blind alley. It appeared in a region that did not have cliffs but did have a long growing season and sufficient precipitation to permit trees there to grow rapidly and attain sufficient size. Reelfoot Lake, in which two of the more recent tree-nesting pairs were found, was created by earthquakes in 1811 and 1812.

5. The use of man-made structures constitutes the peregrine's most venturesome attempt to break with its tradition of nesting on cliffs. Olivier (1953) in his interesting summary of this behavior accepted 24 or 25 reports as authentically proven cases in the last 150 years; but for some of these the evidence surely is incomplete, and the whole phenomenon needs further review. Structures used include: (a) churches in England (Lubbock, 1879; Morres, 1882; and Ferguson-Lees, 1957) and Russia (Dementiev, 1951:95–96); (b) the castle at Heidelberg (Olivier, 1953); (c) ruins and old towers in England (Bolam, 1912:294), Germany (Mebs, 1955, 1960), and Spain (Mountfort, 1958:132); and (d) skyscrapers and public buildings in Philadelphia (Groskin, 1947, 1952), Montreal (Hall, 1955), Nairobi (Brown, 1961), and New York (Herbert and Herbert, 1965). Among the miscellaneous sites are the abandoned stone pier of an unfinished bridge in Pennsylvania (Craighead and Craighead, 1939), a watertower in Hungary (Pátkai, 1947:26), and a barn in Finland (Linkola, 1959). Peregrines around 1900–10 nested for some years on a barrel in a California marsh (De Groot, 1927), for a time withstood the annual depredations of an egg collector, and ultimately transferred their nesting to a platform on an electric-power pole (R. M. Bond, *in litt.*). In general, peregrines have lacked the unobtrusiveness of barn owls and kestrels in their invasion of man's environment; and their reproductive failures here can be traced to a lack of the proper nesting substrate for their eggs, to the birds' noisy intolerance of intrusion when they have young, or to the absence of terrain in which the young can safely make their first flight.

BREEDING DENSITIES

Densities of nesting peregrines seem to vary enormously from one region to another. They seldom are reduced to statistical terms in the literature and then only when the densities are unusually high. The simplest and best-understood index for this species is the mean linear distance of each active eyrie to the next nearest one.

The highest densities involve unusual seacoast situations. For the Queen Charlotte Islands off the coast of British Columbia, where oceanic upwelling supports large nesting colonies of seabirds, the mean distance between about 20 pairs on one island is on the order of 1 mile (1.6 km) (Beebe, 1960). Dense inland peregrine populations in Britain have mean distances from 2.8 to 3.3 miles (4.5 to 5.3 km) in four districts that carry 7 to 26 pairs (Ratcliffe, 1962). For 8 to 11 occupied eyries on an Alaskan river, this distance varied between 7 and 9.6 miles (11.2 and 15.4 km) in different years (Cade, 1960:172 and *in litt.*). Such statistics will differ when smaller samples are selectively considered. For four eyries on the Sussex coast found by Nethersole-Thompson (*in* Ratcliffe, 1962) the distance is about 0.33 mile (536 m). Some of the eyries on Langara Island mapped by Beebe (1960) are apparently even closer. Mean distances for regions that are very sparsely populated by peregrines have not been published, but the faunal literature clearly suggests that in some, such as the Rockies, these distances are very, very large.

In western North America, densities of slightly more than one pair per 2,000 sq miles (5,180 sq km) are estimated by Bond (1946) to hold for regions in which he considered peregrines to be "common"; in mountain and arid regions in which it was rare, Bond describes the peregrine's density as less than one known pair per 20,000 sq miles (51,800 sq km). A similar range density in different parts of Alaska has been reported by Cade (1960:176). Hickey (1942) listed 19 pairs on about 10,000 sq miles (25,900 sq km) around New York City; since landscapes to the east and south of this study area were excluded because they had no breeding peregrines, the density implied has a limited significance. Ratcliffe (1962) has endeavored to surmount the statistical limitations of this situation by calculating density in a precise and arbitrary fashion. His results are essentially an index that should, in time, permit some interesting comparisons to be made between peregrine populations in widely different regions.

Some very interesting biological considerations emerge from this still-incomplete picture. On the one hand, it is by no means clear just what behavioral phenomena enable this species to maintain its low densities in some regions. (This is presumably effected, we suspect, by the important nonbreeding segment of the peregrine population.) At the other extreme, there appear to be behavioral adjustments to different levels of food supply. Ratcliffe (1962) believes that territorial behavior produces a "proximity tolerance" limit between adjacent nesting pairs and that this has evolved in relation to food supply.

COMPETITION WITH OTHER SPECIES

The wide choice of food taken by the peregrine seems to preclude competition with other raptors along these lines. Conflicts at nesting cliffs are frequent in regions where the peregrine's range overlaps those of ravens and golden eagles. In Britain, Ratcliffe (1962) found no known instance of ravens displacing peregrines, several cases of the reverse, and evidence that golden eagles do displace peregrines. Competition or conflict between these three species involves possession of the nesting cliff, and in Scotland breeding densities of the peregrine, as well as the raven, appear to be inversely proportional to those of the eagle. Alaskan evidence presented by Cade (1960:250–254) suggests that gyrfalcons can successfully prevent peregrines from occupying the larger river-cliffs and thus affect their density and distribution. Cade further concludes that peregrines are numerically more successful than gyrs in districts shared by the two species because the peregrines rely on more constantly adequate sources of food, are less restrictive in their selection of nesting cliffs, have a more stable reproductive performance, and escape from the Arctic winter by migration.

METHODS: POPULATION INVENTORIES AND INDICES

INVENTORIES OF PAIRS

The simplest form of peregrine inventory has consisted of single visits to each of a series of known eyries. In the past, those made by egg collectors were carried out early in the nesting season; in more recent decades, bird-banders and falconers have timed their trips to coincide with the median date that half- or three-quarter-grown young might be expected in the eyries. For Britain, Ratcliffe (*in litt.*) has concluded that April is the best month in which to determine whether or not a site is occupied.

The conversion of observations based on single visits into inventories of breeding pairs always entails some risk. Some females are extremely close sitters, and their mates may be off on hunting forays when the observer visits the eyrie. On one occasion (Nethersole-Thompson, 1931), the egg collector did not realize a female was present until he roped down and actually touched the incubating bird in the small cave in which she was brooding. This situation is variously overcome by the observer exploding firecrackers, shooting off guns, dropping rocks on the talus slope, climbing down to traditionally used ledges, or just plain watching. The excretory stains of peregrines (called "whitewash" by many) are conspicuous on some types of rock but not on others. To late-season observers, they often indicate that young are or were present. Freshly strewn feathers of peregrine victims and castings beneath perches are harder to detect on a peregrine cliff, but they can often be found without much difficulty on the smaller cliffs and can be taken as evidence that at least a raptorial bird has been present.

Some peregrines, when sufficiently disturbed, may desert their clutch and roost as much as 5.5 miles (8.8 km) away (Herbert and Herbert, 1965). In Connecticut during the 1930's, an alternative roosting site was on a crag 4–5 miles (6–8 km) from the actual eyrie (Hickey and Spofford, *unpublished data*). Such alternative nesting crags generate confusing speculation that an extra pair is present (Ratcliffe, *in litt.*).

Because they may fail to disclose pairs that have already deserted, single-observation surveys taken late in the nesting season have a tendency to underestimate the actual number of resident pairs (Cade, 1960:174); and the degree of this bias remains to be measured in contemporary research on this species. Late-season surveys can, however, yield reasonably accurate data on the number of reproductively successful pairs and on the number of young reared to various ages in successful nests. Successive weekly or 10-day mortality rates for the nestlings remain to be worked out. The compilation of such rates may require a cooperative inquiry in which, as Cade (*in litt.*) suggests, the data should be segregated by ecological regions.

In the present volume, single-observation surveys are reported by Berger *et al.* in the eastern United States (Chapter 13), by Enderson in the Rocky Mountain region (Chapter 5), and by Beebe in British Columbia (Chapter 3). In Pennsylvania, Rice visited active eyries twice each year and seemingly deserted sites only once (Chapter 12). While it is difficult to establish—from limited field work—that a site is really deserted in a given year (Ratcliffe, 1962), visits repeated over a period of years seem to justify conclusions of desertion. In nonwilderness landscapes, such surveys are frequently buttressed by the field work of other observers, as explained below. In New York State, some deserted eyries are now conspicuously occupied by nesting feral pigeons (Daniel Smiley, pers. comm.).

There is obviously a continuum of time that various observers can invest in peregrine surveys. There is another continuum involving the degree of climbing that investigators deem appropriate for their studies. Some, like the Herberts (Chapter 4) and Mebs (Chapter 16), have felt that climbing may cause some peregrines to desert a clutch or attract too much attention to a given site. Others, like Hagar (Chapter 10) and Ratcliffe (Chapter 21), have climbed assiduously, being especially interested in the fate of the birds' eggs.

It seems pertinent to notice in all these reports that statements regarding net reproductive success or the lack of it are the observer's conclusions. The actual facts in all such cases are what he did, what he observed, and when. The publication of so many details would be enormously expensive, and our failure to do so here needs to be kept in mind when one evaluates some of the statistics reported in this volume.

The difficulties imposed on a single investigator of the peregrine have inevitably led to cooperative studies of the peregrine population on an extensive basis. These have included one on North American peregrines east of the Rocky Mountains to which 147 people contributed notes and observations (Hickey, 1942), a parallel study west of the Rockies involving about 50 cooperators (Bond, 1946), a project of the British Trust for Ornithology to which over 170 persons responded (Ratcliffe, 1963), and a recent survey of rock-nesting peregrines in the German Democratic Republic conducted by Kleinstäuber (1963). There are great advantages to cooperative studies of this kind, as well as occasional difficulties arising from (a) duplicate (up to five) names given to single cliffs and (b) the general lack of observations in remote districts. In the BTO Enquiry, D. A. Ratcliffe and K. D. Smith complemented the cooperative study by two full seasons of intensive field work on their own.

This extensive approach is obviously practical in the more settled regions, and modifications of it involving a limited number of tested and interested cooperators appear in a number of status reports presented in this volume: Virtually all the European surveys involve the cooperative approach. While this is due to the extensive reports asked of participants, many of their statistics are based on small study areas that have received the intensive study of cooperators. In the 1964 survey of the eastern United States by Berger, Sindelar, and Gamble, the single-inventory approach was relied upon and a cooperative survey was complementary. In some parts of western North America and in virtually all of the Alaskan and Canadian Arctic, cooperative studies are usually impossible to work out.

MIGRATORY INDICES

Migratory peregrines in the Northern Hemisphere tend to concentrate along oceanic coast lines (Allen and Peterson, 1936) as well as the shorelines of lakes as large as Lake Michigan (Mueller and Berger, 1961) and Lake Superior (Hofslund, 1966). They may also be seen along mountain ridges like the Appalachians (Broun, 1963). All the above authors report considerable variation in the numbers of hawks seen from one year to the next, and this has led to their interesting analyses of the effects of weather on the numbers actually observed.

Almost no use, however, has been made of such statistics as clues to population trends among breeding peregrines in the north. Among the first to do so has been Kruyfhooft (1964), who published the number of peregrines captured from 1942 to 1963 in Belgium, where raptors and small birds have been legally netted from 1 October to 15 November each year. His statistics (subjected to a slight manipulation by us in Fig. 1.3) indicate that a remarkable decline in peregrine numbers set in about 1955. Many, but not necessarily all, of these Belgium-caught birds can be assumed to have come from Fennoscandia.

Some similar and particularly interesting indices contributed to the present volume are Spofford's analysis of population trends at Hawk Mountain in eastern Pennsylvania (Chapter 27), the brief notes by Berger and Rice respectively on peregrines on the shores of Lake Michigan and Maryland-Virginia (Chapter 24), and Enderson's description of the opportunities for such indices on the gulf coast of Texas (Chapter 23). These reports inevitably lead one to wonder about equal possibilities for this type of research on the eastern coast of the Mediterranean Sea (Meinertzhagen, 1954), the Sinai Peninsula (Cade, *in litt.*), the west coast of the Caspian Sea (M. W. Nelson, *in litt.*), the eastern coastline of China, and the Ural Mountains in the USSR.

The degree to which such statistics can be manipulated safely remains to be seen. Five-year running averages of the migrating raptors seen by

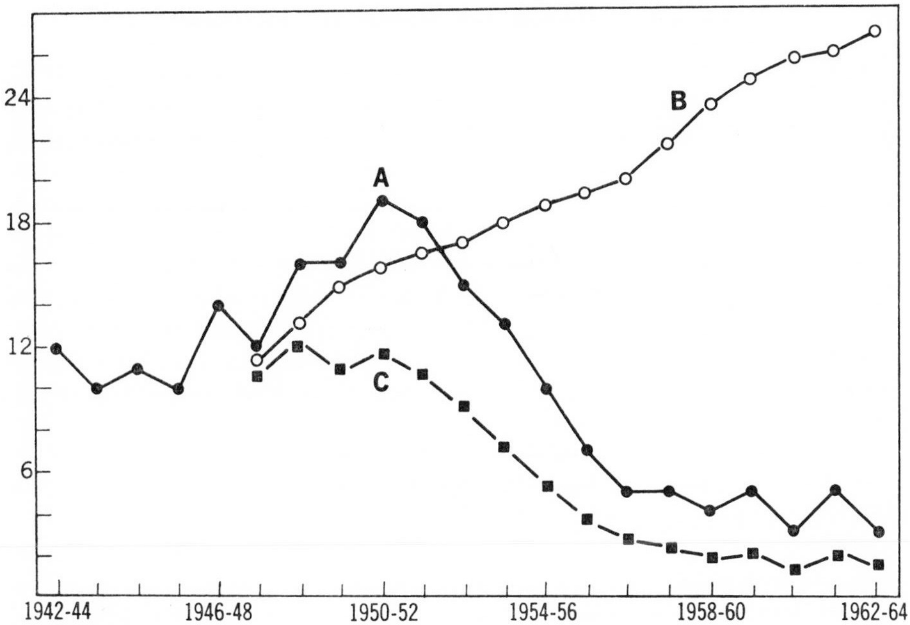

Fig. 1.3. Belgian data on migratory peregrines. Three-year running averages of (A) the number of birds netted each fall, (B) number of netting permits issued (in thousands), and (C) the number of peregrines caught per 10,000 permits issued. Original data from Kruyfhooft (1964 and *in litt.*). UW Cartographic Lab.

Hofslund (1966) and his cooperators at the western tip of Lake Superior show a steady decline in the number of peregrines seen per day from 1.71 in 1951–55 to 0.54 in 1956–60, with small irregular fluctuations after that to 1959–63. The breeding origin of these birds is unknown, and the significance of the running averages remains to be determined. The potential value of indices of migrating peregrine populations centers on the information that they give on the health and behavior of populations that reside in the northern wildernesses of both Eurasia and North America. The significant change in the percentage of immature-plumaged birds found by Maurice Broun for bald eagles passing Hawk Mountain (36.5 in 1931–45 vs. 23.1 in 1954–60) has been an important clue to the profound change that is taking place in that species in eastern North America (Sprunt and Cunningham, 1961). This type of ornithological research is still in its infancy and, as the indices presented in this volume suggest, its utility is bound to increase in the decades ahead.

THE VITAL PROCESSES

Conventional statistics on the percentages of nests successfully fledging young have only minor significance in analyses of peregrine ecology.

The scattered nature of the nesting sites on the one hand, generally makes for samples that—to the statistician—are ridiculously small in studies carried out by a single investigator. A second mitigating circumstance is that peregrine pairs occasionally do not seem to lay any eggs at all. This behavior was pointed out by Hickey (1942) who ascribed it to senescence, a hypothesis that Herbert and Herbert (1965) find unsupported by the egg-laying records of females observed in the 1950's on the Sun Life Building in Montreal and along the Hudson. Bond (1946) also noted pairs that apparently failed to lay at all. The significance of nonbreeding pairs of peregrines remains unknown. It was, of course, nearly impossible to detect in the era of active egg-collecting; and its existence, even in a normal population, requires the calculation of a key statistic—the number of young reared per occupied site. As this may be impossible to calculate in some studies, interest has also centered on clutch size and on the number of young reared per successful nest.

CLUTCH SIZE

Discussion of the significance of clutch-size variation in birds, sparked by Lack (1947–48), has been a particularly interesting development in ecology during the past two decades. Regional gradients in the clutch size of peregrines have been reported by Hickey (1942) and Bond (1946), the former presenting data showing a trend toward smaller clutches as one goes north in eastern North America, the latter showing a quite opposite trend west of the Rocky Mountains. Bond (1946) felt that his own data as well as Hickey's were potentially biased by the tendency of egg collectors to be attracted to the unusual.

This bias has been more recently overcome by the field work of Cade (1960) in Alaska. The bias has been also tested in Germany by Mebs (1960), who found no significant difference between sets in the Museum Alexander Koenig and those observed under modern conditions. The available statistics, set forth in Table 1.1, show clutch size in North America increasing as one goes south from the Arctic and then decreasing as one reaches western Mexico. A clutch size of two to three seems to hold for Australia (Mathews, 1915–16; Serventy and Whittell, 1951).

In view of Beebe's hypothesis presented in Chapter 34 that the eastern United States currently lacks sufficient food for the peregrine, the large numbers of eggs and young in this region take on some significance. Both figures are slightly biased: the former by the exclusion of known second sets (which would be smaller), the latter by the inclusion of young seen as well as fledged. A potential bias enters the British data owing to the inclusion of fresh sets of three eggs that were not rechecked and may have become four (Ratcliffe, *in litt.*).

Gladkow (1941) has made the interesting statement that, on the

Timan tundra, the number of young is four and seldom three. This region lies at approximately 67°30′ to 68°N and 48°31′ to 51°6′E, and the original data need to be presented in detail. Clutch size for peregrines on the oceanic islands seems to be unreported. The entire phenomenon of world-wide variation in the clutch size of this species now invites an ecological review.

In addition to geographic differences, a second variable in clutch size is the number of eggs laid by a female peregrine after her first clutch has been lost to a predator, the eggs collected or simply deserted. Known second sets have fewer eggs, averaging 3.0 for 22 sets in the eastern United States in contrast to the 3.72 cited above.

Age seems to affect the egg-laying capacity of peregrines only slightly: Yearling females either do not lay or lay less than a normal clutch. At a Maryland site in 1936, an immature-plumaged female laid two eggs that were taken by a collector (W. A. Wimsatt, *in litt.*); it is not certain, however, that this set was complete. The yearling Philadelphia-nesting female in 1946 laid three. The Sun Life yearling in Montreal laid none.

Demandt (1953, 1955) has reported clutch size at a site in Westphalia falling in consecutive years from three to two to one and has suspected senescence. Disturbance by egg collectors was ruled out but not disturbance by pigeon fanciers (Mebs, pers. comm. 1964). The 1965 conference did not shed much light on this phenomenon, although it did produce some indirect evidence related to recent trends in mean numbers of young raised per successful female.

Female peregrines of known age are seldom mentioned in ornithological literature. In their interesting paper on Hudson Valley peregrines,

Table 1.1. Geographic Variation in Mean Numbers of Peregrine Eggs and Young

Region	Period	Eggs: No. sets	Eggs: Mean ±SE	Young: No. eyries	Young: Mean ±SE	Reference
Arctic	—	54	2.95±0.95	75	2.45±1.03	Cade, 1960:183, 185
Southern Canada[a]	—	22	3.45±0.94	25	2.60±0.87	Hickey, 1942
British Columbia	1952–58	—	—	25	2.36±0.81	Beebe, 1960
Eastern U.S.A.[a]	—	282	3.72±0.72	124	3.05±0.80	Hickey, 1942
Southern California	—	24	3.58±0.72	—	—	Bond, 1946
Mexico	—	23	3.30±0.93	—	—	Bond, 1946
Finland	1850–1939	117	3.15±0.81	—	—	Linkola, 1959
Northern Germany	—	—	—	14	2.57	Kleinstäuber, 1930[b]
Mark Brandenburg	Ca. 1900	186	3.44±0.60	—	—	Koenig, 1931[b]
Southern Germany	1947–59	24	3.21±0.88	48	2.46±0.80	Mebs, 1960
Switzerland	1935–57	—	—	34	2.44±0.75	Herren, 1958[b]
Cornwall	1930–40	—	—	24	2.4	Ryves, 1948
Great Britain	1945–61	98	3.41±0.57[c]	30	1.87±0.91	Ratcliffe, 1962

[a] East of the Rocky Mountains; young are shown as birds seen, not fledged.
[b] Original not seen; cited by Mebs (1960).
[c] This is a minimum and for the whole of Britain perhaps would be greater than 3.5 (Ratcliffe, *in litt.*).

Herbert and Herbert (1965) report a very strong renesting drive in a female peregrine which laid four (sometimes incomplete) clutches in 1951 and again in 1952, when she was believed to be at least 11 and 12 years old. The best production record of a known-aged female peregrine involves the remarkable falcon on the Sun Life office building in Montreal. Hall (1955) has reported that birds were first seen flying around this building in 1936 and that "pairing" was observed but no eggs seen in the spring of 1937, the pair remaining until late September. Data supplied to Hickey by J. D. Cleghorn (*in litt.* 17 May 1938 and 23 August 1939) contain nothing on the birds' 1936 appearance and state that the female in 1937 was of immature plumage. She was not known to Cleghorn to nest that year, although she and her mate were seen copulating, and they remained on or near the building until 27 September. Cleghorn's notes for 1937–39 are more detailed than Hall's published account, and we accept his version of the early history of this female, who continued to nest on the building through her 16th year. Her number of young reared annually diminished with her age; clutch size did not. Mebs (1960) has argued against the senescence theory on the ground that egg-robbing (in Germany by fanatical pigeon fanciers) is sometimes extremely hard to detect. We also regard egg-eating by the falcon as another factor that may have influenced Demandt's observations. This latter extraordinary behavior, which Ratcliffe (1958 *et seq.*) has done so much to elucidate, remains one of the most mysterious aspects of raptor behavior. It may or may not be associated with peregrine age, and it is discussed at length in the present volume (Chapters 21, 36).

A few words remain to be said about a final factor affecting peregrine clutch size. Abnormally large clutches are occasionally reported, and we take these to be genetically characteristic of the individual females involved. Six-egg clutches have occasionally been found in Britain (Jourdain *in* Witherby *et al.*, 1939); in the United States their frequency was only 1% in 282 cases (Hickey, 1942). Along Iowa's Cedar River Palisades, clutches of six, four, and six were taken in the years 1896–98, the young (from a second clutch) and an adult were killed in 1898, and the site abandoned (Keyes, 1906); it is now a popular state park. Near Otter Creek in southern Wisconsin, the only set of seven eggs ever recorded for this species was collected by L. R. Wolfe and E. B. Ford on 21 April 1933, and a second clutch of six eggs was seen on 11 June (L. R. Wolfe and O. J. Gromme, *in litt.*). There seems to be little chance that this record clutch was laid by two females, and the possibility that very large clutches are indeed the result of isolated mutations or rare genetic combinations appears entirely reasonable. As far as we can detect, local variation in clutch size is rare in this species and not attributable to local differences in the available food. Regional variation within Britain has been asserted by Ingram and Salmon (1929) and by Nethersole-

Thompson (1931); but the original data have not been presented, and they surely require statistical treatment.

RENESTING

As a general rule, the short breeding season in the Arctic prevents most birds from renesting after the loss of their first clutch of eggs in that region. Peregrines follow this rule. Further south, the renesting habit among peregrines has been quite common—at least in healthy populations in the past. In Nethersole-Thompson's (1931) extensive egg-collecting experience in Britain, a second laying took place in two out of three cases where the first set was taken, third (fertile) clutches being known.

When egg-collecting was in its hey-day, second sets were regularly found by collectors. This was true not only in Australia (North, 1912), Germany (Schiermann, 1925), and Great Britain (Nethersole-Thompson, 1931), but also in that part of the United States south of Canada. A surprising development in recent years has been the failure of some peregrines to display this renesting behavior. Demandt (1952), who was a close student of peregrines for 20 years, reported this in Germany, but Herbert and Herbert (1965) found one female on the Hudson River laying four (sometimes incomplete) sets in 1950 and 1951. It is true, of course, that peregrines can best be counted on to renest if their clutch is lost at an early stage of incubation (Hickey, 1942; Mebs, 1960; Ratcliffe, *in litt.*), and that egg collectors tried to be early—if only to beat their rivals. (Among 95 North American sets taken by egg collectors prior to 1941, we have noted that 30 were taken fresh and 20 with incubation just begun.) Mebs (1960) states that most of the old German egg collectors took their sets just as soon as the clutches were completed. In summing his own experience as an egg collector in Britain, Nethersole-Thompson (1931) concluded that a second nesting takes place in two out of three cases "if the first is interfered with." It is hard for us, however, to evaluate the statement of Demandt (1953) that the cliff-nesting peregrines in western Germany have in recent years lacked suitable alternate eyries for renesting sites. In northern Germany, where peregrines nest in the old tree nests of other birds of prey, a scarcity of renesting has been reported by Schnurre (1950) at a time when all large raptors were decreasing, so that alternate sites were presumably less available to the peregrine.

The significance of renesting in peregrine populations not subjected to human interference remains unknown. As a population characteristic, the phenomenon is important to groups of birds like the Phasianidae (Hickey, 1955). It undoubtedly helped the peregrine to survive the era of egg-collecting in both Europe and North America, but its ecological significance in the present era remains to be determined.

YOUNG PER SUCCESSFUL PAIR

Variation in the number of young peregrines fledged at successful eyries in general follows the geographic pattern of variation in clutch size (Table 1.1). The drop from eggs seen or collected to young seen or fledged is 17% among Arctic pairs, 19% in the eastern United States, 24% in southern Germany, and 25% in southern Canada. Some variability in the data may arise from the inclusion of young that did not actually fledge, but we regard this bias as relatively small. We did, however, exclude large downy young in Beebe's (1960) sample for British Columbia. If these are included with birds observed in 1962 and 1964 (Beebe, *in litt.*), the mean number of young for 57 marine peregrine pairs there is 2.37. The samples reviewed in this table are all from populations thought to be stable, the one exception being Ratcliffe's, where the reduction from eggs to young was 45% and indicative of a declining population. For a typically stable population in Britain, Ratcliffe (*in litt.*) believes that a mean clutch of 3.5 would normally be reduced by 29% to about 2.5 young.

NET PRODUCTIVITY

That yearling peregrines usually do not breed is of course well-known, and Dementiev (1957) reports both male and female specimens of *F. p. babylonicus* (evidently yearlings) with undeveloped gonads on 26 April and 17 May. Such specimens may represent the majority of yearlings, seldom seen at occupied eyries.

Since adult-plumaged birds at these sites occasionally may not lay eggs either, it seems necessary to express net productivity as the number of young reared per occupied site. This statistic for 67 British and American sites (Table 1.2) was 1.5. Life-table computations have led Olsson (1958) to conclude that 1.16 young are required of all pairs to balance Fennoscandian populations of the common buzzard—if yearlings do not nest. This statistic must be fairly close to that holding for stable populations of the peregrine, but it is by no means certain that all peregrines begin to breed at 2 years of age.

MORTALITY RATES

Until now, mortality rates for peregrine falcons have not been published. The outlines of population turnover in other raptors, however, have begun to emerge.

In the eastern highlands of Scotland, Brown and Watson (1964) report 34% of the golden eagles from July to September to be immature

Table 1.2. Peregrine Production in British and American Study Areas, 1939–40

	Cornish coast[a]	Around New York[b]	Total
Number of deserted sites	4	8	12
Number of unsuccessful sites	10	17	27
Number of successful pairs	24	16	40
Total number of occupied sites	34	33	67
Young reared per successful pair	2.4	2.5	2.45
Young reared per occupied site	1.7	1.2	1.5
Percent of sites occupied	90	81	85
Percent of pairs producing	71	48	60
Percent of sites producing	63	39	51

[a] Ryves, 1948 [b] Hickey, 1942

and only 16% from September to May, with most of the change occurring between late September (when eaglets leave their parents) and November. For peregrines, this critical period is generally taken to be the first month or two after the young birds leave their parents and search for food themselves. French- and Swedish-reported recoveries of banded common buzzards have disclosed that 79–80% of the reared young die before they reach maturity (Mayaud, 1955; Olsson, 1958). These percentages reflect vulnerability to the gun, and they may exaggerate the proportion of young birds dying from natural causes (Hickey, 1952:28,40).

As a general rule in avian population dynamics, it can be said that the low productivity of birds that do not breed at 1 year of age is offset by low adult mortality rates (Hickey, 1952). In these species, population balance is the resultant of these mortality rates, the productivity of the breeders, and the nonproductivity of the nonbreeders. While a few peregrines do produce young at 1 year of age, it is not even certain that all adult birds are breeding at age 2. It would appear that annual adult mortality rates for birds of this type will be found to lie somewhere between 15 or 17% (as in the herring gull—cf. Paludan, 1951) and 30% (as in the marsh hawk or hen harrier—cf. Hickey, 1952). For the common buzzard, Olsson (1958) has calculated rates that we regard as probably approximating those that should characterize stable populations of the peregrine: 56% for the first year (starting "1 July" but 1 August seems more nearly correct), 22% for yearlings, and averaging 19% per year for adults.

POPULATION BEHAVIOR

POPULATION STABILITY

The general stability of peregrine populations—at least in the Temperate Zone—has been an impressive characteristic to ecologists. Tundra raptors locally fluctuate in response to lemming cycles (Hagen and Barth, 1952; Pitelka, Tomich, and Treichel, 1955) but peregrines—although feeding at times on lemmings—are quite independent of them as food resources (Berg, 1913; Cade, 1960:224, 248).

The concept of stability in peregrines rests on four uneven sets of data: census work on other raptorial birds, similarly local population studies of the peregrine itself, eyrie histories, and a few field estimates of the longevity of adults occupying specific eyries.

1. Wendland (1953) carried out a nesting-raptor census on an area of 52.9 sq miles (132 sq km) just north of Berlin. Here, to cite only his most abundant species, the pairs of common buzzards were given as 28, 29, 30, and 29? in 1941–44 and 29 and 30 in 1950–51. On a Michigan study area, Craighead and Craighead (1956:228) found 63 pairs of hawks and owls in 1942, 66 in 1948, and 65 in 1949. In an increasing population of tawny owls that almost doubled in a British woodland, Southern (1959) found an orderly rate of increase that averaged 5% per year over an 11-year period.

2. Walpole-Bond (1914) was perhaps the first to count nesting peregrines each year on a study area. In Sussex, where the combined frontage of censused cliffs along the English Channel came to little more than 16 miles (26 km), he found nesting pairs to vary from 7 or 8 up to 12. This rather remarkable variation appears to have held from 1904 to 1912, in a part of England where "game preservation" (= "vermin control") may well have increased the mortality rate of adult peregrines and contributed to population fluctuations of this magnitude.

In a 10,000-sq-mile (25,900-sq-km) study area that included New York City, R. A. Herbert, W. R. Spofford, and Hickey found 18 pairs of peregrines and 1 unmated male in 1939 and 19 pairs in 1940 (Hickey, 1942). On a middle section of Alaska's Colville River, Cade (1960:171–172) found 10, 8, 11, and 9 sites occupied in consecutive years. Here, near the periphery of its range where one would expect fluctuations to be maximal, the peregrine's densities varied less than 17% about a mean and tended to be inversely proportional to the number of nesting gyrfalcons that were present. There is no doubt, also, that some of these Alaskan eyries were in a very active state of erosion, and that they lacked the stability one normally associates with peregrine nesting ledges generally. Dementiev (1957) mentions loamy nesting sites in Turkmenia that we suspect may have the same ephemeral attraction to peregrines and perhaps contribute to the fluctuations in observed numbers of this species. On a longer stretch of the Colville River, Cade found 32 pairs in 1952 and 36 pairs in 1959, with 5 unmated adults present in each period.

On the whole, the published census work on nesting peregrines has not been at all extensive, and the papers contributed to the present volume fill a notable gap in our knowledge of this species.

3. The chief evidence of population stability in the peregrine seems to consist of individual eyrie histories. The traditional use of certain cliffs by peregrines year after year, however striking, is not valid evidence of population stability. Falcons from an eyrie on the island of Lundy (off the coast of Wales where two pairs are said to nest) are mentioned as far back as 1243 (Gurney, 1921:60) and have had a special fame among falconers right up to modern times (Gilbert Blaine, pers. comm., 14 January 1937). A Finnish eyrie at Aavasaksa occupied in 1756 was still in use two centuries later (Linkola, 1959). Occupation of the same Soviet site in the seventeenth and nineteenth centuries has been reported by Dementiev (1951). But none of these statements can be relied on to mean continuous use. Mann (1889) has reported the dates on which Sir Hamon Le Strange [or Lestrange] caught 87 peregrines at Hunstanton Cliff in eastern England in 50 trapping seasons beginning in 1604; 65 of these were young birds captured between 29 September and 4 March. Gurney (1921:140) has called these "young ones from the nest," a circumstance that is open to some doubt. Nevertheless, Le Strange was able to secure at least one peregrine from this site in 46 out of the 50 trapping periods. The eyrie was finally deserted about 1818 (Harting, 1890).

It is, however, the study of deserted eyries that has convinced ornithologists of peregrine population stability. After viewing the known history of 408 peregrine eyries in eastern North America, Hickey (1942) concluded that the deserted eyries represented from 10 to 18% of those recorded in this region. Among 17 definitely deserted were 8 that were tentatively labelled "temporary" eyries—sites used briefly by peregrines and not involved in important population changes. Among 20 possibly deserted sites were 4 in Colorado where undefined "ecological changes" may have favored prairie falcons at the expense of peregrines. These changes are dealt with elsewhere in this volume in a fascinating study by Nelson (Chapter 4). After eliminating temporary sites, Ferguson-Lees (1957) estimated that only 57 cliffs were deserted in the 1930's out of a sample of 627 peregrine eyries in the British Isles. For 61 peregrine territories that he censused in Britain during the postwar years, Ratcliffe (1962) found 80% to be regularly occupied in each season for which he had information, 11% to involve either apparently missing birds (possibly at alternative nesting sites) or occupation but no nesting, and 8% apparently deserted in at least one breeding season.

Linkola (1959) makes the interesting statement that, with one exception, Finnish ornithologists have never knowingly observed a nesting site that was being used by peregrines for the first time. The exception, at Porvoo in 1939, involved a yearling female that did not return the following year.

4. Evidence of longevity is somewhat tenuous but still contributes to the idea of stability. This includes such identifiable birds as the Montreal female that was known to reach 18 years, another female that apparently

occupied the same German eyrie for 18 years (Horst, 1937), and three Hudson River birds that attained minimal ages of 17, 18, and 20 years (Herbert and Herbert, 1965). These impressive statistics are clearly exceptions to the probable mean life expectancy of the peregrine falcon. What does emerge from the data available is the picture of a species with a probably low mortality rate, a strong tradition of re-occupying stable nesting sites, a great tenacity to remain in the face of a sometimes quite hostile human population, and a nonbreeding segment that—at least in the past—was generally capable of supplying replacements for the adults that were removed from the nesting population by mortality.

THE RECENT POPULATION CRASH

Population studies of the peregrine falcon have not (to our knowledge) been carried out in the Southern Hemisphere, and the general observations of ornithologists there convey little or no hint of any recent decline in numbers. In western India, however, there has been a general decrease of open-country raptors, including peregrines, beginning as early as 1961 (K. S. Dharmakumarsinhji, *in litt.*).

Recognition of the widespread character of the present decline in peregrine populations of the Northern Hemisphere has been fairly slow. At first, those investigating regional populations of this species were unaware that the decline was not just a local one. In 1953, R. A. Herbert and K. G. Skelton reported to the annual meeting of the American Ornithologists' Union that, in their study area [the Hudson River Valley], virtually 100% of the peregrine pairs were now unsuccessful in their reproductive efforts (Cade, 1960:184). The nearly complete failure of some 14 peregrine pairs in Massachusetts was at this time being attributed by J. A. Hagar (*in litt.*) to predation by raccoons (*Procyon lotor*). By 1962, it was rumored at the XIIIth International Ornithological Congress that not a single young peregrine had been raised that spring in the northeastern states. Many ornithologists dismissed this as unsubstantiated.

In western Europe, study of the peregrine was inevitably proceeding at a different pace in each country, and published reports on the decline appeared in Germany, Finland, and Britain in that chronological order. For some years, a small cliff-nesting population had been followed by Demandt (1937*a*, 1937*b*, 1939, 1940*a*, 1940*b*). Demandt (1953) found a distinct change setting in about 1946 among peregrines nesting in North Rhine-Westphalia, where the breeding pairs normally averaged four but dropped to two in 1946 and 1947, none in 1949, and one in 1950. This occurred in a region where pigeon fanciers were numerous and extremely hostile to the peregrine. A drop in numbers of peregrine eggs laid per clutch in this region was indeed striking, but this could have been due to excessive molestation of the falcons during their egg-laying period (Th. Mebs, pers. comm., 1964). Demandt's pessimistic view of the peregrine's future was expressed in 1955 in a paper appropriately entitled "Wanderfalkendammerung?"

The tree-nesting population on the north German plain at this time was in equally poor straits. Schnurre (1950) was able to establish in Brandenburg (west of Berlin) that, in contrast to the goshawk, the peregrine had not increased during and after World War II, and its decline was associated with a decrease in the numbers of domestic pigeons. Wendland (1953), who had three tree-nesting pairs each year from 1940 to 1944 in his study area north of Berlin, found only one pair resident annually from 1949 to 1951. This was at a time when other German raptor populations were stable or increasing. Annual productivity in this small sample of peregrines averaged only 0.5 young fledged per pair. The decline was abrupt in 1945, and not a single peregrine was seen in 1946–47. Nonbreeding behavior of peregrines elsewhere in Germany became evident in the 1950's, and Demandt (1950, 1957) wondered if this significantly reflected sterility in old birds or was merely the result of more intensive field work.

Finnish research on this species was accelerated by 1,500 questionnaires sent out in the winter of 1958 (Suomus, 1958). Answers to these disclosed that a population decline had set in about 1953, with a sharp drop in the number of nesting birds between 1956 and 1957; mean clutch size, which had varied from 3.0 to 3.3 during different parts of the previous century, had dropped to 2.9 in 1950–54 and 2.8 in 1955–58 (Linkola, 1959). In 1959 it was 2.7, the mean number of young in successful eyries was 2.1, and less than 50% of the nesting pairs fledged any young (Linkola, 1960). In 1961–63, successful eyries were still averaging about 2.1 young per site, and the average number of young fledged per pair ran about 0.9 (Linkola, 1964). Changes in the total peregrine population of Finland are set forth in this volume by Linkola and Suominen (Chapter 15).

Reproductive success of the rock-nesting peregrines in the GDR during this period was particularly low. Kleinstäuber (1963) reported that rock-nesting pairs averaged only 0.59 young per eyrie from 1946 to 1960, that this dropped to 0.39 for 18 eyries in 1961, and that it was down to 0.29 for 14 eyries in 1962. A bulletin calling for a great increase in protective measures for the peregrine was then prepared by Kleinstäuber and Schröder (1963).

In Britain, the story broke somewhat slowly. In 1957, *British Birds* devoted most of its April issue to the current status of the rarer birds of prey in the British Isles, and Ferguson-Lees (1957) summarized a study he had carried out in 1947–50, showing (a) marked recovery in peregrine populations depleted by wartime control and (b) stable numbers in unaffected districts. There was little hint that something unprecedented in the annals of British ornithology was about to take place. Ratcliffe (1958) next described the amazing fact that broken eggs were in 10 of the 59 peregrine nests he examined in 1951–56 in contrast to 1 out of 35 in 1945–50. The story for a stretch of the Cornish coast was related by Treleaven (1961). Only one young was reared at 6 eyries in 1957, no young at 7 sites in 1958 and 1959, and 5 out of 7 sites were deserted (or essentially so) by 1960. The British Trust for Ornithology then launched its important cooperative inquiry, the results of which Ratcliffe published in 1963 and has summarized in this volume (Chapter 21).

The complexity of the whole situation in Europe was further brought out by Linkola (1964), who reported 43 peregrine sites inactive in a Finnish survey and who estimated that the total number of surviving pairs in his country must be less than 50—and perhaps was only 10.

In the United States, it was thus evident in 1963 that the rumor of 1962 had attained the status of hypothesis, and that a survey of our eastern eyries was badly needed. This investigation was made a reality in 1964 by the Richard A. Herbert Memorial Fund. Its results, reported in the present volume by Berger, Sindelar, and Gamble (Chapter 13), were so dramatic as to make an international conference on the population biology of *Falco peregrinus* an absolute necessity.

DECLINING POPULATIONS OF OTHER RAPTORS

That other raptor populations were in trouble at this time was well known to those familiar with the contemporary literature of field ornithology. An excellent background to the present volume can be found in a report on The Working Conference on Birds of Prey and Owls, organized by the International Council for Bird Preservation and held on 10–12 April 1964 at Caen, France. The 22 papers in this report offer interesting insights into the biology and conservation of raptorial birds in western Europe in this period. [The Caen report can be secured from The International Council for Bird Preservation, c/o Natural History Museum, Cromwell Road, London, S.W.7 (price 17/6 postage paid); or c/o Milton Erlanger, Treasurer U.S. National Section, 350 Fifth Avenue, New York, New York 10001 (price $2.50 postpaid).]

Another important background conference was held in Ohio in May 1965. Sponsored by the National Audubon Society, this meeting sought to clarify research problems associated with the dramatic decline of the bald eagle in certain regions.

The picture thus emerging was that a number of raptorial bird populations were inexplicably and simultaneously declining on two continents. Something of this decline in the osprey, bald eagle, gray sea eagle, and the accipitrine hawks is presented in a series of brief reports in the present volume (Chapters 25, 27–30).

THE WISCONSIN CONFERENCE

The interesting questions for population ecologists center, then, on the possibilities that (a) some of these phenomena have a common pattern and (b) others will require quite diverse explanations. It is scarcely necessary to add that animal populations under natural conditions are nearly always responding to a complex of factors, and it is safe to say that the peregrine falcon population is no exception.

The main purpose of the peregrine conference reported on in this volume was to crystallize and evaluate some practical hypotheses to account for the remarkable event in population biology that has taken place: the extracontinental population crash of a species that normally fluctuates less than 10% around its mean. To this end, nearly half of the conference was devoted to describing the status of peregrines in various regions and to recording census and reproduction data that, for the most part, have never been published. From these pages it is now possible to date the decline (or declines) and learn what is known of the ecological events associated with them.

Patterns to be noted by readers of the present volume include variations in the percentage of paired but nonbreeding birds, frequency of egg-eating and broken eggs, possible changes in the ratio of young to old birds, trends in statistics on net productivity, and regional variations in the chronology of population change. It was impossible, of course, for all the contributors to this symposium to supply data on all these aspects of peregrine biology. Nor was it possible to bring together all the world's experts on the peregrine falcon.

While the conference contributors sought to evaluate these data and to formulate hypotheses to account for all these phenomena, readers of the present volume will, we hope, have a more leisurely opportunity to digest the information and reach their own conclusions.

ACKNOWLEDGMENTS

We are much indebted to D. D. Berger, Dr. Antti Haapanen, Dr. Frances Hamerstrom, Dr. Nagahisa Kuroda, and Dr. M. D. F. Udvardy for translations and bibliographic assistance; to Norman Ford and the Van Tyne Memorial Library of the Wilson Ornithological Society for repeated bibliographic help; and to Dr. T. J. Cade and Dr. D. A. Ratcliffe for critical advice in the preparation of this review.

LITERATURE CITED

Allen, D. L., and L. D. Mech. 1963. Wolves versus moose on Isle Royale. Nat. Geogr., 123(2):200–219.

Allen, J. A. 1872. Ornithological notes from the west. Amer. Nat., 6(5):263–275.

Allen, R. P., and R. T. Peterson. 1936. The hawk migration at Cape May Point, New Jersey. Auk, 53(4):393–404.

Ashford, W. J. 1929. Peregrine falcon nesting on the ground in Hampshire. Brit. Birds, 22(8):190.

Audubon, J. J. 1831. Ornithological biography, or an account of the habits of the birds of the United States of America . . . . Edinburgh. 5 vol.

Baker, E. C. S. 1917. Notes on the nidification of some Indian Falconidae. Ibis, ser. 10, 5(2):224–241.

Beebe, F. L. 1960. The marine peregrines of the northwest Pacific Coast. Condor, 62(3):145–189.

Bellrose, Frank, Jr. 1938. Duck hawks nesting in western Tennessee. Wilson Bull., 50(2):139.

Bendire, Charles. 1892. Life histories of North American birds with special reference to their breeding habits and eggs. Smithsonian Inst., U.S. Nat. Mus., Spec. Bull. 6. 446 p.

Bent, A C. 1938. Life histories of North American birds of prey. Part. 2: Orders Falconiformes and Strigiformes. Bull. U.S. Nat. Mus. 170. 482 p. + 92 pl.

Berg, Bengt. 1913. Der Wanderfalke und die Lemmingzüge. Novitates Zool., 20(2):284–288.

Bolam, George. 1912. Birds of Northumberland and the eastern borders. Henry Hunter Blair, Alnwick. 726 p.

Bond, R. M. 1946. The peregrine population of western North America. Condor, 48(3):101–116.

Borg, Karl. 1962. Predation on roe deer in Sweden. J. Wildl. Mgmt., 26(2):133–136.

Boudwin, George. 1877. Peregrine falcon *(Falco peregrinus)*. Forest and Stream, 8(11):161.

Brooks, Allan. 1926. Notes on the status of the Peale falcon. Condor, 28(2):77–79.

Broun, Maurice. 1963. Hawk migrations and the weather. Hawk Mt. Sanct. Ass., Kempton, Pa. 11 p.

Brouwer, G. A. 1927. *Falco peregrinus* Tunst. *en Larus fuscus affinis* Reinh. broedvogel in Nederland. Ardea, 16(1):4–10 [English summary].

Brown, L. H. 1961. The peregrine falcon comes to town. Country Life, 1 June 1961, 129(3352):1280–1281.

———, and Adam Watson. 1964. The golden eagle in relation to its food supply. Ibis, 106(1):78–100.

Butler, A. W. 1898. The birds of Indiana. A descriptive catalogue of the birds that have been observed within the state, with an account of their habits. Report of the State Geologist of Indiana for 1897, [Indiana] Dep. Geol. and Natur. Resources, p. 515–1187.

Cade, T. J. 1960. Ecology of the peregrine and gyrfalcon populations in Alaska. Univ. Calif. Publ. Zool., 63(3):151–290.

Campbell, A. J. 1901. Nests and eggs of Australian birds . . . . Sheffield. 2 vol.

Cheng Tso-hsin [ed.]. 1963. Chung-kuo ching-chi tung-wu chih-niao lei [China's economic fauna: birds]. Sci. Publ. Soc., Peking. 694 p. (translated 20 March 1964 by Joint Publ. Res. Serv., Off. of Tech. Serv., U.S. Dep. Com., Washington, D.C. JPRS no. 23,630, OTS no. 64–21853.)

Cooke, M. T. 1943. Returns from banded birds: some miscellaneous recoveries of interest. Bird-Banding, 14(3):67–74.

Coues, Elliott. 1874. On the nesting of certain hawks, etc. Amer. Nat., 8(10):596–603.

Craighead, F. C., Jr., and J. J. Craighead. 1939. Hawks in the hand. Houghton Mifflin, Boston. 290 p.

Craighead, J. J., and F. C. Craighead, Jr. 1956. Hawks, owls and wildlife. Stackpole, Harrisburg, and Wildl. Mgmt. Inst., Washington, D.C. 443 p.

Culver, D. E. 1919. Duck hawks wintering in the center of Philadelphia. Auk, 36(1):108–109.

Dall, W. H., and H. M. Bannister. 1867–69. List of the birds of Alaska, with biographical notes. Trans. Chicago Acad. Sci., 1:267–310 (original not seen; citation from W. J. Beecher, pers. comm.).

De Groot, D. S. 1927. The California clapper rail: Its nesting habits, enemies and habitat. Condor, 29(6):259–270.

Demandt, C. 1937*a*. Beobachtungen an einem westdeutschen Wanderfalkenhorst. Beitr. Fortpfl.-biol. Vögel, 13(2):99–100.

———. 1937*b*. Wanderfalke bezieht nach Störung seines Felsenhorstes einen Baumhorst. Beitr. Fortfpl.-biol. Vögel, 13(3):115.

———. 1939. Brutbiologische Beobachtungen an einem Felsenhorst des Wanderfalken. Beitr. Fortpfl.-biol. Vögel, 15(3):89–101.

———. 1940*a*. Weitere Boebachtungen an Horsten westfälischer Wanderfalken. Beitr. Fortpfl.-biol. Vögel, 16(1):3–6.

———. 1940*b*. Eigenartige Verzettelung einer Wanderfalkenbrut. Beitr. Fortpfl.-biol. Vögel, 16(5):191–192.

———. 1941. Vom Einfluss der Witterung auf den Beginn der Balz oder des Gesanges einiger Vogelarten. Beitr. Fortpfl.-biol. Vögel, 17(1):9–11.

———. 1950. Gibt es Alterssterilität bei Vögeln? Vogelwelt, 71(5):163.

———. 1952. Beobachtungen an westfälischen Wanderfalkenhorsten. Vogelwelt, 73 (6):208–211.

———. 1953. Brutbiologische Probleme beim Wanderfalken (*Falco peregrinus*). J. Ornithol., 94 (1–2):99–102.

———. 1955. Wanderfalkendämmerung? Ornithol. Mitteilungen, 7(1):5–6.

———. 1957. Rätselhaftes Verhalten von Wanderfalken-Brutpaaren. Vogelwelt, 78(6):183–185.

Dementiev, G. P. 1951. [The peregrine falcon in the USSR], p. 80–100. *In* G. P. Dementiev and N. A. Gladkov [ed.], The birds of the Soviet Union [in Russian]. Soviet Science, Moscow. Vol. 1. 652 p. (Translated 1966 by U. S. Dep. Com., Clearing House for Federal Scientific and Technical Information, Springfield, Virginia. TT 64-11027.

———. 1957. On the Shaheen *Falco peregrinus babylonicus*. Ibis, 99(1):477–482.

———, and V. D. Iljitschev. 1961. Bermerkungen über die Morphologie der Wüsten-Wanderfalken. Falke, 8:147–154.

———, and E[rwin] Stresemann. 1955. Über Wanderfalken und Würgfalken (*Falco peregrinus und F. cherrug*) des Berliner Zoologischen Museums. J. Ornithol., 96 (1):344–346.

Enderson, J. H. 1965. A breeding and migration survey of the peregrine falcon. Wilson Bull., 77(3):327–339.

Errington, P. L. 1933. Food habits of southern Wisconsin raptors. Part II. Hawks. Condor, 35(1):19–29.

Eutermoser, G[ust l]. 1961. Erläuterungen zur Krähenstatistik. Deutscher Falkenorden, 1961:49–50.

Farner, D. S. 1955. Birdbanding in the study of population dynamics, p. 397–449. *In* Albert Wolfson [ed.], Recent studies in avian biology. Univ. Ill. Press, Urbana. 479 p.

Ferguson-Lees, I. J. 1951. The peregrine population of Britain. Bird Notes, 24(6): 200–205, (8) 309–315 [original not seen; quoted by Cade, 1960].

———. 1957. [The rarer birds of prey: Their present status in the British Isles.] Peregrine (*Falco peregrinus*). Brit. Birds, 50(4):149–155.

———. 1963. Changes in the status of birds of prey in Europe. Brit. Birds, 56(4): 140–148.

Forbush, E. H. 1927. Birds of Massachusetts and other New England states. Part II. Land birds from bob-whites to grackles. Mass. Dep. Agric., Boston, 461 p.

Gabrielson, I. N., and F. C. Lincoln. 1959. The birds of Alaska. Stackpole Co., Harrisburg, and Wildl. Mgmt. Inst., Washington, D.C. 922 p.

Ganier, A. F. 1932. Duck hawks at a Reelfoot heronry. Migrant, 3(2):28–32.

Gladkow, N. A. 1941. Beitrage zum Studium der Vögel der Timan-Tundra. J. Ornithol., 89(1):124–156.

Goss, N. S. 1878. Breeding of the duck hawk in trees. Bull. Nuttall Ornithol. Club, 3(1):32–34.

Green, C. de B. 1916. Note on the distribution and nesting habits of *Falco peregrinus pealei* Ridgway. Ibis, ser. 10, 4(3):473–476.

Groskin, Horace. 1947. Duck hawks breeding in the business center of Philadelphia, Pennsylvania. Auk, 64(2):312–314.

———. 1952. Observations of duck hawks nesting on man-made structures. Auk, 69(3):246–253.

Gurney, J. H. 1921. Early annals of ornithology. H. F. & G. Witherby, London. 240 p.

Hagen, Yngvar, and E. K. Barth. 1952. Jaktfalken (*Falco rusticolus* L.): Noen iakttagelser fra Dovre i Norge. Vår Fågelvärld, 11(3):116–125 [summary in English].

Hall, G. H. 1955. Great moments in action: The story of the Sun Life falcons. Privately printed, Montreal. 37 p.

Harting, J. E. 1890. A commentary on Sir John Sebright's observations upon hawking. Zoologist, ser. 3, 14(167):417–421.

Hatt, R. T., Josselyn Van Tyne, L. C. Stuart, C. H. Pope, and A. B. Grobman. 1948. Island life: a study of the land vertebrates of the islands of eastern Lake Michigan. Cranbrook Inst. of Sci. Bull. 27. 179 p.

Herbert, R. A., and K. G. S. Herbert. 1965. Behavior of peregrine falcons in the New York City region. Auk, 82(1):62–94.

Herren, Hans. 1959. Wanderfalkenbruten im Kanton Bern 1957–58. Ornithol. Beob., 56(1):27–28.

Hickey, J. J. 1942. Eastern population of the duck hawk. Auk, 59(2):176–204.

———. 1952. Survival studies of banded birds. U. S. Dep. Interior, Fish and Wildl. Serv., Spec. Sci. Rep.: Wildl. no. 15. 177 p.

———. 1955. Some American population research on gallinaceous birds, p. 326–396. *In* Albert Wolfson [ed.], Recent studies in avian biology. Univ. Ill. Press, Urbana. 479 p.

Hofslund, P. B. 1966. Hawk migration over the western tip of Lake Superior. Wilson Bull., 78(1):79–87.

Horst, F. 1937. Wie gross ist das Jagdgebiet des Wanderfalken? Beitr. Fortpfl.-biol. Vögel, 13(3):98–99.

Ijzendoorn, A. L. J. van. 1950. The breeding-birds of the Netherlands. E. J. Brill, Leiden. 73 p. + map.

Ingram, G. C. S., and H. M. Salmon. 1929. Notes on the nesting habits of the peregrine falcon (2). Brit. Birds, 22(9):198–202.

Jesperson, Poul. 1946. The breeding birds of Denmark: With special reference to changes during the last century. Einar Munksgaard, Copenhagen. 79 p.

Johnson, R. A. 1941. Nesting behavior of the Atlantic murre. Auk, 58(2):153–163.

Jones, F. M. 1946. Duck hawks of eastern Virginia. Auk, 63(4):592.

Kesteloot, E. 1964. Pigeon-fanciers and protection of birds of prey in Belgium, p. 68–70. *In* Working conference on birds of prey and owls. Caen, 10–12 April 1964. Int. Council for Bird Preservation, London. 140 p.

Keyes, C. R. 1906. Prolific duck hawks. Auk, 23(1):99–100.

Klaas, C. 1941. Ein Wanderfalke als Wintergast Frankfurts. Natur und Volk, 71(12):563–570.

Kleinstäuber, Kurt. 1963. Bestandskontrolle und Horstsicherungsmassnahmen für unsere Felsen-Wanderfalken (Stand 1962). Falke, 10(3):80–82.

———, and Horst Schröder. 1963. Der Wanderfalke ist in Gefahr! Arbeitsgemeinshaft für Jagd- und Wildforschung, 18:1–7.

Koenig, Museum A. 1931. Katalog der nido-oologischen Sammlung (Vogeleler-sammlung) im Museum Alexander Koenig in Bonn a. Rhein. 1,122 p. [original not seen; quoted from Mebs, 1960].

Kruyfhooft, Ch. 1964. Serious decrease of the peregrine falcon in Belgium during the autumn migration, p. 70–73. *In* Working conference on birds of prey and owls. Caen, 10–12 April 1964. Int. Council for Bird Preservation, London. 140 p.

Kuhk, Rudolf. 1939. Die Vögel Mecklenburgs: Faunistiche, tiergeographische und ökologische Untersuchungen im Mecklenburgischen Raume. Verlag Opitz & Co., Güstrow. 339 p.

Kuyt, E[rnie]. 1966. Adjoining unusual nest sites of snow goose and peregrine falcon. The Blue Jay, 24(4):171.

Lack, David. 1947–48. The significance of clutch size. Ibis, 89(2):302–352; 90(1): 25–45.

Legge, W. V. 1878–80. A history of the birds of Ceylon. London. 1,237 p. [original not seen; quoted by Wait, 1925].

Lindquist, Thorvald. 1963. Peregrines and homing pigeons. Brit. Birds, 56(4):149–151.

Linkola, Pentti. 1959. Jalohaukan kohtalo Suomessa. Suomen Luonto, 18(1):3–19; (2):34–48.

———. 1960. Jalohaukka 1959. Suomen Luonto, 19(1):20–23.

———. 1964. Jalohaukka 1961–63. Suomen Luonto, 23(1):5–11.

Lubbock, Richard. 1879. Observations of the fauna of Norfolk and more particularly on the District of the Broads. Jarrold & Sons, London. 239 p.

Mann, T. J. 1889. Hawks: how obtained and trained. Trans. Norfolk and Norwich Nat. Soc., 4:650–668 (1 unpaged table).

Mathews, G. M. 1915–16. The birds of Australia. Witherby & Co., London. Vol. 5. 440 p.

Mayaud, Noël. 1955. Coup d'oeil sur les reprises en France de buses variables *Buteo buteo* (L.). Alauda, 23(4):225–248.

McGilp, J. N. 1934. The hawks of South Australia. South Australian Ornithol., 12(8):261–293.

Mebs, Th. 1955. Zum Brut-Vorkommen des Wanderfalken (*Falco peregrinus germanicus* Erlang.) in Süddeutschland. Anzeiger Ornithol. Gesellsch. Bayern, 4(5): 343–362.

———. 1960. Probleme der Fortpflanzungsbiologie und Bestandserhaltung bei deutschen Wanderfalken (*Falco peregrinus*). Vogelwelt, 81(2):47–56.

Mech, L. D. 1966. The wolves of Isle Royale. Fauna of the National Parks of the United States. Fauna Series 7. U.S. Govt. Printing Office, Washington, D.C. 210 p.

Meinertzhagen, R[ichard]. 1954. Birds of Arabia. Oliver and Boyd, Edinburgh and London. 624 p.

———. 1959. Pirates and predators: The piratical and predatory habits of birds. Oliver and Boyd, Edinburgh and London. 230 p.

Momiyama, T. T. 1927. Some new and unrecorded birds from Japanese Territories I [in Japanese and English]. Annot. Ornithol. Orient, 1:1–79.

———. 1930. On the birds of Bonin and Iwô Islands [in Japanese]. Bull. Biogr. Soc. Japan, 1(3):89–187.

Morres, A. P. 1882. The peregrines of Salisbury Cathedral. Zoologist, 6(61):18–20.

Mountfort, Guy. 1958. Wild paradise: The story of the Coto Doñana expeditions. Houghton Mifflin, Boston. 240 p.

Mueller, H. C., and D. D. Berger. 1959. A second peregrine falcon banding return from Uruguay. Bird-Banding, 30(3):182–183.

———. 1961. Weather and fall migration of hawks at Cedar Grove, Wisconsin. Wilson Bull., 73(2):171–192.

Nethersole-Thompson, Desmond. 1931. Observations on the peregrine falcon (*Falco peregrinus peregrinus*). Oologists' Record, 11(4):73–80.

Niethammer, Günther. 1938. Handbuch der deutschen Vogelkunde. Akademische Verlagsgesellschaft, Leipzig. Vol. 2. 545 p.

Nordström, Göran. 1963. Einige Ergebnisse der Vogelberingung in Finnland in den Jahren 1913–1962. Teil I. Ornis Fennica, 40(3):81–124.

North, A. J. 1912. Nests and eggs of birds found breeding in Australia and Tasmania. Australian Museum, Sydney. 2nd ed. Vol. 3.

Olivier, Georges. 1953. Nidification du faucon pelerin sur les edifices. L'Oiseau et la Revue Française d'Ornithol., 23(2):109–124.

Olsson, Viking. 1958. Dispersal, migration, longevity and death causes of *Strix aluco, Buteo buteo, Ardea cinerea* and *Larus argentatus:* A study based on recoveries of birds ringed in Fenno-Scandia. Acta Vertebratica, 1(2):85–189.

Pátkai, I. 1947. Ragadozó madaraink. Nimrod Kiskönyvtär, Budapest. 187 p. [Original not seen; quoted by A. Keve and M. D. F. Udvardy, *in litt.*]

Paludan, Knud. 1951. Contributions to the breeding biology of *Larus argentatus* and *Larus fuscus.* Idensk. Medd. fra Dansk. Naturh. Foren., 114:1–128.

Peck, G. D. 1924. Reminiscences of my egging ground. Oologist, 41(6):65.

Peters, J. L. 1931. Check-list of birds of the world. Harvard Univ. Press, Cambridge. Vol. 1. 345 p.

Peterson, R. T. 1948. Birds over America. Dodd, Mead & Co., New York. 342 p.

Pitelka, F. A., P. Q. Tomich, and G. W. Treichel. 1955. Ecological relations of jaegers and owls as lemming predators near Barrow, Alaska. Ecol. Monogr., 25(1):85–117.

Porsild, A. E. 1951. Bird notes from Banks and Victoria islands. Can. Field-Nat., 65(1):40–42.

Preble, E. A. 1908. A biological investigation of the Athabaska-Mackenzie region. U.S. Dep. Agric., Bur. Biol. Surv., N. Amer. Fauna Ser. no 27. 574 p.

Ratcliffe, D. A. 1958. Broken eggs in peregrine eyries. Brit. Birds, 51(1):23–26.

———. 1962. Breeding density in the peregrine *Falco peregrinus* and raven *Corvus corax.* Ibis, 104(1):13–39.

———. 1963. The status of the peregrine in Great Britain. Bird Study, 10(2):56–90.

Ridgway, Robert. 1895. Nesting of the duck hawk in trees. Nidologist, 3(4–5):42–44.

Ripley, S. D., II. 1961. A synopsis of the birds of India and Pakistan . . . . Bombay Nat. Hist. Soc., Bombay. 703 p.

———, and G. E. Watson. 1963. A new peregrine falcon from the Cape Verde Islands, eastern Atlantic Ocean. Postilla (Yale Peabody Mus. Nat. Hist.), 77:1–4.

Rodriguez de la Fuente, Felix. 1964. Cetreria y aves de presa. Servicio Nacional de Pesca Fluvial y Caza, Ministerio de Agricultura, Madrid. 2 Boleten Tecnico, Serie Cinegetica. 75 p.

Rudebeck, Gustaf. 1950–51. The choice of prey and modes of hunting of predatory birds with special reference to their selective effect. Oikos, 2(1):65–88; 3(2):204–231.

Ryves, B. H. 1948. Bird life in Cornwall. Collins, London. 256 p.

Salomonsen, Finn. 1950. Grønlands fulge: The birds of Greenland. Ejnar Munksgaard, Copenhagen. 608 p.

Schasiepen, H. 1956. Am Felsenhorst des Wanderfalken. Wild und Hund, 59(5): 76–78.

Schiermann, Gottfried. 1925. Wanderfalke und Hühnerhabicht in der Mark Brandenburg. J. Ornithol., 73(2):277–283.

Schnurre, Otto. 1950. Wandlungen in Bestand und Ernährung norddeutscher Wanderfalken und Habichte, p. 396–401. *In* Adolf von Jordans and Fritz Peus [ed.], Syllegomena biologica (Festschrift O. Kleinschmidt). [Akademische Verlagsgesellschaft and A. Ziemsen], Leipzig and Wittenberg. 471 p.

Schüz, Ernst, and Hugo Weigold. 1931. Atlas des Vogelzugs nach den Beringungsergebnissen bei palaearktischen Vögeln. Friedländer & Sohn, Berlin. 160 p. + 149 maps.

Seebohm, Henry. 1901. The birds of Siberia: A record of a naturalist's visits to the valleys of the Petchora and Yenesei. John Murray, London. 512 p.

Serventy, D. L., and H. M. Whittell. 1951. A handbook of the birds of Western Australia (with the exception of the Kimberly Division). 2nd ed. Paterson Brokensha Pty Ltd., Perth. 384 p.

Smiley, A. K., Jr., and Daniel Smiley, Jr. 1930. An unusual duck hawk recovery. Bird-Banding, 1(3):144–145.

Southern, H. N. 1959. Mortality and population control. Ibis, 101(3–4):429–436.

Spofford, W. R. 1942. Nesting of the peregrine falcon in Tennessee. Migrant, 13(2–3):29–31.

———. 1943. Peregrines in a west Tennessee swamp. Migrant, 14(2):25–27.

———. 1945. Peregrine falcons in a west Tennessee swamp. Migrant, 16(4):56–58.

———. 1947. Another tree-nesting peregrine falcon record for Tennessee. Migrant, 18(4):60.

Sprunt, Alexander, IV, and R. L. Cunningham. 1961. Continental bald eagle project. Progress report no. 1. Nat. Aud. Soc., New York. 7 p. (mimeo).

Stresemann, Erwin, and Dean Amadon. 1963. What is *Falco kreyenborgi* Kleinschmidt? Ibis, 105(3):400–402.

Sulkava, Seppo. 1960. Muuttohaukan ravinnosta. Suomen Riista, 13:33–39.

Suomus, Heikki. 1958. Ajankohtaisia kysymyksiä huuhkajasta ja muuttohaukasta. Suomen Luonto, 17(1):5–9.

Swann, H. K., and Alexander Wetmore. 1936. A monograph of the birds of prey (Order Accipitres), Vol. 2, part 14. Wheldon and Wesley, London. p. 353–448 + 2 pl.

Thomasson, L. 1947. On the nesting sites of the peregrine falcon in the countries around the Baltic [in Swedish, English summary]. Vår Fågelvärld, 6(2):72–81.

Thomson, A. L. 1958. The migrations of British falcons (Falconidae) as shown by ringing results. Brit. Birds, 51(5):179–188.

Treleaven, R. B. 1961. Notes on the peregrine in Cornwall. Brit. Birds, 54(4):136–142.

Twomey, A. C. 1936. Climographic studies of certain introduced and migratory birds. Ecology, 17(1):122–132.

Uttendörfer, Otto, G. Bodenstein, and R. Kuhk. 1952. Neue Ergebnisse über die Ernährung der Greifvögel und Eulen. Eugen Ulmer, Stuttgart. 250 p.

Vaurie, Charles. 1961. Systematic notes on Palearctic birds. No. 44. Falconidae: The genus *Falco* (Part 1, *Falco peregrinus* and *Falco pelegrinoides*). Amer. Mus. Novitates, 2,035:1–19.

———. 1965. The birds of the Palearctic fauna: A systematic reference. Non-passeriformes. Witherby, London. 763 p.

Voous, K. H. 1960. Atlas of European birds. Nelson, London. 284 p.

———. 1961. Records of peregrine falcons on the Atlantic Ocean. Ardea, 49(3/4): 176–177.

Wait, W. E. 1925. Manual of the birds of Ceylon. [Supplement of the Ceylon Journal of Science.] Colombo Museum, Colombo. 496 p. + 20 pl.

Walpole-Bond, John. 1914. Field-studies of some rarer British birds. Witherby & Co., London. 305 p.

Wendland, Victor. 1953. Populationstudien an Raubvögeln. II: Bruterfolg 1940–51, untersucht bei 7 Arten. J. Ornithol., 94(1–2):103–113.

Whistler, Hugh. 1926. The birds of the Kangra District, Punjab. [Part II.] Ibis, ser. 12, 2(4):724–783.

Wilson, Alexander, and George Ord. 1808–14. American ornithology; or the natural history of the birds of the United States. Philadelphia. 9 vol.

Witherby, H. F., F. C. R. Jourdain, N. F. Ticehurst, and B. W. Tucker. 1939. The handbook of British birds. H. F. and G. Witherby, London. Vol. 3. 387 p.

Wolfe, L. R. 1938. A synopsis of North American birds of prey and their related forms in other countries. Bull. Chicago Acad. Sci., 5(8):167–208.

PART I

POPULATIONS: STATUS AND TRENDS

The Peregrine Falcon in Western North America and Mexico

CHAPTER 2

BREEDING ALASKAN AND ARCTIC MIGRANT POPULATIONS OF THE PEREGRINE

Clayton M. White

This paper is intended to bring up to date our knowledge of the present breeding status of peregrine falcons in particular areas of Alaska (starting with Cade's account, 1960), to provide more information on migrations of peregrines, and to interpret data gathered by me on the population structure of nonbreeding adults and the stability of the migrant population of this species in the Arctic.

References to peregrines in Alaska and citations mentioning them are numerous; Cade (1960) has given a thorough account of these. His account is accurate and serves as a concise basis on which to develop other studies that he did not have time to work out. One of the valuable contributions Cade made was to emphasize and make known other features of Arctic peregrine biology in need of further study. My studies in Alaska followed Cade's by some 5 years, were based on observations made from September 1962 to September 1963, and from June to September 1964, and were made possible by funds granted by the National Science Foundation and the National Institutes of Health. These funds supported, principally, other studies underway in the Department of Biological Sciences (grant to Brina Kessel) and the Laboratory of Zoophysiology, Institute of Arctic Biology, University of Alaska. Also, the generosity of the geological field parties of several oil companies, that allowed me to accompany them in helicopters, made it possible for me in 1964 to study peregrines in an extensive area on the Arctic Slope.

SPRING ARRIVAL

The spring arrival of peregrines throughout Alaska, save perhaps in the southeast, follows closely that of waterfowl and shorebirds. The fields of Creamers' Dairy, about 1.5 miles (2.4 km) northwest of Fairbanks, lose their snow before other places in the area and therefore are convenient for observations since they attract tremendous numbers of waterfowl and thus peregrines. The numbers of peregrines were highest in the last week of April and first week of May. Brina Kessel, University of Alaska, gives (mimeo. table) 28 April as the earliest date observed between 1950 and 1960. They have been reported on the Taylor Highway southeast of Fairbanks on 24 April (B. Kessel, pers. comm.). The most I saw any one day was seven—four at Creamers', two 1 mile (1.6 km) north of Creamers', and one in flight between Creamers' and Noyes Slough. One of the birds seen north of Creamers' was in the immature plumage. The total number of different individuals that I saw there probably was not more than 12. The birds were not evident in the earliest hours of the morning. On several occasions I was at the field between 5:00 A.M. and 6:00 A.M. (sunrise was about 4:30 A.M.) and failed to see peregrines, whereas the ornithology class from the University of Alaska would arrive at the field about 6:00 A.M., leave about 7:30 A.M., and see one or two falcons.

NESTING NUMBERS

On the Tanana River, at Chena Bluffs, some 3 miles (4.8 km) south of the University of Alaska campus, there was an active eyrie at least from 1928 to 1952 (Cade, 1960). Cade found the birds present in 1959, but not breeding, and falcons were not there in 1963 nor in June 1964. A fish wheel situated directly beneath the eyrie in 1963 and 1964 may have caused inactivity at least in those years. From Chena Bluff along the Tanana River to Nenana, some 50 miles (80 km), there were three eyries in

1963, and probably they were there also in the early 1950's when Brina Kessel made a trip along the river (B. Kessel, pers. comm.). In 1963 these three eyries averaged 1.0 fledged young each.

I have reported elsewhere (White, 1964; also in MS in preparation) my findings on Birch Creek, a tributary of the Yukon River, an area that I feel to be inhabited by perhaps two pairs of tree-nesting peregrines. This area along Birch Creek should be thoroughly searched to obtain corroboration for these nestings. There is a record (Dall and Bannister, 1869) of one site along the Yukon River where the birds utilized a fallen tree. The biology of tree-nesting habits is not understood, but tree nests appear to be prevalent in some peregrine populations and unknown in others inhabiting similar habitats.

The density of peregrines along the Colville River, on the Arctic Slope, has not diminished since Cade's last survey in 1959; in fact, it may have increased. The middle stretch of the Colville River, between the mouth of the Oolamnagavik River and Umiat Mountain, received the greatest attention from Cade. The highest concentration of peregrines on this more-or-less 75-mile (120-km) stretch was 11 pairs in 1958. So large a number was thought to have been possible because no gyrfalcons bred there. Consequently all sections of cliff were available for peregrines. In 1964 I examined this same section of river, part of it by boat with Max and Jon Denton and part by helicopter, except for the upper 2 miles (3.2 km), that is above what Cade called "Upper Crescent Bluff." On this 2-mile stretch of the river, the greatest number of eyries found by Cade in any one year was two. Eleven pairs of falcons were present on the remainder of the river in 1964, although it is not known if all had nests. This is two more than Cade found in any one year. The year 1964 was exceptional in that five pairs of gyrfalcons and a lone individual gyrfalcon also occupied cliffs on the middle section of the river. Peregrines and gyrfalcons occupied three bluffs concurrently.

In the cases of joint occupancy of bluffs, the sites that each species used differ markedly. The peregrines were usually at the brink of a slope or on a bluff to which a person could easily walk, whereas the gyrfalcons were on vertical faces of a cliff, usually under an overhang accessible only with the aid of a rope. The cliffs occupied concurrently by both species were, using Cade's names, Red-stone Pinnacles, Ten-mile Bluff, and Five-mile Bluff. During Cade's study (1960:172, see his Table 1), gyrfalcons were never seen to occupy Five-mile Bluff at the same time peregrines nested there, and only two bluffs ever housed both species in any one year. I think availability of food was responsible for the high population of gyrfalcons, and supporting data for this conclusion will be presented elsewhere (MS in preparation); the reason for the large number of peregrines is unknown. The fledging success of the peregrines was low. At four eyries within 10 miles (16 km) up and down river from

Umiat, only three nestlings were fledged. In the general vicinity of the Colville River, four areas of bluff on the Killik, five on the Anaktuvuk, four on the Chandler, and two on the Nanashuk rivers were examined. All but three of the 15 bluffs were occupied by either peregrine or gyrfalcon, and one was occupied by both. I was able to make a thorough inspection of the north slope mainly because of my association with oil geologists working by means of helicopters. The geology field parties would stop at, measure, and take rock samples from almost every exposed outcrop available, both along the rivers and in upland areas, from the coast to the Brooks Range.

Individual pairs of peregrines that experienced nesting failure on the Colville differed individually in their subsequent behavior; some left the site almost immediately, and others remained for up to 2 months. The falcons at Ten-mile Bluff lost their young about a week after hatching, around 28 June, but remained at the bluff until late August. At Umiat Mountain the last egg disappeared between 20 and 25 June, and the adults were gone by 1 July. At Coal-seam Bluff the young were within a week of fledging on 18 August; on 21 August they had disappeared, and the adults were not evident.

As of 1960 (Cade) no falcons had been reported to nest on the Kenai Peninsula, some 25,000 sq miles (65,000 sq km). However, David Roseneau of Anchorage informed me (pers. comm.) that peregrines are nesting at Moose Pass and Homer on the Kenai Peninsula, and Richard Bishop of the University of Alaska reported them (pers. comm.) in the general vicinity of Seward. These reports would extend the known breeding range considerably in Alaska, at least to the extreme limits of this 25,000-sq-mile area.

Cade mentions a scarcity of peregrines in southeast Alaska, with only seven eyries reported. Other workers have speculated that a high population density should logically extend up along the Alexander Archipelago since peregrines are so numerous on the Queen Charlotte Islands and Forrester Island, where the physiography resembles that along the Alexander Archipelago. In support of Cade's thesis, I offer the following: In my examination of more than 100 immature museum specimens of the subspecies *F. p. pealei*, taken mostly in the breeding season, those from the Aleutian Islands and Alaska Peninsula are more or less uniformly dark whereas those from the Queen Charlotte area range from dark to a pale color type. I do not, however, have statistics on the relative percentages of these phenotypes on the Queen Charlottes. The striking differences in uniformity of phenotypes between the two areas could be interpreted as a result of a hiatus in the geographic range, lack of panmixia, or at least restricted gene flow as would result in an area such as a portion of the northern Archipelago with an extremely sparse population. The difference may, however, be a function of linear distribution and sedentary tendencies rather than density or simply sampling error. It is clear that more data are needed on the population structure and density of this species in southeast Alaska.

FALL MOVEMENT

David Roseneau told me of an island off the Kenai Peninsula where migrants in numbers apparently comparable to those of the Maryland-Virginia and Gulf of Mexico coastlines appear around the first of September. This area should be investigated further. Banding might be feasible and would be extremely helpful in defining the migration route and winter range of this population. Along a 52-mile (84-km) stretch of the Alcan Highway in interior Alaska and a small portion of Canada on 11 September 1963 I saw seven peregrines. Some were soaring, and others were in direct flight. None were seen in company with others, and I assumed that all were migrating. No peregrines were seen on the remainder of the Alcan Highway during the 5-day trip southward to Calgary, Canada, and the route followed by these falcons migrating out of Alaska and adjacent Yukon is unknown to me. It would seem important to know whether the route followed is a coastal, inland, or random movement. One banding recovery (see Lincoln, 1928; bird banded in Yukon ca. 69° N lat. and recovered in the intermountain area [Utah]) suggests an overland route for at least some individuals. Twenty-one pigeon hawks were, however, seen along the highway. They appeared to be following the highway, and it is highly likely that these small falcons follow, and use as a food source to some extent, the thousands of Lapland longspurs that travel the open route formed by the highway as one means of crossing the forested interior of Alaska and Canada.

POPULATION STRUCTURE

Numerical and quantitative data on the percentage of survival of first-year Arctic falcons are wanting. I saw one first-year falcon, and Cade reported that none of the 250 peregrines seen by him at the eyrie was a first-year bird and that only six first-year birds were known to him among all of those that had been collected in Arctic Alaska. Likewise Bond (1946) and Hickey (1942) reported few first-year birds either seen in the field or as specimens. It has been suggested that mortality is extremely high among juveniles during their first fall and winter; see, for example, Cade (1960:187). In November and December 1964, however, I critically examined 29 museum specimens having a mixture of adult and immature plumage. Of those having a mixture of the two plumages, four females and two males had brood patches. They came from all parts of the breeding range; nine were from the southern Hudson Bay area, obtained between July and September. One male taken in July was obtained on an island off the Alaskan Arctic coast nearly 100 miles (160 km) north of the known breeding range. Some individuals, almost certainly from the Arctic migrant population, were taken in July and August in mid-latitudes of the United States. A reasonable postulate, then, also suggested by Cade (1960:187), is that first-year falcons not engaged in breeding may pass their first summer within or at the periphery of their breeding range, and are not obvious because they are not associated with eyrie sites where falcons are most often seen. Probably the numbers of spring-returning immature falcons are larger than heretofore supposed, and the factors just mentioned may account for these falcons not being observed. (In 1966 a first-year female had a nest on the Yukon River. The nest contained two fertile eggs. In 1967 one first-year female was seen on the Colville River.)

Some nonbreeding adults may summer north or south of their breeding range. Evidence supporting this is provided by a female (band no. 49–645790) banded as an immature in October 1951, on the east coast of the United States (the date suggests an Arctic migrant) and reportedly recovered on 5 May, 2 years later, in South America. By 5 May, pairs are establishing themselves at eyries in interior Alaska. Likewise, both adults and year-old immatures have been seen in the past 4 years by Robert Sundell, US National Museum, and myself on Farmington Bay Refuge, Utah, in June and early July. They were not seen in late July or August, a time when, if the adults were breeding, they should have been similarly observed. None of the bluffs along the adjacent mountains that previously supported falcons, or cliffs which could support them, contained active eyries at these times. I believe that the birds observed probably were from the Arctic population and not breeding that year. This idea is consistent with data from collected specimens. Statistics on the percentage of first-year birds lost in migration and answers to the following questions are greatly to be desired. What are the effects of this loss upon the population? What percentage loss can the northern population absorb? The migratory populations are exposed for brief periods in autumn and spring to the same environments as resident populations in the United States and southern Canada, and some individuals apparently are exposed for 6–8 months to this same environment in the southern United States. If pesticidal-spraying operations are indeed a principal cause of the disappearance of eastern peregrine populations, it should by all means be determined to what levels of contaminants the migrants are exposed, and what levels they can tolerate without deleterious effect.

The increased and concerted efforts of geologists and seismograph crews exploring for petroleum on the Arctic Slope of Alaska may have an adverse effect on the cliff-nesting raptor population. Nearly every geologist carries side arms but, at the same time, all of those with whom I was acquainted had a high regard for wildlife. I have heard them remark several times, however, that they would like to kill those noisy hawks. Indeed it can become nerve-racking to have the continuous screaming and incessant stooping of peregrines and rough-legged hawks during the 2 or 3 hours that one is working on a cliff or bluff. I was told by numerous geologists that, while they were working on a bluff, they had observed young raptors suddenly frightened into prematurely leaving their nests only to fall into the river. The survival rate among such birds is unknown. Actual shooting of the birds will occur, of course, but probably will be negligible because of the difficulty of hitting a flying bird with a handgun, and because most workers on the Slope realize that the birds are protected. However, one real threat is this: The bluffs are so low that, when a person approaches them, he is near enough to the eyrie site to excite the birds. In one instance where the helicopter was set down a good 600–700 yards (550–640 m) from the bluff, the falcons began flying and screaming. Undue neglect of eggs or young for extended periods in an area where the environment can become extremely harsh could cause a high mortality.

SUMMARY

The peregrines in Alaska do not appear to be decreasing. No evidence of decreasing population or reproductive capacity was noted there. The number of breeding adults seems to be maintaining itself at a constant level, and the population is considered numerically healthy. The migratory routes and wintering grounds of these peregrines are poorly known. Since the population apparently is not decreasing in Alaska and is convenient to work with, in such places as the Arctic Slope, accurate records should be made of population fluctuations in view of the decreasing trends in other populations.

LITERATURE CITED

Bond, R. M. 1946. The peregrine population of western North America. Condor, 48(3):101–116.

Cade, T. J. 1960. Ecology of the peregrine and gyrfalcon populations in Alaska. Univ. Calif. Publ. Zool., 63(3):151–290.

Dall, W. H., and H. M. Bannister. 1868. List of the birds of Alaska, with biographical notes. Trans. Chicago Acad. Sci., 1:267–325.

Hickey, J. J. 1942. Eastern population of the duck hawk. Auk, 59(2):176–204.

Lincoln, F. C. 1928. Bird banding in America. Ann. Report. Smithsonian Inst. for 1927, Publ. 2942:331–354.

White, C. M. 1964. Comments concerning Alaskan peregrine and gyrfalcon populations. J. N. Amer. Falconry Assoc., 3(1):9–11.

CHAPTER 3

THE KNOWN STATUS OF THE PEREGRINE FALCON IN BRITISH COLUMBIA

Frank L. Beebe

This paper presents the results of some additional explorations, mapping, and census work carried out since my earlier publication (Beebe, 1960) on the marine peregrines of the northwest Pacific Coast. A second objective of the paper is to review the implications of the great gaps in our present knowledge of the distribution of *Falco peregrinus* in the northern wildernesses of North America, for almost all of the mapping of peregrine sites that I have been able to do in British Columbia has been along the coastal strip. I have very little data from other parts of the province and none that is firsthand. But before I go on to discuss the rather small area from which there is recent and authentic information, a brief outline should be made of some of the much larger areas in British Columbia where peregrines are known to occur, but in which no organized effort has been made to locate eyrie-sites, let alone to assess populations.

THE INTERIOR REGIONS OF BRITISH COLUMBIA

The province of British Columbia is interesting in that there are three large areas of wilderness, or near-wilderness, in the interior where breeding peregrines are known to occur, and two almost equally large regions where they are not known to occur at all. The regions where breeding peregrines are known to occur will be outlined first.

The central and southern interior (Fig. 3.1) is an area of relatively dry, sparsely to well-timbered plateaus cut by open, grassy valleys that extend from the United States border northward for some 300 miles (480 km) to the vicinity of Prince George; that is, to about the halfway point, latitudinally, of the province. This region is triangular in shape, widest in the north where it extends some 250 miles (400 km) westward of Prince George to the eastern edge of the Coast Range mountains, but narrowing to only 60–70 miles (96–112 km) at the United States border, and bounded on the east by the complex of very heavily timbered ranges of the Selkirk, Monashee, and Cariboo mountain systems. The plateau area thus defined is drained by generally southward-flowing rivers incised into a land surface that tilts in the opposite direction, with the result that the canyons are much deeper in the south than in the north. Yet even at Prince George the canyon of the Fraser is some 500 ft (152 m) in depth. For the most part the roads in this region avoid these canyons. Even where settlements, farming, and ranching do occur, as in the Thompson and Chilcotin river valleys, there are many sections of the canyons that are so steep and precipitous as to remain almost primeval. By far the most extensive of these canyons is that of the Fraser River, which extends from just south of Prince George for some 300 miles (480 km) to the south, faced on each side with cliffs and badlands averaging about 2,500 ft (762 km) in height. Cutting into the Fraser are the extensive lateral canyon systems of the Thompson and Chilcotin, as well as a multitude of smaller streams, some of which, while short, have fearfully steep, narrow canyons of great depth. Peregrine eyries are reported by British Columbia Wildlife Branch personnel who have flown small aircraft along the Fraser on big-game counts, but there is no information as to numbers. Most of these sites are considered to be almost inaccessible to man. There is one rather well-known site of both peregrine and prairie falcon at Dog Creek Canyon, a small lateral canyon entering the Fraser from the east about 250 miles (400 km) north of the United States border. This site is interesting in that it is the farthest north prairie falcon eyrie site known on this continent.

Two other very large areas of true wilderness suitable to peregrines occur in the more northerly sections of British Columbia. One of these is that part of the province that lies east of the Rocky Mountains and drains eastward to the Mackenzie River by way of the Peace, Sikanni Chief, Fort Nelson, Hay, and Liard rivers. This region belongs to the Great Plains section of the continent and is a vast country of flat-lying boreal forest into which the rivers are incised to a depth of 600–800 ft (183–244 m) in the west, but with the depth of the incision decreasing

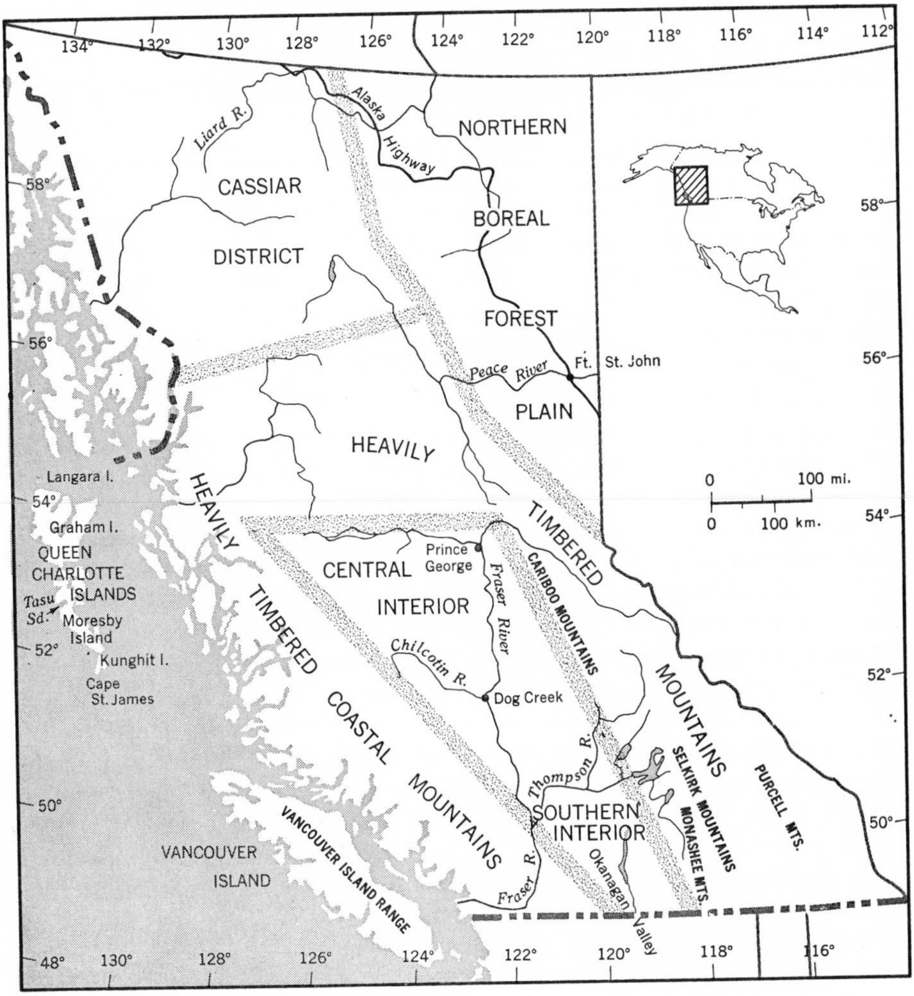

Fig. 3.1. Physiographic regions of British Columbia. UW Cartographic Lab.

toward the northeast. Again, very little is known about the peregrine population of this region except that, unless they are nesting in trees or open muskeg (and of either of these we have absolutely no records), the falcons here are of necessity strictly confined to the watercourses. I know of a brood of young that was taken from the Peace River in 1964 and of two eyries overlooking a small lake near Fort St. John in 1963; also a brood of flying young was seen in 1961 along the Alaska Highway where it parallels the Liard River. The Alaska Highway cuts through the western margin of this area but is the only road in the entire region, the area of which is as large as the entire state of Wisconsin.

An even larger area of equal or even more wilderness character is the region immediately to the westward, including the northern Rocky Mountains and west to the eastern foot of the Coast Range, generally known as the Cassiar District. This is a region of heavily glaciated hills and low mountains, the central highland of which forms the true headwaters of some of the largest rivers of the continent; the Yukon, Skeena, Stikine, Peace, and Liard all originate in this highland. The area is interesting, from the point of view of good falcon habitat, in that most of it is open, the trees being limited to the valley floors. The vegetation and look of the country are definitely subarctic in character, and large numbers of ptarmigan are present. There are reports of falcon eyries in these uplands from Wildlife Branch personnel, but these could be either peregrine or gyrfalcon eyries, or perhaps both. At any rate, there is certainly a good possibility of an upland population of peregrines breeding in this region and northward into the southern Yukon Territory, for extensive ranges of good cliffs are very much part of the scenery. The British Columbia section of this general region, almost all of it wilderness, is larger in area than all of Ireland.

There are three large areas of British Columbia from which, to date, there is no evidence at all of breeding peregrines; and, if falcons do occur in these regions, they must be very widely scattered indeed. These are the regions of heavily timbered mountains: the Coast and Vancouver Island ranges; the Cariboo; the Selkirk, Monashee, and Purcell ranges, and the western slope of the Rocky Mountains; also the broad belt of continuously mountainous country that extends right across the province north of Prince George. The only open areas in these mountains are at relatively high elevations above the timberline, and if there are falcons in such country we have, as yet, no evidence of it.

In only one rather small section of British Columbia where peregrines are known to occur does there appear to be any decline in numbers of breeding birds. This is in the flat-bottomed, glacial Okanagan Valley, the floor of which is highly suitable to agriculture, and into which the river has not cut a deep canyon although the sides of the valley in many places take the form of magnificent cliffs. In the early days of settlement this valley was noted for its peregrines, and Allan Brooks, J. A. Munro, and other naturalists of the generation just passed knew of many eyrie sites. I have reports of two prairie falcon eyries in the valley in 1965 but none of peregrines, and the old site on the high cliff east of Okanagan Falls, occupied almost continuously until about 15 years ago, was completely deserted in 1965. This valley has at once the highest density of human population and the most highly developed agriculture to be found in the interior of British Columbia. With tree-fruits being the main crop, there has been very heavy use of agricultural sprays in recent years. Western bluebirds and western meadowlarks, abundant in the valley 10 years ago, have almost disappeared, but California quail, mourning doves, and starlings abound.

THE COASTAL REGION

Aside from the vanishing population of the Okanagan Valley, the only population of peregrines in British Columbia that has received any really organized attention is the highly concentrated, and in some ways more easily accessible, coastal population. When I wrote of these peregrines (Beebe, 1960), I stated that I thought it to be a saturated population. I have seen nothing since to make me change this opinion. However, some four more expeditions to the Charlottes and the outer Vancouver Island coast since that time, and especially the Wildlife Branch census of eyrie-sites on the Queen Charlotte Islands in 1965, have helped to fill in the pattern of distribution, at which I previously was only able to guess. By 1960 I had mapped eyrie sites along the west side of Vancouver Island and the extreme northwest tip of the Queen Charlotte Islands only. Since then I have been all the way around the Queen Charlottes; so the only part of the Canadian Pacific Coast I have not checked for peregrines is the complex of islets along the mainland coast between the Alaska border and the north end of Vancouver Island.

In 1960 I made a guess, based on the information then at hand, that the main population of peregrines on the Queen Charlotte Islands would be found to extend southward from Langara Island along the outer, exposed coastline. I had some doubts about any significant breeding population being found on the eastern side of the main islands. This has not proven to be the case. The important finding, shown very clearly now, is that in this habitat the falcons are much less closely associated with cliffs, exposed coast, or any other physical feature of the landscape, than they are with a high availability of prey.

Two areas of very high density of population have been found, one on the complex of islets extending southward from Langara Island down the west side of Graham Island on south to the vicinity of Tasu on the west coast of Moresby Island. The other area of high density extends from Anthony Island south to Cape St. James, then northward along the east side of Moresby Island to Cumshewa. Most interesting, in a sense, is that the west coast of Moresby Island from Anthony Island to Tasu was almost devoid of falcons, and this despite a procession of what must be some of the grandest cliffs along the entire Pacific Coast. But this section of coastline is devoid of small islets and this, indirectly, is the reason for the sparse population of peregrines. The two species of small alcids and the two species of petrels that comprise the main food resource for peregrines in this region seem to have an absolute requirement for islands below a certain size. The reason for this is still far from clear, but there are alcid and petrel colonies on both Kunghit Island and Langara Island, the two medium-sized islands at the opposite ends of the Queen Charlotte group; in addition, these colonies have been found on every one of the smaller islets that have been examined on both coasts of the two main islands. I had always thought that there was the possibility that such colonies might also occur on some of the more exposed and cliffy headlands on the west coast of Moresby Island as well, but careful examination has disclosed no evidence of this, and the alcid and petrel colonies do seem to be confined to the smaller islands. The falcons in this region, attached as they are to this food supply, seem to be, therefore, quite closely associated with these same smaller islands and islets.

The Wildlife Branch census of nesting pairs, undertaken in 1965, was originally scheduled to be confined to the Queen Charlotte Islands, and was to be a fairly complete survey of the entire group. However, time and weather did not permit this, and the survey was confined to Moresby and Kunghit islands, and associated islets, only. Along the reasonably quiet and protected waters of the east side, from Cumshewa to Cape St. James, a small, 30-ft (9.1-m) launch was used, which permitted a reasonably close approach to the shorelines and a fairly good count, although even here some pairs were probably missed. Since there was a great deal of mileage to cover and time was limited, the method of counting did not permit much time to be spent at any potential site. The procedure was to run the boat as close inshore as possible under any cliff or open slope that looked like it might be a possible nesting site and there to fire a heavy-calibre rifle bullet against the cliff-face. If two falcons were seen following the shot, the site was listed as being occupied; if only one falcon was seen, the cliff was listed as being probably occupied. The official count, in the areas covered by the census, is based on the number of places where two birds were seen. In the areas farther north, not covered by the census (the west coast of Graham Island and the Langara Island area), it is based on falconers' records.

The official count almost certainly is in error and too low, for it is extremely doubtful if this procedure would locate all pairs. The reasons for error I would list as follows: first, it is known that all peregrines in this region do not necessarily nest on cliffs; second, it is known that some pairs are on cliffs or hill-slopes either so well hidden by timber as to be invisible from the water or sufficiently far back from the water as to make it unlikely that the adults would be disturbed by the shot; third, the birds need not necessarily be in the close vicinity of the cliff at the time the shot is fired; fourth, they may not be on the particular area of cliff that looks good to the human observer and may accordingly be missed even if the shot does put them off at some distance to left or right of the area under close observation. They may be missed in other ways. The shot may fail to put them off, or they may escape being observed even when in plain sight; this last is particularly true in those situations where the report of the rifle puts into the air hundreds, and in some cases thousands, of puffins, cormorants, and gulls.

From Cape St. James northward to Tasu, with the exception of a small area east of Anthony Island, the coast of the Queen Charlottes is very poorly charted and the location of many reefs is not known, nor are water-depths near shore. Due to the great oceanic swells that are a permanent feature of the open water, it was necessary to attempt to survey this strip of coastline from a much larger vessel than was used on the east side of the islands. Here the combination of a relatively large boat, uncharted inshore water, heavy swells or breaking seas, and miles of continuous high cliffs may have combined to make for a considerably greater error in the census than was likely from the east coast. Nevertheless, on 31 May 1965, the weather and seas were such as to permit some 40 miles (64 km) of the west coast of Moresby Island to be worked from a skiff powered by an outboard motor, and this produced a reasonably intimate check of a representative stretch of this coastline. Only one pair of peregrines was seen, and they, significantly, were on a very high, precipitous islet, the only islet in the entire stretch of coastline. Very few alcids or petrels were observed, and the evidence is that the population of falcons between Anthony Island and Tasu is much lower than along other, islet-dotted stretches of the Queen Charlotte Islands coastline.

The census lists some 80 pairs for the Queen Charlotte Islands. My own estimate, based on prior experience, is that there must be at least 100 pairs of peregrines that annually bring off from one to four young; and this in turn must mean a population approximately one-third greater than this that attempts to breed annually, if the nesting failure of these falcons is roughly the same as that observed for other raptors.

This population of peregrines is probably as well situated as any on the continent for any intensive study or research project that might be undertaken in relation to this species. Since this country was depopulated of the aboriginal human residents by smallpox in 1885, the falcons have remained entirely undisturbed. The series of eyrie sites extending from Cumshewa south to Cape St. James, some thirty sites at least, is particularly well located. The northernmost of the series, on the Cumshewa islets, is only about 2 hours by boat from the big airport at Sandpit; the east side waters are relatively safe, and there are always protected anchorages. Most important of all, the entire series can be visited in a single day in calm weather. Since 1962, when this series was discovered by James H. Enderson, Donald V. Hunter, Jr., and myself, it has been regularly visited by falconers, and young birds have been taken under permit from the British Columbia Wildlife Branch. Even if this disturbance is detrimental, which personally I doubt, it has not been of sufficient duration to have, as yet, any significant effect.

ACKNOWLEDGMENTS

The writer wishes to thank the following individuals and officials for their help and cooperation: James Hatter, BC Fish and Wildlife Branch, who made the arrangements which made the 1965 peregrine census of the Queen Charlotte Islands possible; G. Clifford Carl, Provincial Museum, Victoria, BC, for permitting Museum personnel to participate in the census; C. J. Guiguet, Provincial Museum, Victoria, BC, who was in charge of the survey; B. Gates, BC Fish and Wildlife Branch, who participated in the census and officially represented his department; J. H. Fox, BC Fish and Wildlife Branch, who was in charge of the Departmental launch on the trip from Sandspit to Cape St. James; the federal officials who, on request, placed the Federal Patrol Vessel "Sooke Post" at our disposal for the attempt at censusing the outer coast; and Captain Kenneth Harley of the "Sooke Post" and his crew, whose skill and seamanship made the attempt worthwhile.

SUMMARY

Breeding peregrine falcons are present in four major regions of British Columbia, much of which is still wilderness. No studies at all have been made in two very large regions in the north. Little more is known about the central and southern regions except for some evidence that the species has seriously decreased and possibly vanished from the Okanagan Valley in the extreme south. A saturated population of some 80–100 pairs of peregrines in the Queen Charlotte Islands inhabits two areas of very high density and is more associated with availability of prey than with cliffs. No noticeable change in the numbers of these birds has been detected.

LITERATURE CITED

Beebe, F. L. 1960. The marine peregrines of the northwest Pacific Coast. Condor, 62(3):145–189.

CHAPTER 4

THE STATUS OF THE PEREGRINE FALCON IN THE NORTHWEST

Morlan W. Nelson

The purpose of this paper is to review the present status of the peregrine falcon in Utah, Idaho, Oregon, Washington, western Wyoming, and western Montana; and to discuss the ecological factors making for a long-term population change of peregrine in this region.* Utah has been included in this region because of the author's field experience there and the need at this time to review peregrine population changes in as many western states as possible.

The peregrine has always been a rare bird in the intermountain west. At the same time, to those who knew the birds intimately, several nesting sites could be found within a 100-mile (160-km) radius of any of the major cities. In 1938, a trained student of falcons could locate the peregrine falcon's eyrie without too much trouble whether he was in New Mexico, Utah, Idaho, Oregon, or almost any other western state with the possible exception of Nevada. Observations there are too rare to interpret.

FIELD OBSERVATIONS

In 1939, my soil survey work took me to Utah. Within the first 2 weeks of work and observations on the weekends, I found three pairs of peregrines in northern Utah, designated below as eyries U1, U2 and U3.

*The information and opinions expressed in this paper do not represent the official position of the Soil Conservation Service, US Department of Agriculture, but only those of the author.

In the first year of observation, the prairie falcons attempted to take over the U1 site. The aerial battles were spectacular with a fierce and awesome beauty. The prairie falcons seemed to win these battles much to my surprise. The battles were not definite and always ended in a sort of draw, with observers deciding that the prairie falcons won. They had command of the air, but when the birds parted they went back to their respective sites. In this case, the eyries were less than half a mile (800 m) apart. By 1941 the peregrines at U1 did not return to nest, although they were seen near the nesting sites as late as 1946.

During the period 1939–42, I observed from 9 to 14 peregrine eyries depending upon whether some sites were alternate nests of the same pair. In looking back at the situation, I suspect there were only 9 or 10 pairs. The prairie falcons were steadily taking over the nesting sites of these birds, often without a fight of any sort. The peregrines did not seem to come back or did for only a short time. About 50% of these sites were taken over by prairie falcons before 1942. The fighting between the two species had no significance other than being spectacular to watch.

From 1946 to 1948, my headquarters were in Salt Lake City, giving me an opportunity to study the same nesting sites formerly studied in Utah. Only three or four were left, and these birds did not nest each year. By this time, I knew the birds' characteristic behavior of using alternate sites. The birds were not in the same areas. Other falconers were making the same observations. The favorite sites were not occupied, but every once in a while a pair would spend a few days in some unusual place. The prairie falcons continued to take up the old peregrine sites.

In the fall of 1948, I transferred to research in the Soil Conservation Service as Snow Survey Supervisor for the Columbia Basin. This work took me through the states of Idaho, Washington, Oregon, and the western parts of Wyoming and Montana. As the title indicates, a great portion of the work was high in the mountains during both summer and winter.

At this time, I met Richard M. Bond, also working for the Soil Conservation Service as a biologist, stationed in Portland, Oregon. He gave me a list of over 40 peregrine eyries that he and colleagues had checked prior to 1948. All eyries were in the above states, and I began to check them out. Before Bond gave me the list, he stated that he had checked several and that the numbers were going down steadily. He was also a falconer and had followed the nesting pairs along the Columbia River very closely for several years. Another observer, L. L. Schramm of Portland, reported the same steady drop of nesting pairs along the Columbia River and the Oregon coast.

One of the first dramatic changes was on the Malheur National Wildlife Refuge in Oregon (Fig. 4.1). There were three eyries prior to Bond's check; all but one had been deserted sometime before 1952. After 1952, I made several checks for these birds, and they had never been back. The

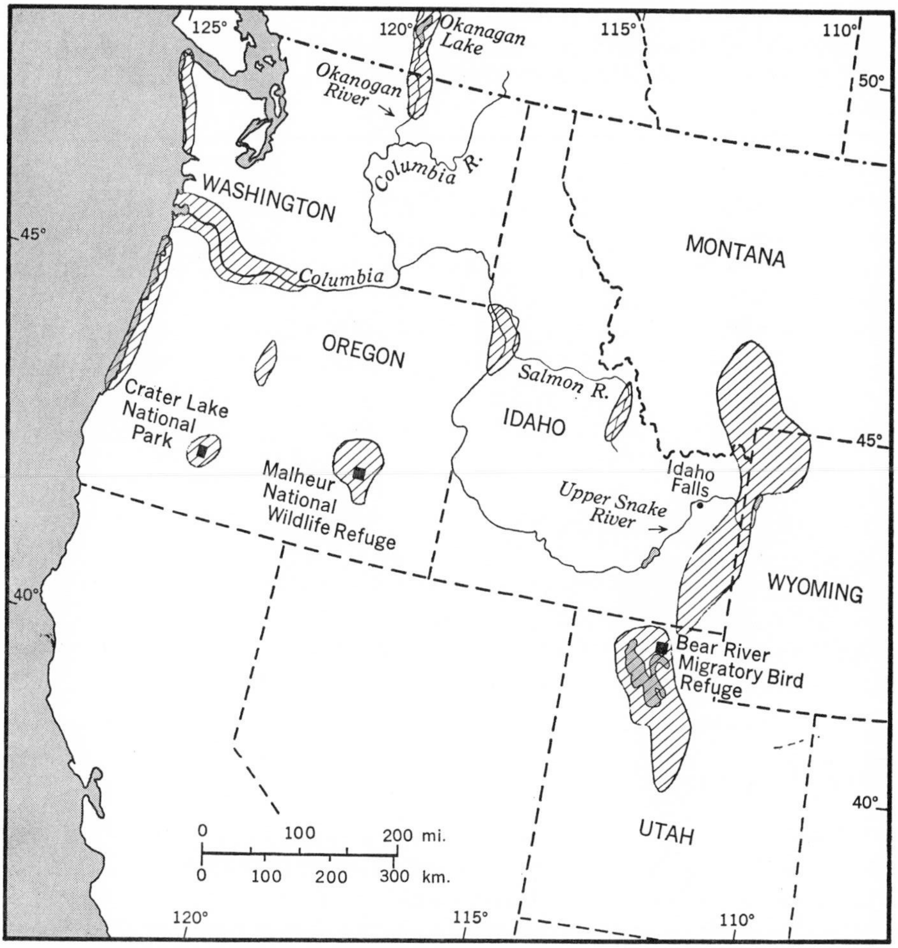

Fig. 4.1. The six-state area included in the present study. The hatched areas are regions where nesting peregrines were formerly found in some numbers. UW Cartographic Lab.

refuge manager knew of these eyries and reported they were not occupied at the time I checked; the birds have not returned since.

This area was once ideal for the peregrine and probably still is in a series of wet years. It has protection, but now lacks water in dry years, and shorebirds are limited. Although there are no peregrines in the area, prairie falcons still nest on the refuge and adjacent to it.

The nesting sites on U1, adjacent to the Bear River Migratory Bird Refuge in Utah, and on the Malheur in Oregon are very similar, and the birds shifted about the same time. In these two areas, we have typical habitat left in limited amount on the refuges. The peregrine falcon was often found with botulism prior to 1950 on both of these refuges. The falcons ate the ducks affected with botulism and lost their power to fly. Thus, they were picked up with the sick ducks. In 1 year, there were six peregrine falcons taken into the Bear River Refuge headquarters with botulism. They all lived and were released. To my knowledge, this has not happened in the past 10 years.

The peregrine sites studied by Bond and Schramm on the Oregon coast and the Columbia River have been reduced in number. Some of these eyries were active in 1952; but the cliffs facing the ocean are very difficult to check, and more field work is necessary.

In 1958, I found three of the old sites along the coast. In 1964, these sites were checked and the birds were not there. The favorite sites, completely protected by the ocean, have not been used consistently. There is no competition from the prairie falcon at any of these sites along the Columbia River west of The Dalles, Oregon, and on to the coast. In fact, the prairie falcon is extremely rare west of the summit of the Cascade Mountains in Oregon and Washington.

Bond (pers. comm.) reported the peregrine to be a common bird along the Okanogan River in Washington and British Columbia in the years prior to 1948. When I checked the area in the middle fifties, there were no peregrines at the old sites. I have not checked in the last 5 years, but qualified observers have not been able to find these birds in that area.

An interesting letter from Allan Brooks written in 1937 (to J. J. Hickey) adds specific observations near and on Okanagan Lake, British Columbia, as follows:

> From 1897 to 1907 the duck hawk was a regular nester in this region. I knew of 5 eyries on Okanagan Lake and about 10 in the region between the south end of the lake and the international boundary.
>
> In 1906 when covering this region, I saw 4 occupied eyries of duck hawks in going down the lake in a canoe. Between Penticton and Osoyoos Lake I saw about 7 others, and other ones were reported to me. In a very high cliff at the foot of Vaseux Lake, there were 3 pairs of duck hawks in about half a mile [0.8 km] of cliff, all nests absolutely inaccessible, nor could the birds be shot as the cliff was 2 gunshots high. I visited this cliff last year, there were no duck hawks but several prairie falcons were seen, though not nesting in this cliff. At a cliff near the north end of Osoyoos Lake in 1906, there were 2 nests of duck hawks and 1 of prairie falcon. I went down to within 6 ft [2.4 m] of the latter, and the female bird was continually swooped at by a male duck hawk, the male of the former never showed up to protect its nest.
>
> In 1922 I visited this cliff, there were 2 pairs of prairie falcons nesting but no duck hawks. Also many praire falcons at other eyries within a radius of 5 miles [8 km].
>
> The last duck hawk to nest near my home here was in 1929, the male was an adult, the female a juvenile; I had her within 10 ft [3 m.] and could see every feather. The following year this eyrie was occupied by prairie falcons.

Other sites in Washington along the Columbia River and the coast that I checked for Bond did not produce nesting peregrines. The great cliffs of the Columbia River are ideal for these birds, but only one or two pairs remain of the 13 pairs once observed. It was not possible to check all of the sites that Bond originally surveyed, and I did not keep the scientific record that is really necessary, believing at the time that my observations were merely a reconnaissance.

The coast birds were the last to change, and they have not been reduced as drastically. It is not possible to check out any of these areas with the same detail as in regions east of the Missouri. There are so many nesting cliffs on the coast of Washington and Oregon and in the intermountain west that we will never know completely. However, one who has spent most of his life observing birds of prey will find them in any area if they are there. To make a scientific check of these birds is a major research problem.

To sum up the situation, I would estimate that 80–90% of the nesting birds in Utah, Idaho, Oregon, Washington, western Wyoming, and western Montana have shifted from their former nesting sites. There were four sites visited in Idaho, five in western Montana, and two in western Wyoming.

CHANGE IN CLIMATE

The change in climate that started about 1876 may be a factor in this change of peregrine nesting habits. Hydrologists, studying the flow of rivers, find a significant shift down, starting in 1933 or earlier. Likewise, average temperatures in the area have been rising (Fig. 4.2).

Idaho observers, who have been here for 60 and 70 years, say that the black-necked stilt and avocet were once common in southwestern Idaho. They have been relatively rare since the middle thirties. It is also true that the swamp area surrounding the thousands of lakes and ponds without outlet in the intermountain west has been significantly reduced, not by drainage, but rather by a shift in precipitation and temperatures.

A slight shift downward in average precipitation, coupled with a rise in average temperature, results in drastic changes in productivity of soils that are critically dependent upon natural rainfall. There is considerable evidence that a drop in nesting populations of shorebirds dependent upon saturated soils in the intermountain west has been similar to that of the peregrine when considered from 1930, or earlier, to the present. The shorebirds are far harder to evaluate, but the general trend seems to be worth studying and may correlate with the peregrine reduction in the same ecologic areas.

There is another consideration with respect to temperature. When spring temperatures rise, cloud cover is less in May, June, and July. In

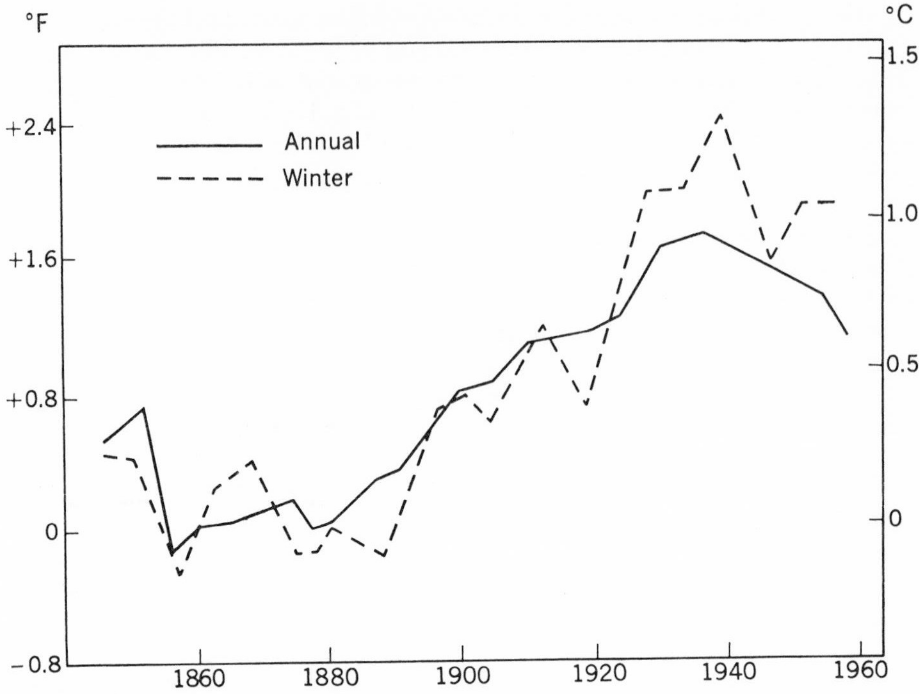

Fig. 4.2. Temperature trends (expressed as departures from the mean) between latitudes 40° and 70°N that appear to have affected peregrine populations. After Mitchell (1961). UW Cartographic Lab.

this region, the direct rays of the sun on birds of prey, just out of the down and into feathers, can kill them in less than one-half hour of exposure between 10:00 A.M. and 5:00 P.M. The temperature must be near 90°F (32°C) for this to occur, but such temperatures are frequent in May and June in the intermountain area below 6,000 ft (1,829 m). Any eyrie of falcon, hawk, or eagle that is without shade during such a day will lose its young birds. Occasionally the death of one young bird will give shade to the other and save it.

It was my grim experience in June 1962 to watch three golden eagle eyries lose all their birds in this way. At the Castle Butte site, my son and I watched the adult eagle stand over the young with her wings spread and her beak open until she could stand it no longer. This was about 3:00 P.M. at an eyrie that would have been in the shade by 4:00 P.M. The two young died before we could climb the cliff and go down to the eyrie. The temperature was unusual, being between 98° and 102°F (37° and 39°C) on that day. We estimated that 30% of the young eagles at 28 eyries we observed were killed by the sun during the hot period. In 1965, there were no eagles killed by direct rays of the sun—we did not have such conditions during the nesting period, and the eagles had an unusually good year. The same was true of the prairie falcons for this year, although they are not as subject to direct rays of the sun as the eagle. They usually nest in deeper holes with better overhangs.

The peregrine eyries that I have found do not show the same respect for the sun as those of the prairie falcon and the gyrfalcon. This is just as true of the birds nesting within the Arctic Circle as in the intermountain area. There is not a serious problem in the Arctic, but below the 6,000-ft (1,829-m) elevation in the mountain states peregrines are doomed to nesting failure in May, June, or July, if exposed to direct rays of the sun.

Furthermore, the peregrines are far more sensitive to heat and cold, and the direct rays of the sun, than either the prairie falcon or gyrfalcon. This is an obvious point with trained falcons and is supported by observations in the wild by the author and other falconers.

The peregrines are late nesters when compared to the prairie falcon, golden eagle, or the gyrfalcon. This late nesting makes the young birds far more vulnerable to heat and the sun than the other birds at the southern latitudes below 50° North. We should consider the possibility that the peregrines moved north or up in elevation, as suggested by Enderson's recent work, at the time when precipitation started to drop and average temperatures climbed steadily, even up into the Arctic areas.

In the intermountain area, falconers, egg collectors, or photographers have not been the problem. There was practically no pesticide problem when the decline started. It is something far bigger and more insidious. At the present time, the precipitation, temperature, and shooting factors are the only parameters which have some possible correlation with the decline. Research may point out that other birds were affected the same way in this region, but a tremendous amount of work remains to be done to test these hypotheses.

On my trip with T. J. Cade to visit the Arctic peregrines and gyrfalcons, I was most impressed by the nesting peregrines along the Colville River. They simply looked crowded and desperate for nesting sites. Those birds living on slopes without a cliff looked like newcomers. The gyrfalcon eyries were far fewer, but none of them had the aspect of a recent site. They all had good overhangs for protection and were on cliffs.

If we eliminated 70 to 80% of the nesting peregrines in the Arctic, the eyries left would seem normal to the terrain. They do not at this time in my opinion, but those of the gyrfalcons do. This may be a significant point, and it needs some consideration by scientists.

POSSIBILITY OF SHIFTING POPULATIONS

There is a good possibility that a large portion of the peregrines in the intermountain area moved north, and to a lesser degree to higher elevations in the same area, starting with the end of the wet periods in 1896.

Our present conditions of precipitation, snowfall, and temperature have changed back to cooler springs in this region (Figs. 4.2 and 4.3), with more snow and precipitation in winter; 1965 was the third year of such a change in our snow records. It is possible that the peregrine may move back down to eyrie sites at lower elevations and back to southern habitats with the present trend. We may not be able to prove the first shift, but we could certainly detect the return if it should occur.

After discussing this with Enderson, I made a check of my data on low- and high-elevation eyries. The change took place at the low-elevation eyries first in all states studied.

In Utah, the first seven eyries to disappear were the lowest in elevation. The last birds nesting were those at the elevation of the lodgepole (*Pinus contorta*) tree line, which here is between 6,000 and 7,000 ft (1,800 and 2,100 m) on the north slopes. The birds still nesting in Utah are almost certain to be above the 6,000-ft level. To check these birds is a very difficult field problem, but this should be done. Recent work by Clayton M. White in Utah bears out this point. Three eyries that he found recently were all near or above the 6,000-ft elevation.

In Idaho, I1, I2 and I3 eyries were not active by 1952. They are also the lowest sites in the state. The peregrines found on the Upper Snake River in 1964 were at alpine fir (*Abies lasiocarpa*), lodgepole pine, and aspen (*Populus tremuloides*) level. In 1965, these birds were not at the

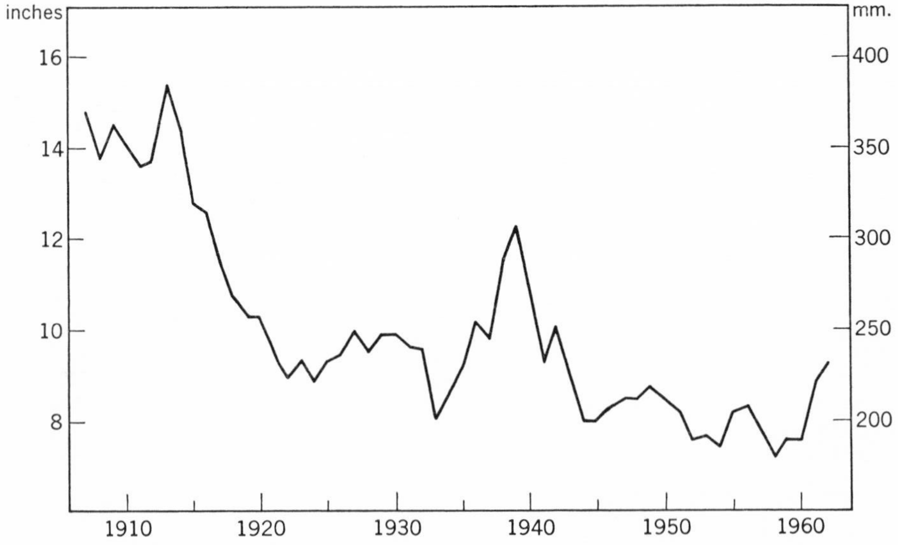

Fig. 4.3. Precipitation trends that appear to be associated with a decrease in peregrine and shorebird numbers in the intermountain area. Five-year running mean of annual rainfall at Idaho Falls, Idaho. Data from the US Weather Bureau (1907–64). UW Cartographic Lab.

two sites that I know. There is a possibility that they were in a third site which I was not able to check. One other site was observed at the rim of Hells Canyon, also at high elevation. The nesting hole was not determined, but adult birds were present. Another similar observation was made below Hells Canyon on the Snake River this year by competent observers. Last year, Gary Ball of Orofino, Idaho, reported observing eggs and, later, young flying from this site.

In Washington and Oregon, the low-elevation nesting sites were also the first to disappear. The eyries on the Malheur National Wildlife Refuge and those along the Columbia and Okanogan rivers are the best examples.

To make a general summary of the four states, I would estimate that 80 to 90% of the pairs studied by many competent observers have shifted their nesting sites. It is possible that new research, following Enderson's technique, would show a larger percentage of peregrines still at the old sites. Only further and more difficult field work can make such a determination. Unfortunately, the nesting possibilities above 6,000 ft (1,800 m) are far less in actual area and nesting cliffs. Therefore, even if the birds did shift to higher elevations, their numbers would be significantly less.

During the same period that the peregrine has declined in numbers in this region, the golden eagle and prairie falcon have remained about the same, with local areas changing slightly. It is difficult to estimate this change, but continuous field work indicates that the numbers of Idaho birds of prey have increased slightly since the law protecting them was passed in 1955.

It is also significant that the reduction in peregrine habitat resulted in better land characteristics for the golden eagle and prairie falcon. These two birds were always common in the intermountain area, and they are today.

The golden eagle is very sensitive to human intrusion during the egg-laying and hatching stage. Yet, there are three highly successful eyries within 75 yards (70 m) of Highway 30 in Idaho. They have been active for the past 18 years and were successful in 1965. The prairie falcon and golden eagle each have over 30 eyries that are within a mile (1.6 km) of major paved roads in Idaho. This same situation exists in Utah, Oregon, and Washington. At one time there were 26 or more peregrine eyries scattered throughout the same nesting sites. There has been an 80 to 90% reduction in the use of these peregrine sites, with no significant change in the other species.

The peregrine is a more tenacious nester than either of the other two birds. It has proven this point throughout many countries, yet it has shifted in this region. Human interference, and particularly shooting, in the Pacific Northwest cannot be evaluated properly because of the remote terrain involved. But if this were a factor, the golden eagle would not be there and the prairie falcon would certainly have been reduced in number.

During the same period, annual precipitation dropped drastically when considered on a "running mean." There are ample data to support this conclusion from records of the United States Weather Bureau on precipitation, and the records of the Soil Conservation Service for snowfall in the mountains of the Pacific Northwest.

The Arctic has had its greatest warming trend of all in the center of the area now densely populated by the peregrine. H. E. Landsberg (1958) writes: "The recent warming of the Arctic has been particularly notable at the edges of the forested regions both in North America and Eurasia. The tree line has been advancing gradually northward. In some areas which have been resurveyed, the forest has advanced two miles [3.2 km] northward over the last thirty years." The area north of 50°N latitude has become a significantly better habitat for the peregrine. The area south of that line has become a slightly better habitat for the golden eagle and prairie falcon.

Let me cite a specific case in Idaho with three peregrine eyries close enough to be affected. The 5-year average annual precipitation at Idaho Falls, Idaho, considered as a "running mean," hit its high point of 15.4 inches (39.1 cm) in 1913, as the middle point of a sliding 5-year average. The annual precipitation dropped steadily, with some fluctuations in the early forties, to a low of 7.2 inches (18.3 cm) in 1958 as shown in Fig. 4.3. Before the end of this period, the birds had shifted. In 1962, I found one eyrie on the Upper Snake River in the lodgepole pine belt with average precipitation more than twice that of Idaho Falls.

The numbers of shore birds in Idaho have dropped with the precipitation and consequent loss of habitat. I do not believe that peregrines could find the food supply they need to raise young successfully in their former habitat at this time. Professional biologists, who have worked for many years in the area, recognize the drastic drop in birds because of low-water years.

Similar climatic changes have occurred in northern and central Europe. The highs and lows were the same in these countries as in the intermountain west for both precipitation and temperature. No correlation coefficients between these data and those for Europe were computed, but the correlation is very high. The same changes were going on in Europe at generally the same time as in North America.

Population extensions to the north are common in this literature as described by Olavi Kalela (1949), Salomonsen (1948) and Siivonen (1952). The changes were most dramatic in Iceland, Greenland, and Finland. Kalela (1952) makes this interesting point: "Among the advancing southern species, the species dependent on shallow eutrophic waters are remarkably strongly represented. One of the factors contributing to this phenomenon may be the drying-up of lakes, in connection with the climatic change, in the *previous* areas of the species, the steppe regions." This very same change in the Pacific Northwest has been measured.

The drop in precipitation and rise in average temperature resulted in this parameter which has been measured accurately since 1870, or before in some cases. In Table 4.1 the surface area of lakes in the Northwest has been tabulated and the reduction in surface area computed by percentage since the maximum lake size was reached in 1870 or close to that year.

These lakes, reduced in surface area of water by 78%, have been relatively big and slow to react to the drop in snow and precipitation that has occurred since 1896. The smaller lakes and ponds, without outlets, dried up sometime between 1907 and 1934. The habitat of the shorebirds, and consequently the peregrine, has taken a similar and even more severe drop.

At the present time, the small-watershed program of the Soil Conservation Service, in building small reservoirs on the headwaters of our rivers, is increasing habitat of this type and is a bright spot for the future. This is also true of the smaller reservoirs built by the Bureau of Reclamation and the Corps of Engineers in some cases. However, these efforts

Table 4.1. Percentage Changes in the Surface Area of Lakes in the Northwest (Data from Bue, 1963)

State and	Maximum size			Present size			% Surface
Lake	sq mi	sq km	date	sq mi	sq km	date[a]	reduction
Oregon							
Goose	186	482	1869 / 1881	ca. 100	ca. 259	[1963]	46
Malheur and Harney	125	324	—	1	3	1961	99
Abert	60	155	—	Dry		1930	100
Summer	70	181	—	Nearly dry		1961	99
Silver	15	39	—	Dry		[1963]	100
Utah							
Great Salt	2,400	6,216	1870	950	2,461	1961	60
Sevier	125	324	—	Dry		[1963]	100
Nevada							
Pyramid	220	570	1869	180	466	1961	18
Walker	125	324	—	107	277	[1963]	14
Carson Sink	250	648	—	Almost dry		[1963]	99
Ruby	37	96	—	Almost dry		[1963]	90
Winnemucca	180	466	1882	Dry		[1963]	100
Mean							78

[a] Dates not cited by Bue are left in brackets and taken as the date of publication.

have a long way to go to change the problem resulting from the wide fluctuations that take place in wet and dry cycles of weather.

It is also interesting to know that many of these lakes have increased in surface area since 1961 which was the low point. Precipitation and snowfall have gone back to previous levels, even to equal those of 1896, and the lakes are gaining in size. They may come back to previous levels within the next 30–70 years.

SUMMARY

The combination of rising average temperatures and drastically reduced snowfall and precipitation, starting sometime after 1870, changed soil conditions, dried up small lakes and ponds, and significantly lowered the surface water area of larger lakes. This caused a critical reduction in habitat for shorebirds and food supply for peregrines. These same factors created a better habitat for the peregrine in the terrain north of 50° N Latitude, and at higher elevations in the same general area covered by this paper.

Of 28–29 peregrine eyries that were active in 1938, not more than 4–6 were subsequently found to be again occupied. It is estimated that 80–90% of the older sites in Utah, Idaho, Oregon, western Wyoming, and western Montana have been deserted by this species, and it is suggested that the peregrine population shifted north and to a lesser degree to higher elevations in the same areas to compensate for the climatic change that has taken place.

LITERATURE CITED

Bue, Conrad D. 1963. Principal lakes of the United States. U.S. Geol. Surv. Circ. 476. 22 p.

Kalela, Olavi. 1949. Changes in geographic ranges in the avifauna of northern and central Europe in relation to recent changes in climate. Bird-Banding, 20(2):77–103.

———. 1952. Changes in the geographic distribution of Finnish birds and mammals in relation to recent changes in climate, p. 38–51. *In* Ilmari Hustich [ed.], The recent climatic fluctuation in Finland and its consequences: A symposium. Fennia, 75. 128-p. reprint.

Landsberg, H. E. 1958. Trends in climatology. Science, 128(3327):749–758.

Mitchell, J. M., Jr. 1961. Recent secular changes of global temperature. Annals N.Y. Acad. Sci., 95(1):235–250.

Salomonsen, Finn. 1948. The distribution of birds and the recent climatic change in the North Atlantic area. Dansk. Ornithol. Forenings Tidsskrift, 42(2):85–99.

Siivonen, Lauri. 1952. On the influence of the climatic variations of recent decades on game economy, p. 77–88. *In* Ilmari Hustich [ed.], The recent climatic fluctuation in Finland and its consequences: A symposium. Fennia, 75. 128-p. reprint.

CHAPTER 5

POPULATION TRENDS AMONG PEREGRINE FALCONS IN THE ROCKY MOUNTAIN REGION

James H. Enderson

This paper reports information obtained during a survey of the nesting activities of peregrine falcons in New Mexico, Colorado, Wyoming, Montana, and Alberta from 27 April to 9 July 1964, and also in Colorado and New Mexico from 15 April to 20 June 1965.

Prior to April 1964, I gathered information on the locations of peregrine nest sites in the Rocky Mountain region (Fig. 5.1) from various sources, mostly by letters to interested persons. I visited as many of these sites as possible to determine if they were still being used by peregrines. Most of the sites were visited only once in the nesting period. The following is an account of peregrine nesting activities recorded in this survey.

SURVEY RESULTS

NEW MEXICO

In 1964, four nest sites were visited in New Mexico, and two were active, fledging four young. Two additional sites were visited in 1965; five of the six eyries were occupied by pairs of peregrines. At least six young fledged in 1965 from the five sites, and the number could be as high as nine. Of the six known sites in New Mexico, one was used as early as 1921, one as early as 1919 (Wetmore, 1920), one as early as 1951, and

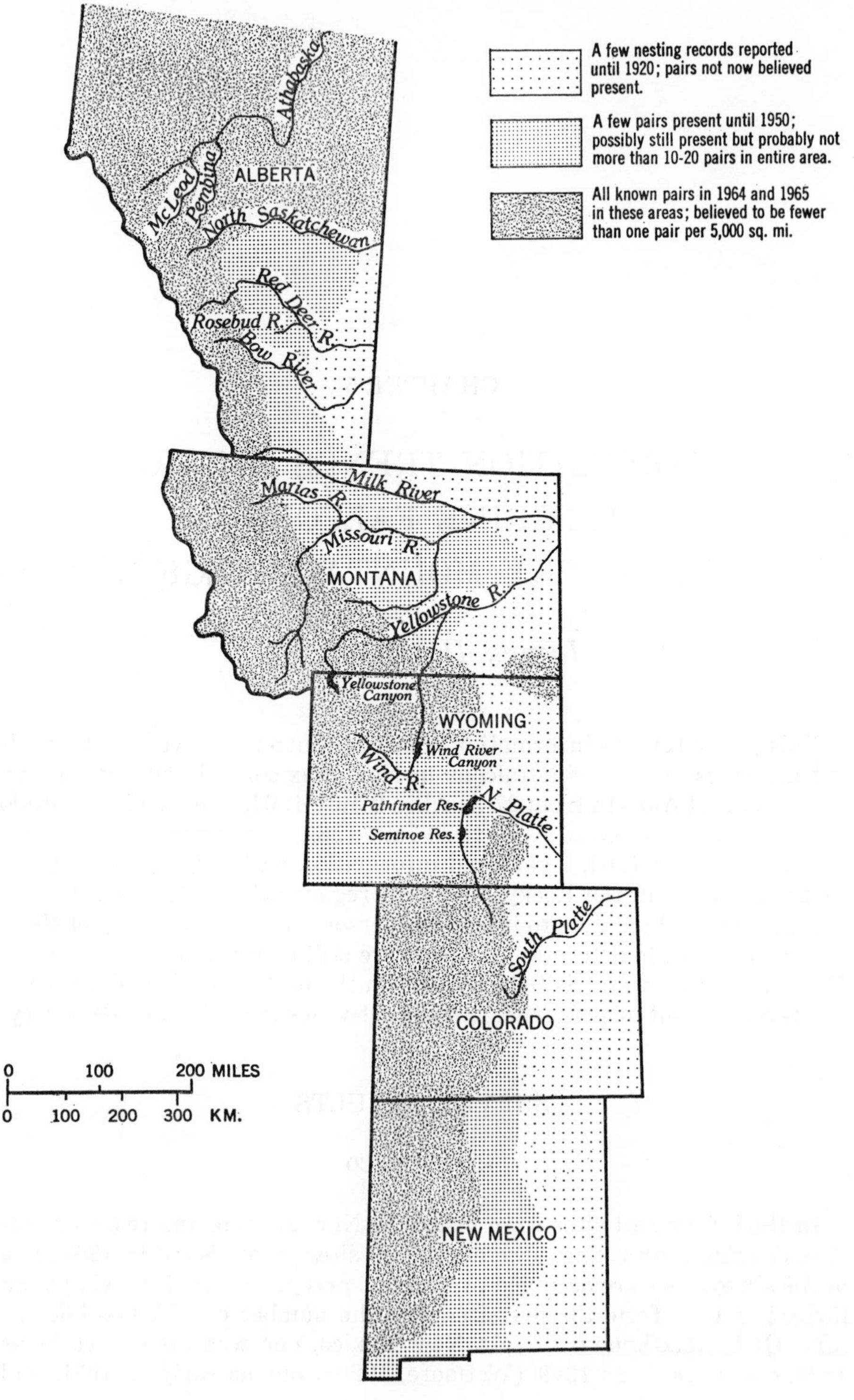
A few nesting records reported until 1920; pairs not now believed present.
A few pairs present until 1950; possibly still present but probably not more than 10-20 pairs in entire area.
All known pairs in 1964 and 1965 in these areas; believed to be fewer than one pair per 5,000 sq. mi.
ALBERTA
Athabaska
McLeod
Pembina
North Saskatchewan
Red Deer R.
Rosebud R.
Bow River
Milk River
Marias R.
Missouri R.
MONTANA
Yellowstone R.
Yellowstone Canyon
WYOMING
Wind River Canyon
Wind R.
Pathfinder Res.
N. Platte
Seminoe Res.
South Platte
COLORADO
NEW MEXICO
0 100 200 MILES
0 100 200 300 KM.

the other four were discovered after 1960. Falconers took two young from one nest in 1964 and 1965, but left one and three young, respectively, in the nest each year. In 1965 they captured one of the adults at this site.

Four of the sites were near streams or lakes, and the other two were in desert country several miles from open water.

COLORADO

In 1964 I visited 12 of 18 known former eyries, and 3 of the remaining sites were visited by other workers. Six of the 15 sites visited were occupied by pairs, while one had a single falcon. Of the 8 unoccupied sites, 5 were used at least until 1960 and another has evidently not been used since the early 1900's. Two others were abandoned in the early 1950's. Eight of the 15 sites were on cliffs more than 70 m high on the tops or sides of mountains. Five were on lower cliffs, usually near a river, and 2 were in canyons whose vertical walls were over 300 m high. A peregrine at one of these canyon sites was seen feeding on a mourning dove. Only 5 young are known to have fledged from the 6 sites occupied in 1964, but there may have been 3 or 4 more.

In 1965 I visited 15 of the Colorado sites; six, possibly seven, were occupied by pairs of peregrines, and a single adult was seen briefly at each of two other sites. One of these sites was later found to be abandoned, but the other was not revisited. There is no information on the production of young, but five of the six known pairs were incubating eggs at the time observations were made.

Four of the six cliffs used in 1965 were used in 1964. One seemingly ideal site in a very deep canyon was used in 1964, but I could not find the birds in 1965.

WYOMING

During field work from 1959 to 1962 I did not encounter nesting peregrines in Wyoming, and in 1964 I visited a few likely places and three former sites. No peregrines were found in the deep North Platte River canyon between Pathfinder and Seminoe reservoirs, and none were seen in the Wind River Canyon south of Thermopolis, Wyoming. A former site in Teton County, active in 1958, has not been used since, and another in the same county was vacant in 1964. Peregrines nested in Yellowstone Canyon, Yellowstone National Park, in the 1950's, but I could not find them there in 1961, 1962, and 1964. At another remote site in Yellow-

Fig. 5.1. Relative densities of nesting peregrines in the central Rocky Mountain region. UW Cartographic Lab.

stone Park, active about 1960, I saw an adult in 1964 and heard a second calling, but could not locate a nest.

MONTANA

I visited 10 eyries in Montana in 1964 and traveled 209 miles (336 km) of the Yellowstone, Missouri, and Marias rivers in areas where peregrines had been seen. I saw only a single adult. It roosted on a cliff used by peregrines in 1911 (Saunders, 1911) and now used by nesting prairie falcons. From the information on hand, it is impossible to determine when the unoccupied sites were abandoned.

I did not visit three other sites in Montana, active in 1955 (three young fledged), 1962 (two young), and 1963 (two young), respectively (J. J. Craighead, pers. comm.).

ALBERTA

In Alberta I traveled 478 miles (769 km) of the Bow, Red Deer, North Saskatchewan, Pembina, McCleod, and Rosebud rivers and flew at low level 185 miles (298 km) of the Athabasca River. Of 21 reported sites, 19 were visited, and many other suitable cliffs were seen. Six of the 19 sites had pairs of peregrines, while 2 others had apparently unmated adults. Of the 11 sites without birds, 6 were used at least as late as 1959.

The six sites with pairs contained 14 young. Food remains found at the eyries were a starling, a robin, a mourning dove, a spotted sandpiper, and Franklin's gulls. One nest had only numerous remains of Franklin's gulls.

All of the nest ledges were on dirt banks less than 13 m high, and two of the active nests were on sheltered ledges on banks less than 4 m high.

DISCUSSION

Of the 51 reported sites in the region from New Mexico to Alberta visited in 1964, only 15 had pairs of peregrines and 4 others had lone adults; only slightly over 33 % of the sites were being used by peregrines. In 1965, 11 New Mexico and Colorado sites out of 21, or about 50%, had pairs of falcons and 2 others had lone adults. Data in the literature on the "normal" number of unused sites in any one year are scanty. Cade (1960: 172) found in a 5-year period that about 55% of the sites were used each year on the Colville River in northern Alaska. However, peregrine occupation of the sites was apparently reduced to some extent through competition by gyrfalcons for use of the same cliffs. Beebe (1960: 173) found about 84% of 61 sites occupied over a 5-year period in the Queen Charlotte Islands, British Columbia. Prairie falcons used

81% of 33 sites in Colorado and Wyoming in 1962 (Enderson, 1960). From this information, it is difficult to draw conclusions on the relative well-being of the peregrine population I studied, but except for New Mexico and possibly Colorado, an abnormally large number of sites are unoccupied each year, possibly pointing to a population decline. According to records in the literature (Cameron, 1907; Taverner, 1919), peregrines once nested along rivers coursing eastward from the mountains across the grasslands in Montana and Alberta. I found only a single unmated falcon in this type of habitat. Equally conspicuous is the reduction of peregrines in a once-forested region of central Alberta. On one river they were to be found about every 10 miles (16 km) in the 1920's (K. Wood, pers. comm.); I found only one occupied site on a 95-mile (153-km) section of the stream. However, four prairie falcon nest sites were found. This new resident has apparently been able to invade the area in recent years due to the clearing of trees and resulting conversion of the region into suitable habitat. Possibly, prairie falcons have been able to occupy the limited nesting sites at the expense of peregrines, because the former winters nearby in southern Alberta and chooses nest sites before the arrival of peregrines in the spring. On another river in Alberta, a 22-mile (35-km) section was said to have six pairs of peregrines in 1958, but I found no birds there in 1964. At two adjacent but very remote sites in Montana that were active in the early 1940's (R. Elgas, pers. comm.), I found no evidence of recent occupancy.

The causes of this apparent reduction are largely unknown. Egg collectors have visited some of the Alberta sites regularly in recent years. Oil-survey crews have traveled the rivers in Alberta during the last decade and have been blamed for shooting peregrines. The young from several sites in Alberta have been taken into captivity. Pesticides apparently have had harmful effects on the peregrines in Great Britain (Cramp, 1963), but it is difficult to understand how they could have affected peregrines in the region I studied, where the similar prairie falcon seems to be thriving.

In the Rocky Mountain region the peregrine exists only where very local conditions are favorable. It is found there near rivers or reservoirs where shorebirds and waterfowl are found and where land birds are vulnerable to attack over water. Other pairs are found on the highest cliffs, often on mountains, where high-flying land birds may be captured. That peregrines in these locally favorable areas are not more numerous than they are may be due in part to the fact that the young disperse into surrounding, unfavorable regions and are frequently lost.

It is difficult to estimate the number of pairs of peregrines breeding in the region surveyed. I found only two previously unknown sites in my travels. It seems very unlikely to me that more than 25 pairs nest in Colorado and Wyoming. Montana probably has no more than this. Alberta has more pairs, perhaps as many as 60, when one considers the large rivers in northern Alberta. However, along one of these, the Athabasca River, I saw little evidence of nesting and no occupied sites.

ACKNOWLEDGMENTS

The 1964 field work was supported by a Colorado College Faculty Research Grant and, in 1965, observations were made under a grant from the American Museum of Natural History.

CONCLUSIONS

In 1964, only slightly more than 33% of the known peregrine nest sites visited in the region from New Mexico to central Alberta were being used. In 1965, about 50% of the New Mexico and Colorado sites were being used. Many of the unoccupied sites fell inexplicably into disuse after 1950.

I estimate that about 25 pairs of peregrines currently nest in Colorado and Wyoming, near that number nest in Montana, and possibly 60 pairs nest in Alberta.

ADDENDUM, 1968

Since my survey was made, several people have commented to me that peregrines are virtually eliminated from the large rivers in the Edmonton-Red Deer-Calgary area of Alberta. In 1966, Berger and I found only four pairs on the entire Peace River in Alberta. In 1967, Dick Dekker (Blue Jay, 25[4]:175–176) reported that, in another Alberta river valley, the breeding pairs had dropped from five in 1960 to two in 1965, and that a single pair returned in 1967 but soon deserted a traditionally used cliff.

LITERATURE CITED

Beebe, F. L. 1960. The marine peregrines of the northwest Pacific Coast. Condor, 62(3):145–189.

Cade, T. J. 1960. Ecology of the peregrine and gyrfalcon populations in Alaska. Univ. Calif. Publ. Zool., 63(3):151–290.

Cameron, E. S. 1907. The birds of Custer and Dawson counties, Montana. Auk, 24(3):241–270.

Cramp, S. 1963. Toxic chemicals and birds of prey. Brit. Birds, 56(4): 124–139.

Enderson, J. H. 1964. A study of the prairie falcon in the central Rocky Mountain region. Auk, 81(3):332–352.

Saunders, A. A. 1911. A preliminary list of the birds of Gallatin County, Montana. Auk 28(1):26–49.

Taverner, P. A. 1919. The birds of the Red Deer River, Alberta. Auk, 36(1):1–21.

Wetmore, A. 1920. Observations on the habits of birds at Lake Burford, New Mexico. Auk, 37 (2–3):221–247, 393–412.

CHAPTER 6

THE PEREGRINE FALCON IN BAJA CALIFORNIA AND THE GULF OF CALIFORNIA

Richard C. Banks

No intensive study of the peregrine population in Baja California has been made. A considerable amount of information on nesting sites is available in the literature prior to 1930, but there has never been an attempt to catalog all sites or to follow trends or fluctuations in the population. Bond (1946) included Baja California in his study of the peregrines of western North America, but wrote little about this segment of the population. He had records of 47 nests in Mexico, presumably all in Baja California or along the Gulf coast of Sonora, as the peregrine does not nest elsewhere in Mexico (Friedmann, Griscom, and Moore, 1950). As Bond (1946:103) pointed out, a large majority of the western nesting records are based on single observations, and the histories and present status of the nests are unknown. There has been extensive field work in Baja California and the Gulf of California in the past 5 years, but this has been of a general survey nature with no concentrated observation of any particular species. Thus the degree of accuracy of estimates of past or present populations here is not as high as, for example, in the eastern United States, where detailed and repeated surveys have been made.

Most of the information on earlier nesting sites of peregrines in Baja California comes from the account in Grinnell's (1928) summation of the ornithology of the peninsula and from the references he cited. Lewis Wayne Walker, of the Arizona-Sonora Desert Museum, has contributed or confirmed the majority of the records for the years between 1930 and

1960. Ed N. Harrison has provided nesting data and locality records from his oological collection and from that of the Western Foundation of Vertebrate Zoology. Sidney B. Peyton has contributed similar information from his collection.

Walker has also given information on the present population in the central Gulf of California, where his field effort has been concentrated in recent years. Additional data on the current status of the peregrine come from my own work in various parts of Baja California since 1960, some 18 field trips.

Early workers in Baja California gave the impression that the peregrine was common. Thus Bancroft (1927:194) wrote that they "are abundant on the islands of both waters [Pacific Ocean and Gulf of California] as well as along the western ocean cliffs as far south as those extend" and that "they are probably the most evenly distributed bird in this region." In summarizing previous works, Grinnell (1928:111) reported the peregrine as a "common resident, chiefly coastwise and around islands, along both sides of the peninsula its whole length," although he qualified his statement by adding that "the more southerly occurrences appear to be mostly of vagrant or non-breeding birds." Bond included most of Baja California and the Gulf in the area where peregrines were "known to be common" (Bond, 1946:fig. 22). As late as 1950, Friedmann, Griscom, and Moore mentioned "numerous breeding pairs northward" in Baja California. All these comments, however, appear to be based on information gathered prior to 1930; aside from Bond's study and references in general works, I know of only three papers since 1930 which mention the peregrine in Baja California.

The breeding peregrines of Baja California and Sonora are referred to the race *Falco peregrinus anatum* (AOU, 1957). There is one winter record of *F. p. pealei* (Friedmann, Griscom, and Moore, 1950).

NUMBER OF NESTS AND POPULATION DENSITY

Bond (1946) had records of 47 peregrine nests in Mexico, presumably all within the area covered by this report. From the literature, from information contributed by Walker, Harrison, and Peyton, and from my own observations, I have prepared a list of 48 localities from which peregrines have been reported. A locality as used in this sense is a rather nebulous thing; it might be an area, a spot, an island, or an island group, and there may be more than one nest reported from a locality.

There are 25 localities on the Pacific side of the peninsula. Of these, four are places where the birds have been seen only, and may or may not nest. The other 21 localities are places where breeding has been reported, and incorporate a reported 38 nests. Four localities in interior Baja California are sight records only. In the Gulf of California and on that side of the peninsula, there are 16 localities. Four of these are sight records only, and the remainder include 15 nests or breeding pairs. Three locality records are available for islands on the Sonoran side of the Gulf of California. One of these is a sighting, whereas the others are records of nesting pairs, with a total of two nests.

Thus, within the area covered by this report, there is a maximum of 55 known nests, and there are 13 additional sight records. Two sight records are for winter months and may represent migrants, but the remainder are presumed to be of birds that were nesting nearby. As many as 66 nests may be involved. It must be emphasized that these records were not contemporaneous, but represent a total for the ornithological history of the area.

Based on a maximum estimate of 64 nests in Baja California (excluding the two Sonoran insular records) in an area of approximately 53,000 sq miles (137,000 sq km), the population density of peregrines would be about one nest per 830 sq miles (2,150 sq km). This figure, however, is quite misleading, as most records and all known nests are coastal or insular. A 5-mile (8-km) strip along both sides of the peninsula encompasses approximately 8,000 sq miles (21,000 sq km), in which there may have been as many as 60 nests; the density calculated on this basis is one nest per 135 sq miles (350 sq km). At the extreme, Lamb (1927) thought that there were six pairs on Natividad Island, which has an area of only about 4 sq miles (10.4 sq km).

CATALOG AND HISTORY OF NESTS

This section is an attempt to catalog all recorded localities of the peregrine in Baja California and the Gulf of California, giving as much of the history of the individual nests as is known. These are, essentially, the data upon which the population estimates given above are based. All references to Walker are to his letter dated 14 May, 1965. Records from the Western Foundation of Vertebrate Zoology and the San Diego Natural History Museum are indicated by the abbreviations WFVZ and SDNHM, respectively. Data given without citations are from my own unpublished observations. Within each series, localities are listed from north to south. Data and references are listed chronologically. The numbers refer to the localities on the map (Fig. 6.1).

PACIFIC COAST

1. *Los Coronados Islands.* Two pairs, one on North, one on South Island, 1910 (Howell, 1910:186); "at least three and probably four pairs

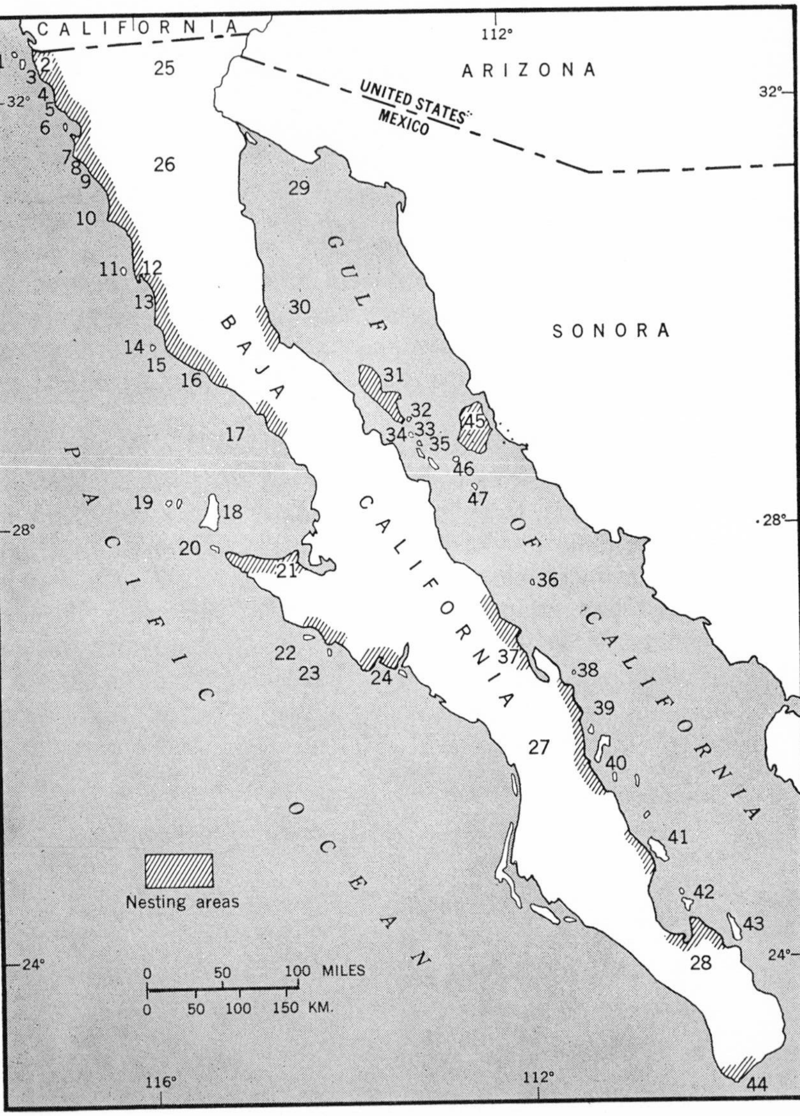

Fig. 6.1. Peregrine distribution in Baja California and the Gulf of California. Numbers correspond to numbered localities in the text. UW Cartographic Lab.

. . . ." (Howell, 1917:56); specimens, juvenile male, 28 May 1916, juvenile female, 28 May 1917, one adult and two juveniles, 28–29 May 1924 (SDNHM); set of four eggs, 19 April 1931 (WFVZ); two (possibly three) pairs on North Island, one on Middle Island, at least four (possibly five) on South Island, about 1932 (Walker); set of four eggs, 11 April 1935, set of two eggs, incubation advanced, 30 April 1940

(WFVZ) ; none seen on Middle and North islands, 9 February 1962, 10 June 1963.

2. *Sea cliffs south of Tijuana.* A pair until at least 1941 (Walker).

3. *Seven and one-half miles south of Rosarito Beach.* A pair using a raven's nest, which raised young often until about 1946 or 1947, when the area became a site for picnickers (Walker).

4. *Descanso.* Three sets of four eggs, 24 March 1923, 29 April 1923, 20 March 1924 (WFVZ) ; a young bird taken from a nest, 19 May 1943 (specimen, SDNHM).

5. *Vicinity of La Misión Lagoon.* Nest found once in 1930's (Walker).

6. *South Todos Santos Island.* A pair nesting, 16 April 1910, four eggs, incubated two-thirds (Howell, 1912:189); nest site seen, apparently occupied (Bancroft, 1932:43) ; female collected about 1936, nest continued at least until 1950 (Walker).

7. *Punta Banda.* Two nests, one deserted soon after 1935, apparently due to use of beach below nest, no definite information on other (Walker).

8. *Vicinity of Santo Tomas.* Two nests, one active until 1949 or 1950, no definite information on other (Walker).

9. *San Antonio del Mar.* Breeding locality (Bancroft, 1927:194).

10. *Cape Colnett.* Breeding locality (Bancroft, 1927:194); one pair, possibly another, 1932 or 1933 (Walker).

11. *Hamilton Ranch, Santo Domingo River.* Set of four eggs, incubation far advanced, 10 April 1926 (Peyton).

12. *San Martín Island.* Male taken as specimen, 10 April 1912 (Willett, 1913:22) ; one nest, 1932 to 1935 or later (Walker) ; set of three eggs, incubation advanced, 10 April 1938 (WFVZ) ; none seen, 10–12 April 1963.

13. *San Quintín Bay.* Two seen flying together, 16 February 1965; one seen, 18 February 1965.

14. *Vicinity of El Rosario.* A pair seen about 1950, presumed to be nesting (Walker).

15. *San Gerónimo Island.* Nesting (McGregor, 1899, *in* Grinnell, 1928:111); common, breeding (Kaeding, 1905:111); "male, female and three badly incubated eggs taken . . . April 13," 1912 (Willett, 1913:22) ; two nests in early 1930's (Walker) ; none seen, 12–13 April 1963.

16. *Punta San Carlos.* A pair about 1954 or 1955 (Walker).

17. *Santa Catarina Landing.* Breeding locality (Bancroft, 1927:194).

18. *Santa Rosalia Bay.* Breeding locality (Bancroft, 1927:194).

19. *Cedros Island.* Common, breeding (Kaeding, 1905:111); several seen (Willett, 1913:22) ; none seen, 14–21 April 1963.

20. *San Benito Islands.* Nesting (McGregor, 1899, *in* Grinnell 1928:111); common, breeding (Kaeding, 1905:111); four nests, two on larger island, one on each smaller island, 1927 and 1950 (Walker) ; two

sets of four eggs, 7 April 1932, set of two eggs, 4 April 1938 (WFVZ); none seen, with good coverage of west and middle islands, 18–19 April 1963.

21. *Natividad Island.* Common, breeding (Kaeding, 1905:111); breeding (Bancroft, 1927:194); "about six pairs resident on the island" in December 1924 (Lamb, 1927:70); set of four eggs, incubation advanced, 3 April 1932 (WFVZ); one pair, about 1948 (Walker); none seen, 21 April 1963.

22. *Scammons Lagoon.* Seen often (Walker).

23. *San Roque Island.* Breeding locality (Bancroft, 1927:194); specimens, adult male and female, 10 April 1927 (SDNHM); nest with two heavily incubated eggs, 20 April 1927 (Huey, 1927*a*:206); present in early 1930's (Walker); set of four fresh eggs, 6 April 1932 (WFVZ).

24. *Asuncion Island.* One pair about 1938 (Walker).

25. *San Ignacio Lagoon.* One seen, 18 April 1927 (Huey, 1927*b*:242); seen often (Walker).

INLAND BAJA CALIFORNIA

26. *Laguna Hanson, Sierra Juarez.* Seen several times, July 1924 (Huey, 1926:353).

27. *La Grulla, Sierra San Pedro Mártir.* Seen 10 and 17 June 1923 (Huey, 1926:353).

28. *San Ignacio.* Rare (Bancroft, 1930:27).

29. *Sierra Laguna, Cape region.* Recorded as present in summer, 1929 (C.C. Lamb, field notes filed at Museum of Vertebrate Zoology); not seen 19–29 May 1965.

GULF OF CALIFORNIA, BAJA CALIFORNIA

30. *Consag Rock.* Breeding (Bancroft, 1927:194, 1932:375); has or had one pair (Walker).

31. *San Luis Islands.* Three pairs, on three islands, no dates indicated (Walker); nesting on three of the islands, set of eggs taken in March 1926 (Bancroft, 1927:194).

32. *Angel de la Guarda Island.* Present at Puerto Refugio, on north end of island, about 15 years ago (Walker); none seen, 15–18 March 1962; one seen, and an apparently old nest found, 19–23 March 1963; a pair seen at Puerto Refugio, early May 1965 (Walker).

33. *Pond Island (at SE point of Angel de la Guarda).* A pair about 10 or 12 years ago, but not seen in last 3 years (Walker); not seen, 18 March 1962.

34. *Partida Island (Norte).* Presence of a pair reported (Bancroft, 1932:351–352); not seen 26 March 1962; two pairs for 25 years or more, seen early May 1965 (Walker).

35. *Raza Island.* Presence indicated (Bancroft, 1932:342); often seen, but nesting only once, about 15 years ago (Walker); not seen, 26 March 1962, 21 October 1964.

36. *Salsipuedes Island.* A pair giving alarm notes near an empty nest, 23 March 1962 (Banks, 1963*a*:54); one pair, did not raise young in 1963 or 1964 (Walker); questionably seen, 24 October 1964.

37. *Tortuga Island.* Presence reported (van Rossem, 1930:223); nest found (Bancroft, 1932:272, 274); seen 30 March 1962 (Banks, 1963*a*: 54); one pair as late as 1964 (Walker).

38. *Conception Bay.* On an island in Coyote Bay (Bancroft, 1932: 252).

39. *San Ildefonso Island.* Set of four eggs, 24 March 1930 (WFVZ); a nest for at least three years, set of four eggs collected, date not given (Bancroft, 1932:237–243) [this is perhaps the set in WFVZ]; one pair until about 1960 (Walker); not seen, 2 April 1962.

40. *Coronados Island.* Seen (Mailliard, 1923:455).

41. *Danzante Island.* Seen (Banks, 1963*a*:54).

42. *Santa Cruz Island.* Seen (Banks, 1963*a*:54).

43. *Espíritu Santo Island.* A pair about 1962 (Walker); not seen on four visits, 1960–65.

44. *Cerralvo Island.* A pair about 1961 (Walker); one seen in 1928 by D. R. Dickey, but not seen by me in extensive time there (Banks, 1963*b*:305).

45. *Cape San Lucas.* One seen, 2 July 1964.

GULF OF CALIFORNIA, SONORA

46. *Tiburon Island.* Seen, 30 December 1931 (van Rossem, 1932:132).

47. *San Esteban Island.* Breeding locality (Bancroft, 1927:194), seen 17 April 1930 (van Rossem, 1931:244); seen in two areas (Walker).

48. *San Pedro Mártir Island.* Breeding specimen, 20 April 1930 (van Rossem, 1931:244); not seen, 21 March 1962; three pairs suspected, one pair found in 1963 or 1964 (Walker).

EGG DATES AND CLUTCH SIZE

Howell (1917) reported for the Los Coronados Islands and Bancroft (1927) for the central part of the peninsula that eggs are laid in the latter half of March and the first part of April. In the records cited just previously in this report, dates for sets in which incubation had just begun range from 24 March to 19 April. Incubation was recorded as advanced in sets with dates from 3 April to 30 April. Of 17 records of clutches with the date of collection available, 14 were taken in April.

Bancroft (1927), drawing on several years of experience in Baja California, commented that there were more often three eggs than four in peregrine nests, but this observation does not correspond with the data currently available. The majority of the 19 records of clutch size compiled in this report are of four eggs. For nest sites along the Pacific coast there are 11 records of four eggs, 3 of three eggs, and 3 of two eggs. In the Gulf of California there are 2 records of clutches of four eggs.

FOOD HABITS

In Baja California, the peregrine apparently lives mainly on pelagic birds. Kaeding (1905) believed that the Cassin's auklet was the principal food source of peregrines on the islands of the west coast. Howell (1912) also mentioned the taking of Cassin's auklets as the peregrines foraged at sea. Lamb (1927) claimed that the peregrines on Natividad Island lived largely on Manx shearwaters, but observed one take a mountain plover. In addition to auklets, Howell (1910) recorded Xantus' murrelet and petrels as food on the Los Coronados Islands. Craveri's murrelets have been recorded as prey in the Gulf of California (Banks, 1963*a*). Bancroft (1932) listed the latter murrelet as well as eared grebes, the elegant tern, and the Heermann's gull as prey in the Gulf, but without indicating specific evidence for predation on these larger birds. Grinnell and Daggett (1903) believed peregrines were responsible for the remains of western gulls found on the Los Coronados.

THE POPULATION DECLINE AND POSSIBLE CAUSES

From the meager data available, it is nearly impossible to say whether there actually has been a decline in the peregrine population in Baja California, and it is absolutely impossible to give any meaningful estimate of any such decline. There are a few instances of known nests being abandoned (Rosarito Beach, Punta Banda), but this does not necessarily mean the loss of a breeding pair. The only figures based on repeated observation of a nesting area apply to Natividad Island, where Lamb (1927) "judged" that there were six resident pairs in 1924, Walker reported one nest about 1948, and I saw none in 1963. Even this set of figures is not convincing; Lamb's comment lacks decisiveness, and it is quite possible to visit an island and not see the birds.

L. W. Walker has spent more time in the northern Gulf of California than probably any other naturalist, and particularly within the last few years his visits there have been frequent. He writes: "In former years, 15 or 20 years ago, my visits to any of these locations after about May 30 would show some young flying with parents—but in four trips at the right dates in the last four years to all the Gulf islands from Tortuga north, I have not seen a single flying immature. . . . So from recent observations in the northern half of the Gulf, I believe that we have almost the same number of nests but reproduction has dropped. . . ."

Walker rules out falconers as a cause of the loss of young birds, and I agree entirely. Natives of Baja California do not, to my knowledge, indulge in this activity, and I have heard no reports of Americans going into that area to obtain birds. If there is any nest robbing for the purposes of falconry, it is most likely along the Pacific coast, from the border south to San Quintín.

To my knowledge, there have been no falcons taken as scientific specimens in Baja California in recent years, nor have oologists been active there recently. There can be little doubt that oologists had some effect on the peregrines in the first third of this century—most writers who have been quoted in the accounts of nests earlier in this paper were avid egg collectors.

In a study of the nesting population of the osprey along the northwestern coast of Baja California, Kenyon (1947) found that the number of birds had fallen markedly in a period of 30 or 40 years, and considered that man was the most important enemy of the osprey. Among the reasons for the latter conclusion were bullets dug from rocks near nests, observations of fishermen target practicing at ospreys and their nests, and the use of chicks and eggs as food by needy fishermen. It is not unlikely that at least the shooting factor applies equally to peregrines. Walker mentioned at least two nests that were abandoned because of disturbance by humans.

In addition to disturbance or killing by native fishermen, the influence of the American tourist must be considered. There has been a tremendous increase in the number of American yachts in Mexican waters in the past decade, and most of these vessels carry firearms. Presumably these weapons are used occasionally, and both ospreys and peregrines would be challenging targets.

Agriculture is relatively unimportant in Baja California, except for three areas near the largest population centers—the Mexicali Valley of the northeast, the northwestern coastal area south to the San Quintín Plain, and the Santo Domingo-Magdalena Plain area of the Cape region. Agriculture is carried out on a small scale in the few places where water is abundant elsewhere on the peninsula, as at Mulegé and San Ignacio. It is unlikely that the use of pesticides is widespread enough in Baja California to affect a bird which is largely restricted to the coast and islands. There may be considerable drainage of pesticide residues into the northern Gulf of California from the Imperial Valley of California and the Mexicali Valley, via the Colorado River, but the dilution factor would be tremendous. Whether there could be enough concentration of residues in the small fish and fish-eating birds to have an effect on the reproduction of peregrines is unknown; there are no data available, to my knowledge, to test such a hypothesis.

SUMMARY

Within the area covered by this report there is a maximum of 66 peregrine nests. This number does not represent the nests active at any one time, but is derived from the ornithological history of the area. Most records were obtained before 1930, and all but a few were obtained before 1960. Noteworthy is the lack of observations of peregrines since 1960, despite extensive field work in areas known to have been occupied by them previously.

Although there are no data on either past or present population levels, the recent lack of observations compared to earlier indications of abundance suggests that a decline has occurred. There is some evidence of lowered productivity of peregrines in the Gulf of California.

This population breeds from mid-March to late April. Most clutches consist of four eggs. The main food source is pelagic birds.

LITERATURE CITED

American Ornithologists' Union. 1957. Check-list of North American birds. 5th ed. Amer. Ornithologists' Union [c/o Museum of Natural History, Smithsonian Institution, Washington, D.C.]. 691 p.

Bancroft, G. 1927. Notes on the breeding coastal and insular birds of central Lower California. Condor, 29(4):188–195.

———. 1930. The breeding birds of central Lower California. Condor, 32(1):20–49.

———. 1932. The flight of the least petrel. G. P. Putnam's Sons, New York. 403 p.

Banks, R. C. 1963*a*. Birds of the Belvedere Expedition to the Gulf of California. Trans. San Diego Soc. Nat. Hist., 13(3):49–60.

———. 1963*b*. Birds of Cerralvo Island, Baja California. Condor, 65(4):300–312.

Bond, R. M. 1946. The peregrine population of western North America. Condor, 48(3):101–116.

Friedmann, H., L. Griscom, and R. T. Moore. 1950. Distributional check-list of the birds of Mexico. Part 1. Pac. Coast Avif. no. 29. 202 p.

Grinnell, J. 1928. A distributional summation of the ornithology of Lower California. Univ. Calif. Publ. Zool., 32(1):1–300.

———, and F. S. Daggett. 1903. An ornithological visit to Los Coronados Islands, Lower California. Auk, 20(1):27–37.

Howell, A. B. 1910. Notes from Los Coronados Islands. Condor, 12(6):184–187.

———. 1912. Notes from Todos Santos Islands. Condor, 14(5):187–191.

———. 1917. Birds of the islands off the coast of southern California. Pac. Coast Avif. no. 12. 127 p.

Huey, L. M. 1926. Notes from northwestern Lower California, with the description of an apparently new race of the screech owl. Auk, 43(3):347–362.

———. 1927*a*. Northernmost breeding station of the Heermann gull on the Pacific Ocean, and other notes from San Roque Island, Lower California. Condor, 29(4):205–206.

———. 1927*b*. The bird life of San Ignacio and Pond lagoons on the western coast of Lower California. Condor, 29(5):239–243.

Kaeding, H. B. 1905. Birds from the west coast of Lower California and adjacent islands. Condor, 7(4):105–111.

Kenyon, K. W. 1947. Breeding populations of the osprey in Lower California. Condor, 49(4):152–158.

Lamb, C. C. 1927. The birds of Natividad Island, Lower California. Condor, 29(1):67–70.

Mailliard, J. 1923. Expedition of the California Academy of Sciences to the Gulf of California in 1921. The birds. Proc. Calif. Acad. Sci., 4th ser., 12:443–456.

van Rossem, A. J. 1930. Four new birds from north-western Mexico. Trans. San Diego Soc. Nat. Hist., 6(14):213–226.

———. 1931. Report on a collection of land birds from Sonora, Mexico. Trans. San Diego Soc. Nat. Hist., 6(19):237–304.

———. 1932. The avifauna of Tiburon Island, Sonora, Mexico, with descriptions of four new races. Trans. San Diego Soc. Nat. Hist., 7(12):119–150.

Willett, G. 1913. Bird notes from the coast of northern Lower California. Condor, 15(1):19–24.

CHAPTER 7

GENERAL DISCUSSION: THE PEREGRINE FALCON IN WESTERN NORTH AMERICA AND MEXICO

HABITAT CHANGE IN THE ROCKY MOUNTAIN AND INTERMOUNTAIN REGIONS

HICKEY: It seems to me that Nelson has put forth evidence for a population change which we must agree has taken place in some fashion. One thing that impressed me in 1940, when I did look at the ornithological literature for this region, was the fact that a number of collectors in the 1870's and 1880's had visited sites in Colorado and reported collecting peregrines and peregrine eggs. My correspondence in 1940 with people like R. J. Neidrach indicated that modern ornithologists were visiting these old sites and were only finding prairie falcons. The population had changed, and it was completely impossible for us to understand why this had taken place. I believe Nelson should be commended for giving us some ecological evidence to explain what until now has been an extremely puzzling phenomenon in peregrine population biology.

NELSON: I know of no evidence that there has been an extension of the peregrine falcon's geographic range to the north. I can say that all the nesting peregrines I have found in Utah, Idaho, Oregon, and Washington since 1938 have been nesting well above the 6,000-ft (1,829-m) level. In Colorado, Enderson is finding the birds up at 8,500 and 9,000 ft (2,591 and 2,743 m). I do not know whether or not these Colorado birds were always there or not. In Idaho they were not.

HICKEY: Bergtold (1928, *A Guide to Colorado Birds*) reported the species to be a "frequent resident . . . up to 10,000 ft." Gold Hill, at which Denis Gale collected a set of four eggs (now labelled peregrine in the US National Museum) in 1889, has an elevation of about 8,500 ft.

NELSON: There is of course evidence that the tree line has shifted to the north in the North American Arctic. The mean temperatures there have risen even more sharply than in the intermountain area. But precipitation in the Arctic has not varied as it has farther south. For instance at Eagle on the Yukon River, annual rainfall on a 5-year moving average dropped from 15 inches (381 mm) down to 7 inches (178 mm). Birds cannot possibly have the same habitat left with rising temperatures and drastically dropping precipitation. Great Salt Lake fell 32 ft (9.8 m) and others as much as 90 ft (27.4 m). I think there is a very real suggestion here that reproductive success must have decreased in the south and increased in the north.

WHITE: In *The Birds of Arizona* (1964), which recently appeared, Monson, Marshall, and Phillips state, giving no basis for their data, that there has been an increase in peregrines in Arizona at the expense of the prairie falcon. According to Dr. Walter Cottam, Utah's veteran plant ecologist, Arizona has the largest fern flora of any state in the Union because of the particular timing and amount of rainfall within the state. Whether this has application here with humidity or not I don't know, but it would be interesting to test that out in Arizona especially.

RATCLIFFE: Nelson, do you think that these precipitation changes to which you referred cover the areas studied by Enderson farther east?

NELSON: Yes, sir, I do. I think that the precipitation, temperature trends, and habitat changed. Now according to Hickey's statement the peregrine density should have been at its best in 1870—a time when everyone agrees that the snowfall, rainfall, and food supply for the peregrine must have been good in this area that we are talking about. Early explorers like Benjamin Bonneville spoke about the peregrine falcon on Silver Lake and on the Warner chain of lakes, not the prairie falcon. At the time I last went there, I found one remaining peregrine and 15–30 prairie falcons in the area. We need to remember that, as the periphery of these great lakes went down—even Abert Lake, which is over 100 sq miles (259 sq km) in extent, went dry in 1934—all the little lakes disappeared. This change increased the habitat in these areas for the ground squirrels, jackrabbits, and all the things that the prairie falcon and the golden eagle live on. Today these two raptors are thriving in these very same areas.

BEEBE: About 4 years ago and after an absence of 30 years, I returned to the old area of my parents' homestead west of Edmonton, Alberta. The whole country has gone over to aspen parkland. What I originally knew as boreal forest muskeg is now in solid aspen. I had to drive 30 miles (48 km) farther north to Whitecourt before I came to the edge of the boreal forest.

HICKEY: This change in Alberta could be due to the drying out of muskegs as a result of lumbering, fire, and land clearing. At this latitude, aspen is the successional species that then takes over the landscape.

CLEMENT: Just to make sure we appreciate how complex this problem is, let me point out that the geologists and the vegetationists are in disagreement as to what may have triggered many of our major landscape changes. One group says the change may have been due to the climatic shift; the other group says it was due to man with, for example, grazing and other land-use practices that affect the landscape.

To emphasize again how important it is to restrict these studies to a regional unit that can be understood so we have some unification of trend, I call attention to the fact that in Canadian Labrador, despite the climatic amelioration, which is rather general, there has been no northward advance of the tree line, whereas in Alaska it is true that the tree line has moved north.

SPENCER: Just to add a little more grist to the mill, dendrochronological evidence shows that between 1927 and 1957 the southwestern part of the United States went through a drought period unequalled in the last 300 years as measured in plant-growth response.

NELSON: This very publication to which Spencer refers was put out by the University of Arizona. It went back to the year 500 and presented evidence of periods of tremendous fluctuation in precipitation in various areas. This picture is very much in agreement with the habitat changes that we are talking about. Likewise, in the soil surveys in this region you can find profiles which are now dry as well as black, indicating that there must have once been appreciable amounts of precipitation in what are now deserts. This former precipitation increased the organic content of the soil and gave it this tremendously black color.

We need more research here, such as a detailed study confined to a river basin like the Columbia. The effect there is more clearly defined than that in a whole continent.

HICKEY: Generally, when a climatic change takes place and when ranges are invaded in one direction, these new ranges are probably invaded by young birds and not necessarily by adults. My concept of avifaunal dynamics is that once an adult nests at a given site or locality, whether it is a warbler or an eagle, it will attempt to stay there for the rest of its life, even though the habitat becomes submarginal and no longer attractive to young or yearling birds that are nesting for the first time.

PEREGRINE NUMBERS IN THE ROCKY MOUNTAINS

BEEBE: Isn't there quite a distinct possibility that, when we know our Rocky Mountain system much more intimately than we now do, a great many more nesting falcons will turn up than we have any idea are there at the present time? I am basing this on the detailed work that has shown nesting peregrines to exist in the interior in the mountain systems of France and Germany.

ENDERSON: Judging from the frequency with which I see them on high cliffs in Colorado, the state I know best as far as peregrines are concerned, I would be very surprised if there are over 20 or 25 pairs of peregrines in the entire state. It may be that more occur, but you can look at a surprisingly large number of very tall cliffs and seemingly ideal areas and not see peregrines.

IRRIGATION EFFECTS ON PEREGRINES

AMADON: I can remember once stopping a few miles north of Boise, Idaho, and seeing this beautifully irrigated area with standing water, hundreds of gulls, killdeers, and huge flocks of Brewer's blackbirds. Hasn't irrigation done as much to increase the food supply for peregrine falcons in one way as the shrinking of some of these desert lakes would have decreased it in another?

NELSON: I think the answer to that lies in the fact that I am speaking of a much broader area than the relatively confined irrigated sections along our western rivers. Furthermore, these birds that are on the irrigated fields are surrounded by barbed wire, by telephone lines, and by power lines. We are seeing a lot more prairie falcons and peregrines that hit the barbed wire fences when they try catching prey in an irrigated area where the fields are relatively small. My point is this: All of the peregrines that I knew were away from the irrigated areas in the first place, such as Gray's Lake, Swan Lake, the Malheur National Wildlife Refuge, and so forth. And from these areas, in the time of high precipitation, there were satellite lakes and shallow ponds extending 40, 50, and 100 miles out in all directions. This is the habitat that I am talking about that deteriorated. At the Bear River Migratory Bird Refuge in Utah, there is enough habitat left to support one pair of peregrines, and there are probably one or two birds remaining in that area; but in the other areas that were farther back in the mountains and below 6,000 ft (1,830 m), the peregrines are gone and so are the birds on which they lived.

THE PEREGRINE FALCON IN CALIFORNIA

GLADING: The method I have used in getting to the heart of this problem is largely that of discussion with people in the California Department of Fish and Game and with falconers in order to obtain an idea as to what is happening to this bird in our state. In addition, I have received the cooperation of the licensed falconers in California; they kindly responded to a questionnaire put out on this subject by me.

First a word in general about the status of peregrines in California. There is no question about it—these birds are in a serious condition if a measure of present numbers compared with past numbers is an indicator of what is happening to the species.

Nesting birds are down materially from the last recorded count of these nests made by R. M. Bond in 1939. According to Bond, there were a certain 65 nesting sites in the state at that time and a possibility of up to 120.

The best that I can possibly estimate, based on the reports of falconers and Department personnel, is from 19 to 32 active eyrie sites in 1965. Bear in mind that this latter estimate is very rough and is taken from falconers reporting nests and birds. The outside figures of 19 and 32 are derived as follows: the minimum figures were calculated on the premise that in instances where two observers each list a nest for a county they are talking about the same nest; the maximum figures are derived on the premise that where two falconers each list a nest for a county they are talking about different nests. The counties that are listed as having birds on this basis are: San Diego 3–6, Orange 2–5, Los Angeles 2, San Bernardino 1, Santa Barbara 1–2, San Luis Obispo 2–4, and Riverside 1. I also have a minimum of 1 each for Del Norte, Mendocino, Humbolt, and Sonora counties and a minimum of 3 for the balance of the north coast with a maximum of 11 for these four counties and the coast. Admittedly, this is a very poor and inexact survey but, again, all we could do with the given time and money.

THE PEREGRINE FALCON IN MEXICO

BANKS: According to the Mexican check-list, the only nesting records for Mexico aside from Baja California are along the Sonora coast.

WHITE: Subsequently, C. A. Ely (1962) published a record in *The Condor* (64:34) of a pair breeding in southeastern Coahuila. He collected an immature specimen at a nesting cliff.

CADE: William A. Wimsatt (pers. comm.) observed an apparently successful breeding pair of peregrines in Tamaulipas on 15 May 1963 at a latitude south of 24°N. The eyrie was some distance from Ciudad Victoria in a narrow gorge transecting the eastern slopes of the Sierras. The nesting ledge, on which young were seen, was in a limestone cliff a good hundred feet (30.5 m) above the talus slope and well under a massive overhang. This is the only eyrie that Wimsatt has seen in Mexico although he has traveled extensively in its southern states.

ADDENDUM: RECENT DATA ON ALASKAN PEREGRINES (1968)

In 1966, 17 pairs of peregrines occurred along 172 miles (277 km) of the Yukon River between Castle Rock, Yukon Territory, and Circle, Alaska (Cade, White, and Haugh, 1968). There were 19 occupied cliffs along this same stretch in 1951, with at least 16 pairs that fledged young. Reproduction in 1966 was high, clutches averaging 3.09 eggs and fledged young averaging 1.8 per starting pair (including nonlayers). Although there has been no significant change in either the size or the reproductive rate of this Yukon population in the last 15 years, total residue levels of DDT and related organochlorine compounds averaged 15 ppm (wet weight) in eggs and newly hatched young, and several hundred ppm in the body fat of adults. The number of pairs and breeding success were similar in 1967, again in association with high residue levels in adult body fat (J. H. Enderson, D. G. Roseneau, and L. G. Swartz, in press).

In 1967, 27 pairs of peregrines were found along 183 miles (293 km) of the Colville River, from the mouth of the Etivluk River to Ocean Point, in Arctic Alaska (Cade, Spofford, White, and Haugh, Final Report to Arctic Institute of North America for 1967). Along this same stretch in 1952 there were 32 pairs, in 1959, 40 pairs (Cade, 1960). Clutch size in 1967 averaged 2.15 eggs, with only one set of four and five single-egg sets in a sample of 19 nests. Fledging success, however, was still better than one young per starting pair, 34 fledglings being produced. By comparison, gyrfalcons and rough-legged hawks bred in maximum numbers with high reproductive success on the same cliffs with the peregrines.

It is too soon to say whether or not a progressive decline has begun in the Colville peregrines, but the small number of eggs laid in 1967 is associated with reduced eggshell weight. Four eggs have shell weights at the *lower range* of values reported by Ratcliffe (1967) for postwar peregrine eggs in Britain, and three eggs taken by White in 1964 show a similar reduction. (White remarks in Chapter 2 that reproduction along the Colville was poor in 1964.)

Considered together and within the total context of information now available on declining peregrine populations, the Alaskan data for 1966 and 1967 indicate that there is an association between relatively high organochlorine residue levels in eggs and body tissues of adult falcons in the far north and lightweight eggshells. I conclude that these northern peregrines are in near jeopardy. They are presently able to persist against the physiological effects of organochlorine contamination, of which change in shell weight can be taken as a measurable indicator, only because they migrate to breed (and to winter, in part?) in regions that are still relatively free of residue build-up in their prey species. Thus, for the time being, residue levels in the falcons can remain at values just below the threshold that induces dysgenic reproductive effects. The fate of these northern peregrines will depend on how organochlorine residues continue to accumulate in the various, geographic prey populations that these long-distance migrants exploit at different seasons of their annual cycle, which takes some of them from the high Arctic of North America to southern South America.—*T. J. Cade.*

The Peregrine Falcon in the Canadian Arctic and Eastern North America

CHAPTER 8

THE PEREGRINE FALCON IN NORTHERN CANADA

Richard Fyfe

The purpose of this paper is to discuss the present status of the peregrine falcon in northern Canada, with particular reference to the area between latitudes 55°N and 73°N. The information was derived from published materials, report files of the Canadian Wildlife Service, personal correspondence and conversations with biologists and naturalists, and my own observations made during 4 years in northern Quebec and in the Keewatin and Mackenzie districts.

GENERAL DISTRIBUTION

The first breeding record of the peregrine in northern Canada was made at Fort Good Hope in 1834 (Preble, 1908). Although early records indicate that peregrines nested throughout the Mackenzie District, MacFarlane believed that they did not nest farther north than 68°N. latitude (Mair and MacFarlane, 1908). This would indicate that the species has either recently moved into the barrens and extended its range northward or that MacFarlane was not aware that it nested along the Arctic coast and the interior barrens. In the eastern Arctic the species was recorded as common in southern Baffin Island by Kumlien (1879:82) and was recorded in the area around the Foxe Basin by the Fifth Thule Expedition in 1921–24 (Hørring, 1937). In the Ungava Bay region it was listed as a breeding bird near Fort Chimo by Turner in 1885 (Manning, 1949).

It is only recently that an accurate map of the range of this species can be drawn for the Canadian north, largely as a result of the investigations of T. H. Manning and several biologists of the Canadian Wildlife Service.

At the present time the peregrine nests throughout the boreal forest, from Alaska east through the Yukon and Northwest Territories, across northern Ontario and northeast into northern Quebec and Labrador. The species is known to breed in the boreal forest zone in the northern parts of all the western provinces with the exception of Saskatchewan, and J. S. Simonyi (pers. comm.) reports that peregrines nest along the Hudson Bay in northern Ontario. In tundra areas, the peregrine nests throughout Arctic Canada from the northern tip of the Mackenzie District, south and east across the barrens to Hudson Bay, along the northern coast of Ungava and north into the Arctic Islands as far as northern Baffin Island and Melville Island (Fig. 8.1).

NESTING HABITAT

As elsewhere, the peregrine in northern Canada is attracted to cliff ledges for nesting sites. In the absence of escarpments or cliff faces, the species will readily nest on cutbanks along rivers or coastal areas, on land forms known as dykes, or on low mounds or boulders. In nearly all instances the nest is located in the immediate vicinity of a body of water, either salt or fresh.

Cliffs are the preferred nesting habitat (Hickey, 1942; Bond, 1946; Cade, 1960), and the greatest densities of breeding peregrines in northern Canada are in areas where there are extensive ranges of cliffs, together with an abundance of food (J. P. Kelsall, pers. comm.; Tuck, 1954; Millar, 1954; Beebe, 1960). My own observations indicate that peregrines in the north will nest on cliffs ranging from 400 ft (122 m) in height to those with ledges only 8–10 ft (2.5–3 m) above the surrounding area. However, the presence of a cliff face does not necessarily mean that

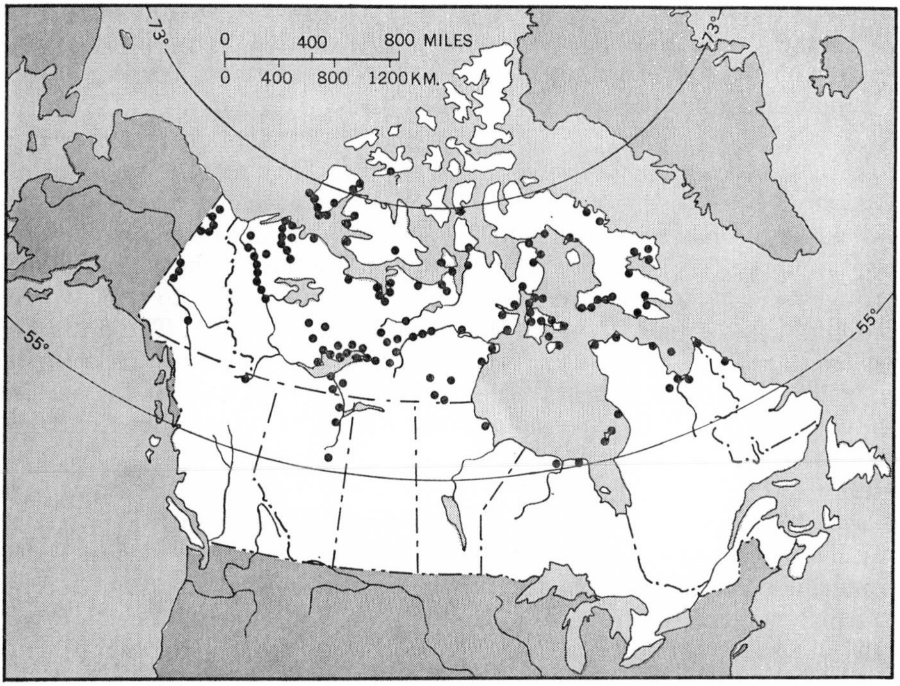

Fig. 8.1. Breeding distribution of the peregrine in northern Canada. The dots represent known breeding locations. One dot may indicate more than one nest site. UW Cartographic Lab.

peregrines will be found breeding in the area (Cade, 1960). If cliffs are not close to water, or if there are not food species available, peregrines will be scarce or entirely absent as a breeding bird.

Cutbanks along rivers or in coastal areas are also used and are a common feature along the rivers and lakes throughout the western provinces, the Mackenzie District, and Yukon Territory. Cade (1960) pointed out that these nest sites are seldom of a permanent nature and that the locations of nests may change from year to year, because of excessive erosion. Nevertheless, peregrines frequently nest on cutbanks, apparently with some permanency. In 1964, I found peregrines nesting on cutbanks along the Anderson River where MacFarlane reported them more than a hundred years ago.

In the central barrens near Contwoyto Lake, land forms referred to as dykes present rocky formations which are elevated over the surrounding countryside. Peregrines and gyrfalcons have found these formations suitable for nesting (Bill MacDonald, pers. comm.).

The most unusual nesting locations in the north are those in the central barrens where land relief is slight. Here peregrines nest on boulders and hummocks as little as 2.5 ft (0.9 m) above the surrounding area (Manning, 1946; Kelsall, pers. comm.). I have also been told by a missionary at Chesterfield Inlet that he has seen peregrines nesting on the ground near Baker Lake.

Cliff nests are typical for the species and are situated on a ledge or in a hole, most often under a protecting overhang. They may be found at almost any height on the face of the cliff. Nests on cutbanks are usually situated in a pothole or hollow under roots at the brink of the bank or in cavities under tree roots or rock outcrops on the face of the cutbank. Peregrines using dykes apparently nest in situations similar to those which you might find on a cliff face (MacDonald, pers. comm.). The nests are located in recesses under an overhanging projection of rock. Those nests on boulders and hummocks are unlike the usual nest sites of the species and are of necessity in exposed locations with little or no protection from above (Kelsall, pers. comm.).

Most of the nests that I visited in northern Canada had scrapes of either earth or gravel. I visited one nest where the eggs were laid on grass, and Höhn (1955) describes downy young as being on a grassy ledge. Three peregrine nests that I have seen in old rough-legged hawk nests had no soft material in the nests, and the eggs were laid on sticks. McEwen (1957) describes five nests observed in the Bathurst area as all being composed of sticks and other plant material.

INTERSPECIFIC COMPETITION AND AVAILABILITY OF FOOD

Cade (1960) suggests that when the peregrine and gyrfalcon are in direct competition, the gyrfalcon is the dominant competitor by virtue of its larger size and its early arrival on the nesting territory. My own observations in the Anderson River area indicate that the gyrfalcon is the dominant competitor, and, as a result, I believe that—in areas where the two species are found nesting during the same season—the gyrfalcon may displace the peregrine from the better nesting sites. Along the Anderson River during the summer of 1964, gyrfalcons occupied all cliff locations, whereas the peregrines nested on the dirt cutbanks. In one instance, the gyrfalcons apparently displaced the peregrines from a pothole which they had occupied the previous year (T. W. Barry, pers. comm.). I do not think that such displacement is a serious limitation for peregrines in the north, though it may limit the number in a particular area during a year of gyrfalcon abundance.

I agree with Cade (1954) that there are few areas in northern Canada where food may be a limiting factor for peregrine falcons. Throughout the boreal forest and tundra regions, passerines, shorebirds, and waterfowl are found in abundance. The exception would be the Arctic desert areas or the relatively barren mountain tops of eastern Baffin Island.

DECIMATING FACTORS

At the present time, little information is available to indicate what factors may be acting to the detriment of the peregrine population in northern Canada. I think the following points are the most important.

1. *Natural hazards.* A late spring, unseasonable storm, or excessive erosion may be critical to the peregrines in the north. Because of the short nesting season, renesting is usually not possible, and a natural catastrophe may end the nesting effort for a particular year.

2. *Human depredation.* It is impossible to determine how many young falcons are taken from the nests for food by native people, and how many are shot by hunters for food or for spite during migration or on the wintering grounds. We do know, however, that some young are eaten and others shot; we also know that northern birds are generally very tame and are included by hunters in that class of vermin called "hawks."

3. *Human interference.* In areas around northern settlements, peregrines are seriously affected by extensive human interference at the nest sites. In some instances (as at Yellowknife in 1964; J. Campbell, pers. comm.), such interference has resulted in almost total desertion of an area by this species.

4. *Insecticides.* We do not know how serious a problem insecticides may be for the peregrine in the north. Certainly, these falcons have some contact with the poisons through those food species that winter in agricultural areas in the south.

PRESENT STATUS

Unfortunately, there are no long-term data available on the peregrine in northern Canada which would indicate either an increase or decrease in the total population. Much of the area is yet to be visited by ornithologists, and most observations that have been recorded have been made during expeditions of but a few weeks duration. A summary of recorded observations made prior to 1960 is given in Table 8.1.

It is apparent that, in general, the peregrine has been observed as a common breeding bird in an extensive area of northern Canada prior to 1960. With the exception of a decrease in the number of breeding peregrines in the immediate vicinity of Yellowknife, all of the recent observations that I have indicate that the peregrine is still a common breeding bird in the north (Table 8.2).

Table 8.1. Early Observations on the Status of Peregrines in Northern Canada

Area	Status of peregrine	Authority
Athabasca-Mackenzie region	Distributed throughout the wooded portion of the region	Preble (1908)
Thelon River, from Timber Rapids to Baker Lake	Peregrines nest wherever suitable sites are available	Clarke (1950) Kelsall (pers. comm.)
Interior Barrens	Widely distributed over the plains area and nesting wherever suitable sites are available	Mowat and Lawrie (1955)
Bathurst Inlet and Coronation Gulf	Common breeding bird	Clarke (1944) McEwen (1957) Kelsall (pers. comm.)
Adelaide Peninsula	Moderately common in the Precambrian country of Adelaide Peninsula	Macpherson and Manning (1959)
Boothia Peninsula	The most common bird of prey on Boothia	Fraser (1957)
Cape Dorset area, Baffin Island	Peregrine falcons were more common in the region in 1954 and 1955 than when Soper (1946) found them	Macpherson and McLaren (1959)
	Common summer resident, breeds	Cooch (1955-56)
Cumberland Peninsula, Baffin Island	Peregrines were more plentiful than gyrfalcons	Watson (1963)
Cumberland Sound, Baffin Island	A regular breeder	Kumlien (1879)
Foxe Basin	Rather common in northwest Foxe Basin	Bray (1943)
Banks and Victoria Islands	Apparently common and breeding wherever suitable nesting sites are found	Porsild (1951)
Banks Island	Unlike the rough-legged hawk, the breeding population appears to be fairly constant from year to year, and the total population is estimated to be 600	Manning *et al.* (1956)

Table continued

Table 8.1.—continued

Area	Status of peregrine	Authority
Interior Ungava	Not uncommon in the interior	Low (1896) (Manning, 1949)
Fort Chimo	Duck hawks were abundant during the summer at Fort Chimo	Turner (1885) (Manning, 1949)
Ungava Bay	Scarcely an island of large size but what has one or more pairs of those hawks breeding on them	Turner (1885) (Bent, 1937)
Akpatok Island	Abundant	Davis (1932)
Newfoundland and Labrador	In view of the few records listed by Peters and Burleigh it would appear to be a rare migrant, which is peculiar as it is fairly common along the Labrador coast	Tuck (1956)

AVAILABILITY AND EXTENT OF SUITABLE NESTING HABITAT

Of 196 recorded nest sites in northern Canada, 77 are described. Sixty-three were on cliffs, 12 were on cutbanks, one was on a boulder (Manning, 1946), and one on a low hummock (Kelsall, pers. comm.). In a check of areas where peregrines were described by observers as being abundant, a study of topographical maps indicated that these were areas of extensive cliff or rocky outcrops. On the other hand, peregrines were absent or sparse in areas of open plains and till, presumably because there is a shortage of suitable nesting habitat.

I have attempted to classify the various areas in northern Canada to indicate the extent of suitable nesting habitat for peregrines. Those areas with which I was familiar were classified and, by working with other observers, we classified additional areas with which they were familiar. Remaining areas were then classified from descriptions in the literature, by the study of air photos, and by the study of 1:50,000 topographical maps.

By relating the nesting habitat to known nesting information, I have classified the areas into three groups as follows:

Group 1. Areas that provide optimum nesting habitat for peregrines, such as cliffs, cutbanks, or dykes, in close association with water (Fig. 8.2).

Group 2. Areas of limited peregrine nesting habitat where there may be cliffs, cutbanks, or dykes locally, but where they are not extensive

Table 8.2. Recent Observations on Peregrines in Northern Canada

Area	Status of peregrine	Authority
Ungava	A common breeding bird in summer along northern coast of Ungava	Father Verspeek (pers. comm., 1963)
Southampton and Coates Island	A common breeding bird in all areas with suitable nesting habitat	Fyfe (pers. obs., 1961–63)
Northwest coast of Hudson Bay	A common breeding bird in Wager Bay also observed regularly along the west coast of Hudson Bay south to Rankin Inlet	Fyfe (pers. obs., 1961)
Great Slave Lake	A common breeding bird on the east arm of Great Slave Lake and in the Precambrian region north and east of Yellowknife	Bill MacDonald (pers. comm., 1963)
Anderson River	A common breeding bird, nesting on virtually every sizeable cutbank	Beebe and Fyfe (pers. obs., 1964)
Inuvik	A common breeding bird nesting wherever suitable habitat was to be found	Beebe and Fyfe (pers. obs., 1964)
Mackenzie River	Common on rock cliffs along most of the river. In some areas pairs of peregrine are very plentiful and were estimated to be as little as a mile apart	T. W. Barry (pers. comm., 1964)

enough to warrant classifying in the first group. Also included in this group are some areas with extensive cliffs or escarpments but which are little known (Fig. 8.2).

Group 3. The remaining areas in northern Canada between 55°N latitude and 73°N latitude. Included in this group are regions with little suitable nesting habitat as well as large relatively unknown sections. These areas represent marginal nesting habitat where some peregrines are known to nest.

The total breeding habitat included in Groups 1 and 2 was then calculated in square miles and square kilometers (Table 8.3).

ESTIMATE OF POPULATION

The number of nesting peregrines observed in the Campbell Lake area by Frank Beebe and myself in 1964 together with John Kelsall's observa-

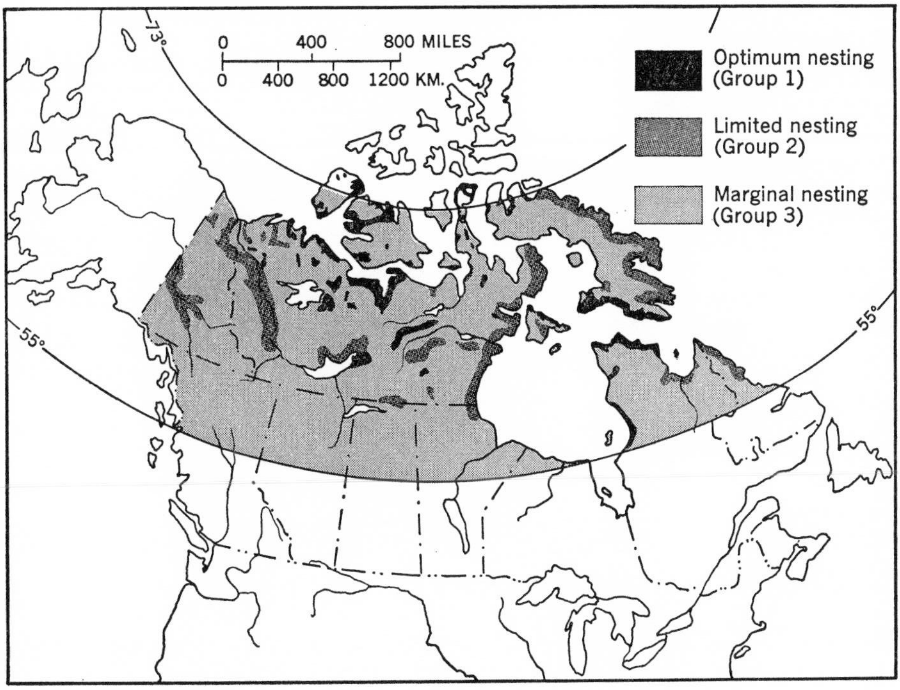

Fig. 8.2. Major breeding areas for peregrines in northern Canada, showing the three types of habitat designated in the text. UW Cartographic Lab.

tions (pers. comm.) for breeding peregrines in the Bathurst Inlet area would indicate a breeding density of approximately one pair of peregrines per 20 sq miles (52 sq km) of suitable nesting habitat. If we can accept this estimate for Group 1 areas, it is possible to obtain a population estimate for those areas with first-class habitat in northern Canada (Table 8.4).

Similarly, my observations on the breeding population of peregrines along the Anderson River in 1964 and the population estimate of Macpherson and Manning (1959) of 125 adult birds for the Adelaide Peninsula would indicate an approximate breeding density of 1 pair per 100 sq miles (259 sq km) in areas with limited nesting habitat. Again if we can accept this estimate as reasonable, it is possible to obtain a population estimate for those areas which I have designated as Group 2 (Table 8.4).

To most observers who are not familiar with the north, this estimate of 7,548 breeding pairs of peregrines in northern Canada may seem excessively high; however, when compared with Cade's estimate of 1,000 pairs for Alaska, and Manning and Macpherson's estimate of 600 birds for Banks Island, it is apparent that the estimate may not be out of line for an area of this size.

Table 8.3. Breeding Areas for Peregrines in Northern Canada

Location	Area in sq miles	
	Group 1	Group 2
Mainland Northwest Territories		
Mackenzie River	1,393	42,107
Anderson River	8,929	2,212
Coronation Gulf	18,842	
Great Bear Lake	6,226	
Great Slave Lake	6,799	13,230
Back River	4,178	
Western Hudson Bay	819	13,844
Boothia Peninsula	6,717	
Queen Maud Islands	1,229	6,062
Melville Peninsula		12,780
Thelon River		9,257
Total	55,132	99,492
Arctic Islands		
Banks Island	4,751	
Melville Island	5,816	
Victoria Island	15,770	
Duke of York Island	369	
Southampton Island	3,604	2,253
Coates Island	123	
Total	30,433	2,253
Northern Quebec and Labrador coast	11,756	6,636
Yukon Territory		9,994
Northern Manitoba		1,024
Northern Saskatchewan		8,765

Table 8.4. Estimate of Breeding Pairs

Location	Group 1 (1 pr per 20 sq miles)[a]	Group 2 (1 pr per 100 sq miles)[b]	Total breeding pairs
Mainland Northwest Territories	2,756	995	3,751
Arctic Islands	1,522	23	1,545
Baffin Island	944	456	1,400
Northern Quebec	588	66	654
Yukon Territory		100	100
Northern Manitoba		10	10
Northern Saskatchewan		88	88
Total	5,810	1,738	7,548

[a] This is approximately 1 pair per 50 sq km.
[b] This is approximately 1 pair per 250 sq km.

ACKNOWLEDGMENTS

I am grateful for the kind assistance of Bill McDonald of Yellowknife for his observations for the central barrens and Yellowknife area, also to John P. Kelsall, Thomas W. Barry, and Ernie Kuyt of the Canadian Wildlife Service, and to many others who have contributed their observations for areas that I have not been able to visit.

SUMMARY

At present the peregrine falcon is known to breed throughout northern Canada north of 55°N latitude from the Alaskan border east to the Labrador coast and north to Melville Island. The distribution and relative abundance of the peregrine appear to be largely determined by the availability of suitable nesting habitat in combination with the abundance of food species. It is apparent that the peregrine in the north is adaptable and that its requirements for nesting are not as rigid as has been suggested for peregrines farther south. Alternately, there is little doubt that cliffs are the preferred habitat in the north.

I have estimated that there are approximately 97,321 sq miles (252,061 sq km) of optimum peregrine nesting habitat together with an additional 128,164 sq miles (331,945 sq km) of more limited peregrine nesting habitat in northern Canada. By applying breeding densities from specific known areas in the north to these estimates I have further estimated that the breeding population for peregrines in northern Canada may well be in the order of 7,500 breeding pairs.

Most observations have indicated that the peregrine is a common breeding bird wherever there is suitable nesting habitat. With the exception of a decline in the immediate vicinity of Yellowknife, there is no evidence to indicate a widespread decline in the population, and recent observations suggest that the peregrine remains a common breeding bird in northern Canada.

ADDENDUM, 1968

Recent field studies that have taken place in northern Canada since the International Peregrine Conference in 1965 present a very confusing picture of the current status of the northern peregrine population. Observations made by C. M. White and J. R. Haugh on the Yukon in the summer of 1966 (White, pers. comm.) and by Ernie Kuyt (pers. comm.) on the Thelon in 1966 and 1967 indicate that the status of the peregrine in these two areas has remained relatively unchanged. In sharp contrast to these findings, the observations of J. H. Enderson and D. D. Berger (1968, in press) along the Mackenzie River and at Campbell Lake in 1966 suggest a sharp decline in the numbers of nesting peregrines in these specific areas, when their findings are compared to the observations during 1964 by Tom Barry, Frank Beebe, and myself for the same areas. In addition to the above-mentioned field studies, I have had personal communication with several other reliable persons, who have visited northern Canada during the past 2 years. Their reports indicate that the peregrine remains a breeding species in areas of suitable habitat in the central and northern Yukon Territory, in the northern Mackenzie District, in the central and northern Keewatin District, and in northern Ungava.

REFERENCES

The unpublished Canadian Wildlife Service reports listed below as C.W.S. Report 139, C.W.S.C. Report 669, etc., are filed in the head office of the Service at 400 Laurier Avenue West, Ottawa 4, Ontario.

American Ornithologists' Union. 1957. Check-list of North American birds. 5th ed. Amer. Ornithologists' Union [c/o Museum of Natural History, Smithsonian Institution, Washington, D.C.]. 691 p.

Banfield, A. W. F. 1951. Notes on the birds of Kluane Game Sanctuary, Yukon Territory. Can. Field-Nat., 67(4):177–179.

Beebe, F. L. 1960. The marine peregrines of the northwest Pacific Coast. Condor, 62(3):145–189.

Bent, A. C. 1937. Life histories of North American birds of prey. Pt. 1. U.S. Nat. Mus. Bull. 167. 409 p.

———. 1938. Life histories of North American birds of prey. Pt. 2. U.S. Nat. Mus. Bull. 170. 482 p.

Bond, R. M. 1946. The peregrine population of western North America. Condor, 48(3):101–116.

Bray, Reynold (with comments by T. H. Manning). 1943. Notes on the birds of Southampton Island, Baffin Island and Melville Peninsula. Auk, 60(4):504–536.

Breckenridge, W. J. 1955. Birds of the Lower Back River, Northwest Territories, Canada. Can. Field-Nat., 69(1):1–9.

Cade, T. J. 1954. On the biology of falcons and the ethics of falconers. Falconry News and Notes, 1(4):12–19.

———. 1960. Ecology of the peregrine and gyrfalcon populations in Alaska. Univ. Calif. Pub. Zool., 63(3):151–290.

Clarke, C. H. D. 1944. Notes on the status and distribution of certain mammals and birds in the Mackenzie River and western Arctic area in 1942 and 1943. Can. Field-Nat., 58(3):97–103.

———. 1950. A biological investigation of the Thelon Game Sanctuary. Nat. Mus. Can. Bull., 96:1–135.

Cooch, F. G. 1956. Birds observed in the vicinity of Cape Dorset, Baffin Island, summer 1955–1956. Can. Wildl. Serv. C.W.S.C. Rep. 462:5.

Drury, W. H., Jr. 1953. Birds of the Saint Elias quadrangle in the southwestern Yukon Territory. Can. Field-Nat., 67(3):103–128.

Eklund, C. R. 1956. Bird and mammal notes from the interior Ungava Peninsula. Can. Field-Nat., 70(2):69–74.

Ellis, D. V., and John Evans. 1960. Comments on the distribution and migration of birds in Foxe Basin, Northwest Territories. Can. Field-Nat., 74(2):62.

Fraser, J. K. 1957. Birds observed in the central Canadian Arctic, 1953, 1955, 1956. Can. Field-Nat., 71(4):192–199.

Gabrielson, I. N., and Bruce Wright. 1951. Notes on the birds of the Fort Chimo, Ungava District. Can. Field-Nat., 65(4):127–140.

Godfrey, W. E. 1953. Notes on Ellesmere Island birds. Can. Field-Nat., 67(2):89–93.

Harper, Francis. 1958. Birds of the Ungava Peninsula. Univ. Kansas, Misc. Pub. 17:1–171, 6 ps. 26 figs.

Hickey, J. J. 1942. Eastern population of the duck hawk. Auk, 59(2):176–204.

Höhn, E. O. 1955. Birds and mammals observed on a cruise in Amundsen Gulf, N.W.T., July 29th–August 16th, 1953. Can. Field-Nat., 69(2):41–44.

———. 1958. Birds of the mouth of the Anderson River and Liverpool Bay, Northwest Territories. Can. Field-Nat., 72(2):93–114.

———, and D. L. Robinson. 1951. Some supplementary bird notes from the general area of the Mackenzie Delta and Great Slave Lake. Can. Field-Nat., 65(3):115–118.

Hørring, Rich. 1937. Birds. Rep. Fifth Thule Expdn. 1921–24. Vol. 2(6–9):1–134.

Irving, Lawrence. 1960. Birds of Anaktuvuk Pass, Kobuk, and Old Crow. U.S. Nat. Mus. Bull. 217. 409 p.

Kumlien, Ludwig. 1879. Contributions to the natural history of Arctic America made in connection with the Howgate Polar Expedition, 1877–1878. U.S. Nat. Mus. Bull. 15. 179 p.

McEwen, E. H. 1957. Birds observed at Bathurst Inlet, Northwest Territories. Can. Field-Nat. 71(3):109–115.

Macpherson, A. H., and T. H. Manning. 1959. The birds and mammals of Adelaide Peninsula, N.W.T. Nat. Mus. Can. Bull. 161. 63 p.

———, and I. A. McLaren. 1959. Notes on the birds of southern Foxe Peninsula, Baffin Island, Northwest Territories. Can. Field-Nat. 73(2):63–81.

Mair, Charles, and Roderick MacFarlane. 1908. Through the Mackenzie Basin. . . . Notes on the mammals and birds of northern Canada. London. 494 p.

Manning, T. H. 1946. Bird and mammal notes from the east side of Hudson Bay. Can. Field-Nat., 60(4):71–85.

———. 1947. Explorations on the east coast of Hudson Bay. Geogr. J., 109(1–3):58–75.

———. 1948. Notes on the country, birds and mammals west of Hudson Bay between Reindeer and Baker Lakes. Can. Field-Nat., 62(1):1–28.

———. 1949. The birds of north-western Ungava, p. 155–224. *In* Mrs. Tom Manning, A Summer on Hudson Bay. Hodder and Stoughton, London. 224 p.

———. 1952. Birds of the West James Bay and southern Hudson Bay coasts. Nat. Mus. Can. Bull. 125. 114 p.

———, and A. H. Macpherson. 1952. Birds of the East James Bay Coast between Long Point and Cape Jones. Can. Field-Nat., 66 (1):1–35.

———, E. O. Höhn, and A. H. Macpherson. 1956. The birds of Banks Island. Nat. Mus. Can. Bull. 143. 144 p.

Millar, J. B. 1954. Murre studies on Akpatok Island, N.W.T. 1954. Can. Wildl. Serv. C.W.S.C. Rep. 910:7–8.

Mowat, F. M., and Andrew H. Lawrie. 1955. Bird observations from southern Keewatin and the interior of northern Manitoba. Can. Field-Nat., 69(3):93–116.

Peters, H. S. 1939. Ornithological investigations made during the 1939 eastern Arctic patrol. Can. Wildl. Serv. Rep. 196:34–40.

Porsild, A. E. 1943. Birds of the Mackenzie Delta. Can. Field-Nat., 57(2 and 3):19–35.

———. 1951. Bird notes from Banks and Victoria islands. Can. Field-Nat., 65(1):40–42.

Preble, E. A. 1908. A biological investigation of the Athabaska-Mackenzie Region. U.S. Dep. Agric., Bur. Biol. Surv., North Amer. Fauna no. 27. 574 p.

Savile, D. B. O. 1950. Bird notes from Great Whale River, Que. Can. Field-Nat., 64(3):95–99

———. 1951. Bird observations at Chesterfield Inlet, Keewatin, in 1950. Can. Field-Nat., 65(4):145–157.

———. 1961. Bird and mammal observations of Ellef Ringnes Island in 1960. Nat. Hist. Papers, Nat. Mus. Can., no. 9:1–6.

Shortt, T. M., and H. S. Peters. 1942. Some recent bird records from Canada's eastern Arctic. Can. J. Res., 20:338–348.

Snyder, L. L. 1957. Arctic birds of Canada. Univ. of Toronto Press, Toronto. 310 p.

Soper, J. D. 1928. A faunal investigation of southern Baffin Island. Nat. Mus. Can. Bull. 53. 143 p.

———. 1946. Ornithological results of the Baffin Island Expeditions of 1928–1929 and 1930–1931, together with more recent records. Auk, 63(2):223–239.

———. 1954. Waterfowl and other ornithological investigations in Yukon Territory, Canada, March 1951. Can. Wildl. Serv. C.W.S.C. Rep. 591:68–71.

Stewart, R. E. (in collaboration with R. P. Allen). 1955. Report on observations of birds and other animals in the Slave-Little Buffalo River Area, District of Mackenzie, Northwest Territories, Canada. Can. Wildl. Serv. C.W.S.C. Rep. 139:1–24.

Sutton, G. M. 1932. The birds of Southampton Island, Hudson Bay. Carnegie Mus. Mem., 12(2):1–275.

———, and D. F. Parmelee. 1956. The rough-legged hawk in the American Arctic. Arctic 9(3):202–207.

Tener, J. S. 1956. Annotated list of birds of part of the Back River, N.W.T. Can. Field-Nat., 70(3):138–141.

———. 1963. Queen Elizabeth Islands game survey 1961. Can. Wildl. Serv., Occasional Paper no. 4. 50 p.

Tuck, L. M. 1954. Murre investigation Akpatok Island. Can. Wildl. Serv. C.W.S.C. Rep. 669:12–13, 34–35.

———. 1956. Observations on Newfoundland birds 1956. Can Wildl. Serv. C.W.S.C. Rep. 765:25.

Watson, Adam. 1957. Birds in Cumberland Peninsula, Baffin Island. Can. Field-Nat. 71(3):87–109.

———. 1963. Bird numbers on tundra in Baffin Island. Arctic, 16(2):87–109.

Wynne-Edwards, V. C. 1952. Zoology of the Baird Expedition (1950). Vol 1. The birds observed in central and south-east Baffin Island. Auk, 69(4):353–389.

CHAPTER 9

NESTING PEREGRINE FALCONS IN WISCONSIN AND ADJACENT AREAS

Daniel D. Berger
and Helmut C. Mueller

The purpose of this paper is to summarize the reproductive history, from 1952 to 1965, of 14 peregrine falcon eyries located along the upper Mississippi River, and to report briefly on the status of nine other eyries in Wisconsin and one nearby in Michigan. Additional eyries have been reported in other areas in Michigan, Minnesota, and Iowa, but are not included in this report.

THE UPPER MISSISSIPPI RIVER

The gorge of the upper Mississippi River undoubtedly represents a significant portion of suitable nesting habitat for the peregrine falcon in this region. Here the river forms the boundary between Wisconsin and Minnesota, and between Wisconsin and Iowa. The river itself occupies only a relatively narrow channel cut in the floodplain, although natural and artificial impoundments occur at intervals. The gorge meanders generally southward through uplands that are primarily unglaciated. Our study area extends from Red Wing, Minnesota, southward to Dubuque, Iowa, a river distance of approximately 320 km (Fig. 9.1). Along this section of the river, the gorge varies from 1.6 km in width to as much as 10.4 km. The bluffs that border the river range in height from 70 m to

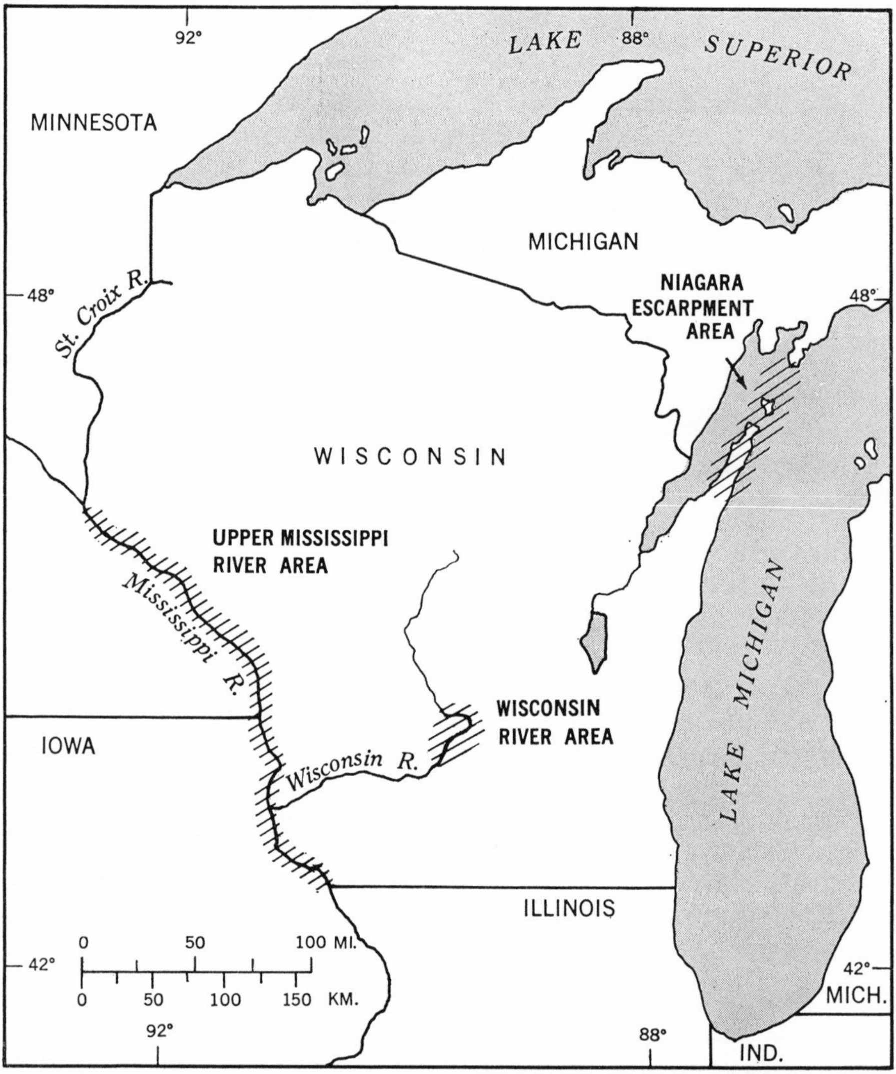

Fig. 9.1. Main breeding districts formerly occupied by nesting peregrines in Wisconsin and adjacent areas. UW Cartographic Lab.

185 m above the floodplain. In most places the walls of the gorge are steep, wooded slopes, but occasionally the river has exposed limestone and sandstone cliffs with a vertical drop of as much as 60 m (Martin, 1932).

In 1952, the first year of our study, we covered approximately 50% of the study area and found two active peregrine eyries, both with young.

In subsequent years we increased our effort and checked more, but seldom all, of the study area, averaging about 75% coverage per year. We almost invariably visited areas in which we had previously seen birds, while previously unproductive areas were visited occasionally, but not every year. In Table 9.1, the eyries are listed in their order on the river from north to south.

The increase in birds counted in the early years of the study (Table 9.1) may represent an increase in our proficiency in finding birds, rather than an increase in the peregrine population. After 1955 (Tables 9.1 and 9.2), the number of occupied eyries began dropping. It appears that, in general, the evacuation began in the south and spread northward. While the southern one-fourth of the study area has a substantial number of suitable cliffs, we were apparently too late to find birds in this area. The US Fish and Wildlife Service (W. E. Green, *in litt.*), however, reports peregrines here prior to 1941 and as recently as 1949. The peregrine count dropped quite steadily until it reached only one bird in 1963 and 1964, and then none in 1965. We recently learned, however, of an eyrie on a tributary river, some 16 km from the Mississippi, that produced two young in 1963. The following year only one adult briefly presided at the cliff, and in 1965 it was abandoned.

In most years we surveyed the river in late May and early June, at which time most of the young are about 18 days old. We travelled the roads that parallel the river below the bluffs. At each suitable-looking

Table 9.1. The Upper Mississippi River Peregrine Eyries 1952–64

A = adult present
c/ = clutch of eggs
P = pair present
P′ = Pair; nesting success unknown
Y = young found
— = no observation

Eyrie	'52	'53	'54	'55[a]	'56	'57	'58[a]	'59[a]	'60[a]	'61	'62[a]	'63[a]	'64[a]
1			2Y	P′	c/3	3Y	P						
2			P	P′	1–2Y	3Y	P	P′	3Y	P	4Y	A	A
3			P	P′	—	1Y	P	P′	1Y	P	2Y		
4				P									
5	1Y	P	P	P									
6		2Y	P	P	P								
7					A								
8		2Y	3Y	c/3	P	P[b]	A[b]						
9	1Y	P	A	2Y									
10			P										
11			P		A				1Y				
12			P′	P									
13		c/1	1Y	P	A								
14				A	A					A			

[a] At least two visits made in these years, including one at egg time. In all other years, only one visit.
[b] Young probably taken or already fledged.

cliff we stopped and looked for signs of occupancy with the aid of binoculars and a spotting scope. Where adults were found, we continued watching until one of the birds was seen taking prey into a cavity or ledge, or until we became satisfied that they had no young. When the nesting ledge was found, we approached the top of the cliff from the rear and, with the aid of ropes and rope ladders, climbed down to band the young.

Since we did little climbing except when we were quite certain of finding young, we have little data on clutch size. In the few cases where we did find eggs, it was always late in the season, and attrition may have reduced the clutch size. Nevertheless, we counted 1 clutch of one egg, 2 of two, and 2 of three. Of a total of 17 broods observed, there were 6 broods of one, 5 of two, 4 of three, 1 of four, and the size of 1 brood was undetermined.

In our peak year, 1955, we made two surveys, one in April, at incubation time, and the other, about 5 weeks later. Of the 13 sites known to us at that time, 11 had at least one bird at the cliff during at least one of the visits. All 11 were checked on the first visit, but only 7 on the second. At only 2 of the 7 sites were the results of observation the same during both visits. In both cases two adults were seen each time. At the other sites there were three cliffs where two adults were seen on the first visit, and none on the second; while at two cliffs none was seen on the first visit, but two were observed on the second check. This suggests that during the earlier years, before the decline, our surveys would have showed more occupied cliffs had we made an early survey in addition to the later one. We might hypothesize that the three pairs that were seen early, but not on

Table 9.2. Summary of Mississippi River Observations on the Peregrine, 1952–64

	'52	'53	'54	'55	'56	'57	'58	'59	'60	'61	'62	'63	'64
No. of sites with at least one adult present	2	5	10	11	8	4	4	2	3	3	2	1	1
Total no. of adults	4	11	18	21	12	8	7	4	6	5	4	1	1
Total no. of young	2	4	6	2	1[a]	7	0	0	5	0	6	0	0
No. of eyries with young	2	2	3	1	1	3	0	0	3	0	2	0	0
No. of young per occupied eyrie	1.0	0.8	0.6	0.2	0.1	1.8	0	0	1.7	0	3.0	0	0
No. of eyries with eggs, but no young		1		1	1								
No. of eyries not climbed, but almost surely no young		1	7	5	6		3			2		1	1
No eggs or young		1		1		1[b]	1[b]			1			
Success undetermined					3			2					

[a] Possibly one more young.
[b] Young probably taken, or already fledged.

the later check, might have been pairs that were unable to lay. Had their first clutch been destroyed, one would have expected them to re-lay, rather than to desert the cliff. In one of the three pairs, two nonproductive years preceded the year of desertion. In the other two, unfortunately, the previous history is unknown since they were not discovered until 1955. At all three sites the desertion was permanent. Early surveys were also made in most years after and including 1958. During this period of reduced numbers, both counts showed a high degree of similarity.

Recoveries have been received on two of the 29 nestling peregrines that we banded. One summer recovery was just 3 years later, only 72 km northeast of the banding site. Another was found dead not quite a year after banding in central North Dakota, approximately 825 km northwest of the birthplace. The former recovery suggests that the birds tend to return to the area of their birth to breed.

Records of peregrines nesting on the upper Mississippi prior to 1950 are fragmentary; therefore, the following figures are of interest. Roberts (1932) estimated that six pairs bred along the Mississippi River in southeastern Minnesota. This includes about one-fourth of our study area. Our data show only four eyries for that part of the river. In 1948, the Fish and Wildlife Service (Green, *in litt.*) estimated 30 peregrines along the entire Upper Mississippi National Wildlife Refuge. This refuge extends for 454 km along the river, and includes about 84% of our study area. In 1949 they put the peregrine population at 20. Incidentally, their report lists two seen on the refuge on 2 December, indicating that some of these birds might be year-around residents. Alternatively, they could be winter residents from farther north.

NIAGARA ESCARPMENT

Apart from the upper Mississippi birds, another breeding peregrine population existed along the Niagara Escarpment in upper Michigan and in Door County in northeastern Wisconsin (Fig. 9.1). We knew of four sites in this area. Our findings are summarized in Table 9.3. The first three eyries are in Wisconsin, and the fourth is in Michigan. All four sites were abandoned by 1958, 7 years ahead of those of the upper Mississippi peregrines.

WISCONSIN RIVER SYSTEM

Most other Wisconsin peregrine eyries are located along the Wisconsin River system (Fig. 9.1). Observations of these sites are scanty. The data were obtained from Hickey (1942 and *in litt.*), and from our own observations.

Eyrie No. W286 produced young peregrines as late as 1939. Being in a state park, it endured heavy disturbance caused by picnickers and rock climbers. The last known clutch was seen in 1953, and only one sighting of an adult occurred since then, in 1956.

Eyrie No. W265 has been known to be occupied since at least as early as 1886. It was abandoned in 1940. Another eyrie site, No. W287, was active from the late 1920's to at least 1933, but was not used between 1907 and 1920. We presume it was inactive after 1933.

Peregrines nested during 3 of 5 years at No. W97, in spite of the fact that the female and all three young were collected in 1921. In 1933 it was unoccupied, and presumably thereafter.

The only definite record for No. W288 was that of a pair without young in 1937, while the only record for No. W272, was 1938 when one young was seen. Presumably these last two sites were abandoned immediately or soon after the reported observations.

It should be emphasized that the Mississippi River cliffs are superior in size to those along the Wisconsin River, and probably suffered less disturbance as well. The peregrines undoubtedly do much of their foraging over the river bottoms which, in the case of the Mississippi, are much more extensive than the Wisconsin bottoms.

OTHER SITES

One other record of a Wisconsin eyrie is one that was "known to early oologists" (Hickey, 1942 and *in litt.*). It was on the St. Croix River, and

Table 9.3. The Niagara Escarpment Peregrine Eyries

Eyrie no.	1951	1952	1953	1954	1955	1956	1957	1958
W2	1 young	Pair; no young	1 adult 1 egg	1 adult; weak response	2 young dead below eyrie	Deserted		
W8		Good sign	2 young	1 young	1 young	Adult heard	Deserted	
W9			1 young	Pair; weak response	1 young	Deserted		
MG18						Pair; succ. unknown	Adult; young taken	Deserted

in 1940 was reported to have two young which were banded. No later observations were reported.

DISCUSSION

According to various estimates, the peregrine falcon could not be considered a common nester on the upper Mississippi River during the last 35 years at least. At best, estimates show one pair to 30 km of one side of the river in the late 1920's. Our highest density was one pair to 64 km of one side of the river in 1954 and 1955. The breeding peregrines are now gone from the study area. The last bird to be seen was in March 1964. Since the pressure of human activity increased only to a minor degree during the duration of our study, we cannot consider it to have been effective in the peregrine decline. Similarly, though some disturbance was caused by falconers, and at least a few young birds were taken, it does not appear that it could account for the decline. It should be noted that disturbances by falconers occurred at only one eyrie; in 1954 two of three young were taken, and in 1957 and 1958 falconers were suspected of taking the young.

The south to north progression of the peregrine disappearance correlates well with a similar phenomenon noted in the eastern United States by Berger *et al.* (Chapter 13).

ACKNOWLEDGMENTS

We gratefully acknowledge the efforts of those who assisted the writers in making the observations. Kenneth H. Kuhn, in addition to his participation in part of the project, supplied us with independently obtained data. Among the many assistants, we are particularly indebted to F. N. Hamerstrom, Jr., F. Hamerstrom, Herman Mueller, R. E. Zarden, A. Hamerstrom, E. Hamerstrom, C. R. Sindelar, D. Seal, R. Anderson, P. Drake, and T. Ennenga.

SUMMARY

On the Mississippi River, where 14 pairs were studied, a decline in the population became noticeable in 1956 and seemed to progress from south to north. Successful pairs averaged only two young per site and were last observed in 1962; the last adult was seen in March 1964. Eyries along the Niagara Escarpment were abandoned by 1958, those along the Wisconsin River system by 1957.

LITERATURE CITED

Hickey, J. J. 1942. Eastern population of the duck hawk. Auk, 59(2):176–204.

Kumlien, L., and N. Hollister. 1903. The birds of Wisconsin. Bull. Wis. Nat. Hist. Soc. Vol. 3, Nos. 1–3. 143 p. reprint.

Martin, L. 1932. The physical geography of Wisconsin (2nd ed.). Wis. Geol. and Nat. Hist. Surv., Bull. 36, Educ. Series No. 4. 608 p.

Roberts, T. S. 1932. The birds of Minnesota. Univ. Minn. Press, Minneapolis. Vol. 1. 691 p. + 49 pl.

CHAPTER 10

HISTORY OF THE MASSACHUSETTS PEREGRINE FALCON POPULATION, 1935–57

Joseph A. Hagar

In 1934, the Massachusetts Legislature passed, and the Governor signed, a statute that extended full protection to all but four of the state's indigenous hawks and owls. Among the protected species was included the duck hawk or peregrine falcon. Several conservation organizations had been active in support of this legislation, and shortly after its passage, their officers made known to the Director of the Division of Fisheries and Game their hope that a particular effort would be made to enforce it with respect to the duck hawks then nesting in the western half of the state. I was delegated to explore the situation, and in due course, to carry out whatever plan of enforcement might develop.

There is no space here to deal with the detail of this project, but I do wish to emphasize the effort that went into it over the next 8 years, to 1942. Forbush had named 7 duck hawk eyries in the state and marked 4 more on a map without indicating their exact location. Of these 11 sites, 10 were found in 1935, and in addition, another 4 for which there was no previous published record. To guard these 14 eyries, I was substantially freed of other duties from mid-March to late June of each year, five district fish-and-game wardens were coached in the most effective ways of keeping part-time watch during the course of their other duties, and in the first 3 years, from two to four deputy wardens were hired to stand watch from early morning to late evening at certain sites where the risk of interference seemed high. One of the results, over the course of 8 years, was a mass of data on nesting habits, interaction of adverse factors, and productivity, which may not have been duplicated elsewhere, and certainly not often. Its particular feature is the amount of almost day-by-day observation from egg-laying to fledging of young.

SCOPE OF PAPER

Given the relatively large amount of material available from the study, the next problem is how to organize it for effective presentation. After consideration of other ways, I have chosen to summarize my data in a series of tables, and my remarks will be largely confined to explanation of the symbols employed, and to pointing out their significance. Nothing will be included which does not bear on *productivity*, and many aspects of that will have to be skipped over lightly. The tables are divided into four sections: horizontally, to compare production figures from six superior sites and eight inferior sites; and vertically, to compare production during the 8-year period of intensive study before the war, with less complete but still revealing figures for the 13-year period beginning in 1945, toward the end of which the breeding population steadily declined. Although my performance must be sketchy, I trust that the outlines of the picture will take shape before I am through.

THE EYRIES AND THE POPULATION

GENERAL DESCRIPTION OF EYRIES

The typical Massachusetts cliff, and none departs very far from the type, is a sheer rock face on the upper portion of a low to medium-high mountain ridge trending north-south and overlooking a river valley; the slopes below the cliff are wooded, the top of the cliff is wooded or semi-open; cliffs are at elevations of 200–1200 ft (60–365 m), their rock faces 40–250 ft (12–75 m) high, and the nesting shelves 10–130 ft (3–40 m) below the top of the face. On the whole, these cliffs are relatively small and low. If it is significant, 11 eyries overlook agricultural land, 2 overlook woods, and the last of the 14 a reservoir.

KNOWN AGE OF EYRIES

A set of eggs taken from Eyrie M5 in 1861 is frequently referred to as the first specific nesting record for the United States, but local history indicates the presence of peregrines at Eyrie M4 in the first decades after 1800 (Richards, 1919). In Table 10.1, the first known record of occupancy at each cliff has been taken from Allen (1869), Bagg and Eliot

(1937), Faxon (1889), Faxon and Hoffman (1900, 1922), Richards (1919), Thayer (1904), Hickey (pers. comm.), and my own field work.

RATING OF EYRIES

Each cliff has been given a *relative rating* (Table 10.1) on the basis of three criteria: height of sheer face above talus slope, disturbance caused by public use (hikers, picnic parties etc.), and the number and suitability of the shelves. Thus, Eyrie M1 is rated AAA; it is a high cliff for southern New England, rarely visited even by local people, and with several very fine shelves. The cliffs with best records of productivity are all rated A for height except M6, which is B for height but an unusual A for disturbance because it is located in the watershed of a reservoir, closed to public entry.

ADULT POPULATION

The six superior sites were always occupied by pairs, and the four to six next best quite regularly so, throughout the 1935–42 period and until at least 1947. The two poorest sites were only occasionally occupied, and the worst of them, never successfully.

Many observations indicate a considerable floating population of unmated females in 1935–42: female vacancies were promptly filled (Eyrie M1 in 1936), and extra females visited cliffs where a pair was already established. Of the latter, some were occasionally fed by resident males, suggesting that they might be subadults raised on the same cliffs the previous season.

A few subadult females were actively mated to resident males; in these instances note that most of them were on low-rated cliffs.

Two adult birds recognizable by special traits of behavior were known to be resident at their respective cliffs for several seasons: a female at Eyrie M2 in 1935–38, a male at Eyrie M1 in 1935–41.

PRODUCTIVITY IN 1935–42

EGGS

Clutches as laid were almost invariably four (Table 10.1); i.e., either four eggs were in the nest when it was examined, or a missing egg could be accounted for, usually in one of two ways. In several instances the first egg of a clutch was laid on one shelf and the remainder on another; the apparent reason was an intervening snowstorm or cold snap which made the first shelf untenable or froze the egg, afterward abandoned. Somewhat more often, there was actual or inferential evidence that a missing egg or eggs had been knocked off a poor shelf by an incubating bird flushing directly and hurriedly from the nest. Only one five-egg clutch was found, at Eyrie M6 in 1945. After the first year, we had only one indication of a clutch taken by egg collectors.

The statistics of egg production for 1935–42 show: at six superior sites, 138+; at eight poorer sites, 68; total, 206. Averages for the six best sites were: per year, 17+; per actual nesting, 3.6+.

YOUNG BIRDS HATCHED

In 1942, all sites were checked to mid-June, but only two of them later for fledged young. In this case, all eggs are entered as of this date and the production for that year *estimated* as the average production at the same cliff in previous years. All such values are probably low.

Of the 138 eggs laid at superior sites, 1935–42, 94± or 68% were successfully hatched (Table 10.2); of 68 eggs at inferior sites, 35± or 51%; all sites together, 129+ of 206 eggs, or 62%.

The circumstances and apparent causes of nonhatching were too diverse for much grouping, but the following comments are offered:

1. The percentage of possibly sterile eggs was low, and some of these may have been, in fact, fertile. Under the same circumstances of severe weather that caused desertion of first eggs, we suspected the fatal chilling of other eggs that upon examination showed no embryo development.
2. A large proportion of nonhatching eggs contained well-developed embryos.
3. As an instance of apparently accidental loss, the four-egg clutch at M8 in 1937 was faithfully incubated for upwards of 6 weeks without hatching; when I finally opened them, the embryos were even-aged, perhaps 10–12 days along. Had the incubating bird been frightened off this open site toward dark of a cold night, and not returned until morning?
4. When the female at M13 was killed at the nest in 1937, the male deserted; when the 1936 female at M1 died after incubating less than 3 weeks, the male alone hatched two eggs, although he failed to raise the young.

On the whole, loss of eggs was spread rather haphazardly over the whole period of incubation, and by the usual standards was rather low.

RAISING OF YOUNG

In contrast to the foregoing, a high proportion of the losses of chicks came in the first few days after hatching, the two principal reasons being:

1. The chicks are apparently quite vulnerable to wet stormy weather while they are getting out of the shell and immediately afterward; Eyries M8 and 10, 1938, are extreme cases, and there were others.

2. In broods of three and four, the last-hatched or smallest bird sometimes failed to grow at the same rate as the others, presumably because of failure to get a fair share of food, and soon disappeared. This was not inevitable, however; some runts caught up with their nest-mates.

By the fifth day the most critical time was over, and further losses low. Somewhat more than two-thirds of the young acquired *Protocalliphora* maggots in their ears, but with no apparent ill effect. The only other disability of any sort involved one bird only, in 1941: about a week after leaving the shelf, it was found sitting on the talus slope in a weakened state, with feathers ruffled and disordered. It could still fly sufficiently to keep out of our reach, but examined through binoculars it appeared to have lesions on its face and inside its mouth.

The statistics from the 1935–42 period were as follows: of 94 chicks hatched at six superior sites, 81 were raised to flying age (86%); of 35 at poorer sites, 26 were raised (74%); the total was 107 flying from 129 hatched, or 83%.

LATER HISTORY

Young birds disappeared from the cliffs 4–6 weeks after flying, and further information came only from band recoveries. Of 88 banded, 14 birds or 16% were reported in later years. Of these, nine died before they were 9 months old—in their first fall and winter—and the other five lived to be, respectively, 1.5, 3.5, 4.5, 6, and 13.5 years. Five recoveries were from Pennsylvania, and one each from Massachusetts, Vermont, Ontario, Connecticut, New York City, New Jersey, Maryland, Virginia, and North Carolina. I conclude from the nature of some of the recoveries that the inexperienced young birds have hard going their first fall and winter, and that southward migration of Massachusetts birds was not very extensive.

SUMMARY OF PRODUCTIVITY IN 1935–42

To sum up, at this point, for the 1935–42 period, I believe the tables give a fairly accurate idea of productivity from the Massachusetts cliffs, and that the conclusions can be extended to the rest of New England and perhaps the middle Appalachians. The major points are:

1. There was regular occupation of the six superior cliffs by mated pairs, and fairly regular occupation of poorer cliffs, although the incidence of subadult females and unmated males was greater. The overall effect was of a nesting population with sufficient reserves to fill in losses on the good cliffs very quickly.

Table 10.1. Egg Production of Peregrines in Massachusetts

Eggs laid
n? = exact number not known
1,2,3 = number of eggs in separate clutches or eggs laid on separate ledges

No eggs laid
M = male
P = pair
IF = female in subadult plumage
F = adult female

Miscellaneous
— = no observations
x = one visit; no birds seen

Eyrie no.	When found	Eyrie rating[a]	'35	'36	'37	'38	'39	'40	'41	'42	'47
Best sites											
M1	1912±	AAA	3+	4	3	4	4	4	4	4	4
M2	19th cent.	ABA	4	4	4	4	4	P	P	P	P
M3	1921	ABA	4	4	3	4	P	P	3	3	4
M4	(1818) 1884	ABB	4	P	P	3	n?	P	4	4	P
M5	1861	ABB	2+	4	4	4	M,IF	P	4	4	4
M6	(1890) 1912	BAA	n?, 2	4	4	4	4	4	4	4	3,4
No. of occupied sites			6	6	6	6	6	6	6	6	6
Total no. of eggs			19+	20	18	23	12+	8	19	19	19
No. nonlaying pairs, birds			0	1	1	0	2	4	1	1	2
Poorer sites											
M7	1888	BAB	1+	1,3	P	P	4	4	3+	4	4
M8	1936	BAC	x	P	4	2,3	P	2	M	P	P
M9	1929	BBB	M,F?	P	3	4	M,IF?	2[b]	M,IF	4	P
M10	1888	BCC	M,IF?	3	P	4	M	M	P	x	3
M11	1906	BCC	3	P	M,IF	P	M	P	M	xxx	—
M12	1902	CBC	—	M	x	3	P	P	4	M	4
M13	1936	CBC	—	3+	4?	M	M?	xxxx	x	xx	M,IF
M14	1926	CCC	M?	M?	xx	—	—	—	—	—	P
No. of occupied sites			4	7+	6	7	6+	6	6	4	7
Total no. of eggs			4+	10+	11−	16	4	8	7+	8	11
No. nonlaying pairs, birds			2+	4+	3	3	5+	3	4	2	4

[a] Relative rating of cliff, based on (1) height of sheer face above talus slope, (2) disturbance caused by public use, and (3) number and suitability of nesting shelves.
[b] Adult female laid two eggs, deserted, disappeared; replaced by subadult female which laid no eggs.

2. The good cliffs as a group produced young birds at the average annual rate of 10+, or 1.7 juveniles per cliff. The poor cliffs produced less regularly, but still contributed to the annual total.

POSTWAR PERIOD, 1945–57

In retrospect, it is unfortunate that the Massachusetts peregrine eyries were not checked more regularly from 1945 on, but the impending decline of the population was not foreseen, and less time could be allotted to the project. The available data are given in Table 10.3. A partial check of the cliffs in 1946 indicated that production was above normal and, indeed, that a greater number of young might fledge than in any prewar year. A more thorough check in 1947 showed good occupation of the cliffs by adult pairs, but in the end production was down to six, well below the average. Furthermore, the pair at Eyrie M6 had a very bad year, losing a

Table 10.2. Production of Young by Massachusetts Peregrines

No eggs laid	*Egg failures*	*Young*
M = male	Usually shown as difference between Tables 10.1 and 10.2	1,2,3 = number reared
P = pair		yd = died or disappeared from the nesting ledge
F = adult female	c/-f = eggs failed	— = no observations
IF = subadult female		
x = one visit; no birds seen		

Eyrie no.	'35	'36	'37	'38	'39	'40	'41	'42	'47	Total young fledged
Best sites										
M1	3	2yd	3	3/1yd	3	1	2	2[a]	3	20
M2	4	2	4	3	3	P	P	P	P	16
M3	1	4	2	3/1yd	P	P	2yd	1[a]	1	12
M4	2 ?yd	P	P	1	c/?f	P	4	1[a]	P	6
M5	2+	2	3	2	M,IF	P	2	2[a]	1	14+
M6	2yd	4	3	1/2yd	3	2	3	2/1yd	1yd[b]	18
Eggs	19+	20	18	23	12±	8	19	19	19	100+[c]
Hatched	14+	14	15	17	9	3	13	9±	6	71[c]
Fledged	10+	12	15	13	9	3	11	8±	5	63[c]
Poorer sites										
M7	c/1?f	2yd	P	P	2	2	3+	1[a]	1	9+
M8	x	P	c/4f	c/2f/2yd	P	1	M	P	P	1
M9	M,F?	P	1	3/1yd	M,IF?	c/2f	M,IF	3+	P	7+
M10	M,IF?	3	P	4yd	M	M	P	x	c/3f[d]	3
M11	c/3f	P	M,IF	P	M	P	M	xxx	—	0
M12	—	M	x	c/3f	P	P	4	M	1yd	4
M13	—	3	c/4?f	M	M?	xxxx	x	xx	M,IF	3
M14	M?	M?	xx	—	—	—	—	—	P	0
Eggs	4+	10+	11−	16	4	8	7+	8	11	56±[c]
Hatched	0	8	1	10	2	3	7+	4±	2	31+[c]
Fledged	0	6	1	3	2	3	7+	4±	1	22+[c]

[a] Estimated on basis of production in previous years.
[b] Two eggs broken out of 3 in first clutch; in second clutch, 2 eggs disappeared during incubation and probably 1 hatched.
[c] For 1936–41 only.
[d] Three eggs taken by egg collector.

first clutch and failing to raise young from a second clutch. This pair was watched more closely than any other in the next three seasons, and their history follows the pattern which is now recognized, belatedly, as characteristic of the decline that was occurring elsewhere. A check in 1951 showed that occupation of the cliffs was now spotty, with production further reduced, and by 1955–57 only an occasional single bird was left.

Although I followed the pair at Eyrie M6 quite regularly in the 4 years 1947–50, because I was trying to photograph them from a blind on the shelf, my notes give little help in accounting for the broken eggs, the disappearing eggs, and the deserted eggs that marked the period. This cliff was closed to all public entry by locked gates at points 2 and 3 miles (3.2 and 4.8 km) away, and since no one was ever at or near the cliff, disturbance cannot have been a factor. The female of this pair was not certainly identifiable by any mark or peculiarity of behavior, but I had the impression that she was the same bird present in 1945 and 1946. Nor did I notice that her behavior was in any way abnormal. There was more sign of

Table 10.3. Miscellaneous Eyrie Histories 1945–57

B = broken	f = failed	x = no birds seen
c = clutch	M = male	y = young
d = dead	P = pair; no eggs	— = no observation
q = fate not known	IF = subadult female	

Eyrie no.	'45	'46	'47	'48	'49	'50	'51	'55	'57
M1	—	—	c/4=3y	—	—	P	c/4=1y	P	—
M2	—	—	P	—	—	P	c/4=3y	M	—
M3	—	4y?	c/4=1y	—	—	M,F?	c/1f	x	—
M4	P	4y?	P	—	—	P	M	—	M?
M5	c/4q	4y	c/4=1y	—	—	1y	P	—	—
M6	4y	c/5=4y	c/3=2B	c/3f	c/1f	c/2B	P	—	M?
			c/4=1yd	c/2f		c/1B			
						c/2-1B			
M7	—	—	c/4=1y	—	—	M?	x	—	—
M8	—	—	P	—	—	—	—	—	—
M9	c/4f	c/2q	P	—	—	P	P	—	M
M10	—	—	c/3f	—	—	P	c/2f	x	—
M12	—	—	c/4=1yd	—	—	—	x	—	—
M13	—	x	M,IF	—	—	—	—	—	x
M14	—	—	P	—	—	—	—	—	—

raccoon (*Procyon lotor*) on the cliff than ever before, and in 1950 fresh raccoon scats and tracks were found within a foot of a scrape containing half of a broken egg. At the time, I was more impressed with the significance of this than I now am; it is wholly unlikely that raccoons could have been the whole story, even in Massachusetts.

SUMMARY

In 1935–42 and in 1947, at the six best sites in this state, initial clutch size was 4 in 33 undisturbed nestings and 3 in 5 others; in 32 verified cases, fledged young averaged 2.50 in successful nests; and in 54 breeding attempts, nonlaying was observed 12 times. At eight poorer sites, nonlaying pairs were noted 16 times in adult-plumaged pairs, 3–5 times with the female in subadult plumage; single males numbered 8–11. Hatching success was 68% at superior sites, 51% at inferior sites, 62% at all sites, egg losses being spread over the whole period of incubation. Chick losses tended to occur in the first 5 days after hatching, 86% of the hatched young fledging at superior sites, 74% at poor sites, 83% at all sites. When one excludes three eyries at which males were doubtfully present, the mean number of young annually produced per occupied site was about 1.59 at the better cliffs (N=54), 0.51 at the poorer cliffs (N=53), and 1.06 at all cliffs (N=107).

Observations were not intensively carried out in the period 1945–57. Sampled reproductive success seemed above normal in 1946, but well below average in 1947 when broken eggs were observed for the first time. By 1951, occupation of the cliffs was spotty, and by 1955–57 only an occasional single bird was left.

LITERATURE CITED

Allen, J. A. 1869. Notes on some of the rarer birds of Massachusetts. Amer. Nat., 3(10):505–648.

Bagg, A. C., and S. A. Eliot, Jr. 1937. Birds of the Connecticut Valley in Massachusetts. Hampshire Bookshop, Northampton. 813 p.

Faxon, Walter. 1889. On the summer birds of Berkshire County, Massachusetts. Auk, 6(1):39–46.

———, and Ralph Hoffman. 1900. The birds of Berkshire County, Massachusetts. Collections Berkshire Hist. and Sci. Soc., 3:107–166.

———, and Ralph Hoffman. 1922. Supplementary notes on the birds of Berkshire County, Massachusetts. Auk, 39(1):65–72.

Forbush, E. H. 1927. Birds of Massachusetts and other New England states. Part II. Land birds from bob-whites to grackles. Mass. Dep. Agric., Boston. 461 p.

Richards, V. F. 1919. The early history of a duck hawk. Auk, 36(3):349–350.

Thayer, G. H. 1904. A Massachusetts duck hawk aery. Bird-Lore, 6(2):47–53.

CHAPTER 11

THE EXTIRPATION OF THE HUDSON RIVER PEREGRINE FALCON POPULATION

Richard A. Herbert and Kathleen Green Skelton Herbert

This paper summarizes the history and reproductive success of the peregrine falcon at eight eyries in the lower Hudson River valley and at a New York City eyrie, and analyzes possible causes of the extirpation of the population in the late 1950's. The behavior of this population has been discussed in a previously published paper (Herbert and Herbert, 1965).

The senior author of this paper made a study of the Hudson eyries from 1930 until his death in 1960. In 1949 the junior author joined in the study, and she assumed the responsibility for gathering and eventually for publishing the data. We are deeply indebted to Joseph J. Hickey, who supplied much of our eyrie histories prior to 1941 and without whose help and encouragement this manuscript could not have been prepared. Thanks are also due to Ernst Mayr for his assistance in the 1940's and to Dean Amadon for his critical reading of an early draft of this manuscript.

The term *eyrie* in this paper refers to a cliff or series of cliffs and nest ledges which are the nesting domain of a single pair of peregrines and their successors over a period of years. The term *cliff* here includes not only natural cliffs, but also abandoned quarries and New York City skyscrapers when used as nesting sites. Each cliff occupied by the birds had at least one nest ledge known to have been used during the period of our study.

The eight eyries of the lower Hudson River, consecutively numbered in this paper from south to north, extended for 55 miles (88 km) north of New York City along the west shore of the Hudson River in New Jersey and New York State, within the boundaries of the Palisades Interstate Park. Here the peregrine was legally protected by the sanctuary status of the Park and by the laws of both New York and New Jersey. A ninth marginal eyrie, situated in a quarry near the No. 5 eyrie was also included in our field observations, although it was not an active nesting site after 1941. (For further description of the eyries, see Herbert and Herbert, 1965).

Over a 30-year period the total number of our nesting-site inspections and wintering observations is estimated to have been on the order of 5,000. We usually spent about 12 hours in visiting the eyries on one field trip, and frequently did not cover all eight in 1 day. The approximate mean for each site inspection of the six lower eyries was 1 hour, and of the two northern eyries (which were visited less frequently) 2 hours. It required nearly an hour to cover the respective nest ledges of the No. 1, 2, and 3 (northern and southern sites), and the No. 4 and 5 eyries.

EARLY HISTORY OF THE HUDSON EYRIES (1877–1940)

Our earliest record for these eyries goes back only to 1877 ("Alianus," 1879) and to Ernest Thompson Seton's story of a racing pigeon taken by a peregrine from the No. 3 eyrie. In the nineteenth century there were other eyries along the 55-mile stretch of cliffs from New York City to Storm King Mountain. Until about 1910, there was an active eyrie on the west shore of the Hudson opposite 125th Street (the late Beecher S. Bowdish, pers. comm.), and at an earlier date the sheer cliff with overhang opposite Manhattan's 79th Street boat basin was an occupied eyrie. There was also an eyrie on the east side of the river in the Yonkers area (Bowdish, pers. comm.). The No. 2 eyrie which we "discovered" in 1947 proved to have been an active eyrie at the turn of the century when, in 1910, Bowdish took the first photographs of a nesting adult at this eyrie (Bowdish, *in litt.*). It had been abandoned for 35 years at the time of its occupancy in 1947. Likewise the southern site of the No. 8 eyrie, which was reoccupied in the 1940's proved to be a long-abandoned nest site.

Thus, even in this limited 55-mile area the peregrine has been retreating under pressure from the human population since the turn of the century. However, in the 1930's the peregrine appeared to be adapting itself to human population pressures with its spectacular appearance on skyscrapers, bridges, and other man-made structures in a number of cities.

On the Hudson the peregrines established eyries in three abandoned quarries on the west side of the Hudson and in one on the east side of the river. But these sites, easily accessible and subject to disturbance, did not prove to be good nesting sites.

In the late nineteenth and early twentieth centuries, the Hudson eyries began to be heavily exploited by collectors, usually egg collectors, although birds from these eyries also supplied museum and private collections. Egg-collecting became a hobby that did not decline until the 1940's. In the 1920's and 1930's the eyries began to be exploited by falconers, who usually took young birds from the nest for training, although adults have also been trapped at the Hudson eyries. However, attrition by falconers did not take a heavy toll of the eyries until the mid-thirties. The seizure of birds by falconers was more disastrous to the peregrines than egg-collecting, because no North American peregrine has been known to hatch two broods in a single season, although it may lay one or more clutches of eggs in replacement.

Pigeon fanciers and gunners also took a heavy toll, particularly of juvenile birds. By the 1930's three of the eyries had become nonproducing, yet the number of adults held fairly constant, any vacancy being immediately replaced.

The early history of these eyries is set forth in an appendix to the present paper, together with a summary of many of our observations. In 1931–40, according to Hickey (*in litt.*), there were about 1.1–1.2 young reared annually, on the average, at each of the occupied eyries along the Hudson for which adequate data are available (Table 11.1). This is similar to the 1.1 young reported for 19 eyries in the New York City region during 1939–40 (Hickey, 1942).

RECENT HISTORY

THE PERIOD 1941–49

World War II provided a temporary respite for the peregrines of the Hudson and the New York City population. Rationing of gasoline and the ban on pleasure driving made some of the eyries inaccessible, and the war effort removed many of the birds' human persecutors. The pairs along the Hudson increased to nine in the early war years, but by 1949 only seven pairs were present. The wintering population in the city increased to 16 in 1946, but by 1952 it had dropped to seven (Herbert and Herbert, 1965).

In three eyries of the lower Hudson, 33 young hatched during the 6 years 1943 through 1948, or 1.83 per eyrie. Eighteen of these young, or 54%, were taken from the nest ledges by falconers; among these 18

Table 11.1. Peregrine Production on Hudson River, 1931–49

Status	1931–40		1941–49	
Eyrie occupied:				
Birds did not breed	4		6	
Birds had no young	5		10	
Eggs laid:				
Clutch failed or deserted	4		2	
Clutch disappeared	3			
Eggs or young disappeared			3	
Hatching known:				
All young lost	1		6	
Subtotal unsuccessful		17		27
Successful pairs:				
Probable	4		5	
Known	11		8	
Subtotal successful		15		13
Total number occupied sites		32		40
Numbers of young				
Died			1	
Disappeared	1		2	
Probably taken			2	
Taken by falconers	3		18	
Subtotal lost		4		23
Probably reared	12±		15	
Known reared	24–25		15	
Subtotal		36–37		30
Reared per occupied eyrie		1.1–1.2		0.75[a]

[a] This would be 1.25 if those taken for falconry had all successfully fledged.

young were five birds banded by the senior author at three different eyries. Only 12 young took wing from the three eyries in these years, a mean of 0.6 per eyrie per year.

However, the mean number of young *probably* reared in the eight eyries of the lower Hudson in the years 1941–49 was 0.75 (Table 11.1). This estimate would be 1.25 if those young taken for falconry had all successfully fledged. Mebs (1960) estimated that a number of fledged young lower than a mean of 1.5 per year was probably insufficient to support the population.

The peregrines of New York City were likewise exploited because of their raids on the pigeon flocks, and they suffered from unfavorable newspaper publicity. One pair successfully nested on two different skyscrapers, hatched 11 young in 1943–48, but was never permitted to fledge a single one. Of the 11 young, 3 were killed by the American Society for the Prevention of Cruelty to Animals, 3 were robbed by falconers, and 5 were turned over to selected, cooperating falconers by conservation officials for rearing and release. Of these 5, 2 died in captivity, 1 was released (fate unknown), and 2 were released and subsequently shot. By contrast, in Montreal, where the peregrine had a more favorable "image" in the press, the pair that nested on the Sun Life Assurance Building hatched 13 young in these years, 1943–48, and 11 fledged (Table 11.2). In the 13 years 1940–52, 26 young hatched, and 22 fledged.

THE PERIOD 1950–61

The year 1950 was the first year, in our experience, in which not one young hatched in the eyries of the lower Hudson. Several factors contributed to the nesting failures of the 1950's, the most obvious being the construction of the Palisades Interstate Parkway, which had been delayed for many years because of the protests of landowners whose land was being expropriated for this "nature preservation" project. Although the Palisades Parkway was not officially opened to the public until 1956, blasting, stripping of trees, and changing of the cliff habitat commenced in 1950, and continually disturbed the nesting cycle of the birds.

As in the 1930's and 1940's, other disturbing factors were falconers and shooting, the latter usually occurring near two of the Park police stations. Weather was also an important deterrent in the nesting seasons of 1950, 1951, 1952, and 1953. Partial reports of our observations for these critical years are given below. Complete field observations for these years are to be given in another paper by Herbert and Herbert (in prep.).

The 1950 nesting season. There were seven pairs present in the eight eyries of the lower Hudson. Eyrie No. 1 continued to be occupied by Male A (present since 1938 and identified by a tuft of white feathers the size of a 25-cent piece on his nape) and Female E, who laid a month earlier than any other Hudson female, and who had been present since 1942 (see appendix to this chapter). Male X, identified by his pale color, dark head, and heavy barring on breast and belly (like a female) had been present since 1940 and continued to occupy the No. 3 eyrie. Other birds could not be individually identified.

The US Weather Bureau in New York City reported abnormal cold and lack of sun throughout the season, but heavy rains, usually a cause of nesting failure in this region, were entirely lacking. In the first week of March, when Female E normally laid, the daily minimum temperature set a record low of 9°F (−12.8°C). April, May, and early June were well below normal in temperature.

As with other species the cold and cloudy spring made for late nesting and decreased chances of success. The No. 6 eyrie, the only one of the

Table 11.2. The Productivity of Two Female Peregrines

	Sun Life female (Montreal)[a]				Female E (Hudson River)[b]			
Age in years	Year	No. of eggs laid	Young hatching	Young reared	Year	Minimum No. of clutches laid	Young robbed	Young reared
1	1937[c]	0	0	0				
2	1938	5[d]	0	0	1942	1	2	0
3	1939[e]	2[d] + 3[d]	0	0	1943	1	3	1
4	1940[f]	4 + 4	2	2	1944	2	0	2
5	1941	5	3	2	1945	1	1	3
6	1942	4	2	2	1946	1	1	3
7	1943	4	4	4	1947	1	2	1
8	1944	4	3	2	1948	1	0	2
9	1945	4[d] + 4	1	1	1949	1	2	1
10	1946	4	2	2	1950	3	0	0
11	1947	4	3	2	1951	4	0	0
12	1948	2[g] (+?)	0[h]	0	1952	3	0	0
13	1949	4	0[h]	0	1953	3	0	0
14	1950	4	3	3	1954	1 (+?)	0	0
15	1951	4	0[h]	0	1955	1	0	0
16	1952	4	3	2	1956	0	0	0
17					1957	0	0	0
Total		69 (+?)	26	22		24 (+?)	11	13

[a] Data from Hall (1955) except as indicated.
[b] This bird was in adult plumage in 1942; her ages shown here are all minimal values.
[c] Female in immature plumage; copulation observed; "did not nest as far as we know"—J. D. Cleghorn *in litt.* to J. J. Hickey, 17 May 1938.
[d] Eggs laid in gutters or on stonework; not incubated.
[e] Data from J. D. Cleghorn *in litt.*
[f] Seven eggs known; an eighth almost certainly taken from a rain gutter by a workman. This was the first year for nest boxes. The falcon appears to have laid her first 2 eggs in rain gutters. She then laid 2 eggs in nest box 1, 2 more in nest box 2, and finally 2 that she incubated and hatched in nest box 1 (Pfeiffer, 1946; J. J. Hickey, *in litt.*).
[g] Observed and photographed by R. A. Herbert.
[h] Eggs evidently eaten by the female.

lower Hudson eyries not occupied in winter, was not even occupied until June. The most remarkable observation of the 1950 nesting season involved the late dates at which the peregrines attempted nesting. Courtship and copulation were seen on 28 June at the No. 7 eyrie; an egg was laid on 5 June at the No. 6 eyrie; and a clutch of eggs was incubated until 17 June at the No. 1 eyrie, where incubation normally took place in March (Herbert and Herbert, 1965). These dates have no parallel on the Hudson.

The 1951 nesting season. Seven pairs were present in the eight eyries. Male A and Female E continued at eyrie No. 1, and Male X at eyrie No. 3. The US Weather Bureau in New York recorded a 4- to 5-inch (10.2- to 12.7-cm) rainfall on 28–30 March, in the vicinity of the No. 1 eyrie, where Female E had been incubating a clutch of two since 11 March.

Construction of the parkway continued, and from 19 March through 28 March blasting occurred each afternoon about half a mile (800 m) north of the peregrines' nest ledge. On 2–12 April daily blasting occurred about a quarter of a mile (400 m) from the nest ledge where the pair was incubating a second clutch; on 13 April one blast was considerably closer to the ledge, and on 17 April we found the ledge abandoned. On 21 April we found Female E incubating on a ledge some 300 yards (275 m) to the south, and on 30 April the blasting site was also moved 300 yards to the south. On 2 May we found that this third clutch of three eggs, one broken, was abandoned. On 14 May Female E was incubating a fourth clutch; in late May the blasting site was moved closer to this ledge, and the fourth clutch was found abandoned. This unusual incubation behavior has been commented on by Herbert and Herbert (1965).

Two young hatched at the No. 2 eyrie, the last young ever hatched on the Hudson. One of these was taken by a Brooklyn falconer.

Road construction disturbed the pair at the No. 4–5 eyries, and caused desertion of the No. 5 cliff during the day, although night perches were occupied. In November 1951 the female of this pair was shot.

The No. 6 eyrie was harrassed throughout the season by "target shooting" by the resident park policeman below the eyrie. On 12 April we saw the female with three primaries missing from her right wing. One fresh, unincubated egg lay on the next ledge at this date; it was later found abandoned.

The 1952 nesting season. In January 1952, there were six pairs at the eight eyries, but prior to the nesting season the male at the No. 2 eyrie was shot, causing desertion of that eyrie. We could not locate the female at the No. 8 eyrie; in March 1952, therefore, there were five pairs, one unmated female at the No. 2 eyrie, and one unmated male.

The nesting season of 1952 was comparable in abnormal precipitation to the spring of 1940, referred to by Hickey (1942) as "the wet, disastrous season of 1940." With 10.11 inches (25.7 cm) as normal for precipitation in March–May, New York City had 16.25 inches (41.3 cm) in 1940 and 16.53 inches (42 cm) in 1952. The spring of 1940 was cool as well as wet, while March and April of 1952 were above normal in temperatures. Despite this advantage no young hatched on the Hudson in 1952, while five young hatched in 1940.

Male A and Female E incubated four clutches, but were disturbed by road building, workmen, trucks, and stripping of trees from above the cliff. They incubated a first clutch for 3 to 4 weeks, a third clutch for 3 weeks, and they are thought to have incubated their fourth clutch until mid-July.

Male X was still present at the No. 3 eyrie, where the pair incubated a clutch until late June.

The female at the No. 4 eyrie, which was shot in November 1951, was replaced in May 1952; but road construction and blasting prevented nesting.

As in 1951, the female at the No. 6 eyrie, disturbed at the one-egg stage, abandoned the egg, which subsequently disappeared. This suggested to us that one of the peregrines may have eaten it.

Although the Palisades Park is a protected sanctuary area, two breeding adults were seen with primaries or tail feathers missing.

The 1953 nesting season. Six pairs were present in the eight eyries at the beginning of the nesting season. Prior to the nesting season a seventh pair was present at the No. 2 eyrie, but construction of the Parkway and blasting caused partial site destruction of this eyrie, and it was abandoned by early May. No young hatched in the eight eyries.

Weather was again a prime deterrent to nesting, particularly at the No. 1 eyrie where Female E normally incubated in March. March rainfall set a record of 7.91 inches (20.1 cm), with 3–5 inches (7.6–12.7 cm) recorded in one storm. Snow flurries occurred on 20 April. Male A and Female E made two, and probably three, nesting attempts.

Blasting and road construction reached the south site of the No. 3 eyrie in late January. On 20 April at the north site, we found Male X incubating one fresh, reddish egg, probably because of the subnormal 34°F (1.1°C) temperature. Five days later this egg had disappeared, only shell fragments remaining on the ledge. This was the only occasion on which we found shell fragments (mentioned by Ratcliffe, 1958), suggesting egg-eating, at any of the Hudson eyries.

Disturbance of incubation or possible seizure of young occurred at the No. 4–5 eyries where the male had been incubating eggs on 23 April, and where we encountered a New York falconer at the cliff. On 16 May the eyrie was deserted; there were no further nesting attempts.

The pair at the No. 6 eyrie had again been disturbed at the one-egg stage, and they abandoned the eyrie by 20 April. The female had apparently been shot at. The disappearance of one egg also occurred at the No. 1 and the No. 3 eyrie in this year, suggesting egg-eating by the falcons.

For the first time in several years we found a pair at the 5A eyrie, situated about one-half mile (800 m) north of the No. 5 eyrie, on 2 June. We presumed this to be the pair from the No. 5 or No. 6 eyrie, both abandoned at this date.

At the No. 7 eyrie the pair incubated eggs in late May and early June, but construction and roadwork beneath the cliff caused the birds to abandon the ledge.

At the No. 8 eyrie a pair was present for the first time in 3 years. We saw courtship but no incubation.

The 1954 nesting season. Six of the eight eyries were occupied by pairs. No young were hatched. Weather was not a factor in the nest failure of 1954. Road work, construction, and blasting continued at the deserted No. 2 eyrie, and at eyries No. 3 and 5. Male X and an adult female were present at the north site of the No. 3 eyrie during the spring, but retreated to the south cliff when disturbed by construction of a large parking lot above the nest ledges of the north cliff. The pair at the No. 4 and 5 eyries attempted nesting, but abandoned the cliff when disturbed by workmen and construction activities. The pair at the No. 6 eyrie did not attempt nesting; on 18 March the female had tail feathers missing, and footprints below the nest ledge of this shallow, exposed cliff suggested that the birds had again been disturbed. The pair abandoned the cliff by 14 May. Male A and Female E at the No. 1 eyrie made only one nesting attempt. Female E had a primary missing on 26 March. The pair appeared to be increasingly shy.

The 1955 nesting season. In 1955 nesting failure was complete among the five pairs remaining in the eight eyries. The No. 6 eyrie was unoccupied for the first time since its occupancy in the 1930's, and the No. 2 eyrie remained unoccupied. Weather was normal.

At the No. 1 eyrie Male A and Female E, the pair which regularly nested the first week of March, attempted nesting in late April. We saw Male A incubating one fresh egg on 23 April, but 4 days later this egg had disappeared. The pair at the No. 3 eyrie (Male X and female) which regularly nested the first week of April, attempted nesting in late April on a ledge far down the cliff, well below the construction of the parking lot on top of the cliff. The pair at the No. 4–5 eyries attempted nesting on the No. 4 cliff early in the season, but failed; they had a scrape on the No. 5 cliff at the late date of 29 June.

The 1956 nesting season. At the beginning of the nesting season, there were four pairs resident in the eight eyries. Male A at the No. 1 eyrie was missing, and the cliff appeared unoccupied, although later in the season we saw Female E. (As reported in Herbert and Herbert, 1965, a lone female seldom retained possession of the eyrie cliff.) Eyries 2 and 6 remained unoccupied. Weather was normal.

Male X and an adult female continued to occupy eyrie No. 3, although construction continued at both south and north cliffs. The pair was incubating on the so-called "black snake ledge" of the south cliff throughout April, and was last seen by us on 28 April. On a ledge near the black snake ledge were a group of pigeons and grain which had been put out for them. These were not the racing pigeons of the Hudson, but a smaller pigeon, the Tippler, bred by pigeon fanciers. Visiting the eyrie in May, we expected to find young, but neither young nor adults were there. We believe that the adults may have been trapped by means of the pigeons. Falconers with New York and New Jersey license plates were known to have visited the eyrie in May. Near the nest ledge we found a metal cleat from a man's hiking shoe.

The pair resident at the No. 4–5 eyries made several scrapes, but did not nest. On 26 May we met falconers at this eyrie.

We saw courtship at the No. 7 and 8 eyries, and the pair at the No. 8 eyrie appeared to be incubating on the south cliff. No young hatched, however, and nesting failure was again complete on the Hudson in 1956.

The 1957 nesting season. Three pairs were believed to be present at the No. 4–5, and No. 7 and 8 eyries in the spring of 1957. The No. 1, 2, 3 and 6 eyries remained deserted. Heavy rains may have delayed nesting. No nesting attempts were made. In two visits to the No. 8 eyrie we did not see either of the pair, but the cliff was occupied, as evidenced by feathers and "whitewash." We again encountered falconers from a distant state at the well-known No. 5 eyrie.

The 1958 nesting season. Eyries No. 1, 2, 3 and 6 remained unoccupied. Weather was normal. On 9 and 10 June we visited all of the eight eyries, but saw not one peregrine. Whitewash at all cliffs was faded.

The 1959 nesting season. Because of the serious illness of the senior author in these years, we made but one visit to the eight eyries. On 10 May we visited all the eyries except the No. 4 cliff. All were abandoned except No. 8, where we saw one bird, and the cliff showed signs of occupancy. The reliable Palisades Park Police sergeant resident below the No. 5 eyrie reported that he had seen a peregrine at the No. 5 eyrie the week before, and that a pair was still resident. At the No. 3 eyrie a tremendous crowd of tourists thronged the newly completed picnic grounds above the nest ledges of the north cliff.

The 1960 nesting season. Because of the death of the senior author we did not visit the eyries in this year.

The 1961 nesting season. With Col. E. L. Hardin of the US Military Academy the junior author visited the eight eyries on 20 and 21 May. At the south site of the No. 3 eyrie on a cedar snag overlooking the black snake ledge, we saw an immature female. The bird circled and scolded, and returned three times to her original perch when flushed. It appeared that she might have eggs on the cliff, although in our previous experience on the Hudson immature females did not breed (Herbert and Herbert, 1965). All other cliffs were abandoned and showed no sign of occupancy *except* the No. 8 cliff where we saw whitewash and feathers but no bird. We encountered falconers at the No. 5 eyrie; they had even visited the relatively unknown eyrie 5A.

On 27 May the junior author visited all the eyries with Herman Goebel of the Adirondack Mountain Club. All of the cliffs were abandoned except the No. 8 eyrie, where we saw a male. At the south cliff of the No. 3 eyrie where we had seen the immature female a week earlier, there was no bird. The car of a New York City falconer whom we frequently encountered at the No. 5 eyrie was parked in the lane—further evidence that these eyries were well-known.

Thus the years 1950–61 saw the gradual extirpation of the peregrine on the Hudson (Table 11.3). In June 1961, only one bird survived on the highest peak of the Hudson, and he subsequently disappeared.

Table 11.3. Last Years for Peregrines at the Hudson River Eyries[a]

Eyrie name	Last year for young	Last year for pair	Last year for single bird	Number of years pairs persisted without young
No. 4	1948?	1949		?
No. 8	1944 or '47	1956	1961♀	9–12
No. 5	1946	1957 or '59[b]		11–13
No. 6	1948	1954	1955♀	6
No. 3	1949	1956		7
No. 7	1949	1957		8
No. 1	1949	1955	1956♀	6
No. 2	1951	1953[c]		
Mean	1948	1955		8–9

[a] A slight error may enter this record in that no field work was carried out in 1960. This may or may not affect the record for the last pair seen at Eyrie No. 5.
[b] Our observations show 1957; but Sergeant Brennan, the local police officer, reported birds present until 1959.
[c] Site destroyed in spring of 1953.

POPULATION ANALYSIS

GENERAL POPULATION DYNAMICS

Various hypotheses have been advanced to explain the widespread decline of the peregrine in the United States, the most frequent being human persecution or poisoning by pesticides, or both. Before discussing factors contributing to the decline of the Hudson Valley population, we should like to review certain generally accepted statistics of peregrine biology.

The peregrine was a widely but thinly distributed species over most of its range in the United States. Small populations flourished in areas of abundant food supply, such as the cliffs of the Hudson River with a year-round supply of racing pigeons, whereas the magnificent cliffs of Nova Scotia and New Brunswick harbored few peregrines.

Secondly, the peregrine is a long-lived species once it attains breeding maturity at the age of 2 years. Three of the breeding birds in the Hudson population were known to have attained ages of 17 to 19 years (Herbert and Herbert, 1965) but, prior to maturity, mortality of young and juvenile birds is very high.

Hickey's (1942) estimate of 1.1 young fledged over a 2-year period at 19 occupied sites in the New York area compares with his average of three downy young hatched at 124 successful sites in the United States south of Canada. Cade (1960:186) in discussing the high percentage of nest losses, gives an average of 1.1 young fledged over a 2-year period at 25 occupied eyries in the Colville area and 20 eyries in the Yukon. He notes changing food supplies (as the result of climatic vagaries) and predators as decimating factors in the production of downy young (1960:186–187).

On the Hudson, food supplies were abundant, and predators, with few exceptions, were conspicuous by their absence. Man, rated by Cade as a negligible factor in nest losses in the arctic, was the major factor in nest losses on the Hudson and in New York City. In these well-known and legally protected eyries a large proportion of young were regularly seized by falconers prior to fledging.

Cade (1960:187) noted that "the universal scarcity of spring immatures suggests that a great mortality must occur among juveniles during their first fall and winter," and he cites Beebe's observations on the Queen Charlotte Islands and museum data reported by Bond (1946) in support of his own observations. In the eyries of the Hudson, as well as in the New York City wintering population, immatures or yearlings were extremely rare, again suggesting a high mortality. Although 24 young were banded by the senior author in the Hudson eyries from 1938 through 1944, none of these eyries was ever occupied by a banded bird. Throughout the years of our study, only two yearlings, both females, occupied Hudson eyries; a third yearling, seen at the No. 3 eyrie in the spring of 1961, was one of the last two birds seen on the Hudson. It disappeared within a week.

Among the banding records extant at Patuxent in 1962, 63 out of 80 recoveries, or 79%, involved immature birds. (Of the birds banded at that time, a few subsequent records of birds recovered as adults presumably have been reported.) Several factors contribute to the high mortality of juveniles, one natural factor being their inability to hunt as well as an adult. (In 1938 a juvenile banded by the senior author was picked up in nearby New Jersey, apparently starving.) But by far the greatest factor in the mortality of juveniles is their unwariness where humans are concerned, and their consequent susceptibility to shooting and trapping in areas with heavily settled human populations.

FACTORS AFFECTING THE HUDSON RIVER POPULATION

As in the 1940's, the peregrines of the Hudson were subject to extreme persecution in the 1950's. Human pressures on the birds included shooting of adults, the trapping of one pair of nesting adults, and repeated disruption of their nesting cycle by visiting falconers, in an effort to secure birds. Only two young hatched during the 1950's, and one of these was taken by a falconer.

During the early 1950's (prior to 1956) when the Park was not open to visitors, we frequently encountered falconers at the eyries with license plates from New York, New Jersey, and Colorado. Falconers operated on the Hudson despite the fact that the Palisades Park is a wildlife sanctuary where police are authorized to arrest anyone interfering with the peregrine, and despite the fact that the peregrine was protected by law in both New York and New Jersey. The eyries of some of the New England states in which the peregrine was not protected, and from which came some of the birds of the New York wintering population (Herbert and Herbert, 1965), were even more open to exploitation by falconers. A documentation of this persisting exploitation is given in a history of the No. 1 eyrie in the 1930's and 1940's in the Appendix to this paper. Loss of young to falconers must be weighed against the high mortality of young from other causes during the birds' first year. It seems extraordinary that, now that the peregrine is known to be an endangered species in the United States, there are few state laws and no national law to protect the bird. In the Middle Ages, often considered the heyday of falconry, there were strict laws protecting the birds; trapping methods were secret even down to the twentieth century, and possession of a falcon was reserved for an earl. Penalties for molesting a falcon or for falcon rustling ranged from imprisonment and mutilation of the left hand to death.

Illegal shooting also played a part in the extirpation of the peregrine in the New York area. Wintering peregrines were shot in the towns of New York and New Jersey, and occasional adults were shot on the Hudson. During the 1950's the pair at the No. 6 eyrie had primaries or tail feathers shot out several times by the resident park policeman charged with the responsibility of protecting them. The male at the No. 2 eyrie and the female at the No. 4–5 eyries were both shot and killed in the winter of 1951–52; both of these cliffs have park police stations below them.

Weather was particularly unfortunate for the peregrines in the critical nesting seasons of 1950, 1952, and 1953 when subnormal temperatures or above-normal precipitation prevented nesting (and at the No. 6 eyrie prevented occupation of the cliff in 1950 until June). Even in 1951 a 4- to 5-inch (10.2- to 12.7-cm) rainfall in the vicinity of the No. 1 eyrie is thought to have caused abandonment of the first clutch laid by the early-nesting female at that eyrie.

Added to these pressures on the peregrines in the 1950's is the possible one of poisoning by pesticides absorbed via their food-chain. Because we made no tests on birds or eggs, we are unable to say whether or not peregrines in this region were affected by pesticides. We would point out, however, that the normal food of all the New York City peregrines (except the Riverside Church and the George Washington Bridge birds, which were close to an enormous starling roost) was the racing pigeon. Racing pigeons also constituted perhaps the major part of the diet of the Hudson River peregrines, although during spring and fall migration they also took other species. Whether or not peregrines feeding exclusively on racing pigeons would come into contact with pesticides in sufficient amounts to cause death or sterility is a moot question. However the peregrines wintering in New York City may have come into contact with pesticides on their summer breeding grounds.

Mebs (1960) estimated that only one-fifth of the fledged young of peregrines reached breeding maturity. As noted in Table 11.1, the mean number of fledged young in the eight eyries of the Hudson in the years 1941–49 was only 0.75; if only one-fifth of these young reached maturity, there were obviously no young to replace adults in the eyries.

Construction of the Palisades Parkway, with its attendant recreation areas above the nest ledges, virtually assured abandonment of many of the eyries. Blasting through the cliffs, bulldozing of trees above the cliffs, and the building of footpaths above favored nest ledges caused continual disturbance from 1950 through 1956. It caused the temporary or permanent abandonment of eyries 1 through 6, and the destruction of the No. 2 eyrie site, where a path led directly to the stone balcony overlooking the most favored nest ledge. Many boys' names were painted on this hitherto-secluded cliff wall. The irony of the Palisades Park was that it was originally conceived as a nature sanctuary, and the peregrine and peregrine eyries figured rather conspicuously in arguments regarding expropriation of the large estates along the Hudson, where the peregrine was, in fact, protected by the no-trespass regulations. In the actual construction of the Parkway the peregrine was ignored; at the No. 1 eyrie the Parkway sweeps out to within 50 ft (15 m) of one of the most favored nest ledges, where a lookout has been established. All along the Parkway a footpath for hikers now threads the very top of the cliff making the ledges below unusable, as the peregrine on these cliffs does not tolerate activity above his nest ledge, although he does tolerate the picnic grounds at the foot of the cliffs, well below his ledge (Herbert and Herbert, 1965). Like many of the "multiple-purpose" recreation areas, recreation took precedence over wildlife, a prime example of this being the enormous picnic grounds and parking lot blotting out the magnificent cliff of the No. 3 eyrie.

Ratcliffe (1963) has pointed out that some raptors in the United Kingdom absorbed organochlorine residues and ate their own eggs, and that subsequent nesting failure was due to this. We have no proof of eggs having been eaten in the Hudson and New York City eyries, but single eggs, and, rarely, a clutch, disappeared. However, the disappearance of eggs also occurred in the early 1940's, when modern pesticides were not in use.

At the No. 6 eyrie, eggs disappeared with some frequency, beginning in 1940, when a clutch of three, which had been marked to prevent its removal by egg collectors, disappeared. At the same eyrie one egg disappeared in 1942, a clutch of four in 1945, a clutch of two in 1947, and a clutch of one in 1950 and 1952. In 1953 a single egg disappeared at the No. 1 eyrie and at the No. 3 eyrie, and in 1955 a single egg disappeared at the No. 1 eyrie.

Ratcliffe (1958) reports seeing bits of broken shell on nest ledges, again suggesting egg-eating. From 1930 to 1960 there was only one occasion on which broken bits of shell were seen on a nest ledge on the Hudson; on 20 April 1953, we found the male incubating one fresh egg (the temperature had dropped to a record low of 34°F (1.1°C) with snow flurries), but on 23 April there remained only broken bits of shell on the ledge.

Although we cannot gauge the possible effect, if any, of the use of pesticides on the Hudson birds, we think that during the late 1940's and 1950's other human pressures on these birds were such that extirpation was inevitable. It is more difficult to explain the disappearance of the New York City wintering peregrine population.

In a general sense all of the pressures—seizure of young by falconers, loss of habitat by road construction, shooting, and even pesticides—may be summed up as resulting from the human population explosion. The human population of the United States expanded from 75,004,575 in 1900 to 179,323,175 in 1960, and a vast road-building and development program has made hitherto inaccessible areas accessible to all. Thus the isolation which the eyries once commanded has vanished.

SUMMARY

In the Hudson River Valley, the nesting peregrine falcon population increased to nine breeding pairs in 1947, the peak number reported in the present century. Productivity averaged about 1.1–1.2 young reared per occupied site in 1931–40 and 0.75 in 1941–50. No young were reared in 1950, and production in this area ceased with two young in 1951, one of which was taken by a falconer. Breeding pairs dropped to seven in 1950, to five (plus one unmated bird) in 1952, to four in 1956, and to none in 1961.

Productivity in the 1940's was importantly affected by falconers who took 50% of the young as well as some incubating adults. Highway construction and blasting destroyed one nesting site in the 1950's and caused repeated desertion of eggs at other eyries. Unfavorable weather appeared to affect reproduction in 1 year, and shooting of the adults additionally contributed to the extirpation of this population.

LITERATURE CITED

"Alianus." 1879. A winter's tramp through the woods. Forest and Stream, 12(3):46.
Bond, R. M. 1946. The peregrine population of western North America. Condor, 48(3):101–116.
Cade, T. J. 1960. Ecology of the peregrine and gyrfalcon populations in Alaska. Univ. Calif. Publ. Zool., 63(3):151–290.
Herbert, R. A., and K. G. S. Herbert. 1965. Behavior of peregrine falcons in the New York City region. Auk, 82(1):62–94.
Herbert, R. A., and K. G. S. Herbert. The extirpation of a peregrine falcon population. MS in prep.
Hickey, J. J. 1942. Eastern population of the duck hawk. Auk, 59(2):176–204.
Mebs, Th. 1960. Probleme der Fortpflanzungsbiologie und Bestandserhaltung bei deutschen Wanderfalken (*Falco peregrinus*). Vogelwelt, 81(2):47–56.
Ratcliffe, D. A. 1958. Broken eggs in peregrine eyries. Brit. Birds, 51(1):23–26.
———. 1963. The status of the peregrine in Great Britain. Bird Study, 10(2):56–90.

APPENDIX

KNOWN HISTORY OF EYRIE NO. 1, 1890–1949

Circa 1890. Clutch collected by egg collectors from Englewood (H.H.C., 1894).
1890. "Full clutch" collected March 30 (Chapman, 1894).
1894. Clutch of 3 collected by some boys about this date (H.H.C., 1894).
1899. Clutch collected and five photographs taken April 23 by W. P. Lemmon (*Abstr. Proc. Linn. Soc. N.Y.*, 12:5).
1907. Pair seen February 12 by G. E. Hix (*Abstr. Proc. Linn. Soc. N.Y.*, 17–19:28).
1908. Clutch taken by Prof. C. C. Trowbridge; all broken (*Abstr. Proc. Linn. Soc. N.Y.*, 20–23:5).
1912. Clutch of 3 collected May 20. Addled (American Museum of Natural History no. 8353. P. B. Philipp).
1913. Pair seen March 30 by L. N. Nichols (*Abstr. Proc. Linn. Soc., N.Y.*, 26–27:3).
1913. Pair seen May 12 by L. Griscom (*Abstr. Proc. Linn. Soc. N.Y.*, 24–25:38).
1916. Pair seen Feb. 16 by G. E. Hix. Male passed pigeon to female (*Abstr. Proc. Linn. Soc. N.Y.*, 28–29:18).
1920. Clutch of 4 eggs (incubated 10–12 days) taken on April 11 by B. S. Bowdish (*in litt.*).
1923. Clutch of 3 eggs taken on April 7 (AMNH no. 8360).
1925. Two young, male and female, taken for falconry (F. B. Lane, *in litt.*).
1926. No young produced (F. B. Lane, *in litt.*).
1927. Two young, male and female, taken for falconry. Both escaped in California (F. B. Lane, *in litt.*).
1928. Two young hatched this year or 1929; 1 fledged, the other taken for falconry (F. B. Lane, *in litt.*).
1931. Three young hatched; 1 taken by a falconer.
1932. New adult female; may or may not have laid eggs.
1933. Pair present February 22. Only adult male present April 9.
1934. New male appeared. Two eggs laid about April 9; 1 infertile, 1 developed almost to hatching when female deserted for the night. Two eggs collected May 30 and given to the American Museum of Natural History.

1935. Female (a large dark falcon) appeared. Clutch laid; female was disturbed and deserted to roost at night on Hunt's Point gas tank about 13 miles (21 km) SE on East River.

1936. Clutch of 4 eggs seen in April; 1 was discarded; 2 failed to hatch; 1 produced a male that fledged in May.

1937. Clutch of 4 eggs failed to hatch.

1938. Male A (marked by white spot on head) appeared. Clutch of 4 eggs disappeared along with female A about April 25. Traps seen on nest ledges.

1939. April 9 pair present. Female B (light-colored, pale falcon) appeared. Clutch disappeared in April; so did female B. Empty scrape seen April 24.

1940. Female C (large, brown falcon) appeared. Pair present April 13. Two eggs marked on April 22 to discourage egg collecting. Pair incubating April 22. Female C taken for falconry May 30 while incubating at night. Male was incubating on June 2, but eggs failed to hatch.

1941. Adult female D (light colored) appeared. Male A still present. March 30 copulation seen. April 7: clutch of 1 seen. April 13, 17, 22, 24, 27, and May 4 and 17: pair incubating clutch of 4. June 7: 3 young on ledge (Cleon Garland, *in litt.*); 1 taken for falconry. June 28: 2 young on ledge. June 29: 2 young flew.

1942. March 1 and 10: male A and female D present. April 4: clutch of 4 seen. April 18: clutch of 4 still on ledge, female missing. Clutch of 4 still on ledge July 15. (Female D found shot.) Female E (very dark, early-laying) replaced her. Female E hatched 2 young, both taken for falconry.

1943. February 17: male A and female E in courtship. April 25: 3 very small young and 1 egg on No. 5 nest ledge. April 29: 4 young on nest ledge. May 20: 4 young, 3 females and 1 male, banded by Herbert. June 3: 3 young discovered taken by local falconers. One young subsequently lost with leash. June 17: 1 young on wing.

1944. March 6: male A and female E on south cliff; clutch of 2 eggs seen. March 8: clutch of 3 seen; incubation commenced. April 10 and 12: female incubating; eggs should have hatched by April 11. April 20: eggs gone, cliff deserted; pair on north cliff. May 14, June 2 and 11: pair incubating clutch of 3 after having incubated first clutch for more than 32 days. June 15: young on ledge. June 26: 2 young males banded by Herbert and H. M. Van Deusen. Two young still on ledge July 26. July 30: 2 young on wing.

1945. April 1: female E incubating on No. 5 nest ledge; male A present. April 19: female E feeding 4 young, hatched about April 12. May 13: 3 4-week females on ledge; evidence that someone had roped down to ledge and taken 1 young. May 31: 3 young on wing.

1946. February 10: male A "ledging." March 10: female E incubating. April 28: 3 young females 2.5 weeks old on ledge; young male believed taken. May 13 and 19: 3 young females still on ledge.

1947. Circa April 20: 3 young hatched by female E, 2 young taken by falconers. May 22: 1 young female about 4.5 weeks old on ledge. June 8: 1 young female on wing.

1948. March 28: female E incubating, male A present. May 31: 1 5-week-old young on ledge. June 12: 2 young on wing, a male and female.

1949. March 5: female E and male A incubating. May: female E and 3 young on ledge in early May, 2 young subsequently taken by falconers. May 17: 1 young on ledge.

KNOWN HISTORY OF EYRIE NO. 2, 1893–1949

1893. Pair reported nesting near Yonkers, N.Y. (F. M. Chapman, in *Abstr. Proc. Linn. Soc.* N.Y., 1894, 5:9).

1909. Pair nested on 2 different ledges. Clutch of 2 seen, 1 egg punctured May 19, nest abandoned; Bowdish was told boy had shot hawks with rifle (B. S. Bowdish, *in litt.*).

1910. Pair found nesting at south nest ledge, May 22. Pictures taken of adult female on nest, May 27, May 30 and June 5: first pictures of adult on nest. June 18: adult female found shot; 3 young on wing, 1 young still on ledge removed by Bowdish and kept until late February when it died "from some throat trouble which prevented it from swallowing" (Bowdish, *in litt.*). The description of the bird's illness suggests trichomoniasis.

1912. Pair seen at nest "opposite Yonkers" (J. T. Nichols, *in litt.*).

1942. January 13: female roosting opposite Yonkers.

1944. March 14: male and whitewash seen on cliff.

1946. February 10: peregrine seen on cliff.

1947. May 6: pair using cliff. May 17: 1 young 2 or 3 days old and 1 egg on nest ledge. May 28: young dead on ledge, probably due to wet weather.

1948. Two young seen May 2.

1949. Three young on ledge in early May; 2 taken for falconry in mid-May; 1 young fledged.

KNOWN HISTORY OF EYRIE NO. 4, 1877–49

1877–78. Pair nested on the Palisades ("Alianus." A winter's tramp through the woods. Forest and Stream, 3:46).

1913. Clutch of 4 collected by P. B. Philipp April 26.

1922. Clutch of 4 collected by P. B. Philipp April 2 (AMNH).

1925–28. Pair apparently raised young every year. (F. B. Lane *in litt.* July 27, 1939).

1932. Pair on north cliff.

1933. Pair raised young.

1934. Pair seen.

1935. Pair on north cliff.

1936. Pair seen.

1937. Three young seen (Herbert, Hickey) on south cliff.

1938. Pair seen, no young. Birds appear to have been egged.

1939. April 9: pair seen. June 25: one young seen. July 2: 3 young seen on ledge.

1940. March 31: pair seen at north eyrie site (Herbert). June 10: no birds present (Herbert, W. D. Sargent). June 16: no birds (M. Brooks, J. J. Hickey, W. D. Sargent). Male X (pale, heavily barred) appeared.

1941. May 25: pair at south cliff at original nest site. June 15 and July 4: much whitewash on cliff; pair not present except at night.

1942. March 22: much whitewash on south cliff. April 4: pair on north cliff.

1943. February 12: 2 males battling for possession of south cliff; male X retained possession; same pair using south and north cliffs. May 3: pair present, no sign of nesting. May 22: pair incubating on south cliff; peeping notes heard from eggs. June 6: 1 young 10 days old on nest ledge of south cliff; female seen dragging black snake off nest ledge (Herbert and Herbert, 1965:86). Suggests second nesting.

1944. March 12: male X and female on north cliff. May 7 and 9: pair on north cliff incubating. June 1: only male X present; eggs or young had been collected.

1945. April 2: 2 females battling high in the air at north cliff, one an adult, the other an immature. Immature was the aggressor, and was the larger bird; she returned and occupied the cliff. Much whitewash on south cliff, where pair probably wintered. April 19 and 26: male X and immature female present, but not breeding. May 26: male X only present.

1946. March 10 and April 28: male X and adult female incubating on north cliff; young later raised.
1947. May 8: male X and female incubating on south cliff. June 8: eggs or young taken, male at north cliff.
1948. May 31: male X and female at north cliff, male "ledging"; probable second nesting attempt.
1949. May 26: male X and female at south cliff; young reported to have been taken from ledge by falconers.

KNOWN HISTORY OF EYRIE NO. 4, 1908–49

1908. Female and 3 young collected by R. B. Potter in May for habitat group in American Museum of Natural History.
1909. No eggs (R. B. Potter, pers. comm.).
1918. Eggs seen in May (R. L. Meredith, pers. comm.).
1921. Five eggs incubated about 11 days collected (AMNH no. 8357). Four eggs, in repeat clutch; then 3 young photographed by Dr. Clyde Fisher (R. B. Potter, pers. comm.).
1922. June 1: 3 young present (R. L. Meredith, pers. comm.).
1923. Four eggs collected, 3–4 days incubated (B. S. Bowdish, *in litt.*). July 4: young taken (R. L. Meredith, pers. comm.).
1924. April 20: 4 eggs collected, fresh (AMNH no. 8364).
1925. Pair nesting (F. B. Lane *in litt.*).
1926. Three young taken for falconry: young male died November 24, 1926, now no. 229072 in AMNH collection; young female also died in captivity; another young female lost in California. (F. B. Lane, *in litt.*).
1927. Pair present (F. B. Lane, *in litt.*).
About 1933. Pair apparently nesting (C. Farley and Herbert).
1937. Pair present.
1938. Only 1 adult seen.
1939. April 9: 1 adult. May 15: old scrape. July 1: male on cliff. Pair assumed present.
1940. April 13: pair "ledging"; 3 scrapes. May 4: pair copulating (Herbert). Eyrie checked throughout spring (February 11, March 10, 30, April 7, 13, 19, 28), and pair found to be nonbreeding (Hickey *et al.*).
1941. February 22, April 20, June 8, 19, and September 7: pair seen; did not breed.
1942. March 8, April 14, and May 3: pair or male present; did not breed.
1943. April 11, 19, and May 26: pair or male present, male in courtship, did not breed.
1944. March 28, April 16, and June 18: pair or male present, male in courtship; did not breed.
1945. April 8, 29 and May 29: pair or male present; did not breed.
1946. February 12 and April 7: male or pair present; courtship seen.
1947. June 8: pair present; no young seen.
1948. June 11: pair seen; may have had young.
1949. Pair present in early June; no young seen.

KNOWN HISTORY OF EYRIE NO. 5, 1923–49

1921. Quarry work ceased.
1923. Pair present; clutch collected (B. S. Bowdish, pers, comm.).
About 1933. No whitewash seen (C. Farley and Herbert).

1935. Pair seen (R. L. Meredith).
1936. Young presumably hatched.
1937. June: pair present; scrape found (Hickey and W. R. Spofford).
1938. July 19: two young present (Herbert and Hickey). One young banded by Herbert; captured in poor condition at Hamilton Township, N.J., September 2, 1938.
1939. April 11: 3 eggs (Herbert). May 14: small tawny adult female and 4 eggs seen (Herbert). June 12: 4 young banded (Spofford). July 1: 1 young recovered when it crashed into house one-half mile distant; replaced on ledge, uninjured (Herbert and Spofford). July 16: 3 young only present on wing (Herbert).
1940. April 19: 4 eggs marked (Spofford and Hickey). May 30: 2 young hatched, male and female (Herbert, Hickey, and Spofford). June 16: 1 young only left on ledge. Young banded (Hickey and Spofford); recovered in nearby New Jersey, October 18, 1941.
1941. April 20: female incubating; clutch disappeared. Clutch of 1 covered by female May 11; deserted May 17 (Herbert).
1942. April 4: clutch of 3 and 1 white egg; clutch marked to prevent removal. May 3: female incubating clutch of 3. May 24: 3 young, 2 male and 1 female, banded by Herbert and A. Klots.
1943. April 19: male present; female incubating on lower ledge. May 26: 3 young on ledge. May 30: 3 young men, using permit of a City College professor, arrested for attempting to steal young.
1944. March 26 and April 16: pair or male present. May 31: 1 young male banded by Herbert; other young reported hatched. June 5: young male, about 26 days old, still on ledge. June 18 and 25: young male not seen all day; adults only present.
1945. April 8: clutch of 2. April 29: female incubating clutch of 4. May 29: one 3-week-old female banded by Herbert; other young had hatched, but had been taken from ledge. Young banded female believed taken from ledge shortly after banding.
1946. April 28: clutch of 3 seen, with possibility of fourth egg concealed. May: 1 young seen.
1947. June 8: pair present; no young seen.
1948. June 11: pair present; no young seen.
1949. Early June: pair present; no young seen.

KNOWN HISTORY OF EYRIE NO. 5A, 1934–47

1934. Pair bred (R. L. Meredith, pers. comm.).
1935. No birds (Meredith, pers. comm.).
1939. No birds (Herbert, Hickey, and Spofford).
1940. No birds (Herbert, Hickey, and Spofford).
1941. April 27: female incubating. May 17: clutch of 3 seen on new nest ledge; pair incubating eggs almost ready to hatch. June 3: eggs still on ledge, bleached and cracked.
1942. April 4: scrape seen. May 3: scrape and bird.
1943. April 11: unoccupied.
1944. March 26 and 29: unoccupied; birds had not been present since previous spring.
1947. May 28: unoccupied; no sign of occupancy.

KNOWN HISTORY OF EYRIE NO. 6, 1933–49

1921. Work on quarry ceased (W. H. Carr, pers. comm.).
1933. Eyrie discovered (R. L. Meredith, pers. comm.).

1934. Young seen; 2 males taken for falconry (Meredith, pers. comm.).
1939. April 21: clutch of 2 seen (Spofford). April 24: clutch of 4 seen and marked WRS (Spofford). July 1: 2 young, male and female, banded; young female remained on ledge, male flew (Herbert and Spofford).
1940. Clutch of 3 marked; 1 egg broken 18 inches (46 cm) away on ledge (Hickey and Spofford). May 18: no trace of eggs or young (Hickey and Brooks).
1941. April 20 and May 11: female incubating clutch of 4. May 17: 3 young and 1 egg on ledge. June 19: 3 young, probably females, still on ledge. Herbert went down to ledge but did not band young because 2 backed up to fly.
1942. April 4: clutch of 4, 1 egg addled. April 26: clutch of 2. May 3: 2 young. May 24: Herbert banded 2 young, both males.
1943. April 11: female incubating. May 26: eyrie deserted; 1 old egg on nest ledge. Young reported taken by falconers.
1944. May 31: three young 2 weeks old on ledge. June 5: 3 young about 18 days old, probably females, banded by Herbert. June 25: 3 young on wing.
1945. April 8: clutch of 4 seen. May 29: pair only present; no whitewash on nest ledge; eggs or young must have disappeared.
1946. April 28: clutch of 2 seen. May 13: 1 young on ledge, about 3 or 4 days old.
1947. April : apparently laid clutch of 2. June 8: incubating clutch of 2 fresh eggs.
1948. June 11: one 4-week-old female on ledge.
1949. Early June: pair present; no young seen.

KNOWN HISTORY OF EYRIE NO. 7, 1884–1949

1884. Young heard and seen on cliffs (E. A. Mearns. 1881. A List of the Birds of the Hudson Highlands. Bul. Essex Inst. 12:124). May refer to eyrie No. 8.
1927. Three young, 1 male and 2 females taken for falconry; 1 female lost in New York State (F. B. Lane, *in litt.*).
1931. Young female taken for falconry; died in 1933, now in AMNH collection (R. L. Meredith, pers. comm.).
1933. Two to three young on the wing (C. Farley, Herbert).
1935. Young present in July (R. L. Meredith and T. Rawls).
1937. Pair seen (Herbert, Hickey); pair in June "acting oddly" (Meredith, *in litt.*).
1938. Pair seen February 18 (W. H. Carr, K. M. Lewis), March 15 (Carr), and in June; did not appear to have young (Herbert, Hickey).
1939. Pair seen April 9 and June 24, nonbreeding (Herbert).
1940. Pair, nonbreeding, seen February 2, March 30, April 14, etc. (Hickey *et al.*). Male, probably from this eyrie, found shot May 26 (Carr, pers. comm.). No male at eyrie in June (Hickey). Pair seen in July (Herbert).
1941. February 22: pair seen, both in *adult* plumage. May 11: pair courting; female an *immature bird* (M. Brooks, Herbert, Hickey). July 4: pair seen, female an *adult*. This suggested that birds were being shot from the nearby West Point shooting stand.
1942. April 4: scrape seen.
1943. May 16: cliff deserted; no sign of occupancy.
1944. June 8: cliff deserted; no sign of occupancy.
1945. April 15: cliff deserted for third year; old whitewash almost gone.
1946. February 12 and April 7: much whitewash on cliff, but no bird seen.
1947. June 8: no bird seen; cliff seems to be used only as night perch.
1948. Eyrie reoccupied; 3 young reported hatched and taken from nest ledge by falconers (Carr and Grierson, pers. comm.).

1949. Young seen on ledge, female carrying food (G. A. O'Dell, Game Protector for N.Y. State, pers. comm.). Four young on ledge were taken by falconers (Grierson, pers. comm.). One adult only seen in late June (Herbert and Herbert).

KNOWN HISTORY OF EYRIE NO. 8 1894–1949

1894. Pair "breeds in the Hudson Highlands" (Guide to the collection of birds. American Museum of Natural History. 1894). May refer to eyrie No. 7.
1914. "Rare resident" (E. H. Eaton, 1914. The birds of New York).
1918. April 15: pair collected by Lt. Wirt Robinson.
1922. Road opened, hewed along side cliff of No. 8 eyrie.
1924 or 25. Four young seen; 2 taken for falconry (Goodwin and F. B. Lane).
1926. Pair said to be nesting (Lane, *in litt.*).
About 1929. Three young almost fledged (Meredith).
1935. Birds reported seen February 11 (H. A. Hochbaum).
1936. Three young raised (W. H. Carr, *in litt.*).
1938. Pair seen February 12 (Herbert). Three young seen in June (Herbert, Hickey).
1939. Pair seen April 9 (Herbert). Three young reported seen July 14 (Carr, *in litt.*). July 16: no birds, much whitewash (Hickey).
1940. May 24: 3 young on ledge. May 30: banded 1 female; 2 young males flew from ledge (Herbert, Hickey, P. T. Olton, Jr., W. D. Sargent, W. R. Spofford, F. Weissner).
1941. February 22 and April 27: no bird seen, but evidence of their presence. Early April: pair seen; female was *immature* (Col. van Gelder of West Point shoots here). May 11 and July 4: pair seen; female was adult. Much whitewash on last year's nest ledge suggests that several young were raised.
1942. April 4: no bird seen (Herbert and Spofford).
1943. May 16: no bird seen, but whitewash on nest ledge suggests young.
1944. June 8: pair present, and 3 4-week-old young; possibility of fourth young on ledge.
1945. April 15: 1 bird seen, probably male.
1946. February 12 and April 7: no bird seen; much whitewash on cliff.
1947. Circa May 27: female acted as though young had left ledge.
1949. Early June: 1 bird seen.

CHAPTER 12

THE DECLINE OF THE PEREGRINE POPULATION IN PENNSYLVANIA

James N. Rice

The objects of this paper are to describe the physical characteristics of peregrine falcon nesting sites in eastern Pennsylvania, to give a picture of the decline of the breeding population from 1939 to 1960, and to record the changes in reproductive success that took place in this period. The study area was roughly 22,000 sq miles (55,980 sq km) in size. Pennsylvania nesting sites are here designated by the symbols P1, P2, etc. Four New Jersey sites in the Delaware Valley are included and designated as NJ1, NJ2, etc.

The records which serve as the basis for this paper were written by me in an "Eyrie Book" after each return from a visit to the eyries. None are from memory. I believe these records to be accurate. I have always been on friendly terms with the falconers who took birds from these nesting sites, and their information was given to me freely at the time. No peregrine population crash was envisioned in the 1940's. I knew that trained falcons were being flown at this time and from where they came.

I believe that others besides the falconers did not take the birds after I had seen them in the eyrie at their late stage of development, due largely to the extreme difficulty of entering the eyries. It took three, preferably four men, skilled with the rope, to reach most of the nesting ledges. Furthermore, any young falconers and the information about their falcons became known to me in due course.

For information needed to complete this report, I am indebted to Morgan Berthrong, T. Halter Cunningham, Joseph J. Hickey, Nelson D. Hoy, the late Benjamin Kane, Richard McCown, Brian McDonald, Alva G. Nye, Arthur S. Richards, Robert M. Stabler, and William F. Turner.

RELATION OF EYRIE-SITE CHARACTERISTICS TO DESERTION

In showing the sharp decline of the nesting peregrine falcon and in examining the reasons for this decline, it is important to note that in many regions such as mine the number of possible nesting locations initially restricts the breeding population to a very low number.

I have listed 39 different sites used in my region at one time or another by nesting peregrines during the past 60 years. Of these 39 eyries, 16 were deserted by 1940 (Table 12.1). One, NJ25, was referred to by Hickey (1942) as a "temporary" eyrie—a site that is seldom used and then only for just a few years. Six of these sites were in agricultural landscapes, four in wilderness areas, one in a recreational area, one was urban in character, and one agricultural-urban.

The three types of cliffs noted in the following tables are described as briefly as possible as follows:

"A" Cliff. Usually an almost sheer rock face over 200 ft (61 m) high from the top to the wooded slope beneath, with more than one good nesting ledge. The cliff is part of a rocky escarpment at least 500 ft (150 m) long, providing lookout points and cover for the falcon. A "good" nesting ledge is one that is protected by an overhang of rock from the direct rays of the sun and direct rain and that contains material, either rock products or soil, in which a slight indentation known as a "scratch hole" can be made by the falcon to contain her eggs.

"B" Cliff. A sheer or jumbled rock face less than 200 ft high and less than 500 ft long with at least one good nesting ledge and other possible fair nesting ledges. The cliff is part of a rocky escarpment of a less extensive nature than that known as an "A" cliff.

"C" Cliff. A cliff consisting of one or more rock outcroppings, one or more of which contains a possible falcon nesting ledge. It is usually part of a short (300 ft [91 m] or less) escarpment of a more continuous nature, different from the continuous "good cover" type cliff known as "A" or "B."

Some of the records in Table 12.1 give an idea of the activity of the various egg collectors and the span of years during which they operated.

The eyries that were deserted by 1940 were, generally speaking, "inferior" to those that lasted until after 1940. All were on "B" or "C" cliffs, and therefore less difficult to locate and enter than those on "A" cliffs.

Table 12.1. Approximate Chronology of the Initial Desertion of Peregrine Eyries in Eastern Pennsylvania and Western New Jersey

Eyrie no.	Type: Cliff	Type: Environ.	Last known date of activity	First known date of desertion
Early desertions				
PO	—	—	Ca. 1841 (Brewer, 1857)	Ca. 1850 abandoned due to railroad (Brewer, 1857)
P28	C	Agric.	1880 Apr. 7 c/4 G. Miller	"No recent records" (Beck, 1924)
P33	C	Wild.	1895 Apr. 5 (Todd, 1940)	[1946 deserted (Rice, Richards)]
Deserted 1911–20				
P26	C	Agric.	1914 Apr. 26 c/4 Gillen	
P38	?	?	1914 May; pair (Todd, 1940)	
Deserted 1921–30				
P30	C	Agric.	1923 Apr. 6 c/4 Harlow	
P27	C	Urban	1920's last clutch robbed (vide Hickey)	1928–39 deserted (Trembly)
P32	B	Wild.	1928 Apr. 18 c/4 Harlow	
P39	?	?	1929 Apr. 3 c/4 Gillen	
Deserted 1931–40				
NJ25	C	Recrea.	1937	1938
P36	B	Agric.	1937 2 young (Case)	1952 deserted (Rice)
P35	C	Agric./Urban		1937 deserted (Rice, Mannix)
P31	?	Wild.	1938 pair nested (Hickey)	
P34	C	Agric.	1938 c/4 coll. by Court	1940 WW seen
P29	B	Agric.	1939 pair? (Wimsatt)	1940 apparently deserted (Rice) 1946 deserted (Rice, Richards)
P37	B	Wild.		1953 deserted (Rice, Richards)

Those that were deserted by 1945 were, to a lesser degree, inferior to the last group that were not deserted until after 1950. Finally, the last four to be deserted were the most "superior" of all the eyries (Table 12.2).

I will qualify "inferior." The most significant quality of peregrine eyries in my region is "accessibility to people." There are three factors that determine this. First is the ease with which people can get near the cliff either from the top or the bottom to disturb the birds. If accessibility to

Table 12.2. Persistence of Peregrines as Related to Cliff Height, Environment, and Accessibility of Nesting Ledges to Man

Eyrie no.	Last year used	Cliff height rating[a]	General landscape	No rope needed	Not difficult with rope	Difficult with rope
P13	1941	B	Coal	X		
NJ6	1941?	B	Recreation		X[b]	
P20	1941?	B+	Agriculture		X	
P11	1942	A–	Agriculture	X		
P17	1946	A+	Agriculture		X	
P12	1947	C	Agriculture	X		
P10	1947	B	Agriculture		X[b]	
P18	1948	C	Agriculture			X[c]
P21	1950	B	Wilderness		X	
P16	1950	A+	Agriculture			X
NJ1	1950	Quarry	Agriculture	X		
P2	1950	A+	Agriculture			X
NJ4	1951	B	Agriculture		X	
P5	1951	A	Agriculture			X
P15	1951?	A	Coal			X
P8	1955	B or Bridge[d]	Recreation			X
P7	1956	B	Wilderness	X		
P19	1957?	A+	Agriculture			X
P9	1958?	A	Agric.; Recr			X
P22	1958	A–	Coal; Wild.			X
P3	1959	A+	Recreation		X	

[a] Highest cliff A+; lowest cliff C

[b] Near road

[c] Low cliff

[d] At least 3 years on abandoned stone bridge piers; at least 1 year on cliff

the bottom of the cliff is easy and the cliff not too high, the birds can be more readily shot. If accessibility to the top is easy, the very presence of people at the top (whether they be falconers, picnickers, or egg collectors) will cause the birds to become nervous, and perhaps desert.

Nearness to a road makes the eyrie more susceptible to marauders than the one near a railroad only. If on a railroad but distant from the nearest road, the eyrie becomes less susceptible to molestation. For example, site P7 is some miles from the nearest road, and lasted until 1956, despite its ready accessibility to people if they ever did get to it.

The second factor in determining the "accessibility to people" of the eyrie is the nature of the cliff and how well its physical qualities protect the birds from people—the height of the cliff and thus the distance between the area used by the birds and possible molesters; for example, although sites P3, P19, and P22 are near roads, they are so high above them that shooting might well be inaccurate. On the other hand, such eyries as NJ6, P10, P11, and P13 are so close either to a road or a railroad that molestation could be more effective, and these eyries were deserted in the early 1940's.

The third factor involving the accessibility of the eyrie to people is twofold: first, the difficulty involved in finding the eyrie site, and second, the difficulty involved in getting into the eyrie. The four eyries just listed are fine examples of eyries easy to locate and easy to get into; and 1941 was the last year for three of these, and 1942 for the other site, P11.

On the other hand, although eyrie P9 was on a railroad not too distant from the road, the length and height of the cliff made locating the eyrie site very difficult. This eyrie boasted a pair of falcons as late as 1957, although, to the best of my knowledge, they never raised any young in 12 years that I found them present. This could be caused partly by the nearness of the nesting ledge to people at the top.

Eyrie P7 is a good example of "protection by distance," since the cliff is not large and the eyrie is easily walked into without a rope. (It lasted until 1956.)

P8 is a fine example of "protection by difficulty of approach." In most years the eggs were laid on old bridge pilings, which are difficult to get to during the normal high water of the early nesting season. (The birds were still present in 1955.)

The physical nature of the cliff itself has a great bearing on this. "A" cliffs are high and long, with more than one suitable eyrie site. Unfortunately for the birds, a few "A" cliffs can easily be climbed and the eyries entered, such as P11 and P17. So they also qualify as being easily accessible and were deserted in the early 1940's, despite their height. The four eyries that existed longest (all were "A" cliffs) had in their favor the fact that all were protected by distance from road or railroad (making shooting the birds more difficult), and all were hard to locate, since all had several good nesting ledges, most of which were very difficult to enter by any but the most skilled and daring climbers, of which there were very few.

THE DECLINE IN NET PRODUCTIVITY

In my opinion the egg collectors reduced by at least one-third a marginal population already restricted by its environment. As Hickey (1942) states, the first clutch in this region averages four eggs; the second, three. Often one egg fails to hatch, from either the first or second clutch; hence the 33% loss.

In some instances the birds did not lay again. I have noted in looking at some clutches taken by eggers that incubation was well on its way when the eggs were taken.

There were, during the present century, four well-known major egg collectors operating in eastern and central Pennsylvania. Their names are well known and some are shown in Table 12.1. Their collections of peregrine eggs are extensive. There are literally boxes upon boxes of eggs in these collections (N. D. Hoy, pers. comm.). Sometimes the eggers operated together, sometimes independently, but over the decade from 1920 to 1930 they certainly effected a great reduction in the peregrine population of Pennsylvania.

By 1940 the number of active eyries was reduced to 21 in the study area. By 1943 the active eyries were down to 14; by 1950 down to 11; by 1955, 5; and by 1960, to the best of my knowledge, all were deserted (Table 12.3). I have what I think is an accurate observation of a single male peregrine seen by Walter Koeller at one Pennsylvania site in mid-March 1965; it was not present later in the season.

There was not much chance of breeding birds moving in from other states either north or south of Pennsylvania. In Vermont, 53 sets of eggs were taken from 1920 to 1934, and many of the eyries were deserted by

Table 12.3. Condensed Eyrie Histories 1939–60: The Chronology of Desertion in Pennsylvania and Western New Jersey

A = 1 adult present
c/ = clutch of eggs seen
D = unquestionably deserted
d = apparently deserted
E = eggs collected
e = eggs eaten
P = pair present
p = pair (immature ♀)
U = unsuccessful pair; eggs failed to hatch
Y = young reared; number unknown (= 2± in Table 12.4)
y = small young seen; not counted in Table 12.4
1,2,3, = no. of young reared
1+2 (etc.) = no. reared plus no. taken by falconers

Eyrie no.	'39	'40	'41	'42	'43	'44	'45	'46	'47	'48	'49	'50	'51	'52	'53	'54	'55	'56	'57	'58	'59	'60
P24	Y	d																				
P23		U																				
P14		A	d					D	A		D	D		D					D			
P13		U	0+1	D	D			D	D		D			D					D			
P11		1+1	U	4	D			D	D	D	d	d		D					D			
NJ6	P	P	Y					D			D				D							
P20		1+2	1					D						D	D							
P17	P	3	d					P	d	d	d			D	D	D	D	D	D			
P12		D	3	d	d			d	P	d		d		d					D		D	D
P10	P	P	P	d				d	A	d	d			d					D			
P18	P	D	D							P	d			d	D	D	D	d	D			D
P21		D						4	P			P	D		D				D			
P16	P	1	2+1					4	P	3	U	P	d	d	D	D	D	D	D			
NJ1										4	1	E	D	D	D			D	D			
P2	P	3	1+3	3	P	2+1	1+?	U	U	P	P	P	d	D	D	D		D	D			
NJ4					1				P		P	P	U	D	D	D	D		D			
P5	Y	3	P	3+1				2	P	P	U	P	P	D	D							D
P15		y	c/3							P	P		P		d	d	d	D	D			
P8		P						U	P	Y	2		P	P	P	P	1	d	d	d	D	D
P7			2+1	4	3+1	2+1	4	4	3+1	2+1	e	e	P	e	D	U	D	2	d	d	d	d
P19	P	1+2						P	D	p	P	1+2	0+2	Y	1+?	Y	P	P	P		D	D
P9	P	P	P	d				P	P	P	P	P	P	P	d	d	d	d	P	P	D	D
P22	E												1	U	P	P	P	d	P	P	d	D
P3	1+1	U	3+1	2	3+1			3	2	P	1	1	1	U	U	d	d	1′	1+?	P	P	D

1940 (Hickey, 1942). The few Connecticut eyries suffered even more than those of Vermont since they were near large population centers. South of Pennsylvania, in Maryland and Virginia, eggers and falconers from the Washington, DC, region took a heavy toll along the Potomac. Even isolated eyries in western Virginia were egged and the young taken by falconers during the 1940's and early 1950's. So the chances of distant isolated wilderness eyries constantly producing to fill the more vulnerable eyries are not as good as might be thought by the unsophisticated falcon-protection enthusiast.

By the late 1940's the adult birds of the 1930's were dying out or getting infertile, as evidenced by the number of active but nonproducing eyries in the early 1950's. Due to the lowering of the population by the eggers, there were not enough young birds to reoccupy all the "B" cliffs, or even the more accessible "A" cliffs. The "A" cliffs lasted until the early 1950's.

By this time the activities of the falconers showed their effects. Between 1940 and 1951, 29 young birds were taken out of a population reduced to the submarginal stage by eggers in the 1920's and 1930's, by shooters at the eyries, and by duck hunters in the south. The consistent pattern of reproductive failure (Table 12.4) set in in 1949.

Of course these 29 were not all potential breeders, due to the recognized great loss of young birds by natural causes during their first year of life. This figure of 29 does not include the 17 which were taken from 6 eyries in 1937 and 1938. This makes a total of 46 birds lost to the population. In the same period at least 105 young falcons flew from our reported active eyries. Three flew in 1938 from the few eyries reported on.

Table 12.4. Summary of Peregrine Reproductive Success in Pennsylvania

	1939–46	1947–52	1953–60	Total
Deserted eyrie (× years)	12	19	50	81
Apparently deserted	9	16	17	42
Nonbreeding				
Adult present	1	2	—	3
Pair present	20	32	14	66
Breeding pairs				
Unsuccessful	9	10	2	21
Successful	35	15	6	56
Total occupied sites	65	59	22	146
Young taken	21	8	—	29
Young reared[a]	81	24±	8±	113±
Reared per occupied site	1.25 (1.45)[b]	0.3 (0.45)[b]	0.4	0.8

[b] Number that would have probably fledged if no young had been taken.

[a] ± = 2 young estimated as reared.

Thus the possible loss due to falconers could be as high as 43%. However, the number of young taken declined sharply after 1941. There was a decline in the number of active falconers in the area of Maryland and Pennsylvania, which at its peak numbered 15. Of those remaining, most have a greater respect for conservation than some of those who took young falcons in the late 1930's and early 1940's. Several have developed a liking for hunting with short-winged hawks, which are more suitable for the terrain of the east.

In defense of falconry—and I repeat some of Hickey's (1942) ideas along with my own observations—I will say that falconers are great propagandists for hawk protection. Through their direct contact with groups such as schools and scouts by way of talks and displays, as well as through an individual approach, they are doing a great deal toward instilling a feeling of admiration for the peregrine falcon, which replaces in many minds a bitter dislike for the bird they have been taught to hate as a pigeon killer or a plain "no-good" hawk! Experienced falconers can and do exert a strong influence toward keeping beginners from practicing with the peregrine falcon.

The North American Falconers' Association is exerting certain pressures through its members to protect eyries from being cleaned out, but not in the geographic area under discussion in the present paper.

Shooting of the falcons at or near the eyrie undoubtedly accounts for some reduction in number. Hickey (1942) records two adults shot out of 19 pairs being studied by him during a 2-year period. I have never seen or heard shooting at an eyrie nor found a dead peregrine at an eyrie, although I found on one occasion (eyrie P6 in 1946) fresh shells below the eyrie, and on several occasions old shells at P9. William Turner and Brian McDonald found a dead female peregrine under eyrie P15 in 1951, and F. J. Trembley reports an adult shot at P13 in 1941.

The fact that some eyries have been deserted for several consecutive years and then successfully reoccupied gives some small hope that this could happen in the future. However, the birds would have to come in from breeding places in the far north, and it is quite doubtful that the strong pull of a high unoccupied cliff encountered on their migration route would be strong enough to overcome their natural instinct to return to their original habitat. Furthermore, most of the northern birds migrate along the coast, thus lowering the chance of their ever seeing a fine unoccupied cliff inland.

The following are good examples of deserted eyries being reoccupied in the period of 1940 to 1959:

P3—deserted in 1954 and 1955, reoccupied in 1956 to 1959.

P7—deserted in 1953, reoccupied and pair unsuccessful in 1954; deserted in 1955, reoccupied and young flew in 1956.

P18—deserted in 1940 and 1941 and perhaps in 1942 through 1947, reoccupied in 1948, pair unsuccessful.

P19—deserted in 1947, reoccupied in 1948 through 1957, raised young.
P22—deserted in 1956, reoccupied in 1957 and 1958, pair unsuccessful.

SUMMARY

1. The normal and natural attrition factors, such as (a) eggs not hatching due to poor nesting site (water or sun entering the eyrie) and (b) raccoons (*Procyon lotor*) or snakes (eating the eggs or young) were of no consequence in the decline of the peregrine population in Pennsylvania.
2. The Pennsylvania population of the peregrine falcon was somewhat reduced in the period from 1920 to 1935 by egg collectors.
3. It was further reduced during the same period by shooting of adult birds at the eyries and possibly of young birds by hunters further south.
4. It was still further reduced between 1937 and 1941 by falconers, who took 34 young in this 5-year period when 45 flew. From five eyries there were only 12 taken from 1942 to 1951; during this same period 59 young flew.

In 1946, in spite of the above-named causes for the decline of the falcon population in the study area, there were still 17 active eyries which, during the period from 1939 to 1946, produced 81 young, or 1.25 young annually per site occupied.

However, from 1947 through 1952, the number of active eyries declined to six. During this period the productivity per pair declined very sharply. There were only 0.3 young reared per year per occupied site.

During the last 7 years (1953–59) of nesting of the peregrine falcon in this area, there were only eight young reared, or 0.4 per pair annually per occupied site. The three pairs remaining in 1958 and one in 1959 reared no young in these years, despite lack of any known disturbance.
5. It is believed that insecticides may have caused the reproductive failure of the falcon, but this has not yet been proven.

LITERATURE CITED

Beck, H. H. 1924. A chapter on the ornithology of Lancaster County, Pennsylvania, with supplementary notes on the mammals. 39 p. reprint from "Lancaster County, Pennsylvania; a history," 1924.

Brewer, T. M. 1857. Smithsonian contributions to knowledge. North American oölogy; being an account of the habits and geographical distribution of the birds of North America during their breeding season; with figures and descriptions of their eggs. Part 1. Washington, D.C. 132 p.

Hickey, J. J. 1942. Eastern population of the duck hawk. Auk 59(2): 176–204.

Todd, W. E. C. 1940. Birds of western Pennsylvania. University of Pittsburgh Press, Pittsburgh, Pennsylvania. 710 p.+23 pl.+1 map.

CHAPTER 13

THE STATUS OF BREEDING PEREGRINES IN THE EASTERN UNITED STATES

Daniel D. Berger,
Charles R. Sindelar, Jr., and
Kenneth E. Gamble

The breeding range of the peregrine falcon covers nearly all of non-tropical North America, although at least in the more settled parts of its range, e.g. the eastern United States, it has been limited to areas where the topographic features are ideal for nesting. Hickey (1942) reported a list of 275 eyries in the United States east of the Rocky Mountains. Most of these were east of the Mississippi River. Hickey concluded that, at least in the more settled regions, the peregrine population had declined by at least 11% by 1940. Since then a dramatic falloff in the peregrine population has become evident in the eastern United States. Early in 1964 Hickey organized a rerun of his 1939–40 survey in order to document the evident decline.

METHODS OF STUDY

The first phase of the project consisted of mapping the location of each eyrie site for a field survey team. This was done by Gamble, who determined which US Geological and Geodetic Survey maps would be needed in the field and transcribed terse eyrie histories and key directions for the field party.

The second phase, which ran concurrently with the first, was a correspondence program carried out by Berger and aimed at determining recent to current nesting of peregrines in the area to be covered by the field survey team.

Phase three was the actual census, carried out by Berger and Sindelar, of the eyrie sites determined in phases one and two. The census, which lasted 3 months, began at the beginning of April 1964 in northern Alabama and Georgia, and proceeded northeastward along the Appalachian Mountains, finishing at the end of June in Nova Scotia and New Brunswick. A total of 14,079 miles (22,526 km) was driven (Fig. 13.1). We used a Volkswagen bus, two 7× binoculars, two spotting scopes (one a 30× and one a zoom scope ranging from 15× to 60×), about 250 US Geological and Geodetic Survey topographic maps, and appropriate rock-climbing equipment.

Our method of operation consisted of stationing ourselves some distance from the nesting cliff, preferably within one-half mile (800 m), but on occasion, with good conditions, as much as 2 miles away (3.2 km), and carefully observing the cliff with binoculars and scope in an effort to discover signs of occupancy—either the falcons themselves, the telltale streaks of excreta ("whitewash"), or feathers or bits of down clinging to vegetation on the cliff face.

Occasionally, where the signs indicated possible occupancy, we discharged a firearm or lit firecrackers in an effort to dislodge hidden birds. We realize that this is merely an accessory device. Failure of this method to reveal birds did not necessarily rule out their presence. Visits to the tops or bases of cliffs were also sometimes made when closer examination seemed desirable.

RESULTS

GENERAL

We had a list of 200 eyries known prior to 1942, plus 36 added sites (Table 13.1); 209 of these (89%) were rated as "valid" or "probably valid" sites. Of those, 146 (70%) were checked in 1964 either by the survey team or by our cooperators. This includes seven sites about which we are dubious due to our inability to find adequate eyrie sites at the locations given.

Of the 63 "valid" and "probably valid" eyries that were not checked, we have good reason to believe that at least 8 (including 3 skyscraper eyries) were inactive. There were a variety of reasons for passing up the 63 sites. Primarily, we had insufficient time to check them all, and knowing this, we passed up scattered eyries all along the way. In some cases cooperators advised us that a given eyrie would be a waste of time to

Fig. 13.1. Route taken in 1964 to survey presence of peregrines at 133 known nesting sites, in the latter part of the nesting season when young would ordinarily be found at the eyries. UW Cartographic Lab.

Table 13.1. Classification of Eyrie Reports in Eastern United States

Class of eyrie report	No. of eyries reported	Number of sites visited in 1964		
		Eyries found	Probably not found	Eyries checked by others
Valid	190	116	7	17
Probably valid	19	12	—	1
Doubtful	12	8	4	—
Invalid	7	6	1	—
Duplicate	6	—	—	—
Other	2	1	—	—
Total	236	143	12	18

visit since it had fallen into disuse due to encroaching civilization, and had been abandoned for years. We passed up other sites due to lack of maps, or because we decided that we had inadequate information for finding the site. A few were not visited because of the extremely long traveling distances involved. We pointedly avoided writing off the more inaccessible sites in order not to bias the data.

In addition to the known sites that we visited, we covered many areas containing good nesting habitat in hopes of finding previously unknown eyries. At known eyries we referred to our topographic maps, and explored most of the places which, from the maps, appeared to be likely alternate eyrie sites.

Our efforts failed to find a single occupied cliff. At best, by estimating the age of excreta on cliffs, we found signs of recent occupancy, say within the last 2 years, at perhaps five or six eyries. One of these may even have had birds earlier in the same year. Recent blasting in the vicinity of this site may have accounted for the desertion. The distribution of the sites surveyed in 1964 is set forth in Table 13.2.

SOUTHERN APPALACHIAN REGION

We will first discuss the southern Appalachian region. The states involved are Virginia, Kentucky, North and South Carolina, Tennessee, Georgia, and Alabama. Northern Alabama and Georgia have long marked the southern limit of the peregrine's nesting range in the eastern part of the United States. Curiously, one of the most recently occupied sites in all the eastern states was in Alabama. This site, a beautiful, isolated cliff, was reported (Rosene, *in litt.*) to be occupied in 1962. By 1964, however, it was deserted. Of four other sites in these two states, the most recent known occupancy was in 1942. Another has not been seen to be active since before the turn of the century.

Table 13.2. Geographic Distribution of Peregrine Nesting Sites

State or province	Validated sites			Probably valid sites		
	No. of eyries reported	Checked in '64 by: Authors	Checked in '64 by: Others	No. of eyries reported	Checked in '64 by: Authors	Checked in '64 by: Others
Alabama	3	2	—	—	—	—
Georgia	2	2	—	—	—	—
Tennessee	16	10	—	1	1	—
South Carolina	1	1	—	1	1	—
North Carolina	5	5	—	3	2	—
Kentucky	1	1	—	—	—	—
Virginia	8	5	1	1	1	—
W. Virginia	3	—	1	—	—	—
Maryland	4	—	1	—	—	—
Pennsylvania	38	26	2	4	2	—
New Jersey	5	1	—	—	—	—
New York	37	11	10	1	1	—
Connecticut	3	—	—	—	—	—
Massachusetts	14	11	1	1	—	—
Vermont	26	23	1	2	1	—
New Hampshire	13	12	1	2	2	—
Maine	7	4	—	3	1	1
Subtotal	186	114	17	19	12	1
New Brunswick	1	—	—	—	—	—
Nova Scotia	3	2	—	—	—	—
Total	190	116	17	19	12	1

Of 14 sites in the Appalachian (or eastern) region of Tennessee, the last-known activity was about 1948. Four sites were still occupied as late as 1947 or 1948. One more was abandoned in 1941 or 1942, and another in 1930 or 1931. Another three were inactive by 1942. The remaining five, which were inactive in 1964, were still occupied in the late 1930's. In most of these, abandonment probably followed shortly thereafter, since positive data are more apt to be reported than are negative data. From this it may be stated that the mean year of desertion approximated 1941.

In South Carolina one of two sites was last seen to be occupied in the late 1800's, and the other in 1933.

In North Carolina, four of eight were last seen active before 1940, although one did not become abandoned until about 1957 and another in 1952 or 1953.

One site in Kentucky still had a pair in 1952 but only a single bird in 1954.

There were nine valid sites in Virginia. One was abandoned in 1936 or 1937, and another in 1952. Most of the rest were not known to be active after the 1930's. One site, however, might still be active. It was heavily marked with whitewash in May 1964, and we strongly suspected that it had had birds earlier in the year, but at least in 1963. It was at this site that we suspected local blasting of having driven the birds away.

MAINE

Since it appears that significant desertions occurred first in the extreme southern part of the range, and subsequently spread northward, we are tempted to discuss the temporal distribution of desertions in the state of Maine—the northernmost of the contiguous states. This analysis is somewhat unsatisfactory since consistent checking of the eyries was seldom done in this region. We are able to say, however, that of 10 valid or probably valid sites, one was active as recently as 1962, another until 1960 or 1961, and a third until 1955.

ANALYSIS

Spofford (1942) has classified southern Appalachian eyrie sites into three types: mountain eyries, canyon eyries, and river bluff eyries. These eyries were not checked often enough in the last two decades to allow the interesting possibility of determining which type of sites might have persisted the longest. Spofford felt that many opportunities for canyon nesting existed in the Cumberland Plateau of eastern Tennessee, but that a scanty small-bird population was probably the main restrictive factor in the utilization of these fine sites by peregrines. In the 1940's he covered a series of tremendous gorges but found only one pair of falcons.

Many possibilities exist as causal factors in the decimation of the peregrine. The taking of young falcons from the eyrie by falconers might result in the desertion of the eyrie. A check of all eyries shown in Table 13.1 revealed that 36 had at least one record of young falcons being taken by falconers or would-be falconers. An additional 22 eyries were listed as "known to falconers," an indication that the production of young at these sites almost surely suffered attrition.

A second, and quite possibly an even more important factor, was the prevalence for some 70 years of fanatic egg-collecting. Many sites in the New England area, and in Pennsylvania, were repeatedly egged, particularly during the second and third decades of the twentieth century. Hickey's (1942 and *in litt.*) survey plus data accumulated during the 1964 survey (*in litt.*) reveal that no less than 69 of the 209 eyries that we rated valid or probably valid were egged at least once. An additional six sites were labelled "known to egg collectors," and, therefore, were almost surely egged. Between 1864 and 1931 a minimum of 49 clutches is alleged to have been collected at a single well-known eyrie in the state of Massachusetts (Hickey, 1942 and *in litt.*). As many as three sets were taken in one season. Frank Flick (1883) said of this eyrie, "I have known 30 persons to visit . . . [the site] in one day looking for the hawk's eggs." In spite of this persistent disturbance, the eyrie remained active until 1952. Although there was no indication of nesting in the last 3 years, the birds were reasonably productive in the preceding 10 to 15 years (J. A. Hagar, pers. comm.). These data tend to conflict with Beebe and Webster (1964) who felt that the practice of egg-collecting "is most discouraging to the nesting birds and generally results in the pair deserting the aerie for the season; and many good aeries have been permanently deserted when so raided year after year." It is pertinent that the disturbance factor caused by falconers diminished sharply during and subsequent to World War II, while the collecting by oologists was largely ended by the mid-1930's.

Two other forms of minor disturbance directly affected the peregrine. One was shooting or collecting birds at the eyrie. We noted 19 sites where this occurred. Secondly, pigeon fanciers are known to be archenemies of the peregrine; however, we know of only two eyries where this element disrupted the nesting.

It appears, then, that in recent decades the peregrine withstood, without drastic effect, the collective assault by oologists, falconers, and shooters.

Other more subtle factors possibly involved in the peregrine decimation have been suggested. Ratcliffe (1963) feels that toxic agricultural chemicals are the probable cause of the decline of the peregrine in England. Nelson (Chapter 4) discusses the correlation between climatic changes and the peregrine population. Beebe (Chapter 34) suggests a suboptimal food supply as the probable cause.

In general, the mode of eyrie abandonment in the eastern states followed a common pattern: Quite often the first indication was the failure of a pair of falcons to hatch their eggs. Secondly, within a year or two, this would be followed by the failure to lay eggs. The next step was desertion of the site by one or both birds. Seemingly the reproductive failure resulted in the lack of birds available for replacement purposes.

We found no indication that the accessibility of the nesting cliff had any relationship to its time of desertion. It is possible that "first-class" cliffs held birds longer than suboptimal ones; however, this was not readily apparent in our study. Hickey (1942) states that "first-class peregrine cliffs are extremely high," and infers that they act as an ecological magnet. In the mid-1930's, the Susquehanna River system in Pennsylvania was dotted with peregrine eyries, yet in our 1964 survey we regarded many of these once regularly-occupied cliffs as only marginally attractive to peregrines. It appears then that some factor or factors other than size and height of cliff must have been effective in attracting the falcons to this region.

In conclusion we would like to emphasize that our failure to find a single occupied peregrine cliff in the eastern states and maritime provinces should not be construed to prove that resident peregrines have been extirpated in this area. We realize the impossibility of thoroughly covering the survey area by a single team in only 3 months. We also recognize that we may have missed peregrines even at sites that we checked, though we feel this is unlikely. We do emphasize that the peregrine falcon, if not extirpated in the United States east of the Mississippi River, is drastically reduced.

ACKNOWLEDGMENTS

This study was the first project of the Richard A. Herbert Memorial Fund. We particularly wish to thank Mrs. Kathleen Green Skelton Herbert for making the study possible, and the US Section of the International Council for Bird Preservation for the administrative work.

We gratefully wish to acknowledge the cooperation of many ornithologists, naturalists, oologists and falconers. Some assisted by supplying data concerning eyrie locations and past history. Others helped by giving direct assistance to the field survey team, while still others checked eyries and reported their findings to us. Regrettably, it is not feasible to list all those who helped in the above manner.

We specifically thank, however, F. N. and F. Hamerstrom for their help in the preparation for the field survey. Mr. and Mrs. B. McDonald helped during the course of the survey. Others deserving specific mention include: K. S. J. Beanlands, R. B. Berry, J. H. Czech, M. G. Edwards, J. H. Enderson, P. G. Favor, A. F. Ganier, S. A. Gatti, W. E. Green, J. A. Hagar, B. D. Kaiman, A. Kaiman, R. B. Lyle, A. G. Nye, E. L. Poole, W. L. Rhein, J. N. Rice, W. R. Spofford, K. A. Stoll, and L. N. Wight. We also received the full cooperation of the Bird Banding Laboratory of the Bureau of Sport Fisheries and Wildlife, US Fish and Wildlife Service, and of the North American Falconers' Association.

This study was conceived and its early stages planned by J. J. Hickey.

SUMMARY

In the eastern United States, 133 formerly used eyries of the peregrine falcon were checked for occupancy by a survey team during the latter part of the 1964 nesting season. None were found to be active.

LITERATURE CITED

Beebe, F. L., and H. M. Webster. 1964. North American falconry and hunting hawks. North American Falconry and Hunting Hawks, Denver, Colorado. 315 p.

Flick, Frank. 1883. Duck hawk. Forest and Stream, 20:323.

Hickey, J. J. 1942. Eastern population of the duck hawk. Auk, 59(2): 176–204.

Ratcliffe, D. A. 1963. The status of the peregrine in Great Britain. Bird Study, 10(2):56–90.

Spofford, W. R. 1942. Nesting of the peregrine falcon in Tennessee. Migrant, 13(2–3): 29–31.

CHAPTER 14

GENERAL DISCUSSION: THE PEREGRINE FALCON IN EASTERN NORTH AMERICA

EASTERN UNITED STATES PEREGRINES AS A DISTINCT POPULATION UNIT

SPENCER: A review of the literature on the peregrine in the eastern United States would seem to indicate that this group of birds may have had geographical race characteristics both anatomical and habitual; and that it was a rather distinct population, in trouble well before the middle of the 1940's. The significantly larger size, the distinctive coloration, and the less defined migratory habit, all point to a separate race. It may also be important that this group of peregrines occupied the southern perimeter of the summer breeding range. The population appears to have been declining prior to the introduction of the chlorinated hydrocarbon insecticides. If this be true, only minor adverse effects would be needed to produce a steep mortality curve.

AMADON: Well I think there was a period 25 or 30 years ago when we were greatly concerned about most of our hawks; and they all seemed to be, and indeed most of them were, declining. But aside from that generalization, I doubt whether it's applicable to say that the eastern peregrine was in serious trouble throughout some parts of its range at least.

THE STATUS OF THE PEREGRINE ON CANADA'S EASTERN COASTS

SPOFFORD: No one at this conference has mentioned Bonaventure Island which, of course, is one of the fabulous colonial bird-nesting places in the northeast in the Maritimes. We all know there used to be three pairs of peregrine falcons on the island, along with the tremendous colony of seabirds. The breeding pairs of peregrines on the island disappeared about 1960. The active pair that Richard Herbert saw on the nearby mainland was in residence more recently than that. John L. Bull, of the American Museum of Natural History, saw a pair on that ledge in the middle of the summer of 1964 and thought they might still be breeding there.

FYFE: Leslie Tuck tells me that nesting peregrines are extremely rare in Newfoundland. In addition to the suggestive report of a pair at Bonaventure, there apparently was one pair breeding in the Maritimes in 1964. For 1965, I have reports of two pairs in Quebec, one of which is apparently authentic. This was by a wildlife biologist who saw the birds in the spring when they were noisy at a nest site.

I went all the way up the north coast of the St. Lawrence this summer (1965) to the Labrador coast, checking the sanctuaries at all of the seabird colonies. I did not see a single peregrine in this area, and there is only one record about 15 or 20 years ago of one bird being seen there in the summer. They have been reported in the past at Anticosti. I am at a loss to explain this absence of peregrines.

Leslie Tuck advises me that peregrines apparently become common as you get farther up the Labrador coast, definitely breeding in northern Labrador. They are breeding at the tip and in the central area of Ungava. They have always been rare in the more southern coastal areas of Canada.

PETERSON: I wonder how much ornithological coverage there was in this area before 1940. This might account for our scarcity of nesting records in this region. Actually there are not too many good seabird colonies there except off the Avalon Peninsula and that would, I suppose, be the area where you would find peregrines. But Leslie Tuck has been a most active field worker there in very recent years.

THE PEREGRINE FALCON POPULATION IN ONTARIO

[Joseph S. Simonyi presented some tables showing his estimates of the abandonment of peregrine eyries in the agricultural, recreational, and wilderness landscapes of Ontario from 1956 to 1965. His report appeared to be based on an enormous amount of field work, the details of which deserve publication. The disappearance of the peregrine in the agricultural and southeastern part of the province appears to be identical to that described elsewhere in this volume for the Middle West and the Appalachians. If this species also is now rapidly disappearing as a breeder in the wilderness regions of Ontario, as Mr. Simonyi believes, changes in even the Arctic populations of this species in North America can be expected.—Ed.]

WINTERING PEREGRINES IN THE NORTHEASTERN UNITED STATES

MRS. HERBERT: Regarding Enderson's comment that the birds presently wintering in the northeast are Arctic birds, I have not checked into *Audubon Field Notes,* for example, to see how many birds are, in fact, wintering in the northeast. As to the 20 or so that used to be in the Greater New York area feeding on pigeons in the winter, I think they have virtually disappeared, so there may in fact not be a wintering population of any numbers there.

ENDERSON: In 1961, 1962, 1963, and 1964, a normal number of peregrines were reported wintering along the seaboard from Cape Cod to Coot Bay in the Everglades. These may be distinct from the population that wintered in New York City; perhaps the birds that wintered in the city were local birds.

THE PEREGRINE DECLINE IN NORTHERN NEW ENGLAND AND NEW YORK

SPOFFORD: Perhaps the data should be broken down into New Hampshire, Vermont, and New York State from the standpoint of the effects of falconry. The Vermont and New Hampshire birds were taken very substantially by falconers, I would gather, but northern New York State birds were not. The collapse or the die-off of the peregrine population occurred at the same time in northern New York State and the Vermont and New Hampshire eyries. My observations are grouped 2 years at a time and represent a very casual type of checking, the percentage of coverage varying greatly from year to year. The young were produced, as you can see (Table 14.1), up through 1957. From then on, there was less coverage on my part, until 1965 when I checked and rechecked a good many places, and found that this sample of the nesting population was entirely extirpated. But I would like to point out one feature of the die-off here: Several eyries here collapsed in a single year. They were raising young in 1957, and the birds failed to return to the eyrie in 1958. This change from successful fledging of young in one year to no birds the next year occurred all through this period.

In the summer of 1965, I found some possibly fresh whitewash in Vermont. I think there may be a bird hanging around this one site. We have had, of course, several records throughout the northeastern area of individual birds being seen in 1965. But it is clear that the real collapse of successfully nesting pairs has taken place.

The Adirondack areas, which I know better, have very high cliffs, when one considers the general area, so much so that sometimes one may see the falcons high in front of the cliffs and at first think they are swallows. These eyries were not bothered during the decline. There was no

Table 14.1. Miscellaneous Observations at 29 Peregrine Eyries in New Hampshire, Vermont, and Northern New York, 1952–65

	1952–53	1954–55	1956–57	1958–59	1960–61	1962–63	1964–65
Eyries with:							
Pair and young	9	11	11	—	—	—	—
Pair + eggs	1	2	2	—	—	—	—
Pair present	4	5	3	1	—	—	—
Single adult		1	3	—	—	—	—
Whitewash	5	17	13	7	3		1?
Old whitewash		1			2	2	7
No sign		1		5	6	10	25
Total eyries	19	38	32	13	12	12	33
Percent coverage[a]	33	66	55	22	20	20	57
Percent active[b]	74	50	59	8		0	

[a] Percent of total eyries observed.
[b] Percent of eyries observed which had at least one bird present ("active sites").

one who ever tried to get to them, and yet the population collapsed at the same time as in New England.

In Table 14.2, from 1952 through 1957, I have summarized the numbers of young produced in 31 successful nestings in this region.

CLEMENT: In view of the evidence which Spofford has just given us, I question the wisdom of trying to use a median date of desertion as Berger gave us, as 1942–43. Our problem is to try to eliminate those nesting sites that we know were abandoned because of disturbance and to account for the disappearance of pairs that were not disturbed, so that the latest dates of nesting are perhaps the most significant ones.

BERGER: I think you're right.

PETERSON: We obviously have several factors operating here.

PEREGRINE FOOD RESOURCES IN THE EASTERN UNITED STATES

BEEBE: I find the Herberts' report absolutely fascinating. There are two things in it which are especially interesting: (1) the evidence of starvation involving at least one young bird that fledged from these eyries and (2) the evidence of the tenacity of the birds in this area where multiple human disturbance was taking place. These two phenomena are, to me, a tribute to the determination of peregrines to breed in spite of everything. That the birds were there at all, as long as they had been, is an amazing thing. The whole pattern suggests to me exactly the thesis presented in my paper (Chapter 34): There was inadequate prey somewhere in this area, and there was a residual peregrine population that was carried on at an artificially high level. Most of the eyries were occupied, and I think the young just were not surviving under those circumstances. I cannot get over that impression.

Table 14.2. Peregrine Reproduction in Northern New England and Northern New York

	Number of eyrie–years			
	1952–57		1958–65	
Pairs with young	31		—	
Pairs with eggs	5		—	
Pairs present	13		—	
Single adult seen	4		—	
Subtotal		53		—
"Whitewash" seen	33		11	
Old "whitewash"	1		11	
Deserted	1		46	
Subtotal		35		68
Percent coverage[a]		88		68
Total		50		29

[a] Percent of total eyries observed.

SPOFFORD: Well, I do know that at least until there were large young on the nesting ledge, the adult birds picked off blue jays and other prey species very consistently all through the area described by Mrs. Herbert. I recall spending one day with, I think, Herbert and Hickey at the Storm King Mountain during the blue jay flights along the Hudson River when the jays would come north up the side of Storm King and then head out across the river to cross to New England; and the adult peregrines were picking off the blue jays one after the other, just after they would get out about 100 yd (90 m) over the water. The peregrines would then go out, pick them off, and bring them back. They were storing them up like nuts on the ledge. They had so many they didn't know what to do with them. That was true all during this spring migration which goes right past all the Hudson River eyries. So until the young birds are fairly large, the adult peregrines do not need the pigeons.

BERGER: I can only speak for our Wisconsin area. You just could not in that area watch the birds that were feeding there and have the feeling that they were having any problem whatsoever getting food. Regardless of how many young they had, they spent their time resting and sleeping. When they felt the need for prey, either for themselves or for their young, it was a matter of 10, 15, or 20 minutes, and they had it.

MRS. HERBERT: On the subject of peregrine prey, I certainly do agree with Dr. Spofford that the adult birds do store them up like nuts in the breeding season. The male takes blue jays, and the female sometimes takes them too. However, when I did count up the various kinds of prey in our observations in the 1950's, I was surprised to discover that the pigeon constituted two-thirds of the birds taken. Even during the nesting season the pigeon was taken more often than blue jays or flickers although they were frequent kills too. Of course this diet was not necessarily for the young because in the 1950's the adult peregrines in our area were not hatching young; but they were incubating, however, and the male was bringing food to the female who would take it from him.

The food of the New York City peregrines, of course, also consisted of racing pigeons but never the house sparrow or the feral rock pigeon. The two wintering birds at the George Washington Bridge and Riverside Memorial Church took starlings because of their proximity to an enormous starling roost. However, the other peregrines did not attempt to take feral city-nesting pigeons; these always take shelter whereas the racing pigeons continue racing and are an easier kill. There was no scarcity of food in our area. I know that my husband and Dr. Hickey at one time had a theory that the male peregrine was more prone to take smaller birds, such as blue jays and passerines. However my husband abandoned this theory. He did always think, and I am sure this was true, that young peregrines had more success in taking insects, for instance. He described to me one young bird that was just off the nest ledge and that just missed taking an insect because it flew through his claws. I believe that young peregrines do take smaller birds and insects. I think that a young bird would perhaps hesitate to strike a pigeon. I don't know of any adult peregrine ever taking an insect, but we did see the young take them.

SPOFFORD: When young peregrines take insects, I don't think it is food that they are seeking. Primarily, they love to play, and they will pick daisies out of a field. They just love to handle things with their feet and they have to learn how to use their feet. During its first 6 weeks or so, a falcon is always reaching a foot out and picking up something. Whether he eats it or not is something else.

BEEBE: This whole discussion indicates to me an absolute dearth of food. I wish you people could see a real abundance of food for peregrines.

CADE: In British Columbia, you have a superabundance of food which is way beyond anything that your falcons can exploit.

BEEBE: Yes it is, but these young ones that you're talking about surely look to me like they are starving to death.

CADE: There were no fewer nesting birds in eastern North America in the present century than there were in colonial times, I'm sure of that.

RATCLIFFE: Surely this theoretical inefficiency of the young peregrines in hunting is, or has been, a constant factor over a long, long time. In this conference we are concerned with changing factors.

BEEBE: I think the passenger pigeon was the change.

GREENLAND PEREGRINES BANDED IN MARYLAND

RICE: During the past 10 autumns, I have banded 171 migrating peregrines on the Atlantic coast at Assateague Island, Maryland (38°N, 75°W). At least some of these birds appear to be part of the peregrine falcon population breeding in West Greenland, as the following recoveries show:

Dates banded and recovered	*How recovered*	*Where recovered*
5 October 1956 November 1959	Shot	Aqugsserniq, Egedesminde District, West Greenland (70° N, 50° W)
10 October 1957 4 September 1958	Shot	Near Umanak, 70° North Latitude, West Greenland (70° N, 20° W)
4 October 1961 5 January 1962	Shot	Near Juacunto Aranz La Pampa, Argentina (43° S, 67° W)
9 October 1956 29 January 1957	Shot	Penal, Trinidad, British West Indies (11° N, 62° W)
3 October 1963 19 February 1964	Not reported	Key West, Florida (25° N, 82° W)
10 October 1954 26 February 1955	Shot	Laguna Rincon, Province of Barahona, Dominican Republic (18° N, 70° W)
1 January 1961 1 April 1961	Killed by car	Cape Hatteras, North Carolina (35° N, 75° W)
10 October 1959 4 April 1960	Shot	Old Harbour, Costa Rica (10° N, 85° W)

The low recovery rate for this sample, 5% up to 29 August 1965, suggests that this population either spends very little time in the United States or that its stay in our country tends to be restricted to coastal districts where shooting pressure is not a serious mortality factor at the time the falcons migrate.

PEREGRINES IN THE SOUTHERN AND SOUTHEASTERN UNITED STATES

SPOFFORD: Berger asked me to say something about Tennessee. I left this state in 1949. Chickamauga Gorge had a pair present and raised young in 1946; Yellow Bluff raised young in 1947; Wolf River had a pair present in 1947; Linville Gorge on the North Carolina side just across from Elizabethton, Tennessee, had peregrines present in the early summer in 1951, so there was possible occupancy there.

The tree-nesting pair at Reelfoot Lake last raised young in 1947; my last check at this tree nest in the big cypress was in 1956 and showed barred owls to be in possession. I did not try at this time to determine whether the peregrines were using a new site. They were known to switch from one tree to another every once in a while.

The other tree-nesting pairs in the state of Virginia have not to my knowledge been checked in recent years. F. M. Jones recorded in 1946 (Auk, 63[4]:592) that these had occupied an area near the coast for at least 20 years. The two nests in 1946 were only 3 miles (4.8 km) apart and both contained young. I have been told by Jones that both these pairs were using nests of the osprey.

The Peregrine Falcon in Western Europe

CHAPTER 15

POPULATION TRENDS IN FINNISH PEREGRINES

Pentti Linkola and Teuvo Suominen

Almost everything that is known at present about the Finnish peregrine falcon is based on the data collected by the Finnish League for the Protection of Nature. In 1958 the League started to pay attention to the fact that the peregrine population was rapidly decreasing. At that time the falcon was not protected in Finland, and the first assumption was that the main reason for the decrease was the active persecution of this bird as an enemy of game. In order to collect facts for protection of this bird, a large-scale investigation was started by the League. Scientific magazines requested all possible information on the peregrine falcon (as well as about two other species, the golden eagle and the eagle owl). At the same time, questionnaires were mailed to many private individuals. These personal requests were sent, among others, to all bird banders, observers of the State Game Research Institute, and other active field biologists. In addition, literature, ornithological archives, museum material, and egg collections were examined. This investigation still goes on, and all reports are collected into a large peregrine archive. Today this archive can be considered as rather complete, and it contains most of the existing information on the Finnish peregrine falcon population.

THE TOTAL POPULATION

Up to now about 400 old or new nesting places of the peregrine falcon have been reported, the exact number being 386 (excluding doubtful cases). As only relatively few nests are reported twice or more, one can conclude that many places have not been reported. Therefore, 386 means a minimum, the actual number being probably much higher, perhaps double this amount, or, possibly, around 1,000 pairs. It is interesting to see that in his work, the grand old man of Finnish ornithology, Einari Merikallio, estimated the total number of Finnish peregrines to be about 800 pairs. His investigations were carried out between 1941 and 1953. At that time most nesting places were probably still in use (Merikallio, 1958).

In Fig. 15.1 the reported, more reliable nesting places are indicated. The distribution seems to be rather even, and the blank areas are mainly due to lack of observations, both negative and positive, in these areas. Thus, for instance, the only two roads in northernmost Finland are clearly shown by the few observations that have been made in this scarcely populated region. There is no reason to assume that the other sections are not equally rich in peregrine habitat.

Peregrine nests situated on rocks are especially frequent in the southwestern islands, on the southern coastline, and in the hill-rich regions of the eastern and northern parts of the country.

A quite different nesting habitat is situated mostly in the western part of the country, and several places are also known in the north: In these regions large bogs are common, and the falcon has been nesting in the open bog. Formerly this kind of habitat was considered to be exceptional, but the more that is known about the birdlife of the bogs, the more common this kind of habitat for the peregrine seems to be. At the moment it seems that this bog-nesting population has been even more common than the rock-nesting one.

For some peregrines, the type of habitat is not known or it is something other than rock or bog. For instance, in two cases the peregrine has been reported to nest on a small open low scar, and in 12 cases in a tree, usually in an old nest of an osprey or other bird of prey. In most cases, however, this extra category in Fig. 15.1 means that the habitat is not reported. This is particularly true in cases where the nest is known only on the basis of museum material and other old information.

On this map altogether 386 places are indicated. Of these, 160 refer to

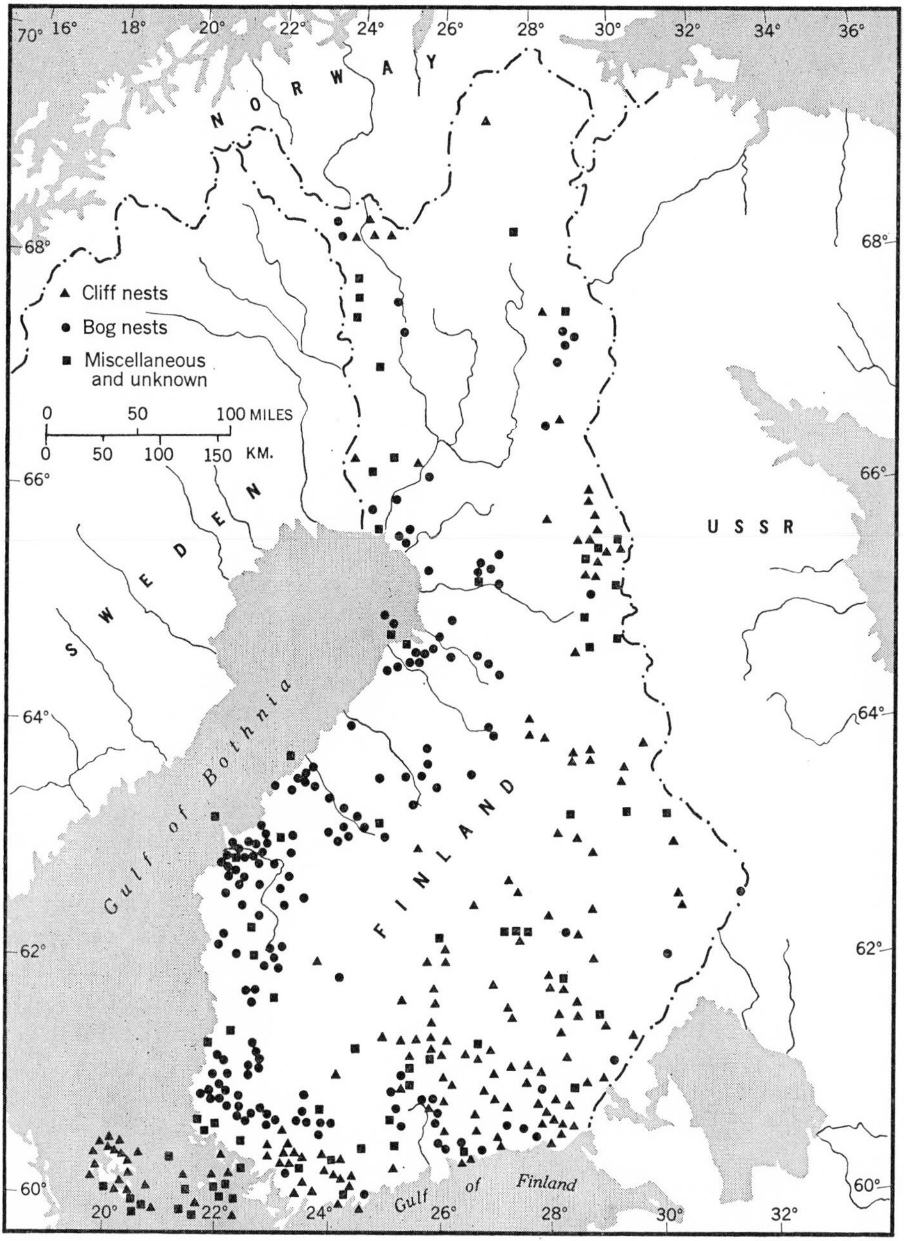

Fig. 15.1. Distribution of former peregrine nesting sites in Finland. UW Cartographic Lab.

rock nests. About the same number, 157, are bog nests. The rest, 69, are miscellaneous or unknown. Thus, rock nesting and bog nesting seem to have been equally common. On the other hand, probably much more is known about rock places, and consequently these places are more completely reported. Certainly there must have been many more bog-nesting birds that have never been discovered. One-third of the area of Finland was originally covered by different kinds of marshes and bogs, and very little has been known about the animals inhabiting them. An active investigation of bog birds has been started only in the last few years, and several new nesting places of the peregrine have been discovered. Thus we can assume that the main part of the Finnish peregrine population has been nesting on bogs. In this habitat the falcon is less visible, and its nest is much more difficult to find. In addition, on the open bog the falcon seems to change the nesting place from year to year more frequently.

Most of the observed places have been in continuous use. If no changes in the environment have occurred, a site may have been used for centuries. The oldest report in the peregrine archive is from 1756, and many are from the nineteenth century. One of these sites, first reported in 1864, was still in use in 1962, 98 years later. A bog nest in the north has been observed by local people for at least 60 years, and their fathers told them that the falcon always nested at the same place. Several bogs and rocks have been named after the falcon. There are still several places called "Falcon Hill," although the falcon itself has been absent for decades. This is particularly true in cases when the human population has come too near to the falcon. This may show that the number of peregrines has been slowly decreasing over a long time. Moreover, the bog-nesting peregrines have also lost their nesting places as a result of the drainage and other utilization of the bogs. In addition, the peregrine has been vigorously persecuted. In several places the nest with the eggs or youngsters has been destroyed every year, and the parent falcons have been shot. Despite this, new falcons have usually appeared the next year, and the nesting has continued. This certainly is an indication of a very high ecological pressure, and almost all possible nesting places have been used from year to year. Only in very few cases have the birds established new nesting places. Temporary nesting places are also exceptional. This means that most of the dots on the peregrine map of Finland indicate permanent and continuous nesting of the peregrine falcon. This was the past.

THE RECENT DECLINE

In 1958 a considerable number of the reported places were examined, 151 altogether. Most of this work represented systematic investigation organized by members of the Finnish League for the Protection of Nature, but part of it was done by others. We can expect that these other observers mainly reported only positive cases, which makes it difficult to evaluate their observations. In addition, the principal observations were made in places where peregrines were known to have been lately nesting. Thus the picture we get must be considered as too favorable. Out of the 151 observations reported in 1958, 35 were positive nesting records. In 8 cases single birds, nonnesting birds, and some fresh sign of the falcon were observed. The remaining 108 cases were negative. The faulty sources mentioned above make it difficult to estimate the actual number of nesting pairs, but we can possibly assume that it is of the magnitude of 100. Compared to the estimate of the original number of nesting pairs, which is of the magnitude of 1000, we reach the conclusion that only 10% of the original amount was left in 1958. This conclusion led to the legal protection of peregrines in Finland in 1959.

Since 1958 the examination of old nesting places has continued from year to year. The decline of population was found to persist, and one place after another became empty. Only in a few cases did a nesting place, once abandoned, become reinhabited later. Usually the vacancy was final. In several cases a single bird without the mate appearing in early spring has preceded the final stage. In the results obtained from 1958 to 1965 (Table 15.1), the population crash is quite evident. As most of the places where birds have been seen in a given year have also been studied during the following years, the observations have be-

Table 15.1. Observations on Known Nesting Places of Peregrine Falcons in Finland 1958–65

Year	Observations: New	Observations: Total	Nesting pairs[a]	Any fresh sign of falcon	Uninhabited
1958	151	151	35	8	108
1959	30	79	31 (10)	7	41
1960	17	68	17 (6)	8	43
1961	6	49	10 (2)	0	39
1962	2	42	8 (1)	3	31
1963	7	43	9 (4)	4	30
1964	24	75	6 (0)	11	58
(1965)[b]	3	18	6 (3)	5	7
Total	240	525	122	46	357

[a] The numbers within parentheses represent the numbers of nesting pairs which have been found in places where no observations have been made during the preceding years.

[b] The last year is not comparable to the others because only 5 reports had arrived at the time this table was compiled, 3 of them including positive cases.

come more and more reliable. This makes the decline shown in Table 15.1 appear less rapid than it actually was. According to von Haartman *et al.* (1963–66), the average clutch, based on old museum material, has been 3.2 (33 cases). Linkola got about the same between 1850 and 1949, 3.1 (130 cases), but only 2.8 (34 cases) between 1950 and 1958. Our present material with 62 cases gives an average of 2.6. There is, however, some uncertainty about the statistics on clutch size because more systematic observations have revealed that in several cases the number of eggs diminished during incubation time. As a result of the active investigation started in 1958, there are now many such observations, while nothing is known of the past. This makes it difficult to say if there is any real decrease in the original egg-number or if the decrease is only due to the fact that all nests have not been found at their early stage. Nothing is known about the reasons which have caused the egg-number to diminish, but in most cases the possibility of human activity must be excluded.

At the present we can assume that the Finnish peregrine population has declined to a level of some few percent, and no change in this process is to be expected. In fact, the situation seems to be still worse when one studies the nesting results. In Table 15.1 altogether 122 positive observations are given. Of these, 102 cases have been observed in some detail. These observations are listed below. Nothing is known about the remaining 20 cases except that the birds probably had nests with eggs.

Nesting success of the peregrine in Finland between 1958 and 1965:

12 cases: the birds abandoned their nests for an unknown reason (total 25 eggs)
4 cases: unexplainable disturbances in nesting (in one case, at least 5 eggs were laid at different places and then abandoned, in others the eggs did not hatch or the youngsters soon died)
30 cases: the eggs or youngsters disappeared (in some cases this is known to be due to human activity, but most cases are unexplainable)
8 cases: observations made only at the egg stage (total 22 eggs)
3 cases: at least small youngsters appeared (3 + 1X)
31 cases: at least big youngsters appeared (50 + 2X)
14 cases: the youngsters are known to have fledged (total 32)

In at least 46 cases an unsuccessful nesting has been established. Of the remaining 56, only 14 cases are known to have been successful. It seems probable that most of the 31 cases where big youngsters have been observed have been successful, as there are only a few observations where big youngsters have not fledged. Nothing can be said of the remaining 11 cases. We can assume that about half of the total number of nestings were successful, and that the average number of youngsters has been slightly more than 2. This means that the average result of all nesting cases is about one youngster per nest.

The fate of adult peregrines is known to some extent through the facts provided by bird banding. During the period 1913–65 altogether 206 peregrines have been banded. Forty-six of these have been found later, that is, about 22%. Most of the birds have been shot down, both in Finland and in other countries. In Finland the peregrine is migratory, and the banding has revealed that the birds have been spending the winter in western Europe, especially in France. There are at least four cases where the bird was already dead upon being found. All these cases are rather recent: the first appeared in 1959, two in 1960, and one in 1963. The banding results up to 1963 are shown in Fig. 15.2.

These facts indicate that at least 22% of the Finnish peregrines are recovered, usually as a result of shooting. Probably many other cases are not reported, especially now when the peregrine is protected in Finland. Four peregrines have been found dead during the last few years. Such birds can be found only accidentally, and very likely many more cases are not found. Nothing is known about the reason for these deaths, but the possibility of biocidal or other kind of poisoning might be kept in mind.

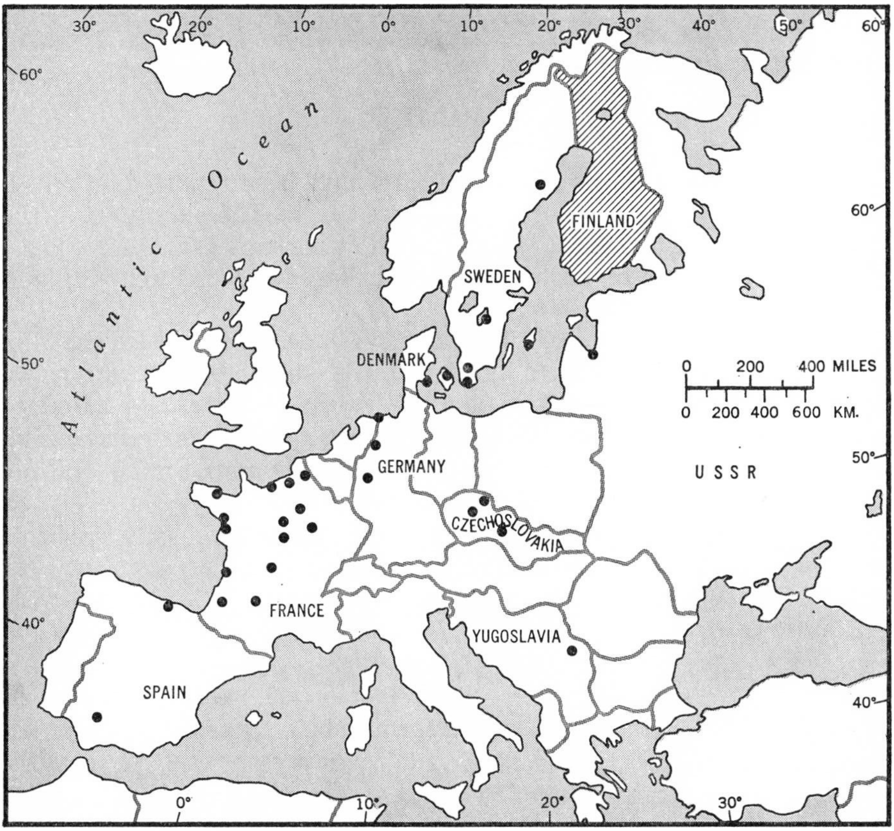

Fig. 15.2. Distribution of recoveries of peregrines ringed in Finland and recovered in other countries (after Nordström). UW Cartographic Lab.

The exact time when the population decline began in Finland cannot be determined. Many observations suggest, however, that in the beginning of the 1950's there were still hundreds of peregrines nesting in Finland. During the years between 1950 and 1958 only small amounts of pesticides were used in Finland, and even now their use is still rather limited. It is hard to believe that the pesticides used in Finland could be the reason for the catastrophic decline in the peregrine population. On the other hand, it must be kept in mind that the peregrines nesting in Finland spend the greater part of the year in their winter regions in other parts of Europe. They arrive in Finland in April, and the autumnal migration starts at the end of August and continues until the end of October. It seems very reasonable to assume that the peregrines may collect biocides in their bodies during the winter. In addition, as a raptorial bird the peregrine might have an additional way to get poisons. Most of its prey are also migratorial, and the prey species, too, might import portions of poisons to Finland from their own winter regions. Up to 1965, no residual determinations of biocides had been made in Finland on peregrines, their youngsters, or their eggs.

SUMMARY

In Finland, 386 peregrine nesting places have been reported, of which 160 are cliff sites, 159 bog nests, and 12 tree nests. The main part of the total population in former times, estimated at perhaps 1,000 pairs, is assumed to have nested on bogs and is now believed reduced to less than a few per cent of its former numbers.

Systematic investigation of 151 known eyries in 1958 revealed that 108 were deserted, 8 were occupied by single birds, and 35 by breeding pairs. Clutch size averaged 3.1–3.2 up to 1949, 2.8 in 1950–58, and 2.6 since then. In 102 recent nestings, about one-half seem to have been successful, the mean number per successful nest being slightly more than 2, and the mean number reared per occupied site about 1.

Of 206 banded peregrines, about 22% were recovered, mostly by shooting.

ADDENDUM, 1968

In 1965, 15 peregrine eyries were known to be occupied, 5 having been discovered for the first time. A single adult was present at 6, a pair without young at 3 more, a clutch of two eggs was seen at 1 (fate unknown), 4 had a total of nine young, and 1 had a very weak chick that soon died. An egg at this last site was analyzed in England and found (Ian Prestt, *in litt.*) to contain 28 ppm of DDE, 2.8 ppm of dieldrin, and 0.2 ppm of heptachlor epoxide. (Aldrin, dieldrin, and heptachlor are not used in Finland.) When 7 of these sites were checked in 1966, 2 eyries each had a single adult present, 1 had a clutch of two eggs (both were later found broken, one of the shells being extremely thin), and at 3 other sites a total of 10 eggs resulted in six young. In 1967, 1 of these 15 sites was deserted, a second had a single adult, and a third had a clutch of three eggs (fate unknown).

An eyrie, discovered for the first time, had a pair in 1966 but no young; another, similarly discovered in 1967, produced one young.

In addition to the above, we now have one record of peregrines reoccupying a bog site. This eyrie lost its birds in the late 1950's. A pair appeared in 1965, laid two eggs, and fledged two young. In 1966, the pair courted but did not nest. In 1967, the eyrie had a single adult that did not stay.

LITERATURE CITED

Haartman, L. von, O. Hildén, P. Linkola, P. Suomalainen, and R. Tenovuo. 1963–66. Pohjolan linnut värikuvin. I. Otava, Helsinki. 439 p.

Merikallio, E. 1958. Finnish birds. Their distribution and numbers. Fauna Fennica, 5:1–181.

Nordström, G. 1963. Einige Ergebnisse der Vogelberingung in Finnland in den Jahren 1913–62. Teil 1. Ornis Fennica, 40(3):81–124.

CHAPTER 16

PEREGRINE FALCON POPULATION TRENDS IN WEST GERMANY

Theodor Mebs

Fifteen years ago West Germany was relatively rich in peregrines. The varied topography presented many ideal eyrie sites. A map of West Germany showing all the eyrie sites used in the last two decades gives the following picture: First is a heavy concentration of these birds in the higher hill-ranges of the Franconian Jura and the Swabian Alps, which are strongly cleft by erosion and have many steep faces on the chalk rock. Also, the northern edge of the northern chalk-Alp zone, as far as it lies within Germany, shows continuous though sparse peregrine eyrie distribution. The falcons nest at the edge of the foothills here and hunt out over the flatlands. Curiously, on the other hand, the whole terrain of the Swabian-Bavarian plateau (between the Danube and the edge of the Alps) has always been without breeding peregrines; presumably suitable eyrie sites are lacking. (However, R. Ettl reports *in litt.* that in 1964 there was a successful peregrine nesting right in the city of Munich!). There have never been any known cases of tree-nesting peregrines in all of southern Germany.

The range of the cliff-nesting peregrines extends over the Black Forest, the hills of Pfalz (the Palatinate), the broken hills of the Rhineland (Hunsrück, Eifel, southern Westphalia), and the Hessian and Weser hills to the Harz Mountains; it thus extends (in the Süntel) a little beyond the 52nd parallel to the north. The eyries within this range, along the Main, the Neckar, and in part along the Weser and elsewhere, are unique in that they are in rock quarries. Here additional eyrie sites have been made available to the falcons within historic times, including ruins, church steeples, and such.

The north German plain with its broad moors, heaths, and wooded areas lies north of the lower mountains all over the center of Germany. Here the peregrines nested exclusively in old pine or beech stands where they utilized old nests of other birds of prey as well as old crow nests for eyries.

METHODS OF COUNTING THE POPULATION

For simplicity's sake the count of eyrie pairs was made by counties. After I had studied the peregrine population of southern Germany (Bavaria, Baden-Württemberg) intensively since 1947 (Mebs 1955, 1960), I had a chance from 1960 on to study and become personally acquainted with the conditions in north Germany (Schleswig-Holstein, Lower Saxony). In the years 1964 and 1965 H. Kramer of Bonn and I arranged for a peregrine population survey of all West Germany to which many people contributed worthwhile data. Space does not permit me to name them, but I extend my heartfelt thanks to them here.

The survey was conducted by checking all formerly known eyries during the breeding season, and some of them several times. Simultaneously, I gathered and tabulated all available observations from former years in order to get as clear a picture as possible of the changes which had occurred between 1950 and 1965. Although we only had observations on most of these eyries for several years or for just 1 year during this time span, in practically every case it was possible to perceive in which year a given eyrie was still occupied. Sometimes our only record was the last year of occupancy, while controls in the following years were negative.

As this table cannot be published here, I am going to draw from it to show population trends—how many eyries were still occupied in 1950, 1955, 1960, and 1965.

RESULTS AND DISCUSSION

In 1950, there were about 320–380 breeding pairs of peregrine falcons in West Germany. The overall reduction in this population by 1965 was about 77%, and it is convenient to discuss the trends in this species according to what happened in seven districts (Table 16.1 and Fig. 16.1).

SCHLESWIG-HOLSTEIN AND HAMBURG

In Schleswig-Holstein the beautiful, old beech stands on the summits of the moraines (in the eastern part of the country) offered peregrines

Table 16.1. The Decline of ***Falco peregrinus*** in West Germany

District (area in sq km)	Region	No. of pairs still present				% Decline
		1950	1955	1960	1965	1950–65
Schleswig-Holstein and Hamburg (16,500)		15–20	12–13	6–9	1–3	89
Lower Saxony and Bremen (47,700)	Heide	ca. 32	ca. 22	ca. 14	2–4	91
	So. Hanover	25–30	ca. 18	8–10	2–4	89
	Harz	ca. 15	10	6	2	87
	Subtotal	ca. 75	ca. 50	28–30	6–10	89
North Rhine-Westphalia (33,950)	No. Rhine	6–8	3–4	1	0	100
	Westphalia	12	5–6	3–4	2	83
	Subtotal	18–20	8–10	ca. 4–5	2	89
Rhineland-Pfalz and Saarland (22,450)		45–50	ca. 40	ca. 25	8–10	81
Hesse (21,100)		25–30	15–20	10–12	3–6	84
Baden-Württemberg (35,750)	Neckar and Hohenlohe	20–25	ca. 15	ca. 10	2–4	87
	Swab. Alps and Upper Danube	50–65	40–45	25–30	18–20	67
	Black Forest and Hegau	20–30	20–25	15–17	6–8	72
	Subtotal	90–120	75–95	50–57	26–32	72
Bavaria (70,550)	Franconian Jura	25–30	ca. 25	15–20	8–10	67
	Main	8	7	3	3	62
	Bavarian and Bohemian Forest	5–6	4–5	3	2	64
	Bavarian Alps	15–20	15–20	ca. 15	10–15	29
	Subtotal	53–64	51–57	36–41	23–30	55
All districts (248,000)	West Germany	320–380	250–285	160–180	70–90	77

ideal eyrie sites. Not uncommonly they nested close to sea eagles and ravens and used their old nests, and they found good hunting over the nearby lakes and moors. In 1950 there were still about 15–20 breeding pairs in Schleswig-Holstein (Fig. 16.2). By contrast in 1965 there were only 1–3 pairs. One pair, which was still nesting and fledged three young in the vicinity of Hamburg in 1964, disappeared in 1965 (J. Dien, *in litt.*). In 1965 only one pair was observed in East Holstein; it was present all spring, but obviously did not breed (D. Richter, *in litt.*). At another place there was a single bird. The population decline here amounts to 90%.

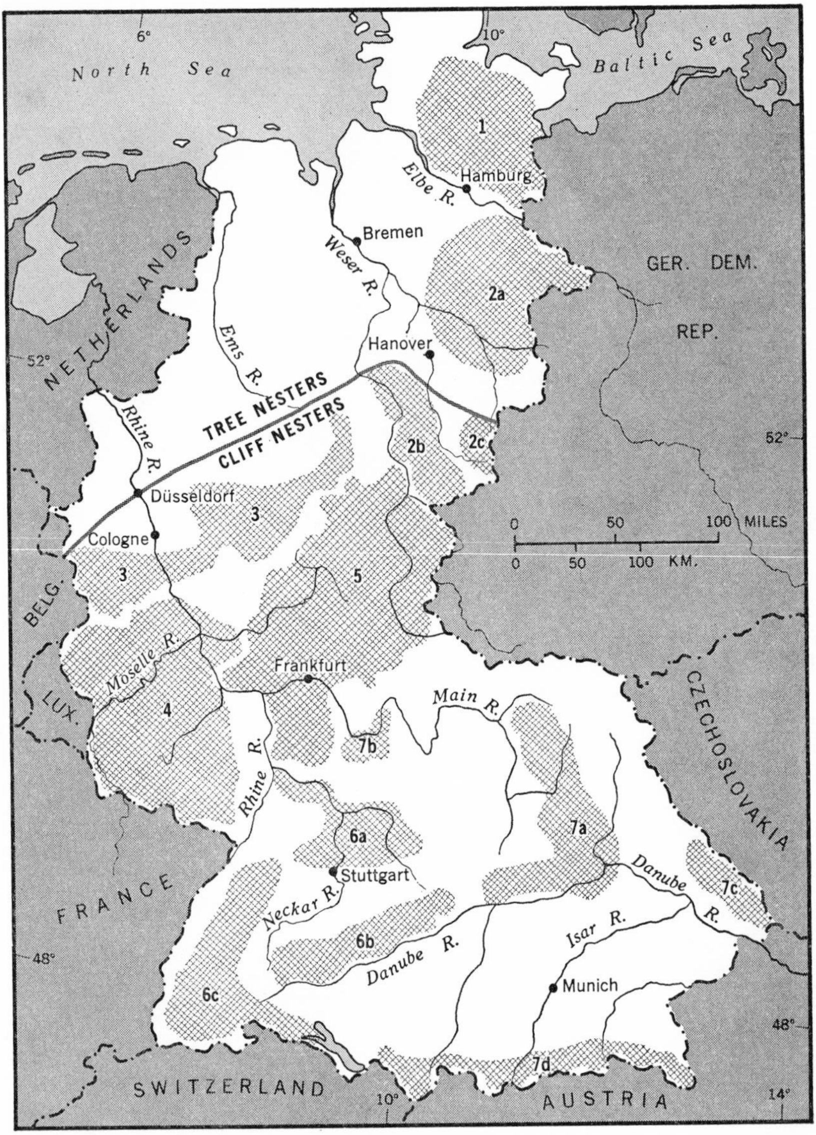

Fig. 16.1. Breeding areas of *Falco peregrinus* in West Germany, where 320–380 pairs nested in 1950, as described in the text. UW Cartographic Lab.

(1) Schleswig-Holstein

Lower Saxony *(2a)* Lüneburger Heide *(2b)* South Hanover *(2c)* Harz

(3) North Rhine-Westphalia

(4) Rhineland-Pfalz and Saarland

(5) Hesse

Baden-Württemberg *(6a)* Neckar and Hohenlohe-land *(6b)* Swabian Alps *(6c)* Black Forest and Hegau

Bavaria *(7a)* Franconian Jura *(7b)* Main *(7c)* Bavarian and Bohemian Forest *(7d)* Bavarian Alps

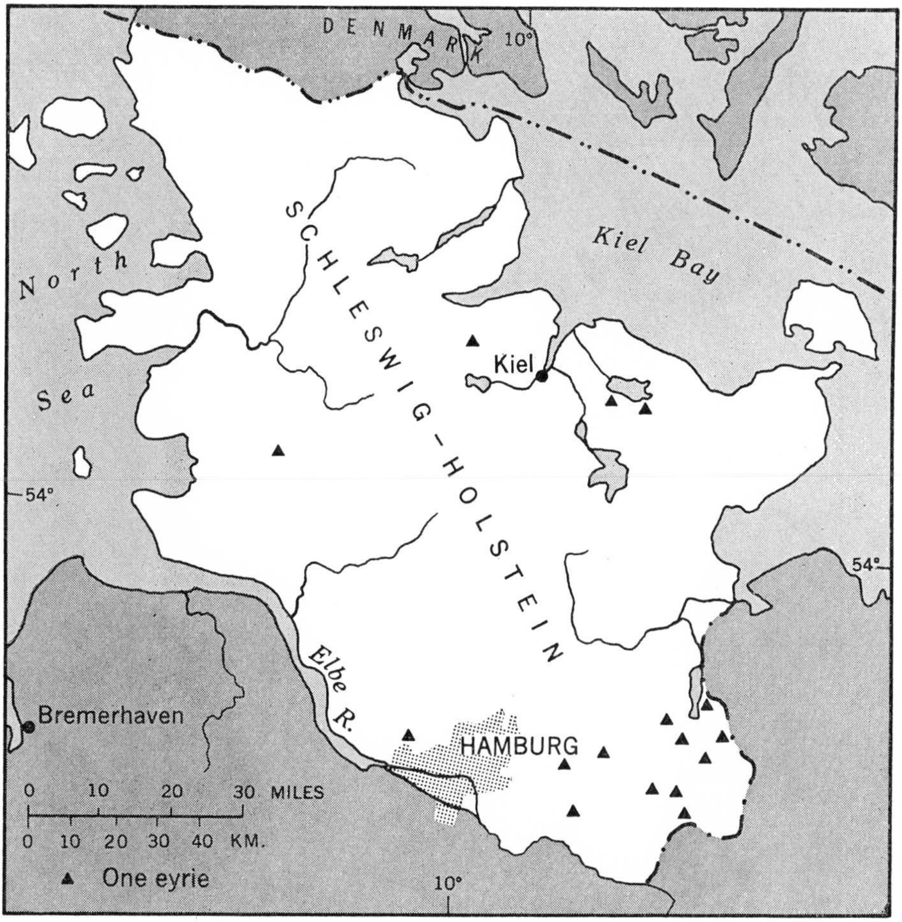

Fig. 16.2. Breeding distribution of *Falco peregrinus* (about 1950) in Schleswig-Holstein, where the birds have been nesting in trees only. The 11 eyries in the southeast (Herzogtum Lauenburg) were in an area of about 800 sq km (309 sq miles)—about 73 sq km (28 sq miles) for each pair, or 1.4 pairs per 100 sq km (3.6 pairs per 100 sq miles). UW Cartographic Lab.

LOWER SAXONY

1. *Lüneburger Heide.* Formerly the peregrine was widespread here and primarily occupied open, old pine stands where it used buzzard, kite, and crow nests as eyrie sites. In Wendland east of Lüchow, in the Göhrde, in the district of Gifhorn, and in the vicinity of Celle it was a regular breeder and appeared locally in relatively great densities (Fig. 16.3) for this species; in the forest district of Fuhrberg near Celle there were up to five pairs (O. Niebuhr, *in litt.*).

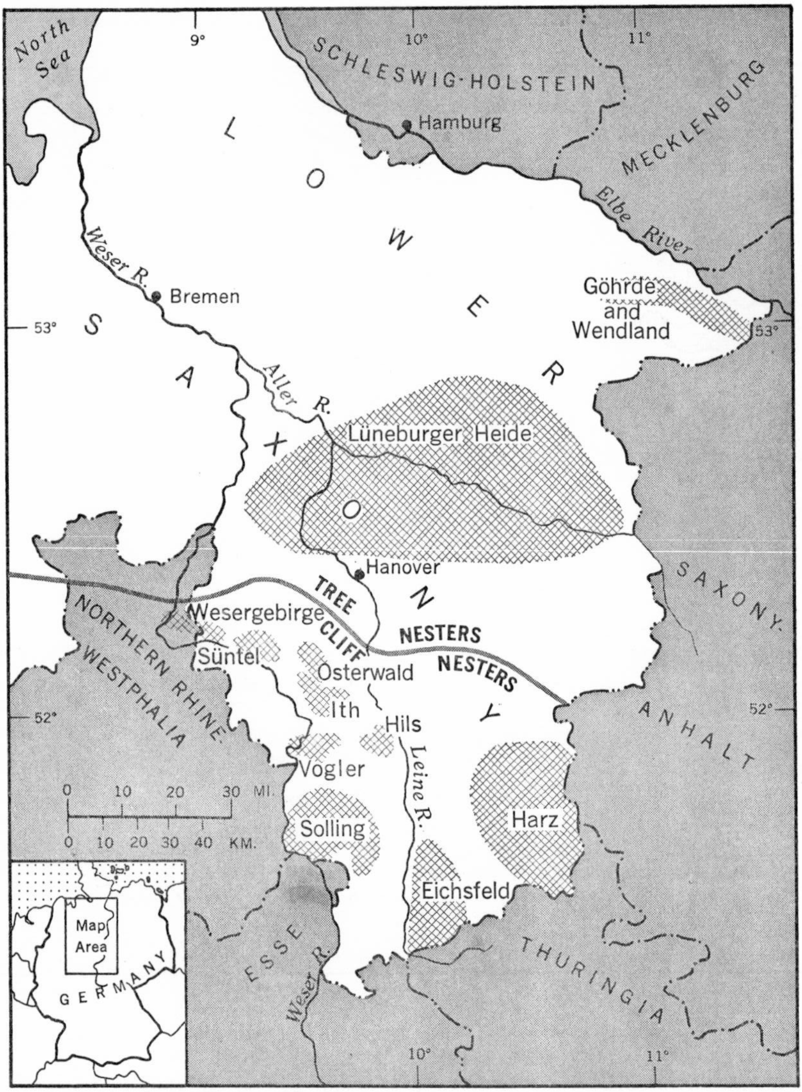

Fig. 16.3. Breeding distribution of *Falco peregrinus* in Lower Saxony (about 1950). Some densities here were as follows:

	N. Lower Saxony		S. Lower Saxony	
	Göhrde and Wendland	Lüneburger Heide	Wesergebirge-Eichsfeld	Harz
Number of pairs	7	23	31	15
Area in sq km	*ca.* 500	*ca.* 3,200	*ca.* 1,800	*ca.* 800
(in sq miles)	(*ca.* 193)	(*ca.* 1,236)	(*ca.* 695)	(*ca.* 309)
Pairs per 100 sq km	1.4	0.7	1.7	1.9
(per 100 sq miles)	(3.6)	(1.9)	(4.5)	(4.9)
Area per pair in sq km	71	139	58	53
(in sq miles)	(28)	(54)	(22)	(21)

UW Cartographic Lab.

Sometimes shooting platforms, long abandoned by deer hunters, were used as eyrie sites. Such platforms are open, but roofed, and were used in four known instances. The last remaining pairs of peregrines several times accepted flat willow baskets as artificial eyries; these L. Müller-Scheesel, previous to 1960, placed in the tips of high, old pines, near formerly used but by then broken-down old nests. Acceptance of these substitutions may show that the tree-nesting population was suffering from lack of suitable eyrie sites. Moreover, old nests easily broke up and fell apart as the result of frequent striking of the nest by the falcons. Not uncommonly the young fell to the ground and readily fell prey to foxes.

In 1950 about 32 pairs bred in the Lüneburger Heide and its vicinity, i.e., in the districts of Lüneburg, Stade, and Osnabrück. By contrast, in 1965 at most 2–4 pairs were estimated. Although I checked all breeding territories used in recent years, no successful nest could be found. There was not one brood, and at only three places did I find a single adult. The three territories which had pairs in 1964 were vacant in 1965. L. Müller-Scheesel knows the peregrines of the Lüneburger Heide as well as anyone; his [translated] letter is typical of the situation.

> I have given up looking for further negative data. We must recognize that *Falco peregrinus* no longer exists as a breeding bird on the Lüneburger Heide. If in this year there should indeed be a breeding attempt, previous experience must be taken into consideration. Next year we'll find a couple of pigeon feathers at best. This has been my experience over and over again. When breeding has once been disturbed, whether by sickness or age, one cannot expect the situation to improve. Indications of such disturbances are small clutches, addled or injured eggs, few young, etc., or also aberrant behavior of the adults. At any rate, I have never known things to pick up in such cases. In so many instances, I have noted that when any of these indicators occur to the slightest decree, it spells doom. I know of no eyries having addled eggs or few young before the war. There were always three or four healthy, lusty young with parents which defended them with strong stooping and screaming. This picture changed about 1950, at first with successive breeding failure and finally with total disappearance.

2. *South Lower Saxony.* The cliff-nesting population in South Lower Saxony (Weser-hills, Solling) which had 25–30 pairs in 1950 (Fig. 16.3), suffered heavy losses from fanatical persecution by pigeon fanciers. The broods were destroyed every year, so that only rarely, and thanks to persistent guarding of an eyrie, did young falcons fledge (A. Daubert, *in litt.*). As the adult birds, for the most part, in spite of all disturbances, remain at their chosen eyrie sites and often behave in a highly conspicuous manner, planned persecution is facilitated. In 1965 there were at most two to four pairs left in this region, which, as in recent years, raised no young. We do not know whether this was due to disturbance or to failure to breed (E. Kratz, *in litt.*).

3. *Harz.* In 1950 the Harz still harbored about 15 pairs (E. Kratz, *in litt.;* Fig. 16.3). The population declined to almost the same extent as in the above-mentioned regions of Lower Saxony. In 1964 there were birds at only two eyries, but no young fledged—a total decline of about 87%. Of eight broods in 1960–62, six failed and only two fledged. Part of the blame can be laid on the pigeon raisers, part to severe disturbance by rockclimbers; in two instances (at the same eyrie), the eggs are said to have been eaten by martens (*Martes foina* or *M. martes*). An eyrie in the southern Harz is typical. In 1962 it still had three young, and an all-out effort was made by conservationists to guard it. Nonetheless the eyrie was found empty one morning, and in it lay a note with the scornful inscription in German:"You've got to keep a better watch." This was the last brood there. The following year the adults did not reappear (K. Engelke and H. Dansberg, *in litt.*).

NORTH RHINE-WESTPHALIA

The decline of the peregrine became obvious in North Rhine-Westphalia soonest, namely in the 1950's. This was clearly pointed out by C. Demandt (1953). Some pairs laid fewer and fewer eggs from year to year, which Demandt tried to explain by superannuation. Finally there were no further clutches, and population increment ceased. Of the 18–20 eyries, originally occupied in 1950, only two remain today. Thus, the decline is about 90%, and the blame is clearly to be placed upon the pigeon fanciers, who, in one case, blasted off the whole eyrie cliff. The two eyries that still had broods in 1964 each fledged two young. The pairs were also there in 1965 but raised no young and apparently did not even breed. A total of seven young fledged from these two eyries in the last 4 years which amounts to 0.9 per eyrie per year (G. Köpke, *in litt.*).

RHINELAND-PFALZ AND SAARLAND

On the Rhine, the Lahn, and the Moselle, as well as on their tributaries in the Eifel, in Hunsrück, and in the hills of Pfalz, 45–50 peregrine pairs still nested in 1950. Of these, 8–10 pairs still remained in 1965—a decline of 80%. A total of 29 breeding cycles was observed at 7 eyries in 1960–64 (K. Röder, *in litt.*), of which 16 were successful (55%); 8 were destroyed, and we do not know why the other 5 did not bring off young. Twenty-seven young fledged from the successful eyries: 1 in each of 6 eyries, 2 in 9, and 3 in 1—an average of 1.69 young per successful brood and 0.93 per pair per year during this period. Man is still an important factor in depressing the reproductive success of peregrines in this region (Table 16.2 A).

PORTRAITS OF THE PEREGRINE

Pl. 1. The Sun Life falcon (1936–1952). This redoubtable female will long remain Canada's most famous peregrine. Marked by a peculiar indentation of the feathering on her breast, which made her readily identifiable from year to year, she appeared as a yearling in 1937 on the Montreal headquarters building of the Sun Life Assurance Company of Canada, remained for 16 breeding seasons, had three successive mates during this period, and reared 21 young. A fearless bird who tolerated no invasion of her family life, she was the most successful peregrine to invade the modern city and the subject of a detailed record of productivity that—for a single raptor—remains unmatched in the annals of ornithology. She had a wise and tolerant landlord as well as a sympathetic and intelligent press, and she left behind a host of admirers. Photo by G. H. Hall 4 June 1941.

Pl. 2–3. The peregrine alighting. No photographer has yet captured the full splendor of the wild peregrine in pursuit of its prey or in its awesome stoop. These graceful pictures of the bird coming in to its nesting ledge were taken in Ontario. The superb powers of flight of the peregrine have enabled it to colonize every continent except Antarctica and to occupy many oceanic islands where its nesting cliffs and food supplies are available. In recent years, however, its populations have been precipitously declining in both western Europe and North America. Photos by R. D. Muir.

Pl. 4. The peregrine at its eyrie. This magnificent picture, long the acknowledged masterpiece among the world's peregrine portraits, was taken at Taughannock Falls, near Ithaca, New York. The ravine is 200–300 yd wide and nearly a mile long. The waterfall has a drop of nearly 212 ft, and the walls of the gorge rise over 300 ft in some places. This wonderful site is now deserted by peregrines. Photo by A. A. Allen (copyright by The National Geographic Society).

Pl. 5–6. Record clutches of peregrine eggs. In southern Wisconsin, the only clutch of seven eggs for this species ever recorded (photographed here by L. R. Wolfe) was collected by L. R. Wolfe and E. R. Ford on 21 April 1933. Twenty-three days later on a different cliff, the falcon's second set numbered five eggs; this new set (bottom) was six when photographed by O. J. Gromme on 11 June 1933. The ability of peregrines to renest helped them to survive the vicissitudes of the egg-collecting era, but renesting disappeared during the great reproductive failures that developed on two continents after World War II. Peregrine eggs are normally laid in a "scrape," and they typically do not touch each other.

Pl. 7. Incubating falcon. Both sexes of the peregrine incubate, and the male faithfully brings food to his mate. This female had her nest in a subarctic bog in Finland where her species is now rapidly approaching extinction. Photo by Teuvo Suominen 1966.

Pl. 8. The yearling male peregrine at a nesting site in Thuringia. At this age, all peregrines are distinctively marked by vertical stripes on their underparts, but they are seldom seen in the breeding season, and their whereabouts at this time is something of a mystery. When paired, yearling females typically lay a small clutch of eggs or no eggs at all. Photo by Camill Gugg 16 May 1932.

Pl. 9. Yearling peregrine on a city feeding ledge. This bird, eating a talpacoti dove in Rio de Janeiro, was undoubtedly reared in the North American Arctic. Peregrines have long found cities to be satisfying wintering sites where pigeons are readily available. As many as 20 different peregrines used to winter in New York City. Photo by Sebastião Pinheiro, 6 March 1959, courtesy *Journal do Brasil.*

Pl. 10–11. Left: The historic hawk house in Dusseldorf, Germany, where for the first time captive peregrines hatched their eggs in 1942–43 and successfully reared young. The adult male was wild-caught, old, and had an injured wing; his 11-year-old mate was hand-reared. "Rittanno," their one downy young in 1943, can barely be seen on the sandy floor.

Right: "Rittanno" in her adult plumage. She caught her first crow on 11 July 1943, became an accomplished hunter, and disappeared in the spring of 1945. Photos by Renz Waller.

PEREGRINE ECOLOGY: TYPES OF NESTING SITES

Pl. 12. Headland sea-cliff: The Clo Mor, a 700-ft Precambrian sandstone cliff near Cape Wrath on the northwest coast of Scotland, occupied by nesting seabirds, peregrines, ravens, and golden eagles. Photo by D. A. Ratcliffe.

Pl. 13. Low, deserted sea-cliff. General view of Hunstanton Cliff on England's east coast where Sir Hamon Le Strange caught 30 male and 57 female peregrines from 1604 to 1654. Abandoned about 1818, the eyrie cannot be precisely identified today. Low-lying cliffs have been gradually deserted by peregrines over a long period. Photo by D. A. Ratcliffe.

Pl. 14. Sea-stack nesting site of the peregrine: Falcon Rock, a detached pinnacle abutting Cabbage Tree Island (foreground), New South Wales. The rock is about 300 ft high, and the island is the home of many petrels on which the peregrines feed. Photo by A. F. D'Ombrain.

Pl. 15. Lake-cliff nesting site: Falcon Crag in England's Lake District, about 700–1,000 ft above sea level. This ancient eyrie, a 300-ft cliff of volcanic rock, is one of at least eight alternative cliffs. The male was found dead in 1961, with no apparent sign of injury, and the territory has since remained deserted. The mean distance between inland pairs in this district was formerly 3.0 miles, compared to 3.0 miles in southern Scotland and 3.1 in parts of Wales. Data and photo by D. A. Ratcliffe.

Pl. 16. River-cliff nesting site of the peregrine: the Yukon River in Alaska. This site, set back from a river and high above a long, wooded talus slope, is typical of many peregrine eyries throughout the world. Only the immediate vicinity is vigorously defended, and the cliff is the "center" of the birds' large hunting area. Rivers provide a favorite hunting area over which peregrines are able to place potential prey species at a distinct disadvantage. Photo by J. R. Haugh.

Pl. 17. Ravine nesting site of the peregrine falcon: The landscape below an eyrie on the Sense River in Switzerland. Smaller cliffs may not be held tenaciously; in regions of increasingly dense human population, they have gradually been deserted by peregrines. In Britain, this process seemed to have been concluded by about 1860, but was still in progress in the 1930's and 1940's in Pennsylvania and Tennessee, obscuring the onset of the great raptor population crash in 1947. Photo by Hans Herren.

Pl. 18. Inland cliff-nesting site of the peregrine: Eyrie Li (Chapter 20) in the Swiss Mittelland, the most densely settled part of Switzerland. The top of this 245-ft sandstone cliff is about 2,430 ft above sea level. Protection of this eyrie goes back to a Berne order dated 22 March 1625, when the nobility sought to license the taking of young for falconry. In Switzerland, the number of young fledged per occupied eyrie dropped from 1.4 in 1951–55 to 0.9 in 1956–60 to 0.5 in 1961-65 and still lower in 1967. Data and photograph by Hans Herren.

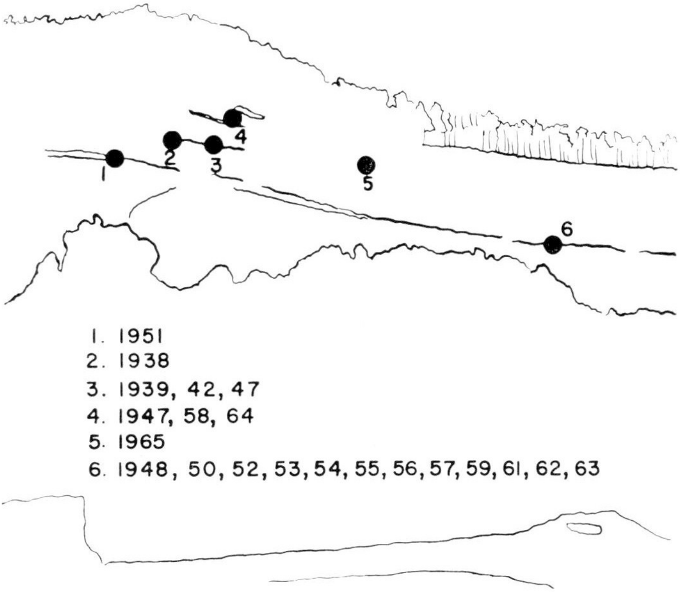

Pl. 19. Use of different ledges at the same cliff. The occurrence of only a single nesting ledge on a cliff or cliff series has been recorded only once in a long series of observations. The eight at Falcon Crag (Pl. 15) appear to be the maximum thus far reported. In this 20-year record the peregrines used ledge number 6 for 6 successive years. Eleven broods averaged 3.0 young at this site in 1935–49, and 10 broods averaged 1.7 in 1951-65. The resident pair raised no young here in 1958–60 but were successful in 1961–64. Data by Hans Herren.

Pl. 20. Inland cliff-nesting site of the peregrine: New South Wales. In Australia, peregrines like other raptors generally lay fewer eggs than they do in the Northern Hemisphere, but they renest as readily. Clutches of three eggs were once taken there from the same cliff on 16 August and on 13 September and were followed by two eggs on 14 October. Photo by K. A. Hindwood.

Pl. 21. Sloping-bank nesting site of the peregrine: Mackenzie. Cutbank nests represent part of the continuum of eyries that ranges from cliffs through slopes to low mounds and level sites. They were once occupied by peregrines as far south as Montana, but their use in recent decades has been restricted to wilderness areas in the far north of both North America and Asia. This nesting site on the Thelon River in Canada's Northwest Territories had four young on 31 July 1963. Photo by Ernie Kuyt.

Pl. 22. Sloping-bank nesting site of the peregrine: Alaska. Old cutbanks have been used in geologically young country, and by their nature are ephemeral. Here the peregrine's eggs and young are often subjected to the danger of slides when the birds select sites under exposed rocks or the roots of trees. M. W. Nelson stands at this site which is about 50 feet above the Colville River. The nest (see also Pl. 47) is immediately below a rock that has fallen down the slope. Photo by T. J. Cade 19 July 1959.

Pl. 23. Sloping-bank nesting site on a Lake Michigan island. The ground nest here (see also Pl. 48) was about 125–135 ft above the water on a 200-ft "cliff" of sand on South Fox Island (about 5.5 miles long and 1.5 wide) and was recorded only once in this region. Photo by Arthur E. Staebler 20 June 1939.

Pl. 24. Tundra-mound site: Keewatin. This low sandy hill in the Canadian Arctic, created by expanding ice of the adjacent lake, has been used by peregrines as long as local Eskimos can remember and certainly from 1951 to 1966. The nest (see also Pl. 50) faced the water but is hidden here by the wild rye *(Elymus arenarius)*. Photo by Ernie Kuyt.

Pl. 25. Bog nesting site: Levaneva, western Finland. About 30 percent of the reported eyries of Baltic peregrines have been on the ground of subarctic bogs and heaths. At this bog site, one of the last to be occupied in Finland, the nest was under the leaning pine. Photo by Urpo Häyrinen.

Pl. 26 (above). Tree-nest—stick type: Germany. Tree-nesting has usually involved the taking over of nests made by other large birds—crows, herons, other raptors. The practice was formerly common in the Baltic area, and the only one used by these birds on the north German plain. The nest here is a man-made one (see also Pl. 60). Photo by L. Müller-Scheesel and G. Synatzsche.

Pl. 27 (right). Tree-nest—broken trunk type: Reelfoot Lake, Tennessee (see also Pl. 52). Here a small population of peregrines was discovered in the 1930's and 1940's. Earlier records of tree-nesting by this species in Kansas, Illinois, and Indiana go back to the 1870's. Photo by R. A. Herbert 20 April 1942.

Pl. 28–29. Tree-nest—hollow-limb type: Tennessee. This cypress was about 130 ft tall and extended well above the forest canopy (see also Pl. 53). The hollow limb was about 90 ft above the water. Hollow limbs were occasionally used in the past by a now-extinct population of peregrines in the Mississippi Valley and are still the eyries of some peregrines in Australia. The practice seems to be unrecorded for the peregrine in Europe; it may have been the basis for an early report of peregrines nesting in southeastern Wisconsin by P. R. Hoy at a time when great beech trees with large holes were found in that region. The supercanopy aspect of the site pictured here is characteristic of many bald eagle nests constructed in great white pines in the Upper Lake States. Photos by W. R. Spofford 25 April 1943.

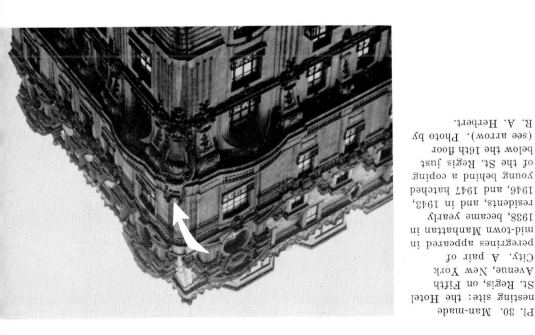

Pl. 30. Man-made nesting site: the Hotel St. Regis, on Fifth Avenue, New York City. A pair of peregrines appeared in mid-town Manhattan in 1938, became yearly residents, and in 1943, 1946, and 1947 hatched young behind a coping of the St. Regis just below the 16th floor (see arrow). Photo by R. A. Herbert.

Pl. 31. Man-made nesting site: the Salisbury Cathedral in southern England (1220-1258). Its spire, the highest in England, reaches 404 ft. Peregrines were reared here in 1864 or 1865, eggs were laid in different rain gutters of the tower at a height of about 193 ft in 1879 and 1880, and two young were taken from the building in 1896. Photo by Herbert Felton, National Monuments Record (Crown copyright).

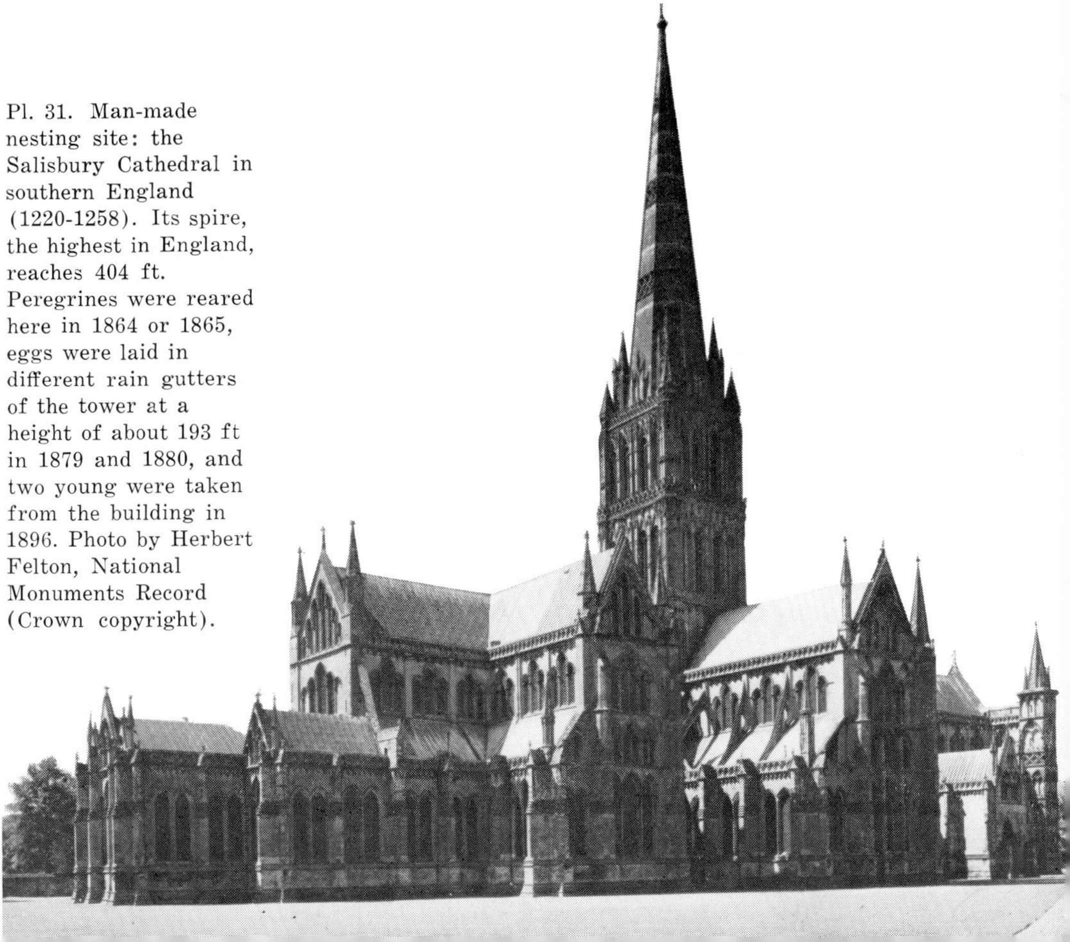

Pl. 32–33. Man-made nesting site: the Mota del Marques, central Spain, where peregrines are reported to have nested for two decades. Kestrels were using the site when it was photographed in 1966. Nesting of this species in 1952, 1956, and 1957 on an old Moorish watchtower on the coast of southern Spain, has also been reported. Great ruins are for peregrines the ecological equivalent of isolated cliffs. Photos by A. S. Leopold. Data by Felix Rodriguez de la Fuente and Guy Montfort.

Pl. 34 (right). Man-made nesting site: Burgruine Liebeneck near Pforzheim, Germany. The ruins of castle Liebeneck (constructed after 1263) were the breeding place of a pair of peregrines until 1960. A single bird was last seen at the eyrie in 1964. The nesting ledge was a wall projection. Data from Th. Mebs; photo by Helmut Wegener.

Pl. 35 (below left). Modern buildings as eyries: the Law Courts in Nairobi, Kenya, where peregrines are said to have nested successfully in 1959 in the recess behind the coat of arms (now removed) at a height of about 60 ft. Photo and data by L. H. Brown.

Pl. 36 (below right). Modern buildings as peregrine eyries: the Montreal office building of the Sun Life Assurance Company of Canada (see also Pl. 1 and 55–58). Height of nesting ledge: 300 ft; main food: pigeons and starlings. Photo by Graetz Bros. Ltd., courtesy of the Sun Life Assurance Company of Canada.

PEREGRINE ECOLOGY: NESTING SUBSTRATES

Pl. 37. "Grassy" substrate on open and exposed site: Northwest Territories. At this eyrie in the Canadian Arctic, with its four young, the vegetation consisted of willow (*Salix* sp.), a sage *(Artemesia Tilesii)*, and *Oxytropis Maydelliana*—none of which are grasses. Photographed 31 July 1963 by Ernie Kuyt.

Pl. 38. Soil and gravel nesting substrates on exposed cliff ledges: an island eyrie in Mexico, close to California's international boundary. Photo by Lewis Wayne Walker, Arizona-Sonora Desert Museum.

Pl. 39. Soil and gravel nesting substrates on exposed cliff ledges: a Finnish eyrie with the adult peregrine identically posed to the California bird above. These birds belong to different subspecies of *Falco peregrinus*. Photo by Teuvo Suominen.

Pl. 40 (left). Old bird nest used on cliff by the peregrine: Northwest Territories. Such nests are fairly common in the Arctic, uncommon in Great Britain, and rare in the United States south of Canada. This rough-legged hawk's nest with its downy peregrine young, photographed by Ernie Kuyt on 29 July 1965 on the Thelon River, was used by the rough-legs in 1963.

Pl. 41 (below). Downy peregrines in rough-legged hawk's nest: Alaska. With many years of use by the falcons, nests such as these gradually flatten and fill up with debris. Photographed on the Colville River in 1959 by T. J. Cade.

Pl. 42 (above). Semi-exposed ledges—tree and shrub cover: Vermont. This site was photographed about 1939 by the late C. A. Proctor and typifies some eyries formerly used in the northeastern United States. Young peregrines were produced in this region up through 1957, and the last few nonbreeding adults were seen at the eyries there as late as about 1965.

Pl. 43 (right). Semi-exposed ledges: Vermont. This nest was in brush and partly under a dead log on a wide shelf passing from forest on to the cliff face. Note the harmless parasitic Protocalliphora in the auditory meatus of the young. Photographed 9 June 1940 by W. R. Spofford.

Pl. 44 (above). Sheltered, overhung sites: New South Wales. This is a favored eyrie of the peregrine where available, and every gradient between exposed ledges and caves seems to have been recorded. This crevice in a low cliff was some 30 ft from the ground. Photographed November 1943, near Waterfall, Royal National Park, Australia, by Norman Chaffer.

Pl. 45 (below). Cave-type peregrine nesting sites: France. Caves (as well as ledges) must be of adequate size if the peregrine's young are to exercise properly and depart from the eyrie in a healthy condition. Sites like this are frequent in limestone, chalk, and sandstone formations and are used by peregrines in many regions. Here the female is tearing up what probably is a jay. Photographed in Burgundy in 1965 by Olivier Le Brun.

Pl. 46 (above). Slope and ground nests—cutbank: Anderson River, Northwest Territories. This scrape well illustrates the ephemeral character of slope nests along rivers in the Arctic. Photo by Richard Fyfe 3 June 1964.

Pl. 47 (below). Slope and ground nests—cutbank: Colville River, Alaska (see also Pl. 22). The peregrine here has typically sought an overhang and the screening of forbs or grasses. Photo by T. J. Cade.

Pl. 48 (above). Ground nests—island slope: Michigan. Close-up of the lake-side eyrie site shown in Pl. 23. The small size of the clutch suggests that the falcon may have been disturbed and shifted to a second site. Photo by A. E. Staebler.

Pl. 49 (below). Ground nests—subarctic bog: eastern Finland. The site appears to be fairly dry and only moderately exposed. Photo by Urpo Häyrinen.

Pl. 50 (above). Ground nests—Arctic mound: Keewatin. This close-up of the site shown in Pl. 24 reveals that the spectrum of exposure found in cliff eyries (Pl. 37–45) is fairly well duplicated in slope and ground nests (Pl. 46–50). Photo by A. H. Macpherson.

Pl. 51 (below). Tree sites—old white-tailed eagle nest: north Germany. Peregrine use of old tree nests of other large birds has been frequently recorded in northwestern Europe, three times only in North America. Photographed about 1949 in Mecklenburg by Jochen Kankel.

Pl. 52 (above). Tree sites—broken trunk: Tennessee. Interior of the cypress-trunk site in a wooded swamp shown in Pl. 27. The hole is 2 ft deep and 3 ft wide. The young, nearly 4 weeks old, are shaded by a small tree growing in the deep litter. The site is known to have been used by peregrines for at least 7 years. Food remains at the eyrie included ducks, herons, songbirds, and a pileated woodpecker. Photo by W. R. Spofford 20 April 1942.

Pl. 53 (left). Tree sites—hollow limb: Tennessee. Interior of the eyrie shown in Pl. 28–29. These eggs on 29 March 1947 were about 85 ft from the ground. The cavity was about 18–20 inches in diameter. This site is known to have been used by peregrines from at least 1943 through 1948. It had four young in 1943; three, in 1944. Spofford found an extra female present in 1945 (in immature plumage) and in 1947 (in adult plumage). Barred owls were using the cavity in 1956. Photo by T. S. Butler and W. R. Spofford.

Pl. 54. Man-made peregrine nesting sites: Pennsylvania. Abandoned stone pier of an unfinished bridge standing in the Susquehanna River. The peregrines using this eyrie had an alternate site on a nearby cliff. This young bird was photographed on top of the pier in 1938 by F. C. Craighead, Jr., and J. J. Craighead.

Pl. 55–58. Man-made peregrine nesting sites: the Sun Life Building in Montreal. Above: flooded-out peregrine eggs resting in rain gutters in 1938 (photos by J. D. Cleghorn). Scattered eggs in 1938–39 led E. W. Pfeiffer and J. S. Luck to install two nesting trays, filled with sand and gravel, on the ledge just below the 20th-floor balustrade. These the birds in time accepted, and they proved essential to the success of this pair. Lower left: nesting tray installed in 1940 (photographed later by Forrest Nagler). Lower right: W. R. Spofford at tray installed 7 April 1947 (photo by R. K. Burns).

EXPERIMENTAL SITUATIONS

Pl. 59 (above). Female peregrine rearing young prairie falcons under experimental conditions: Boise, Idaho. Paired with a captive peregrine male, she produced infertile eggs, but accepted two young prairie falcons. Photo by M. W. Nelson 1966.

Pl. 60 (below). Artificial tree nest: northern Germany. This willow basket is one of 15, filled with decayed leaves and forest-floor litter, installed for peregrines from 1950 on. About five or six were used. Photo by Ludwig Müller-Scheesel and Günther Synatzsche.

Table 16.2. Eyrie Histories for Pfalz and Neckar

D = deserted
Pw = pair without young (at time when it should have them)
Pn = nonbreeding pair
pb = pair breeding but success and eventual young unknown
U = unsuccessful
X = brood destroyed or taken by men; figs. in parentheses = number of eggs (e) or young (y) seen before
1, 2, 3 = number of young reared
— = no observations

A. Pfalz[a]

Eyrie no.	1960	1961	1962	1963	1964
4/35	2	2	1	2	2
4/41	1	1	Pn	Pn	2
4/42	X(e)	X(2y)	3	1	U
4/43	2	Pn	2	2	2
4/48	X(3y)	X(1y)	X(2y)	X(4e)	P(n)

[a] Observations by K. Röder (*in litt.*).

B. Neckar

Eyrie no.	1950	1951	1952	1953	1954	1955
6/2	—	1	X(e)	2	1	Pw
6/3	—	—	2	X(e)	—	Pw
6/4	—	—	—	3	D	—
6/5	—	—	—	2	1	U
6/8	—	—	Pw	Pw	Pw	—
6/9	—	1	X(2e)	Pw	X(3y)	2
6/10	3	X(3e)	U	Pn	Pn	D
6/11	—	1	pb	—	—	—
6/15	—	—	—	—	2	—

HESSE

Of 25–30 breeding pairs in Hesse, only about 3–6 pairs remain—a decline of over 80%. More exact figures on breeding success and results are still lacking.

BADEN-WÜRTTEMBERG

1. *Neckar and Hohenlohe.* The resident peregrine population of the colored sandstone and mussel-chalk cliffs of the lower Neckar and its tributaries still had 20–25 pairs in 1950 (see Fig. 16.4). This population shrank to a minimum comparatively more quickly than the population

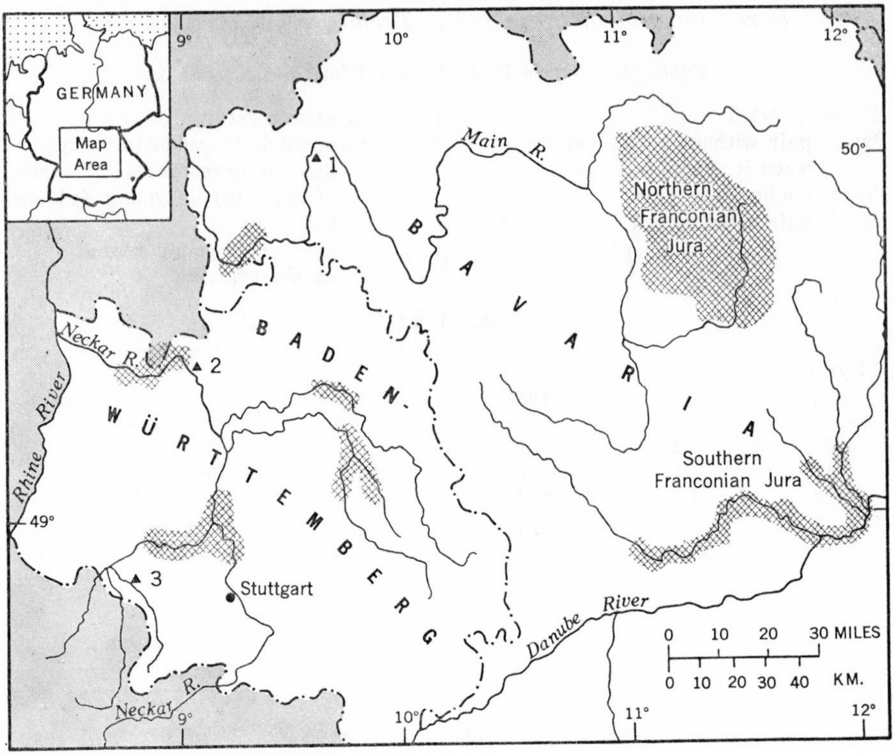

Fig. 16.4. Breeding distribution of *Falco peregrinus* in northern Baden-Württemberg and northern Bavaria. The numbers refer to eyries on the ruins of castles and old fortresses: (1) Ruine Schönrain, occupied until 1952; (2) Zwingenburg, occupied until 1954; (3) Ruine Liebeneck, occupied until 1960. UW Cartographic Lab.

along the Main, which was also nesting on colored sandstone. Whereas the decline along the Main presently stands at 62% (since 1950), it is 87% along the Neckar. Here there are only two—at most four—pairs left, and in 1965 only one pair bred. The population regression apparently started here in the first half of the 1950's (Table 16.2B), whereas along the Main the onset was not until the second half of the fifties (Table 16.3). My observations at an eyrie on the Neckar seem typical: 1953, 3 May—at least two young in eyrie; 1954, 27 May—only one young in the eyrie, still very small, about 12 days old; 1955, 21 May—the falcon is still incubating one egg; 1956—pair present, no brood; 1957—eyrie abandoned. Subsequently, two abandoned eyries were reported to me, from which the adults had probably been shot in 1957 or 1958; before this time local pigeon breeders had destroyed the clutches annually (W. Kost, *in litt.*).

2. *Swabian Alps and Upper Danube.* In 1950, 50–65 pairs of peregrines still nested in this region. D. Rockenbauch, the top authority on peregrines of this region, writes as of 4 August 1965 [translation]:

One keeps coming to the conclusion that the peregrine population of the Swabian Alps, unlike that in the other regions, is still good and less threatened. Unfortunately, the most recent reports force one to give up this sort of wishful thinking. Even nowadays one can still see single peregrines every year in most of the traditional nesting territories, indeed to a large extent there are even pairs present. In 1954, in the Urach-Nürtingen-Geislingen region, four falcons in immature plumage were seen at the beginning of and during the breeding season. Two of these were adjuncts to breeding pairs, one was mated, and the fourth one wandered here and there. It is thus indeed questionable that one can speak of superannuation of the peregrine population in the Swabian Alps. Nevertheless, one must not permit oneself to be deceived by these favorable seeming conditions any longer. The number of broods started is fewer than the number of pairs seen, and brood success is dropping off from year to year. We are now at the point where we can be thankful when at least one eyrie has successfully fledged young!

During the breeding season of 1965 at least 12 peregrine cliffs regularly had birds in the Swabian Alps (exclusive of the area south of the line between Ehingen-Rottweil). At two other places there were single birds for a time. At five eyries at least (probably more) eggs were laid; of these one single-egg clutch was either infertile or abandoned soon after laying (three young fledged here in 1964), another clutch of two eggs was found squashed—cause unknown. In one place the young were killed, presumably by rock climbers. In one place I found two young which, however, disappeared one after another at an age of about one or two weeks. Although access to this eyrie had been treated with marten repellent, the martens (*Martes foina*) probably took these young; they had done so in former years. Only at one eyrie did two young fledge. (In 1964 there were young at at least five eyries and they fledged at two.)

I only have incomplete and in part superficial reports from the rest of the Swabian Alps, mainly from the Upper Danube. It must be assumed with

Table 16.3. Eyrie Histories Along the Main

A = 1 adult present
D = deserted
Pw = pair without young (at time when it should have them)
Pn = nonbreeding pair
pb = pair breeding but success and eventual young are unknown
pp = pair present in early spring, but unknown if breeding or not
U = unsuccessful pair
X = brood destroyed or taken by men; figs. in parentheses indicate number of eggs (e) or young (y) seen before
1, 2, 3 = number of young reared
2± = successful brood but number of young reared is unknown; probably 2
— = no observations

Eyrie no.	'50	'51	'52	'53	'54	'55	'56	'57	'58	'59	'60	'61	'62	'63	'64	'65
7/31	pp	pp	Pw	A	D	D	—	—	—	—	—	—	—	—	—	—
7/33	—	—	—	—	pb	Pw	pp	—	—	D	D	D	D	D	D	D
7/35	pb	—	D	—	pb	Pw	—	A	—	D	D	D	D	D	D	D
7/36	pb	—	Pw	U	X(3y)	pb	Pw	2	—	D	D	D	D	D	D	D
7/38	—	—	—	—	—	pb	—	2±	—	pb	D	—	—	A	D	D
7/32	pb	—	3	Pw	X(3e)	Pw	2	Pw	—	3	pb	Pw	3	Pn	Pn	U
7/34	pp	—	Pw	Pw	Pw	Pw	Pw	pp	—	pp	pp	Pw	Pw	Pn	Pn	2
7/37	pb	pb	Pw	Pw	Pw	Pw	X(2y)	Pw	—	Pw	pp	2	Pw	2	3	Pn

some certainty, however, that the conditions in 1965 were no longer good. In my estimation, there were at most eight pairs and one or two successful broods if as much as that. The peregrine population of the whole Swabian Alps inclusive of the upper Danube Valley must be about 20 pairs at the present. On the average during the last three years one can only calculate two or three successful broods.

3. *Black Forest and Hegau.* Of the original 20–30 peregrine pairs in 1950 there are only 6–8 left today. Exact figures are lacking. The decline seems to have started here in the early fifties and now amounts to about 70%.

BAVARIA

1. *Franconian Jura.* The Franconian Jura region like the Swabian Alps is very often used as a practice area for young rock climbers. One can well look upon this and the associated disturbances as the chief cause of the decline of the local peregrines. Of the 25–30 pairs in 1950 there are now only 8–10, a loss of 67%. The onset of regression was first clearly apparent about 1958, although the majority of the broods had been disturbed or destroyed annually during the preceding decade (Table 16.4), so apparently lack of reproductive replacements played a progressively more important part. Abandoned eyrie cliffs were not reoccupied by new pairs in recent years as they formerly had been known to be, but remained vacant. Of the 8 successful broods observed 1963–65, 1 young was fledged in each of 3 eyries, 2 young in 2, and 3 young in 3—a total of 16 young, while 5 other broods were unsuccessful, giving an average brood success of 1.23 young per brood.

2. *Main.* In both 1950 and in 1951, I was still able to count seven pairs in an air-line 12.5-kilometer (7.8-mile) stretch—an astonishing population density (see Fig. 16.4). (Until 1952 an eighth pair occupied the ruins of the old fortress Schönrain which was about 30 km upstream.) In 1957 there were still five pairs there; in 1959, still four; in 1960–65, only three left (Table 16.3). In summary, there was a decline of 62%. Thanks to the repeated annual checks made during each season since 1961 by W. Hollerbach, we know that in the last 5 years, one pair nested successfully four times (three times rearing two young, and once three young). A second pair bred twice: 1962 successful, three young; 1965 unsuccessful, on 5 June the falcon was still incubating a single egg! The third pair never once brought off young (not after 1950!) and in recent years apparently laid no eggs although much nuptial flight display and several copulations were observed, and the female stayed broodily in a niche until the middle of April. (Unfortunately Hollerbach could not climb to this niche.) In summary, these three pairs fledged 12 young in the past 5 years, which makes a success rate of 0.8 young per occupied site.

Table 16.4. Eyrie Histories for North and South Franconian Jura

A = 1 adult present
D = deserted
Pw = pair without young (at time when it should have them)
pb = pair breeding but success and eventual young are unknown
— = no observations
pp = pair present in early spring, but unknown if breeding or not
X = brood destroyed or taken by men; figs. in parentheses indicate number of eggs (e) or young (y) seen before
1, 2, 3, 4 = number of young reared
2± = successful brood but number of young reared is unknown; probably 2

Eyrie no.	'47	'48	'49	'50	'51	'52	'53	'54	'55	'56	'57	'58	'59	'60	'61	'62	'63	'64	'65
North Franconian Jura																			
7/6				3	X (y)	pb	X (3y)	D	X (3e)	Pw	pb	X (1e)	D	D	—	—	D	D	D
7/4				pb	X (3y)	X (3e)	3	1	X (e)	Pw	pb	pb	Pw	pb	pb	—	—	D	D
7/2					X (3e)	D	A	D	3	—	—	—	—	—	—	—	—	D	D
7/3								A	—	—	—	pb	X (2y)	—	—	—	—	D	D
7/8											X							D	D
7/5	3	X (2y)	X (y)	X (4e)	pb	pb	pb	X (2y)	X (2e)	2	3	1	X (1y)	Pw	pp	pp	Pw	1	1
7/7	4	3	X (4e)	X (3e)	X (e)	D				—	pb	pb	—	—	—	—	—	A	A
7/1				4	2	X (1y)	X (2y)	2±	Pw							X	3	2	Pw
7/9													pb	—	—	2±	X	3	2
7/10																		3	A
South Franconian Jura																			
7/12	—	—	—	—	—	—	—	—	X (3y)	pp	—	—	—	—	—	—	—	—	D
7/13	—	—	—	—	—	—	—	A	X (2y)	pp	D	—	—	—	—	—	—	—	D
7/15	—	—	—	—	—	—	—	X (4y)	X (4e)	X (4y)	—	—	—	—	—	—	—	—	D
7/17	—	—	—	—	—	—	—	—	—	2	—	—	—	—	—	—	—	—	D
7/18	—	—	—	—	—	—	—	X	X	X (4y)	—	—	—	—	—	—	—	—	D
7/22	—	—	—	—	—	—	—	—	—	Pw	—	—	—	—	—	—	—	—	D
7/23	—	—	—	—	—	—	—	—	—	—	—	2±	—	—	—	—	—	—	D
7/25	—	—	—	—	—	—	—	—	—	—	—	pb	—	—	—	—	—	—	D
7/21	—	—	—	—	—	—	pp	X	—	Pw	—	—	—	—	—	—	—	—	pp
7/16	—	—	—	—	—	—	—	pp	—	1+	—	—	—	—	—	Pw	—	—	X (4e)
7/19	—	—	—	—	—	2±	—	—	—	3	2±	—	—	—	—	2±	1	—	X (3e)

3. *Bavarian and Bohemian Forest.* Two of the former five or six pairs are still present. However, nothing is known about their breeding success. One pair is said to have nested successfully in 1964.

4. *Bavarian Alps.* The peregrines in this region live hidden away in wilderness areas which are difficult to get to, so that it has always been hard to study them and the records are incomplete. Nevertheless, through the years, I have gained a fairly adequate picture of their territories, which are pretty well scattered throughout this region. The population, which still consists of 10–15 pairs, is almost entirely unthreatened by human persecution, and therefore has suffered, perhaps at the most, a 30% reduction since 1950. The broods, which are ordinarily reared relatively late, almost always fledge, and thus constitute a good population reserve. The productivity of this population is considerably higher than that reported for areas to the north (Table 16.5).

Table 16.5. Summary of Reproductive Success in Some West German Peregrine Eyries

		No. of			No. of young per	
Region studied	Year studied	Young reared[a]	Successful pairs	Occupied sites[b]	Successful pair	Occupied site
No. Franconian Jura	1947–50	17	5	10	3.40	1.70
	1951–55	9+2	5	20	2.20	0.55
	1956–60	6	3	11	2.00	0.55
	1961–65	15+2	8	15	2.13	1.13
So. Franconian Jura	1952–58	6+6	6	18	2.00	0.67
	1962–65	1+2	2	6	1.50	0.50
Neckar	1950–55	21	12	27	1.75	0.78
Main	1950–55	3	1	19	3.00	[0.2]
	1956–60	7+2	4	11	2.25	0.82
	1961–65	12	5	16	2.40	0.75
Pfalz	1960–64	27	16	29	1.69	0.93
Bavarian Alps	1962–65	15+2	7	7	2.43	2.43

[a] Including successful eyries where the number of young was estimated at 2 each.

[b] Excluding occupied sites where data on reproductive success were incomplete, but including the sites where only one adult was present.

SUMMARY

In 1950, West Germany still had a breeding population of 320–380 peregrine pairs. In 1965 only 70–90 of these remained, which constitutes a 77% decline. In particular, the decline was greatest—about 90%—in the northern districts (Schleswig-Holstein, Lower Saxony, and North Rhine-Westphalia), whereas up until now it has been weaker toward the south: Hesse, Rhineland-Pfalz, and Saarland, 82%; Baden-Württemberg, 72%; and Bavaria, 55% (Bavaria exclusive of the alpine regions—66%). The cause for this difference might be (among others) that, until just a few years ago, the range in southern Germany had reserves in the population and therefore the strong decline set in later than in northern Germany. The real and surely complex factors contributing to the decline have indeed by no means been thoroughly cleared up.

LITERATURE CITED

Demandt, C. 1950. Gibt es Alterssterilität bei Vögeln? Vogelwelt, 71(5):163.

———. 1953. Brutbiologische Probleme beim Wanderfalken *(Falco peregrinus)*. J. Ornithol., 94(1/2):99–102.

———. 1955. Wanderfalkendämmerung? Anomalien im Brutgeschäft des Wanderfalken. Ornithol. Mitteilungen, 7(1):5–6.

———. 1957. Rätselhaftes Verhalten von Wanderfalken-Brutpaaren. Vogelwelt, 78(6):183–185.

Gwinner, E. 1959. Zur Brutbiologie des Wanderfalken in Nord-Württemberg. Vogelwelt, 80(5):156–159.

Mebs, Theodor. 1955. Zum Brut-Vorkommen des Wanderfalken *(Falco peregrinus germanicus* Erlang.) in Süddeutschland. Anzeiger Ornithol. Gesellsch. Bayern, 4(5):343–362.

———. 1960. Probleme der Fortpflanzungsbiologie und Bestandserhaltung bei deutschen Wanderfalken *(Falco peregrinus)*. Vogelwelt, 81(2):47–56.

Schasiepen, H. 1956. Am Felsenhorst des Wanderfalken. Wild und Hund, 59(5):76–78.

Schnurre, O. 1958. Ein weiterer Beitrag zur Ernährungsbiologie der Raubvögel und Eulen des Darss (Mecklenburg). Beitr. zur Vogelkunde, 5(5/6):288-296.

Wittenberg, J. 1964. Über Ersatzbruten bei Raubvögeln. Vogelwelt, 85(3):65–84, (4)105–113.

CHAPTER 17

THE STATUS OF CLIFF-NESTING PEREGRINES IN THE GERMAN DEMOCRATIC REPUBLIC

Kurt Kleinstäuber

GEOGRAPHIC RACES AND EYRIE TYPES

Peregrines occur as breeding birds in all parts of the German Democratic Republic. They belong (Niethammer, 1938) to the race *Falco peregrinus germanicus* (Erlanger) and are found in two different and separate populations that are distinguished from each other by their eyrie type and differing habitat (Fig. 17.1). In the mid-mountain ranges of the south—the Zittau mountains, Elbsandstein Mountains (Saxonian Switzerland), the Erz Mountains, the Franconian Woods, the Thuringian Woods, and the Harz—the eyries are on rock faces (cliff nesters), whereas in the woods northward from this region to the Baltic Sea, that is, in the entire cliffless part of the eastern north German plain, only tree nests are used by peregrines. These nests have been taken over from other large raptors such as eagles, buzzards, and kites, and also from herons, ravens, and crows (tree nesters).

The boundary between the breeding areas of these two populations apparently is maintained constantly. The tree nesters do not penetrate into the terrain of the cliff nesters, although this terrain has just as good woods with suitable breeding territories. Therefore, there will be no making up for the loss if one of these populations dies out sooner. This demarcation of breeding populations stands in sharp contrast to the per-

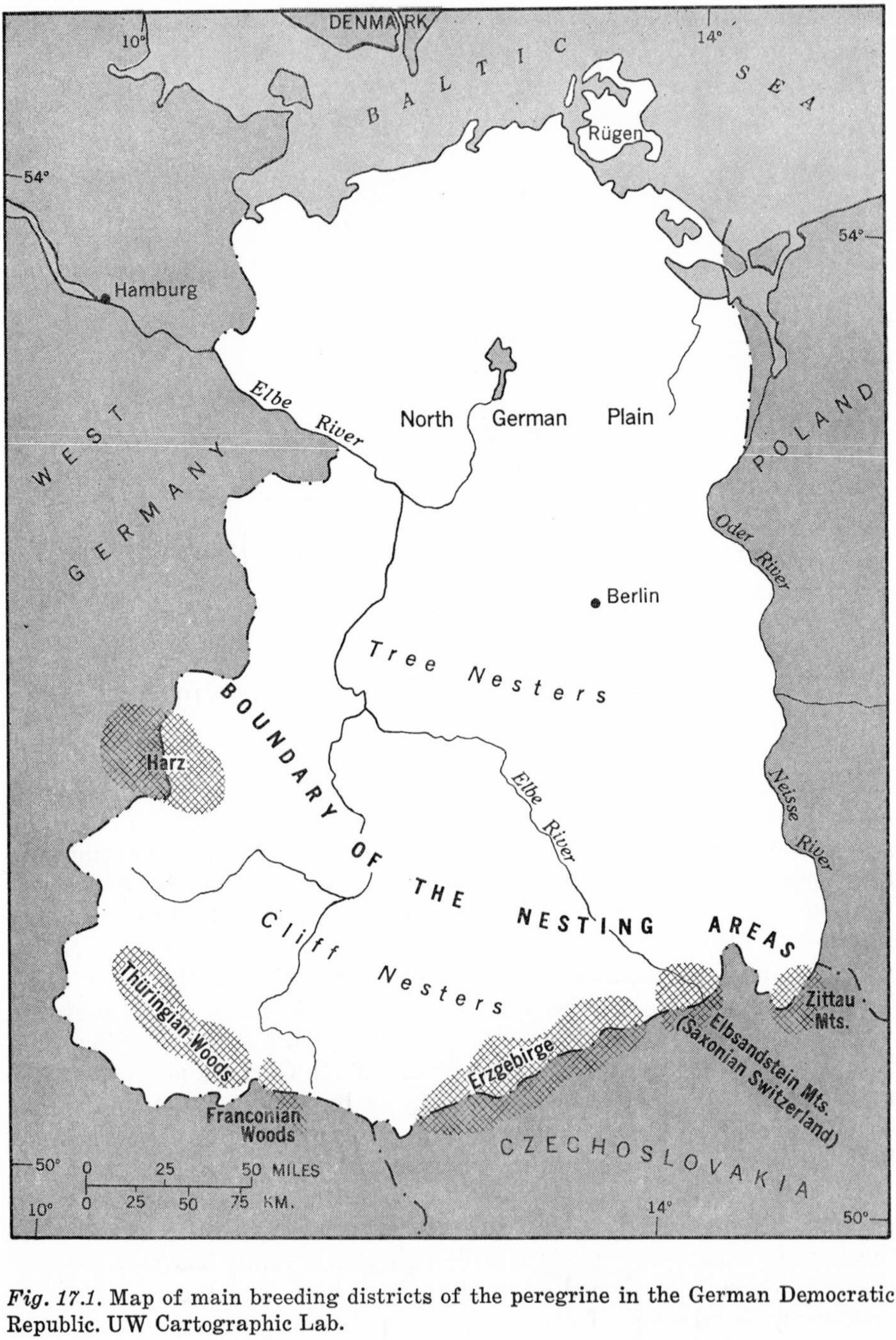

Fig. 17.1. Map of main breeding districts of the peregrine in the German Democratic Republic. UW Cartographic Lab.

egrines of Scandinavia, Finland, and the Baltic provinces, which according to Thomasson (1947) occur as a mixed population of tree and cliff nesters—for these, the variety of their nesting sites is said to bespeak a particularly broad ecological amplitude. But these peregrines belong (Niethammer, 1938) to the race *Falco p. peregrinus* (Tunstall), and it is highly probable that the only cliff eyrie in northern Germany, which became occupied several years ago on the chalk rock of the Baltic Island of Rügen, and which also brought off young in the last 2 years, is being used by a breeding pair belonging to this race. This pair can indeed not be considered as belonging to the cliff-nester type of the south. It is separated from the southern cliff nesters by a distance of 500 km (310 miles), whereas the distance to the southern tip of Sweden is only about 90 km (56 miles).

BREEDING BIOTOPE OF THE CLIFF NESTERS

The breeding range of the cliff nesters covers about 25,000 sq km (10,000 sq miles). They belong—viewed from the standpoint of breeding biology—to the south German peregrine population which, with the exception of a few eyries in abandoned castles, also only nest on cliffs. The breeding density in various parts of the middle mountain ranges is, of course, uneven, being dependent upon the presence of steep cliffs, and particularly upon steep faces, with suitable eyrie niches.

THE CENSUS REGION IN SAXONIAN SWITZERLAND

LOCATION AND EARLY WORK

A part of the Elbsandstein Mountains (the area known as Saxonian Switzerland) was probably always the most thickly populated. This is probably most suitable as an example for the change in the population of the cliff nesters, because it is here that we have the earliest records of numbers, which I wish to present in chronological order. Saxonian Switzerland (Sächsische Schweiz) is a plateau southeast of Dresden, extending along the Elbe River to the Czechoslovak border, and consisting of deeply dissected sandstone rising to craggy cliffs.

In 1916, R. Heyder published the results of a questionnaire sent out to local forestry headquarters, which resulted in turning up nine breeding pairs (Heyder, 1916:314–316). This was followed in 1922 by a survey by R. Zimmermann who established eight sure eyries by direct observation (Zimmermann, 1923).

Directly thereafter, I started to work in a limited part of this area, encompassing 117 sq km (45 sq miles), to establish the presence of all breeding pairs and their annual increment.

To begin with, I found 7–8 occupied eyries and was able to increase the number to 10 in 1929 and 1930 (Kleinstäuber, 1930). Except for natural fluctuations, this population remained at 8–10 pairs until 1938, and this may well have been the optimum population density for this area (Kleinstäuber, Zimmermann, and März, 1938).

APPARENTLY STILL NORMAL CONDITIONS

In the 10 years 1929–38, a total of 109 young fledged from these 8–10 occupied eyries. The counts for individual years were: 18, 18, 9, 13, 9, 12, 7, 5, 12, and 6 young falcons.

It is obvious that, even under those former normal conditions, there were pronounced variations in reproductive success from year to year and also between various breeding pairs within the same year. The average uninterrupted occupancy of a good breeding cliff is about 10 years.

At one of the best eyries, 30 young were fledged between 1926 and 1939. Whether or not and how often breeders changed mates could not be determined. It can be assumed for some pairs by my series of data. Eggs were counted only when it was possible without major disturbance; I cannot give a statistical evaluation here.

The chief prey items of these falcons, according to remains gathered at eyries in April and May and arranged here in the order of their occurrence were: thrushes, domestic and carrier pigeons, Alaudidae, starlings, finches, jays, lapwings, crows, woodpeckers, gray partridges, tits, yellowhammers, ducks and coots. Pigeons took first place in the prey list for the growing young.

THE PERIOD OF REGRESSION

Before I present the breeding conditions of the peregrines in this study area during the years that the population was regressing, I must note that during the war years and the postwar years, 1939–48, it was not possible to make regular and thorough checks. My first survey thereafter was in 1949; only four surely occupied eyries were found, and none of these produced young. In 1950 there were five occupied eyries, and of these only one with two young. In 1951–53 I was seeking eyries in other parts of the mid-mountain range and had to neglect the Sächsische Schweiz. Not until 1954 was the regular survey resumed.

The impression obtained in 1949–50, that the population of the study area was down to about half of what it had been before the war, was confirmed by the subsequent surveys from 1954 to 1964. In these 11 years only four eyries, on an average, were occupied—a loss of about 50%—and during this whole period only 16 young were fledged; the year-by-year count was: 1, 0, 2, 1, 1, 3, 7, 0, 0, 0, and 1 (as compared to 8–10 eyries with 109 young from 1929 to 1938).

For the most part, the old preferred nesting cliffs were occupied; and the low numbers of young produced by these pairs lead one to suspect that old breeding birds may have been involved. On the other hand, a new eyrie, surely occupied by a youthful pair from 1957 to 1964, had the following year-by-year count of young: 1, 1, 3, 3, 0, 0, 0, and 1; that is, approximately normal reproductive success for the first 4 years.

TOTAL POPULATION OF CLIFF NESTERS DURING PERIOD OF REGRESSION

INVENTORY OF 1954–64

Starting in 1954, I worked on the total population in the 500-km-long (310 miles) range from the Zittau Mountains to the Harz and continued the survey with the help of a network of local observers. The results of this 11-year period are presented in Table 17.1.

In the tabulation, 1960 appears to be once more a year of good reproductive success which may be attributable to favorable weather during the breeding season. Then the years 1961–64 show a further rapid decline, not only of breeding pairs but also of reproduction, that cannot be explained by unfavorable weather alone. Finally, in the year 1965, of

Table 17.1. Population of Rock-nesting Peregrines During Decline in the GDR

Year	Eyrie pairs	Young known to have fledged	Young fledging not confirmed
1954	19	6	12
1955	18	16	5
1956	18	6	3
1957	17	6	—
1958	17	3	—
1959	19	6	—
1960	20	11	5
1961	18	6	1
1962	14	4	—
1963	10	1	—
1964	8	2	—
Total	178	67	26

seven occupied eyries, no young fledged; but this year cannot be evaluated in respect to reproductive success, as the natural conditions were disturbed in order to take experimental protective measures. Since before 1939 about 28–30 cliffs were regularly occupied, the drop in the nesting population was about 75%.

EVALUATION OF THE INVENTORY AND POSSIBLE CAUSES FOR THE DECLINE

When one judges the results of the study area in Saxonian Switzerland, it appears that the first phase of the threatening decline of the cliff nesters in this area must have started during the war or in the early postwar years. The particular prerequisites of peregrines need to be examined in retrospect for this time span. Simultaneously the already known causes need to be presented and further possibilities pointed out in detail.

First, let us recall that German hunters and foresters were not permitted to carry guns in the early postwar years; only members of the occupation forces had guns. However, nothing is known about the shooting of falcons at the eyries. On the other hand, the great losses of 1-year-olds by shooting and trapping in their wintering grounds, especially in France, could have continued. Also, the more violent disturbances and destruction by fanatical raptor haters, youths, and mountain climbers may have had their part as well as the robbing of eggs and young by natural enemies such as the marten (*Martes* sp.) and eagle owl. But all these decimating factors occurred before, and they could not jeopardize a healthy population. Pesticides acting upon the breeding adults and on the development of the embryos in the eggs are ruled out for this time period, as DDT and other means of combatting pests were not yet in use in this region. (They could have, if at all, first taken effect during the second phase of the decline after 1961.) Also, infection by one of the many diseases of domestic pigeons, for example paratyphus, is ruled out by a wide margin. During the war and in the early postwar years all pigeon keepers, as well as farmers and also the homing pigeon fans, had reduced their flocks to a minimum because of the scarcity of feed, so that free-flying domestic pigeons were hardly to be seen in the countryside. But, perhaps the very absence of domestic pigeons contributed in hastening the decline of *Falco peregrinus germanicus*! When one considers what a tremendous role the domestic pigeon, the preferred prey, plays in nourishing the highly specialized peregrine, especially during the breeding and rearing season, one can imagine that for the breeding pairs limited to one locality, a food shortage might come about which would have an effect upon reproduction.

The presence of so many pairs, with few or no young, after the war was a bad sign. As long as neither pesticides nor disease can be considered causes, I would like to attribute the decline to the predominance of aging pairs or individuals. The effect of old age does not necessarily need to be sterility, but smaller clutches, lessened brooding intensity, weakened attachment to the eyrie, weaker participation in incubation and rearing, and—in the case of the tiercel—insufficient capacity for bringing in enough food for the family. Perhaps egg-eating and thin-shelled eggs are also indicative of old age. It can be seen from my records that newly founded eyries, which surely mostly arise through young pairs, show a high reproductive rate in the early years that, as the eyrie is occupied longer, then drops off. Sometimes the curve rises again, in which case one may suspect replacement by a new mate. Already in 1949, there was no longer enough youthful replacement in my study area to drive out superannuated breeders. Thus, the latter are able to preempt by far the best breeding areas without, however, bringing forth compensatory replacements.

I believe also that the more often and the longer that human and natural disturbances occur at the eyrie, the sooner do these superannuation factors appear, namely through psychological stresses. The following may contribute: more roads, more trips into the country, tourists and camping, the popularity of rock climbing, photography at eyries, and the curiosity of nature lovers.

Now also, for a number of years there has been the added possibility of harmful pesticide effects (through the prey) upon the reproductive capacity of the falcons. Although very complicated to pin down, I have made a first attempt. In 1964, I took four eggs from two abandoned clutches for analysis by two different institutions. The first analyses were run using *Drosophila* in the laboratory of a chemical factory which manufactures DDT: findings negative. The other analyses were by a public health institute, and the results did not indicate the probability that DDT and BHC were stored within the eggs.

SUMMARY

Breeding peregrines in Saxonian Switzerland (a part of the Elbsandstein Mountains near the Czechoslovak border) numbered 8–10 pairs from 1929–38 and fledged 109 young in this 10-year period, annual production varying from 5 to 18. The population seemed to be down about one-half in 1949–50 and in 1954–64 occupied an average of four eyries and produced a total of 16 young in 11 years.

In the entire GDR, cliff-nesting pairs dropped from 19 in 1954 to 8 in 1965, with 67 young fledged in 1954–64 and 26 not confirmed. One young was fledged by 10 pairs in 1963 and 2 by 8 pairs in 1964. The decline must have started during the war or early postwar years when the only new environmental factor was a shortage of domestic pigeons; this might have affected reproduction. It was seemingly followed by superannuation of the peregrine population, a phenomenon to which other, human stresses may have contributed.

LITERATURE CITED

Heyder, R. 1916, Ornis Saxonica. Ein Beitrag zur Kenntnis der Vogelwelt des Königreiches Sachsen. J. Ornithol., 64:277–324.

Kleinstäuber, K. 1930. Die Wanderfalken horste der Sächsischen Schweiz 1929/30. Mitt. Ver. sächs. Ornithol., 3(1930–32):81–87.

———. 1963. Bestandskontrolle und Horstsicherungsmassnahmen für unsere Felsen-Wanderfalken (Stand 1962). Falke, Publ. A, p. 44–46.

———, R. Zimmermann, and R. März. 1938. Das Vorkommen von Wanderfalk, *Falco peregrinus* Tunst., und Uhu, *Bubo bubo* (L.), in Sachsen. Tharander Forstliche Jahrbuch, 89, no. 11/12.

Niethammer, G. 1938. Handbuch der deutschen Vogelkunde. Vol. 2. Akademische Verlagsgesellschaft M.B.H., Leipzig. 545 p.

Thomasson, K. 1947. Något om pilgrimsfalkens boplatsval. Vår Fågelvärld, 6:72–81.

Zimmermann, R. 1923. Der Wanderfalke in Sachsen. Mitt. Ver. sächs. Ornithol., 1(1922–26):105–119.

CHAPTER 18

THE DECLINE OF TREE-NESTING PEREGRINES IN THE GERMAN DEMOCRATIC REPUBLIC

Horst Schröder

CONCERNING THE POPULATION IN EARLIER DECADES

My report is on the tree-nesting population, which occurs north of Görlitz, Dresden, Leipzig, Halle, and Magdeburg. The breeding range of the tree nesters thus covers over 75,000 sq km (29,000 sq miles). In past decades *Falco peregrinus* was a regular and by no means rare breeding bird throughout Germany. In Naumann's book on the natural history of the birds of Middle Europe, edited by Hennicke (1896–1905), it was stated [translation] concerning the peregrine: "In Germany, it is nowhere rare, least of all in the northern part, and belongs, although not to the very common birds, still by no means to the rare ones." In his book on *The birds of Mecklenburg,* Kuhk (1939) speaks of a marked increase in peregrines in Mecklenburg since the middle of the nineteenth century; I quote him [translation]: "Today *Falco peregrinus* is a breeding bird throughout the province; it prefers to nest in old pine woods, and scarcely a larger stand of this species lacks peregrines." Schalow (1919) in his contribution to the avifauna of the Mark Brandenburg writes [translation]: "In the large, continuous woods, the species is not an uncommon bird of prey at present. In spite of all the setbacks which this falcon has to suffer at the hands of egg collectors, pigeon fanciers, and trigger-happy hunters, one can say that it is still an abundant breeding bird in our province, especially in Mittelmark. Compared with other raptors, as for example the goshawk and the kite, the peregrine population has fallen off least. There is hardly an area from which it has not been reported." O. Schnurre (1953) cites a quotation of L. Schuster's from 1928 [translation]: "Every pine woods in the province has its goshawk and its peregrine." In 1950, O. Schnurre in *Syllegomena biologica* contributed the information that the peregrine population had held at about the same density into the forties. Toward the end of World War II, a noticeable decline set in, which has not halted up to the present time. This fact is applicable for all the GDR. Therefore, as the decline became particularly clear at the end of the fifties, the organization for preservation from extinction of threatened species of the German Academy of Agricultural Sciences in Berlin took this species under its trust.

METHODS OF POPULATION EVALUATION

The current distribution of tree-nesting pairs in the whole range was first assembled in 1960. At the same time the earlier reports could be gathered, which makes the decline since the war clear. The districts were handled by different people: Magdeburg by K. Handtke of Halberstadt; Potsdam, Frankfurt an der Oder, and Cottbus by M. Feiler of Potsdam; Rostock, Schwerin, Neubrandenburg, and others by the author. In 1962, a questionnaire was sent to pertinent people again. In 1964 I personally checked all reported territories in Mecklenburg, and W. Kirmse of Leipzig checked the districts of Magdeburg, Halle, Dresden, and Cottbus. This survey can be considered as rather intensive, and the status of the tree nesters' population from 1960 to 1964 is well known. Not all 1965 reports were available when this paper was written, but the progressive decline is obvious.

DEVELOPMENTS IN THE TREE-NESTING POPULATION 1960–64

In the districts of Rostock, Schwerin, and Neubrandenburg, formerly in the province of Mecklenburg (26,669 sq km [10,297 sq miles], of which 21% are wooded), at least 25 formerly occupied eyries were abandoned between 1946 and 1959. As there were still 23 occupied territories reported in 1960, the decline of the population during the first 15 years after the war amounts to about 50%. After 1950, this negative development reached its high point:

1960 20–23 eyries occupied with 8–10 young
1962 15–19 eyries occupied with 7–8 young
1964 8–11 eyries occupied with 5 young

The pair that was nesting on the chalk cliffs of the island of Rügen is included in the count. If we start afresh giving the 1960 count a value of 100%, this part of the population shrank over 50% within 4 years. In Brandenburg, which contains the districts of Potsdam, Frankfurt an der Oder, and Cottbus (28,013 sq km [10,816 sq miles], of which 36% are woods), in the decade 1950–60 the population also lost 23 to 24 pairs. In the years before 1950, the decline was similar to that in Mecklenburg, but in 1960 there were still 27–28 pairs left for sure. In 1962 there were at least 20 pairs to be reported from this region. In 1964, the picture was not as clear, but much like that in Mecklenburg; there remained at most 10 pairs.

In the districts of Magdeburg, Halle, Dresden, and Cottbus, W. Kirmse was able to make a thorough survey, and clear up a number of uncertainties from earlier years. Thus, the tree-nesting population in this southernmost part of its range was as follows: in 1955–64 there were 26 rather dependable breeding territories in this region. By 1960, 11 had been abandoned. After 1960 an especially sharp decline set in here too, which annually consisted of almost half of the population at the time. In 1964 almost 85% of the population of 1960 was gone (1960, 15 occupied eyries; 1964, 1–3 territories with birds). Conversely, since 1960 only two new nesting sites were established, and since then they have both been snuffed out.

Thus, for the total breeding population the picture of the decline is as follows:

1960	60 ± pairs with 33–40	fledged young
1962	40 ± pairs with 23	fledged young
1964	15–20 pairs with 10 ±	fledged young

Of the total 1960 population, only 25–30% remained in 1964.

In many cases the loss of a pair did not occur from one year to the next. Failure of broods or useless incubation of a clutch often precedes the disappearance of the adult birds by several years. Sometimes only one adult seems to be present for several years at a formerly used eyrie, until, with its disappearance, the eyrie is abandoned. In other cases, the breeding territories became vacant suddenly, even when they had been normally successful in the preceding years.

In evaluating the count of falcon pairs still present, one must consider that the count of actually breeding pairs is still lower, as a large number obviously have not been successful in raising young for years. Such birds are much inclined to wander, and one gets the impression that nonbreeders have but a weak attachment to their territories. This confuses the count. So there is still the possibility, and indeed we will hope so, that we have not found all the pairs. If some pairs have eluded us, it in no way alters the fact of a deplorable and highly alarming decline.

POSSIBLE CAUSES FOR DECLINE

In his report (Chapter 17) on the cliff-nesting peregrines in the GDR Kleinstäuber gave his opinion on causes for the decline based on decades of experience. Most of the suggested causes apply for the tree nesters as well: breaking up of broods by natural enemies; destruction of nest trees, eggs, and young robbed by people; disturbance in the woods by forestry activities and curious visitors; the increase in vacation traffic which is disturbing in general; destruction of preferred nest trees by storms; and in rare cases blundering shooting of adult birds. The losses to the German population during migration and on the wintering grounds are surely not to be underestimated. Kleinstäuber has gone into detail on the subject of superannuation. I can only confirm that the tree nesters, too, usually only had two young in successful broods, three young seldom occur, and one record of four young could not be verified. Of 46 successful broods from 1959 to 1964, of which the outcome was known, 11 fledged one young (24%), 27 fledged two young (59%), and 8 broods fledged three young (17%). Second clutches, which were probably commonly laid in earlier decades when there had been disturbances, are unknown in recent times. In many cases the tree nesters have incubated apparently addled eggs. Dead birds were found only twice in recent years.

Concerning the reduction in available pigeons for prey after the war, Feiler (1964) rightly points out in his paper on the peregrine population in the Mark in the years 1960 and 1962 that, in the early fifties, pigeon breeding took an upswing without a positive influence on the peregrine population. Indeed, the opposite was true because the peregrine's main decline came when there were plenty of available pigeons.

There are a few breeding pairs which have had a rather long history of careful records concerning brood success. G. Creutz, for example, kept records on one eyrie in the Lausitz for 11 years. The clutches were broken up four times, only four times were young reared (1,1,3,1), twice the pair failed to bring off young due to unknown causes, and in 1960 the eyrie was abandoned. Wendland (1953) has reported on 8 years of observations on 17 pairs. The average figure for young fledged was only 0.47 per pair. As 76% of the broods were disturbed or killed, the peregrine stands way at the top in this respect as compared to other raptors. Wendland placed most emphasis for the decline on persecution by man.

But, in the last 5 years, such a sharp regression has set in that it could not have been caused by the above-mentioned factors. There were also direct persecutions by man in earlier decades, surely far greater ones than in the recent past. When one considers falconers, egg collectors, and shooters, these in the last 10 years could have altered the population only in the slightest degree. Kirmse (1964) has ascertained that for the southernmost part of the tree-nesting range, only 20% of the broods were disturbed in any manner. In his 1964 report on the results of the census of tree-nesting peregrine breeding territories in the districts of Magdeburg, Halle, Cottbus, and Dresden, he gives his opinion of this problem, which, in principle, is shared by many ornithologists and conservationists [translation]:

> The population decline of the peregrine [conversely] makes one conclude with great certainty that harmful influences have been at work. These have been increasingly strong since about 1959 but were not previously recognizable. These influences particularly cut down reproduction and due to their severity and great scope cannot be inherently of biological origin only. For populations of species which thinly populate their range and have an almost constant food supply, as for example the bird-eating raptors, are conspicuous in their stability in respect to climatic or biological fluctuations in their habitats. Probably, what we are seeing in the really stable and well-documented population of the peregrine, is how at a particularly vulnerable ecological point, a still hidden harmful influence brought about by man in prolonged alteration of the habitat, has not yet been able to be compensated for by this species. The probability of such an ominous connection should prove alarming to all concerned in having a civilized landscape, especially as well-substantiated reports have come from other countries of the onset of harmful influences and their present ravaging effects on biological balance and therewith upon the fertility of the land. The recent negative results from DDT analyses do not eliminate man-made influences, which, from the speed and degree of the population decline, will probably be far-reaching. Possibly other factors are at work in this case, the influence of which have not been tested, or perhaps the harmful substances have undergone chemical changes (after they have had their deliterious effect) and are no longer evident.

The vitality of the European peregrine population has gone way down as compared with former years. The main causes, therefore, appear to be disturbances which particularly in recent years are directly harmful to health.

WHAT MEASURES WILL BE TAKEN FOR PEREGRINE PROTECTION?

Kleinstäuber suggests that cliff-nesting peregrines be protected by having [eyrie] cliffs set aside as nature reserves, making eyrie niches in appropriate cliffs where they are lacking, shutting off access to eyrie areas, and shutting eyries off from rock climbers. Also, a fencing off of eyries against predatory mammals, especially martens (*Mustela martes*) is proposed. Wherever there is danger of nest robbing by people, an efficient guard should be set up.

For the protection of tree nesters the most important thing, even more than formerly, is to win the foresters over. For this reason, starting in

1965, foresters will be paid a monetary premium of 50 marks for having a successful peregrine nesting in their area. This should spur them on to do everything possible for peregrine protection in future years. It always lies in the forester's power to refrain from any sort of forestry work within 300 m (328 yd) of an eyrie tree from 16 February to 31 July, and to permit no change in the cover within 100 m (109 yd) of the nest by any sort of cutting. These are the measures prescribed by district governments for preserving threatened birds from extinction. These protection measures must without fail be adhered to at peregrine eyries too. The falcon has been placed upon the list of threatened animals. Thus, the opportunity has been given to the conservation authorities to mete out severe penalties to violators. The task of the Federation for the Protection of Threatened Species of Birds has been to appoint for both populations of peregrines corresponding cooperators to conduct the census work and preservation of breeding pairs—often they are the duly qualified district foresters.

Suitable nests of other large birds are as a rule always available in sufficient numbers. Putting up flattish willow baskets would be advisable only where one has the impression that one or another pair can find no suitable nest site.

Inadvertent shooting of peregrines, mistaking them for other hawks, is no longer possible as all diurnal birds of prey have been placed on the protected list in the GDR since January 1965.

As with the cliff nesters, disturbances made by people in the breeding areas must be cut down. The district foresters can assist with this. Photography of threatened birds is prohibited at their breeding places. Exceptions are only permitted by professionals whose research serves for preservation of the species.

The press and magazines, especially the publications having to do with hunting and conservation, will carry series of articles on the need for peregrine protection.

In 1963 a leaflet on peregrines (Kleinstäuber and Schröder, 1963) was published. Five thousand copies were distributed to individuals, scientific bodies, organizations, and specialized groups which might be able to influence the preservation of our bird.

In order to try all possibilities, an experiment was undertaken in 1965: Eggs were taken from four pairs, from three of cliff nesters, and from one of tree nesters, and were taken to the zoo at Berlin-Friedrichsfelde for incubation. These eggs were taken only from pairs which in recent years had probably laid clutches, but never fledged young. We wanted to clear up whether young could be hatched from these eggs or whether they were unviable in general. We wanted to place the young falcons in suitable places for reestablishment afterwards. Unfortunately the experiment was inconclusive: four eggs showed no development whatsoever, the embryos were already dead in three, or they died during incubation. Chemical analyses of the eggs were not available at this writing. This first experiment does not let us draw any conclusions about the viability of such peregrine eggs. Some of these eggs were markedly thin-shelled, which Kleinstäuber seeks to explain by superannuation of the pair.

Before such experiments are tried again with peregrines, we plan to gain experience by gathering eggs from kestrels. As the extirpation of the peregrine in Germany in the wild is hardly to be halted, two nestlings, a male and a female, are to be taken from tree nests to be raised in a large volary, if possible, to become breeders. If this succeeds we will continue along this line. This attempt is entirely for the preservation of the central European peregrine. Of course, the birds will not be trained for falconry.

SUMMARY

Peregrine falcons markedly increased in numbers in Mecklenburg from the mid-nineteenth century and were a common breeding species especially in old pine woods throughout the province by 1939, despite attrition and persecution from egg collectors, pigeon fanciers, and hunters. Toward the end of World War II, a noticeable decline set in and became particularly clear by the end of the 1950's; it extends to all of the GDR and is still in progress. Only 25–30% of the tree-nesting population remained in 1964. Reproductive failures often preceded the disappearance of the adult birds by several years, and about 10 young were reared by the 15–20 tree-nesting pairs remaining in 1964. Second clutches among unsuccessful pairs are now rare, and the mean number of young raised by successful pairs has dropped to 1.9. The decline occurred despite a great increase in the number of pigeons and, in recent years, despite a decrease in habitual disturbance or persecution by man. In some fashion, the health of the adult birds has been impaired and their reproductive efficiency altered.

LITERATURE CITED

Feiler, M. 1964. Der Wanderfalk *(Falco peregrinus)* in der Mark—Ergebnisse von Bestandserhebungen in den Jahren 1960 and 1962. Veröffentlichungen des Bezirksheimatmuseums Potsdam. No. 4, p. 37–47.

Hennicke, C. R. (ed.). 1896–1905. Naumann's Naturgeschichte der Vögel Mitteleuropas. F. E. Köhler, Gera-Untermhaus. 12 vol.

Kirmse, W. 1964. Ergebnis der Kontrolle in den Wanderfalkenbrutgebieten (Baumhorster) der Bezirke Magdeburg, Halle, Cottbus und Dresden. Unpublished MS.

Kleinstäuber, K., and H. Schröder. 1963. Der Wanderfalke ist in Gefahr! Arb. für Jagd- und Wildforschung Merkblatt, 18:1–7.

Kuhk, R. 1939. Die Vögel Mecklenburgs: Faunistische, tiergeographische und ökologische Untersuchungen im mecklenburgischen Raume. Opitz and Co., Güstrow. 339 p.

Schalow, H. 1919. Beiträge zur Vogelfauna der Mark Brandenburg. Berlin. 602 p.

Schnurre, O. 1950. Wandlungen in Bestand und Ernährung norddeutscher Wanderfalken und Habichte, p. 396–401. *In* Adolf von Jordans and Fritz Peus [ed.], Syllegomena biologica (Festschrift O. Kleinschmidt). [Akademische Verlagsgesellschaft and A. Ziemsen], Leipzig and Wittenberg. 471 p.

———. 1953. Über einige Bestandsveränderungen märkischer Raubvögel. J. Ornithol., 94(1):94–98.

Schuster, L. 1928. Einige brutbiologische Beobachtungen aus dem Jahre 1928. Beitr. Fortpf.-Biol. Vögel, 4(6):209–214.

Wendland, V. 1953. Populationstudien an Raubvögeln II. Bruterfolg 1940–1951, untersucht bei 7 Arten. J. Ornithol., 94(1–2):103–113.

CHAPTER 19

THE STATUS OF THE PEREGRINE FALCON IN FRANCE IN 1965

Jean-François Terrasse and Michel Y. Terrasse

The French population of peregrine falcons has never been studied in a systematic manner throughout the entire extent of the country. However, small populations scattered along the length of streams and rivers or in certain massifs have been observed with regularity for about 15 years.

The total population of this falcon must be estimated, before the decline was actually verified, at at least 300 pairs and perhaps 500. Actually, the number of active pairs in 1965 without doubt consisted of between 100 and 150 pairs.

CAUSES OF DECLINE

A detailed analysis of the factors adversely affecting populations of the birds of prey in France has been set forth by J. F. Terrasse (1964, 1965). The following affect the peregrine falcon:

1. Principally la Chasse (Sport): the peregrine falcon is not protected in France, and numerous birds are killed at the nest, captured on pole traps, taken from the nest, and shot on all occasions by 1,800,000 hunters. Not only the departmental federations of hunters but also pigeon fanciers are the primary cause for the destruction of birds of prey.
2. The other causes, such as egg collectors, alpinists scaling cliffs, falconers, interference caused by tourists, etc., do not constitute a decisive factor making for decline on such a large scale.

3. Among the natural causes, one should note fluctuations of the population due, in particular, to bad weather occurring in certain years during the nesting period. The amount of prey species available does not cause much notable change.
4. Diseases. In the large number of eyries visited in the past 10 years, a single case of disease has been reported: a young falcon has been found at the nest infected with trichomoniasis; the second nestling was not infected.
5. Natural competitors. There occasionally is competition with the raven for nesting sites. It is indisputable that the raven is a disturbing factor in the life of the peregrine falcon. Nevertheless, there are numerous examples proving that the two species can nest side by side with success in Britain (Ratcliffe, 1962) and in France and Switzerland too. The eagle owl is in contrast a direct predator, and the peregrine falcon cannot live together with this species in regions where the number of cliffs is importantly limited. The peregrine eyrie in such cases is nearly always located in a deep recess. The eagle owl has considerably decreased in numbers (from hunting, taking of young birds from the nest, overhead electric cables) and has even disappeared in the last 50 years from a large number of regions in which the peregrine falcon has subsequently been able to establish itself.

All these causes have certainly contributed to a considerable degree—and especially hunting—to the decline of the peregrine in France. Nevertheless, this relatively slow decline has been succeeded in certain regions by an extremely rapid disappearance of the species, inexplicable by the above-mentioned causes.

COMPARATIVE POPULATION BEHAVIOR

The peregrine falcon after World War II was a common nesting bird in all regions of France where there were cliffs. It has recently disappeared from the Pays de Caux in Normandy (where there are now probably no pairs, in contrast to 40–50 15 years ago) and in Dordogne. It has also become considerably rarer in the departments of the south where there is now a 50–60% decline.

Without entering into details of the distribution of the peregrine in France, it is nevertheless interesting to compare the populations of this species in three different regions: Normandy, Burgundy, and the western Pyrenees.

NORMANDY

It is in this region of France that the peregrine falcon attained the greatest density.

The lower valley of the Seine regularly supported 14 pairs. Up to 1950–55, the success of the broods was normal despite important destruction. In 1962, there were only two pairs, of which only one had a single young; in 1963, a single pair and no young. In 1964–65, no adults were present.

The Picardy coast, comprising about 150 km (93 miles) of very favorable cliffs where one could find an eyrie about every 3 km (1.9 miles), had a population of about 40 pairs. This population seems to have disappeared completely these last years; a systematic search in 1964–65 did not result in the finding of a single adult.

BURGUNDY

This little-elevated massif is cut by small valleys, hollowed out in the limestone. It is a region principally of forests and cattle-rearing with little cultivation. The peregrine falcon has occupied this region, where it was unknown, since the disappearance of the eagle owl, about 20 years ago. (Initial verification in 1946. According to collected information, the settling of the first pair of peregrines took place between 1940 and 1943.) For the past 15 years, this population of 17 pairs has been regularly studied by the Centre d'Etudes Ornithologiques de Bourgogne (A. Deschaintre and A. Formon, Dijon). From 1950 to 1964, 47 examined clutches contained 139 eggs and supplied 94 young to the fledging stage, or 68% success. At five eyries in 1964, the mean number of eggs was 3, the mean number of young was 2.60, and the rate of success was 87%.

In 1965, on the contrary, among 17 territories visited, 14 were occupied; statistics are as follows:

1. Only 5 pairs had raised some young:
   (a) 1 pair had 3 young;
   (b) 3 pairs each had 2 young (a known clutch of 3 eggs and a clutch of 4 eggs);
   (c) 1 pair had 1 young.
2. The nesting history at 2 eyries where the adults were present could not be verified.
3. Five pairs had clutches but did not have young:
   (a) 2 eyries occupied by the incubating birds (couveurs) had been abandoned without it being possible to know what had become of the eggs;
   (b) the eggs had been found damaged in the 3 other eyries.
4. Two pairs did not lay eggs.
5. Three territories were deserted.

Thus the mean number of young fledged at 12 occupied eyries was 0.8 per occupied site.

PYRENEES

In these mountains of alpine type, covered with forests and pastures, the population of peregrine falcons that we studied in the last 10 years in the western part of the chain has not varied, the sites being reoccupied each year. At least half of the eyries are situated in high cliffs up to 1,600 m (5,250 ft).

In comparing these three regions, one can state that the peregrine falcon:

(1) is maintaining itself very well in the Pyrenees, a high-mountain country without cultivation, in spite of the presence of competitors such as the raven and the eagle owl and the killing by hunters;

(2) is maintaining itself with some fluctuations (perhaps a decline in 1965) in Burgundy, a region of forests and elevation with some cultivation (the use of insecticides limited to the culture of the grape) and in spite of occasional killing;

(3) has slowly declined as the result of systematic killing on the part of hunters and pigeon-lovers in Normandy, a region of intensive agriculture; then has completely disappeared between 1955 and 1960. (The Picardy coast is identical to the English coast on the other side of the English Channel where the peregrine has disappeared in spite of the absence of killing and approximately at the same time.)

In the whole of France, visits were made to 116 territories in 1965 (in this number are included 50 territories abandoned in Normandy), of which 45 were occupied by adults. Of these 45 pairs, 13 have not been studied, 15 did not have young, and 17 had young. At 13 eyries where the number of young was verified, 6 contained one, 3 contained two, and 4 contained three young—an average of 1.84 young per successful eyrie.

In 1965, some very low rates of reproduction have been reported for many of the birds of prey in France: buzzard, goshawk, sparrow-hawk, black kite, kestrel, and Tengmalm's (boreal) owl, perhaps in consequence of the lack of prey (rodents, birds) and in consequence of unfavorable climatic conditions.

With respect to pesticides, no analyses have yet been carried out in France on birds of prey. Five residues of organochlorine pesticides have, however, been found by Ian Prestt, of The Nature Conservancy, in eggs of two species of birds of prey that we have sent to him in Great Britain for analysis. One egg of each species was analyzed, residues in the egg of a hobby exceeding that found in a barn owl's egg (Table 19.1). The hobby's egg contained a dead embryo, near the hatching stage, in which were 98.6 mg of chlorinated residues.

There is therefore little proof to attribute to the use of organochlorine insecticides a role in the decrease or disappearance of the peregrine falcon and other birds of prey in this country. Inasmuch as the destruction

Table 19.1. Chlorinated Residues in Two French Birds of Prey (data from Ian Prestt *in litt.)*

	ppm	
Chemical	Hobby	Barn owl
pp' DDT	0.3	0
pp' DDE	4.35	0.2
pp' TDE	0	0
Dieldrin	0.13	trace
Heptachlor epoxide	0.05	trace
BHC	0.1	trace
Other residues	0	0
Total residues	4.93	0.2

of birds of prey by hunters (shooting and trapping, with the rewards system) is such an important factor of disappearance, all the other factors seem to be insignificant until the present time.

Nevertheless, one can set forth the following circumstantial evidence:
1. The peregrine has disappeared from the agricultural regions of France but even resists repeated killing in the uncultivated zones (Causses, the calcareous tableland of southern France; the Pyrenees; Corsica; Burgundy).
2. The process of disappearance is the same as in Great Britain where chemical analyses have contributed evidence of pesticide residues in the eggs (unhatchability of eggs, then incapacity to lay eggs, and finally disappearance).
3. There has been a parallel disappearance of another bird-eating hawk, the sparrow-hawk, both in Britain and in many parts of France.
4. The disappearance *at the same time* of the peregrine on both sides of the English Channel.

ACKNOWLEDGMENTS

We have to thank all the ornithologists and in particular the Centre d'Etudes Ornithologiques de Bourgogne and the French falconers who were so willing to communicate their observations to us and to permit us to carry out this inquiry.

SUMMARY

Population phenomena exhibited by the peregrine falcon in France have consisted of three trends: (1) a general and gradual decline (shared by other birds of prey) since the end of World War II, brought about mostly by the destructive shooting by hunters all over the country, (2) local increases of nesting peregrines in response to the disappearance of eagle owls; and (3) a relatively recent and extremely rapid disappearance of the nesting population in Normandy, which became complete in 1964–65. In 14 territories in Burgundy, an average of 0.8 young was fledged per occupied eyrie in 1965. The recent process of extirpation appears to be directly related to the percentage of agriculture in three regions that were studied, and the total number of peregrines in the whole country is estimated to have declined in the last 30 years from about 300–500 to 100–150 nesting pairs in 1965.

ADDENDUM, 1968

In France, since 1965, the situation of the peregrine has not changed very much. There is a decrease, but it is slow. Unfortunately, pesticides are more and more used, and peregrines persist only in nonagricultural areas, especially in mountains. The total population is probably now between 100 and 150 pairs, and 100 may be the best approximation.

LITERATURE CITED

Ratcliffe, D. A. 1962. Breeding density in the peregrine *Falco peregrinus* and raven *Corvus corax*. Ibis 104(1):13–39.

Terrasse, Jean-François. 1964. The status of birds of prey in France in 1964, p. 73–85. *In* Report on the working conference on birds of prey and owls, Caen, 10–12 April 1964. Int. Council for Bird Preservation, London. 140 p.

———. 1965. La diminution recente des effectifs de rapaces en France et ses causes. La Terre et la Vie No. 3—1965, p. 273–292.

CHAPTER 20

THE STATUS OF THE PEREGRINE FALCON IN SWITZERLAND

Hans Herren

LANDSCAPE

In Switzerland, three types of landscape run from the southwest to the northeast:

1. *The Jura* is a middle range of chalk, which comprises about one-tenth of the land surface of the country. It ranges in height from 600 m (2,000 ft) in the northeast to over 1,600 m (5,250 ft) in the southwest. The height of the valleys ranges from 300 m (1,000 ft) to 1,000 m (3,300 ft) above sea level. These valleys contain thickly settled areas, both industrial and agricultural, wooded slopes, and high-plateau pastures with sparse spruce woods. Particularly in the ravines, there are cliffs 200 m (660 ft) in height. Average temperatures are 5°C (41°F) in the high valleys, and 9°C (48°F) in protected places. The rainfall is 800–1,600 mm (31–63 inches).

2. *The Mittelland* is the intermountain area, and it extends 30–50 km (18.5–31 miles) between the Jura and the Alps, comprising three-tenths of the surface of Switzerland. Gently sloping toward the Jura, it is a hilly country of 400–600 m (1,300–2,000 ft) altitude in the valleys, with elevations up to 1,400 m (4,600 ft). This is the most densely settled part of Switzerland. The faces necessary for peregrines are along deeply clefted river valleys. They are made of sandstone and conglomerate and go up to 100 m (330 ft) in height. Average temperature is 8 to 10°C (46 to 50° F). Rainfall is 900–1,100 mm (35–43 inches) and locally at the edge of the Alps up to 2,000 mm (79 inches).

3. *The Alps* comprise the southern six-tenths of Switzerland. Peaks are over 4,500 m (14,760 ft) and over large areas have a pronounced alpine character. Thus the human population density is appreciably lower there. As temperature and rainfall vary greatly according to site and altitude, one can give no good figures for any general area. Averages range between 1° and 10°C (34° and 50°F) and between 600 and 3,000 mm (24 and 118 inches) of precipitation. As peregrines only breed in the edges of the Alps, this fragmentary description may suffice.

Since 1948, only one breeding site has been reported in northeastern Switzerland. In southern Switzerland, there was only one suspected eyrie in recent years; this was reported in 1951. All other breeding territories are in the western half of the country. This phenomenon cannot be explained by the biotope and, both in the east and in the west, the birds are equally protected. Perhaps it reflects a lack of observers.

NESTING PLACES

The peregrine is entirely a cliff nester in this region, and there are no eyries either on trees or on buildings in Switzerland. The three landscape types each offer the peregrines nesting sites of a different nature. In the Jura the peregrine occupies the sharply cleft chalk cliffs with many potential eyrie sites. Most are along the ravines, but some are on rock outcrops. In the Mittelland there are also two distinct types: those on the sandstone faces of deeply cleft, narrow canyons (sites Sp, Ro, Vo), and others on faces which rise here and there above the lower hills (sites Yv, Gu). As one nears the Alps, the sandstone is replaced by conglomerate. These rocks offer poorer eyrie sites, often being wet and not steep enough (Fa, Kr).

Without exception, the known eyries of the Alps are on chalk cliffs dominating the flat lands or lakes nearby. The shortest known distance between two simultaneously occupied eyries is 3 km (2 miles). All eyries have the following properties: unobstructed view commanding the area and for landing; ledges and niches with little vegetation; good lookout perches on trees or rocks. Eyries do not seem to be placed in relation to any compass direction.

Other nesters on the same cliff next to the peregrine include the following: raven, jackdaw, stock dove, tawny owl, kestrel, and black redstart.

PRESENCE AND BREEDING SUCCESS

The distribution of peregrine eyries in Switzerland is mapped in Fig. 20.1, and our observations on breeding success are summarized in Table 20.1. The figures on numbers of fledged young are exact minimum

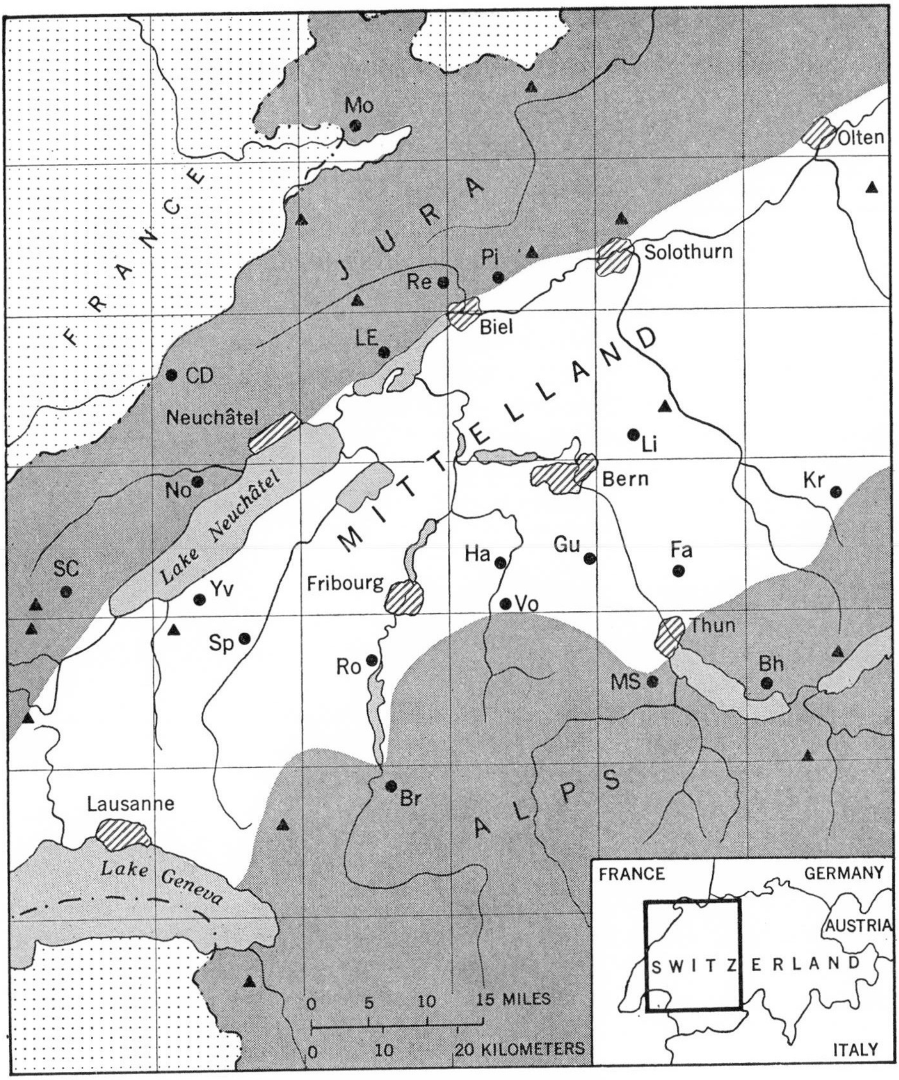

Fig. 20.1. Distribution of peregrine eyries in Switzerland, 1951–65. Solid circles = more or less permanently occupied sites; triangles = eyrie sites occupied only occasionally from 1948 to 1960. Each square is 20 by 20 km (12.4 by 12.4 miles). UW Cartographic Lab.

counts: we may have missed a few, recording only the really seen birds on wing. But as we all used the same techniques from year to year, the results are comparable.

At eyrie Li, an average of 2.99 fledged young was recorded for 11 broods in 1935–49 and 1.7 for 10 broods in 1951–65.

In 1950–59, 1.83 young were fledged in 30 broods in Switzerland; in 1960–65, 1.66 in 21 broods. The really striking changes in reproductive success, however, have involved the number fledged per occupied eyrie (Table 20.2).

FOOD

I found the following 36 prey species of birds in Switzerland:

Teal	Hoopoe	Mistle thrush
Quail	Green woodpecker	Song thrush
Lapwing	Great spotted woodpecker	Blackbird
Woodcock	Sky lark	White wagtail
Black-headed gull	Swallow	Blue-headed wagtail
Stock dove	House martin	Starling
Domestic pigeon	Carrion crow	Hawfinch
Wood pigeon	Jackdaw	Greenfinch
Cuckoo	Magpie	Goldfinch
Swift	Jay	Chaffinch
Alpine swift	Great tit	Brambling
Bee-eater	Coal tit	Yellowhammer

The single mammal, a field mouse (*Microtus arvalis*) may have been caught by the peregrine itself or snatched from a buzzard. Six other species have been reported by Glutz von Blotzheim (1962):

Mallard	Alpine chough
Garganey	Great grey shrike
Nutcracker	Crossbill

The actual diet of the peregrine depends greatly on the hunting region, season, and sex. The commonest prey species are: domestic pigeon, wood pigeon, black-headed gull, starling, jay, mistle thrush, and song thrush.

VARIOUS INFLUENCES ON PEREGRINE POPULATION

There has been strong persecution by pigeon raisers, both private and army. Since 1953 the peregrine has been protected in Switzerland (as have all the birds of prey since 1962). The conservation movement is taking hold, and there is a better attitude towards the raptors. In this connection it is interesting to realize that at eyrie site Li protection was enacted on 22 March 1625 by order of the nobility of Berne. This was, of course, not with nature conservation in mind, but for falconry. The young peregrines were taken from the eyrie and sold for hawking. The nobility licenced those taking the young falcons and pocketed the money. At this same eyrie 21 broods have fledged during the last 30 years!

Table 20.1. Presence and Some Breeding Success of Some Swiss Peregrines 1951–65

D = eyrie examined; no adults present
P = adults present
U = failed in stage of eggs or young
1, 2, 3 = young fledged
B = breeding; result unknown

Eyrie	Elevation (m)	'51	'52	'53	'54	'55	'56	'57	'58	'59	'60	'61	'62	'63	'64	'65
Jura																
Mo	670				P	B				B	3	4	B	P	P	D
Sc									B	B	P	P	1	2	U	U
No														P	1	P
CD	950													2	P	D
LE	600								P	P	1	1	P		D	D
Re	920								P	P	D	2	D	P		D
Pi	550			B	B		P	2	2	1	1	P	P	P	P	D
Mittelland																
Yv	640									B	B	B	B	P	P	U
Sp	580								B	B	B	B	B	B	B	P
Ro	680									P	P	P	P	P	B	B
Ha	710	2	3	3	2	P	B	2	1	1	P	P	P	P	D	D
Vo	850						P		U	2	3	U	2	U	U	1
Gu	820	P	P	1	P	2	1	3	1	1	U	3	2	U	U	P
Li	730	B	2	2	2	1	3	2	U	U	P	1	2	2	2	U
Fa	980			2			P	2	P		P	2		P		D
Kr	900									2		D	P		D	P
Alps																
Br	860										P	P	P	P	1	D
MS	1,260			P			P	B	2	P	P	P	2	P	P	D
Bh	940		P	2			2	B	P	1	1	P	P	P	P	P
Number eyries checked		3	4	7	5	4	8	7	12	15	16	17	16	17	17	19
Number occupied		3	4	7	5	4	8	7	12	15	15	16	15	17	14	10
Adults present, did not breed		1	2	1	2	1	4		4	4	7	7	7	11	6	5
Adults bred																
Result unknown		1		1	1	1	1	2	2	4	2	2	3	1	2	1
Successful		1	2	5	2	2	3	5	4	6	5	6	5	3	3	1
Unsuccessful									2	1	1	1		2	3	3
No adults present											1	1	1		3	9
Number young raised		2	5	10	4	3	6	11	6	8	9	13	9	6	4	1

As there are now new roads into remote areas in Switzerland, shooting with 22's has diminished; going to town on a motor bicycle has become more popular instead.

Owing to increasing population pressure, there is now much demand for recreational areas. Thus, peregrine sites in such reservations receive stronger protection. On the other hand, I examined 14 peregrines found dead or wounded between 1952 and 1965. Of these, 5 flew against wires; 4 were shot; 3 (nestlings) fell down from their eyrie; 2 were wounded, cause unknown; 1 dead male floated ashore below eyrie Bh; and 1 was found without wound, cause unknown. (Wires of various sorts are the main cause of eagle owl fatalities and have resulted in extirpation of these owls in the greater part of their former range in Switzerland.)

Table 20.2. Summary of Reproductive Success of Swiss Peregrines

Status	1951–55	1956–60	1961–65	Total
Classification of eyries				
Birds breeding; no other data	4	11	9	24
Adults present; did not breed	7	19	36	62
Unsuccessful pairs[a]	0	4	9	13
Successful pairs	12	23	18	53
Subtotal: pairs with data	19	46	63	128
Site examined; no adults present	0	1	14	15
Total number of eyries checked	23	58	86	167
Number of young fledged				
Total number	24	40	33	97
Per successful pair	2.0	1.7	1.8	1.8
Per occupied site[b]	1.4	0.9	0.5	0.8
Percent of pairs nonbreeding	42	42	57	49
Percent of sites unoccupied	0	2	16	9

[a] Failed in stage of eggs or young.
[b] Excluding breeding birds on which observations were incomplete.

Military maneuvers, campers, and climbers have certainly caused inadvertent losses. Eyrie Ha was occupied until 1959. In 1960 regularly repeated army maneuvers started in the neighborhood, and no further broods were brought off. Certain fanatical and inconsiderate falconers, operating illegally, may have caused losses too.

As pesticides have not reached such excessive use in Switzerland (nevertheless I should like to know what may be considered an authentic scale), they probably do not have the same role as they do in England (Cramp, 1964). However, we have proof of dead (poisoned) mice poisoning the buzzard, and in 1959 I received a golden eagle fatally poisoned by lead. I can imagine that peregrines are apt to get pesticides by preying upon migratory birds. Swiss peregrines are nonmigratory, and some live in wilderness areas, preying to a certain extent on nonmigratory birds, but they show as high a percentage of unsuccessful broods as do those in other eyries.

The eagle owl is a rare resident in Switzerland. At eyrie Ro, this owl lived on the same cliff with peregrines until 1963. While it was there, the falcons failed to breed successfully. After its disappearance, they fledged young in 1964 and 1965 (Teddy Blanc, pers. comm.). Uttendörfer (1952) lists 15 peregrines in the eagle owl's diet (probably most of them were young birds, which are sometimes referred to as branchers).

We have never seen direct egg-stealing by ravens, but perhaps there is competition between them and the falcons. The raven range contracted into the alpine region after 1850. Since 1950, the range has advanced again, and ravens are taking over peregrine eyrie sites. The raven has the biological advantage of being able to build its own nest and so has many more nest site opportunities. Besides, it nests earlier than the peregrine and is not dependent on such a specialized food supply. At eyries Re, Vo, Gu, Li, Kr, MS, and Bh ravens settled in the last 15 years. The distance between raven and falcon eyries may be only 30 m (100 ft). But this does not mean that the danger to the eggs or to the young raptors is greater. We have seen good success of both ravens and peregrines nesting near each other. The raven is a new intruder in the range of the Swiss peregrine population. Competition may occur until a certain balance has been reached. (It must be remembered that the raven is a common cohabitant with the peregrine in other countries.)

Low temperatures during the breeding season combined with fog may have a bad influence by making hunting by peregrines more difficult; thus the adults are gone from the nest longer. We have no clear evidence on this hypothesis. (Egg-laying normally occurs between 10 and 15 March, fledging about 25 May. Two young flew from eyrie Li as early as 15 May in 1957.) The age composition of the pairs could also have an influence. Females at eyries Li and Kr bred in immature plumage: At Li in 1965 unsuccessfully, at Kr with unknown results. One wonders whether or not this is the result of a lack of adult females that are really in breeding condition. This brings up the question of sexual maturity also raised by Mebs (1955). A photograph (Graumüller, 1939) has shown a tiercel in immature plumage feeding young. We cannot rule out the possibility this might be a substitute parent after the loss of an adult tiercel.

ACKNOWLEDGMENTS

I am indebted to my friend Rolf Hauri, Längenbühl, who shared the field work for many years and besides checked many eyries himself. I am also obliged for personal communications to Cl. Beuchat, L'Auberson (eyrie CD); T. Blank, Missy (eyries No, Sc, Yv, Sp, Ro, Br); J. Cl. Bouvier, Courgenay (eyrie Mo); Dr. U. Glutz von Blotzheim, Sempach; E. Sermet, Yverdon; and Dr. E. Sutter, Basel.

SUMMARY

The breeding peregrine range in Switzerland is, as far as is known, limited to the western half of the country. Eyries are in the Jura, Mittelland, and at the edge of the alpine zone.

Fledged young at successful sites dropped from 2.99 (11 broods) in 1935–49 to 1.83 (30 broods) in 1950–59; and then to 1.66 (21 broods) in 1960–65. Peregrines are protected, but illegal shooting occurs. Frequent losses are due to flying into wires. Some eyries, occupied for many years, have been abandoned because of noise and human disturbance. No young were fledged in an eyrie with eagle owls living nearby.

Pesticides are not used in massive quantities in Switzerland, and it is doubtful that the decline of the peregrine here is attributable to them. It is possible that prey species, mostly migrants, are carrying poisons. Although without conclusive evidence, it is supposed that ravens, newly reinvading the peregrine range, have been causing some disturbance. There had been as of 1965 no marked desertion of frequently used eyrie sites. The number of nonbreeding adults has increased in recent years and represented 57% of the eyries studied in 1961–65. There has therefore been a steady drop in the number of young fledged per occupied site: from 1.4 in 1951–55 to 0.9 in 1956–60 and to 0.5 in 1961–65.

ADDENDUM, 1968

The decline of the peregrine falcon population in Switzerland continued during 1966 and 1967. In 1966, eyrie Vo again had one young; 1 eyrie had a nesting failure; 6 other eyries had a pair present; 8 others had no adults present; and 1 had a breeding pair, result unknown.

In 1967, no young were found; 2 eyries had a nesting failure; 5 others had a pair present; 10 others had no adults present; and 2 had a breeding pair, result unknown.

LITERATURE CITED

Cramp, S. 1964. Predators and toxic chemicals, p. 53–58. *In* Report on the working conference on birds of prey and owls, Caen, 10–12 April 1964. Int. Council for Bird Preservation, London. 140 p.

Graumüller, V. 1939. Mit Kamera und Feder belauschte Vogelwelt, p. 72 + 90. Paul Franke Verlag, Berlin. 268 p.

Hauri, R. 1960. Zur Wiederausbreitung des Kolkraben, *Corvus corax*, in der Schweiz. Ornithol. Beobachter, 57:117–123.

Herren, H. 1962. *Falco peregrinus*, p. 226–229. *In* U. Glutz von Blotzheim, Die Brutvögel der Schweiz. Schweizerischen Vogelwarte, Sempach. 648 p.

Mebs, T. 1955. Zum Brut-Vorkommen des Wanderfalken *(Falco peregrinus germanicus* Erlang.) in Süddeutschland. Anzeiger Ornithol. Gesellsch. Bayern, 4(5):343–362.

Sermet, E. 1959. Grand Corbeau et Faucon Pelerin. *In* Nos Oiseaux (Neuchâtel), 25:133–137.

Uttendörfer, O. 1952. Uhu, p. 101. *In* Neue Ergebnisse über die Ernährung der Greifvögel und Eulen. Eugen Ulmer, Stuttgart. 250 p.

CHAPTER 21

POPULATION TRENDS OF THE PEREGRINE FALCON IN GREAT BRITAIN

Derek A. Ratcliffe

This symposium has come about largely through growing concern at the declining status of the peregrine over a large part of two continents, Europe and North America. My aim here is therefore to review the history of the species in Great Britain right up to the present time, and to examine the possible causes of change in status, particularly the recent serious decline. Some discussion of factors affecting distribution and population regulation is relevant to this theme, but this is in no way intended to be a full account of peregrine breeding biology in Britain.

My information is drawn from numerous sources. Owing in large measure to the energies of egg collectors and falconers, the history and earlier distribution of the peregrine in this country is reasonably well known, and much of this largely unpublished information has generously been made available to me. Numerous enthusiastic field-workers have written short accounts of peregrine breeding biology (e.g. Walpole-Bond, 1914, 1938, and Ryves, 1948), and the results of my own field observations during 17 years, from 1945 onwards, were summarized in a paper on breeding density (Ratcliffe, 1962). Ferguson-Lees (1951, 1957) conducted a postwar inquiry into the status of the peregrine in Britain, and repeated this on a more limited scale later. Then, in 1961, the British Trust for Ornithology launched a full-scale census of breeding population, to which over 170 people contributed, most of them being amateurs whose interests in the peregrine ranged widely. The census was repeated in 1962, and the results were written up by the author, who acted as organizer of the inquiry (Ratcliffe, 1963). Since then I have tried to follow the peregrine situation by means of sample censuses for various parts of Britain, again with the help of many other field-workers, and have published findings for 1963–64 (Ratcliffe, 1965*b*). These last two papers have dealt fully with the probable causes of the recent decline, and the present account is largely a condensation of them.

FACTORS AFFECTING BREEDING DISTRIBUTION AND DENSITY

During the period 1930–39, probably at least 650 pairs of peregrines, on the average, attempted to breed annually in England, Wales, and Scotland. In Ireland, which will not otherwise be included in this account, there were probably at least 200 pairs more. The British Isles were thus one of the strongholds of the species in Europe.

PRESENCE OF SUITABLE NESTING PLACES

The distribution of the peregrine here is limited first by that of suitable nesting places, that is, cliffs, for tree-nesting is unknown in Britain, and pairs nesting on buildings or on the ground are too few and sporadic to be a significant part of the population. I have been able to trace five records of nest sites on buildings during the last hundred years (Salisbury Cathedral, Tay Bridge, Llanelly copper-works chimney stack, Mersey warehouse, and Menai Straits Tubular Bridge). There is occasional nesting in easily accessible sites, on the ground or on steep banks, but mainly in remote areas, unpopulated by man, and this, too, never becomes an established habit in the population because it is usually unsuccessful. British peregrines are thus restricted to precipitous coasts or inland cliffs, mainly in mountainous country. In many districts the species is sparse or absent purely because there are few or no cliffs, even allowing for considerable plasticity in choice. For while tall cliffs are preferred in rugged areas, very small rocks are often accepted if nothing else is available, as on many gently contoured moorlands.

Aspect would appear to be irrelevant to the choice of a nesting cliff. Altitude is more important and, owing to the severity of the climate at high levels, there are very few nesting places above 2000 ft (610 m), though one regularly occupied haunt in the Cairngorms (eastern Highlands) lies at 3000 ft (914 m), in a bleak situation where snow lies late. There is a tendency for the altitude of nesting places to fall towards the far north of Scotland, and the majority in Ross-shire and Sutherland lie below 1300 ft (397 m). The peregrine in Britain is thus by no means a montane species, and the higher levels of the loftier Highland ranges may be regarded as unsuitable terrain, at least for nesting. There are no lower altitudinal limits, though in the more southern districts, very low-lying inland cliffs are often not occupied, because they tend to be too easily accessible to humans. Abandoned quarries have provided a number of nesting haunts in otherwise unsuitable terrain.

Proximity to roads, buildings, recreational sites, and other casual human disturbances does not deter peregrines from breeding when a cliff is high and the nesting ledges inaccessible. But, as Hickey (1942) found in eastern North America, when cliffs are low or broken, with more easily accessible nest sites, such proximity to human activity affects regularity of occupation, and may determine whether a rock is ever used by peregrines at all. Small and unsuitable rocks tend to be occupied only in the remoter, less disturbed areas, but even on the wildest moorlands or coasts, peregrines are seldom to be found breeding on cliffs less than 30 ft (9 m) high.

Suitable cliffs and therefore peregrines are far from regularly distributed over the British Isles. During the period 1930–39, southern England had a large population of at least 100 pairs, almost entirely on sea cliffs along the south coast between South Foreland (Kent) and Lands End (Cornwall) and then along the north coasts of Cornwall, Devon, and Somerset to the Bristol Channel. Wales had about 135 pairs, spread over every county except Flint, and divided almost equally between sea-cliff and mountain; the inland birds were most numerous in the rugged mountains of North Wales, while the coastal ones were densest in the south, in Pembroke and Cardiganshire. Northern England claimed just over 50 pairs, with a coastal minority, mainly in the Isle of Man, and the bulk of the inland population in the Lake District, there being only a sprinkling of pairs in the Pennines and Cheviots. There were probably 50 pairs in southern Scotland, mainly in the western half, Dumfriesshire and Galloway, and rather more of them inland than coastal. The Scottish Highlands supported by far the largest number, something over 300 pairs. I have divided this large region into (1) south and east and (2) north and west, along the Great Glen between the Firth of Lorne and Moray Firth. Of the 140 pairs in the south and east Highlands, only a quarter were coastal, mainly in Argyll; the long eastern coastline has relatively little cliff, and that mainly in Aberdeenshire. The remainder were spread fairly evenly over the extensive hill districts which cover much of the region, though they thinned out on the less rocky moorlands which form the foothills of the eastern Grampians. In the north and west Highlands there were probably about 200 pairs, more than two-thirds of them coastal, mainly on the long ranges of precipice which bound the coasts of the two northern mainland counties, Sutherland and Caithness, and the numerous island groups, particularly Orkney and Shetland. The rest were scattered rather thinly over the interior, and again there were few on the extensive eastern moorlands where cliffs are scarce. Fig. 21.1 gives a general picture of distribution during the period 1900–50.

TERRITORY AND FOOD SUPPLY

Where suitable cliffs are plentiful, peregrines reach a maximum density without occupying all of them, and sometimes there is a large excess of untenanted crags, so that some other factor is evidently limiting numbers. But it is equally apparent that this maximum density is of a different order in different parts of Britain, so that the limiting factor operates with varying intensity. The strongest clues to the nature of this limiting factor are the regularity of spacing of nesting pairs in a "saturated" area, the constancy of this spacing in time, and the existence of a nonbreeding surplus of adult peregrines. This at once suggests territorialism, with each settled pair exerting a repellent influence of similar strength on other members of its own kind, thereby preventing increase in *breeding* population beyond a certain point in any area. Evidence for overt aggression between peregrines is scanty and restricted to the immediate neighborhood of the nesting place—far too small an area to account for the distance between adjacent occupied eyries. However, I believe that it is a territorialism that works more subtly, probably through visual signals or other nonaggressive interaction of the kind described by Ficken and Ficken (1965) for the yellow warbler.

But territorialism is only a proximate factor limiting density and must itself serve some ultimate function; since it evidently varies in strength regionally, the other master controlling factor must be varying too. When one tries to relate regional differences in breeding density (i.e., territorialism) to some corresponding major environmental variation, the only factor which shows a good correlation is gross food supply.

Breeding density for inland peregrines can be measured as an average area per pair, but coastal breeders have a linear distribution, so that the best simple and comparative measure of density is the average minimum distance between each pair and its nearest neighbor. With such an index, the highest density known in Britain was found on the southern sea-cliffs of Kent, Sussex, and Dorset (average minimum distance 1.6 miles [2.6 km]) though one northern Scottish island showed a similar density over a limited length of coast. Over much of England, Wales, and southern Scotland, the figure works out at a fairly constant 3 ± 0.3 miles (4.8 ± 0.48 km), for both coastal and inland nesting grounds. The southern Highlands and many coastal districts of the whole Highlands and islands have only slightly less dense populations (3.4–4.0 miles [5.5–6.4 km]), but with distance northwards in the mountainous parts, density falls off considerably. In the southwestern Highlands and eastern Gram-

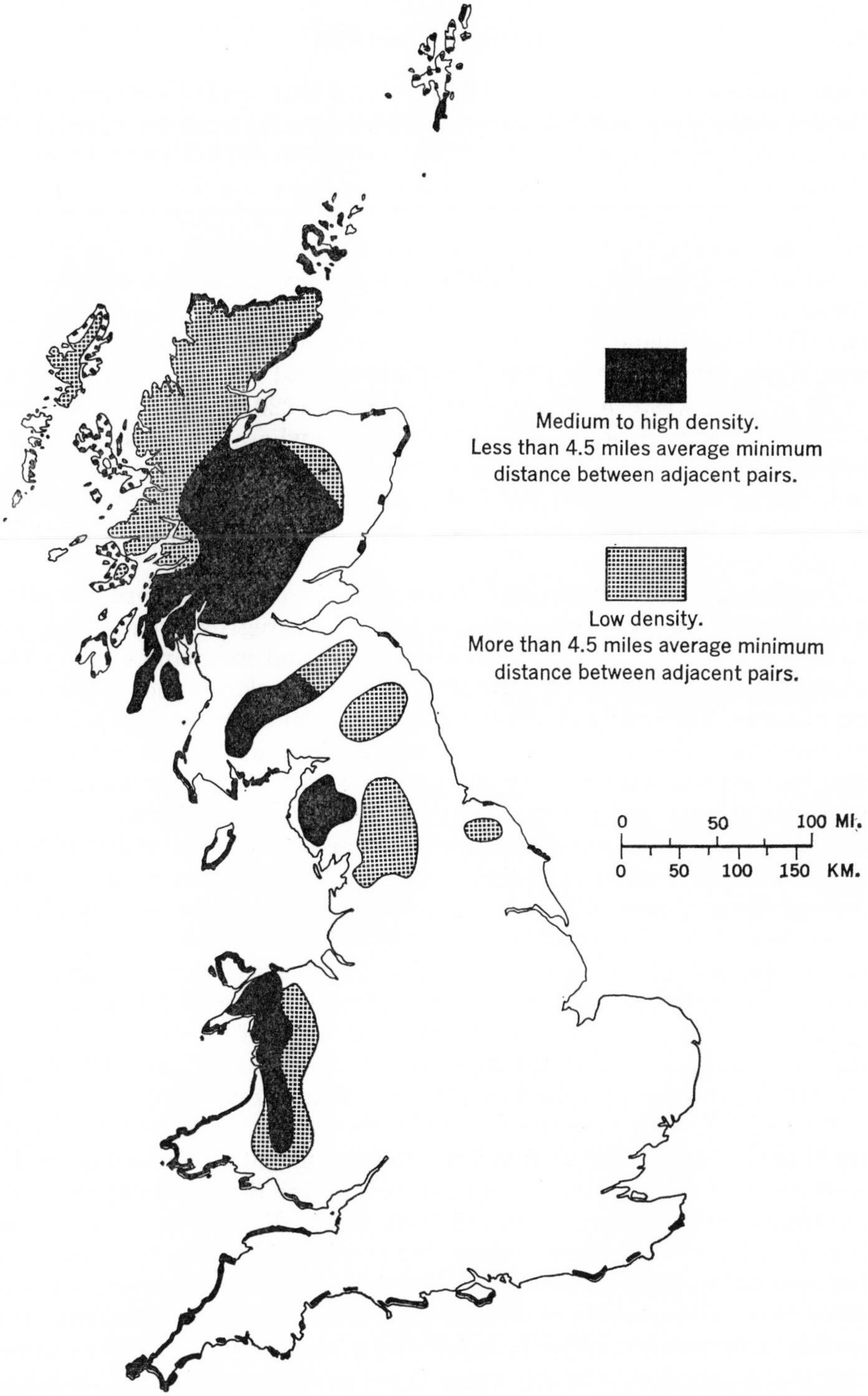

Fig. 21.1. Breeding distribution of the peregrine in Great Britain. UW Cartographic Lab.

pians, pairs are no closer than 4.5 miles (7.2 km), on the average, while for the western and northwestern Highlands, the figure is 6.4 miles (10.3 km); and some coastal districts of the western Highlands have almost as sparse populations at 5.2 miles (8.4 km). Only during the last few years have all the available data been gathered to give a fair assessment of peregrine numbers in the Highlands as a whole, and the total number proves to be far less than one would expect from the size of the area and known densities for more southerly districts. Average area measurements per pair for three inland populations covering the total range of variation are: Wales, 20 sq miles (51.8 sq km); east-central Highlands, 37 sq miles (95.8 sq km); western Highlands, 85 sq miles (220 sq km). I stress that all these measurements apply only to districts where availability of suitable nesting cliffs is not a limiting factor. Highest density is less than that reported by Beebe (1960) for the Queen Charlotte Islands, but lowest density is still greater than that found by Cade (1960) in two districts of Alaska.

Turning now to geographical differences in density of prey populations, we find an obvious parallelism with the peregrine trend, although no actual figures are available. The rich farm and woodland country behind the southern England coastal cliffs supports large and varied bird populations. The coasts of other parts of England, Wales, and southern Scotland, and the mountains of all these regions, are mostly rather less rich, but all are within reach of relatively good feeding grounds with moderate variety and numbers of prey. The southern Highlands border on rich lowlands, but with distance northwards the extent of fertile lowlands dwindles rapidly, and the peregrines become increasingly dependent on the bird populations of the actual uplands. In the eastern Highlands these hill prey densities are reasonably good, with fair stocks of red grouse and other moorland species, but the western and northern Highlands consist of large tracts of particularly barren hill and moor, with very few birds at all. In sharp contrast, some of the sea-cliffs of this sterile region have great throngs of nesting seabirds, although others offer little advantage for food over the bleak interior.

Peregrine breeding density in Britain thus seems to depend on overall food supply. Beebe (1960) found much the same situation on the northwest coast of North America. Yet the peregrine does not appear to be limited directly by availability of food, for in Britain it takes an extremely wide range of prey (about 120 species of birds being recorded) but does not deplete the total prey populations to a point where starvation or even food shortage could occur. Inefficient hunting, selectivity for certain prey species, and other objections have been produced to show that the apparent abundance of prey is not necessarily all *available* to the peregrine, and that the species may at times suffer from effective food shortage. I find these unconvincing as far as the adult breeding population is concerned and see no reason to suspect that available food supply limits the number of pairs that occupy territories at the beginning of the breeding season. Asynchronous hatching is not marked in the British peregrine, and this may be taken as an indication that food supply does not usually vary sufficiently in time to cause serious periodic shortages even for the young in the eyrie. Nor was there formerly evidence for more than occasional nonbreeding in traditional territories.

Even in the barren mountain country of northern Scotland, there is no evidence that the peregrine ever reaches a "ceiling" in its food supply and suffers starvation in consequence. In all regions, its numbers seem to be permanently held at a level well below that which available food supply could potentially allow. Yet this is a predator at the top of the "pyramid of numbers," and it is unlikely that its onetime sole enemies, man and disease, could operate so consistently and effectively throughout its range that numbers never show any tendency to outgrow the food supply. Until recently, mortality was insufficient to prevent the existence of a surplus, nonbreeding population, which appeared to be prevented from breeding by the "saturation" of the nesting haunts. The factor holding numbers down below the "ceiling" of food supply is evidently of a different kind, an internal regulatory mechanism developed by the species itself, and I believe that it is simply the territorialism that has been inferred above.

According to this view, degree of territorialism has evolved as an intermediary device that adjusts peregrine numbers to food supply, by operating on the primary potential for increase, breeding density. The case has been reasoned from geographical parallelism between variations in breeding density and food supply, but the same relationship could also be expected to apply if food supply changed with time.

Other regulatory processes may operate at other points in the life cycle, but if so, these are obscure. Little is known about mortality factors for the adults and flying juveniles, except in the case of human persecution, which will be dealt with as a factor possibly affecting changes in numbers.

POPULATION CHANGES

BEFORE 1950

Only during the last few decades have we any reliable evidence of time trends in the British peregrine population. It has often been claimed that the species declined considerably after the medieval heyday of falconry (when it was protected by harsh penalties as the nobleman's hawk), particularly during the era of game preservation that began after the advent of the firearm and reached its peak in Victorian times. Certainly, there was a great slaughter of the peregrine by game preservers during the nineteenth century, and to a lesser extent since then. But it is far from certain that this caused any permanent decline of breeding population over a period of years, however important a mortality factor it may have been in any one year. Many regional avifaunas mention former low-lying and easily accessible peregrine haunts that have been unoccupied during the last hundred years or so, but these form a small proportion of the total number. In his earlier survey of the British peregrine population, Ferguson-Lees (1951) found that in 1939 at least 570 eyries were occupied in the British Isles, and only 52 once-regular falcon cliffs had become permanently deserted. And out of 49 eyries known to falconers between the sixteenth and nineteenth centuries, 42 were still occupied between 1930 and 1939.

The history of many territories with a long record of persecution suggests that, as a species, the peregrine is able to withstand extremely destructive treatment by man. It was common for many nesting haunts to be occupied without a break for a long period of years, despite nesting failures, due to the killing of one or both adults by shooting or trapping, or the taking of eggs and young, or both. The regularity with which replacements for the victims appeared, even within the same nesting season, has long been a matter of astonishment and comment among ornithologists (e.g. Walpole-Bond, 1914). This in itself suggests that the total British population must each year have produced a considerable surplus, otherwise such losses could not continually have been made good. Some districts, where persecution was less or negligible, evidently had flourishing populations, whose successful breeding maintained this reservoir of recruits for the depleted areas. In other words, deliberate persecution was never on sufficiently widespread a scale to reduce the overall breeding success of the British peregrine population below a critical level.

On the other hand, persecution certainly seems to have been responsible for the failure of the species to recolonize the old, deserted haunts (as well as for their original desertion), and to spread into marginal habitats. Hickey (1942) showed that in eastern North America the tenacity of tenure for a peregrine nesting cliff in the face of deliberate interference was closely related to its psychological attractions in terms of height, inaccessibility of nest sites and other advantageous features, i.e., the less safe the nesting cliff, the more likely it was to be deserted as a result of persecution. Suitability of a cliff thus becomes largely a measure of its safety value to the nesting falcons. Many small and unsuitable cliffs were occupied only in remoter districts where even casual disturbance was slight or absent. The same applies in Britain, where many of the long-deserted cliffs are small or in low-lying, easily accessible situations. Small cliffs, as in grouse moor country, are the most prone to periodic desertion. Yet there are indications, from the occasional and usually unsuccessful attempts at nesting on tiny rocks, or even broken stream banks, in such districts, that the peregrine is sufficiently adaptable to attempt the colonization of marginal habitats. If such attempts were successful, I believe that other birds would follow suit, and the habit of nesting in these accessible places, or even on the ground, would become well established. If this could happen, it would potentially allow a considerable expansion of the British peregrine population. The same would apply to tree-nesting, a habit unknown in this country; should it ever become established, the peregrine's range and numbers here could be enormously increased.

It seems clear that the majority of permanent territory desertions due to human disturbance had taken place by about 1860, and that by 1900, the population had reached a fairly stable level. Since then, more adequate records have established that between 1900 and 1939, the peregrine population in many parts of the British Isles remained almost constant. Then, during the war period 1939–45, the peregrines in many parts of Great Britain were destroyed relentlessly because of the risk of predation on military carrier pigeons. This destruction was almost complete in some former strongholds, such as the whole of southern England and parts of Wales and Northern Ireland, but elsewhere, in northern England and Scotland, it was much more sporadic and ineffective, and the large population of the Irish Republic was unaffected. To compensate for this wartime drain on the population, many districts (particularly in Scotland), where persecution from gamekeepers was previously severe, were left almost undisturbed and enjoyed an unwontedly good breeding success. But any attempts at recolonization in the "controlled" districts were ruthlessly thwarted.

With the end of the war, legal protection of the peregrine in Great Britain was restored, and in many of the decimated districts a rapid recovery of breeding population had taken place by the time Ferguson-Lees completed his postwar inquiry in 1951. This recovery continued and by 1955 had become complete, or nearly so, in some areas, e.g. Cornwall (Treleaven, 1961). It is interesting to find that the original territories and, in many cases, the very same nesting ledges, were reoccupied, and that nowhere did numbers exceed the prewar level, thus indicating that population was normally at saturation level in these areas.

In 1945 I began to study the nesting biology of the peregrine, and gradually worked out the distribution of breeding pairs in four inland, mountain areas, in northern England, Wales, and southern Scotland. By 1955 I was reasonably sure from my own observations, and those of other peregrine watchers, that the breeding populations for these four areas remained relatively constant during this 10-year period. None of the four had suffered more than slight wartime persecution, and fluctuations during the ensuing decade were never more than 7 or 8% above or below a mean value. Although full census data for former years were not available, the earlier records of other workers strongly suggested that this picture of population stability had been maintained for several decades previously. The same impression emerges when the many but scattered records for most other parts of Britain are drawn together.

Only one region, the western Scottish Highlands, does not conform, for there appears to have been a marked decline since 1900. The works of earlier ornithologists (e.g. Gray, 1871) and both the standard regional faunas and unpublished notebooks of J. A. Harvie-Brown make it clear that the peregrine was once a far more numerous species in the deer-forest country of western Argyll, Inverness, Ross-shire and Sutherland, and especially in the Hebrides, than in recent years. It is equally apparent that there has been no comparable decline in the eastern Highlands, nor in certain northern coastal districts, including Sutherland, Caithness, and Orkney. The position in Shetland is less clear, owing to inadequate earlier records, and there may well have been some decline.

This western Highland decline would seem to have been gradual, with territories being deserted one by one over a long period; some were still occupied during the 1920's and 1930's and only forsaken later. An interesting point is that the dispersion of pairs in current occupation still shows its former regularity, at this much reduced density. This suggests that the decline has involved an increase in territorialism, resulting in a wider spacing of nesting pairs. As territorialism is believed to be geared to gross food supply, this presumes that food supply has decreased for peregrines in the western Highlands. There is reason to believe that this has happened. Baxter and Rintoul (1953) have collected a good deal of evidence showing that the populations of many moorland birds, such as the red grouse and golden plover, have declined seriously in this region during the past hundred years. When Harvie-Brown compiled his regional faunas at the end of last century, he even then found clear signs of this decline. The virtual disappearance of the red grouse from much of western Scotland has given cause for speculation and lament amongst many landowners. Some of the Ross-shire and Sutherland moors are now virtual deserts for bird-life, and in some areas it is scarcely an exaggeration to say that the greenshank is the commonest species.

The most probable cause of this decline is the long-continued extractive system of land management for animal crops (sheep, red deer [*Cervus elaphus*], and grouse) which has reduced productivity of much of the hill land almost to that of semidesert. Under an excessively wet climate, the soils, derived from predominantly hard, acidic rocks, were originally of low fertility. Continual heavy grazing and repeated burning of the vegetation have lowered their fertility still further, besides greatly reducing the extent of that important moor plant, the ling heather (*Calluna vulgaris*). As the productivity and character of the vegetation have deteriorated, so have the populations of dependent animals. It would thus have been surprising if the numbers of associated predators had not declined, too. The peregrine appears to have struck a new balance with its food supply in this region by expanding territory size accordingly.

This decline has affected parts of the coast where there are few seabirds and where the peregrines must depend largely on the adjoining moorlands for their food. By contrast, there is no evidence for a comparable decline of peregrine numbers in those western Highland coastal districts where seabird populations were always considerable and have remained so.

An interesting feature of this western Highland decline is that in many areas numbers of the golden eagle have increased as those of the peregrine dwindled. In many instances the former nesting haunts of peregrines have been taken over by eagles. This could be merely a parallel effect of the intensification of land use, with increasing sheep stocks, and perhaps also an increasing mortality of both sheep and deer, as productivity of the land fell. However, in one district where I was able to observe the replacement of one species by the other in four different territories, the eagles appeared actually to oust the peregrines from their nesting crags, instead of taking over those already vacated. In addition to a poorer food supply, competition with the golden eagle may therefore be a significant factor locally in Scotland (this species no longer breeds in England or Wales) in keeping peregrine breeding density at a lower level than that attained elsewhere in the country. The raven is a usual and often close associate of the peregrine in its nesting haunts; only on the smallest rocks does it become a competitor for nesting space, and most doubtfully a dominant one.

AFTER 1950

By the early 1950's the general position was of a fairly stable breeding population over the greater part of Britain. One region, the western Highlands, appeared to have suffered reduction in population due to long-term environmental change, but this decline had terminated, and the only change was in a few other parts of the country, which had experienced a short wartime period of depletion, but were making, or had already made, a rapid recovery to their normal population level.

Then, from about 1955 onwards, it became increasingly clear that the numbers of breeding peregrines in many areas were falling, and that even where there was no actual population decrease, breeding success had often become disturbingly poor. This decline first became apparent in the south of England, reversing the postwar recovery that had looked so promising. In Cornwall, where all breeding peregrines were apparently destroyed between 1941 and 1945, Treleaven (1961) found that in 1955 at least 17 eyries were occupied, but by 1959 this had dropped to 7 and only 2 produced young. In Dorset, only one breeding pair remained in 1946, but by 1956, eight territory-holding pairs were known; in 1958 only five territories were known to be occupied, and by 1960 breeding in this county had apparently ceased (D. Humphrey, unpubl.). Unhealthy symptoms had, however, appeared farther north even before this. Three instances of egg-breakage in peregrine eyries were reported in 1948–49 and in 1951, in 4 out of 9 eyries which I examined in northern Wales, northern England, and southern Scotland, one or more eggs were broken. Egg-breakage continued to occur frequently in these regions throughout the 1950's, and clearly contributed to a generally low nesting success. Two falcons were watched eating their own eggs, one in Lakeland in 1951 and the other in Wales in 1952, and appearances suggested that other breakages were due to the same cause.

Ironically, in 1960, the complaints of pigeon fanciers about increasing predation by peregrines on homing pigeons led the Nature Conservancy to ask the British Trust for Ornithology to conduct an inquiry into the current status and distribution of the species in Great Britain. This inquiry, carried out in 1961–62, was timely, and provided a detailed picture of the extent of the sudden decline (Ratcliffe, 1963). In 1961, in the sample of 431 (60%) out of the 718 known territories visited, 173 (40%) appeared to be completely deserted, and of the rest, only 82 (19%) were successful in rearing young. By 1962, there had been further deterioration, for the sample of 488 territories (68% of the known total) showed 247 (50%) to be deserted; only 68 (13%) were occupied successfully. If one allows for the probability that the former mean level of breeding population was only about 90% of the total of 718 known territories, the scale of decline becomes slightly less. Moreover, in each year nine broods of young were taken by falconers, and there were 17 and 22 eyries that were seen with eggs and not revisited: some of these at least probably produced young. All these eyries were omitted from the successful totals. Yet even when all possible allowances have been made, the severity of the decline for Great Britain as a whole remains obvious; and, since the figures from year to year are directly comparable, the continuation of decline from 1961 to 1962 is equally clear.

The decline showed a wave-like spread in time from south to north, for while it had become severe in southern England by 1960, there was in this year no evidence of decrease in territory-holding pairs in northern England and southern Scotland. In Wales it seems clear that a significant decline in breeding population had occurred by 1960. By 1962 there remained the merest handful of pairs even attempting to breed in the whole of England and Wales, and very few of these were successful (Table 21.1). Southern Scotland was little better, and even parts of the Highlands were affected, with many nonbreeding birds holding territories and with numerous nesting failures. The results of the inquiry are summarized in Table 21.2, while Fig. 21.2 shows the pattern of decline and present distribution.

During the succeeding seasons, 1963–65, I have tried to keep a check on the situation by means of sample breeding censuses, covering all main regions of Great Britain. In 1963 and 1964, data were available for 137 territories that were also visited in 1962. Between 1962 and 1963, the number of occupied territories in this sample of 137 fell from 83 to 62, and the number of successful pairs from 35 to 27. When one uses the 1962 census data for reference, this suggests that in 1963 the number of prewar territories still occupied had decreased from 50 to 38% and successful eyries from 13 to 10%, though these figures must be regarded as approximate. Between 1963 and 1964, the number of occupied territories in the same sample rose from 62 to 66 (40%), and successful pairs from 26 to 35 (13%).

On face value, these figures show that decline continued into 1963, but that by 1964 there had possibly been slight recovery in numbers of peregrines holding territories and of successful pairs. I have not applied tests of significance, believing these to be inappropriate for data of this kind,

Table 21.1. Mean Brood Size 1961–62[a]

Region	Territories visited	Territories occupied	Successful eyries	Young per successful eyrie	Young per occupied territory	Young per territory (total no.)
Southern England	65	13	2.5	1.7	0.3	0.07
Wales	90	23	5	2.2	0.5	0.12
Northern England	55	26	4	2.0	0.3	0.15
Southern Scotland	45	24	4	1.7	0.3	0.16
South and east Highlands	87	71	21	2.2	0.7	0.53
North and west Highlands	119	94	39	1.9	0.8	0.62

[a] Data are based on tables II & III in Ratcliffe (1963) and on unpublished eyrie records for 1961–62. These figures are means for both years, i.e. the data for 1961 and 1962 put together and divided by 2. I did this because mean brood size/successful eyrie would be based on pitifully inadequate data in regions south of Highlands, if the 2 years were taken separately. Again, the differences between regions south of Highlands in mean no. young/successful eyrie are not likely to be significant. Compared with the central Highlands (the middle portion of the "south and east Highlands"), mean no. young/successful eyrie for south and east Highlands is desired because of lower figures for east and west coast and western inland districts.

and merely give the figures for what they are worth. When 1963 is compared with 1961, there is better evidence of continuing decline, over a 2-year period. Since the decline began, some territories have shown recovery, by reoccupation and/or resumption of attempted or successful breeding. In 1964, six previously deserted territories were reoccupied and produced young, and there was a net gain of 10 territories showing improvement compared with 1963. These individual improvements mostly seem to be due to the appearance of new birds, after the original occupants have died, and show that a supply of recruits is still forthcoming. Moreover, at least some of these newcomers bred successfully.

Data for 1965 suggest that the peregrine situation is about the same as in 1964. Certainly, there is no evidence of significant recovery, although numbers of successful pairs remain slightly above the 1963 level. The decline seems to have halted, and this in a sense can be regarded as an improvement. Perhaps it is best to say that, during the last 2–3 years, the peregrine population has reached a new stability, at a much reduced level of numbers and breeding success. No one region has shown any marked change in peregrine status during the last 3 years, and the geographical pattern of territory occupation and successful nesting remains in 1965 broadly as it was in 1962.

Table 21.2. Occupation of Peregrine Territories in Great Britain 1961–62[a]

(1)	(2)	(3)		(4)		(5)		(6)		(7)		(8)		(9)	
		1961						1962							
	No. of territories known	Territories visited		Territories occupied		Successful		Territories visited		Territories occupied		Successful		Different territories visited in 1961–62	
Region		No.	% of (2)	No.	% of (3)	No.	% of (3)	No.	% of (2)	No.	% of (6)	No.	% of (6)	No.	% of (2)
S. England	110	66	(60)	20	(30)	3	(5)	63	(57)	5	(8)	2	(3)	91	(83)
Wales	149	90	(60)	28	(31)	8	(9)	89	(60)	18	(20)	2	(2)	121	(81)
N. England	68	56	(82)	29	(52)	5	(9)	54	(79)	22	(41)	3	(6)	61	(90)
S. Scotland	59	41	(70)	23	(56)	6	(15)	48	(81)	24	(50)	2	(4)	55	(93)
S. and E. Highlands	142	84	(59)	77	(92)	22	(25)	90	(63)	65	(72)	20	(22)	112	(80)
N. and W. Highlands	190	94	(49)	81	(86)	38	(40)	144	(76)	107	(74)	39	(27)	160	(84)
Total	718	431	(60)	258	(60)	82	(19)	488	(68)	241	(49)	68	(14)	600	(84)

[a] A peregrine territory is here regarded as a hypothetical area containing all the nesting places of a breeding pair. All the territories known to be occupied by breeding peregrines for at least one season since 1930 are included in col. 2: a small proportion of these were used irregularly and, allowing for a probable 20–30 further, undiscovered territories, the mean level of regularly occupied territories 1930–39 was probably about 650. The sample of territories visited in 1961–62 was not identical, but there was considerable overlap (see col. 9).

An occupied territory is one in which one or both birds of the pair were present during the breeding season, whether or not breeding was attempted. A successful territory is one in which flying young were reared. Broods taken by falconers and nests seen with eggs but not revisited are not counted as successful. These were, respectively, 9 and 17 in 1961; 9 and 22 in 1962.

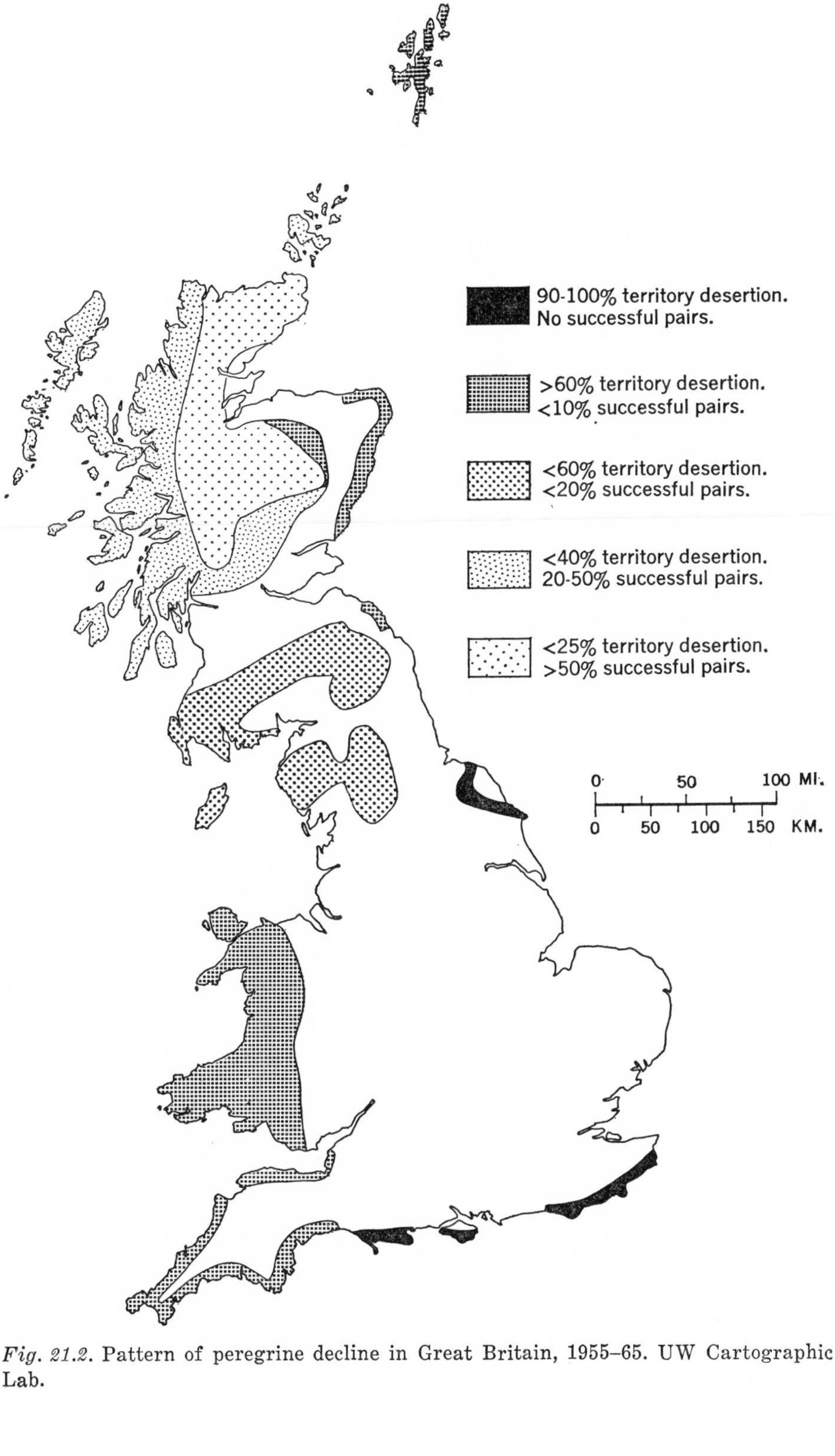

Fig. 21.2. Pattern of peregrine decline in Great Britain, 1955–65. UW Cartographic Lab.

POSSIBLE CAUSES OF THE POST-1950 DECLINE

Decline on this scale and at this rate is quite unprecedented in the history of the peregrine in Britain. An unprecedented cause must therefore be sought.

Dwindling food supply has been suggested as the cause of the long-term but lesser decline in the western Highlands, for there is good evidence of such a change. But in the southern regions where the recent decline of the peregrine has been most marked, there is no reason at all to suspect a significant drop in the total prey populations. The principal prey species here is the homing pigeon, which has certainly not diminished in numbers. Moreover, the western Highland pattern of decline involved an increase in dispersion, with pairs of peregrines still regularly scattered, but at wider intervals; whereas the recent decline elsewhere has been irregular, with no such distribution pattern persisting among the survivors. Food supply is probably still much poorer in the Highlands as a whole than elsewhere, but it is this region which has been the least affected by the recent decline in peregrine population.

Systematic persecution on the wartime scale certainly caused the temporary extermination of peregrines locally, and if extended to a large enough part of Britain might well cause a serious reduction in population, perhaps by reaching the point where the total output of young becomes insufficient to maintain numbers (i.e., mortality is greater than recruitment). If immigration also failed to restore the balance, there could then be a more permanent, progressive decline spreading widely across the country. However, savage though it was, wartime destruction had no effect at all outside the "controlled" districts, and it is highly unlikely that persecution since 1950 has anywhere approached this level. After the war, there was still a good deal of shooting, trapping, and other killing of adults, but most of it local and sporadic, and there has been no evidence of organized destruction on a scale anywhere near sufficient to account for the post-1950 decline. Such activities could scarcely pass unnoticed. Before 1956, taking of eggs and young sorely reduced nesting success in certain districts, but was no worse than during the 1930–39 period, when the species maintained its breeding populations very well in certain districts of England and Wales where a high proportion of all clutches laid was taken annually. The peregrine would appear, in fact, to be one of the most resilient of all species in the face of deliberate persecution.

Two Lakeland peregrine crags have been deserted since at least 1930 because of the continual presence of rock-climbers during the breeding season. Since 1945 this kind of casual disturbance has increased greatly, and there are indications that it would lead to peregrines more and more vacating traditional cliffs. Even so, this effect has been local, mainly in

Lakeland and Snowdonia, and the total number of nesting cliffs involved so far has been quite small—about seven or eight. I know of only one case, in Northumberland, where complete desertion of the territory has inevitably followed, although in most others the alternative cliffs taken over instead are smaller and the nest sites more accessible than formerly. Climbing is, however, predictably a future problem for the conservation of the peregrine in certain areas. Increasing disturbance by holiday-makers and other recreational activities may have begun to threaten some haunts, both coastal and inland, though it is surprising how much casual disturbance peregrines will tolerate when it does not take place actually on the cliff-face, as was evident from the regular occupation of eyries on sea-cliffs within such popular south coast holiday resorts as Hastings and Folkestone, both before and after World War II. While nondeliberate interference by man could thus be responsible for local decline, as a national factor it is insignificant.

We have the example of myxomatosis to show how a vertebrate species, the rabbit *(Oryctolagus cuniculus)*, can be decimated by epidemic disease. Raptors, especially captive birds, are certainly known to have died in circumstances that suggested that pathogens or parasites were responsible. The following diseases and parasites have been reported for the peregrine in North America (Trainer, in Chapter 37): Trained, captive birds—trichomoniasis, aspergillosis, coccidiosis, heart filaria; wild birds—trichomoniasis, botulism, myiasis, lice, tapeworms. In the sample of seven dead peregrine and lanner falcons (four wild, three captive) mentioned by Jefferies and Prestt (1966), five were examined internally, three of them by experienced pathologists. One wild peregrine had died of pericarditis (probably originating from a throat wound); one captive lanner probably died from infestation with a nematode, *Polymorphus boschadis;* but no evidence was found of any disease likely to reach epidemic proportions. The other four birds were unlikely to have died from parasite infection, and no disease was found in the one examined for this possibility. Despite the appearance in Britain shortly after 1945 of two serious epidemic diseases of poultry, infectious bronchitis and Newcastle disease, there is no reason to suspect that these had any effect on the peregrine population. In the absence of any further evidence, it would be quite unjustifiable to presume that such causes of death could reach the plague proportions necessary to account for the recent decline of the peregrine. Nor could such an explanation account satisfactorily for the geographical pattern of decline.

Climatic change cannot be seriously advanced as a possible explanation, despite a superficial similarity between the patterns of peregrine decline and retreat of an animal or plant species during a period of climatic deterioration. Climatic change in Britain during the critical period has been insignificant, especially when one considers the range of climate to which this almost cosmopolitan species is adapted, i.e. the climate of Britain is nowhere marginal for the species.

Of the above possibilities, dwindling food supply, persecution, casual disturbance, and climatic change are clearly untenable as explanations of the problem. Disease cannot be ruled out, but any protagonist must produce acceptable evidence before it can be considered further. There remain only two recent known environmental changes that have been sufficiently widespread and pervasive to merit consideration, namely, increase in radioactive fallout and in use of agricultural pesticides. Environmental contamination by other chemical residues such as detergents and lead from motor fuels is not regarded as relevant to peregrines. Radioactive fallout is so widespread that it shows no correlation with the pattern of peregrine decline, and is, in fact, heaviest in the Scottish Highlands, where decline of the species is least; but pesticidal contamination shows obvious connections.

The geographical pattern of decline and its progress in time show a decided correlation with agricultural land use. Decline began intensified, and reached a virtual extinction point most rapidly in those southern districts that are the peregrine country closest to large centers of arable and fruit farming. Wales, containing a good deal of arable land and bordering on the rich farmlands of the west Midlands and the Evesham fruit-growing area, followed only shortly after; but northern England and southern Scotland, which are farther from extensive arable farming districts, lagged behind and have suffered a less complete decline. The Scottish Highlands, which are bordered only along their southern and eastern edges by this kind of agricultural land, were the last to show symptoms of decline and have been the least affected.

Type of agriculture in turn reflects the scale of use of pesticides. Insecticides, fungicides, and herbicides are applied, as seed dressings and sprays, most intensively in arable and horticultural (including fruit) crop-growing districts (see Fig. 21.3), but essentially in cereal districts. They are used on a much lesser scale on grazing lands, and hardly at all on the permanent pastures which are extensive in the uplands. In some western and upland districts a good deal of oats is grown, but in high mountain country the use of pesticides is restricted to the very small areas of cultivation in the valleys or around the fringes of the hills, and to sheep dips. While some carrion-feeding predatory birds come into direct contact with sheep dips, the peregrine does not, but there may be remoter contact, through contamination of more distant waterways, and finally the sea, from which aquatic birds take up residues.

In theory, of the pesticides used on a large scale, by far the most significant are the organochlorine compounds, which are the most markedly persistent and cumulative in effect. Beginning with DDT, during 1946–47, there has been increasing development and application to agriculture and horticulture of this group of insecticides. Next came γ-BHC,

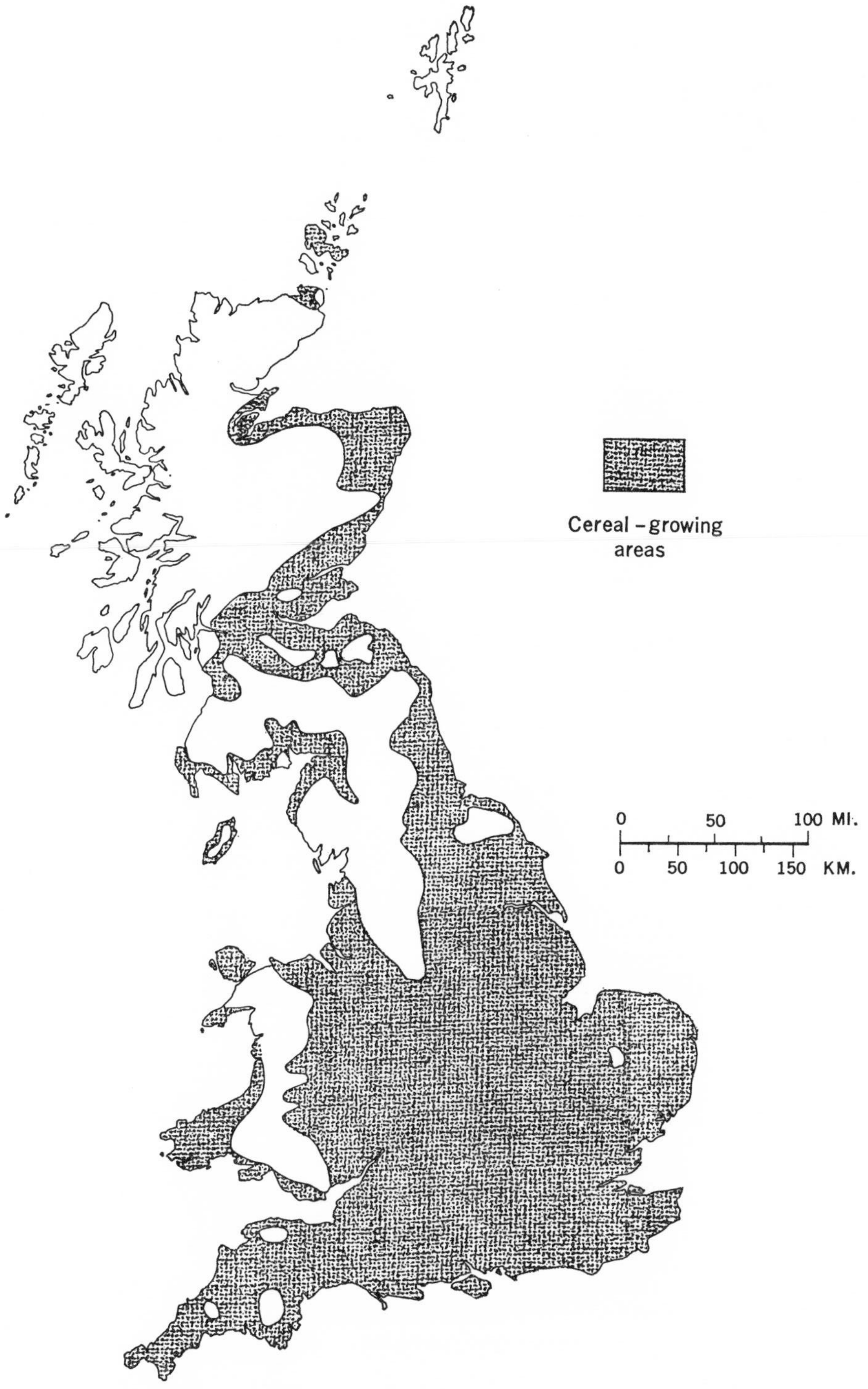

Fig. 21.3. Main cereal-growing areas in Great Britain. UW Cartographic Lab.

and then, during the mid-1950's, the much more toxic compounds dieldrin, aldrin, and heptachlor were introduced, and within a few years found intensive use. These insecticides are used in Britain particularly for the dressing of grain and other seed, thus exposing a large number of the peregrine's prey species to direct risk of contamination. There could be no better example of unprecedented recent change in the peregrine's environment.

The pattern of peregrine decline not only matches the intensity of pesticide use geographically, but also in timing shows close agreement with the development of the organochlorine compounds as the principal insecticides of British agriculture. Unhealthy symptoms, in the form of frequent egg-breakage and reduced nesting success, had been widespread south of the Highlands since 1950, but actual population decline seems to date from about 1955, and had become severe by 1961. The first symptoms correlate with the general introduction and widespread use of DDT and γ-BHC; but the population "crash" corresponds with the advent and rise to prominence of the most toxic chemicals, aldrin, dieldrin, and heptachlor, and also follows the time pattern of the widespread and spectacular kills of wild birds (many of them prey species of the peregrine) which were caused by the use of these substances in particular. Catastrophic bird deaths were noted especially during the period 1958–61.

The widespread contamination of the peregrine by residues of these organochlorine insecticides is now firmly established. In 1961 a single addled egg from a Perthshire eyrie was analyzed and proved to contain residues of DDE (a metabolite of DDT), BHC, dieldrin, and heptachlor epoxide (a metabolite of heptachlor) amounting to a total of 4–5 parts per million (Moore and Ratcliffe, 1962). In 1963–65, 18 eggs (13 fresh) were obtained from 13 different female peregrines in northern England, southern Scotland, and the central Highlands. Every one of these contained all four of these same residues, and usually small amounts of unaltered DDT. Concentrations were as follows, in parts per million of fresh weight of egg contents, and all chemical analyses reported in this paper were carried out by gas-liquid chromatography by the Agricultural Scientific Services of the Department of Agriculture for Scotland or the Laboratory of the Government Chemist, London:

Residue	Range	Arithmetic Mean
pp' TDE	trace* – 0.6	0.1
pp' DDE	2.6 – 30.8	12.7
pp' DDT	trace* – 0.8	0.2
BHC isomers	trace* – 0.8	0.2
Dieldrin	0.1 – 1.8	0.6
Heptachlor epoxide	0.1 – 4.3	1.0
Total	2.9 – 36.1	14.8

*Trace = <0.1

Moreover, since 1963, the corpses of four peregrines found dead in the wild have proved to contain all these same residues (Ratcliffe, 1965*b*; Jefferies and Prestt, 1966). The most contaminated bird, a male found dead on its eyrie on Lundy Island in the Bristol Channel, contained 45.0 ppm DDE, 3.5 ppm dieldrin, 1.3 ppm heptachlor epoxide, and 1.4 ppm BHC isomers in its brain, and 70.0 ppm DDE, 4.0 ppm dieldrin, 1.5 ppm heptachlor epoxide, and 2.0 ppm BHC isomers in its liver.

Analyses have shown that over 50 prey species of the peregrine suffer contamination by these same insecticides (Cramp and Conder, 1961, 1962; Moore, 1965) and even the strictly maritime birds of remote coasts have shown moderate concentrations of residues. Moore (1965) has concluded that a large part of the total environment of Great Britain is contaminated by these substances. This being so, virtually all British peregrines are "at risk" to contamination, and the actual degree of contamination for any individual will be largely a reflection of that for the total prey population with which it has contact. This in turn depends on local scale of pesticide use. In southern England, the tendency will be towards contamination of a high proportion of the prey population, and high (relatively) concentrations of residues per individual; whereas in the Highlands the tendency will be towards low contamination of both populations and individuals. It may well be that the chance (i.e. risk) of taking highly contaminated prey individuals is the really important factor (Jefferies and Prestt, 1966), but this also will increase in the same direction.

It is worth noting here that the part of our peregrine population least affected by decline is in the central Highlands (Table 21.3). Other parts

Table 21.3. Summary of Breeding Success Data 1961–65[a]

Region	Possible total eyries[b]	Occupied eyries	Successful eyries	Young per occ. eyrie	Young per succ. eyrie
Wales	100	34	8	0.5	2.0
Northern England	85	46	10	0.3	1.5
Southern Scotland	55	46	12	0.4	1.7
Central Highlands	50	49	43	2.2	2.5

[a] From data tabulated in the Appendix.
[b] Number of territories examined in the 5-year period.

of the Highlands, especially western coastal districts, have been more affected, if not severely. This difference accords with contamination risks. In the central Highlands, not only do the breeding peregrines feed relatively little on birds from contaminated habitats, but they also appear to have a good food supply in their nesting grounds throughout the year, and so are largely sedentary in the uplands. However, in many western coastal districts the food supply is more seasonal, and when the seabird colonies disperse at the end of summer, some peregrines probably have to move to areas with a better food supply. If the peregrine population here is not sedentary, some individuals are likely to make contact with more contaminated prey populations outside the nesting season. It is also evident now that seabirds are more exposed to organochlorine contamination than those birds that live on hill land, so that even peregrines resident the year round on remote coasts may be more at risk than those of the more productive uplands. Coastal and inland peregrines of the extreme eastern Highlands (an important arable farming area) have also declined considerably.

Having demonstrated that contamination of peregrines by organochlorine pesticides is widespread and that the risk extends to virtually the whole British population of this species, I think it remains to show that the amounts of residue found in the more heavily contaminated individuals are lethal or harmful to reproduction. If this could be done, I believe that an entirely adequate explanation of the decline would be firmly established. The significance of the egg analyses has been discussed in detail elsewhere (Ratcliffe, 1965*a*). The amounts of residue in eggs cannot reflect more than a sublethal dose in the parent bird, so that egg analysis is only of limited value. Since decline began, many territory-holding pairs have apparently failed even to produce eggs, but amongst the remaining part of the peregrine population which still attempts breeding, i.e. lays eggs, further reproductive failure is associated largely with breakage or desertion of eggs, hatching failure of incubated eggs, and death of embryos or hatched young. Egg-breakage has been prevalent since 1951; during the last few years, it has been probably the commonest cause of nesting failure, once eggs have been laid. I have given reasons elsewhere (Ratcliffe, 1958) for regarding egg-eating as the usual cause of breakage and believe that in some direct or indirect way, which I do not pretend to understand, this abnormal and pathological behavior is occasioned by sublethal doses of pesticide residues. One may note that all these forms of breeding failure could result simply from some degree of disturbance to normal breeding behavior, ranging from inability to mate or weakening of the pair bond, to a lessening of the normal parental impulses to care for eggs and young. Such psychological disturbance could occur in birds that showed no evidence of tissue pathology. Although a very few cases of egg-eating were noted before 1945, it is only since organochlorine pesticides that this habit has become prevalent.

Although desertion of eggs, hatching failure of incubated eggs, and death of embryos or hatched young all seem to have become much more frequent during the last few years, there are no figures for an earlier period, and no firm comparison can be made. Of the 17 eyries from which single test eggs were taken, 12 failed to produce young. In 6 of the failures all the remaining eggs were broken, in 3 more, eggs not broken were infertile; in another a single fertile egg was deserted after another infertile one disappeared; and in the last a single fresh egg was deserted. Yet residue concentrations for the eggs from 4 successful eyries showed a mean not significantly lower than those from these 12 failures, and the egg with the highest residues came from an eyrie in which one young bird was reared. But another chick in this successful nest died, and since the egg analyzed was the last laid of the clutch, it may have contained higher residues than the egg which produced the healthy youngster, as a result of increased contamination of the parent during the laying period (see also Ratcliffe, 1965*a*:73). Since 1961, mean national brood size has been lower (2.0 young per successful eyrie) than before 1950 (2.5), but any apparent reduction in clutch-size has been due to frequent breakage or disappearance of eggs, leaving depleted clutches. Mean brood size has, however, remained higher (2.3) in the south and east Highlands than over the rest of Britain (1.9), agreeing with the pattern of adult population decline.

The experimental evidence for other bird species is highly suggestive, but not conclusive. It has been shown (DeWitt, 1956; DeWitt *et al.*, 1960) that sublethal doses of these organochlorine insecticides cause reduced egg hatchability and chick viability in captive ring-necked pheasant and bobwhite quail, but as no egg analyses were included, it is not possible to infer that peregrines would be similarly affected, at the residue levels reported for their eggs. Considerable individual, intraspecific response has been found to a particular pesticide, and it is obvious that at the sublethal range, the limits of harmful dosage are difficult to define. The mean level found in the series of peregrine eggs may be critical for no more than abnormal behavior in the parents, but this alone can lead to substantial loss of reproductive success, which has been a marked feature of the peregrine decline.

There is some evidence that heavier sublethal doses can cause complete sterility. For instance, Post (1951) found that experimental dosage with aldrin (which metabolizes to dieldrin) at between 3 and 8 ppm in the diet, caused the ovaries of ring-necked pheasants to atrophy rapidly. From the failure of many peregrines to lay eggs, sterility (even if only psychological) commonly appears to have been a further stage in deterioration during the decline, before actual desertion of territory occurs. In some territories, one or both of the pair have persisted in occupation for up to 5 years, without laying any eggs. Often, however, territories were found deserted without an intervening period of nonbreeding. From the lack of any positive sign of occupation, many of these territories must be regarded as truly vacant. The simplest explanation of this failure of tenancy is not that the birds left for other places, but that they died and were not replaced. Peregrines are normally faithful to the same territories throughout their life and, in the absence of evidence for an increase in wandering, nonbreeding falcons in other parts of the country, widespread death of the species after 1955 is presumed. The casual finding of dead peregrines certainly seems to be more frequent than in former years, when it was a rare event. In 1961 no fewer than five were reported to the writer, and one in Cornwall showed, before it died, the characteristic tremoring of birds known to be victims of organochlorine pesticides.

The residue concentrations in the Lundy peregrine probably indicate a considerably higher contamination level than that obtaining in the birds whose eggs were analyzed. This bird bore no signs of external injury, and the inference is that it died of organochlorine insecticide poisoning. As in the eggs examined, by far the largest residues were of DDE. Reference to experimental results with captive American bald eagles (DeWitt and Buckley, 1962) suggests that a concentration of 70 ppm of DDE in the liver could well be indicative of uptake approaching lethal dosage. Still more significant are the figures for dieldrin and heptachlor epoxide, two far more toxic residues, and the available data for other bird species, (e.g. DeWitt *et al.*, 1960) make it likely that these substances alone could have been responsible for death. When all residues are taken together, the probability of their amounting to a lethal dose becomes very high.

Using all the analytical data so far available for peregrines and making comparison with those for two trained lanner falcons which suddenly died in captivity, Jefferies and Prestt (1966) have concluded that a combined dieldrin and heptachlor epoxide residue level of 5.2–9.3 ppm in the liver may be regarded as evidence of an acute lethal dose for both species. They have also calculated that the eating of a very few of the more heavily contaminated prey individuals, e.g., pigeons, is sufficient to build up this residue level in peregrine vital organs.

I therefore think it justifiable to claim that organochlorine pesticides caused the death of this Lundy peregrine. And if a peregrine living at least part of the year on an island 12 miles (19.3 km) from the mainland of Devon can accumulate this level of residues, then birds resident in haunts adjoining extensive arable farmland surely stand a strong chance of building up even higher concentrations. I think it likely that greatly increased adult mortality thus played a major part in the post-1955 "crash" of the peregrine population in southern Britain.

Finally, as Prestt (1965) has shown, the peregrine is not alone among British birds of prey in suffering recent and unprecedented decline. The kestrel and sparrow-hawk have shown the same trend, geographically and in time, and decline of the last species has perhaps been even more catastrophic than that of the peregrine. The golden eagle and buzzard have locally shown a marked drop in breeding success since the late 1950's. Though the source of contamination is different, from sheep dips when carrion mutton is eaten, they contain exactly the same residues, but with dieldrin more prominent than DDT/DDE (Lockie and Ratcliffe, 1964; Ratcliffe, 1965*a*). For each of these species, there is a similar weight of evidence to indicate organochlorine pesticides as the principal cause; whereas the simultaneous decline of all these raptors or the reduction in their breeding success, or both, further diminishes the validity of arguments in favor of other possible causes of decline, such as disease, persecution, and failing food supply.

It may well be that other types of pesticide have contributed to this unhappy situation. Organomercurial compounds are widely used and cumulative, but they have not yet been investigated in Britain. Organophosphorous pesticides have caused widespread deaths of wild birds by acute poisoning, but there is no evidence that they have affected the populations of raptors, for they are relatively nonpersistent. Having established that contamination of the population by residues of DDT, DDE, BHC, heptachlor, and dieldrin is general, that sublethal doses are an adequate explanation of reduced breeding success and failure to breed, and that dosage can be high enough to account for death, I feel there is no longer reasonable doubt that these persistent pesticides are causally involved in the recent decline of the British peregrine population. Moreover, whatever the contribution of other chemical pollutants, the impact of the organochlorine group alone would seem sufficient to account for a large part of this decline.

Final proof of this case could only come from controlled feeding trials with captive peregrines or difficult field experiments, although analysis of a larger sample of wild falcons, including nonbreeding, unsuccessful, and successful birds killed in their native haunts, and birds found dead, would go far in this direction. Corpses are only occasionally found by chance and sent in for analysis, and they can, at best, only yield circumstantial evidence of cause of death.

The future could, however, produce some measure of confirmation, merely through the watching of events. If the use of organochlorine pesticides or, at least, the most harmful of them, such as dieldrin, aldrin, and heptachlor, diminishes substantially and is matched by a synchronous recovery in the peregrine population, circumstantial evidence will be complete. A voluntary ban on use of these chemicals for spring-sown grain came into force in Britain in 1961, and at the beginning of 1965 this was extended to cover horticultural uses and aldrinated fertilizer in agriculture. Certainly, the decline seems to have halted; but, while the position of the peregrine population in 1964 may have shown slight improvement on 1963, there is no convincing evidence of further recovery in 1965. If one judges by informal reports, there would still appear to be a considerable use of dieldrin in agriculture, and there is no restriction on current uses of DDT and BHC. Three peregrine eggs collected from different eyries in southern Scotland in 1965 showed a mean level of contamination higher, though not significantly so, than that found in the 15 eggs examined in 1963–64: the figures (in ppm) are 1.6 heptachlor epoxide, 0.5 dieldrin, 16.9 DDE, total organochlorine residues 19.8 in 1965; and 0.9 heptachlor epoxide, 0.6 dieldrin, 11.9 DDE, total organochlorine residues 13.8 in 1963–64. The Cook Report (1964) even envisaged a possible increase in use of DDT as a compensation for loss of other pesticides. In view of the finding that DDT (or its metabolites) already constitute the bulk of the residues in peregrine tissues, and the correlation made between introduction of this chemical and reduction in breeding success, even the complete disappearance of the other organochlorines might not produce marked recovery. Development of resistance to these persistent pesticides by peregrines is no more than a theoretical possibility, and my own view is that, while they continue to be used on the present scale, the peregrine will not regain its former status in Britain. So long as this usage does not increase, the population may remain stabilized at a much reduced level, with only a precarious foothold in England and Wales; and if environmental contamination falls, the population is likely to recover proportionately. The danger of rapid extinction over the whole country may have passed, but the fate of the species is delicately balanced.

I have deliberately ignored information about the status of the peregrine in other countries, since the case I have pleaded for cause of decline in Britain should be strong enough to stand on its own evidence. However, insofar as the British population may receive recruits from or supply them to continental Europe, the population may be interconnected, and not truly separable. Changes here could impinge on the population there, and vice versa. It remains to be seen how far the British findings apply elsewhere, and whether or not the organochlorine pesticides constitute a national problem or a menace to a large part of the peregrine population of the Northern Hemisphere.

ACKNOWLEDGMENTS

I wish to thank again all the many people who have given me information about peregrines; and, as they have been mentioned individually before (Ratcliffe, 1963, 1965*b*), I hope they will excuse the omission of their names here. It is a tribute to the energy and enthusiasm of amateur ornithologists that such a wealth of data about the peregrine in Britain is available. Much of this information was gathered during the peregrine inquiry 1961–62, and I have to thank the British Trust for Ornithology for asking me to organize this survey, and for allowing me to reproduce the results which they have already published. I am grateful to N. Morgan and G. Hamilton of the Agricultural Scientific Services, Department of Agriculture for Scotland, and H. Egan and his colleagues in the Laboratory of the Government Chemist, who are responsible for the analysis of pesticide residues. The pesticidal study was carried out in conjunction with the Nature Conservancy's Toxic Chemicals and Wildlife Section, and I am indebted to N. W. Moore, head of the Section, for his encouragement and help. D. J. Jefferies, I. Prestt, D. Weir, and D. Humphrey have generously allowed me to quote from their unpublished data, and the stimulus of discussion with many other friends and colleagues must also be acknowledged.

SUMMARY

From 1930 to 1939, a fairly stable population of about 650 pairs of peregrines attempted to breed annually in Great Britain. Distribution is limited by availability of suitable nesting cliffs, both coastal and inland, but in suitable terrain breeding density varies widely, and is apparently adjusted to the regionally varying food supply, through strength of territorialism.

Prior to 1950, only three significant peregrine population changes were known in Britain. These were:

1. A postmedieval decline affecting easily accessible eyries in most regions, but complete by about 1860. This was due to persecution and casual disturbance.

2. A slow decline in the western Highlands of Scotland, beginning about 1890–1900 and terminating by 1950. Falling food supply due to extractive land management is believed to be the cause.

3. A temporary extinction or serious decline over much of southern England, and a few other districts, due to wartime persecution 1939–45. Rapid recovery in numbers followed after 1945.

Population stability was otherwise the rule, but after 1955 there was an unprecedented decline, which showed a wave-like spread from south to north; by 1962 the peregrine was almost extinct as a breeding species in southern England and in Wales, and reduced to very low levels in northern England and southern Scotland. The Scottish Highlands, especially in the center, were less affected, but the total British population appeared to be reduced to half the prewar level, and successful eyries to about one-seventh of the former number of breeding pairs. There was often a sequence of deterioration, with egg-breakage, egg-hatching failure, death of young, and failure of adults to lay, preceding actual desertion of territory. Since 1962, the population and its breeding success seem to have stabilized at around this much reduced level.

Persecution, casual disturbance, falling food supply, climatic change, and disease are unacceptable as explanations of this recent and rapid decline. But the increasing use of agricultural pesticides, particularly organochlorine compounds, shows a close correlation, geographically and in time, with the pattern of peregrine decline. Eggs from 14 different females all contained residues of DDT/DDE, BHC, dieldrin, and heptachlor epoxide: it is argued that the concentrations in some are sufficient to account for sublethal effects leading to reduced breeding success. A peregrine found dead contained sufficient of these same residues for them to be the probable cause of its death. Analysis of prey populations has further established that virtually all British peregrines are now "at risk" of contamination by these substances. There is thus a strong circumstantial case for believing the post-1955 decline to be due to agricultural pesticides.

The future of the peregrine in Britain probably depends on the continued scale of use of persistent pesticides, more than on the theoretical possibility of resistance developing. Under existing conditions, its survival at a greatly reduced level of population is feasible.

ADDENDUM, 1968

A sample census of about one-third of the known peregrine breeding territories in Great Britain during each of the years 1965–67 has shown no indication of any further marked change in overall population status and distribution. Since 1963 there has, however, been a slight recovery in occupation of territories in the east and central Scottish Highlands, southern Scotland, northern England, and northern Ireland, and a consequent marginal increase in output of young from these regions. Even so, breeding success of the populations of the southwest Highlands and southern Scotland was lower in 1967 than in 1966. Analysis of 11 eggs in 1967 shows a slight decrease in organochlorine residue levels, especially of dieldrin and heptachlor epoxide, compared with the sample for 1965–66, and confirms that total residue levels are significantly lower in the central Highlands (mean 4.9 ppm) than in other regions to the south (mean 14.8 ppm). Slight recovery of the population in more northerly regions is thus consistent with a decrease in environmental contamination, at least in these more marginal arable farming districts, which were least affected by the original peregrine decline. Egg-breakage has continued to be frequent, and eggshells of subnormal weight were prevalent in most districts with breeding peregrines, except the central Highlands, where breakage was infrequent and eggshells were mostly of normal (i.e. pre-1947) weight.

LITERATURE CITED

Baxter, E., and L. J. Rintoul. 1953. The birds of Scotland: Their history, distribution, and migration. Oliver and Boyd, Edinburgh. 2 vol.

Beebe, F. L. 1960. The marine peregrines of the northwest Pacific Coast. Condor, 62(3):145–189.

Cade, T. J. 1960. Ecology of the peregrine and gyrfalcon populations in Alaska. Univ. Calif. Pub. Zool., 63(3):151–290.

Cook, J. W. [Chairman]. 1964. Review of the persistent organochlorine pesticides. HMSO, London. 68 p.

[Cramp, S., and P. J. Conder.] 1961. The deaths of birds and mammals connected with toxic chemicals in the first half of 1960. Report No. 1 of the BTO–RSPB Committee on Toxic Chemicals. Royal Society for the Protection of Birds, London. 20 p.

[———, P. J. Conder, and J. S. Ash.] 1962. Deaths of birds and mammals from toxic chemicals, January-June 1961. Royal Society for the Protection of Birds, Sandy, Bedfordshire. 24 p.

DeWitt, J. B. 1956. Chronic toxicity to quail and pheasants of some chlorinated insecticides. Agr. Food Chem., 4(10):863–866.

———, and J. L. Buckley. 1962. Studies on pesticide-eagle relationships. Audubon Field Notes, 16(6):541.

———, C. M. Menzie, V. A. Adomaitis, and W. L. Reichel. 1960. Pesticidal residues in animal tissues. Trans. N. Amer. Wildl. Conf., 25:277–285.

Ferguson-Lees, I. J. 1951. The peregrine population of Britain. Bird Notes, 24(6):200–205, (8)309–315.

———. 1957. [The rarer birds of prey. Their present status in the British Isles.] Peregrine. Brit. Birds, 50(4):149–155.

Ficken, M. S., and R. W. Ficken. 1965. Territorial display as a population-regulating mechanism in the yellow warbler. Auk, 82(2):274–275.

Gray, R. 1871. The birds of the west of Scotland, including the Outer Hebrides. Glasgow. 520 p.

Hickey, J. J. 1942. Eastern population of the duck hawk. Auk, 59(2):176–204.

Jefferies, D. J., and I. Prestt. 1966. Post-mortems of peregrines and lanners with particular reference to organochlorine residues. Brit. Birds, 59(2):49–64.

Lockie, J. D., and D. A. Ratcliffe. 1964. Insecticides and Scottish golden eagles. Brit. Birds, 57(3):89–102.

Moore, N. W. 1965. Environmental contamination by pesticides, p. 219–237. *In* G. T. Goodman, R. W. Edwards, and J. M. Lambert [eds.], Ecology and the industrial society: Fifth symposium of the British Ecological Society. Blackwell Scientific Publications, Oxford. 404 p.

———, and D. A. Ratcliffe. 1962. Chlorinated hydrocarbon residues in the egg of a peregrine falcon (*Falco peregrinus*) from Perthshire. Bird Study, 9(4):242–244.

———, and J. O'G. Tatton. 1965. Organochlorine insecticide residues in the eggs of sea birds. Nature, 207(4992):42–43.

Post, G. 1951. A study of aldrin insecticide; its effects on birds and other wildlife. Wyoming Wild Life, 15(9):4–9, 32–36.

Prestt, I. 1965. An enquiry into the recent breeding status of some of the smaller birds of prey and crows in Britain. Bird Study, 12(3):196–221.

Ratcliffe, D. A. 1958. Broken eggs in peregrine eyries. Brit. Birds, 51(1):23–26.

———. 1962. Breeding density in the peregrine *Falco peregrinus* and raven *Corvus corax*. Ibis, 104(1):13–39.

———. 1963. The status of the peregrine in Great Britain. Bird Study, 10(2):56–90.

———. 1965*a*. Organo-chlorine residues in some raptor and corvid eggs from northern Britain. Brit. Birds, 58(3):65–81.

———. 1965*b*. The peregrine situation in Great Britain 1963–64. Bird Study, 12(2):66–82.

Ryves, B. H. 1948. Bird life in Cornwall. Collins, London. 256 p.

Treleaven, R. 1961. Notes on the peregrine in Cornwall. Brit. Birds, 54(4):136–142.

Walpole-Bond, John. 1914. Field-studies of some rarer British birds. Witherby & Co., London. 305 p.
———. 1938. A history of Sussex birds. Witherby & Co., London. 3 vol.

APPENDIX

Occupation and Breeding Success in Peregrine Territories

Data are presented only for those territories visited in each of the five years 1961–65, in four selected regions along the south-north gradient of decline in Britain.

c = eggs
y = young
D = eggs broken or disappeared, young died in nest
R = young reared to flying stage
x = young taken by falconers, but would otherwise have flown
? = size of clutch or brood unknown. Mean brood size is calculated for known values, and unknowns are then given this mean figure
NS = no sign of adult, territory presumed deserted
NN = no nest with eggs or young found, or other evidence of actual breeding
1 Bd = one adult present during breeding season
Pr = one pair present during breeding season

Territory	1961	1962	1963	1964	1965
Wales					
A	NS	NS	NS	NS	NS
B	NS	NS	NS	NS	NS
C	NS	NS	NS	NS	NS
D	NS	NS	NS	1BdNN	NS
E	Pr?	y/3R	PrNN	PrNN	PrNN
F	PrNN	1BdNN	NS	NS	NS
G	y/2R	c/3D	y/1R	c/?D	c/?D
H	y/?R	PrNN	PrNN	y/?R	PrNN
I	NS	NS	NS	y/2-3R	y/2-3R
J	PrNN	1BdNN	NS	NS	NS
K	PrNN	PrNN	PrNN	PrNN	1BdNN
L	PrNN	NS	NS	NS	NS
M	NS	NS	NS	NS	NS
N	NS	NS	1BdNN	NS	NS
O	NS	NS	NS	NS	NS
P	NS	NS	1BdNN	NS	NS
Q	NS	NS	NS	NS	NS
R	y/2R	PrNN	NS	NS	NS
S	c/?D	PrNN	NS	NS	NS
T	NS	NS	NS	NS	NS

Territory	1961	1962	1963	1964	1965
Northern England					
A	PrNN	NS	NS	NS	NS
B	c/3D	1BdNN	NS	y/1R	1BdNN
C	c/3D	c/3D	c/3D	NS	NS
D	y/1D	c/3D	y/2 (1D, 1R)	y/1D	y/1R
E	c/3D	NS	NS	NS	NS
F	NS	c/3D	y/?R	y/2R	NS
G	NS	c/3D	NS	NS	y/2R
H	1BdNN	PrNN	1BdNN	c/?D	y/2R
I	y/1R	c/3D	PrNN	c/2D	c/4D
J	NS	NS	NS	NS	NS
K	y/2R	y/2D	NS	NS	NS
L	1BdNN	NS	NS	NS	NS
M	c/4D	1BdNN	NS	NS	NS
N	c/2D	PrNN	PrNN	y/1R	c/?D
O	c/3D	c/3D	c/3D	c/?D	c/?D
P	1BdNN	NS	NS	NS	NS
Q	1BdNN	NS	NS	NS	NS
Southern Scotland					
A	PrNN	c/?D	c/4D	c/4D	y/2R
B	y/2R	y/2D	y/3R	c/4D	NS
C	y/1R	c/1D	c/3D	c/4D	c/1D
D	PrNN	1BdNN	1BdNN	PrNN	NS
E	PrNN	y/1R	c/4D	y/1R	y/1R
F	y/?R	1BdNN	y/R	y/3R	y/?R
G	1BdNN	PrNN	y/2R	c/3D	c/3D
H	PrNN	c/3D	c/4D	NS	NS
I	PrNN	NS	NS	NS	NS
J	1BdNN	1BdNN	1BdNN	1BdNN	c/?D
K	c/?D	c/4D	1BdNN	1BdNN	NS
Central Highlands					
A	y/3R	y/3R	y/4R	y/3R	y/3R
B	c/?D	y/R	y/R	y/2R	c/?D
C	y/R	y/R	y/R	y/3R	NS
D	y/3^{x}	y/2^{x}	y/2R	y/3R	y/?R
E	y/3R	y/2R	PrNN	y/2R	c/?D
F	y/3^{x}	y/4^{x}	y/1R	y/3R	y/?R
G	y/1R	y/1R	PrNN	y/4R	y/4R
H	y/2^{x}	y/2R	y/2R	y/2R	y/2R
I	PrNN	y/1^{x}	y/3R	y/?R	y/2R
J	y/2R	y/?R	y/2R	y/?R	y/?R

CHAPTER 22

GENERAL DISCUSSION: THE PEREGRINE FALCON IN WESTERN EUROPE

THE STATUS OF THE PEREGRINE IN IRELAND

RATCLIFFE: Before 1939, the whole of Ireland probably had at least 200 pairs of peregrines attempting to breed annually, and the figure could well have approached 300. (I think that the prewar breeding population for the whole of the British Isles could have been around 1,000 pairs.)

The Irish population has clearly been affected by the recent decline and, though the evidence is largely anecdotal, there appears to have been a significant though irregular decrease, more marked in the south and east than in the north and west. The only reliable data are for the northeastern counties of Down, Antrim, Tyrone, Fermanagh, and Derry in Northern Ireland, where 25–28 pairs bred in 1948-49; in Antrim only 4 pairs remained in 1945, as a result of wartime persecution, but the population had risen to 9–10 pairs by 1949 (Ferguson-Lees, 1957). In 1962 Arnold Benington reported that of 24 territories visited, 8 were apparently deserted, and that in the remaining 16, only 8 pairs appeared to be nesting. (I presume he meant they had laid eggs, but he did not ascertain how many were successful.) In 1964, Michael Gilbertson visited or collected data from others on 14 territories in Antrim; of these, 12 were occupied by peregrines, but only two successfully, and most pairs appeared not to nest. In 1965, Gilbertson found 12 out of 17 territories to be occupied, but again most pairs apparently failed to nest, and only two broods were reared.

The agricultural areas of Ireland are in the middle, south, and east, and the presumption is that pesticides are responsible for the decline in this country, too.

THE PARTICULAR SITUATION IN FRANCE

CLEMENT: I would like to ask Terrasse if he agrees with my summing up that the peregrines persist in France despite heavy hunting pressure in nonagricultural areas, but there has been a drastic decline in agricultural areas.

TERRASSE: Yes, that is correct.

PEREGRINE POPULATIONS IN SPAIN

TERRASSE: Spain is a very different country because, of all the countries in Europe, Spain still has a fantastic population of nesting peregrines. This is probably because there are few people, few guns, and few modern agricultural improvements. In the district of Madrid alone, one can find 50 eyries of nesting peregrines. Equal numbers are sometimes found in places smaller than that.

HICKEY: Dr. Felix Rodriguez de la Fuente at the Caen Conference described this population in the same glowing terms. It is now an important source of peregrines for falconers, and its continued reproductive success remains a point of extreme scientific interest.

PEREGRINE POPULATIONS IN SWEDEN AND THE WESTERN USSR

HICKEY: The peregrine story in southwestern Sweden was described in 1964 by Otterlind and Lennerstedt (Vår Fågelvärld, 23:363–415). Here the resident pairs declined steadily from 39 in 1954 to 8 in 1963. This represents a 79% drop in the decade and a mean decrease of 14% per year. According to Lars Wallin (*in litt.*), "There has been a sharp decline in the population of *Falco peregrinus* in Sweden since 1955. In a census performed in 1965 by the Swedish ornithological society and the Swedish society for nature preservation, only 13 pairs could be established in the whole country. Only 6 pairs bred successfully. This is roughly a few per cent of the breeding population in 1955." Peregrine populations in this part of the Baltic thus appear to be identical in their behavior to those in Finland as Linkola and Suominen have described them at this conference.

[Professor Dr. E. Kumari (Zoological and Botanical Institute, Estonian Academy of Science) writes (*in litt.*) that, in the years 1948–58, Estonian ornithologists working under his direction found at least 30 pairs of peregrines nesting in Estonia, a maximum of 40–50 being estimated. On the north Latvian peat bogs, there were at least 20 pairs. Tree nests are generally used in Lithuania and Latvia but are exceptional in northern Latvia and the whole of Estonia where peat bogs involve vast plains with little or no tree growth. Reproduction of this species was still successful in 1948–53 even though some nests had only one fledgling each. Reduced reproduction and desertion of sites appeared in 1954–57. An inspection of some of the known nesting sites in 1965–66 revealed that the majority were deserted, and it is currently estimated (October 1966) that a maximum of no more than 10 pairs of peregrine falcons are nesting in Estonia.]

Kruyfhooft's (1964) population index of migrant peregrines passing through Belgium suggests a population reduction on the order of 80% from 1950–52 to 1958–60. From the data presented at this conference by Linkola and Suominen, I calculate that the mean rate of disappearance of nesting pairs in Finland has averaged 47% a year since 1958. All these reports point to the pending extinction of the peregrine falcon in northwestern Europe. Certainly, one of the interesting problems facing Soviet scientists centers on the question of how far eastward from the Baltic this phenomenon extends into their country.

Migratory Populations of the Peregrine Falcon

CHAPTER 23

COASTAL MIGRATION DATA AS POPULATION INDICES FOR THE PEREGRINE FALCON

James H. Enderson

The purpose of this paper is to call attention to the possibility of developing population indices for Arctic-nesting peregrines by means of systematic counts at certain favorable points where migrants can be readily seen along shorelines in the United States.

The peregrines of North America, excluding the subspecific Peale's falcon of the Pacific Northwest, appear to be separated into two populations on the basis of the degree of migratory behavior they have exhibited. According to band-recovery records, the peregrines of southern Canada and the United States to the south are weakly migratory or nonmigratory. Only one of the 70 resident adult or nestling peregrines banded in that region was recovered south of southern California and central Georgia. That bird, a Colorado nestling, was recovered in central Mexico. None was recovered north of southern Canada. The now-extinct population of peregrines in the eastern United States showed little migratory tendency. Distinct from these southern birds is an apparently large, highly migratory population of peregrines that nests in Arctic regions and winters in the coastal areas of the United States, the West Indies, and Central and South America (Enderson, 1965).

Peregrine band-recovery data from Canada and the United States are the results of the efforts of many people. Among those whose recovery data I have relied heavily upon are W. S. Feeney, J. A. Hagar, C. E. Hall, R. H. Pough, and J. N. Rice.

MIGRATION ON THE GULF COAST

In October 1964, I observed the peregrine migration on two 36-mile-long (58-km) sections of the Texas coast of the Gulf of Mexico. I drove back and forth along the beaches each day, counting the falcons seen and attempting to catch, mark, and band them. Birds were individually marked with dye and by cutting vanes from the shafts of rectrices to create small wing holes as an aid in subsequent identification (Enderson, 1964). In all, I drove 1,052 miles (1,693 km). During the count period the weather was uniform with moderate daytime on-shore winds.

The number of peregrines seen on the two beaches in the 7-day period differed greatly, although these beaches were not over 25 miles (40 km) apart (Table 23.1). In contrast to the first beach (A), the second (B) was deserted of people. Overall, peregrine sightings averaged one every 20 miles (32 km) of travel. All trapped birds appeared in excellent health, with fully developed pectoral muscles showing no signs of weight loss.

Marked peregrines were occasionally resighted or retrapped. Since the positions of the dye mark and wing hole were varied, individuals could be

Table 23.1. Results of a Survey of Migrating Peregrines on the Texas Gulf Coast, 10–17 October 1964

	Beach A	Beach B	Total
Distance traveled			
Miles	698	354	1,052
Km	1,123	570	1,693
Number of Peregrines			
Seen	9	43	52
Trapped and banded	5	10	15
Population index			
Peregrines per 100 miles	1.29	12.15	4.94
Peregrines per 100 km	0.80	7.54	3.07

recognized at a distance. Five individuals were resighted up to 4 days after banding. I saw one of these 65 miles (95 km) north of the banding point.

Although peregrines were seen 52 times, 8 of these were clearly resightings, hence no more than 44 individuals were seen. These included 20 immature females, 16 adult females, 6 females of unknown age, and 2 immature males. No adult males were encountered.

Since peregrines were most numerous just after sunrise and least numerous in the afternoon and evening, it seems likely that many falcons arrive on the beach after sunset, before sunrise, or in the night.

The only peregrine seen with prey was carrying a mourning dove.

PEREGRINE BAND RECOVERIES

A listing of 148 peregrine band recoveries, complete through November 1964, was obtained from the US Fish and Wildlife Service. Nine of these were discarded because the birds had been held in captivity prior to release. Of the 139 remaining, 67 records are of birds banded as nestlings, and 3 are of birds banded as resident adults in the United States or southern Canada. The remaining 69 records are apparently of birds from more northerly regions that were banded in their southward migration.

Only 1 of the 70 nestling or resident peregrines banded in the United States or southern Canada was recovered (in Mexico) south of central Georgia or southern California. None was recovered north of southern Canada. Of the 58 nestling peregrines banded in the eastern United States and later recovered, 45 were recovered before reaching 2 years of age. Of the 58, 31 were shot, trapped, or poisoned.

Most of the 69 recoveries of banded migrants were of birds banded in September, October, and November in shoreline areas. Of these, 39 were recovered some distance away from the banding point before the following summer. Only 4 of these records show that the birds moved northward after banding. All of the others show that the birds traveled to Central and South America (6 records), the West Indies (7 records), or showed conspicuous southward movement. Enderson (1965) gives a mapping of these records.

Of the remaining 30 records of migrants, 11 are of birds recovered within a few months near the point of banding, and 19 are of migrants banded in the fall and recovered after the following spring. Of the latter, 18 have been tabulated in my *Wilson Bulletin* report; the 19th involved a bird banded in Texas on 10 October 1962 and recovered in Texas on 14 October 1964. The birds were presumably southward bound when banded, and most were recovered on some subsequent northward or southward leg of their migration or while wintering in South America.

In view of the fact that it is nearly impossible to obtain a reasonably accurate count of the peregrine population nesting in the Arctic, it seems very urgent that a technique be developed for estimating the relative numbers of these peregrines migrating at certain points in the United States. Conspicuous movements of peregrines occur on the Gulf coast of Texas, on the west shore of Lake Michigan, and on the coasts of Maryland, Virginia, and Florida, and perhaps on the shores of other eastern seaboard states. In view of the variability in the number of observations of peregrines on two similar beaches in Texas (Table 23.1), further study and refinement of the counting is necessary to produce meaningful estimates of abundance of the Arctic population.

SUMMARY

In a 7-day period on the Texas coast, 1.3–12.3 peregrines were seen per 100 miles traveled (0.8–7.5 per 100 km). Marked individuals were sighted up to 4 days later; one, 65 miles (95 km) to the north.

Of 70 nestlings or resident peregrines banded in the United States and southern Canada, only 1 was recovered south of central Georgia to southern California. Southbound birds caught on shorelines have traveled to Central and South America (6) and the West Indies (7) and are regarded as raised in the Arctic.

Variability in the numbers seen on two nearby beaches in Texas suggests that refinement of such counts will be needed to produce meaningful indices of Arctic peregrine populations.

LITERATURE CITED

Enderson, J. H. 1964. A study of the prairie falcon in the central Rocky Mountain region. Auk, 81(3):332–352.

———. 1965. A breeding and migration survey of the peregrine falcon. Wilson Bull., 77(3):327–339.

CHAPTER 24

DISCUSSION: MIGRATORY POPULATIONS

A PEREGRINE POPULATION INDEX ON THE MARYLAND-VIRGINIA COAST

RICE: During the past 12 years, I have been trapping peregrine falcons at Assateague Island in Maryland's Worcester and Accomac counties. My data and those of R. B. Berry for 1964–65 are summarized in Table 24.1.

This index seems to suggest no change in this southbound migratory population during the period of our trapping. During the second 6-year period we used a noose-jacket trapping technique (Woodford, 1966, A manuel of falconry, fig. 9.1) instead of the headset method (the trapper buried in the sand except for his head). When we used this latter method, males had been previously missed. The sex-ratio in these samples

Table 24.1. Peregrine Falcons Caught at Assateague Island, Maryland

	1954–59	1960–65
Number of days of trapping	67	56
Number of birds captured		
Adult males	2	4
Adult females	37	26
Immature males	50	56
Immature females	144	116
Total	233	204
Percent immature	83%	84%
Number caught per day	3.5	3.6

is therefore influenced by a trapping bias as well as by unknown behavioral biases in the birds themselves.

The Arctic nature of this population and its tendency to winter outside the United States have been described by me earlier (see Chapter 14).

A PEREGRINE MIGRATION INDEX IN WISCONSIN

BERGER: At Cedar Grove, Wisconsin, on the western shore of Lake Michigan, Helmut Mueller and I have had fall counts of peregrines which presumably are primarily migrants from the north. From 1951 to 1964 inclusive, we sighted from 8 to 51 peregrines per year for a 14-year mean of 25.9 each fall. The recent counts were 1960, 18; 1961, 19; 1962, 15; 1963, 37; and 1964, 25. This 5-year mean was 22.8.

KRUYFHOOFT'S MIGRATION INDEX FOR BELGIUM

HICKEY: Kruyfhooft's data on the number of peregrines caught each year in Belgium (1964, Working Conference on Birds of Prey and Owls, p. 70–73) convincingly corroborate the decline of peregrines in northwestern Europe described by Linkola and Suominen at this conference. I think the adjusted curves for Kruyfhooft's statistics (see Chapter 1) illustrate the elementary principle that even highly erratic statistics can be used to bring out population trends. In general, peregrine migration is so sparse as to discourage observations by most investigators who might concentrate on this phenomenon alone otherwise. It seems likely that the collection of such statistics for a population index will probably accrue as the byproduct of other efforts like the trapping of raptors by falconers and the mist-netting of passerine migrants by ornithologists.

PART II

CURRENT POPULATION TRENDS IN OTHER RAPTORIAL BIRDS

CHAPTER 25

RECENT POPULATION TRENDS AMONG BRITISH RAPTORS

Ian Prestt

Investigations of the British population of certain raptors and water birds were started in 1964 (Prestt, 1966). These were undertaken following the report of Moore and Walker (1964), which showed organochlorine residues present in the breast muscles of a wide range of bird species, but in greater quantities in the raptorial and fish-feeding birds, and the report of Ratcliffe (1963) demonstrating a recent severe decline in the peregrine.

Large numbers of grain-eating birds died in Britain in the early 1950's following the use of organophosphorous seed dressings, and in the second half of the 1950's following the use of organochlorine seed dressings (Cramp and Conder, 1961; Cramp, Conder, and Ash, 1962; and Moore, 1965). The decline of the peregrine appeared to have started about 1955 (Ratcliffe, 1963). The first investigations had therefore to take the form of historical inquiries to cover this period.

Amateur ornithology is highly organized in Britain by the British Trust for Ornithology (BTO) and the Royal Society for the Protection of Birds (RSPB). It was decided, therefore, to conduct the first inquiry on raptors by sending a questionnaire to regional representatives of the BTO, officials of local ornithological societies, and editors of county bird reports. The questionnaire covered the period 1953 to 1963 and contained eight questions. The first two requested information about the recorders and the area covered, while the remainder were designed to obtain information about changes that may have occurred in the breeding status of the buzzard, sparrow-hawk, merlin, kestrel, barn owl, and tawny owl. Three crows—the carrion or hooded crow, the magpie, and the jay—were included for comparison.

Surveys of this type, which are essentially subjective, have obvious limitations. It should be appreciated, however, that this is one of the few ways to obtain historical information of this kind and, in the absence of research programs, such local records are the only data available. Moreover, the inquiry was straightforward, being only concerned with large-scale changes in the breeding status of a limited number of large, easily identifiable species.

The information received (Prestt, 1965) showed that, in general, all the birds of prey had decreased in numbers: the sparrow-hawk and barn owl extensively, the kestrel severely in the eastern half of England, the buzzard and merlin less severely, and the tawny owl only slightly. In contrast, all the crows had increased generally.

The extent and severity of the decrease of the sparrow-hawk were outstanding. Up to 1950 it was one of the commonest and most widely distributed of the diurnal predators; by 1963 it could no longer be considered a common breeding bird in any county in England. Declines were also reported from parts of Scotland, Wales, northern Ireland, the Isle of Man, and the Channel Islands. The decline was most marked in the eastern, north midland, and midland regions of Britain and was principally the result of a decrease occurring in the late 1950's. The drop in numbers of the kestrel in the eastern half of England was also as a result of decreases occurring in the late 1950's.

The decline of the barn owl was less severe than that of the sparrow-hawk and more widespread than that of the kestrel. It appears to have resulted from both long-term and recent changes and was attributed to a number of causes including severe winters, toxic chemicals, and loss of habitat and nesting sites due to changes in agriculture.

The buzzard was affected by myxomatosis in the early 1950's (Moore, 1957). This caused a general decline and, apart from northern Wales, the number of breeding birds in the traditional areas in the north and west of Britain is still depressed. Some apparently exceptional recent decreases were, however, reported from the northern Pennines, Westmorland, parts of the Midlands, Hampshire, Wiltshire, and southern Dorset.

The diminution in the number of merlins in Britain appears to be as a result of a general deterioration and is not confined to any particular area or time.

The results of the first inquiry suggest that the kestrel, sparrow-hawk, and barn owl now present a conservation problem, so further research programs have been started on them. These are aimed to: (1) investigate further the history of the population, (2) provide further details of the present situation, (3) enable future trends to be recorded objectively, and (4) investigate the causes of their declines. Studies have also been started on the tawny owl, since it appears to contrast with the other three species. Specimens of all four species are being subjected to chemical analysis. To date, analyses have been completed or are in process for 90 kestrels and 30 of their eggs, 40 sparrow-hawks and 35 eggs, 65 tawny owls and 7 eggs, and 60 barn owls.

The following is a short report on the work in progress with preliminary results:

Kestrel. Despite the decrease in eastern England, this species is still common over much of Britain. A method was required, therefore, to enable observations to be used from large areas of the country. Due to this bird's obvious method of hunting by hovering over open ground, it was decided to record its breeding distribution by obtaining records of: (1) confirmed breeding, or (2) suspected breeding, or (3) sight records between mid-May and the end of June, when it is assumed the birds will be in their breeding territories. These records are related to the 10-km national grid. The information is punched onto cards, and a map automatically printed by use of a tabulator.

Unfortunately, the map for 1964 had not been completed at this writing (the delay resulting from the time needed to check map references). The results obtained included information on 300 breeding pairs, 150 possible breeding pairs, and 1,600 sight records. Some confirmation for the results of the first inquiry is already apparent from the small numbers of breeding pairs reported from counties such as Lincolnshire and Huntingdonshire in eastern England. This national survey will be repeated at 3-year intervals.

Tawny owl. This species is still common and widespread. From the work of Southern (1954), it is known that the males establish their territories by calling, usually during October, November, and December. This species was investigated in a similar way to the kestrel, except that records of birds calling in the autumn were substituted for sight records during the breeding season. The results of the 1964 national survey were not available at this writing, but it is already clear that the situation suggested by the first inquiry is correct.

Barn owl. A similar attempt to complete a national survey for this species was unsuccessful, and a new method will have to be devised.

Sparrow-hawk. This species is secretive, particularly during the breeding season. Also, it is now local or uncommon over much of England. A different survey method was, therefore, required. Historical information on breeding density is fortunately available for several parts of Britain. These areas are therefore being used as study areas and searches are being made to determine the current density and breeding success.

A detailed study of the golden eagle is also in progress by Lockie and Ratcliffe, working in Scotland. The first report (1964) was of a study of the reproductive behavior of a sample population in a wide area of the western Highlands of Scotland. It showed a drop in breeding success from 72% rearing young between 1937 and 1960 to 29% rearing young from 1961 to 1963. As with the study of the peregrine, this work is being continued, and the following aspects are receiving attention for a sample population of 22 pairs: (1) breeding success, (2) analysis of a limited number of eggs, (3) a study of the availability of carrion, an important winter and spring food, and (4) an assessment of the breeding density and food of foxes in the same area (these being an important competitor with the eagle for carrion).

SUMMARY

To summarize the position, it can be said that of the ten common species of raptors in Britain, the peregrine and sparrow-hawk have suffered recent severe widespread declines; the kestrel has suffered a marked recent decline in the eastern half of England; the numbers of buzzards, still depressed following myxomatosis, have decreased recently in some local areas; and the golden eagle has shown a recent marked decrease in breeding success in part of its range. The barn owl and merlin appear to have been declining generally over a longer period. Of the three remaining species, the tawny owl is widespread and common; the hobby and little owl have not been studied on a national scale in recent years, but the county bird reports do not indicate a marked change in their status to have taken place.

LITERATURE CITED

[Cramp, S., and P. J. Conder. 1961.] The deaths of birds and mammals connected with toxic chemicals in the first half of 1960. Report No. 1 of the BTO–RSPB Committee on Toxic Chemicals. Royal Society for the Protection of Birds, London. 20 p.

[———, P. J. Conder, and J. S. Ash.] 1962. Deaths of birds and mammals from toxic chemicals, January–June 1961. Royal Society for the Protection of Birds, Sandy, Bedfordshire. 24 p.

Lockie, J. D., and D. A. Ratcliffe. 1964. Insecticides and Scottish golden eagles. Brit. Birds, 57(3):89–102.

Moore, N. W. 1957. The past and present status of the buzzard in the British Isles. Brit. Birds, 50(5):173–197.

———. 1965. Pesticides and birds—A review of the situation in Great Britain in 1965. Bird Study, 12(3):222–252.

———, and C. H. Walker. 1964. Organic chlorine insecticide residues in the eggs of wild birds. Nature, 201(4924):1072–1073.

Prestt, I. 1965. An enquiry into the recent breeding status of some of the smaller birds of prey and crows in Britain. Bird Study, 12(3):196–221.

———. 1966. Studies of recent changes in the status of some birds of prey and fish-feeding birds in Britain. J. Appl. Ecol., 3(Suppl.):107–112.

Ratcliffe, D. A. 1963. The status of the peregrine in Great Britain. Bird Study, 10(2):56–90.

Southern, H. N. 1954. Tawny owls and their prey. Ibis, 96(3):384–410.

CHAPTER 26

THE STATUS OF THE PEREGRINE AND OTHER FALCONIFORMS IN AFRICA

Tom J. Cade

Africa is a large and ecologically varied continent, and an assessment of the populations of diurnal raptors living there represents a formidable and complicated subject, to say the least. The avifauna is especially rich —exceeded in number of species, I expect, only by South America; and the falconiforms are highly diversified. For instance, in southern Africa —that part of the continent lying south of the Cunene, Okovango, and Zambezi rivers, which is the area about which I will have most to say— there are about 800 species of birds (McLachlan and Liversidge, 1957; Mackworth-Praed and Grant, 1962). Of these, some 62 species are in the order Falconiformes as traditionally constituted. Thus, while slightly less than one-tenth of the world's avian species occur in southern Africa, almost one-fourth of the Falconiformes are present there, in an area about the size of the western United States from the Rocky Mountains to the Pacific coast.

Table 26.1 shows the taxonomic distribution of these species. The secretary bird, in the monotypic family Sagittariidae, is questionably placed in the order. The Old World vultures, Aegypiinae, are conspicuous representatives, but I have chosen to exclude them from detailed consideration in this paper. Falcons (family Falconidae) are well represented in southern Africa, with as many as six or seven sympatric species occurring in some areas. The same is also true of the accipiters (Accipitrinae), but the eagles (Buteoninae and Circaetinae) are the most impressive and the most truly characteristic falconiforms of the African scene (see Brown, 1955). To watch several tawny eagles, Wahlberg's eagles, perhaps a single black eagle, one or two martial eagles, and a complement of bateleurs all spiraling up together on a thermal during the heat of midday in the African bushveld is to experience something of primeval Africa, a vestige which one hopes will not perish. Such a sight is readily obtainable in the Kruger National Park.

Other taxa listed in Table 26.1 include several highly specialized species, the phylogenetic affinities of which are by no means settled. The cuckoo falcon and the bat hawk are currently placed with the honey buzzard in the subfamily Perninae, and the curious harrier-hawk, with its "double-jointed" articulation between the tarsometatarsus and tibiotarsus, is grouped with the true harriers (Circinae).

About 80% of the species, 50 in all, are resident African forms (Ethiopian), and about 20% (12) are Palaearctic migrants, which are present only during the austral summer (October through March). A little-studied aspect of raptor ecology in Africa is the way migratory populations that are congeneric, or in some cases conspecific, with resident African forms fit into the complex of predatory niches without serious competition with their relatives. I hope to show that avoidance of competition among these populations is effected in part by distributional adjustments and by differences in habitat associations.

It is only with the greatest temerity that I dare speak about populations and numbers of falconiforms in Africa. So little is published, and my own experience at the time this paper was written was limited to about 5 months of field work in southern Africa, mostly in the arid parts, such as the Kalahari and Namib deserts in South-West Africa. All I can

Table 26.1. Number of Southern Africa Species in Major Taxa of Falconiformes

Taxa	Resident species	Palaearctic migrant species	Total number of species
Sagittariidae	1	—	1
Falconidae	9	4	13
Accipitridae			
Aegypiinae	7	—	7
Milvinae	1[a]	1[a]	1
Elaninae	1	—	1
Perninae	2	1	3
Buteoninae	12	4	16
Circaetinae	5	—	5
Accipitrinae	9	—	9
Circinae	3	2	5
Pandionidae	1	—	1
Total	51	12	62

[a] Two forms: one Ethiopian, one Palaearctic.

try to do is, first, give a kind of thumbnail sketch of the taxonomic, distributional, and numerical status of the peregrine falcon in Africa, in so far as information allows, and then follow this resumé with a somewhat more detailed consideration of the numbers of some falconiforms in South Africa.

THE PEREGRINE FALCON IN AFRICA

DISTRIBUTION AND TAXONOMY

The peregrine is widely distributed in Africa but evidently nowhere very common, except in places along the Mediterranean coast; indeed, it must be considered rare over large regions of the continent, such as the tropical forests of the Congo Basin. Certainly it does not reach densities comparable to those which used to obtain over much of Europe and in Great Britain. In the older literature, the subspecies *brookei, minor* (*perconfusus* of many authors), and *pelegrinoides,* the Barbary falcon, are included as African populations of the species *peregrinus*; but since Vaurie (1961) contends that the Barbary falcon and the red-naped shaheen (*babylonicus*) constitute a distinct species, I shall briefly treat the ranges of the subspecies separately.

An undisputed subspecies of *peregrinus,* the Mediterranean race *brookei,* is said to breed in Africa only on the northern peninsula of Morocco (Tangier and Cape Spartel) and is replaced by *pelegrinoides* in Morocco from the Moyen Atlas southward and right from the Mediterranean coast southward into the Sahara in Algeria and Tunisia; however, *pelegrinoides* has been recorded breeding in Tangier in the range of *brookei.* South of the Sahara, about from Cape Verde in Senegal and the southern Sudan in the east, *pelegrinoides* is replaced by the subspecies *minor* Bonaparte, a large, dark form, some individuals being jet black on the dorsum; but the exact northern limits of the distribution of this race are unknown (summarized from Vaurie, 1961). Evidently *pelegrinoides* is common around Khartoum, but *minor* is unrecorded from there (Meinertzhagen, 1954). The race *minor* occurs through all of equatorial Africa south right to the Cape of Good Hope but is decidedly rare in the tropical forests of West Africa. For instance, Leslie Brown (*in litt.*) saw only two peregrines in 5 years of observation in Nigeria.

The case for specific status of the *pelegrinoides-babylonicus* populations finds its strongest support, in my opinion, on the basis of morphological and ecological differences between these populations and adjacent races of more typical *peregrinus.* The evidence for overlap of breeding ranges is not too good, but field work in critical areas could clear up this matter. The Barbary falcon and the red-naped shaheen are small falcons (there is no overlap in weight with typical *peregrinus* when the sexes are compared), with relatively long wings and short tails, a powerful pectoral girdle, and relatively longer but weaker toes than in typical *peregrinus*. Their plumage is decidedly paler than in races of *peregrinus*, less barred, with much more rufous. The crown is always mixed with rusty red, and the nape is bright rufous chestnut, whereas these parts are black, slaty, or bluish gray in races of *peregrinus*. Unfortunately complicating the picture, *brookei* is a small race of *peregrinus* and also shows some rusty red on the nape, but Vaurie (1961) says it is clearly *peregrinus* and not close to *pelegrinoides*.

The Barbary falcon and red-naped shaheen are basically desert-adapted forms, whereas adjacent and possibly partly sympatric populations of *peregrinus* tend to be either coastal or montane in distribution. I think it is significant that nowhere else in its extensive range, which comes in contact with all the major deserts of the world, has *F. peregrinus* evolved a distinctive desert form. As a whole, the species is not desert-adapted, and populations usually can exist in arid regions only in the presence of large bodies of water—rivers, lakes, or seacoasts (e.g., Baja California). The Barbary falcon and red-naped shaheen are biologically exceptional in this respect.

Since there is some reason to argue for the specific separation of the *pelegrinoides-babylonicus* populations, it is also worth considering the affinities of the Teita falcon within this context. This species seems to embody the extreme expression of those morphological trends away from typical *peregrinus* which are seen in *pelegrinoides* and *babylonicus*—redness in the plumage, especially on the nape, small body size, relatively long wings with an extremely short tail, and a powerful pectoral apparatus. Might not this rare little falcon from East Africa be an arid tropical race of the shaheen? If it could be shown that the affinities of *fasciinucha* are closest to *pelegrinoides* and *babylonicus*, then the question of specific separation of these populations from the peregrines would be settled, because *fasciinucha* is fully sympatric with the *minor* race of *peregrinus*.

PEREGRINE POPULATIONS IN AFRICA

Population studies on peregrines in Africa are virtually nonexistent, and there is very little basis for estimating temporal changes in numbers. Leslie Brown's observations in Kenya are the only ones I know with any historical perspective.

In 1949–52 when Brown (1955) began his intensive studies on eagles in the Embu district of Kenya, he located in an area of about 1,200 sq miles (3,100 sq km) eight nesting pairs of peregrines (Brown, *in litt.*).

Most suitable-looking cliffs in the region seemed to house a pair, and the closest pairs were only about 2 miles (3.2 km) apart. This gives a density of one pair per 150 sq miles (389 sq km), a figure which compares quite well with densities in Arctic and subarctic Alaska (Cade, 1960). It would be most worthwhile to know over how wide a range in East Africa densities of this order obtain. Brown's observations indicate that the population of Embu is limited only by the number of suitable nesting cliffs.

Unfortunately, Brown has not been able to revisit all of these eyries in recent years; but three sites checked in August 1965 either had adult birds present or showed definite signs of recent use (Brown, *in litt.*). Brown feels there probably has been no diminution of breeding pairs in Kenya in recent years.

Brown (1961 and pers. comm.) relates one interesting sidelight about a pair of peregrines in Nairobi. For several years a pair occupied a site behind the British coat of arms on the Law Courts, and they were successful in rearing young at least once. After independence, this symbol of former imperialism, along with many similar objects on public buildings, was torn down, and the nesting site of the peregrines was destroyed. Showing the characteristic adaptability of the species, these falcons then moved a block away to take up residence on a piece of modernistic sculpture stuck onto the side of the former Ministry of Works Building, now the Office of the President. But the unyielding concrete of the sculpture provided no suitable place for eggs, and the peregrines finally moved away, although their splashes were still quite visible on the wall below the sculpture when I visited Nairobi in September 1965.

The peregrine has not been studied extensively in South Africa, and very few nesting sites have been reported in the literature. All evidence points to its being a decidedly uncommon falconiform throughout southern Africa. For instance, Rowan (*in litt.*) has seen peregrines only three or four times in 20 years in the Cape, and she did not record the species once in more than 10,000 miles (16,000 km) of roadside counts (Rowan, 1964); but Siegfried (1966) did record one in a series of 1963–64 surveys covering 1,986 miles (3,178 km). I have seen adult peregrines twice in South Africa—once in the Bontebok National Park in June 1964 and once in the Kruger Park along the Pafuri River in October 1965. For South Africa, I have been able to obtain information on the exact locations of only four eyries, one in the northern Transvaal and three in the Cape. Two sites have been reported in South-West Africa. Peregrines may be somewhat commoner in Rhodesia. The South African Ornithological Nest Record Card collection at the Percy FitzPatrick Institute has entries for five nesting sites in the region of the Selondi Range around

Bulawayo, in an area of not more than 1,000 sq miles (2,590 sq km). In southern Africa, peregrines are essentially birds of remote mountainous regions, coastal promontories, and deep river canyons away from the centers of intensive agriculture and human habitation. Their numbers probably have not changed in recent years, but there is no way to know for sure.

PEREGRINE AND LANNER COMPARED

Over most of Africa, exclusive of the tropical forests, the lanner is the common large falcon, averaging somewhat larger than sympatric peregrines. Any consideration of peregrine numbers must take this fact into account. My general impression is that lanner populations compare well with populations of the prairie falcon in the western United States. Like the prairie falcon, the lanner is essentially a bird of arid and semiarid regions, whereas the peregrine occurs in more mesic environments. For instance, lanners do not occur in the well-watered Embu district of Kenya where peregrines are relatively common; but the lanner is the dominant falcon across the Tana River in the more arid Kitui district, where but one pair of peregrines is known to breed (Brown, *in litt.*). Lanners are common through much of southern Africa, especially in the arid western regions, but at least one pair of peregrines has nested along the Fish River of South-West Africa (Maclean, 1960), and another pair has an eyrie near Gobabis, both very dry areas. One wonders to what extent entry by peregrines into marginally suitable arid habitat is restricted by the numerically superior, more desert-adapted populations of lanners.

ROADSIDE STUDIES OF FALCONIFORMS IN SOUTH AFRICA

GENERAL

Research on raptor population ecology is just beginning in South Africa. To my knowledge, there is no published study on a breeding population of any species covering a specified area and spanning a sufficient number of years to determine trends, although breeding data are being accumulated now by the nest-record card system under the auspices of the Percy FitzPatrick Institute of African Ornithology at the University of Cape Town. Also, the Department of Nature Conservation of the Cape Province has become interested in studying raptor populations in connection with its program of rodent-control. Mr. W. R. Siegfried is in charge of this work, which promises to be most informative. In Rhodesia, a very good start has been made in the granitic outcroppings of the Matopos region near Bulawayo, where 38 pairs of black eagles were located in an area of 160 sq miles (400 sq km) during the 1964 breeding season (Vernon, 1965).

Some roadside counts of falconiforms have been made by several workers, and these studies cover a sufficient span of time—about 15 years—and sufficient area to make detailed comparisons worthwhile to see what trends may be revealed. Unfortunately, each worker or group of workers has tended to emphasize rather different aspects of the information that can be obtained from roadside counts of predatory birds. Rudebeck (1963), who conducted the first published counts back in 1950–51, was mainly concerned with the Palaearctic migrants and only reported on information obtained during the period October through March. Rowan (1964) and Siegfried (1966), who have carried out extensive recent counts in the Cape, place their emphasis on the African species, although their work evidently encompasses the entire year. My own studies in 1964 and 1965 were perforce mostly restricted to the austral winter months when Palaearctic migrants are absent.

Even more disconcerting for one who wants to make comparisons, the raw data, which consist of counts of individuals over specified distances of road, get worked up for publication in a variety of ways, so that considerable recasting of the available information has been necessary. For the sake of future students who may be interested in analyzing this type of information, I would like to make a plea that the minimum standard for the presentation of such data be a simple statement of the total miles traveled, the total number of each species seen, and the dates of travel. I have tried to restate all of the available information in this way, using as an index of density, miles per bird, as the basic unit of comparison. The reverse expression, birds per mile, I find awkward to apply to sparse populations like those of raptors, because a fraction of a bird has no biological meaning.

Many other problems attend the use of this kind of information. Speed of travel, time of day, season, weather, patterns of population dispersion, habits of the species, local superabundance of food, attentiveness and training of the observer, are just a few of the variables which may affect the results of this type of counting. In no way can the figures be taken as an expression of actual population density, but they can be used to establish relative differences within a given species for different times and places and—with exercise of judgment—to compare different species.

Only figures obtained from extensive sampling over hundreds or preferably thousands of miles are worth consideration. Even so, in making such comparisons, the critical question is, what constitutes a significant difference between sets of figures? My guess is that about all one can hope to do is establish long-term trends and order-of-magnitude differences between populations.

STUDIES IN THE CAPE

During the Lund University Expedition to South Africa in 1950–51, Rudebeck (1963) counted falconiforms along the roads. The original vegetation in the area covered by his counts was protea-scrub with some grassland, but the whole region has long since gone under intensive and diversified agriculture, except on mountain slopes. I was able to assemble figures for approximately 1,500 miles (2,400 km) of Rudebeck's travel. The most striking feature of his results is the difference in the numbers of resident African species compared to those of the Palaearctic migrants. While the resident species outnumbered the migrants 13 to 6, the migrants constituted by far the bulk of all individuals counted. The lesser kestrel was most numerous, occurring at a density of one bird per 0.19 mile (300 m) and being two or three orders of magnitude above the resident species and an order of magnitude above the next most common migrant, the eastern red-footed falcon, which occurred at a density of one bird per 11 miles (18 km); but this comparison is in part specious. Over 6,000 of these kestrels were seen at one great roost, and there was nothing approaching a uniform dispersion of one bird per 0.19 miles (300 m). Nevertheless, it seems to be generally true that the lesser kestrel is the most abundant falconiform over much of South Africa during the summer.

Even if the lesser kestrel is omitted from consideration, there is still a large difference between the total number of migrants and the total for residents in Rudebeck's counts. This is a consistent finding, which is seen again and again in all surveys conducted in the agricultural regions, whether in the Cape, the Transvaal, Orange Free State, or Natal.

In 1956, Rudebeck (1963) again visited the Cape, traveling 1,974 miles (3,176 km). Fewer species, and a somewhat different complement of species, were seen—perhaps because these counts were not made in exactly the same areas of the Cape as in 1950–51. The average density for 10 resident species was one bird per 39 miles (63 km); for four Palaearctic migrant species, one bird per 6.1 miles (9.8 km). Lesser kestrels averaged one bird per 11 miles (18 km).

The first impression that numbers were way down from 1950–51 results largely from the fact that fewer lesser kestrels were seen. This may only have been fortuitous; apparently Rudebeck did not encounter a large roosting colony on this trip. The number of black-shouldered kites does seem unusually low, one per 116 miles (187 km); more typically this species averages one per 20–50 miles (32–80 km); but the subtotal for all residents, one bird per 39 miles (63 km), cannot be considered significantly different from the figure for the earlier survey, one per 23 miles (37 km). Figures for the common buzzard are quite consistent between the two counts (one per 32 miles or 51 km in 1950–51, one per 20 miles or 32 km in 1956; also, for the resident jackal buzzard, one per 250 miles (402 km) in 1950–51, one per 329 miles (529 km) in 1956. Eagles are consistently sparse in both sets of data, another general finding from all the surveys in agricultural regions.

Table 26.2 summarizes data obtained by Rudebeck (1963) on a trip through the northern Karoo in 1950. His summertime results are compared with figures which G. L. Maclean and I recently obtained from a short winter trip in similar country. The northern Karoo is a very dry area of scattered low shrubs, succulents, and sparse grasses. Nearly all of the region is stock-grazing land with very large holdings for karakul sheep and cattle. The country is reminiscent of the drier parts of New Mexico, Arizona, and Nevada. The important point to note in this table is that there are fewer Palaearctic migrants than residents in the summer count. This reversal of the situation found so universally in the areas of intensive agriculture is emphasized even more in subsequent tables which summarize counts made in wild lands.

The rock kestrel was unusually common, for the northern Cape, along the road north of Upington in July 1965 (Table 26.2). This area had experienced recent rains; the grass was green, flowering plants were blooming in profusion, and insects were abundant, judging by the number collected on the windshield of our Land Rover. In areas subject to prolonged droughts—a condition which obtains over fully two-thirds of southern Africa—there is no question that locally favorable conditions created by rain concentrate some kinds of falconiforms in large numbers, especially insect and rodent eaters. This is true in the croplands of the Transvaal and Orange Free State, as well as in the stock-raising country of the northern Cape and South-West Africa and in the wilder regions of the Kalahari. As examples, between 14 and 17 October 1961, Prozesky (1964) found red-billed quelea flocking to water in the millions around Lake Ngami in Bechuanaland. In one place, 20 tawny eagles were congregated on the dead trunks of trees. Secretary birds, lanners, greater kestrels, yellow-billed kites, black-shouldered kites, tawny eagles, martial eagles, fish eagles, bateleurs, marsh harriers, and marabou storks were all present and feeding on quelea. He counted 64 falconiforms of several species along 40 miles (64 km) of lakeshore, giving an average of one bird per 0.63 mile or 1 km (Prozesky, unpubl.). Similarly, on 16 February 1965 along one 20-mile (32-km) stretch of the Nossob in the Kalahari Gemsbok National Park, G. L. Maclean encountered 24 lanners, which were feeding on swarms of flying termites.

Mrs. Rowan's (1964) data from the central Karoo provide an even more instructive case in point. As shown in her tables, one bird per 12 miles (19 km) was the overall average for resident falconiforms during a 3-year period of counts covering 2,850 miles (4,586 km). The regularly occurring species were: secretary bird, lanner, greater kestrel, rock kestrel, jackal buzzard, and martial eagle. One bird per 10–15 miles (16–24 km) seems to be the usual average for resident species over much of the northern Cape, but large local deviations from this typical range of density can occur, as shown by Rowan's data. In 1961, following 5 years of

Table 26.2. Falconiforms Seen in Cape Province

A. North Karoo 7–19 November 1950; 675 miles (1086 km); data from Rudebeck (1963)

Species	No. seen	Miles/bird	Km/bird
Residents			
Secretary bird	2	338	544
Lanner falcon	9	75	121
Greater kestrel	10	68	109
Black-shouldered kite	9	75	121
Unidentified eagle	1	—	—
Jackal buzzard	2	338	544
Chanting goshawk	5	135	217
African marsh harrier	1	675	1,086
Subtotal	39	17	27
Palaearctic migrants			
Black (yellow-billed) kite[a]	11	61	98
Common buzzard	1	675	1,086
Montagu's harrier	7	96	154
Subtotal	19	35	56
Miscellaneous			
Unidentified kestrels	7	—	—
Unidentified harriers	3	—	—
Total all Species	68	9.9	15.9

[a] Includes some possibly resident yellow-billed individuals.

B. Between Twee Rivieren and Upington, Northern Cape, 23 July 1965; 215 miles (346 km); T. J. Cade and G. L. Maclean

Species	No. seen	Miles/bird	Km/bird
Residents			
Rock kestrel	13	17	27
Pygmy falcon	6	36	58
Black-breasted snake-eagle	1	215	346
Chanting goshawk	2	107	172
Total	22	10	16

unbroken drought in the region from Beaufort West to the Orange River, the average density of falconiforms was only one bird per 63 miles (101 km). Flood rains occurred in March 1961, and by early 1962 conditions had improved to such an extent that the average density of the diurnal raptors had increased to one bird per 5.3 miles (9.5 km). The following year, the population had settled back to a more usual density of one bird per 12 miles (19 km).

On the other hand, drought may actually favor some falconiforms, especially large soaring eagles and vultures which utilize carrion. Many head of game and stock die under such conditions and provide abundant provender for these scavengers. Such a situation existed in the Kruger National Park in September 1965, following several years of unusually low rainfall, and the abundance of carcasses may well account for the large numbers of eagles and vultures seen in October, although the drought had been broken by then. (These October data are presented later in this paper in Table 26.9.)

Rowan (1964) also did counts in the agricultural districts of the southern and western coastal areas of the Cape. The average for all resident species over a 3-year period covering 6,285 miles (10,091 km) was one bird per 13 miles (21 km). During her study in one part of this region, the so-called strandveld along the west coast, gerbils (*Tatera afra*) increased to plague proportions. Particularly in the area south of the Berg River these rodents became such a serious threat to agriculture that an extensive poisoning program with strychnine and, later, with zinc phosphide was initiated. The poisoning campaign did not extend north of the Berg River, although the rodents were numerous in that area also. The data summarized in Rowan's tables show what happened to the birds of prey in these two areas. In the poisoned area there was a progressive decrease in the number of resident falconiforms counted along roads over the 3-year period, but north of the Berg just the reverse happened. Rowan assumed that south of the Berg the raptors had been killed off by eating poisoned rodents. Although direct evidence for this point was not obtained, it would be difficult to explain her quite clear results in any other way. Evidently the poisoning program had little effect on the gerbil population, which reached a peak in 1964 (Siegfried, *in litt.*).

Subsequently Siegfried (1966) has followed up Rowan's work in this same area. His results show that there was a marked recovery in the number of falconiforms in the poisoned area south of the Berg River. This happy result may be associated with the change from strychnine to zinc phosphide, as the latter evidently is not toxic to raptors in the concentrations usually contained in poisoned rodents. But the continued buildup of the gerbil population was probably the main factor.

Table 26.3, from Siegfried, provides a general picture for selected regions of the Cape for the year 1965. Summer densities (one bird per 11

Table 26.3. Falconiforms Seen in the Cape Province in Summer (December-February) and Winter (May-August) in 1964–65; data from W. R. Siegfried (unpubl.)

Region	Season	Distance		Black-should. kite		Kestrels		All raptors	
		miles	km	miles/ bird	km/ bird	miles/ bird	km/ bird	miles/ bird	km/ bird
Southwestern Cape	S	5,859	9,427	49	79	66	106	15	24
	W	3,035	4,883	29	47	74	119	17	28
Southern Cape	S	2,805	4,513	47	75	5	8	3	5
	W	6,430	10,346	42	67	45	72	16	26
Little Karoo	S	552	888	55	89	25	40	11	18
	W	1,125	1,810	36	58	29	46	13	22
Eastern Cape	S	6,860	11,038	140	225	73	117	23	37
	W	8,308	13,368	166	267	56	90	28	44
Transkei	S	2,732	4,396	137	220	31	51	7	11
	W	1,100	1,770	110	177	40	66	17	27
Karoo	S	1,659	2,669	—	—	9	15	8	13
	W	4,183	6,730	—	—	52	84	28	46
Total	S	20,476	32,762	86	138	35	56	11	18
	W	24,181	37,690	77	123	49	78	20	32

miles or 18 km) average about twice as high as winter ones (one bird per 20 miles or 32 km).

STUDIES IN THE TRANSVAAL AND ORANGE FREE STATE

Data summarized in Tables 26.4–26.6 demonstrate that the composition and numbers of diurnal raptor populations in these regions of intensive agriculture and industrialization—in what used to be the highveld, a grassland with unparalleled herds of game and predators—are much the same as in the southern and western Cape. Resident species are uncommon both summer and winter, but Palaearctic migrants occur in large numbers from October to March. At present, the winter population of residents is quite sparse—about one bird per 20 miles (32 km). Again, this condition seems to be associated with a prolonged drought of 5 years' duration which has affected the whole region of the highveld. By contrast, fiscal shrikes are common, averaging one for about 3–4 miles (5–6 km), although not so abundant as in some parts of the Cape, where the bird may average about one per mile (1.6 km) (Rowan, unpubl.) or as in the Transvaal itself in years of good rain before the present drought (Prozesky, unpubl.).

Malherbe (1963) has reported briefly on an instance in the western Transvaal where a rodent plague—in this case involving the multimam-

Table 26.4. Falconiforms Seen in Transvaal and Orange Free State, October to December 1964, January and November 1955, February 1956; 4,365 miles (7,023 km); data from Rudebeck (1963)

Species	No. seen	Miles/bird	Km/bird
Residents			
Secretary bird	11	397	639
Peregrine falcon	2	2,183	3,512
Lanner falcon	12	364	586
Greater kestrel	27	162	261
Rock kestrel	19	229	368
Black-shouldered kite	88	49	79
Black eagle	1	4,365	7,023
Tawny eagle	3	1,455	2,341
Wahlberg's eagle	1	4,365	7,023
Black-breasted snake-eagle	6	728	1,171
Fish eagle	4	1,091	1,755
Bateleur	1	4,365	7,023
Unidentified eagles	14	312	502
Jackal buzzard	3	1,455	2,341
Gabar goshawk	1	4,365	7,023
African marsh harrier	39	112	180
Black harrier	1	4,365	7,023
Banded harrier-hawk	1	4,365	7,023
Osprey	2	2,183	3,512
Subtotal residents	236	18	29
Palaearctic migrants			
Eastern red-footed falcon	55	76	122
Western red-footed falcon	1	4,365	7,023
Undesignated red-footed falcon	8	546	878
Lesser kestrel	3,184	1.4	2.3
Black kite	843	5.2	8.4
Honey buzzard	4	1,091	1,755
Common buzzard	108	40	64
Pallid harrier	7	623	1,002
Montagu's harrier	15	291	468
Subtotal migrants	4,225	1.0	1.6
Miscellaneous raptors			
Lesser or rock kestrel	87	—	—
Falco sp.	81	—	—
Unidentified harriers	16	—	—
Unidentified raptors	3	—	—
Total all species	4,648	0.94	1.5

Table 26.5. Falconiforms (All Resident) Seen in Transvaal and Orange Free State, July and August 1965; 1,709 miles (2,750 km); data from O. P. M. Prozesky and T. J. Cade

Species	No. seen	Miles/bird	Km/bird
Secretary bird	1	1,709	2,750
Greater kestrel	8	214	344
Rock kestrel	13	131	211
Pygmy falcon	3	569	916
Yellow-billed kite	1	1,709	2,750
Black-shouldered kite	44	39	63
Martial eagle	1	1,709	2,750
Jackal buzzard	5	342	550
Lizard buzzard	2	855	1,376
Gabar goshawk	1	1,709	2,750
African marsh harrier	4	427	687
Unidentified eagles	2	—	—
Total	85	20	32.2

mate murid genus *Mastomys*—was associated with increased breeding densities of falconiforms and owls.

By now the reader is probably wondering what has happened to all the magnificent African species of falconiforms that I mentioned earlier. In the agricultural districts the more frequently seen resident species are indeed few in kind and number—mainly black-shouldered kites, rock kestrels, greater kestrels, jackal buzzards, an occasional lanner or martial eagle, and in the west, chanting goshawks.

The depauperate raptor faunas of these domesticated landscapes stand in marked contrast to the rich and abundant associations of predatory birds still to be seen in the wilder regions—in the mountains and in the larger national parks. There are no good counts of raptors in the mountains (but see Rudebeck, 1956, for some information on the lammergeier, in the Drakensberg), so I shall devote the rest of my consideration to the two large national parks of South Africa, the Kruger and the Kalahari Gemsbok.

Birds of prey in Kruger Park—Lying in the northeastern corner of the Transvaal between the Crocodile River in the south and the Limpopo in the north and bounded on its eastern side by Portuguese Mozambique, Kruger National Park is more than 200 miles (322 km) in length and averages close to 40 miles (64 km) wide, giving a total area of 7,340 sq miles (18,922 sq km) of protected land. Its present limits have been established since 1926, but a portion of the area was proclaimed as the Sabi Game Reserve as early as 1898.

The vegetation can be described in general terms as bushveld—most of it quite enclosed and therefore marginal for the existence of open-coun-

Table 26.6. Falconiforms Seen in Transvaal and Natal Provinces

A. Between Pretoria and Pietermaritzburg, 28 January 1956, 392 miles (631 km); data from Rudebeck (1963)

Species	No. seen	Miles/bird	Km/bird
Residents			
Black-shouldered kite	5	78	126
Palaearctic migrants			
Lesser kestrel	45	8.6	13.8
Black kite	2	196	315
Common buzzard	4	98	158
Subtotal migrants	51	7.7	12.4
Miscellaneous species			
Lesser or rock kestrel	15	—	—
Total all species	71	5.5	8.8

B. Between Pretoria and Pietermaritzburg and country around Rosetta, 19–20 August 1965; 510 miles (821 km); T. J. Cade

Species	No. seen	Miles/bird	Km/bird
Residents			
Secretary bird	1	510	821
Lanner falcon	1	510	821
Greater kestrel	4	128	206
Rock kestrel	2	255	410
Yellow-billed kite	1	510	821
Black-shouldered kite	31	17	27
Black-breasted snake-eagle	2	255	410
Jackal buzzard	3	170	274
Unidentified small accipiter	1	510	821
Total	46	11	17.7

try dwellers such as the falcons and harriers, all of which are uncommon or rare in the park. Five main vegetative associations are recognized: (1) large-leaved deciduous bush in the southwestern corner, (2) mixed rooibos veld over most of the western half north just beyond the Olifants River, (3) knobthorn-Marula parkland in the eastern half north to the Olifants, (4) Mopani veld over nearly all of the northern half of the park, except for the northwestern corner where (5) a well-timbered sandveld occurs (Codd, 1951).

Table 26.7 summarizes what is known about the status of falconiforms in Kruger Park. Forty-six species have been recorded, of which 38 are resident African forms and only 8 are Palaearctic migrants. All of the latter are either uncommon and rare or irregular in occurrence. Twenty-

Table 26.7. Status of Falconiforms in the Kruger National Park, South Africa (Based on Pienaar and Prozesky, 1961, and Prozesky, Unpubl.)

Species	Status	Remarks
Secretary bird	R	Uncommon in open bush and savannah; breeds
Peregrine falcon	R	One sight record (Prozesky)
Lanner falcon	R	Uncommon in the limited open country; probably breeds
European hobby	M	One sight record (Cade & Prozesky)
African hobby	R	Very rare
Red-necked falcon	R	Rare
Eastern red-footed falcon	M	Uncommon and irregular in summer
Dickinson's kestrel	R	Rare, in northern parts only
Greater kestrel	R	Rare in the limited open country
Rock kestrel	R	Rare in the limited open country
Lesser kestrel	M	Uncommon and irregular in occurrence
Cape vulture	R	Uncommon; not breeding
White-backed vulture	R	Commonest vulture; breeds
Lappet-faced vulture	R	Uncommon but widespread; breeds
White-headed vulture	R	Uncommon; breeds
Hooded vulture	R	Common; breeds
Egyptian vulture	R	Very rare
Palm-nut vulture	R	Very rare
Black kite	M	Common but sporadic in summer flocks
Yellow-billed kite	R?	Uncommon, not in flocks; probably breeds
Black-shouldered kite	R	Uncommon in limited open country; probably breeds
Cuckoo falcon	R	Uncommon along forest edges
Black eagle	R	Least common of large eagles
Tawny eagle	R	2nd most common large eagle; breeds
Wahlberg's eagle	R[a]	Commonest buteonine; breeds
Long-crested eagle	R	Uncommon and little known in the park
Booted eagle	M	Uncommon and sporadic in summer; sometimes in flocks
African hawk eagle	R	Fairly common breeder
Martial eagle	R	Common; breeds
Crowned eagle	R	Very rare; probably breeds
Brown snake-eagle	R	Common; breeds
Black-breasted snake-eagle	R	Uncommon; probably breeds
Bateleur	R	Commonest large eagle; breeds
Fish eagle	R	Common; breeds
Jackal buzzard	R	Rare; probably not breeding
Common buzzard	M	Rare and irregular in occurrence
Lizard buzzard	R	Common; breeds
Little sparrow hawk	R	Fairly common; breeds
Black goshawk	R	Uncommon; possibly breeds
African goshawk	R	Uncommon; probably breeds

Species	Status	Remarks
Little-banded goshawk	R	Fairly common; breeds
Gabar goshawk	R	Common; breeds
Dark chanting goshawk	R	Uncommon; breeds
Pallid harrier	M	Rare and irregular
Montagu's harrier	M	Rare and irregular
Banded harrier-hawk	R	Uncommon; breeds
Subtotal resident species		38
Subtotal Palaearctic migrant species		8

[a] Research subsequent to the writing of this paper has shown this species to be an African migrant.

two species are known to breed in the park, and at least 6 others probably breed.

Tables 26.8 and 26.9 give some idea of the species and numbers readily seen along the park roads. Eagles predominate. The bateleur is especially common, and during the late morning and late afternoon it is virtually impossible to look into any quarter of the sky without seeing at least one of these superb soarers. Many accipiters and other forest hawks undoubtedly go unnoticed in the dense bush cover. Even in summer, resident species make up the great majority of all individuals seen. With the exceptions of the bateleur and the white-backed vulture, one is impressed by the diversity of species rather than by the abundance of a few ubiquitous forms.

I did not see a single fiscal shrike during my trips through the park in early August and mid-October, 1965, although the species is occasionally reported and is common along roads within a few miles of the southern entrances to the park. The scarcity of fiscal shrikes in the park—like the uncommonness of all 10 species of falcons occurring there—reflects the extremely enclosed nature of the bushveld. Bush shrikes of several species, especially *Eurolestes melanoleucus* and *Eurocephalus anguitimens,* are common; but in this dense brushy country, the abundant lilac-breasted roller appears to occupy a food-niche much like that of the fiscal shrike in the more open parklands and agricultural districts.

Birds of prey in the Kalahari Gemsbok Park —The Gemsbok Park occupies a portion of the southern Kalahari in a corner formed by the political boundaries of Bechuanaland (now Botswana), the Cape Province, and South-West Africa. From Twee Rivieren at the south entrance to Union's End on the Bechuanaland side in the north, the distance is about 180 miles (290 km) and the total area of the park proper is 3,650 sq miles (9,453 sq km); but at present there is a buffer zone set off in Bechuana-

Table 26.8. Falconiforms Seen in Kruger Park

A. North to Satara, 28–31 March and 16–20 December 1959; 20–28 November 1960; 734 miles (1,181 km); data from O. P. M. Prozesky (unpubl.)

Species	No. seen	Miles/bird	Km/bird
Residents			
Secretary bird	2	367	591
Yellow-billed kite[a]	2	367	591
Black-shouldered kite	1	734	1,181
Tawny eagle	9	82	132
Wahlberg's eagle	4	184	296
African hawk eagle	2	367	591
Martial eagle	3	245	394
Brown snake-eagle	3	245	394
Bateleur	25	29	47
Little sparrow hawk	6	122	196
Little-banded goshawk	3	245	394
Gabar goshawk	4	184	296
Dark chanting goshawk	3	245	394
Subtotal residents	67	11	17.7
Palaearctic migrants			
Common buzzard	3	245	394
Total all species	70	10	16.1

[a] Possibly migrant individuals.

B. Resident species; from Numbi Gate to Punda Milia, 3–7 August 1965, 470 miles (756 km); T. J. Cade

Species	No. seen	Miles/bird	Km/bird
Dickinson's kestrel	1	470	756
Tawny eagle	4	118	190
Black eagle	1	470	756
Martial eagle	3	157	253
Brown snake-eagle	3	157	253
Bateleur	32	15	24
Fish eagle	8	60	97
Unidentified eagles	8	60	97
Little-banded goshawk	1	470	756
Unidentified small accipiter	1	470	756
Gabar goshawk	1	470	756
Dark chanting goshawk	1	470	756
Lizard buzzard	1	470	756
Banded harrier-hawk	1	470	756
Total	66	7.1	11.4

Table 26.9. Falconiforms Seen in Kruger National Park from Numbi Gate to Punda Milia, 19–26 October 1965, 829 miles (1,327 km); T. J. Cade, O. P. M. Prozesky, L. I. Greenwald

Species	No. seen	Miles/bird	Km/bird
Residents			
Secretary bird	2	415	664
Peregrine falcon	1	829	1,327
Rock kestrel	5	166	265
White-backed vulture	523	1.6	2.5
Lappet-faced vulture	47	18	28
White-headed vulture	16	52	83
Hooded vulture	10	83	133
Unidentified vultures	11	—	—
Yellow-billed kite[a]	33	25	40
Black-shouldered kite	2	415	664
Tawny eagle	56	15	24
Wahlberg's eagle	65	13	20
African hawk eagle	11	75	121
Martial eagle	16	52	83
Brown snake-eagle	15	55	88
Bateleur	147	5.6	9.0
Fish eagle	4	207	332
Unidentified eagles	11	—	—
Jackal buzzard	1	829	1,327
Lizard buzzard	1	829	1,327
Little sparrow hawk	1	829	1,327
Little-banded goshawk	2	415	664
Unidentified small accipiters	4	207	332
Gabar goshawk	1	829	1,327
Dark chanting goshawk	12	69	111
Banded harrier-hawk	1	829	1,327
Subtotal without vultures	391	2.1	3.4
Migrants			
Black kite	10	83	133
Miscellaneous			
Milvus sp.	1	—	—
Unidentified hawks	2	—	—
Total all species, excluding vultures	404	2.0	3.3

[a] Possibly includes some migrant individuals.

land, making the total protected area 8,050 sq miles (20,850 sq km). Hopefully the status of this zone will not be jeopardized now that Bechuanaland has received full independence. The park has been in existence since 1931.

In contrast to the diversity of vegetative types in the Kruger, the Kalahari shows a sameness, characteristic of arid lands, over vast stretches. The predominating landform is sandveld—fixed dunes of bright red sand covered with open stands of low thornbush, with such suggestive names as *Acacia detinens* and *A. haematoxylin,* interspersed with sparse shrubs and bunch grasses, which become green only after the infrequent and sporadic rains. After a rain, flowering plants sprout up and bloom in profusion, and for a short period life is abundant in the dunes. During drought the scenery in the dunes is extremely dreary, and one can travel many miles without seeing a single bird.

The uniformity of the sandveld is relieved occasionally by dry river beds, which support open woodlands, mostly camelthorn acacia (*A. giraffe*). In the park, the Auob and Nossob rivers provide such habitats. The birds of prey tend to be concentrated along these riparian woodlands, because the trees offer suitable perching, roosting, and nesting places; consequently, roadside counts along the river beds probably give a somewhat biased impression of the overall numbers in the Kalahari. Greater kestrels, chanting goshawks, and secretary birds are widespread through the dunes, at least during favorable periods after rain, but the latter usually return to the river habitat to roost. Isolated patches of camelthorn or boscia provide opportunities for some tree-associated raptors to remain indefinitely away from the river drainages.

Table 26.10 summarizes what is known about the status of falconiforms in the Kalahari Gemsbok Park. Thirty-two species have been re-

Table 26.10. Status of Falconiforms in the Kalahari Gemsbok National Park, Republic of South Africa (Based on de Villiers, 1958; Prozesky and Haagner, 1962; G. L. Maclean and T. J. Cade, Unpubl.)

Species	Status	Remarks
Secretary bird	R	Common along river beds; "pair or single every 10 miles" (de Villiers); breeds
Peregrine falcon	R	Rare and irregular; not breeding
Lanner falcon	R	Most common large falcon; breeds
Hobby (*F. subbuteo* or *cuvieri*)	?	Seen once; questionable
Red-necked falcon	R	Uncommon but regular along Auob; probably breeds
Greater kestrel	R	Fairly common in open areas, especially dunes; breeds
Rock kestrel	R	Fairly common along river beds; probably breeds
Pygmy falcon	R	Common where sociable weaver nests occur; breeds
White-backed vulture	R	Commonest vulture; breeds

Species	Status	Remarks
Lappet-faced vulture	R	Widespread; not uncommon; about ¼ in numbers of above; breeds
White-headed vulture	R	Rare; status uncertain
Hooded vulture	R	Rare; status uncertain
Palm-nut vulture	R	Rare and irregular; only questionable sight records
Black kite	M	Occasional flocks seen; irregular in occurrence
Yellow-billed kite	R	Occasional individuals seen; status uncertain
Black-shouldered kite	R	Rare in northern sectors only
Tawny eagle	R	Commonest large eagle; breeds in tall trees along river beds
Wahlberg's eagle	R	Uncommon; status uncertain
Booted eagle	M	Very rare; one seen
African hawk eagle	R	Two seen along upper Nossob
Martial eagle	R	3rd most common eagle; breeds in tall trees along river beds
Brown snake-eagle	R	Rare in northern sectors
Black-breasted snake-eagle	R	Uncommon but widespread; probably breeds
Bateleur	R	2nd most common eagle; breeds in tall trees along river beds
Jackal buzzard	R	Rare and irregular in occurrence
Ovampo sparrow hawk	R	One record
Little sparrow hawk	R	One record
Gabar goshawk	R	The common small accipiter along river beds; breeds
Chanting goshawk	R	Commonest medium-sized hawk; breeds
Pallid harrier	M	Rare and irregular
Black harrier	R	Rare and irregular
Montagu's harrier	M	Rare and irregular
Subtotal resident species		27
Subtotal Palaearctic migrant species		4

ported, 27 resident African forms, 4 Palaearctic migrants, and 1 questionable sight record of a hobby. Eleven species are known to breed, and at least 3 others probably do.

Tables 26.11 to 26.13 summarize counts made mainly along the Auob and Nossob river beds. The density indices derived from these counts indicate rather higher numbers of falconiforms than in most other areas —with one exception (Table 26.9)—where similar surveys have been made in South Africa, including Kruger Park. One bird per 2–4 miles (3–6 km) is quite usual. Even taking into account the concentrating effect of the riverine vegetation on the birds of prey, I am still inclined to feel that actual numbers are greater in the Kalahari.

Be that as it may, there is no doubt that both the Kruger and the Kalahari Gemsbok parks provide protected and undisturbed habitats for two of the richest and most impressive assemblages of raptorial birds in all of Africa. The importance of these parks for the preservation of bird life, especially for the preservation of the large birds of prey, is not sufficiently appreciated even in South Africa, where the main concern is for game mammals and carnivores.

Again, as in the Kruger, the Palaearctic migrants are decidedly rare in the Kalahari, and it is the resident African species which are conspicu-

Table 26.11. Falconiforms (All Resident) Seen in the Kalahari Gemsbok Park

A. Along the Auob and Nossob Rivers, 24–27 April 1960; 350 miles (563 km); O. P. M. Prozesky (unpubl.)

Species	No. seen	Miles/bird	Km/bird
Secretary bird	7	50	80
Lanner falcon	1	350	563
Greater kestrel	2	175	282
Rock kestrel	17	21	34
Tawny eagle	2	175	282
Martial eagle	5	70	113
Bateleur	6	58	93
Jackal buzzard	3	117	188
Chanting goshawk	8	44	71
Gabar goshawk	1	350	563
Total	52	6.7	10.8

B. Along the Upper Auob and Nossob Rivers and across the dunes between Mata Mata and Union's End, and from Dikbaardskalk to the Auob, 20 August to 1 September 1964; 339 miles (545 km); data from Cade, Willoughby, and Prozesky

Species	No. seen	Miles/bird	Km/bird
Secretary bird	1	339	545
Lanner falcon	1	339	545
Red-necked falcon	6	57	92
Greater kestrel	15	23	37
Rock kestrel	4	85	137
Pygmy falcon	8	42	68
Tawny eagle	8	42	68
Martial eagle	8	42	68
Bateleur	6	57	92
Chanting goshawk	46	7.4	11.9
Gabar goshawk	10	34	55
Total	113	3.0	4.8

Table 26.12. Falconiforms Observed Up and Down the Nossob River, Kalahari Gemsbok Park, December 1964 and February 1965; 720 Miles (1,158 km); Data from G. L. Maclean (Unpubl.)

Species	No. seen	Miles/bird	Km/bird
Residents			
Secretary bird	54	13	21
Lanner falcon	46	16	26
Greater kestrel	1	720	1,158
Rock kestrel	5	144	232
Pygmy falcon	19	38	61
Yellow-billed kite	2	360	58
Black-shouldered kite	3	240	386
Tawny eagle	52	14	23
Martial eagle	3	240	386
Brown snake-eagle	1	720	1,158
Black-breasted snake-eagle	4	180	290
Bateleur	64	11	18
Gabar goshawk	8	90	145
Chanting goshawk	56	13	21
Subtotal residents	318	2.3	3.7
Palaearctic migrants			
Black kite	2	360	579
Pallid harrier	3	240	386
Montagu's harrier	1	720	1,158
Subtotal migrants	6	120	193
Total all species	324	2.2	3.5

ous. The most ubiquitous and characteristic species is the chanting goshawk, which is widespread through the dunes as well as along the river beds. Another common resident is the pygmy falcon, which occurs as a breeding bird wherever nests of sociable weavers are found. Secretary birds, lanners, greater kestrels, tawny eagles, and bateleurs are all common.

GENERAL DISCUSSION AND CONCLUSIONS

PALAEARCTIC MIGRANTS AND RESIDENT AFRICAN SPECIES COMPARED

The most obvious conclusion from the data summarized above has to do with the marked difference in the numbers and distribution of Palaearctic migrants as compared to resident African falconiforms. It should be remembered that the Eurasian land mass is very much larger than Africa and that almost the whole of its migrant populations of falconiforms moves into Africa to winter mostly south of the Sahara. In

Table 26.13. Falconiforms Seen Up and Down a 25-mile Sector above Twee Rivieren; Data from G. L. MacLean (Unpubl.)

A. On 44 days between October 1964 and March 1965; 2,200 miles (3,540 km)

Species	No. seen	Miles/bird	Km/bird
Residents			
Secretary bird	79	28	45
Lanner falcon	4	550	885
Red-necked falcon	4	550	885
Greater kestrel	11	200	322
Rock kestrel	18	122	196
Pygmy falcon	152	14	23
Yellow-billed kite	4	550	885
Tawny eagle	44	50	80
Martial eagle	16	138	222
Black-breasted snake-eagle	28	79	127
Bateleur	11	200	322
Gabar goshawk	9	233	375
Chanting goshawk	84	26	42
Subtotal residents	464	4.7	7.6
Palaearctic migrants			
Black kite	24	92	148
Pallid harrier	2	1,100	1,770
Montagu's harrier	3	733	1,179
Subtotal migrants	29	76	122
Total all species	493	4.3	6.9

B. On 39 days from April through August 1965; 1,950 miles (3,138 km)

Species	No. seen	Miles/bird	Km/bird
Residents			
Secretary bird	54	36	58
Lanner falcon	4	488	785
Red-necked falcon	1	1,950	3,138
Greater kestrel	24	81	130
Rock kestrel	29	67	108
Pygmy falcon	88	22	35
Tawny eagle	39	50	80
Martial eagle	2	975	1,569
Black-breasted snake-eagle	4	488	785
Bateleur	9	217	349
Gabar goshawk	22	89	143
Chanting goshawk	69	28	45
Total	345	5.7	9.2

South Africa, the Palaearctic migrants predominate in the agricultural regions during the austral summer, whereas resident species are relatively uncommon in such landscapes both summer and winter. The lesser kestrel is by far the most abundant Palaearctic migrant, and the black-shouldered kite is the most widespread and common resident hawk on agricultural lands (except in the Cape, where the rock kestrel is more common); but the migrant kestrel population differs by one or two orders of magnitude in roadside density from the populations of these two commonest resident species.

The resident African falconiforms are mainly distributed in the mountains—such as the Drakensberg—and in the less disturbed regions of bushveld and sandveld. In these regions they far outnumber Palaearctic migrants in summer, and in protected areas such as the Kruger and Kalahari parks rich assemblages of the original raptor fauna still occur in southern Africa. The same is also true of the national parks in East Africa.

One naturally wonders to what extent this interesting distributional separation in the relative numbers of Palaearctic migrants and residents is the result of changes brought about by intensive agriculture. In the Transvaal and Orange Free State, agricultural practices have probably had little influence. The croplands of these provinces occupy what used to be the open grasslands and peripheral parklands of the highveld, which were just the sorts of biotopes with which most of the Palaearctic migrants are associated on their breeding grounds in the Northern Hemisphere. Agricultural practices have created more landscape of a parkland character—fields surrounded by tree plantations—but the general aspect of the region has not changed so much, except around the large urban areas. What the situation may have been like in preagricultural times for resident falconiforms in the highveld is problematical. Secretary birds, lanners, greater kestrels, and some of the large eagles and vultures—exploiters of carrion—were probably more common than now; but I suspect there may always have been voids in raptor niches left by the resident species in the grasslands. These niches were mainly seasonal and dependent upon a high production of prey species in the summer, so that the Palaearctic migrants could annually move in to occupy them in large numbers on a short-term basis. A similar kind of explanation has been advanced to account for the fact that woodland passerine migrants from the Palaearctic spend their African sojourn almost exclusively in savannah or other open country rather than in forest, which would seem to be their more natural preference (Moreau, 1952; Morel and Bourlière, 1962). As a matter of fact, this regimen of the Palaearctic migrants may be disintegrating as more and more grassland is brought under cultivation and more intensive artificial controls are exercised against the insects and rodents which form the bulk of the migrants' food.

The situation seems to be somewhat different in the Cape. Agricultural practices there may have created favorable habitat for Palaearctic migrants where none had existed before by opening up the protea-scrub vegetation. For instance, the lesser kestrel has extended its range from the highveld and eastern grassveld to the southern Cape in recent times (Gill, 1942). At the same time, resident species have probably been reduced, with the likely exception of the black-shouldered kite.

The dispersion of the Palaearctic migrants themselves on the African continent shows some adjustment among species with partly overlapping and slightly competitive niches. In his discussion of Palaearctic migrant falconiforms in Africa, Rudebeck (1963) calls attention to an example among the small falcons. The European hobby, although formerly occurring as far south as the Cape, is rare in South Africa but is still common in Northern Rhodesia (Zambia). The eastern red-footed falcon (*Falco amurensis)* is a common migrant in Nyasaland (Malawi) and the Rhodesias; and large numbers also occur in the Transvaal and eastern Cape, but it is not as common in the latter areas as the lesser kestrel. The main concentration of western red-footed falcons (*F. vespertinus*) occurs more to the north and west of the center of abundance of its close relative *amurensis*. *Vespertinus* is much less common than *amurensis* in South Africa, but the reverse is true in South-West Africa. The lesser kestrel is widespread and very abundant in the highveld of South Africa and in the eastern grassveld of Natal and the eastern Cape, and it has spread into the southwestern Cape in recent times. Migrant individuals of the European kestrel occur as far south as Nyasaland (Malawi), but there are no reliable records for South Africa. Thus, while these five species of small falcons overlap broadly in their African distributions, each has a geographic area of maximum density which is distinct from the others.

POPULATION TRENDS IN AFRICAN SPECIES

There appears to have been no major and irreversible decline in the numbers of resident falconiforms in South Africa over the past 15 years, as far as can be judged by the roadside counts summarized in this paper. Individuals of some species are locally persecuted by farmers, but it is doubtful that shooting has had much effect on any species. Even the martial eagle and the black eagle, which are perhaps most often singled out as enemies of domestic stock, hold their own in fairly well settled stock-raising areas (Siegfried, 1963). The same is apparently true of the less obvious forest-inhabiting crowned eagle in the eastern Cape and Natal (Siegfried, *in litt.*). Drastic, local or regional reductions in numbers of several years' duration are best associated with drought conditions, which are often prolonged in southern Africa. On the other hand, local, short-term superabundance of falconiforms also occurs—usually following rains which affect vegetation and, secondarily, the prey populations on which raptors feed. Continued and ever-accelerating human destruction of natural habitats, as discussed below, is the most serious factor in the reduction of overall numbers of resident African species.

The lammergeier appears to be the only species in southern Africa in serious need of special measures for its preservation at the present time. The last stronghold of this species in southern Africa is in the Drakensberg, especially in Basutoland (now Lesotho). It is also worth noting that the Egyptian vulture, which once enjoyed a very wide distribution in southern Africa, has virtually disappeared from South Africa; but I doubt that human influence has been responsible in this case.

POPULATION TRENDS IN MIGRANT SPECIES

Although Rudebeck's (1963) data for 1950–51 and 1954–56 provide some basis for an assessment, there is not yet enough current information from the agricultural districts to make meaningful comparisons. In the highveld, the general impression in recent years has been one of rela tive scarcity for species such as the lesser kestrel, the red-footed falcons, the common buzzard, and especially the harriers *Circus macrourus* and *C. pygargus* (Prozesky, pers. comm.). A decline in the latter two species has also been noted in Kenya (L. Brown, *in litt.*). Whether this reduction in the numbers of Palaearctic migrants on the highveld is associated with the prolonged drought referred to above or to factors operating on the breeding grounds in Eurasia is open to question. It will be most important to find out what happens when the drought is broken in the highveld.

FALCONIFORMS AND HUMAN LAND USES IN SOUTH AFRICA

Since this conference is primarily concerned with the relationship between the use of pesticidal poisons and the shocking population decline of the peregrine and of certain other species at the ends of long food-chains, in Europe and North America, it is appropriate to consider briefly how pesticides are used in South Africa. As in most other highly industrialized nations, DDT was brought into commercial production in South Africa soon after World War II. Apparently a very large surplus of chloride gas manufactured during the war years provided the initial profit motive for this enterprise.

DDT and many other chlorinated hydrocarbons and organophosphorus poisons are now widely used in South Africa. The following constitute the major control programs in which these materials are involved: (1) control of a wide variety of insect pests on croplands, especially on citrus, garden vegetable, and grain plantings, with DDT and related compounds; (2) aerial spraying with DDT over bushveld for tsetse fly control, chiefly in Zululand; (3) locust control with malathion and related phosphorus compounds; (4) quelea control by aerial spraying of roosts and nesting colonies with parathion; (5) rodent control; and most recently (6) harvester termite control in the Orange Free State with massive applications of dieldrin. For the time being, at least, the locust and tsetse programs appear to have brought these pests under satisfactory control, but very little attention has been given to the effects any of these poisoning campaigns have had on other forms of life, including predatory birds.

If I perhaps sounded an optimistic note in an earlier section where I said there appeared to have been no irreversible downward trends in diurnal raptor populations over the past 15 years in South Africa, I hasten to add that caution should be exercised in accepting this generalization for all species. The very fact that drought conditions coupled with sudden, heavy rains produce such large fluctuations in the numbers of falconiforms over much of southern Africa would tend to obscure the effects of any long-continuing action of a more subtle sort—such as the accumulation of persistent residues of pesticides in the biosphere and their concentration up the various trophic levels. Moreover, our sad experience with peregrines, bald eagles, ospreys, and some other birds of prey in North America and Europe teaches us that certain species are much more vulnerable than others to pesticidal contamination of the environment. In particular, birds of prey at the ends of long food-chains—such as fish-eaters and bird-eaters—are the ones which require critical watching. In South Africa this means, among others, the fish eagle, the peregrine, the lanner, and all of the accipiters, especially the larger species such as *Accipiter tachiro* and *A. melanoleucus*. Intensive, long-term studies on *breeding* populations of some of these symptomatic species are badly needed in South Africa to serve as a monitoring system for environmental contamination in yet another country where, if it has not already done so, the enthusiastic and unbridled use of pesticides could quickly reach dangerous proportions for some species of wildlife.

Although our present major concern for the birds of prey centers on the excessive and inadequately controlled use of pesticidal poisons, in the long run it will be the less insidious and more direct consequences of human occupation of the land that will require our attention. The inexorable changes wrought on the landscape by an ever-increasing human population are all too clearly evident on the African continent. Within its vast distances, there is a great variety of environments—from the bleak but far from lifeless deserts of the Sahara and the coastal Namib in South-West Africa to the lush, tropical forests of the Congo Basin. These environments still support an outstanding array of floras and faunas, beautifully portrayed in Leslie Brown's (1965) new book on the natural history of Africa; but, alas, this richness and diversity of life are rapidly degenerating into the prosaic, uniform, and uninspiring landscapes of intensive agriculture and industrialization. Traveling up the length of the continent by air, one is never out of sight of a road, a cut-over forest, a plot of cultivated ground, or some other sign of human habitation and alteration of the natural scene. "Wildest Africa" is but a wistful memory, to be evoked only by a reading of the narratives and journals of the early explorers, naturalists, game hunters, and voortrekkers. With a human population presently estimated around 280 million and a projected figure of 768 million by the year 2000 (Armitage, 1965), these changes are indeed inevitable, and the present deterioration of the natural scenery can only be expected to worsen in the decades ahead.

In South Africa, I have rated four major categories of human land use according to their impact on birds of prey. First, there are the native reserves—extremely bleak and depressing landscapes—which are badly overgrazed by livestock and overcut for firewood, where sheet and gully erosion have frequently reached irreparable proportions. As an example, the interested reader can consult Cowles (1959) for a chronicle of what has happened to Zululand during one man's lifetime. Crows and kites are the only birds usually seen on these reserves.

Secondly, there are the croplands and industrial wastelands, such as occur around large mining operations. A few species of falconiforms, mostly migrants, hold up well in these areas, and some (black-shouldered kite?) may even have increased in numbers above preagricultural times; but for the most part the raptor fauna of these lands is rather poor in variety and will probably become more so.

The stock-raising lands—mostly in arid or semiarid regions of the western Transvaal, the northern Cape, and in South-West Africa—offer a somewhat brighter prospect. Here the natural vegetation has been less disturbed, and the predatory birds probably occur about in their original numbers and variety. But only a few species are really common in these xerophytic regions.

Finally, there are the protected lands—the game reserves and the national parks. A sample of Africa's former natural splendor may still be witnessed and studied in the larger of these units. South Africa is indeed fortunate to have had political leaders, like Paul Kruger, with the desire and foresight to establish its parks, which are a matter of national pride and which are well managed for maximum "wildness" consistent with public use (for a detailed history of the parks and of nature conservation in South Africa see van der Merwe [1962]). But even larger tracts of land, on the order of 10,000 sq miles (25,900 sq km) or more, should be set aside while there is still time to preserve remnants of natural environments—especially segments of mountain country, grassland, and seacoast.

One of the more unfortunate recommendations of the "Odendaal report" on South-West Africa is that which would turn over the western portion of the Etosha Game Reserve—the largest in the world—for use as a "homeland" for one of the African tribes (see Bigalke, 1964). Surely there is a better solution for both blacks and whites. Responsible government officials, backed by a concerned public, must see to the preservation of these precious scraps of untrampled ground, which will be the last refuges for many of the great predatory birds that once hunted in such grand profusion over all of Africa.

ACKNOWLEDGMENTS

Some of the counts made by G. L. Maclean, O. P. M. Prozesky, E. J. Willoughby, and T. J. Cade were done in connection with field work supported by a grant from the US Public Health Service, ES 00008 (Environmental Health). We thank the National Parks Board, Republic of South Africa, for permission and encouragement to work in the Kruger and Kalahari parks. This paper was written during the tenure of a Senior Postdoctoral Fellowship from the National Science Foundation.

I am much indebted to L. Brown, M. K. Rowan, and W. R. Siegfried for permission to use their unpublished data as freely as I have, but more especially for their critical and constructive reading of the original manuscript.

SUMMARY

African populations of the peregrine falcon are widely distributed on the continent but are mostly quite sparse. The best studied situation is in the Embu District of Kenya, where 8 eyries of *F. p. minor* are known in an area of about 1,200 sq miles (1,900 sq km). There appears to have been little change in this population since the eyries were first discovered by L. Brown in 1949–52. The lanner falcon may be an important factor in determining the distribution and abundance of the peregrine in some marginally suitable arid parts of the latter's range. The North African population of *pelegrinoides* is exceptional among peregrines in showing a high degree of specialization for desert existence; and together with *babylonicus* of the Near East—and possibly also with *F. fasciinucha*—it may form a separate species from *F. peregrinus*.

Sixty-two species of falconiforms occur in southern Africa. Fifty of these are Ethiopian, and 12 are Palaearctic migrants, present only during the austral summer. Since 1950, roadside counts of falconiforms, covering more than 100,000 miles, have been conducted in South Africa. From these counts, the following conclusions have been reached.

1. In the austral summer, Palaearctic migrants far outnumber resident African falconiforms in many areas. The migrants occur chiefly in the agricultural regions, whereas resident species are rather uncommon in such landscapes summer and winter. Resident African falconiforms are mainly distributed in the mountains and in the less disturbed regions of bushveld and sandveld. In these regions they far outnumber the Palaearctic migrants in summer. Thus, there tends to be a distributional segregation between Palaearctic migrants and resident species.

2. The roadside counts, which cover a span of 15 years, reveal no major, irreversible decline in the numbers of resident falconiforms in South Africa. Local and regional reductions in numbers, on a short-term basis, are best associated with drought. Destruction of natural habitats by man is the most important factor in the overall reduction in numbers of resident African species. The lammergeier appears to be the only falconiform in need of special measures for its preservation in southern Africa at the present time.

3. Present indications are that there has been a widespread reduction in the numbers of Palaearctic migrants in recent years, especially in the highveld, which has always been a region where migrant falconiforms concentrated. Whether this apparent change in numbers is the result of the prolonged drought—the worst in South African history—which still gripped the land in late 1965, or to factors operating on the breeding grounds in Eurasia, is a question yet to be settled.

DDT was brought into commercial production in South Africa soon after World War II. Many chlorinated hydrocarbons and organophosphorous poisons are now widely used in South Africa. Intensive, long-term studies on breeding populations of falconiforms at the ends of long food-chains are needed in South Africa to provide a monitoring system for biotic contamination by pesticides in yet another country where enthusiasm outstrips caution in the use of these poisons.

In the long run it will be the more direct consequences of human occupation of the land that will require our attention in behalf of the birds of prey. We must look to the preservation of the larger national parks and game reserves as the last refuges for many of the predatory birds in Africa. The larger these areas are the better from the standpoint of continued self-perpetuation of raptor populations.

LITERATURE CITED

Armitage, J. [ed.] 1965. Britannica book of the year. Encyclopaedia Britannica, London. p. 539.

Bigalke, R. C. 1964. The Odendaal report and wild life in South West Africa. African Wild Life, 18:181–188.

Brown, L. [H.] 1955. Eagles. Michael Joseph, London. 274 p.

———. 1961. The peregrine falcon comes to town. Country Life, 1 June 1961:1280–1281.

———. 1965. Africa: A natural history. Random House, New York. 299 p.

Cade, T. J. 1960. Ecology of the peregrine and gyrfalcon populations in Alaska. Univ. Calif. Pub. Zool., 63(3):151–290.

Codd, L. E. W. 1951. Trees and shrubs of the Kruger National Park. Gov't. Printer, Pretoria. Dep. Agr. Bot. Surv. Mem., 26:3–192.

Cowles R. B. 1959. Zulu journal; Field notes of a naturalist in South Africa. Univ. Calif. Press, Berkeley. 267 p.

Gill, E. L. 1942. Some annotations to Dr. Roberts's "Birds of South Africa." Ostrich, 13:64–69.

Mackworth-Praed, C. W., and C. H. B. Grant. 1962. Birds of the southern third of Africa, Vol. 1. Longmans, Green and Co., London and New York. 688 p.

McLachlan, G. R., and R. Liversidge. 1957. Roberts' birds of South Africa. Cape Times Limited, Cape Town. 504 p.

Maclean, G. L. 1960. Records from southern South-West Africa. Ostrich, 31:49–63.

Malherbe, A. P. 1963. Notes on birds of prey and some others at Boshoek north of Rustenburg during a rodent plague. Ostrich, 34:95–96.

Meinertzhagen, R. 1954. Birds of Arabia. Oliver and Boyd, London. 624 p.

Merwe, N. J. van der. 1962. The position of nature conservation in South Africa. Koedoe, 5:1–122.

Moreau, R. E. 1952. The place of Africa in the Palaearctic migration system. J. Anim. Ecol., 21(2):250–271.

Morel, G., and F. Bourlière. 1962. Relations écologiques des avifaunes sédentaire et migratrice dans une savane sahélienne du bas Sénégal. La Terre et la Vie, 109(4):371–393.

Pienaar, U. de V., and O. P. M. Prozesky. 1961. An amended check-list of the birds of the Kruger National Park. Koedoe, 4:117–140.

Prozesky, O. P. M. 1964. Comprehensive bird concentration at Lake Ngami. African Wild Life, 18(2):137–142.

———, and C. Haagner. 1962. A check-list of the birds of the Kalahari Gemsbok Park. Koedoe, 5:171–182.

Rowan, M. K. 1964. Relative abundance of raptorial birds in the Cape Province. Ostrich, 35(3):224–227.

Rudebeck, G. 1956. Observations on the bearded vulture *(Gypaetus barbatus)* in South Africa, with notes on its behaviour and field characters, p. 406–415. *In* Bertil Hanström, Per Brinck, and Gustaf Rudebeck [eds.], South African animal life; results of the Lund University Expedition in 1950–51. Almquist and Wiksell, Stockholm. Vol. 4. 508 p.

———. 1963. Studies on some Palaearctic and Arctic birds in their winter quarters in South Africa. 4. Birds of prey (Falconiformes), p. 418–453. *In* Bertil Hanström, Per Brinck, and Gustaf Rudebeck [eds.], South African animal life; results of the Lund University Expedition in 1950–51. Almquist and Wiksell, Stockholm. Vol. 9. 516 p.

Siegfried, W. R. 1963. A preliminary report on black and martial eagles in the Laingsburg and Philipstown Divisions. Dep. Nat. Conserv. Prov. Admin., Cape of Good Hope. Investigational Report no. 5:5–15.

———. 1966. Relative abundance of raptorial birds in the South-western Cape. Ostrich, 37(1):42–44.

Vaurie Charles. 1961. Systematic notes on Palaearctic birds. No. 44. Falconidae: The genus *Falco* (Part I, *Falco peregrinus* and *Falco pelegrinoides*). Amer. Mus. Novitates, 2035. 19 p.

Vernon, C. J. 1965. The 1964 black eagle survey in the Matopos, Rhodesia. Arnoldia, Misc. Publ. Nat. Mus. Southern Rhodesia, 2(6):1–9.

Villiers, J. S. de. 1958. A report on the bird life of the Kalahari Gemsbok National Park. Koedoe, 1:143–161.

CHAPTER 27

HAWK MOUNTAIN COUNTS AS POPULATION INDICES IN NORTHEASTERN AMERICA

Walter R. Spofford

Counts of migrating raptors, particularly where the birds are regularly concentrated by favorable geographic features, furnish information reflecting the year-to-year status of populations of hawk species using particular flyways. Moreau (1953) and Nisbet and Smout (1957) have commented upon the decrease in some raptors crossing the Bosphorus not only since the account of Belon (1555) but also in recent decades.

In North America, substantial hawk migrations have been observed along the Atlantic coast (Allen and Peterson, 1936; Barbour and Munroe, 1908; Ferguson and Ferguson, 1922; Trowbridge, 1895); along the Appalachian Mountains (Behrend, 1951; Broun, 1935, 1939; Heintzelman, 1963; Poole, 1934; Pough, 1932); and variously throughout the Great Lakes region (Haugh and Cade, 1966; Hofslund, 1954, 1966; Mueller and Berger, 1961; Pettingill, 1962; Spofford, 1960; Tyrrell, 1934; Wood, 1910). Farther west, great numbers of Swainson's hawks move south across the great plains in autumn (Cruickshank, 1937; Fox, 1956) where they become further concentrated in their annual passage to and from South America (Griscom, 1932:155; Skutch, 1945).

THE HAWK MOUNTAIN OBSERVATIONS

At Hawk Mountain Sanctuary, Kempton, Pennsylvania, annual records of the autumn flight have been kept since 1934 with the exception of the war years 1942–44. The figures of flight numbers upon which the graphs illustrating the present paper have been made are to be found in Broun (1949) for the years 1934–48 and in the annual "News Letter to Members" of the Hawk Mountain Sanctuary Association for subsequent years.

Hawk Mountain Sanctuary is located in eastern Pennsylvania on one of the more southern of the long Appalachian ridges extending generally southwesterly from southern New York State into Maryland, Virginia, North Carolina, and Tennessee. Cross winds against the long ridges cause extensive updrafts favorable for protracted migratory flight. Eagles and hawks ride these "obstructional" air currents for long distances with a minimum expenditure of energy. Usually from 10,000 to 20,000 hawks of 15 species pass along this flyway each autumn, as hawks breeding in eastern Canada and the New England states migrate to more southern wintering grounds.

The graphs prepared from the published Hawk Mountain figures to illustrate this account are better understood with the following qualifications in mind. The numbers of hawks passing each day, and the seasonal total, vary greatly with the weather (Broun, 1963). Most favorable is a strong northwest wind following a temperature drop north and east of the flyway (Broun, 1949). A large number of good flight days results in a high seasonal total, while long periods of windless weather produce small or lowered yearly counts. Thus the yearly figures vary in what appears to be a haphazard fashion (Fig. 27.1).

Again, the various species pass the Lookout at Hawk Mountain at somewhat different periods during the protracted autumnal flight: The broad-winged hawk, bald eagle, osprey, and the American kestrel pass chiefly in September, whereas the sharp-shinned hawk, red-tailed hawk, golden eagle, and common harrier (or marsh hawk) pass later, chiefly in October and early November. It appears that good flight weather in one part of the season and not in another will shift the species percentages in the total count for a given year.

The source of the migrating hawks is a most important consideration. Species with substantial populations breeding in the forests of eastern Canada, such as the sharp-shinned hawk and the broad-winged hawk, pass by in considerable numbers, while other species whose ranges do not extend as far northward, such as the Cooper's hawk and the red-shouldered hawk, are poorly represented. Most merlins and peregrine falcons are coastal migrants, with only a few passing Hawk Mountain. There is no species for which Hawk Mountain figures constitute an index of more than a small part of its continental population, although the figures for the golden eagle are probably a significant part of the remnant eastern North American population of this species.

POPULATION TRENDS

It is clear from an examination of the plots of the yearly figures that some species show a pronounced downward trend; others show no remarkable change over the years; and still others, a small to a considerable increase in numbers.

Although the broad-winged hawk is found throughout much of the suitably wooded parts of eastern America, it breeds extensively in forested eastern Canada, furnishing an autumnal flight of spectacular proportions which may be observed at various vantage points throughout the Appalachians and which passes eventually through Central America. In good flight years over 10,000 may pass Hawk Mountain within a few days. It is clear that the plot of annual numbers (Fig. 27.1) shows no decline over the years and, in fact, some increase. At a similar time, over 50,000 have been counted passing southwesterly along the northern shores of Lake Erie in Canada. Shown in the same figure (27.1) is the annual count of the goshawk, a species that displays occasional irruptive migratory movements lacking a discernible long-time trend.

In contrast are the sharp-shinned hawk (Fig. 27.2) and the Cooper's hawk (Fig 27.3), each of which shows a continued decline remarkably similar in pattern despite the fact that the former is measured in thousands and the latter in hundreds. In each figure the dotted line is a running 5-year average that shows clearly the overall trend without the yearly fluctuation.

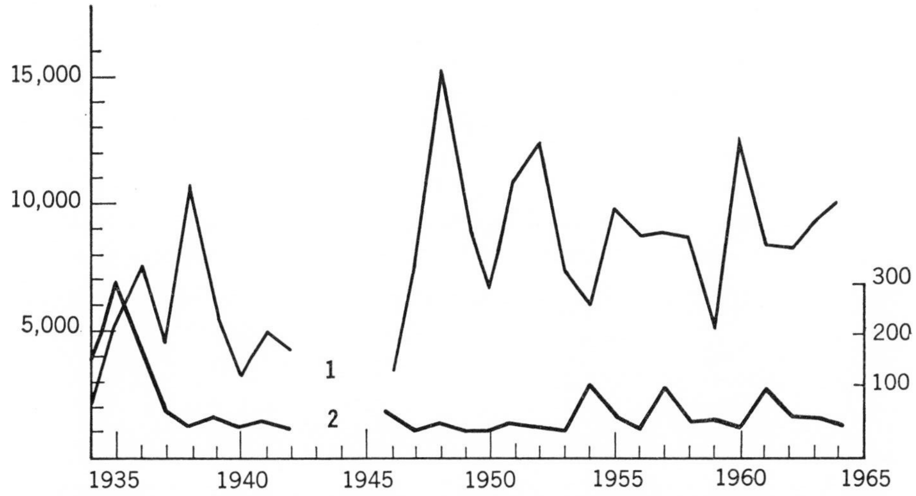

Fig. 27.1. Numbers of (1) broad-winged hawks (in thousands); (2) goshawks (in hundreds) observed each year at Hawk Mountain, Pennsylvania. UW Cartographic Lab.

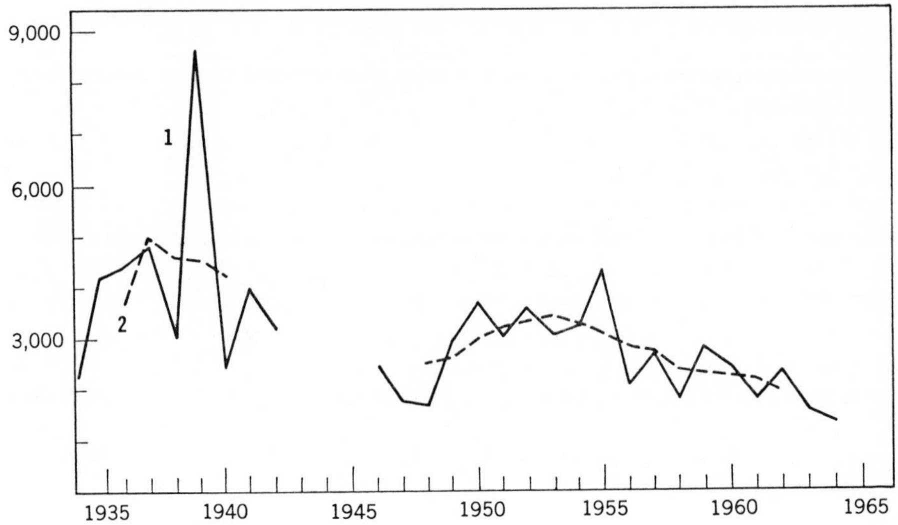

Fig. 27.2. Sharp-shinned hawks observed at Hawk Mountain: (1) actual numbers; (2) 5-year moving average plotted at successive midpoints. UW Cartographic Lab.

Fig. 27.3 Cooper's hawks observed at Hawk Mountain: (1) actual numbers; (2) 5-year moving average plotted at successive midpoints. UW Cartographic Lab.

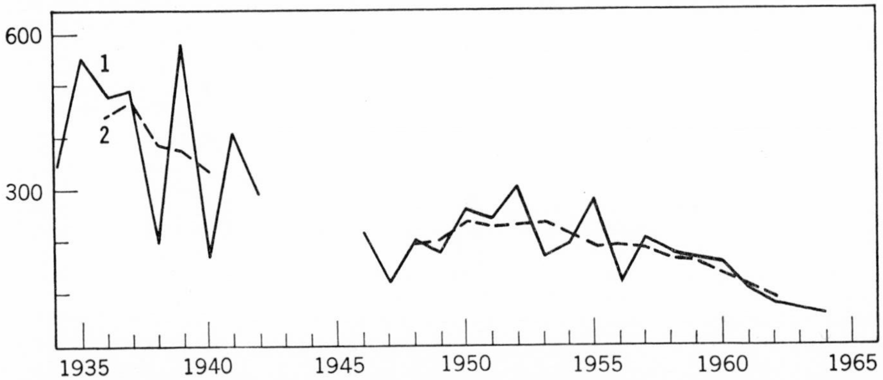

The red-tailed hawk is remarkably widespread over most of North America, occurring in greatly varied habitats from boreal forest to dry desert terrain. The flight figures for a northeastern part of this population (Fig. 27.4) show no continued trend, but it is clear that the numbers after World War II are considerably fewer, dropping from roughly 4,000 to about 2,500 in the last two decades.

Contrary to the preceding, several quite unrelated hawks show a slight to a marked upward trend (Figs. 27.5, 27.6, and 27.7). Most interesting is the osprey, a species whose coastal populations (Connecticut, New Jer-

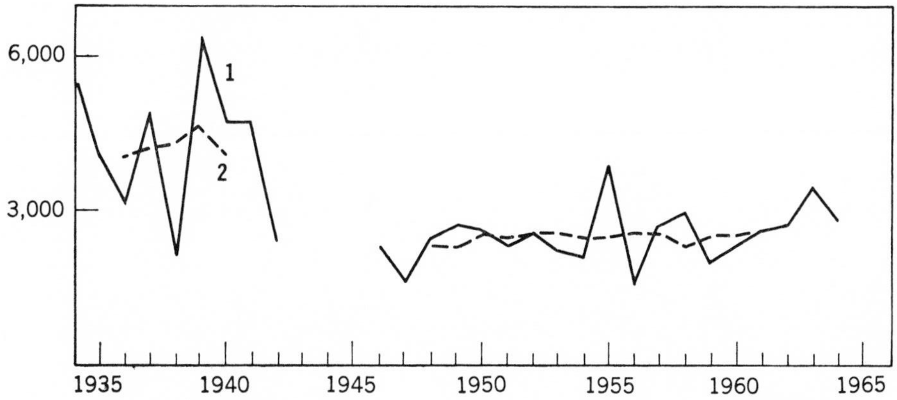

Fig. 27.4. Red-tailed hawks observed at Hawk Mountain: (1) actual numbers; (2) 5-year moving average plotted at successive midpoints. UW Cartographic Lab.

Fig. 27.5. Numbers of (1) American kestrels, (2) ospreys observed at Hawk Mountain. UW Cartographic Lab.

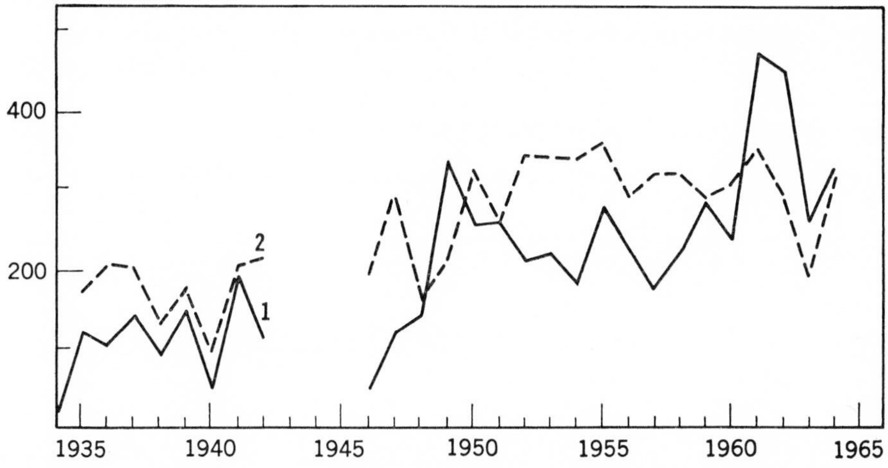

sey, New York) seem to be disappearing. The population passing Hawk Mountain probably is from eastern Canada, for the most part, with some from Maine and the Adirondack Mountains. Since 1950, there has been a remarkable increase in the Hawk Mountain flight, appearing to reverse the downward trend of ospreys from farther south reported by others at this conference. The case of the common harrier is also of interest, for while some of the population in the northern United States appears to be declining, the Hawk Mountain figures show some slight increase. The major breeding area of this species is north of the United States.

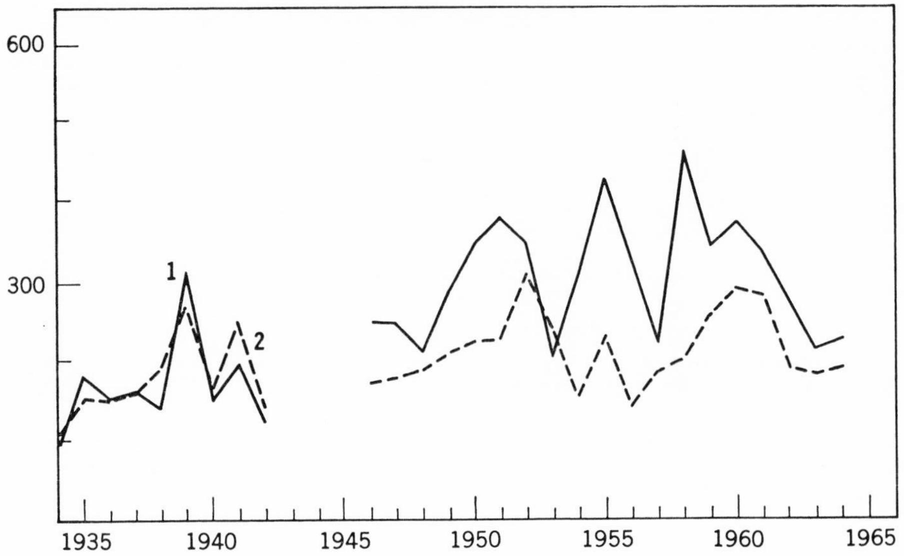

Fig. 27.6. Numbers of (1) red-shouldered hawks, (2) common harriers (marsh hawks) observed at Hawk Mountain. UW Cartographic Lab.

Fig. 27.7. Five-year moving averages plotted at successive midpoints for (1) red-shouldered hawk, (2) osprey, (3) American kestrel, (4) common harrier (marsh hawk) observed at Hawk Mountain. UW Cartographic Lab.

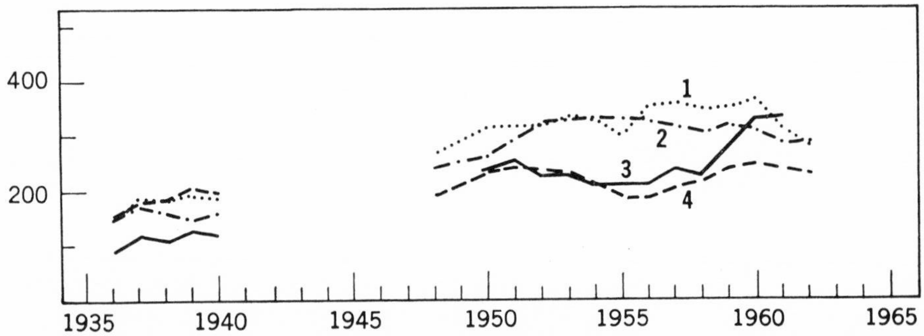

As a breeding species, the red-shouldered hawk is largely located in eastern North America south of Canada. It is widely believed to be decreasing in highly developed areas, but the small group passing Hawk Mountain seems actually to be increasing. I believe some of this apparent increase to be due to better field recognition of this species which, without careful inspection of each bird, may have been overlooked among migrating red-tails. The American kestrel also shows a marked upturn in numbers passing Hawk Mountain (Figs. 27.5 and 27.7).

Three final species to be considered are the golden eagle, bald eagle, and peregrine falcon. Each of these shows a decline in numbers (Figs. 27.8 and 27.9). The migration of peregrines through Hawk Mountain is of a very small group, but this shows loss in numbers of a population that may be northern Appalachian in origin. There is no evidence here of passage of any of the large Arctic population, parts of which are known to migrate along the Atlantic coast.

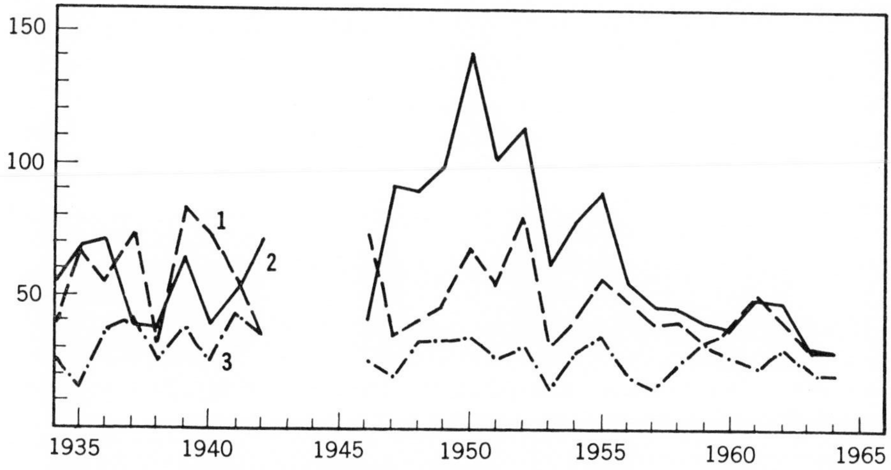

Fig. 27.8. Numbers of (1) golden eagles, (2) bald eagles, (3) peregrines observed at Hawk Mountain. UW Cartographic Lab.

Fig. 27.9. Five-year moving averages plotted at successive midpoints for (1) golden eagle, (2) bald eagle, (3) peregrine observed at Hawk Mountain. UW Cartographic Lab.

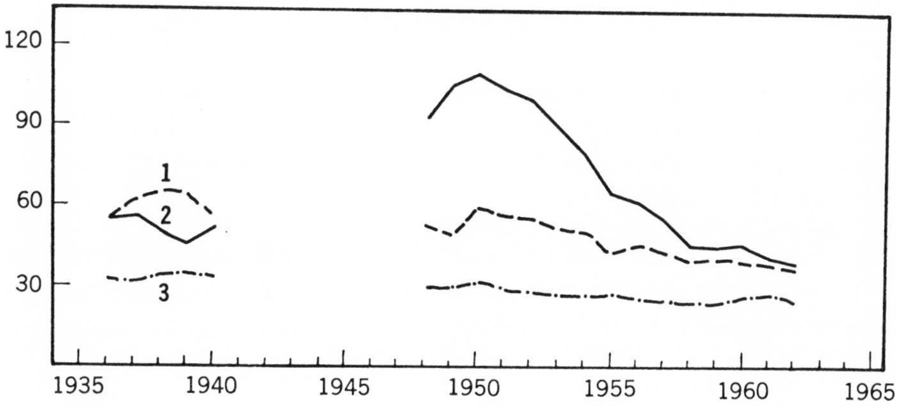

The golden eagles probably are, for the most part, from a formerly more extensive population in eastern Canada. The continuous decline in this flight does not show any indication of a possible recovery from heavy losses during wolf poisoning in the Canadian provinces half a century ago (Baillie, 1958). The bald eagle showed a surprising increase in the years following the war, but this was followed by precipitous decline after the high of 1950. It is generally believed that the source of this eagle flight is birds from the Florida population that move north after breeding in early spring, to summer in New York State, New England, and eastern Canada (Broley, 1947, 1952). These birds return southward in August and September to resume breeding in Florida in November and December. The decline in this migratory population closely parallels the account of the nesting failure in much of Florida (Broley, 1958), but we have no explanation for the marked increase in this flight noted soon after the years 1942–45.

GENERAL COMMENTS

It is clear that the Hawk Mountain indices do not show any general decline in all raptors for the populations concerned. They do show a remarkable and continuous decline in the two smaller accipitrine hawks, and it should be noted here that the food-chains of these species are much like those of the peregrine falcon, that is, they involve small and somewhat larger birds. The failure to find a large decline in the osprey may well be due to the fact that this population is from a northern region as yet not heavily contaminated by environmental pollution.

It is unfortunate that we do not have an observational post in Central America monitoring the whole continental population of broad-winged and Swainson's hawks that pass through this narrow region.

SUMMARY

Five-year running averages of raptors reported each fall migrating in eastern Pennsylvania revealed increased numbers of broad-winged hawks, ospreys, American kestrels, and (to a slight extent) common harriers, since the counts started in 1934. There was no discernible trend in goshawks. Sharp-shinned and Cooper's hawks, bald and golden eagles, and peregrine falcons were all reported in much reduced numbers in recent years. Some of these populations, like the peregrine, come from the northern Appalachian regions; others, from eastern Canada.

LITERATURE CITED

Allen, R. P., and R. T. Peterson. 1936. The hawk migrations at Cape May Point, New Jersey. Auk, 53(4):393–404.

Baillie, J. L. 1958. Six old yet new Ontario breeding birds. Ontario Field Biol., 12:1–7.

Barbour, R., and K. Munroe. 1908. A large migration of hawks. Auk, 25(1):82–84.

Behrend, F. 1951. Fall migrations of hawks in 1951. Migrant, 22(4):53–57.

Belon, P. 1555. L'histoire de la natvre des oyseavx, avec levrs descriptions, & naïfs portraicts . . . . Paris. 28+381 p.

Broley, C. L. 1947. Migration and nesting of Florida bald eagles. Wilson Bull., 59(1):3–20.

———. 1958. The plight of the American bald eagle. Audubon Mag., 60(4):162–163, 171.

Broley, M. J. 1952. Eagle man. Pellegrini and Cudahy, New York. 210 p.

Broun, M. 1935. The hawk migration during the fall of 1934, along the Kittatinny Ridge in Pennsylvania. Auk 52(3):233–248.

———. 1939. Fall migrations of hawks at Hawk Mountain, Pennsylvania, 1934–1938. Auk, 56(4):429–441.

———. 1949. Hawks aloft: The story of Hawk Mountain. Dodd Mead, New York. 222 p.

———. 1963. Hawk migrations and the weather. Hawk Mountain Sanctuary Ass., Kempton, Pa. 12 p.

Cruickshank, A. D. 1937. A Swainson's hawk migration. Auk, 54(3):385.

Ferguson, A. L., and H. L. Ferguson. 1922. The fall migration of hawks as observed at Fishers Island, N.Y. Auk, 39(4):488–496.

Fox, R. P. 1956. Large Swainson's hawk flight in south Texas. Auk, 73(2):281–282.

Griscom, L. 1932. The distribution of bird-life in Guatemala. . . . Bull. Am. Mus. Nat. Hist., 64:1–439.

Haugh, J. R., and T. J. Cade. 1966. The spring hawk migration around the southeastern shore of Lake Ontario. Wilson Bull., 78(1):88–110.

Heintzelman, D. 1963. Bake Oven hawk flights. Atlantic Nat., 18(3):154–158.

Hofslund, P. B. 1954. The hawk pass at Duluth, Minnesota. Wilson Bull., 66(3):224.

———. 1966. Hawk migration over the western tip of Lake Superior. Wilson Bull., 78(1):79–87.

Moreau, R. E. 1953. Migration in the Mediterranean area. Ibis, 95(2):329–364.

Mueller, H. C., and D. D. Berger. 1961. Weather and fall migration of hawks at Cedar Grove, Wisconsin. Wilson Bull., 73(2):171–192.

Nisbet, I. C. T., and T. C. Smout. 1957. Autumn observations on the Bosphorus and Dardanelles. Ibis, 99(3):483–499.

Pettingill, [O.] S. [Jr.] 1962. Hawk migrations around the Great Lakes. Audubon Mag., 64(1):44–45, 49.

Poole, E. L. 1934. The hawk migration along the Kittatinny Ridge in Pennsylvania. Auk, 51(1):17–20.

Pough, R. H. 1932. Wholesale killing of hawks in Pennsylvania. Bird-Lore, 34(6):429–430.

Skutch, A. F. 1945. The migration of Swainson's and broad-winged hawks through Costa Rica. Northwest Sci., 19(4):80–89.

Spofford, W. R. 1960. Hawks over New York. N.Y. State Conservationist, 15(2):14–15.

Trowbridge, C. C. 1895. Hawk flights in Connecticut. Auk, 12(3):259–270.
Tyrrell, W. B. 1934. Bird notes from Whitefish Point, Michigan. Auk, 51(1):21–26.
Wood, N. A. 1910. Bird migration at Point Pelee, Ontario, in the fall of 1909. Wilson Bull., 22(2):63–78.

CHAPTER 28

BRIEF REPORTS: THE STATUS OF THE OSPREY

Population Trends of Ospreys in the Northeastern United States

Roger T. Peterson

In 1954 my family and I moved to Connecticut. We chose Old Lyme because of the many ospreys nesting on the lower reaches of the Connecticut River, near that town. I estimated that there were roughly 150 nests within a 10-mile radius of our home. Some were living in wild, undisturbed areas; others were right in the town, even on telegraph and private poles. In fact the attitude toward the osprey was very much like that of Europeans toward their storks: no persecution whatsoever. There has not been for a generation or two.

I paid the ospreys little attention at first, but in the second summer when I investigated the concentration of nests on Great Island I was puzzled. I looked over the marsh and wondered why there were no young on the nests. The nesting season had been a failure. So was the next year. We found that some of the birds incubated to no avail for 60 and 70 days. The normal incubation of osprey eggs is 30 to 32 days. It was about this time that Peter L. Ames, then a Yale graduate student in ornithology, began his work on the Connecticut River ospreys (Ames, 1961, 1966; Ames and Mersereau, 1964). We cooperated with him.

There were about 20 active nests on Great Island when the studies started. One season this colony fledged six young; the next year three; and the following year one. Ospreys lay three eggs, and normal success should have been close to two young per active nest, perhaps 35 to 40 young normally fledging out of 20 nests.

In 1936 the normal rate of nestling production in ospreys was about 2.3 young per pair per year according to Tyrrell (1936) in the Chesapeake Bay area. Wilcox on Long Island in the early 1940's found an average of 2.2 young per active nest, but in the 4 years from 1960 to 1963, for which I have Ames and Mersereau's (1964) figures, 157 nestings in our area produced 36 young birds, an average of only 0.29 young per nesting, about one-seventh or one-eighth of the norm. A similar drop in reproduction was noted in the Long Island nests by Leroy Wilcox (pers. comm.).

There was erratic behavior. Some ospreys on Great Island were nesting on the ground, in fact on nests without sticks. I saw one nest one year where the eggs were an inch or two under water at normal high tide. And yet the adult bird attempted to brood this clutch. There were some eggs that disappeared in a most puzzling way. It was suggested that the raccoons (*Procyon lotor*) perhaps were a factor. In fact a raccoon was flushed from one eyrie; so we then, in 1960, erected 21 raccoon-proof poles to get the birds off the marsh, off the duck blinds, and onto poles with platforms and sheathed with metal. Most of the birds readily adopted these new sites. The productivity percentages remained the same, however, about 10–15% of the norm. Finally several eggs were chemically analyzed. One chick that had fallen from the nest was analyzed also, as well as samples of fish taken from the nests.

Without proper replacement of young birds the colony has been shrinking. Here are some of the statistics: in 1938, according to John B. Chadwick (pers. comm.), there were 200 nests in the area. My own estimate when we moved there in 1954 was 150 nests. In 1960, by a very precise count, we found that the colony had dropped to 71 nests in which only seven young were raised. By 1961 there were 31 nests and 12 young were raised; in 1962 there were 31 nests, and eight young were raised; in 1963 at 24 nests, nine young were raised; in 1964 at 17 nests, six young were raised. In 1965 at 13 nests, two young were raised. This is about a 33% a year drop, and I think we can predict by the ensuing curve (Fig. 28.1) that the last nesting pair of ospreys will be found in Connecticut in 1973.

The main factor contributing to the decrease of this population has been failure of a high percentage of the eggs to hatch. Nestling losses were small. The seven eggs analyzed for the presence of DDT compounds contained a 35- to 100-ppm (fresh weight) concentration of DDT and its metabolites per egg. And the 5-day-old nestling killed by a fall from the nest contained about 15.9 ppm of DDT and its metabolites. Samples of

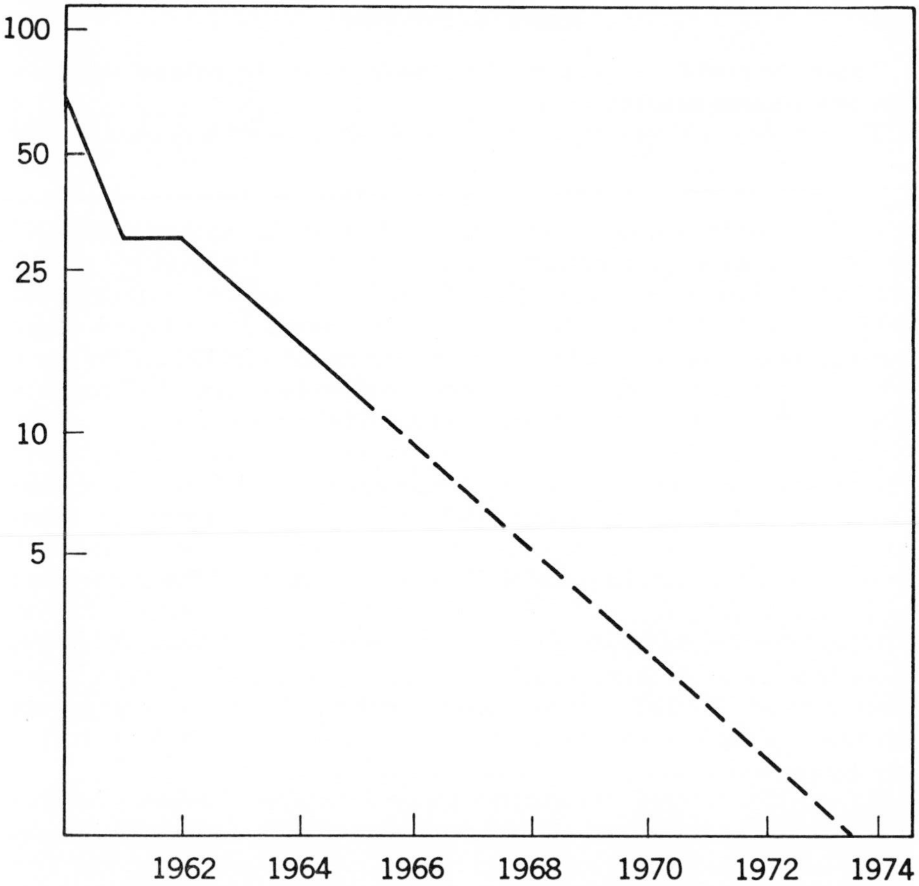

Fig. 28.1. Number of active osprey nests along the Connecticut River. If the rate of decline in 1962–65 remains constant, the last pair to nest should do so in 1973. UW Cartographic Lab.

fish taken at the nest had varying degrees of contamination up to 7.4 ppm.

To quote remarks I have published elsewhere (Peterson, 1965): "There is not much spraying in Old Lyme, but many towns upriver spray. There is undoubtedly airdrift and runoff. We cannot confine these poisons as long as wind blows, water flows or fishes swim. Where we are likely to get the magnification effect [Hunt and Bischoff, 1960] is in the estuarine waters at the mouths of rivers. Traces of poison ingested by little fish upriver—either in the runoff or through poisoned insects—make them easier prey for larger fish. Numbers of affected fingerlings compound their poison in their predators, and it is the large fish that is wobbly, swimming near the surface, that is most likely to be caught by the osprey, which transfers the accumulated poisons to its own tissues."

Hence we might say that what normally would be natural selection has now become unnatural selection.

The ospreys in Connecticut are not the only ones of this species that are in trouble. Very briefly, I will give you some of the others. In New Jersey, there has been a 95% decline since 1960. In 1950 Herbert Mills *(in litt.)* recorded an incomplete total of 253 nests in southern New Jersey with the largest concentration at or near Cape May. Today one cannot find an active nest in Cape May. There still is one strong, though declining, colony at Avalon, New Jersey. On eastern Long Island, there were about 200 pairs in 1945; there are now about 5 in 1965. Gardiner's Island, the most famous colony in our country, had about 300 pairs in 1945 and about 20 pairs in 1965. I will return to that again.

Rhode Island has had a 60% decline in 20 years; Massachusetts and Maine, an 80% decline in 10 years. I have one letter to J. J. Hickey from Leroy Wilcox who perhaps has banded more ospreys than any man in the world, even more than Sten Osterloth of Sweden who has banded 880. Over the years Wilcox has banded 1,340 ospreys on or off the eastern end of Long Island, mostly on Gardiner's Island. He writes (August 1965): "In 1941 there were about 500 nests on eastern Long Island. Today not more than 25 or 30 nests produce young. At Orient State Park, there were formerly 35 nests but now only 1 nest is left, and no young were produced in the last 3 years. There are so few young hatching now that the decline will become even more apparent in the next 10 years."

At one time Wilcox thought the range extension of nesting herring gulls on Gardiner's Island might have had something to do with this decline because the herring gulls would sometimes mob an osprey. But now he is apparently changing his mind. He further writes: "I have no proof that the decline is due to pesticides, but that is my guess. There has been a 90% decline in the black-crowned night herons of the eastern half of Long Island, for probably the same reason. I banded 180 ospreys in 1941, but doubt if I could band over 10 young (in 1965) in the very same area."

SUMMARY

A catastrophic decline of the nesting osprey population on the Atlantic coast has been taking place from New Jersey north to Maine. In Connecticut, the mean rate of annual decline has been 30% in recent years, and extirpation of this population by 1974 is expected. The hatching failure for 185 eggs was 81% in one study area, and this is taken to be the mechanism producing the decline. The failure appears to be brought about by accumulating residues of DDT and its metabolites in the birds' eggs.

LITERATURE CITED

Ames, P. L. 1961. Preliminary report on a colony of ospreys. Atlantic Naturalist, 16(1):26–33.

———. 1966. DDT residues in the eggs of the osprey in the north-eastern United States and their relation to nesting success. J. Appl. Ecol., 3(Suppl.):87-97.

———, and G. S. Mersereau. 1964. Some factors in the decline of the osprey in Connecticut. Auk, 81(2):173–185.

Hunt, E. G., and A. I. Bischoff. 1960. Inimical effects on wildlife of periodic DDD applications to Clear Lake. Calif. Fish and Game, 46(1):91–106.

Peterson, R. T. 1965. Introduction, p. ix. *In* Witmer Stone, Bird studies at Old Cape May. Dover Publications, New York. 2 vol.

Tyrrell, W. B. 1936. The ospreys of Smith's Point, Virginia. Auk, 53(3):261–268.

Ospreys in the Chesapeake Bay Area

William H. Stickel

I would like to expand a little on the situation in southern New Jersey mentioned by Peterson. F. C. Schmid did a great deal of banding in New Jersey in the late 1930's. He had about 25 active osprey nests in nine localities in southern Cape May County. Schmid returned in 1963 and could locate only seven nests. Not one of these was active. Where he had banded about 53 young each year in the late 1930's, he could not find a single young osprey in 1963. The Avalon, NJ, colony was still active in 1963, but Joseph A. Jacobs reported that construction of a road through Avalon Island probably would destroy that colony.

The picture is far brighter in the Chesapeake Bay area. Ospreys are nesting successfully on many offshore duck blinds and other objects in the tidal Potomac. They are relatively abundant on the east side of the Bay in Talbot County. There they have been studied for 3 years by Jan Reese. He found 87 active nests in the county in 1964. Fifty-five young were fledged from the 63 active nests that he studied. This was 0.9 bird per nest. The number fledged per nest with eggs was 0.98. The number fledged per nest with young was 1.6. A major cause of loss was removal of nests from buoys.

Ospreys appear to be common and to be holding up well in the Chesapeake Bay area, but actual population trends are not known. Reese's work may fill this need for an important part of the area. Certainly it merits support on a continuing basis.

The Status of the Osprey in Michigan in 1965

Sergej Postupalsky

When I began my study, very little was actually known about the osprey in Michigan. A check of the literature and the files of the University of Michigan Museum of Zoology revealed less than 30 nest records prior to 1960. During the years 1961 to 1964 I located a number of osprey nests incidental to my investigations of the bald eagle in Michigan. By 1964 I knew of 58 occupied nests in the state. The somewhat incomplete data that I had indicated that nest success was rather low, but no definite population decline could be noticed from the information at hand. In 1965, financial assistance from the National Audubon Society made a more thorough study possible; but despite a greater effort, only 51 occupied osprey nests were found.

With respect to the size of the population in Michigan, I can say that there are probably fewer than 30 pairs in the Lower Peninsula, and in the Upper Peninsula I now know of 27 occupied nests, but there undoubtedly are others not yet discovered. The Upper Peninsula is quite undeveloped in some parts, and the human population is also low; so we can expect more birds up there. Despite the incompleteness of this survey, I believe that I have a representative sample of the osprey population since I have wilderness nests as well as nests in developed areas on my list.

In Michigan, osprey nests are in the northern two-thirds of the state, in other words in the Upper Peninsula and the northern Lower Peninsula. The nest success, unfortunately, is very low. For 50 nests for which the nesting outcome is known (Table 28.1), only 11 (22%) were successful in raising young. The total number of young raised was only 18.

Table 28.1. Reproduction in Michigan Ospreys, 1965

	Osprey				Bald Eagle (Michigan) 1965[b]
	Upper Peninsula	Lower Peninsula	Michigan totals	Virginia 1934[a]	
Number of occupied nests	27	24	51	51	84
Number of occupied nests with known outcome	26	24	50	47	80
Number of productive nests	6	5	11	37	30
Number of young raised	9	9	18	75	39
Percentage of occupied nests productive	23.1	20.8	22.0	78.7	37.5
Young per productive nest	1.50	1.80	1.60	2.04	1.30
Young per occupied nest with known outcome	0.35	0.38	0.36	1.60	0.49

[a] Adapted from Tyrrell, 1936.
[b] Postupalsky, unpubl.

Therefore the young per successful nest was 1.60 as against the 2 or 2.3 that has been mentioned (Tyrrell, 1936; Ames and Mersereau, 1964) in what is considered a normal situation; and the number of young per occupied nest was only 0.4.

One thing that I have been able to determine is that the nest success is equally low in both peninsulas—in the highly developed Lower as well as the less developed Upper Peninsula. Also my data indicated that there was no significant difference in nest success between the accessible or exposed sites and the more isolated wilderness sites. In Michigan, ospreys nest primarily in two different types of habitat; one involves large artificial impoundments or floodings such as the one in Wisconsin described by Berger and Mueller (Chapter 28); and the other habitat type is in deep conifer swamps where the birds nest on top of dead stubs or on pine ridges within the swamps.

The ospreys are failing even in the inland western Upper Peninsula, an area where the bald eagle is doing fairly well. The 22% nest success in the osprey in Michigan compares with a success of between 30 and 42% in the bald eagle over the last few years in the same region.

This lower production is due to high egg losses or the failure of eggs to hatch. Nestling losses are small. Compared with the bald eagle, the lower production in ospreys is really not surprising if pesticides are the factor involved. The osprey feeds almost exclusively on fish, which are known to be highly contaminated in some areas (Burdick *et al.*, 1964; Mack *et al.*, 1964; Hickey *et al.*, 1966); and due to the osprey's migratory habit, it appears to have more opportunity to pick up contaminated food during migration to its winter quarters. Bald eagles will, however, feed on nonfish foods on many occasions (Oberholser, 1906; Broley, 1947; Imler and Kalmbach, 1955; Hancock, 1964). My data indicate that human disturbances, although they may be significant locally, are not a major factor on a state-wide basis.

In summary, low nesting success is leading to a population decrease of ospreys in Michigan. Of 56 nests that I knew to be occupied in 1964, 15 were found in 1965 to be unoccupied. This indicates a decline of some 27%. Observations over several successive years are needed to see if this decline persists. More study is needed in some of the neighboring areas like Wisconsin, Minnesota, and Ontario to see what the osprey populations are doing there.

ADDENDUM, 1968

Reproductive success in Michigan ospreys continues at greatly reduced levels. In 1966 only nine (18%) out of 50 occupied nests produced a total of only 15 young. There was some improvement in 1967 when of 62 occupied nests 17 (27%) were productive, and 30 young were raised.

LITERATURE CITED

Ames, P. L., and G. S. Mersereau. 1964. Some factors in the decline of the osprey in Connecticut. Auk, 81(2):173–185.

Broley, C. 1947. Migration and nesting of Florida bald eagles. Wilson Bull., 59(1):3–20.

Burdick, G. E., E. J. Harris, H. J. Dean, T. M. Walker, Jack Skea, and David Colby. 1964. The accumulation of DDT in lake trout and the effect on reproduction. Trans. Amer. Fisheries Soc., 93(2):127–136.

Hancock, David. 1964. Bald eagles wintering in the southern Gulf islands, British Columbia. Wilson Bull., 76(2):111–120.

Hickey, J. J., J. A. Keith, and F. B. Coon. 1966. An exploration of pesticides in a Lake Michigan ecosystem. J. Appl. Ecol., 3(Suppl.):141–154.

Imler, R. H., and E. R. Kalmbach. 1955. The bald eagle and its economic status. Fish and Wildl. Serv., U.S. Dep. Interior, Cir. 30. 51 p.

Mack, G. L., S. M. Corcoran, S. D. Gibbs, W. H. Gutenmann, J. A. Reckahn, and D. J. Lisk. 1964. The DDT content of some fishes and surface waters of New York State. N.Y. Fish and Game J., 11(2):148–153.

Oberholser, H. C. 1906. The North American eagles and their economic relations. U.S. Dep. Agr. Biol. Surv. Bull. No. 27. 31 p.

Tyrrell, W. B. 1936. The ospreys of Smith's Point, Virginia. Auk, 53(3):261–268.

Ospreys in Northern Wisconsin

Daniel D. Berger and
Helmut C. Mueller

Rainbow Flowage is an artificial reservoir of approximately 15.5 sq km near the headwaters of the Wisconsin River in northern Wisconsin at 45° 50′ N latitude, and 89° 30′ W longitude. The reservoir was filled for the first time in 1936. In 1950 we discovered a colony of nesting ospreys, which were utilizing the dead trees that protruded above the water surface to build their nests. Beginning with the following year, we surveyed the colony each year with the exception of 1964. In most years we made only one visit, and that was in mid-July when the young are of banding age. As a result we have no data on hatching success.

Table 28.2 shows productivity at the colony for 1951 through 1965. We suspect that at the beginning of our study we were witnessing a colony that was still growing. It is interesting to observe that the decline in the number of adults was not preceded by a decline in productivity. Owing to inefficient counting methods in the early years the table does not effectively depict the precipitous decline in the adult population that took place after 1955. The reproductive rate held up reasonably well for another 4–5 years. It can be seen from the table that production fell off

Table 28.2. Productivity of the Osprey Colony at the Rainbow Flowage, Wisconsin

Year	Total no. of nests	No. of successful nests	No. of adults seen	No. of broods of 1	No. of broods of 2	No. of broods of 3	Total no. of young	Young per active nest
1951		7		2	3	2	14	2.0
1952	20[a]	10	28[a]	1	5	4	23	2.3
1953	19[ab]	14	36[a]	7	3	4	25	1.8
1954	20	10	42[a]	4	5	1	17[c]	1.7
1955	27	12	50	5	4	3	22[c]	1.8
1951–55								
Mean	21.5	10.6	39				20.2	1.9
Percent				36%	38%	26%		
1956	15[b]	5[d]	26	3	2	0	7	0.7
1957		9		2	2	5	21	2.3
1958	14	10	24	3	4	3	20	2.0
1959	13	7	27	3	4	0	11	1.6
1956–59								
Mean	14	7.8	25.7				14.8	1.9
Percent				35%	39%	26%		
1960	14	8	26	5	2	1	12	1.5
1961	15	4	25	3	1	0	5	1.25
1962	17	4	25	3	1	0	5	1.25
1963	14	3	19[a]	3	0	0	3	1.0
1965	7	1	15	1	0	0	1	1.0
1960–65								
Mean	13.4	4.0	22.0				5.2	1.3
Percent				75%	20%	5%		

[a] Minimum number.
[b] Nests with at least 1 adult in attendance.
[c] There were possibly 1 or 2 more young.
[d] Bad storm at nest-building time.

markedly in the 1960's. It is pertinent that the trees available for nesting in the flowage began suffering heavy attrition after about 1956, although we feel that it was not serious enough to become a limiting factor until perhaps 1961 or 1962.

We wish to acknowledge the field assistance provided by the following persons: K. H. Kuhn, F. Hamerstrom, F. N. Hamerstrom, Jr., A. Hamerstrom, E. Hamerstrom, H. Meinel, J. Jaeger, and Herman Mueller.

On the Osprey Situation in the German Democratic Republic

Karl Heinz Moll

At present about 60 pairs of ospreys nest in the GDR. The population shows a weak declining tendency. In one censused region on Müritz Lake

Table 28.3. Breeding Pairs of Ospreys, Percentage of Unsuccessful Broods Due to Disturbance of the Adult Birds at the Nest, and Size of Broods Raised

Broods	1959	1960	1963	1964	1965
Pairs					
Number	11	12	10	11	12
Percent unsuccessful[a]	11	33	20	9	0
Size of broods					
3 juveniles	37%	28%	14%	12%	0%
2 juveniles	50	57	86	44	42
1 juvenile	13	14	0	44	33
0 juveniles	0	0	0	0	25
Mean size of brood	2.2	2.1	2.1	1.7	1.2

[a] Due to disturbance.

Table 28.4. Number of Young at Individual Eyries[a]

D = disturbed

Eyrie no.	1963	1964	1965
1	3	2	1
2	D	D	1
3	2	2	0
4	2	3	2
5	D	2	1
6	2	1	0
8	2	1	2
9	2	2	1
10	2	1	2
11[b]	—	1	2
12[c]	—	—	0
Number of young raised	15	15	12
Young/occupied eyrie	1.7	1.5	1.1

[a] Eyrie no. 7 has been excluded. Although it was occupied throughout this period, the reproductive success of the pair was not precisely determined.
[b] Occupied for the first time in 1964.
[c] Occupied for the first time in 1965.

the count of breeding pairs has remained relatively stable since 1959 (Table 28.3).

The count of young ospreys in the census area is declining markedly as the years pass. In 1959 the average number of young fledged per successful nest was 2.2. In 1965 it was 1.2.

Through 1964 the reported lack of success was due to disturbance of the adult birds at the nest. The reduction in numbers of unsuccessful nests is attributed to (1) intensive promotion of osprey protection and (2) an admonition of the Forestry Department forbidding forestry operations during the breeding and rearing season near nests. All failures were reported to have been due to disturbances in 1959, 1960, 1963, and 1964; and this did not occur in 1965 according to reports.

In addition to the decline in the number of young raised per successful nest (Table 28.3), there has also been a reduction in the number of young raised per occupied eyrie (Table 28.4).

The decline in numbers of young ospreys is probably due to the effects of pesticides, and very probably, also due to jets breaking the sound barrier and killing the embryos.

CHAPTER 29

BRIEF REPORTS: THE STATUS OF EAGLES

Problems of the Golden Eagle in North America

Walter R. Spofford

The golden eagle in North America is sparsely but widely distributed over much of the wilder open uplands, extending in the west from low arctic regions of Alaska and Canada southward into the highlands of central Mexico, while in the east a remnant population extends from Quebec into the Appalachians. Eagles are largely absent from our eastern woodlands and the great agricultural lands of the central basin.

Problems relating to the golden eagle have become more familiar in the last few years through the publicity given the aircraft shoot-offs of eagles conducted by pilots hired by sheep and goat industries in the southwestern states. In the late 1930's, ranchers, having discovered that eagles could be approached easily in light airplanes and shot down, formed eagle clubs that hired pilots to kill eagles over substantial areas of our southwestern mountains and plains.

During winter months, individual pilots scored 25 and on occasion up to 38 eagles in one day. While yearly scores of 500 and even 1,000 claimed by some pilots may be somewhat exaggerated, it is now clear that for over 20 years at least 1,000 and perhaps 2,000 golden eagles have been killed from airplanes each winter and spring in far-western Texas and southeastern New Mexico. Eagles are seldom congregated, most kills averaging one in 20 or 30 sq miles (52 or 78 sq km). The large number killed is due to the fact that, after each shoot-off, other eagles gradually move in from more remote areas to occupy the vacant territory. Since such numbers of eagles could not possibly be local residents, their origin becomes a matter of interest.

Although ranching interests state that these are "Mexican" eagles that come across the Rio Grande into American sheep country, the fact is that southern latitude eagles are resident, being largely confined to their general breeding areas; and such few were soon virtually eliminated.

On the contrary, the eagles that are shot each winter consist largely of birds that appear over the range country in late autumn along with other migrant hawks and buzzards moving from the northern winter down into the snowless southwestern uplands. Most of our golden eagles breed in the more northern and western parts of the continent, and considerable numbers breed in Alaska and northern Canada. Such subarctic and boreal eagles feed to a great extent upon ground squirrels and marmots that begin hibernation in early fall. Faced with sharp curtailment of food supplies, most northern eagles move southward toward warmer wintering grounds. In Wyoming, as many as 40 eagles in an hour have been counted along a flyway in early November, and probably many of these reach our southwestern states and Mexico. Ranchers state that eagles first appear over the range in late fall, often following the passage of a "norther." In the east, eagles of the Quebec remnant pass southward along Hawk Mountain, Pennsylvania, to wintering grounds in Tennessee and the Carolinas.

The point to be recognized here is that the shoot-off of eagles is not a local situation but has implications that require continent-wide concern. To this end, the US Fish and Wildlife Service is now engaged upon a 5-year study of the biology and ecology of the golden eagle.

It seems clear that the extent of the shoot-off is of such proportions as to cause a severe drain upon birds breeding widely over half the continent. We know too little of eagle populations, particularly those of boreal regions, to be able to measure their decline, but actuarial considerations of this slow-breeding species demand an investigation of means to halt what appears to be senseless slaughter endangering significant parts of our North American golden eagle population.

It may be added that the passage of a federal statute in 1962, giving some measure of legal protection to the golden eagle, and a departmental regulation prohibiting the use of airplanes in "eagle-control" are helpful measures. But the fact remains that ranchers, convinced, however mistakenly, that eagles menace their livelihood, continue to destroy eagles. (Many of these ranchers are former military pilots and several told me individually that they had killed as many as 200 eagles each winter before hiring professional pilots to do the shoot-off.)

Although it is conceded that wintering eagles may and probably do take some lambs and kids, the claim made by ranchers—that they feed chiefly upon livestock—is certainly not the case, and it now seems clear that the jack rabbit *(Lepus)* is the principal food of wintering eagles in the sheep country, just as is true of nesting eagles in states immediately to the north.

While the golden eagle, with its wide if thinly-held foothold upon extensive upland country of our continent, does not seem to be in immediate danger of extermination, yet the airplane shoot-off of migratory eagles carries a threat imminent in the drastic efficiency of the method itself. Further details on this problem are set forth in Audubon Conservation Rep. 1 (47 p.) published in 1965 by the National Audubon Society, New York, NY.

Population Trends of the Bald Eagle in North America

Alexander Sprunt, IV

Since 1960, the National Audubon Society has been engaged in a study designed to learn more about the status of the bald eagle. This effort, with others that have been carried out over a longer period and still others recently initiated, has now resulted in a much better picture than was formerly available. The present paper summarizes in part a detailed series of reports, mostly unpublished. A more complete publication is planned.

EVIDENCE FOR DECLINE

The bald eagle population has probably been declining slowly for a great many years as the human population has increased. Accurate figures for primeval populations are nonexistent, but indications of the trend are common. It is of interest to note that Kumlien and Hollister (1951) wrote of southern Wisconsin in 1903, "The summer resorts about our lakes have gradually driven this species from its former nesting haunts. Bred about Lake Koshkonong 25 years ago . . . . In southern Wisconsin today the eagle is mainly a spring and fall migrant . . . . " That this slow decline has taken place over many parts of the range of the species is an undoubted fact, but it is most difficult to document accurately.

Since World War II a trend of a different sort has developed in certain portions of the bald eagle's range. A decline has occurred which has been much more rapid and drastic. A few instances of this can be quickly given. In four counties on the west coast of Florida, Charles Broley, (pers. comm.) reported that the breeding population dropped from 73 pairs in 1946 to 43 pairs in 1957. This trend has continued, and we know of only 35 pairs as of 1964. On Merritt Island on Florida's east coast, the population has dropped from 100 pairs to 12 pairs (W. Foster White, pers. comm.), and in a neighboring area Howell (1962) reports a decline from 24 pairs in 1935 to 5 in 1965. Walter R. Spofford (pers. comm.) has documented the loss of the bald eagle in New York from about 12 pairs to none. New Jersey had 35 pairs in 1937 and had only 2 in 1965 (Frank W. McLaughlin, pers. comm.). In the northern Lake States, there has been a definite loss of population, particularly from the shores of the Great Lakes and from the islands in the lakes. Studies by Sergej Postupalsky in Michigan and by Sprunt and Ligas (1963) in Wisconsin confirm this.

So far this report has dealt with breeding eagles. There is also some evidence from migrating and wintering birds. The Hawk Mountain (Pennsylvania) and Cape May (New Jersey) figures for migrating eagles show a sharp decline in the past 20 years. In Virginia, groups of up to 25 individuals used to be found along the ocean beaches in winter, but only an occasional single bird can be seen today (Fred R. Scott, pers. comm.).

One of the phenomena that runs through these cases of rapid decline is a marked lowering of reproductive success. What might be considered the "normal" reproductive success of bald eagles is unknown with any degree of certainty, but from studies in Everglades National Park, some of Broley's early work, and current studies in British Columbia and Alaska, it would appear that a success rate of 50–75% might be expected. In none of the areas where sharp declines have taken place is the figure reached (Table 29.1). Because productivity varies widely, it would be pertinent to list several areas and give the percentage of nest success. For this study the percentage of nest success is derived by dividing the number of active territories into the number of territories that produce at least one fledged young. We have information on some 12 segments of the eagle's population.

In addition to these areas there are significant eagle populations in the Rocky Mountain states, in northern Canada, and in the maritime provinces of Canada; but we have such fragmentary data from these places that it is impossible to draw any conclusion about eagle trends at this time.

Table 29.1. Relation of Nesting Success to Population Status of the Bald Eagle, 1965

Area	No. of nests[a]	Nest success[b]	Population trend	Investigator
Alaska (Kodiak Is.)	125	63%	Stable	R. J. Hensel and W. A. Troyer
British Columbia	175	73	Stable	David A. Hancock
Lake States				
Great Lakes nests	19	4	Declining	A. Grewe, F. J. Ligas,
Interior nests	148	45	Declining	and S. Postupalsky
Maine	30	18	Declining	C. M. Brookfield
New Jersey	4	25	Declining	F. W. McLaughlin
Chesapeake region	44	13	Declining	J. M. Abbott and F. R. Scott
No. and So. Carolina	10	43	Declining	Several observers
Florida				
Central	60	61	Stable	George Heinzmann
East Coast	24	35	Declining	W. F. White *et al.*
West Coast	40	45	Declining	Several observers
Everglades National Park	50	51	Stable	W. B. Robertson, Jr.

[a] The approximate number being studied each year is of course declining steadily.
[b] Obtained by dividing the number of active territories into the number of territories that fledge at least one young.

Along with the figures that show a low reproductive success for certain areas, there has been a decline in the percentage of immature birds in the population. The best data showing this decline are from the Hawk Mountain Sanctuary in eastern Pennsylvania. During the years 1931 through 1945, 36.5% of the bald eagles passing the lookout in fall were immature. This percentage declined to 23.1 for the years 1954 through 1960 (Broun, 1931–60). During the winters of 1961, 1962, and 1963, the National Audubon Society conducted counts of bald eagles in all parts of the contiguous United States. The overall numbers reported varied very little over the 3-year period, but the percentage of immatures steadily declined from 26.5% in 1961 to 23.7% in 1962 and 21.6% in 1963 (Sprunt and Cunningham, 1961, 1962; Sprunt and Ligas, 1963). The constant decline in spite of irregular fluctuation of other variables gives grounds for concern.

To sum up then, it can be said that the overall population of the bald eagle has declined slowly over a long period of time. Since World War II a decline has taken place at a considerably accelerated rate in some portions of the eagles' range. This has been best documented in the eastern part of the United States and has been most serious on both coasts of Florida and on the entire Atlantic coast as far north as Maine.

REASONS FOR THE DECLINE

There are no doubt several reasons for the decline that has taken place. These can be quickly summed up under a few headings. The first is human disturbance. This has been operating over many years but has become more acute recently. The urban sprawl and the proliferation of waterside housing that has come with increasing affluence have worked against the eagle. Another factor that is becoming more of a problem every year is the increase of outdoor recreation with its attendant crowding of areas that were left in virtual isolation only a few years ago.

A second factor is habitat loss. This can be tied closely with human population growth but goes one step further. The cutting of timber has done away with many suitable nesting sites over the years, and the alteration of much of our waterside areas for housing, recreation, and industrial use has become more commonplace.

Shooting of eagles is also a continuing drain on the population. We have had no concrete figures on this until recently, and they are still very preliminary. In its Region III, the Bureau of Sport Fisheries and Wildlife of the US Fish and Wildlife Service has gathered some figures on eagle mortality, and this indicates that shooting was the cause of death in 54% of the cases of mortality that have been recorded (Henry M. Reeves, pers. comm.). Other data, of not as high a quality as those of the Bureau, suggest that the percentage of birds shot may be even higher.

All of the factors mentioned so far are of a direct nature, disturbance, habitat loss, shooting, and while all of these have been operating they do not seem to be adequate to explain all of the conditions surrounding the recently accelerated decline of the bald eagle. There is pretty firm evidence of other factors also having an effect. Their exact nature is presently being investigated.

SUMMARY

Since 1946, the marked decline of breeding bald eagle populations has exceeded 50% in some regions, reached 90–100% in others, and has been accompanied by nesting failures of 55–96%. The proportion of young has shifted from 36.5 to 23.1% in the large population migrating through eastern Pennsylvania and from 26.5% in 1961 to 21.6% in 1963 among eagles wintering south of Canada.

Eagle populations in the Rocky Mountain states, maritime provinces of Canada, and northern Canada are still present in significant numbers and they appear to be stable wherever nesting success exceeds 50%. Research on factors producing the decline is still in progress.

LITERATURE CITED

Broun, Maurice. 1931–60. Annual reports of Hawk Mountain Sanctuary, Kempton, Pa.

Howell, J. C. 1962. The 1961 status of some bald eagle nest sites in east-central Florida. Auk, 79(4):716–718.

Kumlien, L., and N. Hollister. 1951. The birds of Wisconsin. Wisconsin Society for Ornithology, Madison. 122 p.

Sprunt, A. IV, and R. L. Cunningham. 1961. Continental bald eagle project. National Audubon Society, New York. Progress Report No. 1:1–7. (Mimeo.)

———, and R. L. Cunningham. 1962. Continental bald eagle project. National Audubon Society, New York. Progress Report No. 2:1–11. (Mimeo.)

———, and F. J. Ligas. 1963. Continental bald eagle project. National Audubon Society, New York. Progress Report No. 3:1–6.

Population Trends in the White-Tailed Sea Eagle in North Germany

Günter Oehme

At present three areas in Germany have resident sea eagles. The lake flats and coastal regions of Mecklenburg have been a center of spread, as have the lake regions of Brandenburg to a lesser degree. Sea eagles have been present at least since 1948 in the eastern part of Schleswig-Holstein, where there were seven pairs in 1960.

At the beginning of the twentieth century, there was immediate danger of extirpation. From 1920 until after World War II, there was a gradual increase in the population (in Mecklenburg, from about 24 pairs in 1913 to about 86 pairs in 1945 and to about 88 pairs in 1952). This was brought about by the institution of protection measures. Since the twenties the sea eagle has been legally protected in the breeding areas. Formerly, up until 1906, bounties had been paid for shooting them.

In the twenties and thirties and up to 1945, there was exemplary protection of the nest biotope against disturbances, including forestry practices deleterious to sea eagles. After World War II the population scarcely rose again. Increased casualties (between 1946 and 1957 there were records of 104 dead sea eagles, of which 50% had been shot illegally and from 1958–67, 115 dead specimens) and disturbances through forestry practices and of other sorts in the breeding territories led to stagnation and gradual regression of the numbers of breeding pairs. In 1957, 81 breeding pairs were still counted in Mecklenburg. Thereafter the count of pairs slowly diminished, above all because the adult eagles had very few young. In the meantime, in spite of frequent difficulties, attempts were partially successful to prohibit all forestry activities within 300 m of the eyries during the breeding season and, inasmuch as possible, not to disturb the cover within 100 m of the eyrie at any time. Thus, it may be hoped that man-made disturbances will be kept to a minimum.

As stated, the losses are high. In 1964 alone three eyries were orphaned when the adult eagles were killed. In addition to illegal shooting, there is more recently an appreciable additional danger through poison (especially phosphor eggs and corn soaked in Wofatox-concentrate [methyl parathion] which is used for crow control). In 1964, 20 sea eagles were picked up dead—an especially high number. In five instances the deaths are surely attributable to poisoned prey as this method of control was being used in the immediate vicinity at the same time. In many other instances, it was not possible to determine the cause of death, but the majority are not due to shooting or crippling. At present one cannot say whether other pesticides (and which?) are playing an important role in threatening the population, nor whether or not they are the cause for the many dead birds found or for the poor reproduction.

Pesticides could account for this to the same degree as the frequent breaking of the sound barrier at low elevations by jets in the birds' breeding territories (death of embryos?). In past years, at least, man-made disturbances such as forestry operations played an appreciable role in this complex of factors.

The possibility of jeopardizing the population by use of pesticides (for example, DDT and other chlorinated hydrocarbons), which are being used in the German breeding areas in ever-increasing quantities, is to be feared in the future, even though we have no direct evidence for this at present.

LITERATURE CITED

Oehme, Günter. 1961. Die Bestandsentwicklung des Seeadlers, *Haliaeëtus albicilla* (L.), in Deutschland mit Untersuchungen zur Wahl der Brutbiotope, p. 1–61. *In* H. Schildmacher. Beiträge zur Kenntnis deutscher Vögel. Fischer, Jena. 295 p.

———. 1966. Die Seeadler-Verluste in unserer Republik. Der Falke, 13(2):40–47.

CHAPTER 30

BRIEF REPORTS: THE STATUS OF CERTAIN OTHER RAPTORS

Breeding Populations of Diurnal Birds of Prey in France

Jean-François Terrasse

Of the 38 European species of diurnal birds of prey, 22 breed in France. Thousands of these raptors also migrate through the country, or winter there.

Destruction of these birds has in the recent past gone on at all seasons, by every means, and at all levels of society. Rewards were paid annually for killing at least 100,000 each year. Competitions were held for the destruction of noxious animals. Pigeon fanciers were active in killing peregrines. Overhead wires, motor traffic, and toxic chemicals are also important decimating factors.

In respect to the 100,000 birds of prey killed each year in France, I based this figure in 1963 on the reports from hunters themselves. There are in France 94 "Départments" in each of which is an official "Fédération Départementale des Chasseurs" (state hunters' association). All these Federations depend on the "Conseil Supérieur de la Chasse." Each year these Federations give rewards for the destruction of noxious animals (foxes [*Vulpes vulpes*], wildcats [*Felis sylvestris*], feral cats, badgers [*Meles meles*], crows, magpies, and birds of prey, etc.). For each bird of prey they gave 1.00 Fr or 1.50 Fr to everybody showing a beak or legs.

Naturally they gave a reward for all birds of prey, protected or not, because they were absolutely unable to distinguish the difference and, for quite all hunters in France, all birds of prey are verminous! One must remember that there are *1,800,000 hunters* in France (more than in all the rest of Europe), and a lot of them are still shooting at everything that moves from small birds to big ones, especially in the south. The shooting season is from 14 July to 31 March with another short season of 3 weeks in May for migrating waders along the sea coast—now discontinued—and for doves. There are still many installations in the southwest to catch birds with nets. In a single department (Gironde), there are about 6,000 of these net-catchers of birds, and each of them catches in a season some birds of prey (sometimes 5 to 10).

Each year, these Fédérations Départementales des Chasseurs have published the amount of money given as rewards for the killing of noxious animals. In many of the 94 departments there were more than 1,000, sometimes up to 3,000 rewards for birds of prey. And all birds of prey killed or trapped were not shown for the reward. So, I estimate that at least 100,000 and probably 200,000 birds of prey were killed annually in France in the years up through 1963. Nearly all birds of prey of western Europe travel through France at fall and spring during their migration, and many winter there. Today the number of birds of prey killed is probably fewer because there are fewer and fewer of them each year.

Table 30.1 summarizes my estimates of the situation with respect to breeding diurnal birds of prey. A more detailed account of these population trends appears in a report that I made at the conference at Caen (Terrasse, 1964). A statistical representation of the decline from 1960 to 1964 has been published by Ash (1964).

ADDENDUM, 1968

The situation for raptorial birds has changed in France since this paper was prepared in 1965. Protection for these birds has been gaining each year. Many are now protected throughout the year (all eagles, vultures, ospreys), and others are protected in certain areas (kites, peregrines, harriers, etc.). A few raptors are still on the list of noxious species. Some of the Fédérations des Chasseurs have ceased to pay rewards for birds of prey, but many are still paying up to 3.00 Fr.

Birds of prey, however, are still decreasing, and there is still a lot of shooting. There is still a very important destruction of birds of prey in migration in the departments of the southwest, where not less than 50,000 may be killed annually during the shooting and netting season. The Institut National de la Recherche Agronomique has now found organochlorine pesticides in the eggs of all the raptorial birds that have been examined in France, including the booted eagle, common buzzard, sparrow-hawk, black kite, peregrine, hobby, and kestrel.

LITERATURE CITED

Ash, J. S. 1964. A reduction in numbers of birds of prey in France. Bird Study, 12(1):17–26.

Terrasse, J. F. 1964. The status of birds of prey in France in 1964, p. 73–85. *In* Working conference on birds of prey and owls, Caen, 10–12 April 1964. Int. Council for Bird Preservation, London. 140 p.

Table 30.1. Estimated Status of Diurnal Birds of Prey in France

Species	Estimated decline in 30 years %	Estimated present no. of nesting pairs	Remarks
*Griffon vulture	—	40–50	Protected and generally respected
*Egyptian vulture	70[a]	50	20 pairs in western Pyrenees
*Bearded vulture		9–10	Eggers, poisoning, and zoos are a danger
*Golden eagle	60–70	60–70	Depressed in part by myxomatosis
*Bonelli's eagle	75	30–50	Depressed in part by myxomatosis
*Booted eagle		<100?	Confused with the buzzard by shooters
Common buzzard	>50	—	Subject to fierce persecution
Honey buzzard		—	Being destroyed everywhere
Goshawk	>60	<1,000	Many are pole-trapped
Sparrow-hawk	60–80	—	Considerably reduced everywhere
Red kite	60–70	<1,000	Vulnerable to poisoned carcasses
Black kite	None	—	Increasing (pollution of rivers?)
*White-tailed eagle	100	0	Last single adult observed 1959
Marsh harrier	>50	<400	Persecuted everywhere
Hen and Montagu's harriers	>50	—	Almost extinct in certain regions
*Short-toed eagle	60–75	<500	Now protected; killing continues
*Osprey		<10	Still nesting in Corsica
Peregrine falcon	50–80	150	Many destroyed by pigeon fanciers, keepers
Hobby	>40	—	Now very rare in the whole Paris basin
Kestrel	>50	—	With the buzzard, suffering from the destruction of "noxious birds"
Lesser kestrel		<100	Egg collectors are a danger

[a]Except in the western Pyrenees.
*Species protected throughout the country all year.

The Status of Cooper's Hawks in Western Pennsylvania

Earl C. Schriver, Jr.

The Cooper's hawk in the late 1940's was the commonest hawk to be found in western Pennsylvania. It is today one of the rarest. The following information was taken from my records of personal observation of nests. The total number of hours spent searching for nests has gone up as the number of nests found has gone down. There was a break in records from 1951 through 1954 due to time when I was away in military service.

Nest C-A was located on a 99-acre (40.1-ha) sanctuary, owned by Dr. Frank W. Preston, located about 8 miles (13 km) west of Butler, Pennsylvania. It is typical second-growth timber composed of oak (*Quercus*), maple (*Acer*), and wild cherry (*Prunus*) trees, approximately 50–90 years old. The surrounding countryside is mixed woodland of the same type and open areas of homes and farms. This nest was active from 1947 up to and including 1959. The Cooper's hawks did not always raise young, but did make an attempt every year. In 1949, the nest was built, but there was no sign of eggs. Again in 1952 the birds nested just outside the fence, and someone shot up the nest but did not kill the female. My records show a production of 24 young from this nest from 1947 through 1959, excluding 1951–54. In the years 1955 through 1959, the same female occupied this nesting territory. This female was very large and had a habit of soaring over the nest when disturbed. She disappeared just before hatching the eggs in 1959. The male hatched one of the two remaining eggs. I had taken two eggs for experimental purposes. Before the nestling was 2 weeks old, the male attracted a new mate, an immature female. She laid two eggs alongside the young hawk but did not incubate. This was the last nesting of Cooper's hawks at the sanctuary. In 1962, a pair of red-shouldered hawks moved into the territory and have nested there every year since.

Nest C-B was on Tindall's farm. This is in typical mixed woodland. I first found this nest in 1949, located about 90 ft (27 m) up in a large white oak (*Quercus alba*) tree. This was the only nontypical site this bird used. In 7 years, excluding 1951–54, she raised 18 young. The nest was destroyed only once, in 1958. I found a raccoon (*Procyon lotor*) on the nest and suspect it ate the eggs. The last nesting was in 1959, when the female raised three young. There has been no sign of Cooper's hawks here during the nesting season since then.

Nest C-C was located in my home woods. This consists of approximately 2,500 acres (1,000 ha) of mixed woods located in southern Butler

County. This woodland was occupied by sharp-shinned hawks from 1945, or before, until I went into military service in 1950. When I returned in 1955, I found that they had been replaced by Cooper's hawks. I believe that this was their first year in this territory as I was unable to find any old nests in the area. This pair was successful in 3 out of the 5 years they nested. The nest was destroyed in 1957, when something, probably a crow, ate the first egg. The nest was again destroyed in 1959, when a raccoon ate the four young at about 10 days of age. Early in the spring of 1960, I found several remains of Cooper's hawk kills, yellow-shafted flicker, and ruffed grouse, but have not found a Cooper's nest in those woods since 1959.

Nest C-D was found in 1957, near Renfrew, Butler County. From my car, I watched the female building. She was the largest Cooper's hawk I have ever seen. She built a nest, but then laid four eggs a hundred yards (91 m) away in a previous year's nest. One of these was only half size. I was very curious whether or not this one would hatch, but the eggs disappeared, probably being taken by raccoon. This bird then built a new nest on top of the original new nest, by this time an imposing structure, and laid four eggs. She raised all four young, but they did not leave the nest until August. The same female (if one may judge by her size) used this nest in 1958 and 1959, raising three young in 1958 and four in 1959. There has been no sign of Cooper's hawks here since then.

By much hard searching in 1960, I found one Cooper's hawk nest. This was in northern Butler County, and the female was incubating three infertile eggs. I finally destroyed the eggs in hopes that she would renest, but she did not. I have only had the one case, Nest C-D, in 1957, that renested after the eggs had been destroyed.

The winter of 1959–60 seems to have been the crucial time for the Cooper's hawks. I have had nests since that time, but they are few and far between. The nests from 1961 on have shown no sign of fertility loss. This leaves me with only one conclusion. We had a massive winter kill. The same thing happened to the eastern bluebirds, and at the same time.

We had a very open winter in 1959-60 until 19 February. We then had about 16 inches (41 cm) of snow and very cold weather until late April. I believe the Cooper's hawks came north early and were hit with the bad weather.

I had one nest in 1961, which raised four young. Two nests in 1962 raised five young. Four nests in 1963 raised three young; one had the eggs taken, and two nests of young were eaten by raccoon. I only found one pair of Cooper's in 1964, but could not find the nest. In 1965, I did not find any, but my field work was quite limited. A summary of these nesting histories is given in Table 30.2.

Paralleling this phenomenon among nesting hawks is my experience with hawks trapped near Pymatuning, Pennsylvania. Here approxi-

Table 30.2. Nesting of the Cooper's Hawk in Western Pennsylvania

A = at least one adult present for a time
D = deserted territory
P = pair present; no sign of eggs
P′ = pair present; could not find nest
r = territory occupied by a pair of red-shouldered hawks
s = territory occupied by a pair of sharp-shinned hawks.
U = unsuccessful nesting
? = suspected nesting (from old nests)
1, 2, 3 = number of young fledged

Site	'47	'48	'49	'50	'55	'56	'57	'58	'59	'60	'61	'62	'63	'64
C-A	3	4	P	3	3	4	3	3	1[a]	D	D	r	r	r
C-B			3	4	3	2	3	U	3	D	D	D	D	D
C-C	s	s	s	s	3	4	U	4	U	A	D	D	D	D
C-D							4	3	4	D	D	D	D	D
C-E										U[b]	D	D	D	D
C-F									?	?	4	3	U	D
C-G									?	?	?	2	3	D
C-H								s	s	s	—	—	U	P′

[a] Two eggs removed for experimental purposes.
[b] Eggs infertile; finally destroyed by me.

mately 50 to 60 of this species were trapped at the Conneaut Lake Marsh pheasant holding pens of the State Game Commission in the early 1950's. During the last few years, almost no Cooper's hawks have been trapped at these pens.

SUMMARY

Of 32 nests, 24 were successful and averaged 3.2 young fledged per nest from 1947 to 1964. In 1947–57, there were 2.9 young fledged per occupied territory; in 1958–64, 1.9. The abrupt desertion of three territories in 1960 followed a hard winter and suggested a massive winter kill of adults. This was followed by the desertion of five more territories under study. Although the commonest hawk in western Pennsylvania in the late 1940's, the Cooper's hawk is now one of the rarest. The disappearance of eight nesting pairs on study areas paralleled the sharp decline in the numbers reported trapped at a pheasant-rearing farm.

ADDENDUM, 1968

In 1966, I found three nests which showed very definitely either a loss of fertility or embryonic death within a few hours. These were on three new territories. One (C-I) had four eggs, all "infertile"; C-J had four eggs, two "infertile"; and C-K had four eggs, all of which hatched.

In 1967, I had six nests, two of which involved reestablishment of old territories. C-B had an immature female that cackled at me near a new nest. However, she built two nests but did not lay in either one. C-D had a new nest this year about one-third mile (0.5 km) south of the old nesting site. When I found this, a raccoon was lying on the nest, and broken eggs were on the ground. C-J had five eggs, two of which were "infertile." She raised three females. C-K had two eggs, both "infertile." She incubated 5 weeks and then deserted. C-L was incubating when I found her nest. Broken eggs were later found on the ground. One, still in the nest, had what appeared to be a hole caused by the beak of a crow. C-M had four young when found. The trunk of the tree was immediately tinned with a raccoon guard, and the pair raised all four. Thus six pairs in 1967 produced a total of seven young.

Population Trends in Utah Raptors

Clayton M. White

As a result of concentrated egg-collecting activities in the past, raptor populations in Utah have had a rather long history. Numerous eyrie sites provide a record of historical occupancy and are thus fairly good indexes to densities. Since raptor eggs are highly prized, seldom is there an accessible area of land unsearched by the collector. Woodbury (MS) has compiled Utah egg-collecting data, running from the late 1800's to the present, of such collectors as Treganza, Wolfe, Hutchings, and Bee.

FALCONS

In 1910 Treganza collected eggs from six prairie falcon eyries that were active concurrently in Bell's Canyon, a box canyon some 2 miles (3.3 km) in width and perhaps 6 miles (10 km) deep, overlooking Salt Lake City. He also mentions (Woodbury, pers. comm.) at least four peregrine eyries overlooking the Bear River marshes in the 18 miles (30 km) from Ogden to Brigham City. The prairie falcon eyries in Bell's Canyon were inactive by 1940 (Charles Lockerbie, pers. comm.), and the peregrines were apparently gone by 1959. Of ten known prairie and peregrine falcon eyries in the 64 miles (107 km) on the western slope of the Wasatch Mountains from Salt Lake City to Brigham City, only two and a possible third prairie falcon eyries are still active (1965). Homes now occupy locations directly under many of the eyrie sites, and human habitation expansion and activity are undoubtedly responsible for most of the raptor inactivity noted at these eyries. However, one golden eagle nest within 3 miles (5 km) of downtown Salt Lake City was active as late as 1958.

Wolfe (1929) reported on a prairie falcon egg-collecting trip made in 1927 in an area southwest of Salt Lake comprising a territory about 70 by 85 miles (117 by 142 km). He mentions some 29 eyrie sites visited in which adults were in attendance. Although his exact route has not been entirely retraced, a project I plan to undertake and report on in the near future, a good portion of the sites have been revisited, and only 9 of the 17 visited are active. Since Wolfe's trip, at least one peregrine occupied an old prairie falcon site in the area and was last present in 1954. Human activities, specifically the activities of falconers, are felt to have caused the permanent inactivity of at least 4 of these sites.

OSPREYS

Ospreys are reported (Behle, 1944; Woodbury, Cottam, and Sugden, 1949) to be a casual resident with the data apparently based on the 4–5 known nests located near mountainous lakes (see also Bee and Hutchings, 1942). Recent explorations on the Green River in northern Utah have shown that at least 6–8 other sites exist along the river (White and Behle, 1960; Marvin Meyer, pers. comm.). The osprey seems to be holding its own as the old nesting sites are still active, although Boyd Shaffer (pers. comm.) reported that a "dozen" were shot in the spring of 1950 and 1953 at a state fish hatchery. These, however, were taken during migration and possibly were not Utah-breeding birds.

EAGLES

Robert Bee knows of one active bald eagle nest in Utah (J. Clyde Ward and Gerald L. Richards, pers. comm.) and, since the time of Treganza at the turn of the century, several have been reported, but corroboration of these reports is lacking. The breeding status apparently has not changed to any extent during the present century. During migration, however, there is an influx generally into the state. In mid-March 1961, 1962, and 1963, the late Gary Lloyd and I saw large numbers of bald eagles soaring over the highway in the Willard–Bear River Refuge area. In 1961, 12 adult and seven immature bald eagles, and two golden eagles were seen at 9:30 A.M. as they were apparently leaving a roosting area. Swisher (1964) has published a detailed report of this area for the years 1963–64. This appears to be a locality where, at least in some years, bald eagles concentrate, perhaps as a result of the influence of the refuge. This area should be carefully observed over a long period, a job that could be conveniently undertaken by refuge personnel.

BUTEOS

Red-tailed, Swainson's, and ferruginous hawks are showing a decrease, with about 25% of the eyries known to me since 1948 being inactive. The evidence points at human hunting pressure, which could be curbed if the responsible state agencies would undertake a proper publicity program. In 1959 Gary Lloyd and I entered a cattle-grazing area, under a 99-year government lease, encompassing several hundred square miles in northern Utah. The area is fenced, thus keeping out hunters and others. Lloyd and I originally estimated that an 8-mile (13-km) long canyon in the area supported a red-tailed hawk population of about one active nest per 0.6 linear mile (1 km). A detailed study of a portion of this canyon undertaken by Lloyd in 1963–65 showed this estimate to be of the right order of magnitude. (Cooper's hawks in the same canyon are of approximately two-thirds that density, their habitat being restricted.) Two factors for the high populations are thought to be (1) lack of pressure from human hunters and (2) high rodent populations resulting from the favorable conditions produced by cattle-grazing.

Migrating rough-legged hawks suffer high road kills throughout Utah, mainly as a result of their feeding on road-killed jack rabbits. An area where this is most prevalent is on a 162-mile (270-km) stretch of highway US 91 from Levan to Cedar City. In the last week of December 1961, Guy Musser, Gary Lloyd, and I picked up 4 freshly killed hawks and counted 15 freshly killed hawks and 8 dead great horned owls. The road is such that many more individuals could have been in the borrow-pit and passed unnoticed. A Dixie College student who regularly travelled this stretch of highway has reported similar kills during at least the past 2 years (Dennis Manning, pers. comm.). It is not known what part of the Arctic population these hawks are from. This problem has no obvious solution. Rough-legged hawks are very common as wintering birds in some years. In the winter of 1959–60, Gary Lloyd and I surveyed a 12-mile (20-km) stretch of metal high-tension utility poles west of Salt Lake City. A total of 27 hawks was seen in the most favorable 5- to 6-mile (8.5- to 10-km) section. This number varied somewhat and went as low as 14 hawks when the last count was made in the middle of January 1960.

OWLS

Calvin Wilson, Tracy Aviary, Salt Lake City, told me of an area on Farmington Bay Waterfowl Refuge, separated from the Great Salt

Lake by dikes, where during World War II, 12–14 territories of short-eared owls were present. When he and I visited the area in 1961, only two owls were seen. I visited the area again in 1965, and only two owls were present then. Wilson attributes much of the disappearance of owls to hunters, but it may be worthy to mention that an immediately adjacent tract of marsh is heavily sprayed in mosquito-control programs.

SUMMARY

In Utah, then, breeding populations of raptors are maintaining high densities locally but decreasing generally. The biggest single factor may be indiscriminate shooting, while nest robbing by young people and would-be falconers is causing considerable localized disappearance of accipitrine and falconine species. Human habitation encroachment has only limited and localized effect and then only on certain species such as falcons that are intolerant of humans.

LITERATURE CITED

Bee, R. G., and J. Hutchings. 1942. Breeding records of Utah birds. Great Basin Nat., 3(3 and 4):61–85.

Behle, W. H. 1944. Check-list of the birds of Utah. Condor, 46(2):67–87.

Swisher, J. F., Jr. 1964. A roosting area of the bald eagle in northern Utah. Wilson Bull., 76(2):186–187.

White, C. M., and W. H. Behle. 1960. Birds of Flaming Gorge Reservoir Basin, Utah and Wyoming. Anthropol. Papers, Univ. Utah., 48(3):186–208.

Wolfe, L. R. 1929. Collecting rent from falcons and ravens. Oologist, whole no. 501, 46(2):16–20.

Woodbury, A. M., C. Cottam, and J. W. Sugden. 1949. Annotated check-list of the birds of Utah. Bull. Univ. Utah, 39(16):1–40.

Prairie Falcon Nesting Success in Colorado in 1965

James H. Enderson

The prairie falcon nests commonly throughout Colorado; as many as 300 pairs may be present in the state (Enderson, 1964). Population trends in this relatively abundant falcon may parallel those of the much rarer peregrine, and for this reason the following information on the reproductive performance of the prairie falcon in 1965 is presented. These two species generally occur in dissimilar local habitats in Colorado.

I obtained data on the nesting success of 26 pairs of prairie falcons. Since this field work was done late in the nesting period, mostly by other workers, only nests remaining active were visited. Enderson (1964) found that only about 41% of pairs of prairie falcons were successful in fledging at least one young in Colorado and Wyoming in 1960–62. Therefore the 26 pairs observed in 1965 probably represent only the successful minority. In the 26 nests, 79 young were produced, but 17 were taken by falconers reducing the number that finally fledged to 62. The average number fledging was 2.4 young per pair. This figure is lower than a 3-year average of 2.9 for 25 successful nests in Wyoming and Colorado (Enderson, unpublished data). However, the 26 nests studied in the present paper are in an area of higher human population where falconers are more numerous. Under these conditions prairie falcons seem to have experienced a normal year based on performance in 1960, 1961, and 1962; and from my field experience in different times of the year in Colorado, it does not appear that this species is declining.

LITERATURE CITED

Enderson, J. H. 1964. A study of the prairie falcon in the central Rocky Mountain region. Auk, 81 (3): 332–352.

PART III

BEHAVIOR AND GENERAL ECOLOGY

CHAPTER 31

A HARRIER POPULATION STUDY

Frances Hamerstrom

The primary purposes of my study have been to determine whether or not American harriers (*Circus cyaneus hudsonius*) return to the same breeding area year after year and whether the pairs remain mated for life. Such a study depends on marked birds, and adult harriers are difficult to catch in summer. Indeed, except for the fact that they can be caught while defending their nests, my study would have been impossible. Nest finding was thus essential, and in the course of this a considerable amount of information on breeding behavior was obtained. It was also necessary to census my study population each year in order to relate the behavior of banded birds to the population as a whole. I have thus been led into a wider population study as well.

The study was begun in 1959 and is not yet complete. This paper deals with the population aspects of the study from 1959 through 1965, and is based on 99 nests, 533 harriers banded, and 7 years of census. Some additional data for 1966–68 have been parenthetically added in table footnotes and to the legends of the figures as this paper went to press. It is my hope that my findings may give insight into the population dynamics of other raptors, particularly the peregrine.

STUDY AREA

The study area is about 40,000 acres (16,000 ha) in size. It lies mainly within the Buena Vista Marsh in Portage County, Wisconsin, but includes also some of the surrounding upland. Before settlement, the "marsh" was primarily a tamarack (*Larix laricina*) swamp with some open marsh in the center; pine (*Pinus* spp.) and oak (*Quercus* spp.) predominated on the sandy uplands. The marsh has been drained, and both it and the upland parts of the study area are now mostly farmland with a high proportion of nonmarshy grassland, particularly on the drained peat (Hamerstrom, Mattson, and Hamerstrom, 1957). The low spots tend to become sedge (*Carex* spp.) and willow (*Salix* spp.) swales, in which 61% of the nests were found (54 of 89 nests for which cover type was recorded).

In the last two or three years, potato growers have reduced available nesting areas by new plowing, especially in the northern part of the study area. Land under management for prairie chickens has increased harrier habitat in the southern part. It is my impression that the total acreage of good habitat has remained essentially constant, although its distribution within the study area has changed.

TECHNIQUES

Harrier nests were found by (1) watching for food transfers, after which the female returned to the nest, although often not directly; (2) following males carrying food; (3) looking for preening females, which tend to take perches about 7:00 A.M. (Central Daylight-Saving Time) and thence are apt to return to the nest; and (4) investigating stooping harriers, for persistent stooping indicates that there is probably a nest nearby. When examining nests, we made it a point to walk past, thus leaving a scent trail for mammalian predators to follow beyond and away from each nest.

In spring we trapped with bal-chatris baited with starlings (Berger and Hamerstrom, 1962). Almost all the breeding adults, however, were caught in a dho-gaza set over a tame horned owl (Hamerstrom, 1963). Breeding adults were not only banded, but after 1961 marked as well with strong, brightly colored plastic jesses attached around the tarsi with rivets, so they could be recognized in later years without the need for retrapping. For recognition until the next molt, they were imped (Hamerstrom, 1942) with feathers dyed with Diamond or Rit dye. The feathers which proved most satisfactory for imps were primaries from small white domestic ducks for female harriers, and primaries of large white domestic pigeons for the males. We imped two adjacent primaries, in each case those most recently grown in and hard and bloodless at the base. The feathers to be replaced were cut off near the body of the bird so as to leave the hollow base intact. The butt of the dyed feather was dipped in Duco household cement, inserted into the hollow base, and held for a minute or two until the glue set. Thus it was easily possible to recognize marked individuals with the naked eye at a quarter-mile (0.4 km) throughout the summer, and one could sometimes detect the faded imps when the birds returned to the area the following spring.

Of the 553 harriers banded on the study area, 92 were breeding adults, 217 were nestlings, and the remainder were migrants and birds which were apparently nonbreeders.

We censused nonbreeders by coming to know their hunting territories. Had we not used colored imps on breeding birds, we would probably not have been confident of our ability to count the nonbreeders. After the migration was over and as the summer advanced, the latter tended to hunt the same fields day after day. They could often be recognized by field marks, and their presence was predictable. I do not believe them to be birds that had had nearby nests broken up. We have had experience with the behavior of 8 marked males and 12 marked females following nest failure in the egg stage or at hatching; in every case the adults left the area within 24 hours. We cannot wholly rule out the possibility that apparent nonbreeders may still have had some sort of attachment to a set of addled eggs, for we have one example of a female who persisted in incubating four eggs with well-developed dead embryos. I doubt, however, that many of the supposed nonbreeders were anything but what they seemed to be.

SPRING MIGRATION

We have recorded every raptor which we have seen on the study area since the spring of 1959. The harrier count from early February to mid-May, 1959–65, is given in Fig. 31.1. Occasionally, a few adult male harriers winter on the study area, but most of the population is migratory. Among the migrants the adult males are normally the first to arrive in spring, usually during the second half of March. Excluding the exceptionally early records—single birds that probably were wintering—the movement of adult males through the area during the seven springs began on 19 March, 29 March, 8 February, 19 March, 14 March, 19 March, and 19 March, respectively. Brown harriers were generally not seen until 5–10 days after the adult males, with the one exception that the first harrier seen in 1964 was a brown one. Even during the uniquely early migration of 1961, which began during the second week of February, the usual order of arrival obtained.

Brown harriers in spring include adult females and subadults of both sexes, and it is often impossible to differentiate among them in flight. In the hand, however, they are easily recognized. We have records of 87 brown harriers trapped during the period of spring migration, ranging from 4 to 26 per year. In every year except 1965 the first of the brown harriers to be caught were adult females. The first subadults, generally females, were caught 2–10 days later in the 3 years (1959, 1960, and

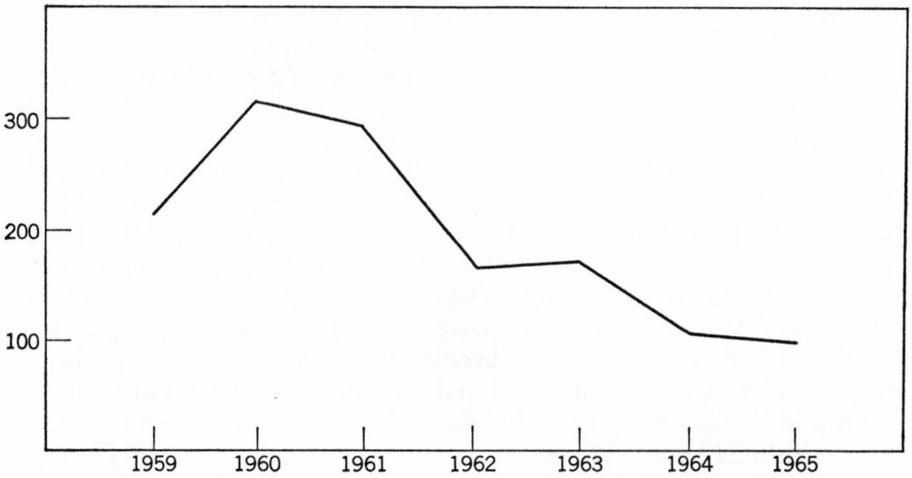

Fig. 31.1. **Numbers of harriers seen on spring migration, 1959–65. [These dropped to 90 in 1966, to 82 in 1967, and to 34 in 1968.] UW Cartographic Lab.**

1962) for which we have an adequate sample of trapped birds; only once, in 1965, the first subadult was trapped before the first adult female, by 10 days, but the sample was very small (four birds).

The study area is not on a major hawk migration route, and I have no reason to suppose that the pattern here differs from normal broad-front migration of harriers over suitable breeding range throughout the state. An exceptional flight day occurred on 3 April 1960, the only one of such magnitude that we have seen here. On that day we saw 6 sharp-shinned hawks, 4 Cooper's hawks, 51 red-tailed hawks, 27 rough-legged hawks, 8 unidentified buteos, 40 harriers, 1 peregrine, and 11 kestrels. Even if we delete the big flight of harriers on that day, the spring of 1960 still remains the top year for numbers of harriers seen on the area.

There has been a pronounced and continuous decline in the numbers of harriers seen on spring migration since 1960 (Fig. 31.1). The drop is 70%.

BREEDING BIOLOGY

MATING

For convenience I am considering a male which brings food to a nesting female, or which is the chief defender of the nest against intruders, to be the mated male at that nest. Actually, however, mating is by no means so simply to be understood, as the following discussion will show.

Sky dancing has been presumed to be involved in mate selection and indeed it may be, but male harriers also sky dance over likely-looking nesting areas on migration. In 1959, with increasing bewilderment, I tried to recognize the plumage and style of dancing of what I believed to be the resident male in a small marsh in front of our house. Simultaneously we attempted to trap our resident pair. From sight observations it became plain that quite a few different males sky danced over this marsh during the spring. We actually trapped 29 harriers, 11 males and 18 females, near this small marsh (big enough for only one territory) in our attempts to catch and mark the "resident pair." The female which finally brought off young in the marsh in July was first caught on 17 April; her mate, however, was not one of the 11 males previously banded there and, as our trapping attempts through the spring had been intensive, I suspect that he moved into this territory after the migrating sky-dancing males had passed northward.

I am pretty well convinced, therefore, that at least during migration a sky-dancing male is not necessarily advertising the territory he has selected for nesting, nor is he necessarily close to mate selection. American woodcock and common snipe similarly display while on migration. This is not to say that sky dancing has no relationship to territory and mating. For example, once, on 26 June 1961, after a nest had eggs, a female was either killed or injured in trapping, and the male sky danced within 1 hour and 29 minutes, presumably to attract a replacement mate.

We have seen too few copulations to know when or where they normally occur. Despite many days of field work and repeated observations of nest building, we have seen only three copulations during this study, one on 10 April, one on 6 May, and one on 13 July when the pair already had two young flying well. We cannot even state unequivocally that harriers do not copulate promiscuously before the pair bond is formed. We have only once seen a marked female copulate. Her partner was unbanded, but 4 days later she was flying about with a different, and marked, male. I do not know whether this was a case of pre-pairing copulation, or loss and replacement of a mate.

Defense of nest would seem a clear indication that the pair bond had been established, but even this is fraught with uncertainties. Our trapping technique during the breeding season, using a horned owl near the nest, gave us many excellent opportunities to watch territorial defense, especially when we failed to net the adults promptly. When the male was not present, the female tended to exhibit a rather standard pattern of behavior, alternating between stooping at the owl, sitting in *trees* (in itself unusual), flying away from time to time, and most interesting of all, what I have termed "distress circling."

Distress circling is soaring in circles, often at great altitudes, and appears to serve the function of drawing in the male to help. Most often her mate comes to join in stooping at the owl; however, the presence of any other harrier on the wing often causes her to stoop with greater vehemence. One particularly persistent and hard-to-catch female by distress circling successively attracted three males: her own mate, another male (probably her mate of the year before and now known to be mated to another female), and still another male, a marked bird. Thus three different males defended this site, but I consider only the one which was usually present, and which drove one of the others away, to be her mate. At another nest, where I was holding the female ready for weighing and was trying for the male, a foreign adult female appeared and stooped at the owl. Possibly she was attracted by the male's stoops.

We have seven cases of certain or almost certain bigamy. Four were among nests that were clumped together, and three were single males each defending two nests that were isolated from other harrier nestings. One male, with red imps in both wings, practised "trigamy."

To add to the confusion, robber females should be mentioned. I have seen males forced to give up food to females which came up from the ground and, crabbing, took it from them. These may have been simple cases of bigamy, with the less popular wife trying to get her due. In no case were marked birds involved, but it is my impression that these females were simply taking advantage of a male carrying food over their nesting areas. Thus I fear that even a food transfer is not surely a sign of a mated pair.

Altogether, the pair bond in harriers appears to be both flexible and imprecise, and further study of marked birds is needed.

NESTING

This was not a nesting study in the usual sense. The material gathered on nesting was largely a by-product. In order to keep disturbance to a minimum, I have avoided early visits to nests and so have relatively few data for the laying and incubation periods. I do, however, have almost as complete data on the annual production of young as a detailed nesting study could have given.

We tried to find all the nests on the study area each year. In 12 cases we were unable to find the nest itself but knew its approximate position by the presence of free-flying young, which characteristically are conspicuous and remain in the close vicinity of their nests for several weeks. By using such young as telltales, I believe that we probably found virtually all nests and nest localities in all years except 1959, when we were not able to cover the whole area. An unknown number of unsuccessful nests may have eluded us, but we did find 34 of them, including 21 which failed in the egg stage or at hatching.

In total we found 99 nests and nest localities (hereafter simply lumped as nests), averaging 15.3 per year. In 1965 we found only four nests despite intensive search. It was the latest spring during the study (in fact, the latest in many years), the mouse population was low, and the count of spring migrants was the lowest among our records (Fig. 31.1).

Table 31.1 gives the total of nests found and their production for the area as a whole, and Table 31.2 the success of 80 nests found before fledging. It is necessary to exclude nests found after fledging in calculating nest success, for we would not have known of these nests except for the fact that they were successful as shown by the already fledged young. Despite the possibility that the number of nests may be in error because of the omission of some unsuccessful nests that were not found, the variation in the number of young fledged on the area as a whole (Table 31.1) is real. The decline in production from 1963 through 1965 is striking and incontrovertible.

The suspected causes of nest failures were as follows:

Nest failure *before hatching,* 19: Eggs disappeared, 6—two of these nests each contained only two white (i.e., well-incubated) eggs when found, leading me to suspect that a vertebrate might be removing eggs one by one; another became vulnerable due to a path beaten by children; the other three, cause unknown. Eggs broken, 8—one nest each because of deer *(Odocoileus virginianus),* skunk *(Mephitis mephitis),* trapping, and trampling by cattle; unknown, four, of which one was probably doomed because the cover of thin quack grass *(Agropyron repens)* was wholly inadequate. Eggs deserted, 5—one each because of haying nearby and lethal cover (an oatfield mowed before hatch); unknown, three.

Nest failure *at hatching,* 2: At one nest the female was brooding a putrefying chick about 1–2 days old with three eggs that failed to hatch; at another, all chicks appeared weak and lacking in vitality, and all died shortly after hatching.

Nest failure *after hatching,* 13: At one nest the young were killed by a raptor and at another by a skunk; at one the downy young were eaten alive by carrion beetles (Silphidae); unknown, 10. One of the unexplained failures was perhaps caused by disease: the half-grown decomposed nest-

Table 31.1. Harrier Nests Found and Young Fledged: All Data

	1959	1960	1961	1962	1963	1964	1965	Total[a]
Total nests found	7	18	19	13	25	13	4	99
Fledged at least one young	7	10	8	7	20	10	3	65
Nests failed	0	8	11	6	5	3	1	34
Total young fledged	At least 27	At least 28	34	At least 22	At least 60	At least 28	13	At least 212

[a] [Five, 3, and 2 nests were found in 1966, 1967, and 1968. All fledged at least one young each; total fledged: 12, 5, and 5. No unsuccessful nests were found.]

Table 31.2. Success of Nests Found Before Fledging[a]

	1960	1961	1962	1963	1964	1965	Total[b]
Nests found before fledging	15	19	9	23	10	4	80
Failed at egg stage	6	8	2	3	1	1	21
Failed at young stage	2	3	4	2	2	0	13
Total failed	8	11	6	5	3	1	34
Total successful	7	8	3	18	7	3	46
Percent successful	47%	42%	33%	78%	70%	75%	58%

[a] 1959 has been excluded because the nest census was incomplete, and all nests were found very late.

[b] Two nests were found before fledging in both 1966 and 1967, and one in 1968. All 5 were successful and fledged a total of 5, 5, and 2 young.

lings were still being fed, and there was a substantial amount of fresh and old food at the nest. Trapping may have been the basic cause of six of the unexplained failures, especially in the case of nests at which we used bownets. We tried very few bownet catches, perhaps three, but began to suspect that a net swinging over the female from above is far more apt to cause desertion than dho-gaza catches.

Of course I wondered to what extent I caused nest failures. If one excludes 1959, when all nests were found late and less complete records were taken, 80 nests were found before the young were free-flying and presumably rather well able to evade enemies: 34, or 43%, failed. At first blush I was inclined to blame myself for nest failures, and made up a vulnerability chart (Fig. 31.2) as a test. In this I am making the following assumptions:

1. A laying period of 9 days. The average size of 42 completed clutches was 4.5 eggs. Eggs appear to be laid at about 2-day intervals, based on my own relatively few records and Balfour's (1957) statement that eggs are normally laid at 48-hour, but sometimes longer, intervals.
2. An incubation period of 31 days. Balfour (1957) gives the average incubation period of 23 eggs as 31.26 days; Breckenridge (1935) determined the incubation period in two instances as 31 and 31–32 days.
3. A nestling period of about 30 days, during which the young remain on the ground in and near the nest and after which they begin to fly, becoming relatively more secure thereafter. Hammond and Henry (1949) reported a nestling period of 30–35 days.
4. The period of vulnerability is thus at least 70 days.
5. Back-dating of eggs and young is often possible. Fresh-laid harrier eggs were pale blue and turned white in 2–3 days. (Balfour, 1962, found the bleaching period to be somewhat longer, up to a week in length.) Thus I was able to estimate the laying of the first egg rather closely if

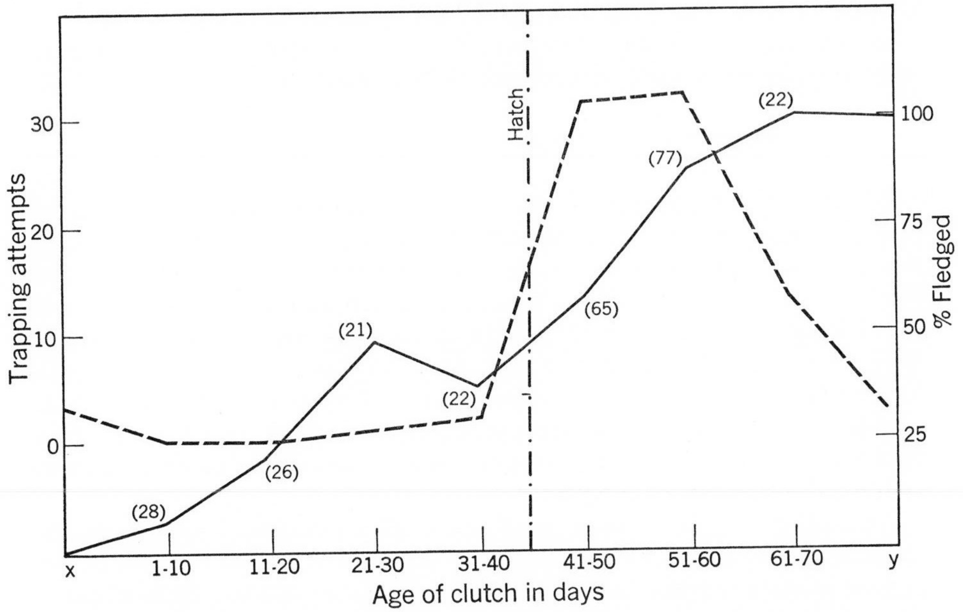

Fig. 31.2. Fledging success of eggs or nestlings found at different stages of the 70-day period of vulnerability and in relation to trapping. UW Cartographic Lab.
Solid line = percent of success of clutches found at different times during period of vulnerability. Sample size for each age class given in parentheses.
x = 37 eggs of unknown age.
y = 34 young already flying when found.

there were any blue eggs in the nest. For nests that were already hatched when found, I made up an age scale based on the length of the longest remex. Young harriers having thick tarsi and chocolate irises are females and those having slender tarsi and a greyish cast to the irises are males.

Fig. 31.2 is an attempt to explore the relationship between fledging success and disturbance caused by trapping. It is based on 92 nests, for 66 of which I knew or could interpolate the date of hatching of the first egg; 1959 is again omitted. This figure shows fledging success in relation to the time the nests were found, plus the number of trapping attempts through the nesting period. As one might expect, the later in the vulnerability period a nest was found (hence the fewer days of vulnerability that still remained), the higher was the percentage of fledging success. At present I cannot account for the relatively high mortality in the period just before the hatch. This is not the time of our most frequent visits to nests. It has been our policy (with the exception of six nests, all of which failed), to visit nests only often enough to band the young and, where possible, the adults; and to trap adults only after the eggs have hatched.

It appears from Fig. 31.2 that we did not cause excessive disturbance by trapping after the hatch: the period when we visited nests was most often the period of high and increasing nest success.

PARENTAL FACTORS AFFECTING SURVIVAL OF YOUNG

Whether or not polygyny is involved, male parents not infrequently either partially or completely desert the growing young. Sometimes, as the interest of the male wanes, he sits on a fence post near the nest, and the female chases him away as though urging him to provide for the family. I know of no case in which the male alone reared the young, nor have we ever seen a male at the nest. At a few nests we did not see a male in the nest vicinity after the young were half grown. With such a large area to cover, we seldom had time to watch individual nests to count male food trips; however, it is my impression that assiduous fathers augured well for the survival of the young.

Assuming weight to be a good index of condition, I compared the weights of 35 males and 55 females with their brood success. Males ranged in weight from 304 to 361 g, females from 432 to 621 g. Eight of these males had nests that failed: their weights were scattered through the range 329–349 g. Thus, nest failures were not associated with either the heaviest nor the lightest males. By contrast, nests of 6 of the 7 heaviest females failed, and all of the 17 unsuccessful females ranged from 464 to 621 g. While not conclusive, these data suggest that the heaviest females were less successful than the others, perhaps because they took better care of themselves than of their eggs and young.

Superannuation has been suspected as a cause of breeding failures in the case of the peregrine. I now have data on 46 harrier nestings involving birds of known age or known minimum age, ranging from subadults to at least 5 years old (Table 31.3); several individuals were known to breed in more than 1 year and are counted more than once. It is interesting that the 14 subadults bred with the same degree of success (79%) as

Table 31.3. Nest Success of Banded Harriers of Known Age

Success	Age and no. of individuals		At least		
	Subadult	2[a]	3[b]	4[b]	5[b]
Reared at least one young	11	7	9	6	3
Failed	3	1	4	0	2
Percent successful	79%	88%	69%	100%	60%

[a] Two birds banded as nestlings, 6 identified by plumage and eye color.

[b] Minimal age in years.

this group as a whole (78%). There is no lessening of success through the fourth year; the drop to 60% among the 5-year-olds is based on a sample which is probably too small to be significant.

Breckenridge (1935) points out that the smaller nestling harriers often fail to survive due to their inability to secure food in competition with their larger nest mates. I too have noticed this. It appears astonishing that the tiniest could survive such competition. I should like to suggest that there may be compensating mechanisms at work. One, which I observed with Cooper's hawks rather than with harriers, is a visual signal. Watching the adult bringing food to the partly grown young, which I had tethered on the ground, I noticed that whichever young hawk had been least recently fed held its feathers so as to display the maximum amount of white down among the dark feathers, and that this was the one that was fed first by the adult (Hamerstrom, 1957). The display of white down appeared to act as a releaser, and may also do so in the case of young harriers. The second mechanism, which I have noticed with young harriers, is an auditory releaser. The hunger call of a very young harrier causes its older brethren to scuttle away as though they could not abide the sound. The mere presence of a very young harrier does not have this effect. These two phenomena seem worth further investigation.

FIDELITY TO MATE AND TO NESTING AREA

Fidelity will be discussed in more detail in another paper. Results thus far may be summarized by saying that, although breeding harriers did commonly return to the study area, pair fidelity was extremely rare. Only one female was known to mate with the same male more than once, but she also had mated with a second male. Of 217 nestlings banded, only three have been known to return to the area (2 years later). Certain aspects of the fidelity study are pertinent to the population data and are introduced here.

Banding shows that those harriers which have nested successfully are more apt to return in a later year than those whose nests failed. A total of 92 adults has been banded at the nest, but four must be excluded because they were banded in 1965 and at this writing have not yet had a chance to come back. Most (72%) of the remaining 88 birds did not return at all. Twenty-six of them, 9 males and 17 females, did return in a later year. Of this group, to my astonishment, all of the females and all but one of the males had successfully reared young in the past. Further, the success of repeat breeders was unusually high. Of 7 males that had fledged young in the nest at which they were first caught, 6 fledged young again when they came back another year; 1 of them returned still another year, but this time his nest failed. And of 10 females that had fledged young, 9 were again successful when they returned. For one of these we had a 4-year history: after two successful seasons she failed in the third, but nested successfully again in the fourth year.

It is a virtual certainty that more birds returned than these figures show. We saw six banded but not color-marked birds that we could not trap. They were probably returning adults that had been banded before we started using colored jesses, as only three banded nestlings have been known to return.

GENERAL DISCUSSION

Perhaps the most striking finding of this study was the drastic decrease in the number of nests in 1965. How to interpret this decrease is not wholly clear. Strong annual fluctuations seem not uncommon. Balfour (pers. comm.) has kindly given me the number of hen harrier (*Circus c. cyaneus*) nests on his 13-square-mile (33-sq-km) study area in Orkney, Scotland, from 1944 through 1965. His nesting density was higher than mine but roughly the same number of nests per year was involved (Fig. 31.3). Balfour's data and mine both show a fairly wide range in number of nests from year to year. I cannot account for my extreme drop in 1965, beyond anything in Balfour's data.

On my study area the downward trend in numbers of nests from 1963 to 1965 is comparable to the trend in numbers of harriers seen on migration (Fig. 31.1). However, we have kept count of the potential breeders on the area each year (Fig 31.4), and although there was some decrease in the number of adults present in 1965, there were plainly enough present for a normal breeding season. The birds either failed to breed, or their nests were broken up so early in the season that we could not find them. For reasons already explained (see Techniques, above), I do not think that early failure is the answer. It seems reasonable to assume that the low number of nests found in 1965 reflects failure to breed. Although Table 31.1 suggests compensatory reproduction at the lower nesting density, fewer young were fledged on the whole area than in any other year.

At this point Daniel Q. Thompson (pers. comm.) kindly gave me his figures on the abundance of meadow voles (*Microtus* spp.) as determined by forage utilization counts in Wisconsin, northern Illinois, and southeastern Minnesota (Fig. 31.5). The close agreement between harrier productivity on my study area and vole abundance in the larger geographic region is striking. The vole index, however, did not drop as sharply in 1965 as the number of harrier nests. [For 1966–68, see Addendum.]

Food may thus be implicated. Harriers prey on both birds and mammals, and are not dependent on either group alone. For example, Errington and Breckenridge (1936) found that 49% of 557 summer food items

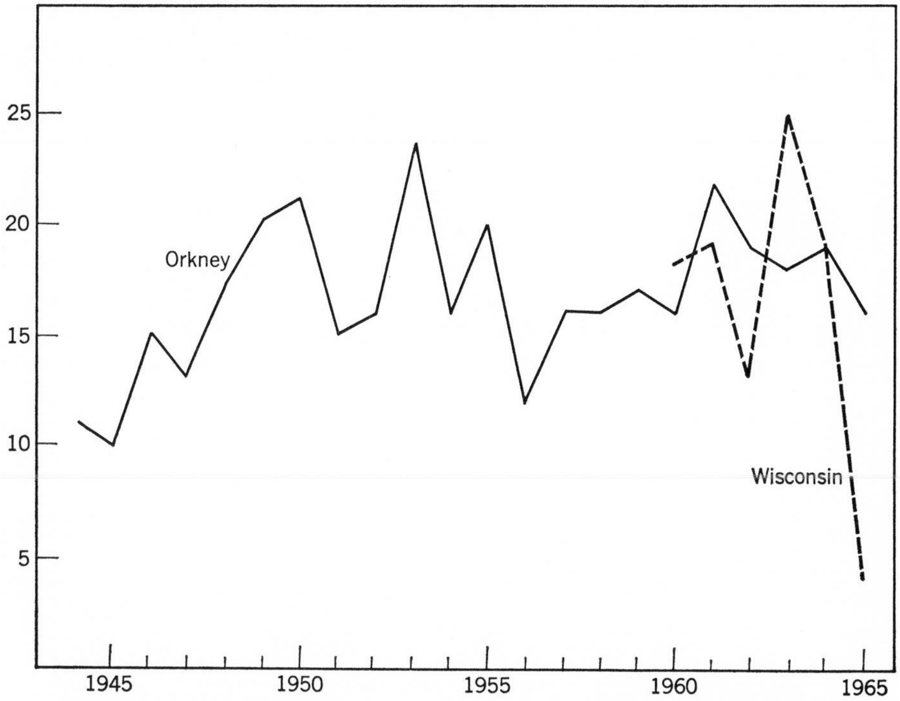

Fig. 31.3. Annual nest censuses on study areas in Orkney, Scotland (Edward Balfour's data) and in Wisconsin, USA (Hamerstrom). UW Cartographic Lab.

in Iowa consisted of birds, while only 4% of 74 items were birds in an exceptionally high vole year in Wisconsin. In no year of my study did there appear to be any scarcity of such foods as red-winged blackbirds, eastern and western meadowlarks, and thirteen-lined ground squirrels (*Citellus tridecemlineatus*). Quantity of prey did not seem to be lacking; therefore we can explore the idea of quality. One might postulate that there are two forces at work, one through the avian component of the harrier's diet and the other through the microtine component. Voles may be high-quality food for harrier production, either voles *per se* or perhaps the flora of their long digestive tracts. Alternatively, a deleterious element in the avian component of the harrier's diet may be responsible for their decline, and scarcity of voles is important mainly as it leads to increased feeding on birds.

Certain changes in behavior during the last 3 years may have a bearing. From time to time we have noticed that not all aerial transfers of food are of the classic type, with the male flying high and dropping the prey to the female who catches it in the air beneath him. Sometimes the male fails to gain altitude and the transfer is at close range with the

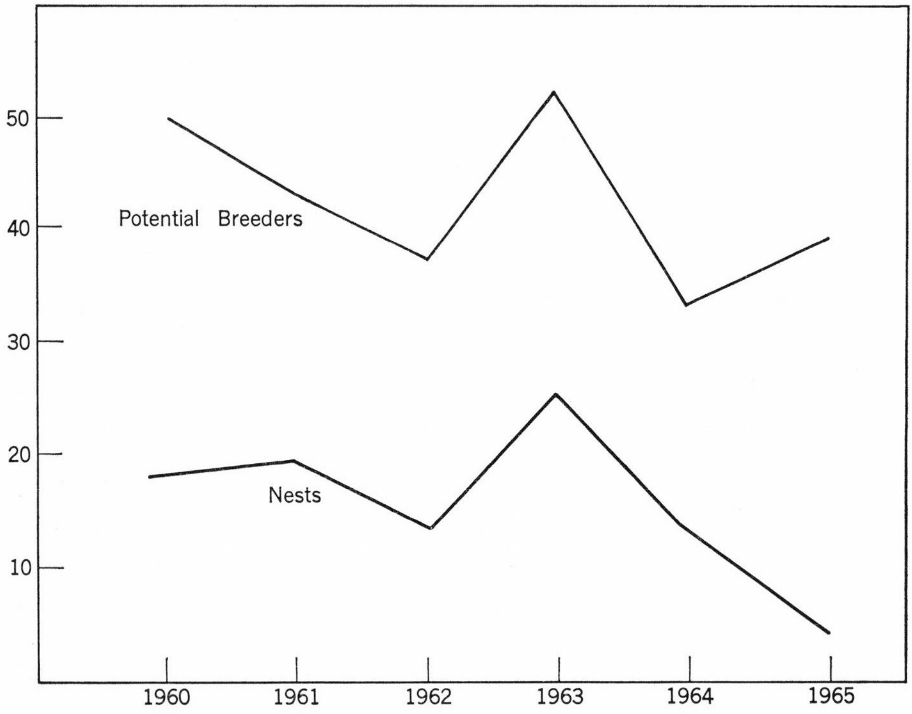

Fig. 31.4. Nests found in relation to breeders on the study area, 1960–65. [In 1966, 32 potential breeders produced 5 nests; in 1967, 40 produced 3 nests; in 1968, 30 produced 2 nests.] UW Cartographic Lab.

birds even touching each other. In 1963 Don Follen, who was banding harriers about 40 miles (64 km) west of my study area, told me that he was seeing many almost frantic talon-to-talon transfers, often involving actual crabbing. I saw the same thing as a common occurrence for the first time that summer, and such atypical transfers seemed more common in 1964 and 1965 as well.

Again, although there seemed to be an adequate breeding population on the area in 1965, sky dancing was sharply reduced. In fact in 1965, for the first time in some 24 springs in central Wisconsin, I did *not once* see a harrier sky dance, either during migration or in the nesting season.

In summary, the low nesting density in 1965 was associated with (a) an exceptionally late spring, (b) a decrease, continued over a period of several years, in the number of spring migrants through the study area, and (c) two behavioral anomalies, i.e., atypical food transfer and a dearth of sky dancing, the latter on a scale unprecedented in my experience. The paucity of nests was not associated with any comparable decrease in the number of adults on the study area during the breeding sea-

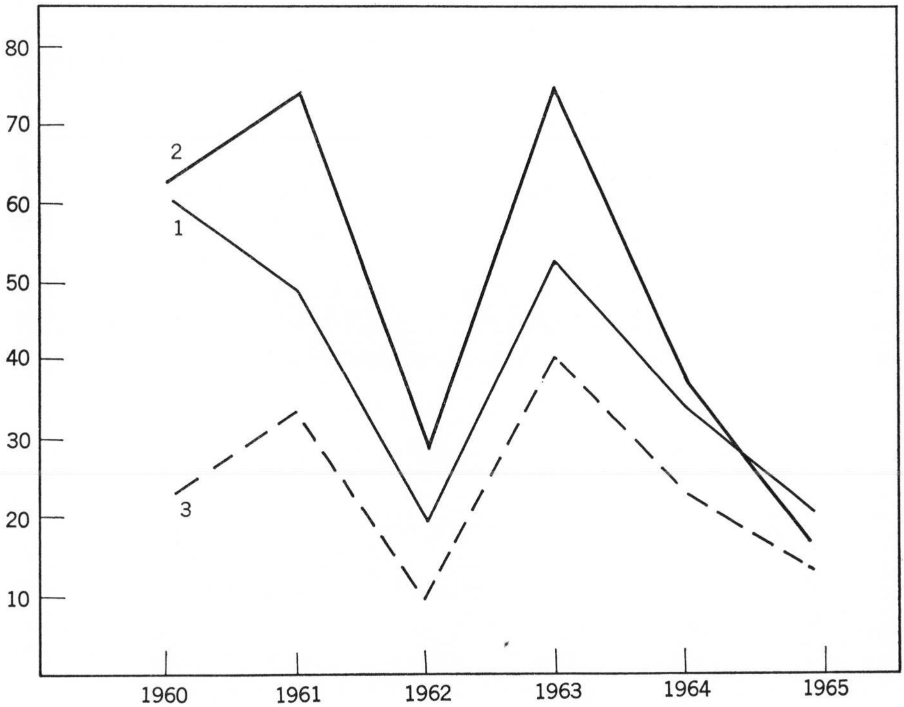

Fig. 31. 5. Harrier productivity in relation to regional vole abundance.
(1) Percent of stems cut by voles in sample plots in Wisconsin, northern Illinois, and southeastern Minnesota (Daniel Q. Thompson's data).
(2) Number of harrier eggs found on the study area.
(3) Number of harriers fledged on the study area.
[The stems-cut-by-voles index rose to 51.6 and 62.9 in 1966 and 1967. Local trapping since 1964 also showed a strong increase in voles in 1966 and 1967, but the number of young fledged did not increase. The local vole population in 1968 was extremely low.] UW Cartographic Lab.

son (although some decrease did occur), nor with any apparent overall shortage of food (although meadow voles were regionally at a low level), nor was the breeding season so strongly curtailed as to rule out the possibility of successful nesting. The birds simply seemed to have returned from the south without the normal sexual drive, suggesting that the trouble may have begun in the wintering quarters.

There are suggestive parallels with the "pesticide story" as developed elsewhere in this symposium. Certainly pesticides are heavily used on the harrier's wintering range in the southern United States, and it is to be expected that prey animals will pick them up. The postulated deleterious element in birds as a source of food on my study area might well also be pesticides. Thus, returning to the area in a year of vole scarcity, a higher than usual proportion of birds in the diet might continue and intensify an exposure begun on the wintering grounds and lead to unsuccessful breeding as in 1965. This is speculation: I have not had funds nor manpower to explore the possibility. The fact remains that the cause of the decrease in nesting is still unknown. The season of 1965 could have been no more than an aberrant year—but the *degree* of departure from the other years seems out of proportion. It is too soon to know whether or not this harrier population, like the peregrine of the eastern United States, is slipping into limbo.

(Recent counts suggest that it is. The population did not respond to two years of increased vole abundance in 1966 and 1967; in 1968 it was at the lowest point of the ten-year study period.)

ACKNOWLEDGMENTS

I wish to express my gratitude to the many people who have helped, and in particular to Raymond K. Anderson, Daniel D. Berger, Lawrence D. Crowley, Paul Drake, Jr., Frederick N. Hamerstrom, Jr., Joseph Platt, William Scharf, and Charles Sindelar, Jr., and my appreciation for financial help from the Josselyn Van Tyne Research Fund in 1960 and from a Frank M. Chapman Grant in 1964. Those who helped with the field work in its first years have been acknowledged in an earlier paper (Hamerstrom, 1963).

SUMMARY

American harriers were studied on a 40,000-acre (16,000-ha) area in central Wisconsin from 1959 through 1965. Conclusions are based on a 7-year census, 99 nests, and 553 harriers banded, including 92 breeding adults.

The population is migratory. Adult males are the first to return, followed next by adult females and then by subadults.

The pair bond seems imprecise and flexible during a given breeding season, and pair fidelity from year to year was extremely rare (one instance) although 26 of 88 banded adults did come back. Polygyny sometimes occurred. The success of 80 nests found before fledging was 58%; the trapping and banding of adults at the nest after the hatch did not appear to increase nest failure, but such disturbance before hatching may have done so. There was some evidence that the heaviest females tended to be less successful in nesting than the others, but this did not seem to be the case in males. Subadults were as successful in nesting as older birds.

Harriers that had nested successfully were more apt to return in later years than those whose nests had failed, and the success of such returning breeders was higher than the average.

There was a 70% decrease in the number of migrants through the area from 1960 through 1965. There was a similar decrease in the numbers of nests, eggs, and young fledged, although the potential breeding population was adequate each year. Nests decreased 84%, from a high of 25 in 1963 to 4 in 1965. The abundance of nests appeared to fluctuate with the abundance of voles (*Microtus* spp.) in the region from 1961 to 1965. The cause of the harrier decline is unknown, but there is suggestive evidence that pesticides, acting through the avian component of the harrier's diet, may be involved.

ADDENDUM, 1968

Since this paper was written, abnormalities in breeding behavior have seemingly continued to shortstop most harriers before egg laying. The percentage of harriers failing to nest has risen to 87 in 1968.

The parallelism between vole abundance and harrier productivity from 1961 through 1965 completely broke down in the period 1966–68 (see footnote to Fig. 31.5).

LITERATURE CITED

Balfour, E. 1957. Observations on the breeding biology of the hen harrier in Orkney. Bird Notes, 27(6–7):177–183, 216–224.

———. 1962. The nest and eggs of the hen harrier in Orkney. Bird Notes, 30(3):69–73.

Berger, D. D., and Frances Hamerstrom. 1962. Protecting a trapping station from raptor predation. J. Wildl. Mgmt., 26(2):203–206.

Breckenridge, W. J. 1935. An ecological study of some Minnesota marsh hawks. Condor, 37(6):268–276.

Errington, P. L., and W. J. Breckenridge. 1936. Food habits of marsh hawks in the glaciated prairie region of north-central United States. Amer. Midl. Nat., 7(5):831–848.

Hamerstrom, F. N., Jr., O. E. Mattson, and Frances Hamerstrom. 1957. A guide to prairie chicken management. Wisconsin Conservation Dep., Tech. Wildl. Bull. 15. 128 p.

Hamerstrom, Frances. 1942. Dominance in winter flocks of chickadees. Wilson Bull., 54(1):32–42.

———. 1957. The influence of a hawk's appetite on mobbing. Condor, 59(3):192–194.

———. 1963. The use of great horned owls in catching marsh hawks. Proc. Internat. Ornithol. Congr., 13:866–869.

Hammond, M. C., and C. J. Henry. 1949. Success of marsh hawk nests in North Dakota. Auk, 66(3):271–274.

CHAPTER 32

RINGED PEREGRINES IN GREAT BRITAIN

C. J. Mead

Twenty recoveries have been reported from the 214 peregrines ringed in Great Britain since 1920; in addition, eight foreign-ringed birds have been recorded. Table 32.1 shows the annual distribution of the British ringing and recovery totals. These records yield information on movement and survival/mortality.

MOVEMENT

Recoveries of British-ringed peregrines (all of British-hatched birds) do not show any consistent long-distance migration but a rather confused

Table 32.1. Annual Ringing and Recovery Totals of Peregrines in Great Britain

No records were kept of the annual totals before 1920. Only 5 of the grand total of 214 are recorded as having been ringed whilst free-flying: all other birds were ringed as nestlings. The asterisks indicate the number of recoveries reported in each year.

	Year of decade									
Decade	0	1	2	3	4	5	6	7	8	9
1920	—	—	—	3	—	*	4*	—	10	5
1930	8	11	5	7	1	3	5	—	4	15
1940	3**	6	3*	3*	—	3	11**	*	5*	5
1950	6*	5*	7*	7*	3*	5**	4	7	3*	2
1960	3*	3	13	1	8					

pattern of dispersal from the breeding sites (Thomson, 1958). One long-distance recovery, from northwest Scotland to southern Ireland, of 445 miles (712 km) south reported in January of the bird's first year is the only record comparable in distance to even the shortest of the eight Scandinavian-ringed birds reported from the British Isles. These nine records are plotted in Fig. 32.1. Other recoveries showing movement seem biased,

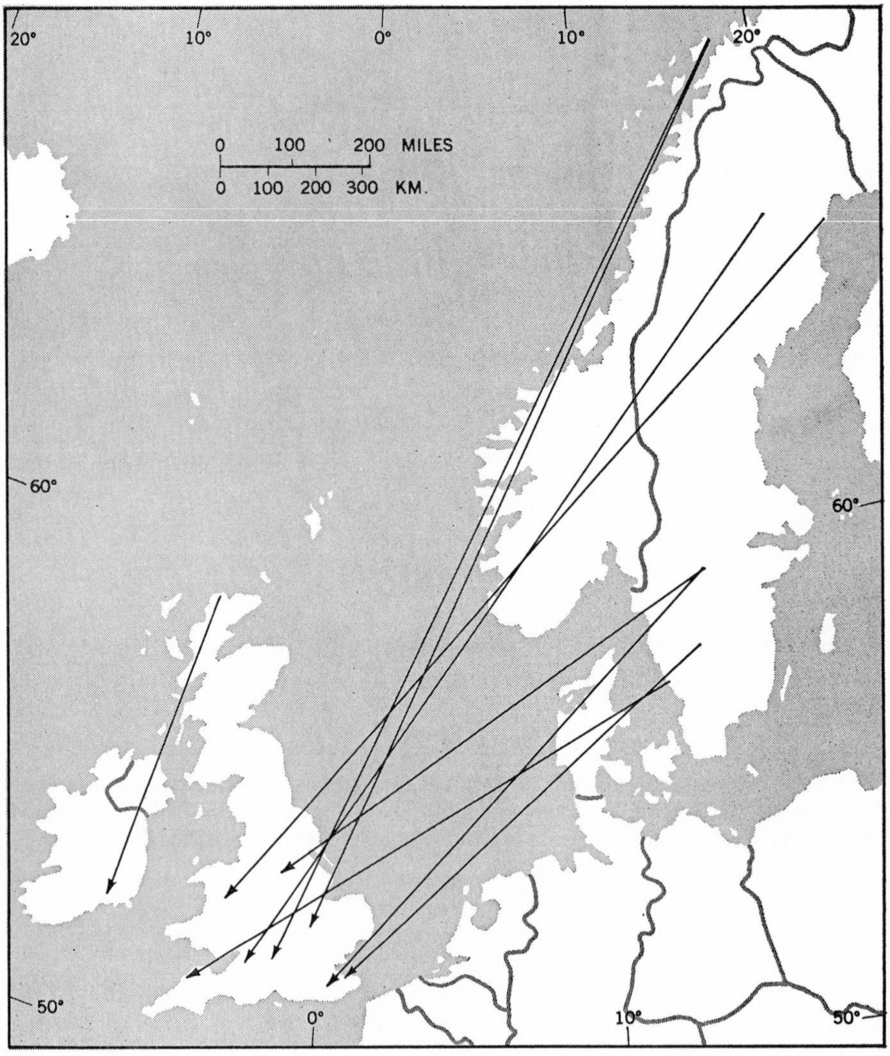

Fig. 32.1. Peregrine recoveries in Great Britain: 8 foreign-ringed birds and 1 long-distance movement of a native-ringed bird. UW Cartographic Lab.

at all times of the year, to the north. Fig. 32.2, in which are plotted the distances and directions of recoveries for the half-years April-September and October-March, shows this very clearly. Since disproportionate numbers of peregrines are ringed to the south of their main stronghold in the northern half of Scotland, a ringed bird is far more likely to find a vacant territory to the north of its birthplace than to the south.

One other aspect of movement is illuminated by a ringing recovery. This concerns a nestling common curlew ringed in Sutherland in 1964 and found dead 8 or 9 miles (13 or 14 km) away in an occupied peregrine eyrie. The time between ringing and recovery and its age when ringed are such that the curlew's maximum contribution to this movement would be of the order of a few hundred yards. This illustrates the distance a nesting peregrine will travel while feeding young.

SURVIVAL/MORTALITY

Of the 20 British recoveries listed (Table 32.2), 16 are recorded as being dead, one was "trapped accidentally," and another was found in-

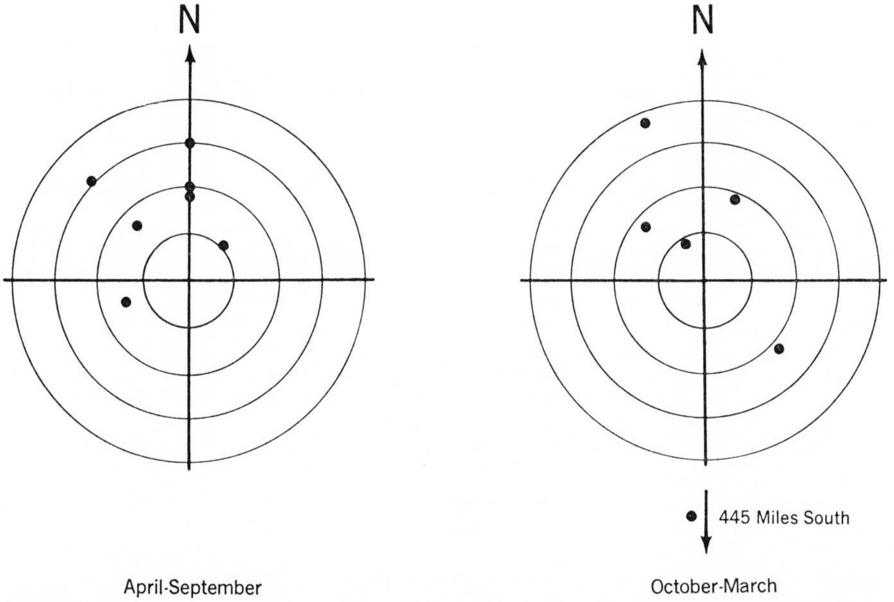

Fig. 32.2. Distances and direction of movement of peregrines ringed in Great Britain. The concentric circles represent movements of 50, 100, 150, and 200 miles respectively (roughly 80, 160, 240, and 320 km). Movements of less than 40 miles (64 km) are omitted. UW Cartographic Lab.

Table 32.2. Recoveries of Peregrines Ringed in Great Britain

Localities are all given by county alone. Recoveries are arranged chronologically by ringing dates. Four birds, all from one Cornish brood in 1914, which failed to fledge are omitted. The initial line lists ringing data; second line, recovery data. The manner of recovery is given by the following symbols:

Pull. Pullus, young still in the nest
Juv. Juvenile (in both cases near their nest site)
v caught or trapped, and released with ring
\+ shot
x found dead or dying
xA found long dead
() caught or trapped and not released, or released with ring removed
/?/ manner of recovery unknown

102.603	Pull.	29. 5.23	Westmorland		
	x	5. 5.24	Westmorland	Sexed ♀	5 miles
102.612	Pull.	29. 5.23	Same brood as 102.603		
	/?/	Spring 1925	Perthshire		ca. 100 miles N.
27.624	Pull.	9. 6.26	Somerset		
	+	25.11.26	Somerset	Sexed ♂	Local
402.306	Pull.	9. 6.35	Cumberland	Brood of 2	
	+	1. 4.43	Westmorland		12 miles S
404.244	Pull.	9. 6.38	Yorkshire	Brood of 2	
	+	20. 4.42	Argyllshire	At nest	152 miles NW
404.631	Pull.	0. 5.39	Selkirkshire	Brood of 4	
	+	0.10.40	Kincardineshire		95 miles NNE
404.632	Pull.	0. 5.39	Same brood as 404.631		
	x	0. 5.40	Berwickshire		51 miles NE
404.257	Pull.	15. 7.40	Yorkshire		
	xA	0.10.47	Yorkshire		15 miles SE
404.810	Pull.	29. 5.43	Breconshire		
	/?/	11.10.46	Montgomeryshire		49 miles NNW
404.716	Pull.	21. 5.46	Cumberland	Brood of 2	
	()	9.12.46	Ayrshire		85 miles NW
404.715	Pull.	21. 5.46	Same brood as 404.716		
	+	0. 4.52	Isle of Man		72 miles WSW
406.002	Pull.	22. 5.48	Isle of Man		
	+	8. 6.48	Isle of Man		Local
404.260	Juv.	5. 7.49	Yorkshire		
	x	11. 8.50	Fife	On tide-line	150 miles N
407.257	Pull.	27. 6.50	Sutherland	Brood of 2	
	+	23. 1.51	Wexford (Ireland)		445 miles S
407.258	Pull.	27. 6.50	Same brood as 407.257		
	x	ca. 22.10.54	Banffshire		110 miles SE
408.037	Pull.	2. 6.51	Kirkcudbrightshire		
	x	11. 4.55	Renfrewshire		48 miles N
408.783	Pull.	25. 5.53	Inverness-shire	Brood of 3	
	x	7. 9.53	Inverness-shire		12 miles N
408.782	Pull.	25. 5.53	Same brood as 408.783		
	x		Ross-shire		80 miles NW
409.462	Pull.	31. 5.53	Lundy Island (Devon)		51°12′N, 4°40′W
	x	ca. 17. 3.58	Louth (Ireland)	Apparently drowned	190 miles NNW
408.421	Juv.	1. 7.60	Inverness-shire		
	()	31. 7.60	Morayshire	Injury to wing	28 miles NE

Recoveries in Great Britain of Peregrines Ringed Elsewhere

Göteborg	Ad. ♀	5. 6.35	. . . (Västergötland) SWEDEN	ca. 58°00'N, 13°00'E
23.514 D	/?/	18. 1.37	Birchington (Kent)	51°23'N, 1°19'E
Stavanger	Pull.	5. 7.38	Bleik, Andöy, Lofoten Islands, NORWAY	69°18'N, 16°00'E
30.260	v	4.11.38	West Ilsley, near Wantage (Berkshire)	51°32'N, 1°19'W
Stavanger	Pull.	9. 7.43	Bleik (as above)	
30.521	+	2.12.43	Swaton Fen, near Sleaford (Lincolnshire)	52°56'N, 0°19'W
Stockholm	Pull.	1. 7.45	Kanevare, Jokkmokk (Norrbotten) SWEDEN	66°32'N, 20°00'E
TA 3346	( )	22. 2.46	near Stow-on-the-Wold (Gloucestershire)	51°56'N, 1°44'W
Göteborg	Pull.	16. 6.46	Stråvalla, near Åsa (Halland) SWEDEN	57°17'N, 12°10'E
D 39.413	/?/	30. 1.47	South Molton (Devon)	51°01'N, 3°50'W
Stockholm	Pull.	20. 6.46	Hällefors (Örebro) SWEDEN	59°47'N, 14°30'E
TA 6613	/?/	6.12.46	Yalding, near Maidstone (Kent)	51°14'N, 0°26'E
Stockholm	Pull.	20. 6.46	Same brood as TA 6613	
TA 6614	/?/	11.11.47	Escrick (Yorkshire)	53°52'N, 1°03'W
Stockholm	Pull.	6. 7.47	Luleå (Norrbotten) SWEDEN	65°35'N, 22°10'E
TA 4193	/?/	28.11.51	Onslow, near Shrewsbury (Shropshire)	52°45'N, 2°18'W

jured and given to a falconer. Recovery details are lacking for the Scandinavian-ringed birds. Seven of the 16 dead birds were reported as being shot: three of these during the war when peregrines were being shot by order of the Air Ministry. Additional details of three of the shot birds state that one was "shot at nest by keeper" (1942), another "whilst stooping at wooden pigeon decoys" (1940), and the last "whilst attacking young turkeys" (1952). None have been reported shot since the peregrine received protection by Act of Parliament in 1954 but, of course, some of the birds "found dead" may well have been shot. No. 102.603, a 1923 pullus, was reported dead by her ringer, Dr. Moon, on 5 May 1924, and his letter may be of interest:

> The Peregrine was found on a crag about two feet [61 cm] below the nest which contained one broken egg. The bird was decomposed, and I can give no suggestion as to the cause of death beyond stating that the local hunt lost two hounds from poison and many carrion crows have been found dead in that district. Though I believe the dead bird was the occupier of the nest, it is possible that she was the loser of a fight with the real owner. There are three eyries in this district, and every year I have one or more dead peregrines brought to me usually dead from injuries obviously the result of fights and not a trap or gunshot.

Dr. Moon obviously believed this 1-year-old bird capable of breeding. D. A. Ratcliffe (pers. comm.) suspects that more thorough post-mortem examinations would have revealed that such birds had really been shot.

Fig. 32.3 shows the months of recovery of all birds reported in the British Isles (except one recorded as "Spring"). There are two peaks of recoveries of old, British-bred birds—in April and October. The April peak coincides with the start of the breeding season, but the October peak seems less easily explained. Since only one of the four recoveries

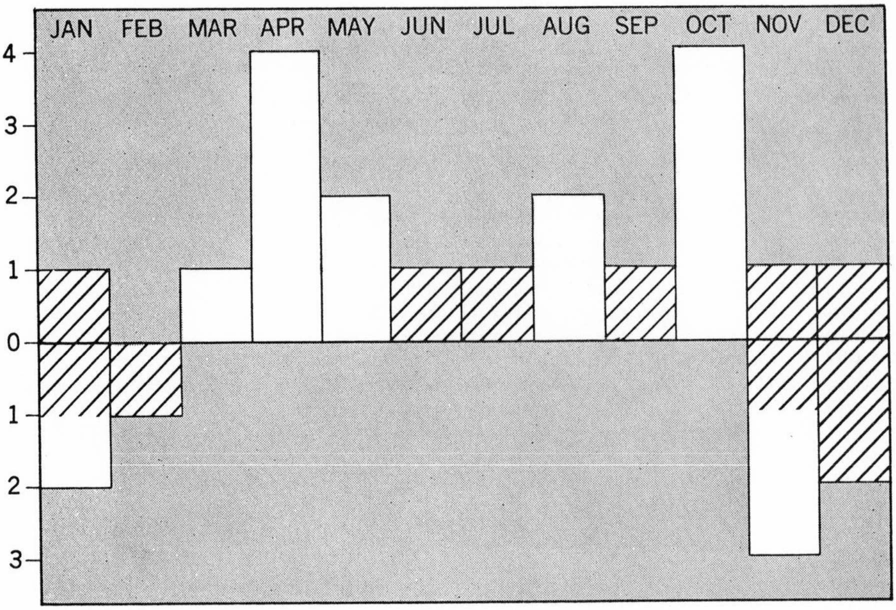

Fig. 32.3. Distribution of peregrine ringing recoveries by calendar months in Great Britain. Recoveries above the line are of British-ringed, native-bred birds; those below the line are of winter visitors to Great Britain ringed in Norway and Sweden. Cross-hatching indicates birds recovered during first year of life. UW Cartographic Lab.

was a shot bird, it is not directly connected with the shooting season but may be related to a change in food supply.

The age distribution of dead birds in completed years after their first January 1st is as follows:

Age in years	0	1	2	3	4	5	6	7
No. of individuals	5	1	0	3	1	1	1	1

The oldest bird was 7 years and 10 months old. These sketchy figures, coming mostly from the more vulnerable parts of the British population, give a further life expectation of about 2.5 years for each bird that reaches its first January 1st. This could mean that, if all first-year birds pair and attempt to breed, each pair of peregrines must raise about one young to independence each year for the population to maintain itself.

LITERATURE CITED

Thomson, A. L. 1958. The migrations of British falcons *(Falconidae)* as shown by ringing results. Brit. Birds, 51(5):179–188.

CHAPTER 33

IS THERE A GENETIC CONTINUITY CONCERNED IN EYRIE MAINTENANCE?

Clayton M. White

These remarks are the results of my analysis of data gathered from the examination of over 850 North American peregrine specimens (part of a geographic-variation study). The data are at best suggestive, and I present them for what they are worth. I make no passionate nor fanatical defense of them because of the lack of definitive proof based on a sample of adequate size; however, since the purpose of this conference is to evaluate hypotheses and crystallize ideas to account for the present status of the peregrine, I will present them. All possible explanations for the phenomenon we are witnessing should be briefly explored in the interest of the scientific mind. The answers and correct interpretations of the problem of genetic influence on maintenance of eyries, if it is real in certain populations, may be moot since the eastern North American population, which could be conveniently experimented with, no longer exists.

The impressions I received from the specimens examined are partially a function of what I consider my ability to recognize differences and similarities between individuals or populations. The peregrine, at best, is a highly variable species, but phenotypic differences, a reflection of genotype, can be very marked and constant. Before the data can receive a full scrutiny by the participants, a brief and general assessment of their morphological variation in North America is in order. (For a more complete analysis, see White, 1968.) It might be said that eastern North American peregrines differ from both western continental North American (not Pacific coast *pealei*) and Nearctic populations by being larger, with longer wings, and proportionately longer tails. Adults from the east are generally alike in that the white forehead band tends to be lacking or restricted and the head and shoulders are dark blue or blackish. The underparts are variable. Arctic specimens are lighter on the head and shoulders and usually have a very broad white forehead band. Underparts are likewise variable. It is the immature birds, however, that are distinctive. Arctic specimens are rather uniform and tend to be lighter brown with wide light edgings to the feathers on the dorsal side. They have a yellowish to buffy overwash, and the streaking on the underparts tends to be narrow and elongate. Crowns of the heads tend to be lightly marked, and prominent ocelli are present on the nape.

It is the eastern immature peregrines that are significant. They tend to range from a light-headed type with prominent ocelli to a very dark-headed bird with no ocelli; from an individual with a reddish overwash to one with a grayish overwash. The variation includes other characters in various combinations. One characteristic that tends toward uniformity is the streaking of the flanks which gives a mottled, rather than lanceolate, appearance. The extremes in the variation are usually localized rather than generalized. Birds from given areas tend to look alike in amount of pigmentation. The indications are that if the sources of data were extensive enough, recognizable demes within the population might show up as particularly manifested by the immatures.

I will not imply that a concept which applies to one segment of a population is valid for the entire species, since morphologically different populations are a product of their evolution and contain perhaps unique properties dictated by conditions. These remarks concern mainly the eastern North American sedentary populations which, from all indications, lack extensive panmixia.

The picture presented [at the conference; not reproduced here—Ed.] shows an individual from Stag Lake, New Jersey.

This individual conforms to the general eastern-type peregrine, but it is distinct as an individual. My first impression of this bird, since it was so distinctive, was that it was a dirty, sooty bird, not unlike some birds of the *pealei* population in color, but a scrutiny of the feathers showed them to be not sooty. This individual was collected on 5 May 1923, as a year-old-bird. There are two other individuals from Stag Lake that are in every detail so near alike that all of them appear to be "identical triplets." The other two specimens were taken in the early fall, one in 1915 and one in 1916. In the interim between the 1916 and 1923 specimens, an apparently breeding adult male, was also taken in late May. Even though an apparently breeding adult male was taken between the fall 1916 and spring 1923 immatures, the extreme similarity of the immatures suggests (1) that a link exists between them and a continuity of their genotypes and (2) that the collection of the adults did not break the genetic history existing at the eyrie.

As a result of information obtained from A. E. Eynon, via Hickey (pers. comm.), I am able to state the following: Three eyries were spaced around Stag Lake, ranging from ca. 13 to 18 miles (21 to 29 km) in distance from it. There was no eyrie at the lake itself. J. von Lengerke used the lake as a shooting stand for migrating hawks. This latter point is important since the chance of obtaining local birds from this point, over other localities, is increased. The immature bird, AMNH 129274, taken 10 October 1915 (wing 330 mm) is of the eastern type and not from the Arctic migrant population (wing 301–22 mm), and the fact that local birds were taken during the migration period seems to be a function of there being a shooter present and does not unequivocally reflect migration on the part of the falcon. That three eyries were so close to the lake lessens the chance, however, that all of the three immatures mentioned are from any single one of the three given eyries.

Again, it should be stressed that there are certain characteristics that make all eastern peregrines alike. The morphological variation is not constant except within limits, and yet, where there is a continuous record of individuals from a given locality, the variation from the whole of the population is constant. This same local consistency, within the labile context of population variation, is seen in a record of numerous specimens from the Fort Verde area in northern Arizona and the vicinity of Great Falls, Montana, and the Okanagan Valley, British Columbia. (Likewise, six males from the Okanagan Valley have wing lengths ranging from 302 to 305 mm while the overall wing length of males in western North America, of which the Okanagan birds are a part, varies from 291 to 318 mm.) Within highly migratory Arctic populations, however, where panmixia appears more complete, the color variation is much less but still within limits.

I will discuss another facet and then will try to correlate these points. Three of the several outstanding works on North American peregrines, i.e., Hickey (1942), Bond (1946), and Cade (1960), have commented on traditional use of the eyrie sites; and all three have attributed this to different sets of conditions and further, from what Enderson (1964) intimates, the criteria stated by these authors do not necessarily apply to prairie falcons. What is clear is that we really do not know all the factors responsible for traditional eyrie use. Since Cade had access to both the philosophies of Hickey and Bond, and was therefore able to analyze and integrate what he thought appropriate, I will draw from his work. Concerning Hickey's concept, Cade says that from Hickey's point of view a first-, second-, and third-class cliff cannot be distinguished by physical characteristics only; one must also know what kind of occupancy and breeding performance obtained as a result of peregrines having been attracted to the cliffs. That is, if the classes of cliffs can be defined only in terms of the history of their occupancy, and if that history cannot be clearly correlated with any physical dimension of cliffs, then it follows that something in addition to the cliff is operative in producing the observed history. Cade feels that first-class cliffs (those most likely to have historical occupancy) are ones occupied by a pair of "effective breeders," in other words, a pair able to fledge one or more young each year because the mates have made the necessary adjustments for a strong pair bond. This implies that the same pair returns yearly to a cliff and their return is contingent on fledging young. Cade remarks that successful mates require a history of association together at a nesting cliff.

Cade then gives an example of the famous Taughannock Falls peregrines that disappeared from the cliffs around 1948, apparently as a result of the systematic killing of one of the adult members, thus reducing "effectiveness." The adults, however, were rapidly replaced up until 1948. That rapid replacement occurs in peregrines is widely attested (Hickey, 1942; Ratcliffe, 1962), and these replacements purport to come from a "floating, nonbreeding population." Yet this "floating" population is not effective enough to maintain the "ideal" eyrie especially where killing reduces "effectiveness" of the breeding adults and results in a failure to produce young. Likewise the replacement appears not to be uniform throughout the range.

Some peregrine tree sites in the United States, for example, seem to have been localized and apparently had short histories where persecution prevailed (the collection of eggs, adults, and so forth). But the accounts of these locations indicate that trees of the type used were widespread over large areas and yet they were not used. What happened in the disappearance of the tree site is not clear. Removal of these "giant" trees doubtless had effect on the disappearance of these birds; however, as the Neosho Falls, Kansas, eyrie was only ± 50 ft (15m) up in the tree, the tree size is apparently not important. Was it the actual tree that was important then, or some other factor such as the "effectiveness" of the adults which dictated the use of trees?

A synthesis of the above, then, might well be that eyries are thought to be maintained as a result of the "effectiveness" of breeders which is dependent on whether or not young are raised. Is it that the adults (excuse the anthropomorphism) are satisfied and content with having raised young and thus return, or is there a "pool" of young that return for a brief period yearly to their homesites and are thus available if adults do not return or until they establish themselves at some other site? None of the above, however, rules out the effectiveness of a cliff in its role as an "ecological magnet."

As mentioned earlier, the collection of a year-old spring individual from a locality where identical early fall birds were taken 7 years earlier, may indicate a return to the same eyrie site of spring returning young. The fact that they are "identical" in morphological appearance, in a variable population, indicates some genetic relationship. The same parental adults may have been responsible for this, but an apparently breeding adult was taken in the interim between 1916 and 1923. The sedentary behavior of eastern peregrines is one point in favor of this postulate. The phenomenon of genetic demes within populations could conceivably be the factor responsible for the variation and number of apparently nonvalid races named in the European sedentary population. (Various names, such as *germanicus, brittanicus, rhenanus, scandinaviae,* and *cornicum,* have been given to the nominate *F. p. peregrinus* race [see Peters, 1931; Vaurie, 1961]. These names for the most part indicate local areas. Regarding this very situation, K. H. Voous [*in litt.* 5 January 1967] states, "The subspecific situation in Europe is very complex, and seems to be defined by family-groups, or at least family-tradition [both as regards nesting and distribution]. Thus there is a most remarkable homogeneity in plumage characters—[for example] in the Rhine Valley.")

The data presented above are tenuous, and the nearest banding record that comes to their support is that of an individual retaken during the spring 5 years later, 20′ lat. 00′ long. from the point at which it was banded as a nestling.

A problem of this sort would be dictated by conditions, population pressure being foremost. There are many points discordant with the idea set out above, and we are not dealing with a fixed, hard-fast phenomenon; if it were, we could not account, for example, for new eyrie sites being established (like the postwar repopulation in Britain) nor for banded birds breeding hundreds of miles distant from the place where they were raised. If there is such a "pool" of young returning to their homesites, how many years will they return before establishing eyries of their own?

The application of this problem with regard to the eastern population and its disappearance could be significant, especially if the effectiveness of the adults, for sundry reasons, is nil. Once a population is in an unstable condition of recruitment, the effects of the above problem might come into play. This could act as a final blow to a declining sedentary population, in terms of sites becoming unoccupied, especially if no replacement from more northern unaffected areas occurred. Again the variables in eyrie maintenance appear to be manifold.

SUMMARY AND CONCLUSIONS

Different geographical populations of a species (in some cases best regarded as subspecies) tend to show different biologies as a result of the factors imposed during their evolutionary histories, as graphically demonstrated in Canada geese (Hanson, 1965). Peregrines also show interpopulation ecol-physiological differences. Dementiev and Gladkov (1951: 87), for example, have demonstrated that the spring development in the gonad cycle of Eurasian peregrine populations is correlated with breeding phenology on their breeding grounds (dictated by climatic conditions in northern populations) and may not necessarily reflect the photoperiodic effect imposed on them in their wintering and prenuptial grounds. Likewise, eastern United States peregrines would conceivably have biological limits different from those of Arctic and subarctic breeding populations. Eastern populations tend to be resident or even sedentary whereas Arctic peregrines are highly migratory, and my data even indicate that the smallest individuals may go the farthest south and make the longest migrations (specimens from Chile and Paraguay). The sedentary tendency in eastern populations is probably important in their population dynamics.

Eastern populations tend to show color variation that is locally consistent within the labile context of the entire population variation; Arctic peregrines show less color variation on a population basis. The local consistency of the temperate-latitude, resident peregrines would tend to support the idea that there indeed may be "demes—the interbreeding community" (Mayr, 1963) within the population. Loyalty to the eyrie site, in both young and adults, is essential to the concept. Such loyality, in varying degrees, might possibly have resulted in defunct eyries, given nonreproducing adults and low population pressure. The latter would tend to oppose reutilization of distant defunct eyries and population maintenance in the face of the ever-present selection factor—pesticides.

LITERATURE CITED

Bond, R. M. 1946. The peregrine population of western North America. Condor, 48(3):101–116.

Cade, T. J. 1960. Ecology of the peregrine and gyrfalcon populations in Alaska. Univ. Calif. Publ. Zool., 63(3):151–290.

Dementiev, G. P., and N. A. Gladkov. 1951. Birds of the Soviet Union [in Russian]. Soviet Science, Vol. 1. Moscow. 652 p.

Enderson, J. H. 1964. A study of the prairie falcon in the central Rocky Mountain region. Auk, 81(3):332–352.

Hanson, H. C. 1965. The giant Canada goose. Southern Illinois Univ. Press, Carbondale. 226 p.

Hickey, J. J. 1942. Eastern population of the duck hawk. Auk, 59(2):176–204.

Mayr, Ernst. 1963. Animal species and evolution. Harvard Univ. Press, Cambridge. 797 p.

Peters, J. L. 1931. Check-list of birds of the world. Harvard Univ. Press, Cambridge. Vol. 1. 345 p.

Ratcliffe, D. A. 1962. Breeding density in the peregrine *Falco peregrinus* and raven *Corvus corax*. Ibis, 104(1):13–39.

Vaurie, Charles. 1961. Systematic notes on Palearctic birds. No. 44. Falconidae: The genus *Falco* (Part 1, *Falco peregrinus* and *Falco pelegrinoides*). Amer. Mus. Novitates, no. 2035:1–19.

White, C. M. 1968. Diagnosis and relationships of the North American tundra-inhabiting peregrine falcons. Auk, 82(2):179–191.

CHAPTER 34

PASSENGER PIGEONS AND PEREGRINE ECOLOGY

Frank L. Beebe

It would be very interesting, in view of the decline in the population of peregrines in the eastern United States and southeastern Canada, to know much more than we now do about the population of these falcons in this region under truly primitive conditions: not the conditions of 50 or 60 years ago, or even of a century back, but upwards of 200 years ago. When one reads that in 1805 Audubon (1831:325) saw schooners at the wharves of New York City loaded in bulk with passenger pigeons that had been caught up the Hudson, and which sold at one cent each, one wonders how many falcon eyries were along the Hudson River then. But even then New York was a city; certainly the disappearance of a biomass as great as was that of the passenger pigeon must have had a profound effect, not only on the peregrines, but on every raptorial bird in the region this species occupied. The random placement, from year to year, of the great breeding colonies may have precluded their universal use by all peregrines breeding in this region in any one year, but just as certainly the presence of a breeding colony anywhere near a peregrine eyrie would have meant the raising of large broods, and perhaps more important, this species must have ensured a very high survival of the young of all peregrines raised to flying age and located anywhere within 100 miles (160 km) of such a colony. Brewster (1889) accepts the statement of S. S. Stevens, the veteran Michigan pigeon netter, that the passenger pigeon continued laying and hatching during the entire summer, the entire colony always moving from 20 to 100 miles (32 to 160 km) after each brood of young, and in years of plentiful food three and even four broods being raised in one season. It seems to me as being as close to a certainty as anything possibly can be, that the original primitive population of peregrines in southeastern Canada and the eastern United States was built up on and largely sustained by the great biomass of this now-extinct species.

It is known that the peregrines of this region have been in long-term decline; but the duration of this decline is not known, and it is entirely possible that this species was already much reduced from the truly primitive population by the time it was first noticed by the early ornithologists of this continent. The only place in the world where peregrines are known to live in proximity to a colonial-nesting species of anything like comparable numbers is on the northern Pacific coast, and the numbers of falcons here, and the proximity of the nesting pairs, are, when compared to most other regions, considered to be somewhat phenomenal. Just how much, and how quickly large-scale human utilization of one of the important prey-species would reduce the peregrine population in this region would be difficult to say; but that it would have a profound effect, in time, is almost a certainty. Even so, the total disappearance of one such species in the northwest coastal region might be less disastrous to the falcons in this area than the very rapid extermination of the passenger pigeon must have been to the eastern birds, owing to the presence, on the Pacific coast, of substitute prey-species of very similar size and habits.

To support this view further, it should be pointed out that in western Oregon, western Washington, and southwestern British Columbia there is an area of some considerable size from which peregrines appear to be largely absent as a breeding species, and from which, moreover, they appear to have been always largely absent. This area extends from a little south of Eugene, Oregon, northward some 800 miles (1,280 km) to about the halfway point of Vancouver Island. It is essentially the first long interior valley inland from the mountains facing the open Pacific; the northern half, however, is a drowned valley and is filled with the salt water of Puget Sound. Many large valleys open to the eastward, the most important of which are the valley of the Fraser River and that of the Columbia River. Although much smaller in size, this region is in many ways singularly like that of the eastern United States. There are minor differences in climate, the winters being somewhat warmer and wetter than those of the east, the summers cooler and drier. Like the eastern United States this region was in its primitive state covered with dense forests, primarily conifers, however, instead of deciduous woods; and like the east, it has been subjected to very rapid change by man. It now supports a human population of several millions, and of course the country has been opened and diversified in a pattern of woodlots, hillside forests, open agricultural lands, towns, and suburban and city development. The birdlife of this region, especially in summer, is almost identical to that of the eastern USA, robins, flickers, and jays being the more abundant passerines. A large wild pigeon, the band-tailed pigeon, moves northward from California to breed in the region, but this species reproduces as isolated pairs in hillside forests instead of in dense colonies. The region abounds in mountain cliffs, cliffs overlooking agricultural land, cliffs bordering lakes and large rivers, and cliffs rising from the saltwater of the Gulf of Georgia. Yet this region (see Addendum) has apparently had few breeding peregrines. This seems the more remarkable when only 200 miles (320 km) northwestward peregrines are abundant, as has been pointed out, and also across the mountains to the eastward. One must conclude that this region, in the primitive state, was unlike that of the eastern USA in that it had no species that occurred in sufficient numbers over a long period of time to permit the build-up of a breeding population of peregrines in a region where, originally, all land areas were closed by timber.

It is perhaps significant too, that this same region does support a fair number of wintering peregrines, which, in a way, makes the lack of a breeding population even more meaningful. This is because the low-lying lands tend to flood in winter, and at that season to support large flocks of widgeon, teal, pintail, mallard, and shoveler ducks, while the marine areas fill up with wintering marine ducks—bufflehead, golden-eye, and old-squaw—as well as red phalarope and some of the smaller alcids. All these except the mallards leave the region by early May; the alcids for the outer coast, the waterfowl for the subarctic and Arctic. At this time the peregrines vanish from the area too, as should be expected. Yet the region supports a high population of those raptors that are well-oriented to the prey species, the Cooper's hawk being particularly abundant. In 1956 five breeding pairs were found in the woods surrounding a small lake only 2 miles (3.2 km) long and just 6 miles (9.6 km) from the center of the city of Victoria.

As a species the peregrines on this continent appear to be divided into three reasonably distinct populations. Of these, one appears to have its center of abundance somewhere in the Arctic, probably in the central barrens west of Hudson's Bay but possibly somewhat farther north in the southern half of the Canadian Arctic archipelago. The Northwest Coast maritime population may have its greatest abundance on the Queen Charlotte Islands and the Alexander Archipelago; but more likely it is along the chain of the Aleutians. The present-day center of abundance of the inland or continental population is almost certainly in the boreal forest of the Canadian Northwest and south interior Alaska. Just as certainly its primitive center of abundance was in southeastern Canada and the eastern USA. It may or may not be entirely coincidence that it has virtually disappeared from that part of its former range that coincides, almost exactly, with the former range of the passenger pigeon, but the magnitude and rapidity of the environmental changes brought about by man in this region make it quite impossible to say just what combination of stresses have been really responsible.

The Arctic and North Pacific populations, and to only slightly lesser extent the northwestern segment of the continental population, appear to be little changed from the primitive condition, even as the regions they occupy remain little changed. These regions, moreover, far from being attractive to widespread permanent human habitation, are being more or less actively depopulated of such thin and scattered populations of hunters, trappers, and fishermen as they once had. There is somewhat of a paradox here in that the human populations in the north and northwest are, in fact, increasing, but the pattern of development is such that all of this population tends to be increasingly concentrated in a few major settlements instead of being very widely scattered and living off the land as was the case 30 to 50 years ago. Whatever the social consequences of this modern trend may be, it does appear to be a very good thing for much of the wildlife of the north, removing, as it does, almost all human pressures from some very large areas.

ADDENDUM, 1968

In the region of few peregrines mentioned above, one old record from Waldron Island has been discovered, and two eyries were found in 1967 and 1968.

LITERATURE CITED

Audubon, J. J. 1831. Ornithological biography . . . ., Vol. 1. Edinburgh. 512+15 p.

Brewster, William. 1889. The present status of the wild pigeon (*Ectopistes migratorius)* as a bird of the United States, with some notes on its habits. Auk, 6(4):285–291.

CHAPTER 35

RESEARCH NEEDS IN REESTABLISHING LOCAL RAPTORIAL BIRD POPULATIONS

Morlan W. Nelson

In every country in the world competition is increasing for living space and the natural products of the soil as a result of the human population explosion. The birds of prey are particularly vulnerable to this change and resulting problem because they need greater understanding and space than required by most other birds. Research and work with the raptorial birds is difficult, but public opinion now seems to be in favor of these birds. Work must be started immediately to prevent further reductions from the many causes now apparent. I would like to propose new research for consideration.*

In many years of working with Walt Disney Productions on their films and TV releases, I was forced into situations, not ordinarily considered by falconers, that may be useful in research. The first was with a peregrine falcon that became so much a part of my family that she began to lay eggs and eventually it became obvious that the peregrine could be raised in captivity. I knew that it had been done in other countries on rare occasions. This old peregrine laid many eggs and raised two young prairie falcons when her own eggs did not hatch. However, at the time, it seemed to me such work was one hundred years ahead of our needs in falconry. Now, as this conference implies, we may be thirty years behind time for the public at large and falconers.

*The information and opinions expressed in this paper do not represent the official position of the Soil Conservation Service, US Department of Agriculture, but only those of the author.

The peregrine is the easiest one of the raptors to reestablish in a new site, then the prairie falcon, and finally the golden eagle. I did not follow out the same techniques with the bald eagle, but from the few that were worked, the same principles are almost certain to be successful.

Two basic possibilities have been developed. First is outright propagation in captivity, which has been done but needs much more research to become practical. It is extremely important for our future populations of the birds of prey and for falconry.

The second is to use existing populations—still holding their own or gaining slightly—to reestablish birds of prey in areas where they have been gone for years. The reestablishment possibilities hold out great promise for immediate action to restore populations of the golden eagle, peregrine, and bald eagle where suitable habitat and protection now exist. If there are other problems such as the pollution factor in all phases, or loss of habitat, these should be solved before restoration is attempted.

The golden eagle is suggested for the first reestablishment attempt because there are areas in other countries where the birds were killed off and the habitat has not changed significantly. However, it is possible that a similar attempt should be made with peregrine falcons without regard to habitat, just to work out the problems and determine practicability of the reestablishment technique. The nesting sites of this species in the Arctic could provide young falcons for this attempt without danger to the future population of adult birds. At least one young falcon must always be left in each eyrie to make certain that the adult birds are not disturbed too much.

Restoration would also be most effective if research attempts were made in other countries first, so as to broaden the base of reactivated breeding sites and thus to counteract the pressure of human population increases and use of land on these species.

As a suggestion for research, I would propose that we take three pairs of immature golden eagles from their eyries in the United States northwest and reestablish them in their former habitat in the highlands of England, or any other country with a similar situation and interest.

The general plan would be as follows:

1. Locate 30 to 100 eyries in the northwest; this has been completed, as I know of this many nesting sites and there may be other persons with similar knowledge.

2. Do not make detailed checks of the sites until after the eggs are hatched because the adult birds desert eggs as a result of even slight intrusion.

3. In April or May, after the eggs are hatched, determine the number of sites with two or more young. Determine the sex of young birds in each eyrie and plan pairs of eagles with several back-up sites. Plan to

consider leaving one eagle in each nest, although in order to obtain the right sex, it may be necessary to change eagles of roughly the same age from one nest to another. This is no problem to the adult birds; they do not seem to object to the change in any way. When there is a big age differential among the young, relocate birds so as to be of similar age and size in the various eyries. This eliminates the killing of the smallest eagle which is very common when one eaglet is 5 days or more younger than the older. By using the technique of relocating eagles, it is possible to take six from the nesting sites without actually reducing the number of birds that would be produced in the wild in that year. The relocation is a formidable cliff-climbing problem but well within the limits of modern mountain-climbing knowledge.

4. Use knowledge of former eyries in the country selected for population restoration to make a reconnaissance of the area and construct, or rebuild the old eyries with covered routes of access. At the actual site, install one-way glass so that men could (a) observe the condition and actions of the eagles on the eyries without being seen by the eagles and (b) also feed the eagles without human association with the food.

5. The food given to the transferred young should have enough natural items such as rabbits, starlings, reptiles, etc., so that there is no question of dietary deficiencies. At the moment, we do not know the answer to a diet for young birds except with natural food, fortified with vitamins in light amounts. The food should be almost all natural but can be frozen to make the supply a practical possibility.

6. At the right point in the mental and physical development of the young eagles, fly them to their new sites. This point is just about a week and a half before the birds fly—when they are fully feathered. Special shipping boxes must be made and extremely careful handling of the birds is necessary to eliminate (a) the mental problems that can develop with an eagle mishandled at this age and (b) the damage to feathers that are still developing.

7. As the birds fly from their new eyrie, they would need to be fed and watched for at least 2 years. Biologists and falconers could watch the birds and trap them if necessary for treatment of any disease that might develop. Constant observation is not necessary, just during feeding or for special reasons.

8. When the birds began to select mates, it might be necessary to trap one bird that would locally interfere with a mated pair. This would probably start after the second year, but food should be available at the original site for 5 years, although it might not always be used. There is no problem of them becoming dependent on the eyrie food from my experience, except when they cannot get wild quarry. The food being available at the eyrie would eliminate migration or shifting in bad winters. It would also attract wild eagles and tend to create a new population in the

area, with a firm base of food. The wild mated pairs of eagles in the northwest do not migrate, although their young do in unknown distance or direction.

9. A 16-mm film record of the original eyries in North America and in their new country should be made for scientific purposes and to help finance an expensive operation.

10. Construct observation sites and make telescopes available for the public to watch the progress of the eagles. This would create the understanding that is necessary for the birds' protection and survival. The funds secured from this enterprise may also be used to continue similar operations with the birds of prey in general.

The techniques described above would work with the peregrine falcon, prairie falcon, bald eagle, or other birds of prey with adjustments for their individual variations and needs. Likewise, according to experience with imported falcons from Asia such as the saker, it is highly possible that subspecies would make the adjustment to new habitat. The most obvious possibility in North America is that of the Alaskan bald eagle being able to adjust to areas out of its normal range. In my opinion, it is probable that the Alaskan birds will adjust to all of North America except the humid south and southeast, and they may have a chance there. Only an actual reestablishment attempt will answer these questions in any habitat.

One great factor rises against the reestablishment possibility—public understanding and appreciation of the birds themselves. Laws alone will not protect these birds, as we already know. We must have the active participation of educators, conservation clubs, sportsmen's clubs, state and federal organizations, falconers, and finally the majority of the public at large. We fight the prejudice of the ages and the current problem of too many people in the field with guns, who do not know what to do with them and have no training. Personally, I believe in the right to bear arms at all times without restriction—but that freedom should carry an obligation of knowledge and appreciation of nature in general. It should be an obligation of the state fish and game departments in licensing hunters, and the added duty of education to present to every student the principles of ecology as well as the conservation of our soil and water resources, which is the most active part affecting habitat.

In 1965 the United States Congress appropriated funds for the Fish and Wildlife Service to study and work on many of the problems brought out in this conference. This fact is a very encouraging one, in view of all the problems that are obviously already present.

This conference has great technical significance because on an international basis it recognizes the problem of the peregrine falcon and the birds of prey in general. It represents the first step in solving the problem. The second step, which should be an outcome of the conference, is that imaginative research and action will take place to determine the extent that management of the birds of prey is possible. The cooperation that is necessary between private, state, and federal organizations is exemplified by this conference. It will take all of these interests vigorously participating to accomplish the task ahead in limited management and conservation of the birds of prey.

The staggering problem represented by the understanding of the shooting public could negate all of the technical work that has been accomplished. The various media that we have today for extending public information must be carried out in an organized and well-directed manner. If the public is not convinced of the value of this work, it would be impossible for us to accomplish it. The quickest, most obvious mass media we have today are television, films, and finally writing. The technicians read the written word, but many already have the proper understanding and background. Television and films hit the public quickly and forcefully. In my opinion, these are the media that will change public opinion to a point of understanding that will allow us to accomplish our task. Whatever one thinks of the Walt Disney Productions' nature series in film and on television, from a technical standpoint, it must be conceded that the public at large has been swayed significantly in the direction of general appreciation and understanding of nature.

The hawks, eagles, and falcons have been an inspiration to people of all races and creeds since the dawn of civilization. We cannot afford to lose any species of the birds of prey without an effort commensurate with the inspiration of courage, integrity, and nobility that they have given humanity with very little but persecution in return. If we fail on this point, we fail in providing the basic philosophy of feeling an *understanding part* of our universe and all that goes with it. Every person needs this now, more than ever in history.

CHAPTER 36

GENERAL DISCUSSION: BEHAVIOR AND GENERAL ECOLOGY

BIAS IN PEREGRINE CENSUS DATA

RATCLIFFE: In an appendix to my 1963 peregrine report [Bird Study, 10(2):56–90], I made a lot of qualifications to indicate that allowances have to be made for various snags in the population-census data. One would need several visits by an experienced observer to each territory before the data could be claimed as really reliable, and seldom was this requirement fulfilled. I am quite sure that many territories put down as deserted were still held by at least one nonbreeding bird (not seen by the observer), that many apparently single birds were actually still paired, and that many apparently nonbreeding pairs had laid eggs which had already disappeared before the first visit. In an earlier paper [Ibis, 104(1):13–39], I stressed the necessity of carefully examining the whole territory if a regular pair appears to be absent (i.e., the difficulty of proving a negative) and think that in some apparently deserted territories, the pair were merely nesting in an alternative cliff unknown to the observer. In at least one case I did myself put down a haunt as deserted because the tight-sitting female refused to leave her eggs, and the true picture only emerged when another man went there after the birds had hatched! Censuses undertaken late in the season may give a completely false idea of the number of attempted nestings or occupations earlier in the year.

But for all these shortcomings, I do not think that census data of this kind are too unreliable. We had a certain amount of cross-checking by different observers reporting on the same haunts. And one just has to use the available information to get anywhere. It gives the general picture, and since the errors are probably roughly constant, it gives perhaps an even better comparative index between one year and the next.

TRADITIONAL USE OF NESTING SITES

MRS. HERBERT: We discovered an eyrie which, for the first time in our experience, had a pair in 1947. This was our No. 2 eyrie (Herbert and Herbert, 1965). However, the late Beecher S. Bowdish identified the nest ledge which the birds used in 1947, 1949, and 1951, as the one on which he had taken his first photograph of adult peregrines back in 1909 to 1912. That eyrie had ceased to be occupied in 1912. As it was not reoccupied until 1947, there is something in these traditional preferences. Likewise at another eyrie Mr. Bowdish identified the ledges that the peregrines were using in the forties and fifties as the same ones that they had used back in 1912. This is rather puzzling because it involves a span of years longer than the life of one bird. We do not know what makes peregrines select these nest sites instead of other ledges which to us appear to be just as good. Feeding perches, including fallen cedars, are also traditionally used in my experience.

RATCLIFFE: V. C. Wynne-Edwards has some comments on the same thing in his recent book *Animal Dispersion in Relation to Social Behaviour.* He believes that all these perching and nesting places are identifiable by the birds themselves. They leave their marks. In Britain the places are usually identifiable by means of the green wash or stains that are produced down below. Nitrogenous matter washes down the rock, and this area in turn is colonized by small green algae that produce a green streak. This can be used by the peregrine investigator to track down nesting sites, as he can spot these streaks at a long distance. Old eyrie ledges often also have a particularly luxuriant growth of grass (e.g., *Anthoxanthum odoratum*) and are conspicuous on those cliffs where the prevailing ledge vegetation is of a different kind. Wynne-Edwards believes that the birds themselves spot these streaks and that over a long time there is a tendency to use these places merely because the birds themselves can recognize the signs. In parts of western Scotland, lichens grow down the rock instead of algae.

When the peregrine population of Cornwall was virtually exterminated during the war by the Air Ministry, no young were produced there for several years; but there was rapid recolonization of many vacant sites immediately afterwards. It is certainly true in our country too that no matter what lapse of time there is in occupation of a nesting haunt, the selfsame ledges are the ones that are usually reoccupied when birds come back. There may be a lapse of 40 or 50 years, but the old nesting ledges are the ones they go for first.

[Relative to the growth of lichens on rocks used by birds and discussed above, John W. Thomson, lichenologist at the University of Wisconsin, reports (pers. comm.) that this phenomenon is common throughout the North American Arctic as well as in Eurasia. The lichens are *Caloplaca elegans, C. sorediata,* and occasionally *C. murorum.* Thomson regards the color as brilliant yellow and not green. He has seen it on the Pitnegea River north of Cape Sabine (Alaska), at Coppermine, NWT (Canada), on rocks in Lake Winnipegosis (Manitoba) and Lake Superior, and on Northern Lights Lake near the end of Gun Flint Trail, Minnesota. The phenomenon in Greenland has been described by Lynge (1934, Rhodora, 36:133ff). It also is extremely common in prairie country, is produced by gulls as well as falcons, and appears to be a plant response to the availability of calcium. Tikhomirov (1959, The interrelationships of the animal life and vegetational cover of the tundra; translated from Russian 1966 by USDA and Nat. Sci. Found. 67 p.) likewise mentions nitrophilous growth near the nesting sites of gyrfalcons, peregrines, merlins, and gray sea eagles in the mountain tundra of the Soviet Arctic, but he does not specify the plant species involved.—Ed.]

RATCLIFFE: The very *green* streaks and washes on rocks below peregrine (and raven, kestrel, and buzzard) eyries, perches, and roosts, are produced by organisms different from those of the yellow-orange bird rocks which are well-known in the north and often mentioned in botanical studies of the Arctic. In Britain these green "stains" are mostly produced by green algae, both unicellular and filamentous, but in the northwest Highlands the stringy gray-green lichen *Ramalina scopulorum* often takes their place below eyries (including those of golden eagle too). These effects are not often noticed on sea cliffs, where lichens and algae are usually abundant anyway, but they are very characteristic of inland nesting places. The yellowish "ornithocoprophilous" lichens, such as those mentioned by Thomson, are different, and occur mainly on the tops of boulders and projecting rocks used as perching places, often right away from cliffs.

Regarding the reoccupation of the south coast eyries in England after 1945, I have no first-hand acquaintance with events there, but gathered that they returned to the very same cliffs, and sometimes the same ledges which were occupied before 1939. Ryves (1948) has something on this in his book, *Bird Life in Cornwall.* Being coastal, the sites here are perhaps less obvious to the human eye (green stains not localized), but I don't doubt that they are as easily recognized by peregrines as on inland cliffs.

I can confirm what Mrs. Herbert said about use of identical eyrie ledges after lapses in occupation of territory. In the Lake District, three different territories were deserted for 10–15 years, though at different actual times, and when they were reoccupied, the eyrie ledges which had been favorites during the earlier periods were again the ones most often used. In many cases, such a bowl has been made on a ledge that it would persist for many years and so be recognized by falcons; and, when raven nests are used (as they so often are in Britain), it is merely a matter of *that* species using the same ledges. As I tried to show previously [Ibis, 104(1):13–39], the ecology of these two species in Britain is similar indeed, and what applies to continuity of occupation of territory and sites in one is, I feel sure, good for the other.

GENETIC CONTINUITY AT PEREGRINE EYRIES

RATCLIFFE: White does not define what he means by "genetic continuity," but he evidently intends this to mean closeness of relationship between pairs successively occupying the same eyrie, with the tacit assumption that they belong to, or constitute, a population which is genetically distinct from other localized populations. Such a thesis can only be supported by proving that there is *no* recruitment from other populations, and it is not sufficient to show that some birds do return to the vicinity of their birthplace to breed. I do not doubt the evidence for this last tendency, but all this shows is that continuity of occupation is more likely to be maintained by birds reared in the vicinity than by birds from elsewhere. It does not seem really relevant to the question of what makes a particular cliff and particular ledge in one place so attractive to peregrines whereas other cliffs and their ledges elsewhere are less attractive or unattractive.

There clearly is a question of the importance of genetic continuity, but this seems to be geographically broader in its relevance, i.e., an issue of *population* maintenance rather than eyrie maintenance, and I think White has taken both together. For instance, taking the British Isles as a single region, it is obvious that, if eyrie maintenance depended on locally produced offspring, the south coast of England would have remained completely depleted or shown only very slow recovery, when persecution ceased after 1945. Yet the complete absence of tree nesters and scarcity of ground nesters here would suggest that birds from regions of Europe where these habits are common do not come to Britain, or at least do not stay to breed.

This matter of regional races is of obvious importance regarding the possibility of recolonization of a depleted region by falcons from one less affected. Cade, in conversation with me, made the important point that it is unlikely that the Canadian Arctic peregrines could recolonize the depleted eastern United States because of different physiological adaptation, e.g., more important than any difference in clutch size is the difference in time of breeding, the southern (United States) birds having eggs while the northerners are still migrating northwards through the same region (the same situation as northern and southern races of golden plover in Britain). Difference in migratory habits would also be involved.

Thus genetic differences are perhaps important on the regional but not on the local scale; but where the local ends and the regional begins is another question!

Then, on the question of continuity depending on survival of one of the pair actually in occupation, which Cade seems to favor, undoubtedly the destruction of both of a pair at the same time did not prevent a good many British eyries from being occupied without a break over a long period. Witness also William Rowan's 1921 account of a pair of merlins being shot each year for 19 consecutive years at the same site (British Birds, 15:122–129). One Lakeland peregrine eyrie known to an older friend of mine had a curious sequence. During the 1920's it was robbed repeatedly and few if any young were reared; yet it was occupied continuously. Then about 1930–33, young were reared every year, but in 1934 the haunt was deserted and remained so for many years, though it was eventually retenanted; the reason is mysterious.

The continuity of eyrie occupation seems to involve the whole obscure issue of psychological adaptation to external visual stimuli, and the degree of genetic fixation which this involves. To me, one of the big questions in avian biology (and so far the most ignored) is "How is geographical spread limited?" Migration only emphasizes that birds are essentially mobile creatures potentially capable of extending their range rapidly and widely. Yet over long periods the majority of species show static distributional patterns (even when they are migratory) and especially in regard to breeding distribution. Now and then one species begins to spread or retreat, and at any one time any region usually has several species changing their distribution. Yet the majority only do so in response to gross climatic change, and this is usually over a fairly long period. Why are they so conservative? I am, of course, not counting geographical changes clearly related to fairly direct human influence.

I am not sure how far this problem can be separated from that of limitation of ecological range, i.e., distribution within the geographical range. Insofar as the two can be separated I feel that with a cosmopolite such as the peregrine we are dealing more with ecological restriction of range. Here the fixity of psychological response to the visible attractions of the habitat is surely important, and this comes right back to Hickey's original concept of the magnetism of the nest-cliff. Cade is right in saying that one must judge the "quality" of a cliff by one criterion, i.e., size and appearance *or* continuity of occupation and breeding success, otherwise it becomes a circular argument. If you take the second criterion, it would seem in Britain that a third-class cliff in one district (big cliffs plentiful) may be a first-class cliff in another (moorland, few cliffs at all), so everything depends on the choice available.

In one part of Lakeland, there is a gap in regularity of peregrine distribution, although a range of small crags (regularly occupied by ravens) lies right in the middle of the gap. Peregrines have never been known to nest here, despite the suitability of the position, and I feel that if only the crags were bigger, they would surely have done so. Crags as small as this hold breeding peregrines in moorland areas such as the Cheviots, but here there are virtually no big cliffs. In Lakeland, nearly all the peregrines are in biggish cliffs, and so it seems that the limits of acceptability are determined by the established pattern for the particular district. But at what point in any district do the attractions of a cliff fall below a threshold? And how does one account for the regional variation in strength of this threshold? I think one is right in saying or implying that this threshold has evolved in relation to its survival value in terms of breeding success, and so will be different in unpopulated Arctic regions compared with our areas of denser human population. But I also think that there is individual variation in the threshold level of acceptability, and that this is concerned in the occupation or desertion of marginal nesting cliffs. If both of a pair at a marginal haunt die (or perhaps only one of them), it may be quite a while before an individual with the necessary low threshold chances to arrive at the place. Other "normal" peregrines may ignore it, and so the place stays deserted for some time.

One of the most extraordinary events (to me) in European ornithology, and one which shows both ecological and geographical extension of range, is the recent and sudden "colonization" of the Dutch polders by breeding dotterel. Little groups have turned up in several areas, I believe, totaling perhaps 100 pairs or more. For a bird known previously as a purely Arctic-alpine species this is very remarkable. This low-level nesting is so far unknown in Britain, where the species is known only on high mountains of the north. Could these events in Holland result from a true genetic mutation, affecting psychological response to habitat? Once the first difficult step has been taken by one bird or a pair, others seem easily to follow suit, and the new habit snowballs. So it was with titmice and milk-bottle tops.

On the other hand, I feel that there is something in this recognition of existing signs left by predecessors as well, and that this is involved in the psychological stimulation.

It seems to be true that very long-deserted peregrine cliffs have a tendency to stay deserted, even when they are eminently suitable in appearance, setting, and so on. Here, all signs of former occupation have presumably vanished. Perhaps in the raven it is more noticeable than in the peregrine that there is an apparent inhibition to the recolonization of long-lost ground. This is particularly true in the Pennines and eastern Highlands, where it seems that the raven really has lost ground since nineteenth-century persecution became heavy. Much of the ground is very suitable, and these are almost the only inland areas of Britain where peregrines do not usually (one can almost say invariably) share their nesting cliffs with ravens. We know that ravens reach these districts, and there are a few nesting pairs, but there is still much persecution from grouse preservers, and there is little or no evidence that the species attempts to breed at some of the long-deserted haunts, though unsuccessful attempts are made at others.

I was always puzzled by the history of peregrine occupation at two haunts not far from my home. Both were in moorland country, one Pennine and the other Southern Upland, and both were the only breeding place for many miles around, owing to absence of other suitable cliffs. The first has ravens nesting irregularly, and the second was never known to be without nesting ravens in any year. Both had long spells (up to 25 years) of desertion by peregrines, for no apparent reason, but both were reoccupied by breeding pairs, in 1954 and 1959. Moreover, both were visited by peregrines, which sometimes roosted there, during these spells of desertion. Yet there was no known nesting attempt during these periods. What happens? Do some individuals need the proximity of other settled breeding pairs before they are themselves stimulated enough to breed? Or is it that these rather small and undistinguished cliffs (one haunt is a shut-in ravine) lie at the limits of acceptability, so that only a few individual peregrines can be stimulated to attempt breeding there? Once nesting actually takes place, such haunts may well remain tenanted until both of the occupying pair die so close together (in time) that no remating (to preserve continuity) is possible. Then again, I was always impressed by a comment of Walpole-Bond's (p. 239, in his *Field Studies of Some Rarer British Birds* [1914]), that a certain breeding haunt was held by a barren, female peregrine for years, the bird driving away prospective newcomers. In the end the owner of the ground deliberately shot this barren bird, and at once a pair came and nesting was resumed. It was a presumption that the bird was barren.

POPULATION TURNOVER AND FIDELITY TO PREVIOUS SITES

BEEBE: With respect to the permanency of pairs in the peregrine, I believe Enderson has some contrary data relating to prairie falcons. Certainly the impression I get on the Queen Charlotte Islands in British Columbia is that there are different pairs occupying specific eyrie sites from one year to the next. The most convincing instance I would cite was one involving a small island in the Queen Charlottes at which there was once a pair in occupancy that was not identifiable, but the next year there was a pair in occupancy, and the female was lacking one leg. She was still breeding effectively. One year later I observed that there was a pair on this site but it did not include that one-legged female. When you revisit an eyrie two or three years in succession on the Queen Charlottes, there is a noticeable difference in the behavior of birds that you can detect:

shyness as opposed to extreme aggressiveness and that sort of thing. I think—and these are only impressions—that in the highly saturated populations there is a considerable exchange of eyrie sites among individual birds and much shifting around.

ENDERSON: I think one has to be careful in assuming that individual birds return to the same site year after year. In the prairie falcon, out of a sample of 14 instances, only 43% were the same birds, where the same individual returned to the same site in the following year (Enderson, 1964, Auk, 81[3]:332-352). Now if you think then in terms of both members of the pair, it seems very improbable that in the prairie falcon the same pair will be nesting together in subsequent years at the same site.

RETURN OF YOUNG TO NEST NEAR THEIR HATCHING SITE

ALDRICH: I am wondering whether or not there is any evidence that the young—although they were not found going back to the same general region where they were fledged—went anywhere else farther away. Can we assume then that they did nest far away from their place of origin, or were they merely part of this nonbreeding population "beating around" and waiting for an opportunity to utilize an eyrie that had become unoccupied in the area where they had originated? In other words, there would be a floating population—which I think has been suggested a number of times—and, when one of the members of the pair at an eyrie has been killed, it is replaced by another bird fairly quickly. This could go on repeatedly until eventually it is seen that this floating population is all used up, and then this eyrie is abandoned. Then, with no recruitable population left, the tradition of nesting in that area would be broken, and it would take a long time to reestablish that eyrie. Thus, sites would go uninhabited, as they seem to do, for long periods of time. But in this paper of White's, we have the very intriguing idea that the hereditary subunit of population is tied in with a given eyrie; possibly in areas where eyries or suitable nesting sites are relatively scarce, this sort of situation would be more obvious. If there were more closely spaced good sites, why maybe this population would expand to those. I think this has potential for interesting possibilities in management of these birds. We ought to try to get more information on the history of the birds based on definite banding.

ENDERSON: I think also one must be careful in assuming that young birds, and I'm speaking again of my prairie falcons, will return to the same region to nest in subsequent years. There are only two instances of prairie falcons that I know of where the young fledged in previous years in a given locality returned to that area to nest. One was a female that did nest within 22 miles (35 km) of where she was fledged. Another one was a second-year female that returned to attempt to nest within a mile (1.6 km) of where she was fledged; however, she was displaced by the resident female at that site.

BEEBE: With this high record of reproduction on the Sun Life Building, why was there no return of young to that eyrie? The high incidence of peregrines feeding on pigeons suggests to me now, for what it's worth, that experienced adults can sustain themselves on this type of quarry, but I think that those young birds that fly and become independent of their parents just lose out on that type of quarry. I don't think there are enough other prey species or just pigeons to support them in an urban environment. If 22 young were fledged in 13 years on the Sun Life Building, why didn't some come back and reoccupy that site? Birds traditionally go back to the area from which they were hatched; presumably there should have been some survival.

MRS. HERBERT: We assume that the same phenomenon was happening all over the eastern one-third of the United States: that various human pressures began in the 1940's to affect the age structure of the peregrine populations in this region. We did not know in the 1940's that we only had old birds left, but that was the case.

HICKEY: The second of the three male adult peregrines at the Sun Life Building was a banded bird that was never captured and hence was of unknown origin. It is possible that this male could have come from the many young that were banded at this site.

BERGER: At the Sun Life Building in Montreal, production fell off in the last few years. This obviously means that the last birds produced were not going to be sitting around waiting for the site to be deactivated. They would have taken up residence somewhere else; and presumably they would then stay there and not move to the site vacated by a deceased parent.

BEEBE: You are assuming that the high hatch of birds in previous years would have wandered off somewhere?

BERGER: They would have settled wherever they could.

BEEBE: I don't think that's necessarily so. I think they could have just as well hung around waiting for their turn. Why not?

BERGER: It is possible, but it is not reasonable to assume that.

BEEBE: But it is unreasonable not to assume it.

CADE: At one time in the population, there must have been a reservoir of nonbreeding birds that were somewhere around close by.

BERGER: There undoubtedly were unmated birds. I think one should not assume that these constituted a major portion of the population, but rather a minor portion.

CADE: It couldn't have been too minor with some populations where we heard about continued replacement in Europe.

BEEBE: And the Hudson River eyries.

CADE: Then too, the fact that they are not seen does not mean they are not around. Except at migratory concentration points, the only place that you can count on seeing a peregrine is where peregrines are occupying a nesting area.

BERGER: Where a pair suffers the loss of one, the remaining bird gets a brand new mate. The mate could come from a similar situation elsewhere.

HICKEY: I have a very clear impression that a bird tends in an exponential fashion to return to the site at which it was raised. About five studies show this when one plots on the x-axis of a graph the distance that a bird nests away from the place where it was hatched and on the y-axis logarithms of the density of birds breeding in the concentric circles surrounding the point where the birds were hatched. On semilog graph paper this relationship is a straight line: The density of birds breeding in each of these circles decreases at a constant rate as you go out from the point at which they were fledged. Probably in the peregrine we are dealing with a species where the distance that the birds nest will be much farther away from their birthplace than it would be (say) in a robin or a house wren.

The importance of this is, when we try to envision the possibility of the eastern breeding range being recaptured by this species in the United States, I think that this is going to be a very slow process and that we will not find birds are coming into the southern Appalachians ahead of birds in New England. The species will have to recapture its former range from wherever it now is and move in by invading concentric rings or zones.

The other intriguing thing about such an invasion of vacated range is this: What will happen if this vacated range is invaded by northern birds that have a clutch size of three going into a range where peregrines formerly had a clutch size of four? Apparently this can happen.

RATCLIFFE: It depends on whether or not clutch size is genetically fixed.

HICKEY: Well, if we accept David Lack's conclusions in *The Natural Regulation of Animal Numbers,* it's genetically fixed.

EXTRA FEMALE AT A NESTING SITE

SPOFFORD: We used to wonder a great deal about whether or not an Arctic peregrine could possibly be drawn into one of the vacancies among the Appalachian eyrie sites. Our thinking was that since the breeding cycles were so far apart, perhaps such a replacement would never be effective.

In 1945, the pair at my biggest tree nest at Reelfoot had a changeover in the female. The old female disappeared and, when I came back in the spring, there were two females there. One of them was a very small female; not really any larger than a tiercel. The only way we really knew it was a female was that it persisted in coming in and out of the scrape site even when I was right on the tree. Sometimes when I was almost in front of the hole, it would come in right between my feet and get into the hole. It turned out there was another female present. This was a big dark 1-year-old bird. The male bird would pay no attention to the small, light adult female but would always bring in food, feed the big dark female, and just ignore the little one. There were no eggs laid that year.

The next year when I inspected this site, there were still three adults there, but the female on the eggs was a big, dark, more or less Appalachian type, as we used to call such birds at that time. When I climbed the tree, out she went; and before I had even gotten out on the limb near the nesting cavity, this small female came along and got on the eggs. She just got on as the big one got off; but as soon as the big female returned, this little bird had to get off. Well, I don't know whether this was an Alaskan bird or a babysitter!

SEX RATIO OF UNPAIRED PEREGRINES

MRS. HERBERT: On the Hudson we found that, if the male was killed, the female might frequent the eyrie for a month or two but she usually disappeared. For instance, in one winter, the male at our Eyrie No. 2 was shot, the female remained until March, and she then disappeared. Likewise the male at our Eyrie No. 1 disappeared in 1955, and the female we saw there just once during the spring. On the other hand, when the female was shot, the male retained possession of the eyrie and usually attracted a female.

HAGAR: I think it is more or less accepted that the male peregrine has been the one that was attached to the cliff. My experience was that, if nothing happened to the male and in the absence of a female, he occupied the cliff from the latter part of February through the nesting season and the whole summer until the early part of December. The males cited in my Massachusetts report were not supposed males; they were absolutely identified as males, all of them.

They might not always be seen, but they always came back. They tended to come back to roost at night, waiting until the latter part of the afternoon, and the male would often show up.

WHITE: On lone eyries in the Arctic, where you find only one bird, it usually is the female. I am wondering if perhaps there is a differential of males versus females in specific areas.

BEEBE: I have three observations of lone females occupying cliffs on the Queen Charlottes. None of males. The same situation is true of the Arctic.

CADE: In Alaska, I had one female that was quite atypically colored. Although she was an adult, she was almost as brown as an immature bird, particularly on the back. She occupied a site in 1952, and she was still there in 1956 and in 1957. She did not have a mate in any of these 3 years. In 1958, a new female took over that cliff, and it became an active nesting site for the first time in my experience.

EGG-EATING AND SMALLER CLUTCHES OF EGGS

PRESTT: One has to be very careful about the question as to whether a smaller number of eggs has been laid or whether no eggs have been laid. I have now started a fairly intensive population study of the European sparrow-hawk and, as an example of what can happen, in one particular area in the first year, I recorded that in two of the 10 territories a pair of birds was present but I concluded they had not attempted to breed. I visited the study area rather late in the season that first year. The next year I came earlier in the season for my first survey, and a pair of birds was still present in each of these two territories; but, as I was earlier in the season, I found each had a nest with four eggs in it. When I came back a fortnight later, neither of the nests had any eggs in it. One of the birds we found in the act of destroying one of her eggs.

Since we have extended this study, we find that sometimes the birds will lay a full clutch and destroy the full clutch within a few days after laying it. However, we also had a bird which laid six eggs, sat on all six for nearly a month, and only then started destroying them. She had destroyed four when we came and took the last two for chemical analysis. So one has to be very careful when, if you are not visting nest sites at frequent intervals, you assume that no eggs were laid or only small numbers were laid. It may be the full clutch was there in the first place.

MUELLER: John T. Emlen has some data on egg-eating. His group was experimentally manipulating the eggs in gull nests and giving the birds fresh eggs after they were well advanced in the cycle of incubation. After the birds had been incubating for the normal length of time, there was an increasing tendency for the gulls to eat their eggs. Hence this egg-eating or egg-breaking by the peregrine may be a result of infertility or arrested development in the egg.

RATCLIFFE: It has been our experience that peregrine egg-eating can occur in any stage of the incubation. It can be with a completely fresh egg before the clutch is completed, and it can be at any stage thereafter. It can involve either one egg or the whole set.

BEEBE: How much of egg-eating is really due to the disturbance caused by the observer? There is a factor in here that I think we all tend to ignore. When we make these observations, we make no allowance for the fact that our very observing is a disturbance factor.

RATCLIFFE: It has been a constant factor over a long period of years, but egg-eating has only recently become frequent.

CADE: It's not though, exactly. For instance, I could give an example that bears on the lines of what Beebe is talking about. When I carried out my surveys on the Colville River in Alaska, I did not realize this until I looked back over the data in later years, and I did not report it in any publication. In order to cover as much of the river as possible, I would start early on the upper part of the river when the birds had just about completed their clutches and, by the time I finished at the end of the river, the falcons there had well-developed young. If I made a second trip down the river, on reanalysis of my notes, the nest failures on the upper part of the river that I visited first, when the birds had eggs, proved to be much higher than the nest failures that occurred lower on the river where I visited eyries that had young.

HICKEY: Beebe's question concerns a point that has worried me. Many observers of the peregrine have deliberately refrained from roping down to nest ledges to check on the status of the birds' eggs. Both Hagar and Ratcliffe belong to the school of investigators who regard this disturbance as exaggerated. Hagar found no evidence of broken eggs during the most intensive part of his study. The significant thing about Ratcliffe's observations (as well as Prestt's) is that the broken eggs have been frequently found on the observer's first visit to a nest. I think we must conclude that disturbance at the nesting site is not an important factor in modern egg-eating by adult raptorial birds.

REACTIONS OF NESTING RAPTORS TO INTRUSION

NELSON: Leslie Brown told me of raptors in Africa, which—in response to people who were down below watching—would crouch over their eggs and hide with their head behind a branch. I think that these birds can be disturbed, but I do think they build up some sort of a tolerance. A classic example of this occurred in Idaho in 1965. There was a golden eagle that nested close to a canal and about 10 ft (3 m) above the top of the canal. You could walk down the canal, and about 30 yards (27 m) out you were looking 10 ft up at the female eagle in the tree nest. Golden eagles usually nest in this area in cliffs, but this bird nested in a cottonwood tree, and I have watched her for a good many years. She successfully raised young with the ditch rider and all kinds of children going up and down the ditch within not more than 40 ft (12 m) from the eyrie and not more than 10 ft differential in height. In 1965 a young boy came along with a rifle. He fired three shots at the bird on the nest, missing with the first two. The bird crouched and put its head behind a branch. On the third shot he hit the bird and knocked it off to the base of the tree. Now the golden eagle is one of the most sensitive species to human intrusion, and yet here was a bird so accustomed to people that it remained at 30 paces under gunfire.

There are at least three golden eagle eyries and prairie falcon eyries in Idaho above Highway 30 which are within 50 yards (46 m) of the highway. There must be 100,000 people going beneath them in motor cars annually; some get out and walk around. But those birds have consistently been successful with this kind of activity going on.

PETERSON: This was true for years with the Florida bald eagles around Tampa and Sarasota. I remember seeing young eagles being successfully raised in a nest 20 ft (6 m) from a schoolroom window through which children could watch. In southern New Jersey, I also recall an osprey's nest that was on a schoolhouse chimney years ago. This occurred at a time when numbers of noisy children were going in and out of the building.

FYFE: We had a situation on the Anderson River in Canada's Northwest Territories where we had four nests in a sequence. We had gyrfalcons with young, successful nests below a certain point, and when we got to a certain point going down river we had four successive nests in which we found eggs or else evidence—like dropped feathers from the adult birds—that the falcons had been there. In two instances there were eggs in the nest. When we were talking later about this, we could not understand why all of a sudden there was a stop in nesting success. The birds were still present around these nests. Well, on talking with some people later in this area, we found out that trappers had been through the nesting area in the first week of May, which would have been the time that the falcons were just first sitting on the eggs. We did break open the eggs on these nests, found that they had been fertile, and concluded that the birds had been disturbed. The gyrfalcons up in this region are very, very shy. Upon being disturbed, they do not hang around the nesting site and make a racket as peregrines usually do; instead they just slip away—you may not even see them leave the nest. Sometimes they will come back and cackle at you; sometimes they will not. Now, this is strictly, should I say, circumstantial evidence or something: men went through this area trapping. They stopped at lakes along the river at points right beneath these nests. We know of one nesting place where they definitely did trap. At the second place they camped for 2 days. This I submit was enough to disturb those falcons so that the eggs addled.

PETERSON: Then why did the Sun Life birds in Montreal stand up to all the crowds that leaned over and watched them?

FYFE: There is this difference: The falcons on the Anderson River are wilderness birds that are not used to this human interference, whereas perhaps the city-dwelling birds, I think from what we've heard at this conference, will take an awful lot of disturbance after they are conditioned to the situation.

PART IV

POPULATION FACTORS

Pathogens, Parasites, and Peregrine Falcons

CHAPTER 37

DISEASES IN RAPTORS: A REVIEW OF THE LITERATURE

Daniel O. Trainer

A prerequisite to any discussion concerning the role of infectious disease as an ecological factor affecting peregrine falcon populations is a reexamination of the part infectious disease plays in limiting avian populations. This will be followed in the present paper by a review of the literature on diseases of raptors and finally by a resumé of our knowledge regarding diseases of the peregrine falcon.

AVIAN DISEASES

There are at least three general methods by which infectious disease affects wild avian populations.

EPIZOOTICS

There are many examples of epizootics that have caused significant mortality of hundreds, thousands, and even millions of wild birds. In

Wisconsin, a cecal fluke *(Sphaeridiotrema globulus)* occurs periodically in migrating American coots and causes mortality of 300–500 birds per year (Trainer and Fischer, 1963). The seasonal occurrence of the fluke and associated losses of birds has been regular and predictable.

A well-documented example of an epizootic affecting thousands of birds is avian cholera *(Pasteurella multocida)*. A review of this disease (Trainer, 1965) illustrates that as many as 40,000 waterfowl have been lost at a single site in 1 year (Rosen and Bischoff, 1949).

Botulism (*Clostridium botulinum* type C) occurs in many areas of North America and affects all species of waterfowl. Losses of waterfowl to botulism have been in the millions (Sciple, 1953).

INDIVIDUAL MORTALITY

Nonepizootic avian losses, often called "natural mortality," are commonly encountered in the literature. Interesting studies of individual mortality involving large numbers of birds in Great Britain are those of Keymer (1958) and Jennings (1961). The latter reported the cause of death of 1,000 birds whose carcasses were examined in the laboratory. In these 1,000 cases the diagnosis was: 18% infectious disease, 5% parasitic disease, 29% trauma, 10% poisons, 11% adverse weather conditions, and 20% not determined. Other studies (Herman, 1955; Keymer, 1958; Quortrup and Shillinger, 1941) revealed a similar variety of causes of death. Some of the infectious diseases that have caused individual mortality include aspergillosis, avian pox, ornithosis, and tuberculosis.

There has been a great deal of discussion concerning the role of pesticides as a mortality factor in wild birds. Past studies illustrate that multiple etiological factors are present in almost every instance of increased mortality. Every effort should be made to ferret out all the factors when one is investigating the population decline of any wild species.

INAPPARENT DISEASES

Probably, the most important role that disease plays in wild populations involves an area about which we know the least. Many infections produce inapparent or mild disease that is not easily detected or recognized in the field, which may result in impaired reproductive success as a result of infertility and low hatchability, in stunting and reduced growth rate, abnormal behavior, and a shortening of the life span. Although not as spectacular as epizootics with high mortality, these inapparent infections might well be the most significant.

Numerous avian diseases directly affect fertility. For example, pullorum disease *(Salmonella pullorum)* can reduce production of a laying pheasant flock by 75%. It can also adversely affect nestling birds (Biester and Schwarte, 1965). Other *Salmonella* species, such as *S. typhimurium,* produce intestinal disorders that can result in severe mortality among nestlings. Trichomoniasis *(Trichomonas gallinae)* can cause high mortality in dove nestlings, yet not grossly affect the parents.

The effect of disease on behavior in wild species has not received much consideration or study. Speculation concerning the effect of pesticides on behavior can be quite interesting. Infectious diseases are known to affect behavior, but the significance of these behavior alterations to survival of wild species has never been fully evaluated.

One of the chief signs utilized in disease diagnosis is the observation of abnormal animal behavior. Botulism is commonly called "limber neck" because of the strange behavior pattern observed in infected birds. A synonym of pseudorabies is "mad itch" because of the behavior exhibited by its victims.

It was proposed earlier that pesticides may cause raptors to abandon their nests, resulting in mortality of the embryos. A large number and variety of subclinical diseases may produce sufficient illness, to result in nest or young abandonment, or both. Even an alteration in the body temperature of the setting parent, caused by infectious disease, could affect embryo survival since the incubation temperature of embryonated eggs is so critical.

It is obvious that a variety of diseases can affect avian populations in a number of ways and that disease is another ecological factor warranting consideration in the investigation of wild avian population changes.

RAPTOR DISEASES

A summary of the infectious diseases of hawks that have been reported in the literature is categorized by causative agent (bacterial, viral, and parasitic) in Table 37.1. Because of time and space limitations, only some of the more interesting and potentially important maladies will be discussed briefly and others simply acknowledged as occurring.

BACTERIAL DISEASES

Of the bacterial diseases known to occur in hawks, fowl cholera provides a very interesting epizootiological picture. As discussed earlier, fowl cholera is recognized as a cause of epizootics in wild waterfowl. Gulls that often feed on infected waterfowl also become exposed and succumb to the disease. The carcasses of dead ducks and gulls are scattered over a wide area. Wild mice find and feed on these infected carcasses. As the mice and birds develop signs of disease, they apparently become

Table 37.1. A Summary of Infectious Diseases of North American Raptors

Bacterial	Viral	Parasitic
Fowl cholera	Ornithosis	Myiasis
Tularemia	Eastern viral encephalitis	Trichomoniasis
Plague	Western viral encephalitis	Tapeworms
Botulism	Newcastle disease	Trypanosomes
Tuberculosis	Fowl paralysis	Trematodes
Pseudotuberculosis	Fowl pox	Nematodes
Erysipelothrix	Mycoplasm	Coccidiosis
Aspergillosis		Plasmodium
Anthrax		Leucocytozoon
Salmonellosis		Hemoproteus
		Sarcocystis
		Ectoparasites[a]

[a] Including lice, mites, ticks, and fleas.

more susceptible to predators including the marsh hawk, or hen harrier, which in turn develop fowl cholera (Rosen and Morse, 1959). This interesting interspecific food-chain involving waterfowl, rodents, and raptors illustrates the complexities of disease transmission and the necessity of knowing the epizootiology of a disease.

Tularemia *(Pasteurella tularensis)* and plague *(P. pestis)* are two bacterial diseases considered to be associated primarily with wild rodent populations. The "normal" method of transmission from rodent to rodent is via fleas or other ectoparasites. It has been documented that these infections can alter the behavior of the rodents and render them more susceptible to predatory hawks that in turn contract the disease (Jellison, 1938, 1939). Although the virulence of these microorganisms in avian species is generally low, they provide additional examples of maladies that can affect avian predatory species. Birds of prey have also been incriminated in the spread of plague and tularemia by mechanical means, i.e., picking up and dispersing infected fleas (Hull, 1963).

Botulism *(Clostridium botulinum)*, although not a truly infectious disease, is a recognized important mortality factor in wild waterfowl (Sciple, 1953). Infected waterfowl exhibit altered behavior patterns; they become weak, less active, lose their fear of natural enemies, and exhibit signs associated with central nervous system disorders. These altered actions render infected waterfowl more susceptible to predatory birds. Predators after feeding on infected waterfowl themselves become victims of botulism. An alternate method of botulism exposure occurs in young hawks that drink and bathe in areas of heavy concentration of botulism toxin (White, 1963).

Predatory birds have developed erysipelas and anthrax from feeding on diseased mammalian carcasses (Hamerton, 1942).

Other bacterial and mycotic diseases such as tuberculosis, pseudotuberculosis, aspergillosis, and salmonellosis have been reported in raptors maintained in captivity (Blair, 1910; Steinhaus and Kohls, 1942; Ainsworth and Rewell, 1949). The occurrence and significance of these agents in wild birds is unknown.

Although the significance of bacterial diseases to raptor populations is for the most part unknown, Table 37.1 presents an extensive list of bacterial diseases that have occurred in raptors.

VIRAL DISEASES

The number of viral diseases of raptors (Table 37.1) is not as extensive as the bacterial or parasitic diseases listed, but their potential as an ecological factor is just as great.

Newcastle disease, one of the most important domestic poultry diseases of the world, is widely distributed in wild avian populations (Gustafson and Moses, 1953). The virus has been isolated from the osprey (Keymer, 1958) and owls (Ingalls *et al.*, 1951). This malady merits specific consideration when one is discussing population declines of raptors because of its recognized importance as a direct mortality factor, its ability to affect reproduction, as well as the timing of its introduction into North America.

More than 127 species of birds, including hawks, are listed as hosts of ornithosis. This severe infectious disease of avian populations and man is a significant disease of pigeons and ducks (Hull, 1963).

Avian populations have long been considered the natural reservoir of some of the viral encephalitides. Both eastern viral encephalitis (Karstad *et al.*, 1960) and western viral encephalitis (Kissling *et al.*, 1955) have been reported in hawks, but their importance in these populations is unknown.

Fowl pox has been reported from many wild avian species (Biester and Schwarte, 1965: 675–770). It is an important cause of mortality in the mourning dove and pigeon (Locke, 1961), and its potential for hawks is obvious. Other avian viral diseases have been observed in captive raptors, but their natural occurrence has not been reported.

PARASITIC DISEASES

An extensive list of parasites of raptors has been reported in the literature (Table 37.1), and both myiasis and trichomoniasis are important, recognized mortality factors.

Myiasis, or infestations with fly maggots, has been recorded regularly in hawks of North America. In the east, Sargent (1938) reports that, although many raptor nestlings are myiasis-infested, mortality is rare;

whereas White (1963) in the west observed instances where 100% of the nestlings succumbed to the infection. In both the east and west, myiasis is a problem only during certain years, i.e., wet, damp years are conducive to the development of myiasis in nestling hawks, whereas dry, arid nesting seasons result in a lack of the disease. Although the impact of this parasitic disease on continental hawk populations is not known, it is important locally and potentially could be quite significant.

The parasitic disease that appears to have considerable potential for affecting hawk populations is trichomoniasis. Documented accounts of this malady occurring and causing mortality in hawks are numerous. Stabler discusses this situation in Chapter 38.

An interesting illustration of an interspecies relationship of parasitism is the case of the tapeworm *Cladotaemia* (Scott, 1930). This adult tapeworm is found only in the intestinal tract of the ferruginous rough-legged hawk. Here it lays its eggs which are excreted in the hawk's droppings onto the ground and vegetation. The prairie dog (*Cynomys ludovicianus)* feeding on contaminated vegetation consumes the eggs which develop into larvae within the animal. Another hawk then feeds on larval-infected prairie dogs, the larvae develop into adults in the hawk, and it becomes the final tapeworm host. The prairie dog and rough-legged hawk are the only two species involved in the maintenance of this parasite.

A wide variety of parasites have been reported for raptors (Table 37.1). All of the major groups of endoparasites have been documented for hawks (Chandler, 1941; Herde, 1942; Rausch, 1947; Schultz, 1939; Wood, 1931; Williams, 1947). Most of the blood protozoa of avian species have been observed in hawks: *Plasmodium, Hemoproteus,* and *Leucocytozoon* (Coatney, 1936, 1937; Herman, 1944). Whenever ectoparasites were diligently looked for, they were found (Malcomson, 1960).

Although a wide variety of parasites exists in raptors, again their significance to wild populations is for the most part unknown. The presence and prevalence of a wide variety of numbers and kinds of parasitic, bacterial, and viral agents illustrate the potential of disease as a possible ecological factor that warrants consideration when one is studying raptor population dynamics.

PEREGRINE FALCON DISEASES

A summary of our knowledge regarding infectious diseases of the peregrine falcon is illustrated in Table 37.2. The diseases have been classified as those reported for captive birds and those observed in the wild.

Of the diseases known to occur in peregrines naturally, botulism and myiasis are recognized mortality factors that could be important. In Utah, both have definitely affected local breeding populations (White,

Table 37.2. A Summary of Infectious Diseases of the Peregrine Falcon

Captive	Wild	
Trichomoniasis	Trichomoniasis	Tapeworms
Aspergillosis	Botulism	Mallophaga
Coccidiosis	Cestodes	Mites
Heart filaria	Myiasis	Fleas
	Filaria	Ticks

1963). Their significance might not be geographically limited, and both merit future consideration as significant ecological factors.

Trichomoniasis has been reported in both wild and captive populations and is a known mortality factor of peregrine falcons (Table 37.2).

The presence of aspergillosis, coccidiosis, and heart filaria in captive birds is of interest but of little apparent importance. A variety of endo- and ectoparasites occur in both wild and captive peregrines, but their significance is unknown (Langton and Cobbold, 1881; McIntosh, 1940; Crisp, 1854).

This literature review of diseases of raptors, and specifically those of the peregrine falcon, was undertaken to provide a basis for a discussion of infectious disease as an ecological factor to be considered in the decline of the peregrine falcon. Despite the fact that raptors have not been studied intensively, a rather lengthy and variable list of diseases has been reported. These include viral, bacterial, fungal, and parasitic agents that can affect the host in a variety of ways. Although the significance of these agents to wild raptor populations is for the most part unknown, their potential as mortality factors does exist. It would appear that disease is another ecological factor that should be included in a study of the decline of the peregrine falcon.

LITERATURE CITED

Ainsworth, G. C., and R. E. Rewell. 1949. The incidence of aspergillosis in captive wild birds. J. Comp. Pathol., 59(1):213–224.

Biester, H. E., and L. H. Schwarte. 1965. Diseases of poultry. Iowa State University Press, Ames. 1382 p.

Blair, W. R. 1910. Reports of the veterinarian and pathologist. Ann. Rep. N.Y. Zool. Soc., 15:101–109.

Chandler, A. C. 1941. A new spiruroid nematode *Habronema americanus* from the broad-winged hawk. J. Parasitol., 27(2):184.

Coatney, G. R. 1936. A check-list and host-index of the genus Haemoproteus. J. Parasitol., 22(1):88–105.

———. 1937. A catalog and host index of the genus Leucocytozoon. J. Parasitol., 23(2):202–212.

Crisp, E. 1854. Filaria in the heart of a peregrine falcon. Trans. Pathol. Soc. London, 5:345.

Gustafson, D. P., and H. E. Moses. 1953. Wild birds as possible spreaders of Newcastle disease. Proc. Amer. Vet. Med. Ass., 90:281–285.

Hamerton, A. E. 1942. Report on the deaths occurring in the Society's gardens during the year 1941. Proc. Zool. Soc. London, 112:120–137.

Herde, K. E. 1942. A new spiruroid nematode, *Thelazia buteonis,* from Swainson's hawk. J. Parasitol., 28(1):241–244.

Herman, C. M. 1944. The blood protozoa of North American birds. Bird-Banding, 15(3):89–112.

———. 1955. Diseases of birds, p. 450–467. *In* Albert Wolfson [ed.], Recent studies in avian biology. University of Illinois Press, Urbana. 479 p.

Hull, T. G. 1963. Diseases transmitted from animals to man. Charles C. Thomas Publishing Co., Springfield, Illinois. 967 p.

Ingalls, W. L., R. W. Vesper, and A. Mahoney. 1951. Isolation of Newcastle disease virus from the great horned owl. J. Amer. Vet. Med. Ass., 119(892):71.

Jellison, W. L. 1938. The possible role of birds in the epidemiology of sylvatic plague. J. Parasitol., 24(1):12.

———. 1939. Sylvatic plague: Studies of predatory and scavenger birds in relation to its epidemiology. Public Health Rep., Washington, D.C., 54:792–798.

Jennings, A. R. 1961. An analysis of 1000 deaths in wild birds. Bird Study, 8(1):25–31.

Karstad, L. H., S. Vadlamudi, R. P. Hanson, D. O. Trainer, and V. H. Lee. 1960. Eastern equine encephalitis in Wisconsin. J. Infect. Dis., 106(1):53–59.

Keymer, I. F. 1958. A survey and review of the causes of mortality in British birds and the significance of wild birds as disseminators of disease. Vet. Rec., 70(36):713–720.

Kissling, R. E., R. W. Chamberlain, D. B. Nelson, and D. D. Stamm. 1955. Studies on the North American arthropod-born encephalitides. Amer. J. Hyg., 62(3):233–254.

Langton, H., and T. S. Cobbold. 1881. Siptutanious worms in a peregrine falcon. Zool., 5:309.

Locke, L. N. 1961. Pox in mourning doves in the United States. J. Wildl. Mgmt., 25(2):211–212.

McIntosh, A. 1940. A new taenoid cestode *(Cladotaenia foxi)* from a falcon. Proc. Helminth Soc. Washington, 7(2):71–74.

Malcomson, R. O. 1960. Mallophaga from birds of North America. Wilson Bull., 72(2):182–197.

Meyer, K. F., and B. Eddie. 1952. Reservoirs of the psittacosis agent. Acta Trop., 9(1):204–214.

Quortrup, E. R., and J. E. Shillinger. 1941. Three thousand wild bird autopsies on western lake areas. J. Amer. Vet. Med. Ass., 99(776):382-387.

Rausch, R. 1947. *Bakererpes fragilis* N.G., N. Sp., a cestode from the night hawk *(Cestoda: Dilepididae).* J. Parasitol., 33(5):435–438.

Rosen, M. N., and A. I. Bischoff. 1949. The 1948–49 outbreak of fowl cholera in birds in the San Francisco Bay area and surrounding counties. Calif. Fish and Game, 35(3):185–192.

Rosen, M. N., and E. E. Morse, 1959. An interspecies chain in a fowl cholera epizootic. Calif. Fish and Game 45(1):51–56.

Sargent, W. D. 1938. Nest parasitism of hawks. Auk, 55(1):82–84.

Schultz, R. L. 1939. A new tapeworm from Swainson's hawk. Trans. Amer. Microscop. Soc., 58:448–451.

Sciple, G. W. 1953. Avian botulism: Information on earlier research. U.S. Dep. Interior, Spec. Sci. Rep.: Wildlife, 23:1–13.

Scott, J. W. 1930. The development of two *Cladotaenia* in the ferruginous roughleg hawk. J. Parasitol., 17(1):115.

Steinhaus, E. A., and G. M. Kohls. 1942. Isolation of an acid-fast bacillus from a hawk. J. Amer. Vet. Med. Ass., 101(781):502.

Trainer, D. O. 1965. Workshop symposium on avian pasteurellosis. Bull. Wildl. Dis. Ass., 1(2):11–13.

———, and G. W. Fischer. 1963. Fatal trematodiasis of coots. J. Wildl. Mgmt., 27(3):483–486.

White, C. M. 1963. Botulism and myiasis as mortality factors in falcons. Condor, 65(5):442–443.

Williams, R. B. 1947. Infestation of raptorials by *Ornithodoros aquilae*. Auk, 64(2):185–188.

Wood, M. 1931. Intestinal parasites in sharp-shinned hawks. Auk, 48(2):265–266.

CHAPTER 38

TRICHOMONAS GALLINAE AS A FACTOR IN THE DECLINE OF THE PEREGRINE FALCON

Robert M. Stabler

Literally for centuries the pigeon fancier has been plagued by a disease known as canker; and the falconer, by one known as frounce. The cause of both of these maladies is a small protozoan organism known as *Trichomonas gallinae.* First described in 1878 by an Italian veterinarian named Rivolta, the parasite has caused the loss of millions of dollars worth of pigeons, thousands of infected mourning doves annually, and, what is pertinent to this conference, countless trained hawks. (For a complete review of *Trichomonas gallinae,* see Stabler, 1954.) The organism lives mainly in the upper digestive tract of the host, frequently swarming in the mouth, throat, and crop. It does not occur in the feces. It is in the mouth and throat, when a nonimmune bird picks up one of the more virulent strains, that the typically yellowish, cheesy, undermining lesions occur. Death may be due to a blocking of the passageways as the lesions assume massive proportions, or to an excess of toxins produced in viscera by the more invasive strains.

The existence of strains of *T. gallinae* varying greatly in pathogenicity is a most important facet of this parasite's epizootiology. There are strains that produce no serious disease and yet, when present in a bird, cause the production of a strong, protecting immunity. This is known as premunition and, as long as the bird remains infected, it is completely protected against the highly pathogenic strains. Because of the extremely valuable protection of a premunitive infection, one should never completely eradicate the low-level, immunity-producing infections. Fortunately for the avian hosts, these virulent strains are greatly in the minority, so that the uninfected, nonimmune bird normally acquires a sublethal strain, recovers from its disease, and retains the parasite in a beneficial, immunity-preserving, premunitive state. This is probably the situation as it occurs normally in the wild.

Doves and pigeons, the normal hosts for *T. gallinae,* frequently recover from infections with the fairly virulent strains of the parasite. They may, of course, live for years harboring the trichomonad, which loses none of its disease-producing ability as the years go by. The organism is passed on in this virulent state to the offspring, some of which die, some of which live to pass on the disease. It is these recovered birds that are the source of infection for susceptible predators that might consume them. The writer has seen fatal frounce from time to time in his own birds including the peregrine, gyrfalcon, American kestrel, pigeon hawk, goshawk, Cooper's hawk, red-tailed hawk, red-shouldered hawk, and golden eagle, all infected inadvertently or deliberately with virulent strains from domestic pigeons. These deaths occurred, of course, before the advent of Enheptin as a trichomonacide (see Stabler and Mellentin, 1953). There is today no excuse for a captive hawk's dying with trichomoniasis. The cure is at hand in Enheptin.

But what of the wild bird, that hawk which is capable of catching and devouring a feral pigeon or dove? It should be remembered that some three-quarters of all wild common pigeons and virtually 100% of all commercial ones (those raised for squabs) are carriers of *T. gallinae,* many of them with highly virulent strains. Furthermore, the mourning dove is also a natural host of *T. gallinae,* and the alarming epizootics of dove trichomoniasis in the southeastern United States (see Stabler, 1954) attest to the presence of highly virulent strains in these birds which also serve as prey for the larger, faster hawks. Published information on the influence of *T. gallinae* on the wild raptor is extremely difficult to find. In fact, it appears to be virtually nonexistent. Cade (1960) puts it very well when he states, "The most critical period of survival for young peregrines comes after they leave their parents. It is only a guess what happens at this time. Certainly, as every falconer knows, there are many diseases that are lethal to falcons, especially juveniles—three of the commonest ones are frounce (trichomoniasis), aspergillosis, and coccidiosis—and these diseases must take a toll of the wild juveniles as well." It is unfortunate that Cade did not have concrete evidence to support his suggestions, at least so far as *T. gallinae* was concerned.

To the writer's knowledge the only published account of the presence of *T. gallinae* in the wild hawk involved the finding of the parasite in the mouths of two 10-day-old peregrines that were still in their eyrie (Stabler, 1941). Appropriate culture tubes were taken to the eyrie site, which overlooked the Delaware River in Pennsylvania. The small falcons' mouths were swabbed out, the material placed in the cultures and later incubated. Rich growths of *T. gallinae* were obtained from each bird. Both birds were taken into captivity and were quite healthy when last seen; one was banded and released at 4 months, the other flew away at 2 years.

So what may we conclude regarding the possible effect of *Trichomonas gallinae* on the large, bird-catching hawks in general and the peregrine falcon in particular? It is the writer's opinion that this parasite has not in the past, nor will in the future, have any appreciable effect on the survival, either generally or locally, of any of the pigeon- and dove-eating populations of feral hawks. Even the highly columbiphilic, strictly urban populations of peregrines must have suffered only the minutest losses from trichomoniasis. Had their diet been 100% pigeons, it must be remembered that not all pigeons harbor *T. gallinae,* that most strains of the parasite are nonvirulent, and that, should an individual peregrine acquire one of the more virulent strains and survive its bout of trichomoniasis, it still would stand only the merest chance of passing its infection on to its possible offspring. Even though the female peregrine proffers small tidbits of pigeon to the very young chicks, unless these pieces are contaminated with *T. gallinae* of themselves, there would be a very small chance, indeed, of her fouling them with *Trichomonas*-bearing saliva. This is in sharp contrast with the feeding methods of the columbiforms, where all food received by the squabs for several weeks is delivered entirely by regurgitation. Furthermore, many peregrines now long gone from their former eyrie sites were known to feed only occasionally on a pigeon or dove. The writer, in examining the avian remains in numerous now-deserted, out-of-the-way eyries when these were being occupied year after year, noted the feathers of blue jays, meadowlarks, red-winged blackbirds, and prey of this type, with the pigeon being an uncommon article of food. No, it just does not seem that the case for *T. gallinae* as a factor in the decline of the peregrine can be made, especially since the epizootiological evidence is all on the other side.

LITERATURE CITED

Cade, T. J. 1960. Ecology of the peregrine and gyrfalcon populations in Alaska. Univ. Calif. Pub. Zool., 63(3):151–290.

Rivolta, S. 1878. Una forma di croup prodotta da un infusorio, nei polli. Giorn. Anat., Fisiol. e Patol. Anim., 10(3):149–158.

Stabler, R. M. 1941. Further studies on trichomoniasis in birds. Auk, 58(4):558–562.

———. 1954. *Trichomonas gallinae:* A review. Exp. Parasitol., 3(4):368–402.

———, and R. W. Mellentin. 1953. Effect of 2-amino-5-nitro-thiazole (Enheptin) and other drugs on *Trichomonas gallinae* infection in the domestic pigeon. J. Parasitol., 39(6):637–642.

CHAPTER 39

THE POSSIBLE ROLE OF INFECTIOUS AGENTS IN THE EXTINCTIONS OF SPECIES

Robert P. Hanson

THE PARASITIC CONTINUUM

One of the points made in Stabler's chapter concerns the variation that occurs in the degree of virulence of trichomonads. This variation has been documented not only for protozoa, but also for bacterial and viral parasites. Rare is the parasite that does not have strains that are highly virulent, of lesser virulence, and almost lacking in virulence—a continuum. We presume that the avirulent ones usually predominate in nature as these are the ones that are found in carrier animals and consequently are most readily perpetuated.

If suitable samples were to be taken from the participants in this symposium, a good many viruses could be isolated, viruses which are not inconveniencing their hosts appreciably. Nevertheless, some of the viruses that could be recovered would be fully capable of producing human fatalities. One of them is Herpes simplex virus, found in the lips. Herpes is capable of causing fatal infections of babies or of causing fatal infections in individuals of any age, if certain barriers are circumvented by the inoculating needle. This kind of situation, involving the presence of potentially lethal viruses in apparently normal individuals, is not unique. All animals have such viruses.

HOST-PARASITE RELATIONSHIPS

Two kinds of host-parasite relationships need to be contrasted. There are population-dependent diseases in which transmission is from one to another individual of a single species, and there are population-independent diseases in which transmission is from one to another individual of the same or a different host species. Most important to our consideration is the fact that one or more of the host species of a population-independent disease can be eliminated without disturbing the perpetuation of the parasite.

Measles in man is a population-dependent disease, being readily transmitted among children. Hog cholera in swine and myxomatosis in rabbits are other examples.

Botulism, an intoxication produced by a saprophyte multiplying in tissues of dead animals, is population-independent. The toxin is ingested with food or water. Death of the intoxicated animal has no bearing on the perpetuation of the bacterium. Equine encephalitis, known as a disease of horses and man, is transmitted to them by mosquitoes. It is perpetuated in nature as a systemic infection of certain birds which it does not seriously harm. The dying horse and ailing man are incidental hosts and have no bearing on the perpetuation of the virus.

The epizootic nature of these two types of disease differ. The dependent disease is transmitted most rapidly in populations of high density. Such diseases are short-lived in small populations: a 50-hen coop, a rural family, or a herd of 20 cows. They are long-lived in large populations: a chicken broiler flock that adds 10,000 day-old chicks per week, the children born into a city, or recruits in a military reception center. The nature of the recruitment to a population frequently determines the epidemic wave. Measles occurs in a 4-year wave, which is related to the size of the susceptible preschool crop of children. On the other hand, repetition of identical influenza serotypes in an adult population may be as infrequent as once every 60 years.

Population-dependent diseases are transmitted most effectively by aerosols and by pollution of food and water supplies. Such diseases are rare in wildlife populations. The result in instances in which they occur may be a drastic decrease in population, but it is most improbable that such diseases will destroy the host population. Black death and human cholera killed one out of four and perhaps one out of two individuals over whole nations. But people were left, and communities were rebuilt.

Myxomatosis is a mild infection of Brazilian cottontails (*Sylvilagus brasiliensis*) that will, when introduced into European rabbits (*Oryctolagus cuniculus*) cause 100% mortality. When the virus was introduced into Australia to reduce the feral European rabbit population, it killed 99% of the hundreds of thousands of rabbits infected by mosquitoes.

After 10 years, it now kills more than 50% but less than 90%. The population has been greatly reduced. Some observers estimate that the present population is less than 1% of the original population in many areas, but no one believes that the rabbit will be eradicated from Australia by the virus. Both the rabbit and the virus have been modified by their association.

POPULATION-INDEPENDENT DISEASES

The nature of population-independent diseases is different. Transmission is controlled only by the size of the reservoir. Consequently, it can affect very dispersed populations, be they isolated jungle tribes, a dozen hens on a remote farm, or solitary animals like the peregrine. The disease may appear in these hosts at infrequent intervals. Equine encephalitis was observed in horses on Long Island in 1840 and then it was not reported until 1926. Since then, it has been reported at much more frequent intervals. Murray Valley encephalitis of man was reported in Australia in 1917 and then not again until about 1950.

Transmission may be by vectors (encephalitis), by water (leptospiroses), by food (botulism), and sometimes by several routes. Theoretically, this kind of disease could eradicate a species since the pathogen input continues irrespective of the size of the remaining population. Continued input of irradiated males is the basis of the screwworm-control program in the southern United States, a campaign which has been quite successful in eliminating the species from the southeastern part of the country. Presumably, if historical accounts are accurate, certain Indian and Polynesian tribes were eliminated by the repeated introduction of smallpox by resistant white carriers.

What are essential factors in a disease-induced catastrophic population decrease? First, a population that has no prior experience with the pathogen. Second, introduction of the parasite by a carrier species capable of maintaining and disseminating the parasite.

SOURCES OF INFECTION FOR THE PEREGRINE

The peregrine, on the basis of many of the discussions I have heard, might be considered more susceptible than most predators are to their prey parasites, as it prefers prey on the wing, which may be presumed to be less parasitized than carrion.

What prey species might be a source of parasites for the peregrine? It could be a newly introduced prey species or a long-standing prey that has become a carrier of a new disease.

I am not in a position to give a definitive answer to this question, but I can suggest some possibilities. We have introduced into the United States birds which were not part of our fauna in the past, like the coturnix quail, the starling, and the English sparrow. There have been changes in the abundance in some of the species upon which the peregrine preys. The red-winged blackbird, for example, has greatly increased in numbers. In fact, changes in abundance of prey species have occurred in all areas in which the peregrine decline has occurred. These changes must have inevitably induced changes in activity patterns of the peregrine.

THE PIGEON AS A SOURCE OF NEW PARASITES

What is the possibility that a new parasite has become established in prey that has long been available to the peregrine? I am going to take the example of the pigeon, as it has been adequately documented that the pigeon constitutes a part of the diet of the peregrine in areas in which man is present. In Wisconsin, there are 23 pigeon clubs with some 4,000 members, and it has been estimated there are double that number of owners of pigeons. Lofts usually range in size from 12 to 500. This is a sizable population that probably is typical of other regions.

It has already been mentioned that pigeons have canker (trichomoniasis). They are also infected with fowl cholera, coccidia, and pigeon pox. They can be infected by *Salmonella pullorum* and *S. gallinarium*. Psittacosis is not uncommon, as five of six groups of feral pigeons collected in Wisconsin a few years ago were demonstrated to be positive for that disease. Similar reports are available for other parts of the world. Among respiratory diseases, we find pigeons susceptible to Newcastle disease, mycoplasmosis, and aspergillosis. Pigeons have a variety of mites, lice, and roundworms.

What changes have been made in the management of pigeons? Pigeons are still fed much the same type of diets that they have been fed for the past hundred years. This is very different from the situation that exists in production of chickens that regularly and almost universally receive additives to their diet. Pigeons are given occasional treatment with antibiotics or NF-180. While overdosage of individually treated birds may not be uncommon, antibiotics are not a regular constituent of their diet. Vaccination practices common to poultry are rare among pigeons.

In pointing out these differences, we must remember that pigeons, reared in close contact with man, are also frequently in close contact with poultry. Furthermore, some pigeon dealers accumulate flocks of 500 to several thousand birds in crowded quarters. Observers report that such flocks always contain sick and dying birds. Spares (a term for inferior birds), usually including some sick birds, are sold to trainers of hunting dogs. Some escape in the field only to fall prey to predators. This provides an avenue for continued introduction of diseases of pigeons and their domestic associates into wild populations.

EMERGING PATHOGENS OF BIRDS

What are some of the emerging pathogens of poultry which may be getting into pigeons and from pigeons into wildlife? Several changes have occurred in the last 20 to 30 years. The widespread use of antibiotics in poultry feed has led to selection of some antibiotic-resistant parasites. Salmonella, resistant to streptomycin, occurs now in poultry populations. Forms resistant to antibiotics may also be altered in some of their other properties such as pathogenicity for nondomestic birds.

Vaccine viruses have been substituted for wild viruses that are pathogenic for poultry. Stabler pointed out that virulent canker did not kill many of the pigeons because prior infection with a mild strain of canker protected them. This is natural vaccination. Avirulence for chicken of the prevalent vaccine strains does not necessarily mean that these viruses are avirulent for other species. I can cite two examples. A Newcastle disease vaccine strain which is avirulent for chickens and widely used as a vaccine is just as pathogenic for man as any of the virulent strains. Furthermore, one of the vaccine strains is highly pathogenic for goose embryos, although it is of low virulence for chicken embryos.

Newcastle disease was first recognized in 1926. It became prevalent in Europe in the 1940's. About 1946 it reached eastern United States, and by 1949 it was common throughout the country. Bronchitis and laryngotracheitis were recognized before 1940, and mycoplasmosis was recognized after 1950. Since 1960, an adenovirus of chickens, GAL, has been found to be extremely widespread in domestic birds. It does not induce a recognized disease in chickens, but one strain induces a severe disease in quail.

MANIFESTATIONS OF DISEASE

What are consequences of infection? Disease agents need not induce fatalities to reduce host populations. They can cause infertility and fetal defects. German measles does the latter in man. Newcastle disease can produce similar teratogenic defects in chickens. Psittacosis can do the same in sheep and has been reported to do it in birds. Newcastle disease also induces muscular dystrophy—droop of the wing, twist of the neck, which would interfere with survival. Abnormalities in the nervous system, caused by equine encephalitis virus, produce the so-called dummies in horses. Much milder behavioral defects in wild species would disturb mating patterns and lead to a failure to survive.

Peregrines may be susceptible to some of these diseases. The disease agent need not induce rapid death in peregrines to reduce the population. The loss could be catastrophic from a disease transmitted by a carrier-prey species and continually presented to the peregrine.

To find out what part infective disease may play in the decline of peregrine populations, serological and microbiological methods can be utilized. Specific antibodies can be readily identified from blood of birds or yolk from eggs. It is possible, without injuring the bird, to take rectal or tracheal swabs or draw blood from which viruses and bacteria can be isolated. An answer could be obtained by a well-planned, adequately staffed, and well-financed program.

REFERENCES

Carrère, L., J. Roux, and F. Maury. 1952. Flore microbienne intestinale des cobayes traités par divers antibiotiques. Rev. Immunol., 16:406–411.

Darlington, C. D. 1960. Origin and evolution of viruses. Trans. Royal Soc. Trop. Med. and Hyg., 54:90–96.

Garnham, P. C. C. 1959. The evolution of the zoonoses. The Medical Press, London. p. 251–256.

Lwoff, André. 1959. Factors influencing the evolution of viral diseases at the cellular level and in the organism. Bact. Rev., 23(3):109–124.

Marshall, I. D., and F. Fenner. 1960. Studies in the epidemiology of infectious myxomatosis of rabbits. J. Hyg., 58(4):485–488.

Shope, R. E. 1964. The birth of a new disease, p. 3–22. *In* R. P. Hanson [ed.], Newcastle disease virus: an evolving pathogen. Univ. Wis. Press, Madison. 352 p.

CHAPTER 40

GENERAL DISCUSSION: PATHOGENS AND PARASITES

THE PIGEON SITUATION IN BRITISH COLUMBIA

BEEBE: I had some 6 years on plague, tularemia, and associated work in British Columbia during the war years. I have also flown falcons for a number of years. The members of this panel will recognize from my reports that in my area we have, if not the largest, certainly the densest population of peregrines reported so far anywhere on this continent. This population of peregrines comes freely in winter down into Puget Sound where pigeons have been available to them for the past century. The falcons certainly are showing no decline. Need I say more? We have pigeon fanciers and pigeon racers in British Columbia too, and pigeons are regularly shipped into British Columbia and the Puget Sound area from all over this continent, including California and the eastern USA. If pigeons were in any way involved in the transmission of disease to the peregrine population, we would have seen a major decline in peregrines on the Queen Charlotte Islands and on the associated west side of Vancouver Island. This has not happened.

HANCOCK: One thing in regard to the Peale's peregrines, though, is that they have no access to pigeons while the falcons are young. Similarly, the Arctic peregrine is presumably passing through this country and has access to pigeons but is not known to be declining. The decline involves the population of peregrines in contact with the pigeon at the time at which the falcons are feeding their young.

BEEBE: That could be a possibility, I agree. There might possibly be an infection of the young in the nest, although we hear reports of young fledging in affected areas all the time. The young seem to get off the nest and fledge all right, even while they are being fed pigeons. I cannot but think that, if there were any serious pathogenic organism present in domestic pigeons being fed into the wild peregrine population, it would have showed up in my area, as well as elsewhere in North America.

TRICHOMONIASIS IN THE GOLDEN EAGLE

NELSON: Starting I believe in about 1934, the domestic pigeon began to nest in the cliffs of the American west. By about 1952 or 1953 it had gone all the way up to the Columbia River and reached the summit of the Cascades. All at once it was in the home of the golden eagle, where there had been no pigeons. I am sure that the golden eagle before this time did not have the opportunity to or could not catch the pigeon except one that may have been very sick. But what has happened now? The pigeons now go out and live right in the cliffs. Sometimes there will be 300–400 pigeons living on the same cliff site with the golden eagle, or in the same canyon. The golden eagle catches the fledglings that jump out of the nest and cannot fly very well. It also goes to the pigeon nesting holes in the cliffs and reaches in with its long feet to pull out one of the young. When we took six eagles from six different eyries, at five of which there were about two birds each, all six eagles came down with trichomoniasis within about 3 or 4 weeks. I did not know whether I had fed the birds something after we had taken them or whether they had gotten the disease before I took them. This still has not been established. We did find a young eagle dead with holes in the roof of its mouth, a young eagle that was killed by the heat. I think that we did establish that the eagle has this disease. Although I have kept as many as nine eagles a year, I never had one before that had the frounce. This particular strain of disease did not cure like it does with our falcons. We first had to go through the Enheptin routine of therapy which took the disease down for a while but did not stop it. Then we called the people who make Enheptin, and they said, "Well you'd better try aureomycin," and we called Stabler and talked with him. Finally we did save all of the eagles, except one and that one died from an overdose of Enheptin. Thus I believe that eagles are not as tolerant of Enheptin as are the falcons. Eagles now have a method of getting trichomoniasis which they did not have before in their historical homes. It remains to be seen what this all means in the wild.

DISEASE AND INTERSPECIFIC POPULATION DECLINES

GLADING: Generally speaking, I think we can rule out a pandemic disease by virtue of the evidence that we have heard here in the last couple of days. The population drops have been worldwide in certain habitats. They have not been restricted to one species of bird; they have tended to all occur about the same time. We cannot really point to a disease that has acted this way. It is almost unbelievable that trichomoniasis would all of a sudden begin to catch on to all these birds, ospreys, and the whole complex of bald eagles, Cooper's hawks, sparrow hawks, and European kestrels.

BEEBE: The band-tailed pigeon is distributed from British Columbia, Utah, and north central Colorado south to northern Nicaragua; its fossils are reported in the pleistocene of California and Nuevo Leon. It has been available to peregrines for a long time.

RATCLIFFE: One could say that the case against pesticides has been based on carefully reasoned, circumstantial evidence. I think Hanson has made a very ingenious case, but I think there are one or two vital links missing.

For instance, we have found dead peregrines that contained amounts of pesticide which we believed were large enough to be responsible for their death. We have yet to find dead peregrines which had actual symptoms or other evidence of these diseases. Four of the peregrines which were found dead in Britain were examined by veterinarians and pathologists, and they did not show any of these symptoms of pathogens of any kind which are identifiable.

Another point is that there is no disease evidence from ornithologists and falconers who have seen young in the nest, or from falconers who have taken birds and have observed them soon after they have taken them. (I think one cannot infer too much after birds have been in captivity a while.)

In addition we are concerned here with the synchronistic declines of different species. One would find it rather difficult to believe that two or more different species in Britain—peregrine, sparrow-hawk, and golden eagle—were suffering the same symptoms of decline and all being affected by the same organism.

There are other possibilities which at first sight show the same possible correlation with the peregrine population decline. Radioactivity has been mentioned. I think in Britain it does not show too good a correlation when one looks into it further—there are geographical differences in population effects that do not square up.

PIGEONS AS PEREGRINE PREY

HANCOCK: It is probably not the trained homing pigeon which the peregrine takes, but the feral pigeon which is not fed by the pigeon fancier.

MRS. HERBERT: Along the Hudson River, peregrines did not take the feral bird; the city pigeons were much more difficult to catch. The feral pigeon takes cover. The racing pigeon behaves differently, and therefore it is a much easier prey. The racing pigeons are raced for exercise from their lofts; they are let out every afternoon to fly over the roofs of New York. Therefore, peregrines always take the racing pigeon; they do not try to take the feral pigeons which nest on the same buildings several stories below them but are far more difficult to catch.

HANSON: I understand pigeons are fed a grain rather than a mash, and this is one reason why they do not get these antibiotic mixes. Now it is true that grain, in certain places, does contain some residues. Now this I do not believe is particularly significant because insecticides are ordinarily not put on grain crops. They are used only as a secondary treatment.

THE EVALUATION OF POST-MORTEM FINDINGS

HANSON: I want to make one comment here in relation to these previous discussions of the finding or not finding of microorganisms in birds. I believe that it is impossible to take a bird and not find a parasitic organism present in it. Now this doesn't mean, and I don't want to allege, that these are causes of mortality, but I will not accept the statement as completely valid that you do not find pathogens. I would prefer, and I think the case would be stronger for insecticides, if you admit that you more frequently find pathogens present in some of these birds, because this is the characteristic thing when a thorough examination is made.

PRESTT: I would bear you out. In my discussion (Chapter 42) I gave the veterinary result which said they could find no cause of death. In most cases there were *Escherichia coli* present, and a number of parasites were in fact isolated but were not considered to be harmful.

HANSON: That's right. Because ordinarily, if you take a dead specimen of a bird and give it to a parasitologist, he will find parasites. If you give it to a microbiologist, he will find microbes. If you give it to a virologist, he will find viruses. If you give it to the person who is doing work on chemistry, he will find residues. This is just inevitable; this will happen in every species. Now what is the cause of death is still another matter.

GEYER: In connection with our discussion, let us bear in mind that we are trying to explore all possible avenues and, regardless of what our evidence may be from the aspect of pesticides—and I don't intend to minimize this—let us not bias our thinking from the standpoint that we fail to look for other evidence. I myself was a victim of bias at one time, involving a case of anaplasmosis in cattle. Repeatedly I made the statement while in Ohio that we did not have this disease in cattle in that state. Finally I decided to take the blood samples that we were routinely collecting for brucellosis testing. When these were subjected to a test for anaplasmosis—lo and behold, we found reactor after reactor. Now why didn't we have an active disease? The only basic reason that we could explain was that we did not have the necessary intermediate host, the tick, to serve as a transmitter. These are things that I think we must keep in mind. Let us not be biased in our deliberation on this, lest we lose sight of something that is very valuable.

TRAINER: I would certainly agree. For example, my list of diseases was not presented to say that all these factors are killing these birds. This was not the intent. In fact, most of the pathogens were found, but their significance was not known. There were a few cases in which I tried to point out where pathologists did know there was mortality due to a particular organism, but these actually are very few in number. Hence we were not coming up here trying to say: Look at all this; this is killing your falcons; this is your answer. This was not the intent, but my understanding was that this was a conference to get ideas and explore the various possibilities. Hence it was our hope that we could throw these things out and discuss them and see whether or not they did or did not fit in this whole picture.

Now when people are saying: Well, we looked at this, and we did not find a pathogenic organism that caused the die-off, I like to mention the case where at one time brucellosis was causing all the abortions in our cattle. The dairy industry cleaned up all the brucellosis, and all of a sudden leptospirosis was causing abortions. It was there before but, because they were looking at brucellosis and were trying to control it, they looked no further. I don't know what this proves except that one has to look continually and consider all factors. I don't think it's all just a simple one-cause type of relationship.

GEYER: I would like to make one other comment after looking at the Beebe and Webster book, *North American Falconry and Hunting Hawks*. I notice that they listed some diseases and parasites encountered. Now when we think of disease, disease is anything that is in violation of a norm. A fractured leg is a disease, in essence, if you are going to be technical.

BEEBE: Are not pesticides the most insinuating disease of all?

GEYER: Their presence is a disease, absolutely.

BEEBE: The difference is that these factors have been present for centuries, presumably. The new thing is what we are talking about.

RATCLIFFE: Whenever epidemic disease appears among wild species, some measure of resistance has developed. We have had the decline of the peregrine with us now for approximately 10 years, with—as far as I know—no indication that developing resistance has as yet come to light.

HANSON: I think the best answer to that, of course, is the experience with myxomatosis, because this has been unquestionably the most carefully studied of any pathogen introduced into a population, both in Australia and in Europe. In both instances there has been evidence of some degree of increased resistance in the host populations as well as appearance in the parasite population of varying strains that were less virulent. Actually, there is more evidence of the latter than there is of increased resistance in the host population.

GEYER: Another factor that one ought to have to include would be the presence of antibodies to certain diseases. If antibodies were present, this would be indicative that the bird had been exposed to a disease.

MORTALITY IN CAPTIVE FALCONS

PRESTT: In Britain we are still very much continuing our searches and do not feel by any means that we can understand all the results we have been shown. Three other falcons were in the mews of W. G. Fisk at the time of the death of his lanners (see Chapter 42), though they were kept in buildings separated by 200 yd (183 m). These were two peregrine falcons, male and female, and a female gyrfalcon. All three were fed on the same diet as that of the lanners. The female peregrine, a young bird in 1963 that had been flown successfully during the year, also fell ill at the same time as the lanners and died shortly after them. Unfortunately this bird was not chemically analyzed after A. R. Jennings' examination. His examination showed, however, that the bird had a very severe infection with *Polymorphus boschadis,* a nematode worm known to be parasitic in water birds, which causes very severe anemia and emaciation. Dr. Jennings expressed the opinion that the parasite was the immediate cause of death but suggested that there was the possibility of chronic poisoning by insecticides as well. A male peregrine and gyrfalcon, both 3–4 years old at the time, also fell ill during the same period. The peregrine became very ill and the color of his feet went pale before he started eating normally again. Both of these birds later recovered, though the peregrine moulted badly.

THE PUZZLE OF SYNCHRONIZED POPULATION DECLINES

CLEMENT: The real puzzle in this situation is the synchrony of population decline in such diverse species as the osprey which is a fish-eater, the Cooper's hawk which is a woodland-bird eater, the peregrine which is of a different ecosystem if you will, and the sparrow-hawk of Europe. This is the real puzzle, to most of us, that there should be a synchrony of declines in such a wide array of species. Now, is there some pathogenic possibility to account for this, which would not simply be a multiplicity of pathogens involved?

HANSON: I would say that we would be hard put to find a pathogen that would be capable of running through a group of food-chains as diverse as the osprey, which feeds on fish, a bird that feeds on other birds, and one that feeds on rodents. I think this would be difficult. I think it's also difficult, as several have pointed out in another discussion, to follow insecticides readily through these diverse chains. The argument for pathogens would have to depend on a pathogen which is peculiar to a prey species upon which all of these particular predators prey.

PETERSON: I think that, if we assume that it is pesticides, one could almost predict the species that would be affected and where those various species would be in trouble.

CAUSES OF REPRODUCTIVE FAILURE

SPRUNT: Could sublethal doses of botulism type E produce reproductive failures in bird species? Like the bald eagles, for instance?

HANSON: Well, I don't think we know the answer to that. We have been talking here about only agents that are going to go right out and kill the bird right away. I would guess that perhaps, if disease is involved at all with the disappearance of some of these species, it might be some of these sublethal cases where it is producing some sort of stress on the bird. Perhaps something else comes along and triggers the actual mortality. I don't know. Theoretically this could happen.

GEYER: It is possible that infertility may come in ranch mink as a result of their eating fish that have botulism E or high residue levels of insecticides. Both of them are involved in the mink food-chain, and it is going to be necessary to determine which one is the important factor. Ranch mink are in trouble in some areas where fish makes up a sufficient part of their diet.

MRS. HAMERSTROM: Obviously one of the things that concerns us here is the birds' failure to breed. Now I wonder whether Dr. Trainer or some of you could check which of all those various things in one way or another directly or indirectly might be causing a reduction in breeding.

TRAINER: Newcastle would very definitely be involved. This is one of the most serious problems in domestic poultry, as far as breeding is concerned. All we can do is use other examples. We certainly don't know what they do in hawks, so that the ones I would check would be ones that, again from evidence in either domestic poultry or in wild birds in captivity, do affect the birds' reproduction. With any parasitic or chronic infections, certainly the latter, the whole general health of the bird goes down to the point that reproduction is a stress and strain on it, and one could have potential failures at that point.

GEYER: I would make one comment that, if the literature fails to cite this, it is indicative that perhaps we've never been looking.

TRAINER: This is certainly true. We at the University of Wisconsin perform a diagnostic service for the State Conservation Department for all wild creatures, and we get in roughly 400 or 500 specimens during the course of a year. If we get one hawk, this is unusual, so that we certainly do not have, from our own experience, anything to contribute to this discussion. I think this may be fairly typical throughout the country: you just do not get opportunities to look at these raptorial species.

SYNERGISM: PATHOGEN AND PESTICIDE

McCABE: I would like to suggest, as has been mentioned here before, that these two agents, one a pathogen and the other a pesticide, each at sublethal levels, when combined in a single bird, could cause death. Then one would have to assume that this could be done experimentally, but this is very difficult to carry out. On several occasions it has been mentioned that, when we tested for certain kinds of pesticides, we could not kill the captive bird with large dosages of pesticide. Possibly these particular birds, kept in aviary conditions, were so free from disease organisms that the investigator could not have this combination of disease and pesticide.

TRAINER: Well I think the members on the panel would agree that there are circumstances involving lowered resistance wherein certain organisms become pathogenic. Certainly, man has suffered in this way with septic sore throats for many, many years. Only under certain circumstances of stress do we then have the advent of the disease. This is the type of thing that I think we are attempting to explore here.

VACCINE EFFECTS

RATCLIFFE: Is there some possibility that the viruses used in the new vaccines in the poultry industry, for example, might have become pandemic but be expressed only in a few susceptible species? Is this at all sensible as an idea?

TRAINER: Well, I am not sure that I follow exactly what you are asking, but it is certainly true that some of the vaccine strains that are used in the United States in poultry have become widespread in the poultry population. They have replaced the virulent strains in the chicken population. Now whether or not they exist in other species is quite another matter. Most of the studies in the past have always shown association with just a few birds in contact with poultry. We are finding an amazing number of reactors to Newcastle virus among Canada geese, which we had not anticipated. This seems to be an appreciable population of reactors. Now what significance this has we do not know.

NEED TO STUDY LIVING ANIMALS IN THEIR ENVIRONMENT

TRAINER: One comment I would like to make is that all of our information here is on carcasses. In any other study one usually tries to go out and study the animal in its environment or at least as it is living, and this gives one much better clues as to what is going on. No one has ever checked wild birds' eggs for various pathogens. The information is certainly just very fragmentary.

GLADING: I would agree certainly that there is a remote possibility of some disease that can cause some of this decline. However, my personal feeling is that I would not look for it in any of the diseases listed by Trainer. I would look for it in a new viral disease.

STRATEGIC CONSIDERATIONS IN RESEARCH PLANNING

PRESTT: May I return to Hanson's remark, with which I fully concur, that when a chemist looks he finds some chemical residue, when a parasitologist looks he finds parasites, and so on. Now this is a problem with so many aspects to it that one could go on almost indefinitely examining all these aspects. At the moment, we are analyzing literally hundreds of birds' eggs and birds themselves for organochlorine chemicals. In Britain this costs something like $70 for an egg or a piece of tissue. This is only for the organochlorines. Organophosphates have been used in Britain, and now we have found most of the organochlorines other than DDT (or TDE or DDE). At the moment our chemists are unable to carry out an analysis for organophosphate. The Swedes, as we have heard, having several years ago reported it was not likely in their opinion to be a wildlife hazard, have now decided that mercury is in fact a considerable wildlife hazard; and it is probably causing a decrease in the Swedish birds of prey. Now if you talked to an ecologist or a biologist, he would say it is not good just considering some one aspect of the peregrine falcon; you have got to consider its entire ecology. I am sure in the light of all this we would all agree that the intelligent thing to do is at least to try and follow the most obvious clue. Now suppose no one ever thought there was a possibility of pesticides being involved, but we had produced all the evidence of the change in the birds' prey, their sudden decrease, and this lack of breeding success. Would you have felt that it was worth following up any particular line of disease, would it even have occurred to you that this would have been a reasonable explanation, or are we perhaps being a little academic in trying to search every conceivable possibility? I do not mean this facetiously at all. I mean there has to be a limit to this. We in The Nature Conservancy have a whole team of 20 people working full-time on it, and we are still not touching all the aspects.

GEYER: I think this is basically the attitude that you take when you are confronted with a problem that is present and unanswerable. Certainly within the domestic animal field, we have been confronted with this type of problem repeatedly where we have a situation for which we do not know the answer. And so we explore all aspects. In other words, whether or not you involve yourself in bacteriology, virology, or toxicology, you run the whole gamut. This is the only thing you can do, because you are searching for one thing, an answer.

PRESTT: Would you feel that the evidence from the different parts of the world would not make any difference to this? Suppose someone else had not thought of parasites; would you feel that a disease could perhaps provide this answer?

GEYER: I really feel, as a matter of fact, that—if we had known the information about the insecticides—a very plausible case, not necessarily a true situation, could have been built for a number of happenings, and this would have been accepted as a valid situation by most of the scientific community. Now this does not mean that it is the true ideology. But a very plausible case could be built, and I think we frequently do this. I think you can find evidence of this in the scientific literature, where a particular hypothesis has been created, people have gone out and found evidence in support of it; this has then been accepted for years, until new techniques come along that have subsequently established that another ideology was actually true.

PRESTT: Yes. All of the independent veterinary laboratories in Britain have now examined a fair number of wild birds of prey, and not one of them has been able to produce a disease explanation for this widespread general decline of raptors in the country. Is that still asking too much?

GEYER: I'm not in any way making any aspersions against their professional capability, because I know that they are doing an excellent job. But I would not expect anyone, anywhere, to be able to tell you yes or no in relation to a pathogen, because this depends on the technical efficiencies that one has available at a specific time. Certainly what we would have done 5 years ago is not what we would do today. We would examine a problem with different tools and different techniques today, and we would come up with different answers today, just the same as a chemist in the past could not have detected low residue levels of the chlorinated hydrocarbons as he could today. Let us not forsake all other aspects for fear we will get into trouble with something else.

Pesticides as Possible Factors Affecting Bird Populations

CHAPTER 41

PESTICIDE RESIDUES IN FISH AND WILDLIFE OF CALIFORNIA

Eldridge G. Hunt

About 20% of the pesticides used annually in the United States are applied to farms and forests in California (Rollins, 1963). The effect of these compounds upon wildlife has been actively investigated in recent years (Rudd and Genelly, 1955, 1956; Genelly and Rudd, 1956; Hunt and Bischoff, 1960, 1962; Bischoff and Hunt, 1961; Hunt, 1961, 1963, 1964; Hunt and Keith, 1962; Keith, 1963, 1964, 1965; Abbott, Craig, and Keith, 1965).

These investigations have contributed to the overall knowledge of wildlife-pesticide relationships, but their scope has been somewhat limited. The need for an environmental pesticide-monitoring program in California is widely recognized. The report of Governor Edmund G. Brown's Committee on Pesticide Review (State of California, 1964) contains a recommendation that an environment-monitoring program be established to supplement the existing program of monitoring pesticide residues in raw agricultural commodities. This committee, composed in large part of the governor's own cabinet officers, was established in 1963 to make an intensive study of the state's programs relating to pesticides. Of particular concern to the committee was a review of all available evidence as to the adequacy of these programs to discharge the state's total obligation to its citizens.

The statewide environment-monitoring program as proposed had not been set in operation at the time of this conference. However, the California Department of Fish and Game has been and is involved in studies aimed at selecting appropriate plant and animal species for monitoring purposes. A review of these findings provides an indication of the extent and types of pesticidal contamination occurring in the wild environment in our state.

We have contracted for more than 750 residue analyses during the last 2 years. Included in the sampling programs were tissues from more than 50 animal species, terrestrial and aquatic plants, water, and mud or sediments. The animals sampled were marine and freshwater game fish, shellfish, waterfowl, fish-eating waterbirds, raptors, big-game species, and upland-game species. In general, the selection of species to be analyzed was made on the basis of their importance in animal food-chains or their exposure to pesticides in a particular ecosystem. However, some of the results reported were from analyses made of animals involved in die-offs from suspected poisoning.

DDT or its metabolites or breakdown products were found in all samples analyzed for chlorinated hydrocarbons that contained residues. Residues of dieldrin, endrin, aldrin, toxaphene, heptachlor, BHC, chlordane, Thiodan (endosulfan), mercury, Baytex (fenthion), parathion, arsenic trioxide, and strychnine were detected in one or more tissue samples.

Most of the analyses involving fish were of striped bass (*Roccus saxatilis*) taken from the Sacramento and San Joaquin river systems. The average residue levels in fat of the 128 fish sampled were 20 ppm DDT, 28 ppm DDE, 15 ppm TDE, 0.7 ppm dieldrin, and 0.11 ppm endrin. Roe from 16 stripers averaged 1.7 ppm DDT.

A total of 20 adult salmon (*Oncorhynchus tshawytscha*) taken from the Pacific Ocean, San Francisco Bay, and the Upper Sacramento River were collected, and flesh and ova samples were analyzed. Residue levels in all samples were less than 1 ppm of the DDT complex.

We had nine samples of catchable rainbow trout (*Salmo gairdnerii*) from one of our hatcheries analyzed. An average of 7.9 ppm of DDT was detected in the fat of these fish. Fifty-six samples of prepared trout feed contained an average of 0.68 ppm DDT.

Shell fish were collected from the major bays of California. Residues averaging 0.1 ppm DDT were found in these marine animals although no pesticides were detected in most of 10 species sampled.

Fat from 10 species of waterfowl collected in northeast California contained an average of 5 ppm DDT. Four species of ducks taken from San Francisco Bay had an average of 13 ppm of DDT in adipose tissue.

Six species of shorebirds from San Francisco Bay contained residues in fat ranging from 1.9 to 45 ppm of DDT. The highest level found was in a short-billed dowitcher. Avocet and killdeer eggs from the Sacramento Valley contained an average of 13 ppm DDE. The DDE content of eggs of common egrets and black-crowned night herons taken from the same area averaged 56 ppm.

Samples of agricultural drainwater contained chlorinated hydrocarbon insecticides in the range of 5–250 parts per trillion (ppt). Analyses were made of 1-gallon (3.8-l) grab samples of unfiltered water. Levels found in bottom mud from these drains were higher but always less than 1 ppm.

Of particular interest to conservationists are the residue levels found in raptors. We have had residue analyses made on tissues from birds of this group that were accidentally killed or killed by poachers. An adult bald eagle contained 1 ppm of DDT and 60 ppm of DDE in its body fat. Another adult bald eagle had 2,800 ppm of DDE and 13.0 ppm of dieldrin in its body fat. Similar samples from a Swainson's hawk contained approximately 1 ppm of DDT, and fat from two nestling prairie falcons had 5.0 DDE, 1.9 ppm DDT, and 0.18 ppm dieldrin. A California condor killed accidentally had 18 ppm DDT and 30 ppm DDE deposited in its fat.

In the spring of 1965, we began a program of sampling residues in birds' eggs. The levels found should indicate the degree of contamination in various bird species. Most of the eggs will be from raptors and water-associated birds. To date, 211 eggs have been collected from 95 nests, representing 34 species of birds.

The eggs that have been analyzed so far were collected in several locations in Lassen County in the northeastern part of California. There is very little pesticide use in the areas where these eggs were taken. In all cases the analyses were made of egg yolk only. The levels of DDE in eggs from two osprey nests were 24 and 35 ppm, respectively; DDT levels in the same samples were 4.3 and 3.5 ppm. Red-tailed hawk eggs from a single nest contained 8.3 ppm DDT, 21 ppm DDE, and 1.3 ppm of dieldrin. DDT and DDE at levels below 2 ppm were detected in sparrow hawk (North American kestrel) eggs. Similarly low levels were found in the eggs of a long-eared owl, a great horned owl, and a marsh hawk. The highest levels found in this series of egg analyses were in a sample of snowy egret eggs which contained 44 ppm DDE, 39 ppm DDT, and 0.18 ppm dieldrin. Residue levels in eggs from two black-crowned night herons' nests averaged 36 ppm DDE, 1.7 ppm DDT, and 0.52 dieldrin.

This cross-section of our residue figures shows that pesticide contamination in the wild environment is widespread. This type of information can be helpful in selecting a so-called problem area for special study or, if collected systematically over a period of years, can provide trends in pesticide contamination of the environment. However, it would be misleading to attach significance to the residues reported in terms of their real or potential hazard to the contaminated animals.

I feel that there is a great deal more to assessing the hazards of the persistent chlorinated hydrocarbon insecticides to animals than measuring the pesticide load in their bodies.

An assessment of hazard should include not only data on the toxicological and physiological effects of the contaminants on the animals exposed but more importantly should be based primarily on an understanding of the interrelationships between the pesticide, the living organism, and the environment. Pesticides do not behave the same in different environments. We have seen many times that the same pesticide has a different impact in one ecosystem than in another and may also have different effects on the same animal species when they are found in different habitats.

For example, some lakes treated with toxaphene may become nontoxic to fish soon after treatment, while other lakes remain toxic to reintroduced fish for years. Water chemistry, water depth, water temperature, bottom type, weather factors, and animal and plant life occurring in the lake all may influence the chronological span of toxicity of this pesticide in lakes.

The direct effect of DDT on robins, as reported in studies made in Wisconsin (L. B. Hunt, 1960) and Michigan (Wallace, 1960) was much more severe than the effects of DDT on robins at Knox Mountain in California (Keith, 1965). In the Michigan and Wisconsin studies mortality was reported; at Knox Mountain no adverse effects were noted. The differential effect on robins that can occur in a single type of application (Dutch elm disease control) was explained by Hickey and Hunt (1960). The number of factors that influence differential effects are undoubtedly compounded when pesticide applications are made in a different manner and in different types of habitat. In the eastern states much of the DDT application was made from ground applicators to deciduous trees; at Knox Mountain aerial applications were made to coniferous forests.

Studies in California have demonstrated that a member of the DDT family of insecticides applied to an aquatic environment shows up in animal food-chains to a greater degree than a similar compound in an arid terrestrial system. Therefore, we would expect the greatest problems to occur when these chemicals go into an aquatic community.

What we have been saying here is that, as ecosystems vary, the involvement of pesticides with the various components of the environment also varies, and the potential for pesticides to affect various species of wildlife varies accordingly.

Our evaluation of the pesticide-peregrine situation in California is summarized as follows:

1. We feel that pesticides are a potential threat to peregrine populations, as a source of pesticide contamination is present in the normal prey

species of this falcon, e.g., ducks and shorebirds. However, there are insufficient data available to determine how serious the threat might be or even how pesticides might be affecting falcons.

2. What we need now is information on the interrelationships of the peregrine with the various environments in which it lives. All the major factors believed responsible for the decline of the falcon should be evaluated. To give proper emphasis to evaluating the hazards of pesticides, ecosystems should be selected for study where comparisons of maximum and minimum exposures to pesticides could be made.

When information is available on the amount and types of pesticides associated with the life cycle of the peregrine, we will be in a better position to plan detailed studies to determine the effects of pesticides on the population of this bird. The studies should provide detailed data on food habits and (ideally) should involve controlled experiments on the effects of pesticide residues on reproduction. Such a program of research on the peregrine falcon will be difficult to accomplish in some regions due to the current depleted population of this species.

SUMMARY

In 1963–65, 13 different pesticides were found in more than 750 samples of Californian animals and their environment. In body fats, the ppm of DDT ran 5–13 in waterfowl, in shorebirds 1.9–45, in a prairie falcon 1.9, in a California condor 18, in osprey eggs 3.5–4.3, and in red-tailed hawk eggs 8.3. Dieldrin ran 1.3 ppm in the latter, and 13 ppm in eagle fat. DDE ran 60 ppm in the fat of one eagle specimen, 2,800 in another. As pesticides represent a potential threat to peregrine populations where ducks and shorebirds are normal prey, research workers need to evaluate maximum and minimum exposure of peregrines to pesticides and (ideally) to carry out controlled experiments on reproduction.

LITERATURE CITED

Abbott, U. K., R. M. Craig, and J. O. Keith. 1965. Effects of malathion spray on embryonated chicken eggs exposed under field conditions at Tuolumne Meadow, Yosemite National Park. Poultry Sci., 43(5):1297.

Bischoff, A. I., and E. G. Hunt. 1961. Conservationists concerned about pesticides. Outdoor Calif., 22(3):4–5.

Genelly, R. E., and R. L. Rudd. 1956. Chronic toxicity of DDT, toxaphene, and dieldrin to ring-necked pheasants. Calif. Fish and Game, 42(1):5–14.

Hickey, J. J., and L. B. Hunt. 1960. Songbird mortality following annual programs to control Dutch elm disease. Atlantic Nat., 15(2):87–92.

Hunt, E. G. 1961. Effects of pesticide use in forests. Outdoor Calif., 22(9–10):6–7.

———. 1963. Pesticide residues in fish and wildlife populations. Proc. 43rd Ann. Conf. West. Ass. State Game and Fish Comm., p.129–132.

———. 1964. The cooperative approach to handling wildlife-pesticide problems. Proc. 44th Ann. Conf. West. Ass. State Game and Fish Comm., p. 344–348.

———, and A. I. Bischoff. 1960. Inimical effects on wildlife of periodic DDD applications to Clear Lake. Calif. Fish and Game, 46(1):91–106.

———, and A. I. Bischoff. 1962. Insecticides and pheasants. Outdoor Calif., 23(10):11–12.

———, and J. O. Keith. 1962. Pesticide-wildlife investigations in California—1962. Proc. 2nd Ann. Conf. Use of Agr. Chemicals in Calif., Davis. 29-p. insert.

Hunt, L. B. 1960. Songbird breeding populations in DDT-sprayed Dutch elm disease communities. J. Wildl. Mgmt., 24(2):139–146.

Keith, J. O. 1963. Chemical approaches in co-ordinating wildlife management and mosquito suppression practices. Conf. for Co-ordinated Program on Wildl. Mgmt. and Mosquito Suppression: Yosemite Nat. Park, Oct. 15–18, 1962. p. 77–80.

———. 1964. An approach to the solution of pesticide-wildlife problems. Proc. 44th Annual Conf. West. Ass. State Game and Fish Comm. p.353–356.

———. 1964. Wildlife problems resulting from the use of insecticide in California. Report of the Fourth Agr. Aviation Research Conf., U. Calif., Davis: USDA, ARS, July 9–11, 1962. p.113–115.

———. 1965. Problems in the development of tailor-made insecticides: insecticides and wildlife. Bull. Entomol. Soc. Amer., 11(2):76.

———, and E. L. Flickinger. 1964. Fate and persistence of DDT in a forest environment, p.44–46. *In* The effects of pesticides on fish and wildlife. U.S. Dep. Interior, Fish and Wildl. Serv. Circ. 266. 77 p.

———, M. S. Mulla, and A. F. Geib. 1963. Relative toxicity of five organo-phosphate insecticides to mallard ducks, p.49–50. *In* Pesticide-Wildlife Studies, 1963. U.S. Dep. Interior, Fish an Wildl. Serv. Circ. 199. 130 p.

———, M. S. Mulla, F. A. Gunther, and A. F. Geib. 1964. Persistence and effect of parathion in marsh habitats, p. 42–44. *In* The effects of pesticides on fish and wildlife. U.S. Dep. Interior, Fish and Wildl. Serv. Circ. 226. 77 p.

———, R. A. Wilson, and G. H. Ise. 1963. Agricultural pest control: Crop insects in the Klamath Basin, p. 56–57. *In* Pesticide-Wildlife Studies . . . . U.S. Dep. Interior, Fish and Wildl. Serv. Circ. 167. 109 p.

Rollins, Robert Z. 1963. Federal and state regulations of pesticides. Amer. J. Public Health, 53:1427.

Rudd, R. L., and R. E. Genelly. 1955. Chemicals and wildlife—an analysis of research needs. Trans. 20th North Amer. Wildl. Conf., p. 189–198.

———, and R. E. Genelly. 1956. Pesticides: their use and toxicity in relation to wildlife. Calif. Fish and Game, Game Bull. 7. 209 p.

State of California. 1964. Report on pesticides in California (Edmund G. Brown's Committee on Pesticide Review), 121 p.

Wallace, G. J. 1960. Another year of robin losses on a university campus. Audubon Mag., 62(2):66–69.

CHAPTER 42

PESTICIDES AS POSSIBLE FACTORS AFFECTING RAPTOR POPULATIONS

SUMMARY OF A ROUND-TABLE DISCUSSION AND ADDITIONAL COMMENTS BY THE CONFEREES

Chairman: John L. Buckley. *Participants*: Joseph J. Hickey, Ian Prestt, Lucille F. Stickel, and William H. Stickel

The main purpose of this discussion, Buckley said at the outset, was to review what we do know about the effects of persisting insecticides on raptorial birds as well as to bring out what we do not know. The discussion concentrated almost entirely on seven chlorinated hydrocarbons and some of their breakdown products:

DDT 2,2-bis (*p*-chlorophenyl) -1,1,1-Trichloroethane
TDE (DDD; "Rhothane"; a metabolite of DDT)
  2,2,-bis (*p*-chlorophenyl) -1,1,-dichloroethane
DDE (a metabolite of DDT)
  1,1,-dichloro-2,2-bis (*p*-chlorophenyl) ethylene
Dieldrin (HEOD; the oxidized metabolite of aldrin)
  1,2,3,4,10,10-hexachloro-*exo*-6,7-epoxy-1,4,4a,5,6,7,8,8a-octahydro-1,4-*endo, exo*-5,8 dimethanonaphthalene
BHC (benzene hexachloride; in the gamma isomer: lindane)
  1,2,3,4,5,6-hexachloro*cyclo*hexane
Heptachlor (commonly metabolized to heptachlor epoxide)
  1,4,5,6,7,8,8-heptachloro-3a,4,7,7a-tetrahydro-4,7-*endo*methanoindene
Endrin 1,2,3,4,10,10-hexachloro-6,7-epoxy-1,4,4a,5,6,7,8,8a-octahydro-*exo*-1,4-*exo*-5,8-dimethanonaphthalene

At the time of this discussion, these compounds were known to be lipid soluble and tended to be stored in the fatty portion of vertebrate organ tissues, the highest residues occurring in the fat itself; and lower residues in breast-muscle tissues. Similarly in the eggs of birds, residues are present in the yolk but little or none in the white. Throughout the discussion, the conferees (with one stated exception) confined their ppm statistics to fresh-weight calculations, which are obviously lower than those cited for dried tissues.

The discussion began on the hypothesis, chairman Buckley said, that many scientists are of the opinion that these insecticides are biologically active materials that can be expected to have some kind of an effect on living organisms—certainly upon those against which they are applied and possibly against other organisms as well. While the occurrence of small residues of these compounds in the environment is generally referred to in this discussion as "contamination," many speakers explicitly did not wish to add attachments that such residues are necessarily disadvantageous to the organisms in which they are reported.

ENVIRONMENTAL CONTAMINATION TODAY

WIDESPREAD DISTRIBUTION

At the time of this conference, the widespread monitoring of pesticides in nature was only in the planning stages in the United States. Hunt's remarks (Chapter 41) on residues in California's birdlife represent a preliminary exploration of residues in a region where approximately 20% of the pesticide usage in the United States is now concentrated.

It was the view of MRS. STICKEL that the general contamination of wildlife in the United States is difficult to appraise from data of the past because most specimens analyzed were taken from areas that had been treated, and in fact many of the animals were ones that had been found dead after treatment programs. And until recently there has been little dependable information concerning the proportions and kinds of pesticides that animals contained. This was because of analytical problems. Colorimetric methods required separate samples for each pesticide, and if a liver was analyzed for DDT, the entire sample was used up, and analyses could not be made for dieldrin, for example. Gas chromatography permitted multiple determinations, but introduced further problems. For example, DDE (one of the less-toxic breakdown products of DDT) has many times been confused with dieldrin in whole or part. The confusion can go in either direction; it can exaggerate the proportion of dieldrin in some cases and the proportion of DDE in others.

The validity of DDT-dieldrin ratios, in MRS. STICKEL'S opinion, is therefore somewhat tenuous. She gave a few examples from data she believed to be satisfactory. One example is the contamination of rivers. Pesticide residues have been found in all major river basins of the United States (Weaver *et al.*, 1965). Dieldrin occurred most frequently, followed by endrin, DDT, and DDE. This was partly a matter of differential solubility. There were regional differences, however. For example, DDT was found more frequently in the western states, which have extensive irrigation works. At the 11 stations (considering the entire United States) where the quantities of dieldrin were greatest, DDT products were not detected at 3 and were detected below quantifiable limits at 7. At 4 stations where both DDT and dieldrin were measurable, the DDT products were 1–2 times the dieldrin. At the 11 stations where quantities of DDT products were greatest, dieldrin was not detected at 3. At 8 stations where both were measurable, quantities of DDT products were 3–22 times those of dieldrin.

Differences in DDT-dieldrin ratios related to locality were conspicuous in some Canada goose samples. Four fat samples from Wheeler National Wildlife Refuge in Alabama, for example, contained 12–40 times as much DDT product as dieldrin, and one sample contained equal amounts of the two. Effluent from a DDT-manufacturing plant formerly reached a river near there. DDT products also predominated in the seven Horseshoe Lake, Illinois, samples, but measured only 3–6 times the quantity of dieldrin. In contrast, dieldrin predominated in samples from Swan Lake in Missouri; DDT products measured only 0.6–0.8 the quantity of dieldrin in seven samples; DDT products were predominant in one sample.

In animals found dead after dieldrin treatments, MRS. STICKEL continued, dieldrin tends to predominate. Whole-body residues of dieldrin exceeded those of the DDT products in 19 of 32 samples of birds found dead in Virginia following dieldrin treatments, but in all cases the quantities of DDT and dieldrin were not far apart (Stickel and Heath, 1965). In Tennessee specimens found dead after dieldrin treatment, the DDT products were always small fractions of the dieldrin residues. These specimens were eastern cottontail rabbits *(Sylvilagus floridanus)*, cotton rats (*Sigmodon hispidus*), and meadowlarks. Residues in animals (living or dead) taken in treated areas soon after application are not a very satisfactory reflection of general environmental contamination, but neither can they be ignored, for more and more areas are being treated. Some very good data on contamination of wildlife species and their foods are being gathered in California. Data have been published for Connecticut (Turner, 1965; Tompkins, 1964), and work is underway elsewhere. The National Monitoring Program will attempt to establish levels and trends of pesticide residues in many portions of the environment, including fish and wildlife (Dustman, 1966).

HICKEY pointed out that at a study institute in England in July 1965 Dutch investigators (Koeman and van Genderen, 1966) reported quantities of the more toxic chlorinated hydrocarbons which were higher than he expected in the American environment. Brain residue levels in dead and dying hawks ran 4.4–6.7 ppm of dieldrin and 3.2–17.7 ppm of BHC. Mesenteric fat of some raptors contained up to 3.0 ppm of heptachlor epoxide, 15.7 of endrin, 17.0 of dieldrin, and 89.3 of BHC. A buzzard in heavy convulsive seizures had about 10–10.8 ppm of dieldrin in its breast muscle.

In Michigan, Wallace, Nickell, and Bernard (1961) mention eight species of diurnal raptors that were seen with the symptoms of insecticide poisoning. Brain levels of DDT in three of these were found by the Schechter-Haller test to be low or medium, although one red-shouldered hawk contained 48 ppm in its breast muscle and 37 ppm in its liver. These tests were run before gas chromatography was available, and the breakdown of DDT to its metabolites in these birds is unknown.

PRESTT reported that in Britain, as in these Dutch examples, there invariably is a whole range of the chlorinated hydrocarbons including DDT and/or its metabolites. Almost without exception, if some are present, all are present. In 1963 and 1964 a survey included eggs of 17 species of seabirds collected at four different sites on the British coast. Dieldrin and DDE were detected in all the 90 eggs collected; 70 of the eggs contained DDT and TDE; and 47, traces of BHC which in no case exceeded 0.2 ppm. In addition, 48 also contained small amounts of heptachlor epoxide (Moore and Tatton, 1965). From this and previous surveys, it was concluded that:

(1) residues of the organochlorine insecticides may be widely distributed in small amounts in British waters;

(2) the total organochlorine insecticide residues found in the eggs of different seabirds are nearly all of the same order, most of them lying in the range 0.4 to 3.5 ppm;

(3) there was no evidence of an increase in contamination from 1963 to 1964; and

(4) since there is little or no spraying of British coastal waters with insecticides, the residues detected must derive either from the contamination of rivers or from aerial drift.

Data on contamination of the British environment have also been reported by Lockie and Ratcliffe (1964), Moore (1965*a*, 1965*b*), Moore and Walker (1964), Ratcliffe (1965), Taylor and Brady (1964), and by others. Levels in the breast muscles of aquatic birds appeared to be appreciably higher than those in terrestrial birds (Moore and Walker, 1964).

In addition to this British evidence of contamination in the North Atlantic, HICKEY added, there is an interesting set of data on residue levels in Pacific fish reported by the Food and Drug Administration at the hearings of the United States Senate (Larrick, 1964). Analyses of crude oils of fish taken off the coast of California disclosed residue levels of 15–340 ppm in 6 out of 11 species. The maximum level involved 80 ppm of DDT,

60 ppm of TDE, and 200 ppm of DDE. [Contamination of the world's marine environment by these compounds is now also known to extend to the Antarctic. Tissues from Adelie penguins and a crabeater seal (*Lobodon carcinophagus*) have been analyzed by the Patuxent Wildlife Research Center and found to contain low levels of chlorinated hydrocarbons. Six penguin livers ran from 0.016 to 0.115 ppm of DDT, TDE, and DDE, and four penguin fat specimens from 0.024 to 0.152 ppm (Sladen, Menzie, and Reichel, 1966). An independent study by George and Frear (1966) disclosed up to 0.18 ppm DDT in penguin fat and up to 2.8 ppm DDE in the kidney tissue of a skua (George and Frear, 1966). There were no residues in 15 samples of snow nor in 7 samples of invertebrates from four phyla.]

HICKEY cited residue levels in Lake Michigan fish to show that this large body of water was seriously contaminated. Among specimens taken as much as 5.5 miles (9 km) out from the Wisconsin shore, alewives (*Alosa pseudoharengus*) averaged 3.3–3.4 ppm of DDT-complex, 10 chubs (*Leucichthys* sp.) 4.52 ppm, and muscle tissue in 5 whitefish (*Coregonus clupeaformis*) 5.60 ppm (Hickey, Keith, and Coon, 1966).

[In Sweden, where liquid mercury seed dressings are heavily used, extensive contamination of the agricultural environment is evident in the residues of mercury found in the liver and kidney tissues of the many species of animals found dead in the countryside and subsequently analyzed by the State Veterinary Medical Institute. Residues there in these organs have been as high as 45 mg/kg in pigeons, 100 in raptors, 110 in corvine birds, 136 in finches, 140 in pheasants and partridges, and 270 in the tawny owl (Otterlind and Lennerstedt, 1964; Borg, Wanntropp, Erne, and Hanko, 1965).]

As a general principle, it seems certain that many of the world's environments are now contaminated by somewhat substantial levels of the new biocidal chemicals and that this is particularly true where the peregrine falcon and certain other populations of raptorial birds have been decreasing in the past 10–15 years.

PERSISTENCE OF INSECTICIDES

W. H. STICKEL described how, after *pp'*-DDT is given to experimental birds, TDE can be quite soon found in the liver and—long after the birds are taken off dosage—DDE can still be found in the birds' tissues. The first metabolite is formed rather quickly; the second, rather slowly. DDE apparently can persist for months on a declining basis.

BUCKLEY mentioned that there were fascinating and marked differences in persistence between the individual animal and the system in which it lives. Clear Lake, California, was last treated with TDE for gnat control in 1957. A continuing study by California's Department of

Public Health and Department of Fish and Game, GLADING reported, shows that fat residue levels in 1958 and 1963 changed from 126 ppm of TDE to 16.8 in white catfish, from 56 to 12 in largemouth bass, and from 1161 to 808 in western grebes. While some of the 1963 values could of course have been reinforced by subsequent aerial drift or runoff into the lake, many of the grebes could also have picked up insecticides on other bodies of water.

[Persistence in poultry also varies with each compound. Stadelman *et al.* (1965) supplied the equivalent of 10–15 ppm insecticide in the food of chickens for 5 days. Residue levels in body fat and egg yolk were then checked at subsequent intervals of 1, 5, 10, 17, and 26 weeks. Detectable amounts of each compound were found in both tissues as follows: BHC —10 weeks; DDT—17 weeks; dieldrin, heptachlor epoxide, and DDE—26 weeks. Administration of the insecticides in this experiment was by capsules, a method that does not lend itself to uptake and incorporation of the toxicant into body tissues quite as efficiently as even distribution of the insecticide in the birds' daily food.]

The principle emerging at this point seems to be that persistence of the hydrocarbons in nature is very much greater in marine and aquatic ecosystems than in terrestrial environments.

PESTICIDE CONCENTRATION BY BIOLOGICAL MECHANISMS

GLADING reviewed the dramatic build-up of chlorinated hydrocarbons in Californian lakes. Working up layer by layer in each ecosystem, TDE had finally wiped out a breeding colony of western grebes at Clear Lake (Hunt and Bischoff, 1960). At the Tule Lake National Wildlife Refuge, over 1,100 birds belonging to 10 species were found dead between 1960 and 1962. The indicated mortality agent was toxaphene which was locally used only in 1950–60, and which entered the refuge attached to suspended material carried in irrigation water. This toxaphene later ran 0.0–0.2 ppm in sediment and invertebrates, and up to 8.0 ppm in whole fish. Carcasses in some of the fish-eating birds ran 9.2, 9.5, and 10.0 ppm of this compound. Others contained no detectable residues of toxaphene —and up to 459.5 ppm of DDT in their fat (J. O. Keith, 1966).

In a part of Lake Michigan, HICKEY reported that DDT + TDE + DDE averaged 0.014 ppm in bottom sediments, some of which were taken at depths of 96 ft. Invertebrates (*Pontoporeia affinis*) living in these muds ran 0.4–0.5 ppm. Fish living on this amphipod were averaging from 3.4 to 5.6 ppm, and herring gulls that fed at least part of the year on these fish averaged 99 ppm of the three compounds in their breast muscle and 2,441 in their body fat (Hickey, Keith, and Coon, 1966).

In marine ecosystems, RATCLIFFE said, this stratification was also evident although the residue levels off Britain were much lower. Eggs of plankton-feeding kittiwakes ran 0.3 ppm; those of the omnivorous herring gull, 0.9; those of auks, which feed on small fish, 3.5; and those of the shag, which feeds on large fish, 7.8 (Moore and Tatton, 1965). Another British study disclosed that this concentration phenomenon also extended to terrestrial ecosystems. Egg-residue levels for 36 birds in the family Corvidae varied from 0.4 for the magpie up to 2.1 ppm in the raven. Among 30 samples in the families Accipitridae and Falconidae, the levels were 1.0 for 4 kestrel eggs, 2.5 for 4 common buzzard eggs, 2.6 for 7 golden eagle eggs, 6.2 for 2 merlin eggs, and 13.8 ppm for 13 peregrine eggs (Ratcliffe, 1965). The kestrel eggs were from birds living in hill country and feeding largely on *Microtus* and other voles. Ravens, highest in the Corvidae, were largely feeding on sheep carrion, while the other crows were vegetarians or omnivores.

PRESTT added that The Nature Conservancy did collect some small mammals and found no residues in them. Since there was a considerable gap between (a) the time these had been able to feed on dressed seed and (b) the time they were trapped for chemical analysis, an effort was now being made to collect mice at earlier dates. The picture in British birds has been shown by Moore and Walker (1964) to involve some marked differences in residue content between raptorial and fish-eating birds on the one hand, and herbivores on the other, the latter being much lower, and omnivores being intermediate.

HALE gave some results from a Wisconsin study that was still in progress. In a forest ecosystem where 1 lb of DDT had been applied per acre (1.1 kg/ha) in May, one *Microsorex* had 267 ppm of DDT complex in its fat in June; another in July, 436. A healthy goshawk collected in July had a fat reading of 247 ppm.

Another major principle, emerging in the present decade, thus centers on the biological concentration of the new biocidal chemicals in the upper levels of regional ecosystems. This phenomenon, which is reviewed in detail by Rudd (1964), involves the transportation, concentration, and delayed expression of persisting chemicals—and it tends to leave the world's raptorial bird populations in a particularly vulnerable position.

THE SIGNIFICANCE OF RESIDUE LEVELS

In general, very little attention was given at the conference to the serious effects of pesticide treatments on field populations of local birds and mammals. For a documented set of these examples in the United States, most of which occurred in the past 10 years, see Dustman and Stickel (1966).

DIRECT MORTALITY

Establishment of the usefulness of tissue residues in the diagnosis of death has been a particular concern to many investigators. MRS. STICKEL began by stating that this is a difficult problem. When birds are found dead in the field, there often is no way of knowing what chemicals, if any, they have consumed, nor the quantities, nor the time of exposure. Hence, we have felt that if a tissue is to be used in diagnosis of death, its residues must be, insofar as reasonably possible, independent of time, and independent of dosage levels. In other words, the birds that die in a short time from feeding on a diet containing 5,000 ppm should have the same representative levels in a diagnostic tissue as ones that die after a longer time of feeding on a diet containing 500 ppm. In one study with brown-headed cowbirds, some died during dosage, but some died in tremors up to 40 days after they were put on clean food. Residue analyses showed that levels of DDT + TDE in brains of all of the birds that died, regardless of the length of time they were on dosage, or whether they died after dosage was over and they were eating clean food, were all of the same magnitude. They also were similar to brain levels of DDT +TDE in bald eagles that died when dosed experimentally, and in several other species studied by other workers (Stickel, Stickel, and Christensen, 1966). Residue content of other tissues, in contrast, tended to increase with time. Whole-body residues were a little higher in the survivors than they were in birds that died, as well as increasing steadily with time. So the whole-body analysis, as far as diagnosis of death is concerned, would not appear to be especially useful, and MRS. STICKEL suspected that fat is in the same category. There is no reason to think it would not be.

The actual range of DDT + TDE in the brain of animals killed in dietary experiments with DDT is from 35 to 181 ppm (Stickel, Stickel, and Christensen, 1966). In general, brain levels of 30 ppm of these two compounds offer a useful approximation of the lower limit that may be taken to represent serious danger and possible death.

PRESTT discussed residue levels in lanner and peregrine falcons that had died either in the wild or in captivity. The post-mortems, described in detail by Jefferies and Prestt (1966), led to the following conclusions. Five birds with 5.3–9.3 ppm of dieldrin and heptachlor epoxide in their livers died from organochlorine poisoning; two others with 0.8–2.0 had not. In four of the allegedly insecticide-killed birds dieldrin plus heptachlor epoxide in the brain ran from 3.0 to 7.8 ppm.

MRS. STICKEL commented that these dieldrin residues (excluding the heptachlor epoxide) are very much the same as those found in the livers of dogs killed experimentally. These were 3.3–7.4 ppm in six dogs that died or were killed *in extremis* (Harrison, Maskell, and Money, 1963);

liver levels of dieldrin were 8 and 12 ppm in two dogs that died in another study (Kitselman, Dahm, and Borgmann, 1950). Livers of certain animals found dead in a dieldrin-treated area in Tennessee contained somewhat greater amounts: 5 meadowlarks contained 8–16 ppm, 5 cotton rats contained 15–37 ppm, and 5 eastern cottontails contained 28–103 ppm (Patuxent Wildlife Research Center unpublished data; analyses by Stoner Laboratories, California). Two pheasants killed experimentally contained 14 and 115 ppm of dieldrin in their livers (McEwen *et al.*, 1963).

[Swedish scientists appear to regard mercury levels of 25 mg/kg as lethal levels in the liver. When 41 goshawks were shot or trapped in their country, 10 had levels ranging from 25 to 53 mg/kg (Borg *et al.*, 1965). Among six white-tailed eagles found dead in Finland, liver levels of this compound ran 4.6, 12.2, 19.0, 19.8, 24.7, and 27.1 mg/kg (Henriksson, Karppanen, and Helminen, 1966). As relatively small amounts of alkylmercury seed dressings have been used in Finland, these Finnish investigators believe their birds picked up the residues elsewhere.]

RESIDUE LEVELS IN DIET

PRESTT described an exploration of residue levels that Jefferies and he had carried out on some prey species of falcons in Britain. Three mallards and 1 pheasant contained very small residues; only 2 out of 6 moorhens possessed detectable residues; 6 wood pigeons had very small or no residues, but 3 others all had high residues. In one of the latter birds, dieldrin ran 9.00 ppm in breast muscle tissue. It thus appears that residues lethal to the falcons could be obtained by ingestion of a few highly contaminated prey rather than a large number of prey with small residues (Jefferies and Prestt, 1966). There is also evidence in Britain that a wood pigeon can pick up an LD_{50} dose of dieldrin by feeding for less than 5 hours on dressed grain (Murton and Vizoso, 1963). Prestt further pointed out that the situation is probably made worse by peregrines taking the weaker and probably more heavily contaminated birds that they encounter in flocks (Eutermoser, 1961; Saar, 1961).

W. H. STICKEL related how, when the fire-ant-control program began in 1958, fear was expressed for the future of woodcock, for this bird feeds largely on earthworms, and Barker (1958) had shown that worms will concentrate large amounts of DDT. It was assumed—correctly, it was later proved—that they would concentrate other poisons. The US Fish and Wildlife Service decided to learn how vulnerable woodcock were to the main fire-ant chemical, heptachlor, and certain other insecticides to which they were exposed.

The first trials were made by giving woodcock capsules containing different amounts of chemical. This proved to be completely futile with both heptachlor and DDT for, although many formulations were tried, large single doses simply did not kill cage-adapted birds in full flesh (Stickel, Dodge, *et al.*, 1965). The chemical quickly passed through the intestinal tract, and less than a lethal dose was absorbed by the body. This was true whether a wettable powder or an oil solution was used. Even underweight birds were killed only by heavy doses. It became clear that to answer the question of danger in the field many small doses had to be administered in the food.

The woodcock were therefore fed worms that were artificially contaminated with heptachlor. This yielded drastically different results: woodcock died within a few weeks when fed worms that contained an average of 2.86 ppm of heptachlor epoxide. (This figure was determined from analysis of worms from each lot fed. All figures are on a dry-weight basis.) At this level of food contamination, 2.86 ppm, whole bodies contained an estimated mean of about 13 ppm. At a lower level of heptachlor intake, 0.65 ppm, woodcock did not die. They did, however, have a slightly higher mortality than controls when subjected to starvation. Those that succumbed under starvation contained an average of 3.7 ppm (Stickel, Hayne, and Stickel, 1965). These feeding levels of 2.86 and 0.65 ppm take on meaning when compared to the many samples of worms taken from fields treated for fire-ant control; the average in these was about 4 ppm.

THE SIGNIFICANCE OF DDE

PRESTT discussed some calculations that led to the hypothesis that something like 70 ppm of DDE has a toxicity equal to 1 or 2 ppm of dieldrin. DDE is much less toxic to rats and mice than the DDT from which it is derived.

Another point raised by Prestt, concerning DDE, MRS. STICKEL also felt to be extremely important. DDE is the form that often predominates in fish, so that if a bird contains a lot of DDE it does not necessarily mean that it consumed DDT. The bird could have transformed the DDT to DDE itself or could have obtained DDE directly from its prey; looking at the residues in fish one suspects that often it is the latter.

Now this discussion of residues, MRS. STICKEL continued, so far concerns only residues that indicate death. The more important question is whether effects on behavior or effects on reproduction, or on reproduction through behavior, can be postulated on the basis of residues in eggs. We have very little definitive information on this subject. As far as absolute levels are concerned, one would have to hypothesize rather tremendous differences in sensitivity of the species in order to feel that the DDT residues in eggs of the Connecticut ospreys could have had anything to do with their demise, because they were very low compared with Keith's gulls or Hunt's California pheasants. The osprey eggs from Connecticut and Maryland had similar and small amounts of DDT and TDE, although the Connecticut eggs had somewhat more DDE. There is some evidence concerning the relative importance of the different metabolites in eggs. Residues of TDE and DDT were higher in Keith's dead gull eggs than in live eggs, but this was not true of DDE.

In the New York lake trout study (Burdick *et al.*, 1964), there was no correlation between DDE residues and death of the fry. In contrast, an amount of DDT (plus TDE) in the eggs that would be equivalent to 2.9 ppm in the fry produced substantial mortality, and no fry survived with as much as 5 ppm. However, DDT and TDE are rarely present without some DDE, and hence, Mrs. Stickel concluded, their effects cannot be completely separated, and the effect of DDE alone has not been sufficiently studied.

REPRODUCTIVE FAILURES

PRESTT described the regional variation in the population decline of British sparrow-hawks and how these differences were each associated with reproductive failure. In Hampshire, where the population was unaffected, clutch size averaged 3.8 eggs; and the mean number of young per nest was 3.1. In northern Scotland, where only a very slight decline was evident, 4 out of 5 nests were successful in 1964, and reproduction was reasonably high in 1965. In northwestern England, where a severe decline had taken place, only 1 out of 11 regularly held territories produced young. In Cumberland, four eggs disappeared halfway through the incubation period, and a small fragment of the eggs was found at the bottom of the nest. In northeastern England, where 8 regularly occupied territories were checked in York, the only nest with eggs failed in 1964, and its addled eggs were collected after 5 weeks. No nests at all were found there in 1965.

RATCLIFFE stated that peregrine population decline in Britain was not a simple process. It involved a sequence of deterioration in which actual disappearance of the bird was only the final stage. There was a characteristic sequence in which nesting failure began with eggs that were laid but failed to hatch. This was the first stage of deterioration and was followed by the apparent inability of the birds to lay eggs, i.e., eggs could never be found although the birds usually were in residence. This was followed by the final stage which was the disappearance of the birds. The sequence was very variable. Sometimes there was a complete step from nesting success or successful nesting in one year to complete disappearance of the birds the next. Sometimes it was much more drawn out, and the birds would lay eggs for several years in succession but fail every year to hatch them before the eggs disappeared. Some birds have remained only at that stage, and others have gone through the whole range of the sequence of deterioration.

These effects are obviously not being caused by something which is lethal. They were sublethal effects of something. RATCLIFFE felt they posed three questions, none of which we can properly answer yet. First is how they relate to the decline of the population as a whole, and how they relate to disappearance of the individual birds. Obviously, a failure of reproduction is not going to help the population to maintain its numbers. The second point is how far they are significant with regard to the particular issue, the contamination of the species by pesticides. The third question is: how far other people's data and observations of similar phenomena can be compared or equated with these observations. He concluded with the comment that it is very fascinating at this conference to hear people, one after another, from different parts of these two continents that we have been discussing, putting forward this same picture, a repeated sequence of deterioration in which eggs were found broken, pairs failed to lay eggs, and then the pairs finally disappeared.

LEVELS IN ADULTS AND THEIR EGGS

W. H. STICKEL reviewed some of the pesticide aspects of the osprey colony at Old Lyme, Connecticut. (For changes in the numbers of breeding pairs, see Peterson's account in Chapter 28.) Peter L. Ames studied this colony for several years, with some assistance from the Fish and Wildlife Service in 1963 and 1964 (Ames and Mersereau, 1964). In 1963, he collected local fish for analysis, some actually from osprey nests. He also collected one osprey egg from each nest. Analyses were made at the Patuxent Wildlife Research Center. Ten analyses of fish of seven species revealed that DDT+TDE averaged 2.06 ppm (range 0.66–3.5), wet-weight basis. The less toxic metabolite, DDE, averaged 0.63 (range, trace to 2.0). In 21 osprey eggs, DDT+TDE was down to 0.47 ppm (range 0–1.3) and DDE was up to 5.97 ppm (range 3.1–10.4). Figures for residues in these eggs are adjusted to the basis of fresh wet weight (for this adjustment, see Stickel and Heath, 1965: 5).

Thus we see that in going from fish, through bird, to egg, DDT + TDE was reduced by about four times, while DDE increased by about 10 times. There was little of the DDT group present to begin with. By the time the two more toxic forms reached the egg, they were down to about half a ppm, and DDE was accumulated only to about 6 ppm.

A similar study was made in the Potomac at the same time. Residues in fish and osprey eggs ran a little lower (Stickel, Schmid *et al.*, 1965), but the DDT residues in both areas really were small. The dieldrin residues were also small, from 0 to 0.5 ppm in Connecticut fish and from 0 to

0.1 ppm in Potomac fish. Unfortunately, the osprey eggs were not analyzed for dieldrin. There is increasing evidence, STICKEL felt, that dieldrin is present in eagles and ospreys in more than trace amounts; clearly, this highly toxic chemical must be given more attention now that problems of analyzing for it are being overcome.

KEITH reported that herring gull eggs collected by him in northwestern Lake Michigan were slightly less in DDT and TDE content compared to breast muscle tissue of adult birds, and appreciably less in DDE. DDT-complex averaged 227.5 ppm in live eggs, 98.8 in adult breast muscle, and 2,441 in adult fat (J. A. Keith, 1966; Hickey, Keith, and Coon, 1966). The birds' fat in this case was an obvious source of contamination in the formation of the eggs.

MRS. STICKEL commented that when a person takes a drug, it doesn't stay with him forever. It is continuously lost by chemical breakdown and excretion. Loss of chlorinated hydrocarbon pesticides proceeds in the same manner, but very slowly for DDT and for dieldrin. For example, DDT residues of 76 ppm in fat of cattle declined to 9 ppm after 566 days on clean feed (Bovard *et al.,* 1961). Rates of loss may be greater when the concentration is higher, but it is clear that these chlorinated hydrocarbons will persist in the animal body for a very long time. Greatest concentration is in the fat; when a bird or small mammal loses weight rapidly, death may result from pesticide poisoning. This has been shown in various studies. However, quite independently of release of stored pesticide, a bird that is thin or in poor condition is more vulnerable.

The storage of pesticide in fat can be considered a protective mechanism, allowing time for the normal slow processes of metabolism and excretion. Emergencies of food shortage may turn the protection into a hazard.

VERY LOW RESIDUE LEVELS

MRS. STICKEL stated that the effect on vertebrate animals of pesticides in combination is very little studied. Yet animals analyzed usually contain DDT products, dieldrin, traces of heptachlor epoxide, and traces of benzene hexachloride. The question is whether or not one chemical enhances the toxicity of another. This is well known to occur with certain combinations of organophosphate chemicals. However, evidence concerning chlorinated hydrocarbons suggests an opposite effect. For example, dieldrin storage in rats is reduced by exposure to DDT (Street, 1964). In another study, dosages of aldrin or chlordane reduced the toxicity of parathion to mice; that the protection took time to develop was postulated to be a result of the time necessary to stimulate the production of detoxifying enzymes (Triolo and Coon, 1963).

The possibility that egg-breaking by raptors may be due to low residue levels was raised at this conference by Prestt and Ratcliffe. MRS. STICKEL submitted that egg-breaking may be a generalized stress response. Pesticides could be a stress factor, but so also could numerous other things, such as other toxic substances, confinement, crowding, and disturbance. Egg-eating is not rare among captive birds. The Patuxent Wildlife Research Center has a colony of 41 pairs of sparrow hawks; 40 of them laid eggs, and many of these ate their eggs or young. None of these birds was on dosage. MRS. STICKEL also has a colony of 48 pairs of Coturnix quail; both dosed and undosed birds break and eat their eggs; at the time of this meeting (1965), she had not assembled the data to see whether egg-eating was more prevalent among dosed birds. MRS. STICKEL mentioned an example of an effect of DDT on behavior. Exposure of Atlantic salmon parr (*Salmo salar*) to sublethal doses of DDT for 24 hours prior to testing in a horizontal temperature gradient resulted in a shift in the selected temperature. The direction of the shift depended upon the concentration. At 5 ppb DDT the shift was towards the cold end; and the shift reversed itself at 10 ppb and continued to rise toward the warm end as the DDT concentration was raised until a maximum effect was reached at about 50 ppb DDT. So far these shifts of the selected temperature have spanned a total range of about 17°C (63°F). The implications of a 17° shift in the selected temperature in wild salmon leads to fear for their survival in some waters (Solman, 1963; Ogilvie and Anderson, 1965).

HICKEY mentioned that behavioral changes in goldfish had been reported at the Monks Wood Conference by Warner, Peterson, and Borgman (1966). The changes involved 96-hour exposures to 1.8 μg of toxaphene per liter of water at 25°C (77°F).

W. H. STICKEL began his discussion of low residue levels by commenting on the oft-repeated suggestion that very low residues may be highly significant. This may be true, he felt, if one is speaking of endrin, dieldrin, or heptachlor. He believed, however, that in thinking of birds and mammals we should not attribute great importance to low levels of the DDT group, especially DDE; and he knew of no test in which small DDT residues have been convincingly associated with a drop in reproduction. Small residues are easily stored, metabolized, and excreted without apparent harm. Large residues, especially of DDE, are often found in birds and eggs that seem perfectly healthy. Even impressively large residues may be associated with no known effect. In other studies, massive residues may be associated with partial mortality and/or partial reduction of reproduction. STICKEL illustrated this point by reviewing the following examples.

In J. A. Keith's herring gull study of 1964 (Keith, 1966), nine living eggs were analyzed. In these there were 19 ppm of DDT, 6 of TDE, and 202 of DDE—all this in good eggs. Residues in dead eggs were a little higher. Yet reproduction of the colony was only partially suppressed, not virtually eliminated as one might have expected. To clinch this point, reproduction in the colony was normal in 1965 despite the fact that residues remained high (Keith, *in litt.*). Clearly, herring gulls can reproduce successfully in the wild even when they and their eggs contain very high residues of the DDT group. We must conclude that it is not safe to attribute great behavioral effects to small DDT residues. We also see that it is not safe to blame every drop in reproduction on pesticides alone.

The recent California pheasant experiment (Azevedo, Hunt, and Woods, 1965) is also convincing. Birds were placed on 10, 100, and 500 ppm DDT 5 weeks before laying and were kept on dosage. The 500 level proved lethal and had to be reduced. There were several deaths at 100. Small differences in reproductive success appeared in hatchability and chick survival, but overall reproductive success, as measured by production of 46-day-old chicks, was as good in the 10-ppm group as in the controls. And what were the residues in eggs? Eggs of the 10-ppm group averaged 20.6 ppm of DDT and those of the 100-ppm group averaged 129. These figures are based on wet weight of yolk, and they include only DDT itself, not its metabolites. It is clear that substantial DDT residues do not necessarily lead to dead eggs and dying chicks.

In another California pheasant study, hens and complete clutches were taken from a heavily treated area and from an area that had not been directly treated (Hunt and Keith, 1963). Eggs were artificially incubated. Clutch size and fertility were normal. But mortality and crippling of chicks totaled 72% for the treated area as compared with 40% for the control area. Here residues were huge (106, 406, and 1,020 ppm of DDT proper in yolks of three eggs), dieldrin was also present, sometimes in substantial amounts, and birds had been exposed to pesticides to varying degrees for their whole lives. We cannot know what affected the chicks of this study so severely, but we can see that some reproduction is possible even when there are massive DDT residues in eggs.

Genelly and Rudd (1956) placed pheasants on heavy dosages of DDT, dieldrin, and toxaphene 2 weeks before laying began. Despite the severity of dosage, reproductive success did not drop below half that of the controls. Losses of reproduction occurred all along the line from egg production to survival of young. Part of the problem appeared to be poor condition of females caused by repellency of treated food. Certainly, however, there was little magic in DDT residues, for birds receiving 100 ppm of DDT in their diet were only 8% below controls in reproductive success although their eggs contained 162 ppm of residues (in unstated form). Birds receiving 400 ppm of DDT had reproductive success only 26% below that of the controls although eggs contained 349 ppm of residues.

In a test of effects of BHC on pheasant reproduction, Ash and Taylor (1964) found the chemical repellent to pheasants, but they conditioned the birds to treated feed and got as much BHC into them as they could.

Residues in different batches of eggs averaged 3.4, 7.6, 9.3, 10.5, and 12.6 ppm, generally higher than in the field, where 5 ppm was relatively high. The test revealed no effect on reproduction other than a slight suppression of egg production and a short delay in the beginning of egg-laying. Hatchability was fully as high in treated as control eggs. As BHC had been suspected in Britain of causing failure of hatching, these results were important. It was also found that BHC, unlike DDT or dieldrin, was rapidly lost from the body and that egg production quickly picked up after dosage ceased.

These examples, supported by certain unpublished work, STICKEL said, lead to several tentative conclusions:

1. Birds may have normal or nearly normal reproductive success when there are relatively large DDT residues in eggs. This can occur even in the wild, which shows that behavioral effects are not always present to a critical degree when egg residues are high.

2. There is no evidence that a few parts per million of DDT compounds in eggs cause reproductive trouble. The question is still open as to whether such small DDT residues in eggs may be directly correlated with adverse behavioral effects, but at present this possibility does not seem strong.

3. Chlorinated hydrocarbon dosages that do clearly reduce avian reproduction are, with possible exceptions, not far below those that will kill some of the birds if long continued. The idea that reproduction is inhibited by doses that are far below lethal levels is based partly on misinterpretation of data, partly on correlations that may prove spurious, and partly on the paucity of really long-term studies. It is not surprising that dying or endangered birds do not reproduce well or that chicks loaded with toxicant do not survive well. Rather, it is surprising that they perform as sturdily as they do.

4. Long-continued intake of small doses is far more lethal than we once thought. We see many examples of mortality in long-term, low-dosage work at Patuxent. We now know that birds receiving 25 or 40 ppm of DDT in oil throughout the year are living dangerously. So are birds receiving a few ppm of endrin, aldrin, dieldrin, or a little more heptachlor. They may seem healthy for long periods, but some may die whenever the group is moved to another cage or is otherwise stressed. As mortality goes up, reproduction naturally tends to go down, but aside from this, the reproductive effects of low, long dosages are so complicated by variability as to be hard to measure. To date, however, we know of no good example of great reduction of reproduction by a dosage that was well below lethal levels.

5. Declines of avian reproductive success under insecticidal dosage are almost always partial, are often small, and are rarely eliminative. This seems to hold even when toxicant levels are high enough to kill a signifi-

cant percentage of parents. It is not characteristic of insecticides, from what we know of them, to cause drastic reproductive failure while killing few if any adults. The typical effect, as we now see it, is a percentage decline in reproduction as dosages approach lethal levels.

6. It is not characteristic of DDT, dieldrin, or most other chlorinated hydrocarbons to kill birds or to block reproduction without leaving residues that are substantial in relation to the toxicity of the chemicals involved. We can be reasonably confident that DDT levels representing serious damage to birds will be well above two or three ppm of total residues. We know little of the danger levels of other chemicals, however, especially those that may be correlated with subtle behavioral effects.

STICKEL felt it necessary to deal with these questions at length because there is still a strong tendency to attach much importance to small DDT residues, and he knew of nowhere else that evidence to the contrary is assembled. There is also a tendency, now a habit, to blame pesticides for all avian declines, even where the evidence does not support the belief.

The tragedy of this is that we are in danger of missing the real causes. Let us agree that pesticides kill wildlife and may cause population declines. But so do many other things, and most of us are not even looking for them. Disease for example is the apparent cause of death for thousands of loons and other waterbirds in the Great Lakes. There is no doubt that disease is an important factor in many avian deaths and die-offs. Often the disease is not easy to diagnose or even demonstrate as illustrated by the case of the loons.

Metals such as lead and mercury must also be given much consideration. Mercury is considered the major factor causing enormous declines of birds in Sweden (Otterlind and Lennerstedt, 1964; Borg *et al.*, 1965). We have hardly started to look for it in this country, but mercurial seed dressings are commonly used here, as they are in Sweden. Mercury can also be a pollutant from industry of various kinds. Mercury can accumulate in the system and may have irreversible behavioral effects, as the minamata episode in Japan demonstrated (Gerarde, 1964). Lead is currently the subject of a lively controversy about its public health aspects, for worrisome amounts are spread over the landscape from combustion of leaded gasoline, and no doubt much is released as industrial pollution. Arsenic too is sometimes a severe pollutant. We know it can accumulate in the body, but what do we know of it in wildlife? The same can be said of many metals. Even copper and zinc can be toxic to fish at low concentrations. What about birds? Does anyone know and is anyone looking?

One thing clear is that any of these pollutants is likely to be found, perhaps concentrated through the food-chain, in organisms in estuaries of streams draining industrial areas, and in such areas the eagle-osprey problem is acute. The need of work is evident, but there is an enormous difficulty in learning what levels of metals are natural and which are toxic, and also in learning which of the many organic compounds—methyl, phenyl, or what have you—of metals are most dangerous. The water-pollution and fisheries people have a good start in this field, but wildlife workers have hardly touched it, except for mercury in Sweden.

It is often pointed out that avian declines have accelerated since 1945, and that this has been the period of modern pesticides. We must remember that it has also been a period of more industry, more pollution, more people, and fewer areas of good avian habitat. It is very likely that declines have different causes.

Much time, work, and money may be needed to determine the cause of a single decline. No one is close to launching the necessary medical, chemical, and ecological study of any decline. If specific pollutants come under suspicion, the Fish and Wildlife Service is in a good position to test them, insofar as lethal and reproductive effects are concerned. Each test of this sort is a big undertaking, however. The Service is currently testing all of the common chlorinated hydrocarbon insecticides, including DDT and dieldrin, which are common pollutants, and experimental work with lead is getting under way. We are beginning to have field-collected birds and eggs analyzed for mercury, but it is still difficult to have this done. The Service is also financing some study of behavioral effects of pesticides. More than this we cannot do at present.

No one knows where the trails will lead, STICKEL concluded, but the time is short for many forms of life; it is important that we follow the hottest trails we can find and avoid barking up the wrong trees.

SOME RESEARCH NEEDS

In MRS. STICKEL's opinion, many more wild species should be tested than have been so far. For the most part, test animals have been those easily kept in captivity. These include game species, but most of these are very hardy or adaptable species—they must be in order to be game species. As discussed earlier, however, we should not expect differences of hundreds of times. For example, a conspicuous difference in response of Coturnix quail and brown-headed cowbirds to DDT was encountered in some of the studies carried out at the Patuxent Wildlife Research Center. On a dosage of 500 ppm DDT in the diet, all cowbirds were dead in about 2 weeks. Yet about half the Coturnix quail given 900 ppm still were alive at the end of 2 weeks. Bats (*Eptesicus fuscus*) proved to be far more susceptible to DDT than are other mammals (Luckens and Davis, 1964); none survived a dosage as great as 40 mg/kg whereas the oral LD_{50} (median lethal dose) has been reported as 400 mg/kg for mice, 150 mg/kg for rats, and 300 mg/kg for rabbits. Yet this was not true of the response of these same bats to dieldrin or endrin (Luckens and Davis, 1965).

MRS. STICKEL commented on the problem of collecting eggs for analysis. She suggested that, before these are analyzed, one take the volume of the egg in its shell, because this will help with the interpretation later. It often happens that eggs collected for analysis are old and rotting because they have remained in the nest long past hatching time. This is especially true with rare species. High residues in these eggs may be merely artifacts of computation. Personnel at the Patuxent Wildlife Research Center had a good example of this from the field in eggs that were collected by Peter Ames in Connecticut. One egg was collected from each nest early in the season. Subsequently five of these nests continued to hold eggs that did not hatch, so that there were both early and late eggs from five different nests. Parts per million computed on a wet-weight basis showed a very big difference between the early eggs and the late eggs. However, when volumes were used to make adjustments back to a fresh-weight basis, the later eggs had lower residues just as often as they had higher residues. The reason for the problem is simply that eggs lose weight during incubation and during decomposition (Stickel, Schmid, *et al.*, 1965).

Concerning the problem of determining the lethal amounts of residues in hawks, MRS. STICKEL believed that the only way to do this is experimentally—that is, by feeding the birds a diet that contains pesticides and maintaining suitable controls. Captive hawks will die from many causes, and even if much time were spent on autopsy and studies involving bacterial and viral culture transmission, it would not always be possible to know whether diseases or parasites were the cause. Pesticide analysis of these birds would show what was present but would not show whether the quantities were harmful. The same principle prevails for birds found dead in the field independently of known pesticide applications. However, these probably should be considered somewhat differently, for they at least would show the extent of natural field exposure.

SUMMARY

Since their introduction in the 1940's, chlorinated hydrocarbon insecticides have become virtually universal contaminants of the world's environments, often including ecosystems in remote areas. There is some regional variation in residue levels, DDT and its metabolites are particularly present, mercury levels are especially high in Sweden, and the general spread of dieldrin remains to be evaluated.

In general, the residues found tend to be quite low, but they are invariably concentrated in the successive layers of animal pyramids and tend to be highest in aquatic ecosystems. Persistence in some areas may be for years, with DDT breaking down into DDE (now quite widespread) and

TDE. Delayed expression of chlorinated insecticides has unquestionably killed many birds and lowered the reproductive success of at least a few.

Residue levels that can be taken as evidence of death from pesticides are now being recognized. The lower level for hazard from DDT + TDE is about 30 ppm in the brain. Dieldrin plus heptachlor epoxide measured 5–9 ppm in the livers, and 3–8 ppm in the brains of one group of birds that died. For mercury, about 25 ppm in the liver proved fatal. At the present time, the significance of levels causing reproductive failure in birds is unknown. Many species seem able to reproduce in spite of rather high levels, especially of DDE.

In Britain it appears that a wood pigeon feeding on dressed seed can pick up an LD_{50} dose of dieldrin in 5 hours, and a falcon can obtain lethal amounts by feeding on a few highly contaminated prey. Earthworms in fire-ant-control areas carried levels of heptachlor epoxide lethal to woodcock. In passing from fish to adult osprey to egg in a marine ecosystem, DDT + TDE was reduced by about four times, while DDE increased about ten times. Among herring gulls, egg levels of DDT and TDE run about 5% of those in adult fat; while DDE is about 10%. Storage of these compounds in animal fat allows for a slow process of excretion, but it is hazardous in emergencies and in birds is subject to transferral to their eggs.

In general, the sublethal levels of insecticides being found in raptors are not readily interpretable because of the lack of experimental work along comparable lines. Egg-breakage and egg-eating occur among captive birds not on dosage. Behavior changes are however reported in laboratory fish. Many captive birds seem to reproduce quite well on relatively high diets of DDT, and there is no evidence that a few ppm of this compound in eggs cause reproductive trouble. Long-continued intake of small doses of more toxic, persistent pesticides is, however, often quite lethal.

The effects of dieldrin, mercury, lead, and other known pollutants on avian reproduction all invite research at this time. Many more wild species need to be studied under controlled conditions that permit the determination of cause-effect relationships.

LITERATURE CITED

Ames, P. L., and G. S. Mersereau. 1964. Some factors in the decline of the osprey in Connecticut. Auk, 81(2):173–185.

Ash, J. S., and A. Taylor. 1964. Further trials on the effects of gamma BHC seed dressing on breeding pheasants. The Game Research Ass., 4th Ann. Rep., p. 14–20.

Azevedo, J. A., Jr., E. G. Hunt, and L. A. Woods, Jr. 1965. Physiological effects of DDT on pheasants. Calif. Fish and Game, 51(4):276–293.

Barker, R. J. 1958. Notes on some ecological effects of DDT sprayed on elms. J. Wildl. Mgmt., 22(3):269–274.

Borg, K., H. Wanntorp, K. Erne, and E. Hanko. 1965. Kvicksilverförgiftninger bland vilt i Sverige. Rapport Från Statens Veterinärmedicinska Anstalt, Stockholm. 50+3+34 p.

Bovard, K. P., B. M. Priode, G. E. Whitmore, and A. J. Ackerman. 1961. DDT residues in the internal fat of beef cattle fed contaminated apple pomace. J. An. Sci., 20(4):824–826.

Burdick, G. E., E. J. Harris, H. J. Dean, T. M. Walker, Jack Skea, and David Colby. 1964. The accumulation of DDT in lake trout and the effect on reproduction. Trans. Amer. Fisheries Soc., 93(2):127–136.

Dustman, E. H. 1966. Monitoring wildlife for pesticide content. Nat. Acad. Sci., Nat. Res. Council, Pub. 1402:343–351.

———, and L. F. Stickel. 1966. Pesticide residues in the ecosystem. Amer. Soc. Agronomy Spec. Pub. no. 8. p. 109–121.

Eutermoser, G. 1961. Erläuterungen zur Krähenstatistik. Deutscher Falkenorden, 1961:49–50.

Genelly, R. E., and R. L. Rudd. 1956. Effects of DDT, toxaphene, and dieldrin on pheasant reproduction. Auk, 73(4):529–539.

George, J. L., and D. E. H. Frear. 1966. Pesticides in the Antarctic. J. Appl. Ecol., 3(Suppl.):155–167.

Gerarde, H. W. 1964. Toxicology: organic. Ann. Rev. Pharmacol., 4:238–240.

Harrison, D. L., P. E. G. Maskell, and D. F. L. Money. 1963. Dieldrin poisoning of dogs. 2. Experimental studies. N.Z. Veterinary J., 11(2):23–31.

Henriksson, K., E. Karppanen, and M. Helminen. 1966. High residue of mercury in Finnish white-tailed eagles. Ornis Fennica, 43(2):38–45.

Hickey, J. J., J. A. Keith, and F. B. Coon. 1966. An exploration of pesticides in a Lake Michigan ecosystem. J. Appl. Ecol., 3(Suppl.):141–154.

Hunt, E. G. 1966. Studies of pheasant-insecticide relationships. J. Appl. Ecol., 3(Suppl.):113–123.

———, and A. I. Bischoff. 1960. Inimical effects on wildlife of periodic DDD applications to Clear Lake. Calif. Fish and Game, 46(1):91–106.

———, and J. O. Keith. 1963. Pesticide-wildlife investigations in California—1962. Proc. 2nd Ann. Conf. Use of Agr. Chemicals in Calif., Davis. 29-p. insert.

Jefferies, D. J., and I. Prestt. 1966. Post-mortems of peregrines and lanners with particular reference to organochlorine residues. Brit. Birds, 59(2):49–64.

Keith, J. A. 1966. Reproduction in a population of herring gulls (*Larus argentatus*) contaminated by DDT. J. Appl. Ecol., 3(Suppl.):57–70.

Keith, J. O. 1966. Insecticide contaminations in wetland habitats and their effects on fish-eating birds. J. Appl. Ecol., 3 (Suppl.) :71–85.

Kitselman, C. H., P. A. Dahm, and A. R. Borgmann. 1950. Toxicologic studies of large animals. Amer. J. Veterinary Res., 11(4):378–381.

Koeman, J. H., and H. van Genderen. 1966. Some preliminary notes on residues of chlorinated hydrocarbon insecticides in birds and mammals in the Netherlands. J. Appl. Ecol., 3 (Suppl.) :99–106.

Larrick, G. P. 1964. Presence of DDT in fish oils, p. 193-197. *In* Coordination of activities relating to the use of pesticides. Part 1: Hearings before the Subcommittee on Reorganization and International Organizations of the Committee on Government Operations. United States Senate, Eighty-eighth Congress, First Session. U.S. Govt. Printing Office, Washington, D.C. 390 p.

Lockie, J. D., and D. A. Ratcliffe. 1964. Insecticides and Scottish golden eagles. Brit. Birds, 57(3):89–102.

Luckens, M. M., and W. H. Davis. 1964. Bats: sensitivity to DDT. Science, 146(3646):948.

———, and W. H. Davis. 1965. Toxicity of dieldrin and endrin to bats. Nature, 207(4999):879–880.

McEwen, L. C., J. E. Peterson, M. H. Mohn, and G. H. Ise. 1963. Ring-necked pheasants: toxicity and tissue residues of aldrin and Sevin, p. 50, 68. *In* Pesticide-wildlife studies: A review of Fish and Wildlife Service investigations during 1961 and 1962. Fish and Wildl. Serv. Circ. 167. 109 p.

Moore, N. W. 1965*a*. Environmental contamination by pesticides, p. 219–237. *In* G. T. Goodman, R. W. Edwards, and J. M. Lambert [eds.], Ecology and the industrial society: A symposium of the British Ecological Society. John Wiley and Sons, New York. 395 p.

———. 1965*b*. Pesticides and birds—A review of the situation in Great Britain in 1965. Bird Study, 12(3):222–252.

———, and J. O'G. Tatton. 1965. Organochlorine insecticide residues in the eggs of sea birds. Nature, 207(4992):42–43.

———, and C. H. Walker. 1964. Organic chlorine insecticide residues in wild birds. Nature, 201(4994):1072–1073.

Murton, R. K., and M. Vizoso. 1963. Dressed cereal seed as a hazard to woodpigeons. Ann. Appl. Biol., 52(3):503–517.

Ogilvie, D. M., and J. M. Anderson. 1965. Effect of DDT on temperature selection by young Atlantic salmon, *Salmo salar*. J. Fisheries Res. Bd. of Canada, 22(2):503–512.

Otterlind, G., and I. Lennerstedt. 1964. Den svenska fågelfaunan och biocidskadorna. Vår Fågelvärld, 23(4):363–415 (with English summary: Avifauna and pesticides in Sweden).

Ratcliffe, D. A. 1965. Organo-chlorine residues in some raptor and corvid eggs from northern Britain. Brit. Birds, 58(3):65–81.

Rudd, R. L. 1964. Pesticides and the living landscape. University of Wisconsin Press, Madison. 320 p.

Saar, C. 1961. Der Krähenfalke "Mara." Deutscher Falkenorden, 1961:47–49.

Sladen, W. J. L., C. M. Menzie, and W. L. Reichel. 1966. DDT residues in Adelie penguins and a crabeater seal from Antarctica: ecological implications. Nature, 210(5037):670–673.

Solman, V. E. F. 1963. Biocides and wildlife. Minutes and papers of the 27th Federal-Provincial Wildlife Conference. Canadian Wildlife Service, p. 45–51.

Stadelman, W. J., B. J. Liska, B. E. Langlois, G. C. Mostert, and A. R. Stemp. 1965. Persistence of chlorinated hydrocarbon insecticide residues in chicken tissue and eggs. Poultry Sci., 44(2):435–437.

Stickel, L. F., and R. G. Heath. 1965. Dieldrin, DDT, and heptachlor epoxide in birds found dead in an area treated with dieldrin, p. 15. *In* The effects of pesticides on fish and wildlife. U.S. Dep. Interior, Fish and Wildl. Serv. Circ. 226. 77 p.

———, F. G. Schmid, W. L. Reichel, and P. L. Ames. 1965. Ospreys in Connecticut and Maryland, p. 4–6. *In* The effects of pesticides on fish and wildlife. U.S. Dep. Interior, Fish and Wildl. Serv. Circ. 226. 77 p.

———, W. H. Stickel, and R. Christensen. 1966. Residues of DDT in brains and bodies of birds that died on dosage and in survivors. Science, 151(3717):1549–1551.

Stickel, W. H., W. E. Dodge, W. G. Sheldon, J. B. DeWitt, and L. F. Stickel. 1965. Body condition and response to pesticides in woodcocks. J. Wildl. Mgmt., 29(1):147–155.

———, D. W. Hayne, and L. F. Stickel. 1965. Effects of heptachlor-contaminated earthworms on woodcocks. J. Wildl. Mgmt., 29(1):132–146.

Street, J. F. 1964. DDT antagonism to dieldrin storage in adipose tissue of rats. Science, 146(no. 3651):1580–1581.

Taylor, A., and J. Brady. 1964. Chlorinated pesticide residues in wild bird eggs. Bird Study, 11(3):192–197.

Tompkins, W. A. 1964. A pesticide study on the Westfield, Farmington, and Connecticut River watersheds, July 1, 1963–June 30, 1964. Conn. River Watershed Council, Inc., Greenfield, Massachusetts. 11 p.

Triolo, A. J., and J. M. Coon. 1963. Effects of aldrin and chlordane on the toxicity of organophosphates and hexobarbital sleeping time in mice. Fed. Proc., 22:189 (abstract).

Turner, N. 1965. DDT in Connecticut wildlife. Conn. Agr. Exp. Sta. Bull. 672. p. 1-11.

Wallace, G. J., W. P. Nickell, and R. F. Bernard. 1961. Bird mortality in the Dutch elm disease program in Michigan. Cranbrook Inst. Sci. Bull. 41. 44 p.

Warner, R. E., K. K. Peterson, and Leon Borgman. 1966. Behavioural pathology in fish: a quantitative study of sublethal pesticide toxication. J. Appl. Ecol., 3(Suppl.):223–247.

Weaver, L., C. G. Gunnerson, A. W. Breidenbach, and J. J. Lichtenberg. 1965. Chlorinated hydrocarbon pesticides in major U.S. river basins. Public Health Reports, 80(6):481–493.

CHAPTER 43

GENERAL DISCUSSION: PESTICIDES

ADDITIVE EFFECTS AND INTERSPECIFIC VARIATIONS IN TOXICITY

SPENCER: I am very much interested in this potentiation or additive effect. A great many pesticide formulations now carry more than one active ingredient. Mixtures of DDT and dieldrin are actually antagonistic. Dieldrin is not stored in the fat of animals ingesting it when DDT is included in the diet. Generalizations on the additive effects of different chlorinated hydrocarbons can be misleading.

Now I would like to suggest two things that are being overlooked. We have laid great stress here on the fact that the birds that are endangered are those that are feeding upon other birds and on fish while the birds that are feeding upon mammals are in no danger. I suggest that this assumes that birds accumulate greater levels in their fat than do mammals. This has not been established.

I would also suggest that there are differences in tolerance to the chlorinated hydrocarbons among the various species of birds that may determine why some species tolerate a condition while others do not. This is a point that Stickel made earlier: we need toxicity data on each species. Whenever the US Department of Agriculture registers a new chemical, lethal-dosage studies on the *species in question* are required.

Certain species of birds will accumulate fair levels from feeding on treated insects, other birds will not. For example, if you were to offer two species, let's say a broad-winged hawk and a peregrine, treated food of the same type, I suggest that you would find that the peregrine may be adversely affected, while the broad-wing will not. Both will have taken in the same amount of poison. Sharp differences in susceptibility to poisoning are common.

Perhaps you would like to know that many of the objectionable uses of pesticides are being phased out. We're not as far behind as some of you might think. Let me put it this way: In Britain they have done a thorough job of assessing their problem and associating cause and effect. They have compiled and documented this evidence and presented it to their governing bodies. This is what we have to do. This is what we have not done.

PESTICIDES ON REFUGES IN THE UNITED STATES

MRS. STICKEL: In the Department of the Interior, we of the Bureau of Sport Fisheries and Wildlife are concerned with the degree of pesticide contamination of wildlife refuges. Results of two recent studies may be of interest to you.

The first of these concerned the Everglade kite, the United States population of which is threatened by extinction. Its dependence on snails for food raised the question of pesticide content of the snails. The Loxahatchee Refuge is one place where a few birds have been seen recently; hence, snails were collected there for residue determinations. Analysis for chlorinated hydrocarbons was made of three groups of 10 snails each. Residues of DDT averaged 0.11 ppm; DDE averaged 0.07 ppm, and benzene hexachloride 0.006 ppm, all low levels that would seem not to be hazardous. No other chlorinated hydrocarbons were detected.

The second study arose from the suspicion that Canada geese might be accumulating deleterious amounts of pesticides on their wintering grounds. Hence just before northward migration in the spring of 1965, adult female geese were collected at the Horseshoe Lake and Union County Game Refuges and the Crab Orchard National Wildlife Refuge in Illinois, at the Wheeler National Wildlife Refuge in Alabama, and at Swan Lake National Wildlife Refuge in Missouri. It was gratifying to learn that the birds contained only very small amounts of pesticides. Even in fat, where residual pesticides concentrate, the whole DDT group averaged only 1.18 ppm for the Wheeler flock and less than half this amount for the other groups. Residues were far lower in liver, muscle, and ovaries. Small amounts of dieldrin and heptachlor epoxide (less than 1 ppm) also were detected in fat samples.

PESTICIDE USAGE IN UNDERDEVELOPED COUNTRIES

W. H. STICKEL: Some speakers have implied that when birds leave the United States, they virtually leave pesticide dangers behind. Actually, pesticide use probably is better controlled in the United States and Britain than almost anywhere else. In underdeveloped countries, pesticides are often splashed around at rates we consider horrifying. There are places where dieldrin is sold in unmarked paper bags and where the authorities do not dare warn people it will kill fish, for that is what they would then do with it. Dr. Cade tells me that the agricultural strip along the coast of Peru and Chile is very heavily treated. In South Africa, thousands of acres are treated with dieldrin to kill subterranean termites that are preventing revegetation of arid rangeland. Elsewhere in Africa, large areas are sprayed with dieldrin to kill tsetse flies. In all underdeveloped countries, farmers are under pressure to produce more food, and pesticides are always mentioned as one of the main tools. Our migrating birds may encounter pesticides wherever they go, unless they seek out wilderness.

PETERSON: South of the United States border, pesticides are an environmental factor to be reckoned with. About a month ago I was in Colombia, South America, with Carlos Lehmann, one of the leading Colombian ornithologists. I did not see the large numbers of new, interesting species of birds I had expected. Indeed, I saw fewer species than I would in a day's birding about my home in Connecticut. However, among other things we did visit a large colony of cattle egrets. We were under a large ceiba tree blossoming with cattle egrets' nests and, while I was photographing them, a bird flopped to the ground at my feet, went into shudders and died a short while later. I inquired "What's this?" and was told "This happens constantly; this is due to the chemicals they are putting on the fields."

There are many kingfishers in tropical America, six species in Colombia. I wanted to see them. But we saw not one in the week we spent in the field. I asked "Where are the kingfishers?" I was told that chemicals in the food-chain had apparently eliminated them. Mind you, this was Latin America—Colombia—relatively "undeveloped."

Actually, Colombia is not so underdeveloped; I saw with my own eyes the fleets of planes that spray the fields in the Cauca Valley. There was a great lowland forest in that valley not so many years ago; it is now one great sugar plantation.

Cade has suggested at this conference (Chapter 45) that a big section of the North American continent ought to be set aside for research purposes where one could not apply persisting insecticides. This would still not take poisons out of the area's ecosystems, because as long as poisons drift, as long as winds blow, or fishes swim, or birds travel, these chemicals will move about; and we know that some of these chemicals have now reached the ends of the earth.

POTENTIAL PESTICIDE CONTAMINATION IN THE GULF OF CALIFORNIA

SPRUNT: In respect to the possible sources of pesticides in the Gulf of California, I think Banks is quite right in saying that there might be drainage from the Imperial Valley; but there is a considerable and heavily used agricultural belt all along the southern coast of Sonora and Sinaloa and down as far as Nayarit, and there are large insecticide-processing plants and mixing plants and so on in this region. Hence there could be quite a bit of runoff from the eastern side of the Gulf of California too.

GLADING: Generally speaking, the pesticides we are worried about really are not carried through the water, they are carried in organisms or attached to soil particles. Even almost immediately after an application, it is difficult to find any quantity of the chlorinated hydrocarbons in the water. At Big Bear Lake in California, we just could not find these chemicals in the water, but we were getting dead birds all over the place for a number of weeks. The lethal compound proved to be toxaphene in the food-chain.

L. W. WALKER: Throughout most of the year, pelagic birds are the primary foods of peregrines in the Gulf of California, and the supposition that the dilution of waterborne insect sprays would be so great as to have no effect is more than just logical. If it is not, we can bid goodbye to falcons in the Gulf area. However, in the fall of the year the Gulf is an important migratory flyway for passerines. Orioles, doves, and even tremendous flocks of lark buntings use the islands as stepping stones; and, after being harried by several peregrine near-misses, they get the idea that humans are the lesser of the two evils (how wrong can they be), and a person can almost step on them before they will fly. From my observations I believe these migrants, direct from the poisoned fields to the north, are preferred foods when they are available in the fall. Whether a month or a year of feeding on chemical-impregnated birds could cause sterility I do not know, but it is a thought that should be considered. In the past few years I have found peregrine eggs in late July which is about a month or so after the young should have been flying [*in litt.* to J. J. Hickey, 20 October 1965].

THE POSSIBLE SIGNIFICANCE OF DIELDRIN

W. H. STICKEL: Our British colleagues have shown convincingly that some British peregrines were killed by dieldrin. Could this have happened here? Ratcliffe tells me that the peregrines get much of their dieldrin from domestic pigeons, which get it from eating dressed seed.

In the United States, Spencer tells me, many different seed dressings are sold, and most of them contain dieldrin or aldrin that soon becomes dieldrin. They are used in various parts of the nation, primarily in the South, but there are large areas in which they are not used, according to Spencer. The problem may be spotty. It is reported, for example, that aldrin used on seed rice in Texas killed fulvous tree ducks. There is reason to think that it is used partly because it does kill rice-eating birds. Dieldrin and aldrin are used in this country for many purposes other than seed treatment. Thus, there is a real possibility that dieldrin may be affecting raptorial birds in America.

Dieldrin is extremely toxic, as you know, and it is extremely stable. It tends to persist as dieldrin for long periods in soil, water, or animals. Dieldrin is the pesticide found most often in American rivers (Weaver *et al.*, 1965, Public Health Reports, 80:481–493). It is often found in fish. When we analyze eagle or osprey eggs, we find one or two ppm of dieldrin. What effect does it have in these eggs? We do not know, but tests now underway at Patuxent may tell us. Bobwhites, pheasants, and mallards are being kept on long-term, low-level dosages of common hydrocarbon insecticides, including dieldrin, to study effects on reproduction and to learn the significance of residue levels in the eggs. In the first breeding season, after 3 or 4 months of dosage, no gross, obvious effect appeared. This is by no means conclusive, but it does bear out the idea that one should not expect magic of these compounds in birds and mammals; it takes more than traces to have measurable effects.

REGIONAL USE OF SPECIFIC CHEMICALS

SPENCER: Up to this time it has been very fruitful and very useful to speak in terms of pesticides. But we have come to a point now where this term should be dropped, and we begin to look at the problem directly. In the United States there are over 800 basic chemicals that are classified as pesticides, formulated into approximately 60,000 registered products. These pesticide products include sanitizing agents that you use in your home, algaecides used in water-cooling towers, slimicides used in paper mills, as well as agricultural products used on field and forest. I think the reference to "pesticides" should be dropped, and from now on we should speak of "chlorinated hydrocarbons" because these are what we have been referring to. Of the chlorinated hydrocarbons, we should identify the five or six that are actually involved. It is also important to look at the problem from a regional standpoint because, depending upon the crops grown in the country involved and the registration practices of that country in accepting certain pesticides and refusing others, peregrines are going to be subjected to different chlorinated hydrocarbons. Our British colleagues have pinpointed their problem because they know the pesticide used and the timing of the field applications. The tests to be run for accumulation of pesticides at the mouth of any river or tributary will depend upon the pesticides that have been applied in the upstream drainages or on crops of the area. Thus chlorinated hydrocarbon "X" may be responsible in one area, chlorinated hydrocarbon "Y" in another. We also may be making an error in considering only the chlorinated hydrocarbons. This has been brought out by a statement that mercurials are also suspect. Eight hundred pesticide chemicals can have an infinite number of effects on the animal kingdom.

Predation, Shooting, and Other Factors

CHAPTER 44

GENERAL DISCUSSION

PREDATION BY RACCOONS AND GREAT HORNED OWLS

ALDRICH: With respect to osprey nests, Peterson mentioned that the raccoon has been initially considered a possible predator of significance in Connecticut. I know that the raccoon has been occasionally suspected of predation on the bald eagle nests in the Chesapeake Bay area. We have evidence that the raccoon has increased considerably in the eastern United States, at least over the years, as a result of its fur being of little importance any more. Waterfowl biologists have also noticed that it has increased as a predator on waterfowl nests in Manitoba. I am wondering whether there is any further evidence that this increasing raccoon population has become serious for any of the birds of prey.

HANCOCK: In northwestern Washington, I have seen raccoons on two occasions sleeping in bald eagle nests. The raccoons did not appear to have harmed that particular eagle, because eagles were nesting in an alternate nest nearby. But this does not mean, of course, that they would not eat young bald eagles if they were to find them in a nest.

SPOFFORD: A bald eagle population has been under study by the Pennsylvania Game Commission over a number of years. They have actually found the raccoon feeding on the young. Their evidence seems to be that they have seen the young eagles in the nest, and the next morning, raccoons in the nest and no eagles remaining. Whether or not they have actually examined the stomach contents of the raccoon, I do not know. But they feel quite certain that raccoons do eat young eagles. This year (1965), all three nests had incubating females in March, and all three of them failed in May.

AMADON: I think there is another aspect to this, too. Some years ago when Heinz Meng was studying the Cooper's hawk in central New York, he was losing many nests, and I believe he demonstrated that the raccoons were actually tracking him through the woods and climbing the nesting trees. Another thing occurs to me in connection with these easily accessible falcon eyries that we were shown in Alaska: foxes or possibly even wolverines (*Gulo luscus*) might follow a person around so that a nest that had been visited, particularly one in which the young were handled and banded, might be far more susceptible to predation than one that was not visited.

POSTUPALSKY: I have another comment on predation on osprey. I have two records of predation on low osprey nests which were preyed upon by a mammalian predator that swims and climbs, probably a raccoon. In one case a set of three eggs disappeared overnight, and in the same nest this spring three young ospreys aged between 9 and 12 days were destroyed. The heads and feet were found in the morning. Roy Latham has described a nest on Long Island where the young were destroyed by raccoons in three successive seasons. This record appeared in The Kingbird in 1959.

PETERSON: I have known both osprey nests and eagle nests to be occupied by great horned owls. Charles Broley said that one nest out of 20 during his period of study around Tampa Bay would be occupied by great horned owls. But he did have one extraordinary case where he had a great horned owl and a bald eagle incubating not more than 3 ft apart.

SPRUNT: I think that this 5% or less figure would be a pretty good estimate of this predation on the bald eagle generally. Great horned owls do affect bald eagle nests to a certain extent; but, in many cases when such an eagle nest is taken over by a great horned owl, the bald eagles will use an alternate nest nearby.

PETERSON: For many years, we have had one pair of great horned owls nesting on Great Island in Connecticut and, although they sometimes will be in osprey nests, they always raise their three young.

AMADON: I was once taken to a little rocky stack offshore near Anchorage, Alaska, where we found the remains of a peregrine on a rock, with the wings and the skeleton mostly cleaned. I couldn't imagine what on earth could have happened to it there. Then, as we worked a little farther around the island, an old horned owl flew out from the edge of the rock.

There were no trees at all on this little island, and this bird flew across the water to the mainland. It is possible that *Bubo virginianus* may take some falcons here in North America just as *Bubo bubo* does in Europe.

THE EFFECT OF SHOOTING ON RAPTORS

BEEBE: The widespread use of firearms in the USA is one of the things that anybody coming across the line from Canada finds absolutely appalling. American tourist boats when they cross our border into Canada have firearms in every place, hung on their owners' hips, and everywhere else. They seem to be needed down in the United States. One thing that makes me pleased that I'm living in Canada is the absolute obsession with firearms that I see in the States as opposed to what I find across the line in my own country. When I went out to look at the situation regarding peregrines on the Olympic Peninsula, I very rapidly came to the conclusion, even before I looked, that I would find no peregrines. There were dozens of fellows going out in boats fishing, and every one of them was loaded down with heavy sidearms and cartridge belts buckled around them. You would have thought they were really going into the wilderness! They were going to shoot anything they saw!

L. W. WALKER: Carl Kenyon's report on an osprey decrease in the Gulf of California is absolutely correct, dishearteningly so, but in a quarter century of travel in the gulf area I find that it is the low nests that are no longer occupied—the nests that are easy targets for a .22-caliber rifle from a rocking boat. Those on islands that are situated on the uppermost crags are still going strong. To my mind the osprey decrease in this region is due to target practice of thoughtless Americans, eliminating one part of the Gulf atmosphere that drew them there in the first place. Water-borne insecticides passing through a food-chain and finally lodging in ospreys would be stretching a point in regard to these marvelous birds. But with the peregrine falcons—maybe so [*in litt.* to J. J. Hickey, 20 October 1965].

SONIC BOOMS AND EMBRYONIC MORTALITY

SPRUNT: Sonic booms have been suggested a number of times as a source of mortality for bald eagle embryos, but I have had no data to confirm this hypothesis. For the past 2 years we have had a number of low-level jet flights by military aircraft in the Florida Keys practically every day, and some of the pilots occasionally break the sound barrier. Despite these low-level sonic booms, the osprey population has been reproducing very well, as has the bald eagle population in that area.

NELSON: We have used the sonic boom as a research tool to start avalanches. It was very embarrassing that, in contrast to a single avalanche which takes just 40 lb of dynamite to set off, we have induced 23 avalanches with a single sonic boom in Glacier National Park—to such an extent that we had to refrain from using this technique. We were avalanching places we did not want to. This was over Murdock Lake where the pilots were instructed to come down over the lake, level out, and crack the sonic boom. This is different from the sonic boom that comes as a drag from a high elevation. I do not think the high booms could ordinarily break an egg or an egg membrane. Occasionally, as when a pilot makes a mistake in the air and the sonic boom is directed down, I don't think there is any doubt but what you could damage an egg. When one looks at what you can do with an avalanche on a head-on sonic boom and the tremendous force on a mountain, one is bound to be impressed.

GLADING: In California, one of our two remaining state game farms is about 3 miles (5 km) from one of the most important overseas air bases, and we have not had any differences in pheasant production before and after this technical development. At this farm we are also rearing red-legged partridges with no trouble.

HICKEY: Frank L. Cherms of the Department of Poultry Science at the University of Wisconsin tells me that Americans have at several times had to consider the possibility that sonic booms have an effect on the hatching poultry. There has been a good deal of research on this and our poultry scientists are convinced that there is no effect.

GEYER: Poultry producers using mass-production techniques in the United States have been far more concerned with helicopters—particularly Sikorsky rotors—than they have with sonic booms from jet aircraft. The poultry industry even put a lot of pressure on the federal government to approve the use of tranquilizer drugs to be fed to their broilers.

THE HUMAN POPULATION EXPLOSION IN CALIFORNIA

GLADING: We have one peculiar thing in California. The white-tailed kite which 25 years ago was put on the list of endangered species has now exploded and become a very common raptor in the Sacramento Valley, the Delta area, and elsewhere in California. This bird is a much easier target than the peregrine falcon. We need to understand why one bird goes down and the other bird goes up.

PETERSON: One ecological difference between the white-tailed kite and the peregrine is that the kite has literally no food-chain, or it is very short—it eats insects, and it must eat a lot, whereas the peregrine, being on a longer food-chain, is exposed to the pesticide magnification effect initially reported in an aquatic food-chain by Hunt and Bischoff (1960, Calif. Fish and Game, 46: 91–106). I think this is a thing to keep in mind.

HICKEY: California has had perhaps the greatest population explosion that we have here in the US. I wonder what one would say about the effect of this population explosion on nesting sites of the peregrine falcon?

GLADING: I really do not think that it has been any big factor. Most of the falcon nests that I know of are in pretty remote parts of California. While it is true that in wild environments a lot of people are out wandering around that were not wandering around before, a lot of these peregrine nests are on private ranches that are still pretty much closed. I just do not believe, while I would not discount it entirely, that man's interference with the nesting cycle is proportional to the population decline of the peregrine falcon.

BANKS: I would tend to put a lot more emphasis on the increase in human population, particularly in southern California, than Glading did. Virtually from Santa Barbara to the international border at San Diego the region is becoming more and more completely developed. It is true that the big increase in population is in metropolitan areas. These, like San Diego, are spreading out more and more to the coast so that houses are now right over the bluffs in many instances, even falling over the bluffs at times. Hence they are getting much closer to the sort of habitat that the peregrines along there would presumably like. With additional people, there is a lot more usage of the beaches immediately under these cliffs.

CADE: Can I just verify what Banks has just said? There formerly were at least six coastal peregrine eyries between San Diego and Los Angeles. Dana Point was one famous one; there were several around the present artists' colonies, and so forth. These nesting sites have been deserted for quite a number of years, I am sure due just to the factors to which Banks has called attention, namely, the building up of the seaside communities on the tops of the bluffs.

GLADING: While I agree that in southern California there are a number of old peregrine nesting sites that are just too civilized now, many of the areas that Bond indicated as active nesting sites in 1939 are in uncivilized parts of California and have no nests in them now.

PART V

POPULATION DYNAMICS AND SIGNIFICANCE OF TRENDS

CHAPTER 45

ROUND TABLE DISCUSSION

Introductory Remarks

Dean Amadon

Almost everything bearing on peregrine or other raptor populations is, in the final analysis, ecological. One might think of natural ecological factors like climate or food, or purely artificial ones, man-produced, like pesticides or radioactive fallout. I don't think that we can make a clear distinction between these. Actually, every aspect of the environment, even in the Arctic or in the less settled regions, is in our time to some extent influenced by human activities. I am personally well convinced that pesticides may be the answer to the specific problem that confronts us, namely the catastrophic decline in certain bird-eating and fish-eating raptorial birds, in areas where they are especially likely to pick up pesticides. However, I assume that, since we had such a thorough discussion of pesticides, we are to go back and think once again about some of the other things that have been presented to the conference or that may occur to us as the discussion goes along. I think it is important to do this because, even if pesticides are the factor we are looking for, the fact remains that, with the human population explosion, the vast increase of industry, the use of areas for recreational purposes and so forth, there will be continuing pressure on these raptors. Some of these pressures will in large areas be disastrous regardless of whether pesticides are present or not.

POSSIBLE FACTORS AFFECTING RAPTOR POPULATIONS

Let us just briefly consider, mainly by recapitulation, a few of these other possibilities, and then they can be brought into this discussion further. One possible factor that might be affecting populations and distribution of raptors is *long-term climatic change.* A few years ago, much was being said about a warming trend—for example, some of the marine commercial fishes of the North Atlantic moving north, being taken off Greenland, and disappearing farther south; and then, when we were told that the peregrines in North America were doing so well farther north and so poorly farther south, I thought that possibly this was reflecting some such long-term climatic change. I am now inclined to doubt it. There seems to be some evidence for a recent reversal of this warming trend, at least in some localities, and furthermore, the peregrine falcon is not a particularly good species on which to hang such a hypothesis, since —as we have noted before—it does occur in the tropical parts of the world. On the other hand, we could keep in mind that, from a geological point of view, we know that vast numbers of species have become extinct only a relatively few thousand years ago. There were all sorts of fancy big eagles and vultures in California which rather rapidly became extinct as a direct or indirect effect of the climatic vicissitudes accompanying the Ice Ages.

Now another possibility is *disease,* which was considered rather thoroughly earlier in this conference. Certainly at times disease or parasites can be of crucial importance. For example, in the Hawaiian Islands, there initially were no mosquitoes. When they and avian malaria were introduced, half a dozen or more native species of birds became extinct almost overnight. At least that is the most plausible reason for their extinction, which occurred before there had been any noticeable deterioration in the environment. While it is unlikely that widespread species like the bald eagle or osprey are going to be totally exterminated by the appearances of a new disease or a more virulent disease, nevertheless it is obvious that they could be decimated over vast areas by such factors just as we have seen in the case of European rabbits *(Oryctolagus cuniculus)* with myxomatosis in Australia. Closer at home, we have examples of the catastrophic declines in the species of trees like the American elm *(Ulmus americana)* and the American chestnut *(Castanea dentata)* when new viruses or other diseases became prevalent in North America. I think also we should keep in mind that species sometimes seem to become dominant and start spreading rapidly, for example the cattle egret, which has increased so tremendously in North America. This is not merely a matter of being introduced on a new continent because the cattle egret has been spreading also in parts of Africa and so forth. It is probably true that for equally obscure reasons certain species can, so to speak, "hit the skids" and begin a decline which surely is linked with some genetic change or some change in the ecology upon which we may not be able to put a finger.

Food shortage or change in the food supply is another possible factor controlling species of raptors. However, we are concerned here with the decline of a number of species of rather differing food habits and, despite Beebe's ingenious theory as to the passenger pigeon, I do not think that a diminution in food supply can be the real answer to the problem that confronts us.

We then, perhaps, have to turn to the various ways in which *man* is affecting the ecology of these birds, and—needless to say—these ways are numerous. One of the most obvious is direct shooting or poisoning to get rid of the birds. This can be disastrous when it involves a geographically restricted population. One species of North American falcon, not a very good one for falconry, the Guadalupe caracara, was exterminated in short order when it was supposedly preying on the grazing goats on Guadalupe Island off the western coast of Mexico. Such total extermination again is less likely in a widespread continental species but can certainly remove species from large areas. Other influences of this sort are egg collecting, trophy collecting, falconry if not properly regulated, and rock-climbing, increased use of areas for various recreational purposes, deforestation, and mere disturbance resulting from the increasing population with more people, more cars, and more noise and disturbance of all sorts.

IMPORTANCE OF A MULTIFACTORIAL APPROACH

Now regardless of our conclusions as to pesticides, I think it is important that we keep these other factors in mind and do what we can about them, for several reasons, the first of which is that—as was pointed out by W. H. Stickel in our panel discussion of pesticides (Chapter 42)—it is just barely possible that we are missing the boat and that, although pesticides, say, quite obviously are killing adult birds or reducing the productivity of these raptors in certain areas, it may be we are mistaken if we conclude that pesticide use is the overall factor involved. I think it is obvious that persisting pesticides are not going to be eliminated overnight. All we can hope for is a diminution in their use, more careful regulation, and an attempt to use chemicals that are less toxic or less dangerous to these birds. For example, one might imagine a situation in which the use of pesticides was reduced to the point where, let us say, the productivity of the osprey or the peregrine falcon was reduced by 50%. In such a situation it would be necessary to give the most careful attention to every other means of conserving these birds in order to maintain a population.

We all know the proverb "It was the last straw that broke the camel's back." In some of these species that are subjected to all sorts of adverse influences, the populations may get along after a fashion, but then a cumulation of various things increasing their mortality in one way or another just subtly reaches a point of no return, and the populations disappear even though the situation in some cases may not have deteriorated in any obviously new manner. We have a moral responsibility to save these birds for future generations and to do so we must consider every possibility—no matter how unlikely—and pursue every means of conserving and increasing their numbers—no matter how difficult.

The Northern Peregrine Populations

Tom J. Cade

I would like to begin by saying that I second Amadon's broad use of the term ecology, and I follow Fraser Darling's estimation of ecology as encompassing all that interests ecologists. By that I would include not only biology and environment, but also where appropriate politics, sociology, philosophy, and ethics. I will confine most of my remarks to the northern situation but will draw some comparisons between the northern populations in North America and populations as we presently know them in temperate regions.

THE UBIQUITY OF THE PEREGRINE

When I first started my studies of raptors some years ago, I was working mostly at that time with Frank A. Pitelka at Berkeley; and he used to like to annoy me occasionally by stating that in his opinion the peregrine was a weed among hawks. This never really bothered me at the time; I was inclined to agree with him that the peregrine is indeed a kind of weed because, as we have heard from some previous discussions at the meeting here, it has a very wide range, it formerly, at least, was almost ubiquitous, and as the most cosmopolitan species of raptor was approached only by the osprey in its total worldwide distribution. It occurs in a wide variety of habitats, different populations being readily adapted to different kinds of nesting situations, all the way from nests flat on the ground to those a thousand feet up on a cliff, and so forth. And although not especially profiting by man's alteration of the earth—like a good weed should—the peregrine has nevertheless been highly tolerant of the close proximity of human activities in many portions of its range.

RESILIENCY OF PEREGRINE POPULATIONS

More important is a point that our British colleagues have continually stressed, and that I think is important for us to keep remembering when we look at the present sick population of peregrines in the temperate regions: It is the fact that peregrine populations have, at least historically, been resistant and resilient to a very wide range of mortality factors including, as we have heard, persistent shooting in France and during the war along the coast of Great Britain. Yet in the face of this kind of mortality, the eyries tended to be reoccupied in short order once the mortality factor was reduced. This, to me, is the main reason why it is so difficult to explain the present catastrophic crash of Temperate Zone populations on the basis of any of the more commonly experienced mortality factors that we ecologists are used to talking about when we discuss populations. The peregrine falcon is not a lemming, does not exceed its food supply, and then die off in large numbers. Ratcliffe has explained very well in one of his papers (1962; Ibis, 104:13–39) how the territorial system of the peregrine tends to keep the population reduced well below the limits that could be set by its food.

As we saw in an earlier discussion (Chapters 37–40), I think there is no known disease that could reasonably be invoked to explain such a population crash. Everything that we have heard about so far in this conference, it seems to me, argues very convincingly for the operation of some sort of—if I might say—insidious or unnatural factor or constellation of factors affecting these populations. I will not at this moment say anything more about the use of persistent pesticides. That will come up later on. Now, not only is this one of the most remarkable events in population ecology, as Hickey called to our attention in announcing this conference; to me it is also one of the most disturbing in its implications for the conservation of an aesthetically desirable species that most of us would like to keep on our continent. It is also extremely foreboding in its implication that man has already reached an unsafe limit of contamination with the products that he puts into the environment.

CRITICAL IMPORTANCE OF THE ARCTIC ENVIRONMENT

I am convinced, from what we have heard at this conference, that the peregrine falcon will be extirpated from the North American continent, at least south of the 50th parallel. I don't think that there is anything we can now do about it, even if we stopped all pesticide usage immediately, as of today. This means that we are in all likelihood going to end up with only (1) a highly migrant population of Arctic peregrines that breed in the boreal forests and tundra, pass over this country in the spring and fall, and winter in some rather vaguely defined part of tropical America, and (2) the marine coast peregrines about which Frank Beebe told us (Chapter 3).

Now I would like to emphasize a point about these surviving populations, one to which we have alluded but which has not been sufficiently stressed, in my opinion: these are wilderness populations. The future of these populations ultimately depends in my opinion on the preservation of wilderness areas. I am much less impressed than Frank Beebe is by the absence of man in the Arctic. Human population is not decreasing in the Arctic; it is increasing, although becoming more centralized in certain communities. But more important than that, it is not necessarily the resident human population in the Arctic that we need to consider as a serious factor in changes which are going on up there. White (Chapter 32) has referred to some undesirable features of oil exploration which I think should be checked on in the Arctic. One should add that the influence of the scientific investigators themselves on the Arctic slope of Alaska has in some cases had deleterious and lasting effects on the environment. I think we need to watch these things much more carefully in the Arctic than in some other areas. When Fraser Darling was in Alaska he used the expression "tender environment"; the tundra is very easily disturbed. If a lichenous tundra is overgrazed by reindeer *(Rangifer* sp.), or if it is burned by fire, it takes on the order of 50 to 75 years to recover—if it recovers—and there are apparently some cases in Alaska where it is not going to recover. Different kinds of vegetation come back, like willow scrub *(Salix* sp.*)*.

I would like to put to you that the minimum requirement for the preservation of some of these areas in our American Arctic would be the setting aside of the entire Arctic Slope of Alaska as a wilderness refuge and the restriction of any permanent human habitation north of the Brooks Range. I would also include the entire upper Yukon drainage system in this, including the Yukon Flats, which our friends in the Corps of Engineers would dearly like to make into a second Lake Erie—flooding out no one knows how many peregrine eyries that exist in the watersheds around the Yukon Flats. I feel it necessary to state this proposition as an extreme position for the effect; but wilderness preservation in the Arctic, I am convinced, requires the setting aside of very, very large tracts of land indeed. This can still be done today with a minimum of inconvenience to human populations. The whole of the Arctic Slope of Alaska could be set aside with inconvenience to probably not more than 3,000 people.

RESEARCH NEEDS ON NORTHERN PEREGRINES

As has been abundantly pointed out by our Canadian colleagues and by White (Chapter 2), most of what has gone on in the Arctic in the way of research on falcons has involved quick surveys, very superficial in their treatment, of tens or hundreds of thousands of square miles of country in which we know there are a lot of peregrines; but we do not know precisely how many there are. We need immediate surveys to find out how far north in America the present population decline is occurring, and we need to know how far north the present reproductive abnormalities in these sick populations are occurring. This sort of information can still be obtained by river surveys of the sort that most of us have made. We need to have some intensive studies done on productivity of what we hope are still normal, healthy peregrine populations in the southern part of the Arctic. And we need, as was mentioned by Aldrich, an intensive banding program primarily, I would say, to determine more about what the wintering range of the population of peregrines is, because indeed this is still very poorly understood. And I think that the needed information can be obtained probably only by banding recoveries.

This kind of ecological research would be invaluable, I believe, in providing a background of information on the still relatively undisturbed and healthy populations of peregrine falcons. With this information we can evaluate more clearly the factors that are responsible for the decline of our Temperate Zone populations.

Peregrine and Prairie Falcon Life Tables Based on Band-Recovery Data

James H. Enderson

An estimate of the annual decrement of a selected sample from the peregrine and prairie falcon populations in the United States and southern Canada can be obtained from band-recovery data. In these calculations the birds banded as nestlings and subsequently recovered are taken to represent the general populations. Bias may appear in the life tables from several sources. Many band recoveries are from shot birds, and since immatures may be more vulnerable to shooting than adults, these data tend to exaggerate the observed mortality rate of immatures because death due to other causes may not occur in the same immature-adult ratio. Another source of error is in the choice of the date taken as the beginning of the first year. If the banding date of the nestling is used as the start of the life table, there will be a tendency for the first-year mortality rate to be too low, since the first recovery may not be made until middle or late summer. If the date of the first recovery is used as the beginning of the first year in the life table, there is a tendency for the calculated rate of mortality of first-year birds to be too high because all mortality taking place in the *next* 12 months is related to that age group. A third source of bias is the loss of bands from falcons. Band loss tends to increase the apparent rate at which the younger segment of the population is recovered, since it lowers the number of older banded birds reported. This elevates the calculated mortality rate. In view of the considerable possibility of band loss in falcons, calculations of adult mortality rates from band-recovery data can be regarded at least as upper estimates of mortality. A fourth source of inaccuracy stems from using incomplete recovery information. Falcons may live to be 20 years old, and hence one can be certain that reports of such longevity will not occur until birds have been banded 20 or more years ago. If recoveries of birds banded since that time are used, they tend to increase the calculated mortality rates for the younger age groups in life tables derived by Lack's method (Lack, 1943).

It is apparent from the recovery data that some immature individuals of both species were recovered in their first summer, soon after banding, at rates not apparently distinct from rates in certain other fall and winter months (Table 45.1). In view of this, the date of banding of these nestlings may be used as the beginning of year one, with less tendency for the calculated mortality rate of this age group being biased too low.

Of the 44 recovered North American immature peregrines, 22 were reported shot; 7 of the 21 recovered as adults were shot. Of the immature prairie falcons recovered, 41 of 61 were reported shot, and 9 of 20

Table 45.1. Monthly Recoveries of Peregrine Falcons and Prairie Falcons Banded as Nestlings

Age when recovered	May	June	July	Aug.	Sept.	Oct.	Nov.	Dec.	Jan.	Feb.	March	April	May	Total
Peregrines														
Immatures	1	3	2	6	10	7	1	4	1	5	2	1	1	44
Adults	0	0	0	0	2	4	7	0	3	0	0	2	3	21
Prairie Falcons														
Immatures	0	1	5	12	5	10	6	5	4	7	1	3	0	59[a]
Adults	1	1	2	0	0	2	2	3	3	4	1	1	—	20

[a] Does not include two others reported as "recovered in fall."

adults were recovered by this means. Immatures appear to be more vulnerable to shooting.

Two sets of figures appear in the life table for each species (Tables 45.2 and 45.3). Those without parentheses are calculations based on banding and recovery-reporting periods to 1962–64. Those in parentheses are based on recoveries of birds that were banded prior to 1951 or prior to 1953. Thirteen years is the longest period between banding and recovery for either species, and life-table calculations allowing that recovery period may be considered very nearly complete.

The immature mortality rate, allowing a 13-year recovery interval, is 70% and 74% for the peregrine and prairie falcon, respectively. The average annual adult mortality rates for these birds are both 25%. These latter rates may be compared to 23% for the great horned owl, 28% for the barn owl, and 30% for the marsh hawk calculated by Hickey (1952).

If one assumes that the 25% average annual mortality rate is a good estimate of that rate for the general population, then an immature mortality in the order of 70–74% is representative of a declining population. On the assumption that these falcons do not breed until the end of their

Table 45.2. Peregrine Falcon Life Table Based on Recoveries of Birds Banded as Nestlings

Age interval[a] (years)	No. of recoveries[b]	No. alive at start of period[b]	Annual mortality rate (%)
0–1	44 (40)	65 (57)	68 (70)
1–2	6 (5)	21 (17)	27 (25) (ages 1–14)
2–3	4 (3)	15 (12)	
3–4	2 (2)	11 (9)	
4–5	2 (2)	9 (7)	
5–6	3 (2)	7 (5)	
6–7	1 (1)	4 (3)	
7–8	1 (0)	3 (2)	
8–9	0 (0)	2 (2)	
9–10	0 (0)	2 (2)	
10–11	0 (0)	2 (2)	
11–12	0 (0)	2 (2)	
12–13	1 (1)	2 (2)	
13–14	1 (1)	1 (1)	
Subtotal excluding age 0–1	21 (17)	81 (66)	27 (25)
Total	65 (57)		

[a] Date of banding taken as beginning of age interval 0–1.

[b] Numbers without parentheses are based on banding data through 1964; thus this part of the table is incomplete. Numbers in parentheses are based on falcons banded prior to 1953.

Table 45.3. Prairie Falcon Life Table Based on Recoveries of Birds Banded as Nestlings

Age interval[a] (years)	No. of recoveries[b]	No. alive at start of period[b]	Annual mortality rate (%)
0–1	61 (53)	81 (72)	75 (74)
1–2	8 (7)	20 (19)	
2–3	5 (5)	12 (12)	
3–4	3 (3)	7 (7)	
4–5	1 (1)	4 (4)	
5–6	1 (1)	3 (3)	26 (25)
6–7	1 (1)	2 (2)	
7–8	0 (0)	1 (1)	
8–9	0 (0)	1 (1)	
9–10	0 (0)	1 (1)	
10–11	0 (0)	1 (1)	
11–12	0 (0)	1 (1)	
12–13	0 (0)	1 (1)	
13–14	1 (1)	1 (1)	
Subtotal excluding age 0–1	20 (19)	55 (54)	26 (25)
Total	81 (72)		

[a] Date of banding taken as beginning of age interval 0–1.

[b] Numbers without parentheses are based on banding data through 1962; thus this part of the table is incomplete. Numbers in parentheses are based on falcons banded prior to 1951.

second year, it is possible to estimate the total number of young produced by the birds in the table. By summing the figures in the "number alive at start of period" column (Tables 45.2 and 45.3), beginning with age group 2–3, an expression of the number of adults entering each successive breeding season is obtained. Actually, these falcons start to breed in the early spring before they are 2 years old, and hence more birds may actually breed in that year than appear in age group 2–3. When one considers the data in parentheses in the two life tables, the values are 49 and 35 for the peregrine and prairie falcon, respectively, or about 25 and 18 pairs. If annual production of each species is assumed to be 1.2 young per pair, then 30 and 22 young were produced by these peregrines and prairie falcons, respectively. These figures are well below the 57 and 72 birds entering age group 0–1; the represented populations are not reproducing themselves and are declining. The likelihood that immatures are most easily recovered by shooting has probably exaggerated the band recovery and mortality of first-year birds with the result that the expected productivity of the adults will not be able to balance losses in this sample population.

On the other hand, band loss from adults produces an erroneously high rate of adult mortality in the sample and lowers the calculated adult productivity.

In summary, life tables based on North American band recoveries show a calculated immature mortality rate of 70% and an average adult mortality rate of 25% for peregrines. For prairie falcons the respective rates are 74% and 25%. These rates for both species are representative of sharply declining populations. However, these figures may be biased by several factors.

LITERATURE CITED

Hickey, J. J. 1952. Survival studies of banded birds. U.S. Dep. of Interior, Fish and Wildl. Serv., Spec. Sci. Rep.: Wildlife No. 15. 177 p.

Lack, David. 1943. The age of the blackbird. Brit. Birds, 36(9)166–175.

An Ecological Appraisal of the Peregrine Decline

F. N. Hamerstrom, Jr.

It has been suggested that we must examine *all* possible causes of the peregrine decline. This is silly. Certainly we must not limit our investigations and our thinking to pesticides alone, but I believe it is utterly impossible to examine all possibilities. I do not think anyone ever does, really; on the contrary, one has to be selective. Literally to investigate all possible aspects of a problem would be an astronomically inefficient operation. Instead, one looks at a problem and says, "Well, where can I get hold of this?" Or, most particularly, "What seem to be the really important aspects?" Other aspects that seem to have a more remote importance are set aside for later attention. Work on the peregrine problem is being done on a selective basis now, and I think properly so.

SIGNIFICANT ASPECTS OF THE PEREGRINE DECLINE

Large area involved. From an ecologist's point of view, what are the important lines of approach in this problem? What are we looking for? For one thing, there may be something involved which kills directly. Over a very large area, there has been a very great decrease in numbers. Sometimes the decrease has been 100%; reductions of 90% and 80% are not uncommon. This is drastic. There are not many killers that have operated simultaneously over such an enormous area, involving both hemispheres, in the past. This in itself should narrow the field of possibilities.

Reproductive failure. It is especially interesting that from one part of the world to another the story is the same: a decrease in production of eggs, a lowering in hatching success, and a time during which eggs seem to be either broken or eaten—but at least in some way physically destroyed. Then one of the adults disappears, the second one disappears, and the eyrie is empty. Not always, of course; the changes in some eyries have been abrupt, but it is striking that the reports of so many people are so similar. This in itself may help to identify the unknown that we are looking for because again there probably are not many things that act in this manner. Behavioral disturbances are often involved. Egg-breaking may well be a behavioral matter but, in any case, along with the decline in clutch size, hatchability, fertility, and the like, there are disturbances in overt behavior.

Involvement of other species. Another promising lead is the fact that population losses are not limited to the peregrine. Other raptors show similar declines. Disease is often more specific than this. Here is something that affects not one species or a few closely related species but a much larger group. All, however, are related to one another by a common bond in food habits: all are flesh eaters, at the top of long food-chains.

Pesticide correlation. One of the approaches now being followed is to go after such positive correlations as the foregoing, as exemplified extremely well by what is being done in Britain. Ratcliffe showed very clearly that the timing of the introduction of pesticides and their geographic distribution tie in directly with the present decline not only of peregrines but of other raptors as well in Great Britain. Both chronology and geography are pointing in the same direction. British investigators have established the presence of pesticides in the tissues of the animals with which they are concerned, and they have established that pesticides can kill these animals. This approach will be continued vigorously.

ANOMALIES IN THE POPULATION PICTURE

To try a different tack, I am struck by the anomalies in the situation. In addition to the positive approaches, it seems worth while to look at the things that *do not* seem to fit. Not with the idea that, if there are exceptions, the proposal made so far must be wrong; quite the contrary. The places that do not seem to fit offer an exceptionally fine chance to dig in and find out *why* they do not, and in this way to come closer to an understanding of the whole problem. I suspect that pesticides best fit the situation as we now see it. On the other hand, I realize that our present definition of the problem is dependent on what we already know. There may be some pieces of the puzzle that we have not found yet, that we do not even know exist, but that may perhaps lead to a different interpretation in the end. Nevertheless, to look closely at the anomalies should help to find the correct interpretation, whether it be pesticides or something else.

Differences between North America and Europe. The geographic distribution of the decline and the exceptions to it are a useful line of attack. Fyfe reports that in North America our northern peregrine population is doing well (Chapter 8). It is the southerly population which is by far in the worse situation and which Cade said we may lose. Why the difference? On the other hand, from what we know so far of Europe, the northern population is hard hit and the southern birds are in the better shape. Latitude *per se* can hardly be the answer. We need to know how peregrines are faring in Russia, but perhaps can use the peregrine figures from Finland as the only data we have at the moment that are geographically close to the USSR. The Finnish data show the most drastic decline of all, directly contrary to our experience in arctic North America.

Perhaps these hemispheric differences reflect that on this continent our more southerly breeders have wintered mainly within the United States, while the birds from farther north pass through this region to winter in Central and South America where pesticides are not yet as thoroughly in use; whereas in Europe the relationship between breeding and wintering areas is otherwise. Pesticides are lightly used or not at all in the Finnish breeding range, but many Finnish peregrines winter in France, a highly developed country which is more comparable to the United States than to the southern part of our hemisphere. There is thus suggestive evidence, worth following further, that in the geographic anomaly between the decline in Europe and North America there is support for the hypothesis that pesticides are the cause.

"Islands" of better productivity. These are intriguing. The high productivity in the Queen Charlotte Islands of British Columbia may be, as Beebe has suggested (Chapter 3), simply the direct result of an exceptionally good food supply. This would be an excellent population from which to learn how well-situated peregrines get along. What is its productivity and its general life pattern? The central Highlands of Scotland represent a geographic exception to the rest of Britain of immediate interest. To what extent do those birds move out of the highlands? It appears that they do not and so are less exposed to pesticides than many other populations are. If this is the case, it strengthens the pesticide hypothesis, but verification depends on the kind of banding Cade has suggested.

The one place in Germany where peregrines are doing best is again a wilderness or semiwilderness area. One cannot really call it wilderness. I remember being there several years ago with a friend. We got on top of a beautiful mountain, and he took a deep breath and said, "Wonderful! Wilderness! Nobody here!" There was no one else there at the moment, but one had only to look at any rock to see the scratches of hobnails that had been there before. Still, from the standpoint of peregrine nesting, it might be wilderness enough; at least, there are no farms and no farm pesticides in that mountainous region. This, however, is no guarantee for the future, for pesticides are increasingly used for the "control" of forest insects. We are already approaching the day when the wilderness may be more dangerous to birds of prey than the food-growing regions of the world: Restrictions against crop residues are less strict or do not apply at all to the products that we do not eat, such as trees and cotton.

Terrasse spoke of the fine population of peregrines breeding in Spain (Chapter 22). Why so? This again may tie in with a less thoroughly developed agriculture, or it may not. It is a place to look at, for something is happening there that is working in the direction that we want rather than the opposite.

Interspecific comparisons. Suggestive comparisons can be made with other species, for example, peregrine and osprey. Here are two species that are not much alike in many respects, but in many areas they are going the same road. Hanson pointed out that in studies of disease the search for a carrier is important, and that prey species could act as sources of infection (Chapter 29). What disease would be transmissible through prey to both the peregrine and the osprey? Simonyi said, "Ospreys don't eat pigeons." He is correct: What is a common denominator? Once again pesticides are a logical answer—not necessarily the only one, but certainly worth a look. In Finland there is a dramatic contradiction to the general trend. There the peregrine is strongly decreasing, but the osprey is increasing. What could make such a difference? Suominen showed me a sketch map demonstrating that peregrines, as they moved out of Finland on migration, flew in a generally south and westerly direction, ospreys generally in a south and easterly direction, suggesting that the two winter in different regions. This may be of extreme importance as a line of approach. In contrast, how shall we explain Postupalsky's finding that in Michigan ospreys are apparently failing even where bald eagles are doing well? An explanation of this anomaly might be very illuminating.

Again, Peterson told a gruesome story of the osprey situation in Connecticut, while Spofford reported a slight increase in the numbers of ospreys migrating south past Hawk Mountain in Pennsylvania. These birds originate farther north than Peterson's Connecticut population. Why do they differ?

Other species show anomalies that may bear on the peregrine problem. Why is the bald eagle doing so poorly along the Atlantic coast from Florida north, and by contrast so well in the Pacific Northwest and moderately well in parts of the Lake States? Even within these generalities, however, there are exceptions. Sprunt says there are two populations in Florida which, if not thriving, at least are doing much better than the others there (Chapter 29). And the bald eagle is doing far better in the interiors of the Lake States than around the shores of the Great Lakes themselves. Why? Perhaps this is a matter of greater persecution along the Great Lake shores, where they are perhaps a little more vulnerable, but that explanation will hardly account for all the differences in eagle productivity across the continent.

Schriver reported (Chapter 30) that the Cooper's hawk has almost disappeared from western Pennsylvania, and Spofford reports a major decline of this species in New York. Curiously, however, Spofford has pointed out to me that in parts of New York the goshawk is increasing as the Cooper's hawk decreases. Here are two species very closely related taxonomically and in other ways. Yet they do have differences, and in food habits the Cooper's hawk is closer to the peregrine than the goshawk is.

Finally, the tawny owl in Britain does not fit the general picture of raptors in decline there, as pointed out by Prestt (Chapter 25). Why should the tawny owl differ from the rest? Why not the tawny owl too? Here again the fact that a difference is there makes one wonder why—and questioning is a first step toward learning.

We are of necessity dealing largely with circumstantial evidence. Some controlled experiments are being set up—witness the Stickels' work. Such experiments will have to be few in number and slow in giving results. We are already short of time. The anomalies outlined above involve not only peregrines but also other species placed at the ends of long food-chains; they are characteristic not of a limited area but of two continents. I suggest that in these anomalies and others like them we have a series of natural experiments already in operation which could be exploited to give some of the answers which we need so desperately and so soon.

Hypotheses on Peregrine Population Dynamics

Howard F. Young

The purpose of my discussion is to bring out the magnitudes of change that we might expect when peregrine populations vary in their rates of mortality and productivity. In order to simplify my remarks, changes will be carried out only over 3-year periods.

DYNAMICS OF A STABLE POPULATION

Let us say that we have 100 adults, that these are going to produce some offspring that we will call the first-year birds, and that these 100 adults previously have produced offspring which are now second-year birds. In my discussion, I am having 25 of these second-year birds present. As far as I can determine, at least the bulk of the peregrine population does not breed until the end of the second year, so such birds in a given year would be added to the adult population of the next year. Put a year down here, say this is going to start in 1950, which perhaps was a crucial year. Now what about the productivity of the 100 adult birds? The productivity figures that have been given at this conference vary quite exceedingly. In most cases I am sure they are nowhere big enough for adequate replacement and population stability. I am talking now about an undisturbed peregrine population of the good old days, and I have used a figure of 2.5 young fledged per successful pair per year. This is higher than I think has recently been found in the United States. Mebs in his 1960 paper (Vogelwelt, 81:47–56) had a productivity of this sort. Herren at this conference (Chapter 20) had a productivity of 3.0 per successful pair for one group of eyries, so that this hypothetical figure of 2.5 certainly is not impossible. Then the question comes up about what percentage of the adults are successful in breeding. And this was hard to get at. What I did was to refer to Hagar's conference paper (Chapter 10) on an area where the wardens were protecting the eyries, and I included both his "good" eyries and his poorly producing eyries. From these data I computed that 47% of the adults were successful in their breeding attempts, but I did not use this figure. I stepped it up, and I am using here a figure of 60% to represent successful nests.

The selection of some of these statistics was for the purpose of establishing a uniform population, but at the same time I wanted to use calculations which had some approach to reality. Hagar's population, I am sure, was not under 24-hour protection, and it was in a relatively civilized area, so I believe that at least sometime in the past it may have had 60% success.

Now let us see what happens. We have 100 adults with an assumed even sex ratio here. This would give us 50 pairs; with 60% of these successful, we have 30 pairs, each producing 2.5 young. This would yield 75 fledglings.

The next question involves mortality. Here the figures are probably weakest of all. Again referring to Mebs's paper: he had an estimate of 80% first-year mortality, but he did his computations, as far as I can figure, on the basis of all successful pairs. He also estimates 20% adult mortality. I have accepted this second figure. Where I use the 20% adult mortality rate, this would involve the second-year birds too—in other words, mortality other than that of the new fledglings. Then, if the first-year mortality is set at 66.7% for birds that have fledged (a figure that possibly is low), a uniform population results. We have in 1950 a total of 200 birds. Now these second-year birds can be added to the breeding population next year. By including the 1950 adults, we have 125 birds; but only 80% of them survive to the next year, and that comes out at 100 adults again. One-third of these 75 fledglings will survive to become the second-year birds of 1951, and the 1951 adults will produce 75 more young, so you go back to your 200 population (Table 45.4). Well, we can go through 1952 and keep on going. If we accept any of this, we will wind up with the same population all the time. Now I am not maintaining that this is the breeding biology of the peregrine. What I am trying to do is to establish a base and then say: What if something happened to this population? What would be the results? If we do use these figures here, I feel that, according to the paper by the Herberts (Auk, 82:62–94) and from my discussion recently with M. W. Nelson, an extreme life span in the wild of 20 years would be reasonable. On this basis, starting with a cohort of 100 fledglings and the mortality rates as indicated here, the population would be reduced to about 0.4% at the end of 20 years. That fits the pattern fairly well, I think.

Regardless now of the factors that are involved, whether human disturbance, pesticides, shooting, or disease, these various factors of environmental deterioration could affect a population like this in a variety of ways. One way might be to increase the mortality, another one might be

Table 45.4. Hypothetical Stable Peregrine Population

Assumptions

(a) Longevity—20 years in the wild (Herbert & Herbert, 1965 Auk)

(b) Yearling mortality—66⅔% per year

(c) Adult mortality—20% per year

(d) Nesting success—60%

50 pairs × 0.60 successful = 30 pairs × 2.5 young per pair = 75 first-year birds

(e) Productivity—2.5 fledglings per successful pair per year (Mebs, 1960 Die Vogelwelt, 82:47–56)

Population Structure

Year	Adults	1st year	2nd year	Total population
1950	100	75	25	200
1951	100	75	25	200

Population Characteristics

(a) Turnover period—0.4% of population remaining at end of 20 years.

(b) Average age at death—2.8 years; of those surviving 1st year—4.6 years; senility probably not a factor (Hall's record of 18-year-old female producing young).

to decrease the productivity of the successful pairs, or another one might be to reduce the number of nesting attempts which were successful. What I want to do now is to examine these three different things and see what results.

EFFECT OF INCREASED MORTALITY RATE

First of all, let us take increased mortality. I have used an increase of 10% in each case to keep things comparable. If we increase the adult mortality by 10%, we now have a 22% adult mortality, and in the first-year birds, 73%. I have done some rounding, I might say, on these. I have rounded off some of the birds too. (If I had 23.4 birds ready to come back, I did not figure that the 0.4 of a bird would migrate!) In Table 45.5 we start with the same population as in Table 45.4. Now we are going to say something has happened so that a 10% increase in mortality occurs. So, if we take these 100 adults and 25 second-year birds, and show a 78% survival, we have 98 adults returning in 1951. These 75 first-year birds, surviving at 27%, will produce 20 second-year birds. The 98 adults of 1951 (49 pairs), 60% of which will be successful, would produce 72 birds, and our population would total 190, which is 95% of the original population. A 10% increase in mortality causes a 5% drop in the population in this one-year period. Going on to 1952, one may follow the same pattern. At the end of 3 years the total population would be 88% of its original size. Since we had 50 breeding pairs, there would have been 50 eyries occupied in 1950; 3 years later we would have 87 adults present, and this divided by two gives us 43, with one bird left over. This would mean six eyries deserted and maybe a single bird occupying an eyrie, which seems to fit the pattern of some of the observations made over a period of time and reported at this conference: certain eyries are not occupied, or in some cases are occupied by only single birds.

Table 45.5. Hypothetical Population with Mortality Increased by 10% to 22% for Adults and 73% for Yearlings; Other Factors as in Table 45.4

Year	Adults	1st year	2nd year	Total population	
				No.	%
1950	100	75	25	200	100
1951	98	72	20	190	95
1952	92	69	19	180	90
1953	87	65	19	176	88[a]

[a] Of 50 eyries originally occupied, 6 deserted, 1 single bird (1953).

In their report on Wisconsin, Berger and Mueller (Chapter 9) mention situations such as parks being built and roads being cut near eyries, but they believe that the decreased peregrine population certainly was not due to a lack of suitable eyries. If we had the birds here, these eyries or nearby cliffs would be occupied. The progressive decrease of occupied eyries, I think, is not due primarily to deterioration of the nesting site, but rather to the loss of the birds. The 10% increase in mortality over a 3-year period results in approximately a 12% drop in total population.

DECLINE IN PRODUCTIVITY

Now let us go back to the original mortality rate, and assume that whatever environmental factor or factors were involved did not act through mortality, but instead reduced productivity by 10%.

Here we refer to Table 45.6, and we have 2.3 young per pair instead of 2.5 young per pair. You would have mortality as in Table 45.4 but because of the reduced productivity the adults would produce only 69 young. Note that in 1953 there is 94% of the original population, including 98 adults. If a male and a female were lost, you may have only one deserted eyrie in this case, or you may have two eyries with single birds on them. A 10% decrease in productivity results in only a 6% decrease in population, about half the loss that the direct mortality caused, so in comparing those two it would appear that the direct mortality would be a more important factor.

DECLINE IN NESTING SUCCESS

Now let us say that the pesticides or disease or disturbance, whatever it was, did not affect the productivity of successful nests, nor affect the mortality, but instead increased the number of unsuccessful breeding at-

Table 45.6. Hypothetical Population with Productivity of Successful Nests Decreased by 10% to 2.3 Young per Pair per Year; Other Factors as in Table 45.4

				Total population	
Year	Adults	1st year	2nd year	No.	%
1950	100	75	25	200	100
1951	100	69	25	194	97
1952	100	69	23	192	96
1953	98	67	23	188	94[a]

[a] In 1953 there would be one deserted eyrie, or two eyries occupied by single birds.

tempts. Table 45.4 assumed a 40% failure in nesting attempts. If I increase this by 10%, it gives me 44% failure, and 56% success. Table 45.7 shows the results. In 1953, you wind up with 98 adults, 189 total population, 94.5% of the original. This is exceedingly similar to Table 45.6, and again there would probably only be 1 deserted eyrie.

CONCLUSIONS

It would appear to me that in a bird like the peregrine, mortality would be the most important of the effects compared here. And I think this is related to the fact that some of the population consists of the nonbreeding subadults. If one turns to a bird like the bald eagle, which may not mature until the fifth or sixth year, and makes similar computations, one finds an even more striking difference between the effects. Mortality seems to take the eagle down in comparison at a faster rate; it is more important in the eagle than, say, sterility, for example. If one turns to a short-lived bird like the robin which breeds at 1 year of age and is a more rapid breeder, then you find that sterility will decrease the population faster than mortality. Certainly it is possible that a pesticide or some other environmental disturbance could affect more than one of these things simultaneously. So in Table 45.8, combining a 10% reduction in productivity of successful nests with a 10% increase in nest loss, you wind up here with 180 birds, 90% of your original population, and this is interesting, 97 adults. This again would mean that there might be a deserted eyrie and a single bird, or perhaps 3 single birds. Recall that mortality of the same magnitude by itself would reduce the population to 88% of the original. Finally, to put this in the worst possible situation we may increase mortality by 10% also, as shown in Table 45.9. In a 3-year period ending in 1953, we wind up with 156 birds, 78% of our original population, and 85 adults. So we are short 15 birds, that would be 7 pairs, 7 deserted eyries, and a single bird. It seems to me that we are here ap-

Table 45.7. **Hypothetical Population with 10% Increase in Nest Losses (Nesting Success = 56%); Other Factors as in Table 45.4**

Year	Adults	1st year	2nd year	Total population No.	Total population %
1950	100	75	25	200	100.0
1951	100	70	25	195	97.5
1952	100	70	23	193	96.5
1953	98	68	23	189	94.5[a]

[a] In 1953 there would be one deserted eyrie, or two eyries occupied by single birds.

Table 45.8. Hypothetical Population with 56% of Pairs Successful, Producing 2.3 Young per Successful Pair per Year; Combination of Tables 45.6 and 45.7

Year	Adults	1st year	2nd year	Total population	
				No.	%
1950	100	75	25	200	100.0
1951	100	64	25	189	94.5
1952	100	64	21	185	92.5
1953	97	62	21	180	90.0[a]

[a] In 1953 there would be one deserted eyrie, and one occupied by a single bird, or three eyries occupied by single birds.

Table 45.9. Hypothetical Population with Adult Mortality 22%, Yearling Mortality 73%, 56% of Pairs Successful, Producing 2.3 Young per Successful Pair per Year; Combination of Tables 45.5, 45.6, 45.7

Year	Adults	1st year	2nd year	Total population	
				No.	%
1950	100	75	25	200	100
1951	98	62	20	180	90
1952	92	61	17	170	85
1953	85	55	16	156	78[a]

[a] In 1953 there would probably be 7 deserted eyries, plus 1 occupied by a single bird.

proaching the magnitude of loss which has been reported in some places in the United States. One of the things that was interesting to me was that 10% is not a particularly spectacular figure, but with a bird of the breeding biology somewhat of this nature, it is conceivable that a relatively moderate change in the environment could bring about very decided changes in the population.

The Significance of the Decline

Gustav A. Swanson

At the expense of a little recapitulation I will try rather briefly to bring out two or three points that have particularly impressed me during this conference.

THE ADAPTABILITY OF THE PEREGRINE FALCON

One of the things that has impressed me again and again during the discussion is that, before the recent decline, the peregrine falcon certainly was considered a successful species—not one which, like some of our endangered or recently extinct species, was in any serious danger. If you think of such species as the passenger pigeon, the whooping crane, and the California condor, I think you will see what I mean. All of these species had inherent characteristics that made them particularly vulnerable. The whooping crane even in Catesby's time was a rare species. The passenger pigeon, though extremely abundant, had a mass psychology, nesting in tremendous quantities in very limited areas that made it particularly vulnerable to man and his market hunting. At least in our time, the California condor has had a very limited population in a very limited area, and the peregrine does not fall into any of these categories at all. Until recently we would not have considered that it was in any danger. It is a highly adaptable species and a species that taxonomists have recognized by dividing up into quite a number of different recognizable races. It is a species that we have heard nests successfully in a large variety of places. All of us from this side of the Atlantic were astonished to learn of the bog situation in Finland where so many of these birds were nesting. In that same connection, it seems to me we have heard some possible misinterpretations presented. It does not seem to me very likely that there is the clear-cut boundary between the tree-nesting and the cliff-nesting birds that our friends from East Germany seem to feel so sure about. The birds clearly have wide adaptability and, if we think merely of tradition instead of genetic influences, I think we can easily explain these differences in nesting-site selection.

RESISTANCE AND BREEDING POTENTIAL

The peregrine falcon, then, has been until recently a very successful and very persistent species. It has, however, had a rather low rate of reproduction so that it cannot be looked upon as in the category of a species that could genetically develop a resistance to something widespread, such as disease or pesticides, as we have found in some of the invertebrates that have an extremely high rate of reproduction. So these are a couple of points that I think fortify Ratcliffe's very clear conference statement that we are dealing here with an unprecedented decline in recent times. Our data are not very good; they are not equally good all over the world, but it is clear that we have an unprecedented decline in the last 20 or 25 years, and to explain that we do need an unprecedented change because we are dealing with a species that has been very successful. I would plead, however, for an open mind and a recognition of the fact that many, many different factors have been shown during the conference to have caused mortality and population reduction, and that we would be on much safer ground if we were thinking of one factor superimposed upon another, rather than trying to explain everything in terms of just one.

BAND-RECOVERY RATES

One of the statistics, which impressed me and which was mentioned only once as I recall, was the one from Finland where 22% of the banded birds were recovered, mostly from France and presumably mostly as a result of shooting. This is a very high percentage of recoveries, if we assume that this is an absolute minimum and that there are many of these banded birds that have been killed or found dead by people who have not reported the recovery. This we have certainly found in the case of our waterfowl banded and then shot here in North America.

SUPERIMPOSED FACTORS

In support of the idea that we should look for factors superimposed on factors, I should like to call attention again to Nelson's very intriguing statistics on precipitation changes. The thought that there could be a precipitation change from 15.4 inches (39.1 cm) down to 7.2 inches (18.3 cm) of rainfall in a wide area occupied by our peregrines, was a surprising one to me. This, combined with an increase in temperature, must have had its influence. The fact that this decline in precipitation was very clearly reflected in a reduction in the area of lakes in the vicinity by itself must have had a very definite effect on peregrines. But then he showed also that eyries that were perfectly suitable under normal conditions of sunshine and nebulosity would become unsuitable because the birds would be so much more exposed when you had a higher degree of clear, hot weather. This, it seems to me, is an example. Clearly it was reflected over a long period of time. It is not the catastrophic kind of thing we are looking at here. But the aggregate effect of these many different factors needs to be considered very carefully.

CHAPTER 46

GENERAL DISCUSSION: POPULATION BIOLOGY AND SIGNIFICANCE OF TRENDS

Biology of the Peregrine and Other Raptors

PIGEONS, PIGEON FANCIERS, AND PEREGRINES

MEBS: Pigeons are distributed throughout the whole of Germany. At the time when the female peregrine is incubating her eggs, the male claims blackbirds and other native species as its prey. When both sexes are hunting, they take mostly pigeons.

HICKEY: Kesteloot (1964) in the report of the Caen Conference on Birds of Prey and Owls has estimated that about 50% of the world's pigeon fanciers are located in Belgium and Germany, the number in Belgium being 165,000, which is 8% of the human male population of that country. This concentration of the people with the same hobby has its fringe element which is absolutely fanatical in its persecution of the peregrine.

BEEBE: It does seem to me that this very group of people may be providing peregrine falcons with an important source of food in that region. They may hate them, but they are feeding them.

MEBS: Yes, they have done so over the years, but now they have turned the tables.

BERGER: It does not follow, however, that, if the pigeons were absent in this region, the peregrine would be absent too.

CLEMENT: I would like to ask Mebs whether or not he feels that there has been an increase in the fanaticism of the pigeon fanciers in these last

10 years to account for this rapid decline. Now pigeon fancying has been active in western Europe for some 50 or more years. I am puzzled that we should have this post-1950 peregrine decline partly ascribable to pigeon fanciers and to rock climbers. I am aware that rock climbing has perhaps increased a great deal since World War II.

MEBS: The pigeon fanciers became very active about 1950. In the last 15 years in Germany they have had more time and more money to spend on their hobby.

PETERSON: It is going to be the wobbly pigeon that has eaten seed dressing that is the easiest for the peregrine to catch. In effect, this represents a kind of natural selection, now the unnatural selection in the case of peregrines. They are selected in and selected out. But they belong in the food-chain of peregrines.

BEEBE: Has there been any research done on the tolerance of the domestic pigeon to pesticides? Does it have an extremely high tolerance? From the great use of pigeons by these peregrines in every country reported so far at this conference, it seems to me that the pigeon requires study as the potential carrier of these persisting chemicals to the peregrine.

RATCLIFFE: It is true that, in a lot of the areas where the peregrine is most affected, the pigeon is the principal prey; but I do not think one should place too much emphasis on the significance of the species. I think that, whatever the food spectrum happened to be in the contaminated area, falcons would get pesticides just as much from other species. It is because the whole prey population is contaminated that the amounts, and therefore the effects on peregrines, reflect this level of contamination.

BEEBE: Is the whole spectrum contaminated, or are you only assuming that?

RATCLIFFE: No, the whole prey population. We have data for over 50 different species that are preyed upon by peregrines at times.

MRS. HERBERT: I should like to ask Dr. Ratcliffe how carefully fed racing pigeons would come into contact with pesticides?

RATCLIFFE: They often stop during a race and feed on the farmland. A large number also do not return to their lofts but go wild. And they may then go on, or they may just live at large in the countryside. The peregrine is therefore feeding both on birds being raised and on ones that are feral.

MRS. HERBERT: In some of our cities, there are a number of racing pigeons flying about, and they usually get back to their lofts unless they are taken by the peregrines. Today there are not enough peregrines to take them. I do not see how they would come in contact with pesticides. They don't go out into the country.

RATCLIFFE: The grain that their owners feed to them may also be contaminated. I think it frequently is to some degree, but we don't know how much.

MUELLER: In Europe, there are also pigeons that are not being raised, that are not being fed and fostered by pigeon fanciers: wood pigeons, stock doves, turtle doves, collared doves, and the wild rock doves. It seems to me that these form a variable proportion of the food of the peregrine. In other words the pigeon fanciers are not supplying Europe with peregrines. There are other pigeons which are also supplying food to these falcons.

BOTULISM AND SALT SECRETION

CADE: I was interested to hear that botulism has been reported in some hawks. That reminded me of the recent study by Cooch, reported in The Auk (1964; 81:380–393), on the relationship between avian botulism and nasal salt secretion in waterfowl and some shorebirds which live around alkaline waters in western and central North America. He first of all demonstrated that a number of these birds associated with alkaline waters do indeed have functional salt-secreting glands as do marine birds. He further brought forth some evidence, not completely convincing but at least highly suggestive, that the botulism toxin in sublethal titers interferes with the functioning of the nasal glands. Conceivably, some birds sick with "duck disease" could die from osmotic stress resulting from malfunction of their nasal glands and thus indirectly as a result of a level of the toxin which is usually considered sublethal.

Now, let me just add a further detail to bring this story back to the hawks. We have recently discovered in our laboratory at Syracuse that quite a number of falconiforms, including the peregrine, have functional salt-secreting glands (Cade and Greenwald, 1966; Condor, 68:338–350). Except for the aegypine vultures and the bateleur, falconiforms produce the secretion in rather small volumes; but it is just as concentrated in NaCl as in many of the marine birds, around 500 to 600 millimoles per liter. It appears that nasal salt secretion is a functional feature of falconiform organization, because the urine of hawks is typically hypotonic or isotonic to their blood for NaCl. So they need an extrarenal mechanism for excreting the salt acquired in their carnivorous diet. Now, whether or not one can tie botulism in with salt gland secretion as one cause of mortality in hawks, I do not know; but I point this out as an interesting possibility that could be explored further. The discovery of functional nasal glands in the falconiforms is a good example of how little is really known about the biology of hawks, and our lack of intimate knowledge is, in my opinion, the best reason for hoping we can keep some of them around for future generations to study.

RAPTOR POPULATION MODELS

MUELLER: One practical difficulty in drawing up population models for raptors is that most of the field data, on which these models must currently rest, are not sufficiently extensive.

ENDERSON: Another problem is that, under natural circumstances, raptor mortality and reproduction do not remain constant over a period of years.

YOUNG: This is especially true where density-dependent factors affect such populations. My impression now is that perhaps direct mortality in the case of the peregrine has been more important than interference with reproduction.

GLADING: Young's first table with its fairly small loss of adults certainly fits the picture of California condors, as deduced by Miller and the McMillans in their 1966 status report on this species (National Audubon Society Research Report No. 6). Their particular population has a production that is fairly normal; its decline is due to a small but regular loss of adults. If I were to attempt a mathematical model of our present peregrine populations, I would take the nesting success figures and apply a 90% reduction to them. I think we could then rapidly come up with the types of population losses that have been demonstrated at this conference.

AMADON: Regardless of the detailed accuracy of Young's models, I think the most impressive thing is that they do show that relatively modest changes in mortality and reproduction can have a cumulative effect.

PEREGRINES AND MAMMALIAN GROUND PREDATORS IN FINLAND

SUOMINEN: The fact that so many Finnish peregrines nest on the ground raises some questions about changing numbers of predators that might affect this segment of the peregrine population. Today, we have more foxes in Finland than, say, 20 years ago. But there are no observations of foxes destroying peregrine nests. If one can judge from the behavior of dogs feeding up close to peregrine nests, I do not think that foxes are probably significant in peregrine ecology.

Two new predators have been introduced in Finland. One of these is the mink *(Mustela vison)*, but it is common only on the seashore. The other species is the raccoon dog *(Nyctereutes procyonides)*, which was introduced in the USSR near Finnish waters. It does not feed on birds, and it is not common. Some single animals are seen in widely scattered places in Finland. Perhaps one should repeat that the enormous decline of peregrine falcons in Fennoscandia has involved not only ground-nesting birds but tree-nesting and cliff-nesting populations as well.

REPRODUCTIVE POTENTIAL OF THE SPARROW-HAWK

PRESTT: We have in Britain the remarkable coincidence of two bird-feeding birds of prey involved in this tremendous population crash at almost the same time. The breeding biology of these two is not the same. Whereas it is probably true to say for the peregrine that it has a relatively low productive rate, I do not think this could be said for the sparrow-hawk. The normal clutch of the sparrow-hawk in Britain is considered to be four to six eggs. They can breed in their first year. I believe that the second-year breeders represent the more normal circumstance, but undoubtedly 1-year-old birds have been found successfully breeding at their nests. Hence I think we could classify this as a relatively rapidly breeding bird. I would also remind you again that the sparrow-hawk was extremely common. It could be said of many counties in England that the English countryside has a lot of fields and lots of small woods. Almost every wood in these areas—before this decline—would carry a pair of sparrow-hawks. And the kill must have been enormous in a very short space of time. You will remember that I reported what still appeared to be a successful breeding population of sparrow-hawks in Hampshire. Now this is in an area we call the New Forest; it is an area completely isolated from agriculture—its woods are separated by heathland, and it has many peculiarities. For example, it has a population of the common buzzard, and this was one of the few populations of the buzzard in Britain that was not indirectly affected by the spread of myxomatosis—probably because the buzzards in the New Forest fed on squirrels and jackdaws in contrast to the rabbit-feeding habit of most of the buzzards in the rest of the country. Hence this population wasn't affected when myxomatosis wiped out the rabbits. I think we could say that 100 sq miles (259 sq km) represent the area of the forest which is completely free from any pesticide effect.

It is interesting that, while within this area the sparrow-hawk population is still apparently normal in numbers, the sparrow-hawk is now extirpated on agricultural areas abutting the forest all around. In one of my study areas eight dead sparrow-hawks were found at one time. This was unfortunately about a year before I started my work, and the Forestry Commission did not attempt to have these birds analyzed for toxic chemicals.

I think it is important to reflect on the different biology of these two species, and yet the same final population effect has been produced.

GOLDEN EAGLES IN THE UNITED STATES

SPOFFORD: I don't see any real problem, at least from the pesticide point of view, involving the golden eagle in much of North America, because the food-chain of this species is so short in our western country. Here in the east in the Appalachian Mountains, where we have just a small handful of golden eagles, the food-chain of these Appalachian birds is much longer. The golden eagle in Maine, for instance, will eat barred owls, red-tailed hawks, broad-winged hawks, and such things as that. It will also eat great blue herons and American bitterns—bitterns, in fact, by the dozen. The pair of eagles at one eastern nest, which contained one young in 1957, is still building or rebuilding a nest every year, but as far as I can tell has not laid an egg since 1957. One other eastern pair succeeds in producing about one young every 3 years.

LONG-TERM POPULATION TRENDS IN RAPTORS

PRESTT: Population changes in raptors occurred, of course, long before modern pesticides were ever thought of. This has been well brought out for the buzzard in the British Isles by Moore (1957; Brit. Birds, 50:173–197). In 1800, this species was a common breeding bird throughout Britain. By 1865, a serious decline had taken place. By 1900, the buzzard was confined to the western part of Scotland, England, and Wales. By 1954, its distribution had extended somewhat farther east, and its total population in the British Isles was estimated to lie between 20,000 and 30,000 birds. Moore showed that these changes were closely correlated with the fortunes of "game-preservation" in both time and space. At the moment, we do not think that the buzzard has been seriously affected by toxic chemicals. So, while I am sure we are right to be concerned about these compounds, it does not do, I think, to allow them to dominate the problems of conservation completely.

Another species that historically declined in Britain is the red kite. In the fifteenth century this was an abundant species, even in the streets of London. By 1900, two pairs were known in the central region of Wales, and there were possibly a few other pairs at that time. With protection this population reached 6 pairs in 1948 and in 1950 9 pairs, with 8 young produced. By 1965, these had grown to 14.

RATCLIFFE: There has also been a long-term decline in the merlin population in Great Britain, dating back quite probably prior to the onset of the organochlorine period; and we are not sure about the causes.

PRESTT: We have analyzed only one death of a wild merlin, and it had moderate amounts of all the persisting organochlorines.

Significance of Conference Data

THE CONTAMINATION OF FOOD-CHAINS

PETERSON: If we are to assume the economical hypothesis that widespread residual poisons, whether they be chlorinated hydrocarbons or others, are involved, and that the effects would show up most critically in birds of long food-chains, we could predict (1) what species would be most likely to be in trouble; and (2) what portions of their populations would be in trouble. Almost everything I have heard here during this meeting has justified that assumption, including the anomalies that were so masterfully presented by Hamerstrom (Chapter 45).

In short, the most likely food-chains to be contaminated and to affect the top predators would be chains involving birds and fishes. In other words, the bird-eating birds and fish-eating birds would be most vulnerable. Mammal-eating birds of prey would be less affected, but I would say that even in this category there would be some that might be involved. For example, a bird of prey that ate shrews would, for obvious reasons, be in more trouble than one that ate *Microtus:* the shrew being an insect eater, *Microtus* a vegetable eater.

Now, if this effect is possible to predict, why not go down the list of birds of prey?

In doing so I'll try to discuss further some of the anomalies that Hamerstrom has brought up. First, I will point out that our discussions here have shown the danger of taking a provincial stand. If there is some factor affecting our local birds, it is tempting to apply it to populations throughout the whole range of the species. Actually, quite different factors may be operating against certain birds of prey locally. But there is one thing that seems to cut straight across almost on a world basis, and this is the pattern of pesticide use and the way pesticides get into the ecosystems.

OSPREYS AND BALD EAGLES

It was brought out that in Finland the ospreys are doing well. I must say I have visited osprey nests in Finland—when I speak about them I am not just imagining conditions. I have been there. And what kind of lakes do they live in? They are in lakes that are not in any great river system where the magnification effect of pesticides can build up. Their ecosystems involve pure water.

But on the Connecticut River, as I have reported, it is a very different story. Actually there is relatively little spraying at the mouth of the river, but there are many cities upriver. The river goes through Massachusetts, Connecticut, New Hampshire, and Vermont, and we get the greatest magnification effect in the estuary at the end of the river system where the ospreys live. Our Connecticut ospreys are on the way out.

On the other hand, ospreys are doing well in the southern tip of Florida. Recently Frederick K. Truslow came up from Florida to show me a large number of beautiful osprey transparencies that he took in Florida Bay and the Everglades National Park. Even the park biologist there, W. B. Robertson, until recently had a hard time believing that things could be so bad for this species elsewhere, because he noted that ospreys were still raising their three young successfully each year in his region. It is tempting to dismiss a phenomenon when it is not occurring in one's own bailiwick. But all we have to do is to look at the setup in southern Florida. There is no draining of poisons into the lower Everglades as yet. And the bald eagle is doing well there too. I can also see why the bald eagles in the outer fringe of the Everglades and on Florida's Kissimmee Prairie are doing well, being where they are. On the other hand, the ones along the west coast of Florida (Tampa Bay, etc.) are in trouble. This is all very logical in view of the way the chemicals travel.

GOLDEN EAGLES

Look at that terrific pounding this bird has been given by aerial gunners in western Texas. It must be a drastic drain on the wintering population and yet, so far as we can learn, reproduction is good in Montana and elsewhere where the species nests. The golden eagle is standing up well under persecution. Here I would like to point out that the golden eagle is a mammal eater. It is not a fish eater, and therefore we would not expect it to be in as serious trouble as the bald eagle. But in Scotland a most extraordinary thing has happened since 1960. Nests that had been producing normally suddenly went into a sharp decline. When I visited Scotland a year ago, I climbed to two golden eagle nests. One was empty, and in the other the eggs had failed to hatch. This was puzzling until it was explained to me that these highland birds were apparently getting dieldrin from sheep carcasses. The sheep get the dieldrin in sheep dips. These Scottish birds are, in part, carrion eaters and thus, even in what we call a relatively undisturbed area, they are not immune from the products of the pesticides industry.

On the whole, in North America, I would expect the golden eagle to survive the pesticide syndrome better than the bald eagle.

ACCIPITERS

Earlier at this conference I briefly discussed the interesting anomaly regarding this group. These birds we would expect to be very seriously affected. This I predicted several years ago, and it is showing up unmistakably in the population trends for the Hawk Mountain area observed by Maurice Broun and reported by W. R. Spofford at this conference (Chapter 27). However, there is danger in comparing data from Hawk Mountain too literally from one year to the next: in fact, at any migration point, the number of birds you are going to see in any single year is quite fortuitous. The number depends on wind direction and how it focuses the migrants against certain land contours. If you do not have a northwest wind during the week of the broad-winged hawk flight in September, you do not see as many broadwings, etc. But we certainly can take 5-year blocks of data and come up with something indicative, as Spofford has done. Broun has given us more than 30 years of matchless migration data that now disclose some significant population trends. The Cooper's hawk is now down to less than 10% of its former numbers. If we go back to the earlier figures, 700 or more were reported each year; the tally is now on the order of less than 100. The same trend is reflected at Cape May, New Jersey. The Cooper's hawk has become a rare bird along the seaboard. It is a pleasure to go to the far west and still see Cooper's hawks with some frequency. In the east I now see them rarely.

The sharp-shinned hawk, a smaller bird eater, I would also expect to be in trouble, and the graphs show that it is.

People ask why our third accipiter, the big goshawk, is not in trouble. Here again, the answer is in the basic food. This species is not a bird eater, except for grouse, which in turn are bud eaters; in North America the goshawk feeds principally on snowshoe hares (*Lepus americanus*). It exhibits a cyclic population phenomenon that is pretty much tied in with snowshoe hares and, so far as we can see, the goshawk is not affected by food-chain contamination. Cooper's and sharp-shinned hawks are.

HARRIERS

The marsh hawk is one we should watch. It is a borderline species, using some bird food and some small mammals. But we must watch this species. We have recently lost the marsh hawk as a breeding species in our Connecticut River area. But we did not really have enough of a population to represent a significant sample. We had only two pairs. Bitterns are gone, fish eaters too. Night herons are almost gone.

Leslie H. Brown, formerly the Chief Agricultural Commissioner in Kenya, told me that he has noticed a marked drop in migrating harriers in East Africa. They also have a resident harrier in Kenya, but the ones that migrate down from the heavily farmed agricultural areas in the Ukraine and Russia are noticeably scarce.

CADE: That is also true in South Africa.

BUTEOS

PETERSON: I would not expect the buteos to suffer as much from food-chain poisoning. Basically, they are eaters of small animals. The red-shouldered hawk is the one to watch. In New England it has dropped precipitously in numbers. But there is an indication at Hawk Mountain that there are still fair numbers of red-shoulders coming through.

The bird of prey that I would expect to have the least complicated, most successful life today is the broad-winged hawk. This bird has four things in its favor: (1) it does not eat birds; pesticides do not, so far as I know, get into its food-chain; (2) there is more good habitat for the broad-wing in the northeastern United States than existed 50 years ago because it is a bird of second-growth woodland. Connecticut, for example, now has about 70% of its area in woodland. Fifty years ago woodland was less than 30%. This same shift in land-use pattern has also taken place in much of New York State. Poor land, marginal for agriculture, has gone back to forest and is now available for more broad-wings. (3) The broad-wing migrates in a "mob" about 15 September. The whole population gathers together and moves down the Appalachian ridges before anyone has taken a shotgun into the woods. Even the habit of travelling in a group helps this species because a gunner on the ridge could pick off, say, one lone red-tail after another; but, if he shot one broad-wing, the others of the flock would tower out of reach. This is in its favor. At any rate, the species makes a quick journey out of Canada and the United States. (4) There may also be less competition on the wintering grounds. This was brought home to me in Colombia recently. Today, I am told, half of all the birds of prey that one sees in winter in that Andean country are broad-wings. I spent a week trying in vain to see some of the endemic raptors which live there in forests that are now almost gone. The broad-wing can fill a niche that has been vacated by some of the endemics as a result of the destruction of the primeval forest.

Thus, the broad-wing is the one raptorial bird in the New World that seems to have everything in its favor, and the migration figures show it. The population indices include not only the one at Hawk Mountain but also another on the North Shore of Lake Ontario. It is the one species that I do not worry about.

HAGAR: Yes, I think that is true. It does not seem to be vulnerable the way the others are.

PETERSON: The rough-legged hawk I would not expect to be vulnerable to the chain effects of insecticides because it is largely a mouse eater. It is an Arctic-breeding species and probably quite cyclic. We do have years of periodic population depression, but then we get a good year and a lot of rough-legs.

The red-tailed hawk, a mammal eater, I would not expect to be seriously affected.

OTHER SPECIES

The peregrine is, of course, the bird that we are most concerned with at this conference. I am not going to go into all the anomalies concerning the peregrine that we have touched on at this conference. Many have already been discussed; but I might say that the anomaly of a good population of peregrines in Spain is interesting because there is also a relatively large population there of the European white stork. Conversely, the last white stork to nest in Sweden did so in 1952; the last white stork in Switzerland, about 1950. Of course these were marginal populations anyway. Actually, the stork decline had started before the widespread use of modern pesticides. The decline has continued and, in some countries such as Holland and Denmark, it has accelerated. But my last information on the population in Spain was an estimated 14,000 nesting pairs. This too may change because Spain is now becoming more affluent.

POSTUPALSKY: I have a comment on bald eagles in the Lake Michigan area, prompted by a remark by Keith. Back in 1941, the Michigan Department of Conservation attempted an eagle survey, during which a number of nests were located in Michigan's Lower Peninsula. Looking over these reports, as well as contemporary records from other sources, I noted that the greater number of active nests at that time was in the western part. In contrast, active nests remaining in Lower Michigan today are distributed in just the opposite fashion. The majority, namely about three-fourths, are found in the east. Very few nesting eagles are left in the western half today, and in the Grand Traverse area in the northwest—a former stronghold—none are left whatsoever. Let me remind you that western Lower Michigan is noted for its fruit-growing industry, which relies heavily on pesticides. In 1965, I knew of only one pair of bald eagles nesting on the shores of Lake Michigan, while in 1961 there were still about eight pairs. Ten years ago there were about 20. The species has disappeared completely as a breeding bird from the Beaver Island group in northern Lake Michigan. The region I speak of here is the same general area where high pesticide residues have been found in herring gulls; and bald eagles do take gulls on occasion. These gulls have been shown to contain residues of DDT compounds averaging close to 100 ppm (wet weight) in breast muscles and as high as 2,400 ppm in body fat. It should not take too many such gulls to poison an eagle. Dosage experiments conducted by the United States Fish and Wildlife Service have shown that the bald eagle can be killed by food containing as little as 83 ppm (dry weight) of DDT (Stickel *et al.*, 1966, Trans. No. Amer. Wildl. and Natur. Resources Conf., 31:190–204). This level is lower than the contamination—if you'll pardon the word—now present in the wild herring gull population in northern Lake Michigan.

BEEBE: I am going to say this rather seriously. As a Canadian, I take serious objection to the spread of these poisons which are originated and manufactured in the United States and are being spread across the length and breadth of this continent to the degree that they are. It has been shown to the satisfaction of everyone here, and I think a big broad percentage of the public too, that they are detrimental to the health of not just the peregrine falcon but many other species of animals as well. On the basis of what has been done in Britain, aldrin, dieldrin, and heptachlor should not be "phased out"; their use should be stopped.

CHLORINATED HYDROCARBONS AND ANIMAL BEHAVIOR

W. H. STICKEL: If you ask about the possibility of avian behavior being affected in subtle, injurious ways by pesticides, I must say that this is entirely probable. The chlorinated hydrocarbons are believed to kill by their action on the nervous system; nonlethal amounts may well have other effects on the nervous system. Certainly many birds have sublethal amounts in their brains. Finally, it has been demonstrated by Ogilvie and Anderson (1965, J. Fisheries Res. Bd. of Canada, 22:503–512) and by Warner *et al.* (1966, J. Appl. Ecol., 3[Suppl.]:223–247) that pesticides at very low levels have behavioral effects in fish. Research of this sort with birds is greatly needed, but only a small start has been made. I suspect that even in work of this sensitivity, demonstrable effects in birds and mammals will be found only when readily measurable residues—not mere traces—are in the nervous system.

Dieldrin is not the only chemical requiring study. Endrin is famous for its extreme toxicity and is actually used to kill orchard mice. It was number 2 in frequency in our rivers. DDT, number 3, is everywhere and is long-lasting. At high levels, it can kill birds outright, as the Dutch elm studies have shown dramatically. No one knows what levels of DDT or its metabolites in the brain correlate with behavioral changes. Heptachlor, famous as a wildlife killer in the fire-ant program, is found in many animals. Toxaphene and chlordane are also widely used residual chemicals. Even parathion persists longer than we often think.

DISEASES REPORTED IN RAPTORS

TRAINER: Table 37:1 (Chapter 37) is a checklist of diseases that have been reported for hawks. A report of the presence of disease in a host does not necessarily mean that it was the cause of death. There were instances, as with botulism, myiasis, etc., where disease unquestionably was responsible for mortality; however, in the other instances, pathogenic organisms were isolated, but their significance was unknown. This list of diseases was presented to provide a basis for a discussion on the possible role of disease in the decline of the peregrine falcon.

This review of diseases in raptors was presented merely to offer for consideration one more factor that might be involved in this population decline. All of the diseases listed are capable of affecting reproduction, and several are specific diseases of the reproductive tract. Viral agents that can cause reproductive failures include Newcastle disease, fowl pox, and ornithosis. None of the bacterial agents listed directly affect the reproductive tract, but several cause chronic infections that can adversely affect reproduction. The parasite infestations are usually chronic and affect the entire general health of a bird, and therefore can alter normal physiological functions such as reproduction.

The diseases reported in the literature which caused appreciable mortality in raptors were myiasis, botulism, and fowl cholera. Losses due to these diseases were severe, but geographically limited. The remaining reports of disease involved individuals or small numbers of birds.

ONSET OF THE PEREGRINE DECLINE

HICKEY: To me, the critical thing in Kleinstäuber's paper (Chapter 17) was his statement that this decline of the peregrine falcon started during the war years. Mebs, do you agree that the decline of the peregrine in Germany started in the war years?

MEBS: No, I don't agree.

COVER: Isn't it correct that in Germany after the war there were even some new peregrine nesting sites established that were not known earlier? And that this occurred during a time when guns were not available to the civilian population?

MEBS: Perhaps. I have written that the peregrines increased in the war years, the years of 1942 or '43 to 1946 or '47. They increased because

(1) there was no one who had time for hunting, (2) the hunters had no weapons to shoot the peregrines, and (3) there were no rock-climbers and only a few pigeon fanciers. I had the impression that in these years between 1943 and '47–'48 there was an increase of the peregrine, perhaps to 1950, and then came the decline.

HICKEY: It has been pointed out by Rice (Chapter 12) that the desertion of peregrine eyries in Pennsylvania was accelerated in the late 1930's. During this very period, peregrines were taking up new nesting sites in cities like Montreal, New York, and Philadelphia. Indeed during the 1940's, the peregrines along the Hudson River probably reached a 25-year peak (Herbert and Herbert, 1965). The desertion of some eyries can be considered normal even in a stable population spread over a large region like the Middle Atlantic States. Some "temporary eyries" will be occupied or reoccupied for a few years; other temporary eyries will be abandoned. Given enough years, a peregrine population study should show an increasing number of deserted sites—even though there is no substantial overall change in the nesting population each year. Thus, in a fairly large region, some eyrie desertion must be regarded as normal. This phenomenon tends to obscure the onset of the great population crash we are considering. It seems to me quite probable that the acceleration in desertion reported by Rice was due to local disturbance. The significant desertion of cliffs that were difficult to climb with a rope started in Pennsylvania in 1948 at a low cliff and in 1950 at high cliffs (Table 12.2, Chapter 12).

The interesting thing that has come out of this meeting, I think, is the fact that the modern decline of the peregrine and other raptors is uniformly associated with the reproductive failure of the birds. Some adult mortality due to pesticides seems to be in the picture, but its role is evidently minor in North America.

Early in the 1940's, it was apparent that the desertion rate for peregrine eyries east of the Rockies was on the order of 11–18% during recent decades. Some eyries remained in use despite highways and railroads built below the faces of the cliffs. Others did not. Picnicking on top of the smaller cliffs seems to have been an important factor in some of these desertions. The growth of cities may have affected others. The restriction of the peregrine population in this region certainly was very gradual. The dramatic thing about the present crash is that somewhere after 1950 this population went down so rapidly. Moreover, it went down on two continents. We have had nothing like this in the known history of bird populations.

PEREGRINES AND PESTICIDES

AMADON: Regarding the fact that the East German peregrine population declined before modern pesticides were used in that region, I would assume that the situation was the same as Suominen pointed out in Finland in that these birds or at least the young ones were wintering in areas which were possibly affluent enough to have begun to use pesticides at that time.

In thinking about these European reports as a whole, it seems to me that the English situation described by Ratcliffe is especially significant because we have a peregrine population there that has been subjected to strong pressures for centuries—by falconers, by the most dedicated egg collectors perhaps in the world, and by the greatest concentration of game keepers. During the war the government even attempted to shoot all the peregrines because they were killing pigeons used by the military services. But despite all this the peregrine population showed great resiliency and, when they were temporarily knocked out of southern England by this wartime persecution, they came back rather rapidly. Thus, despite all of these things, the peregrine population held up, until all of a sudden it went down. When in these other instances in Europe we are trying to blame the decline on pigeon fanciers or other persons, I think we may be misled by something that is temporary or local. It is in this British account that we really get the true slant on this decline: that it is tied up with pesticides that we now know are so pervasive in our environment.

RATCLIFFE: I think we need direct evidence of the responses of such birds to these chemicals under carefully controlled experimental conditions—and with a control population. These experiments are extremely complicated to carry out. The work being pursued by the Stickels with their kestrels at the Patuxent Wildlife Research Center is the nearest approach to this that one can make with raptorial birds.

HICKEY: Hunt (Chapter 41) has pointed out some rather high levels in the fat of six shorebirds in California. Shorebirds lingering in mosquito-controlled coastal marshes represent one potential source of pesticidal contact for peregrine falcons. It is true to this extent: some of these preys will be taken by peregrines in the Arctic; others, during their migration.

MRS. HAMERSTROM: It has been suggested that the best way to get rid of carnivores is to give them oral contraceptives. Pesticides may act precisely as contraceptives. The effect that Young has demonstrated hypothetically may be more pernicious than would seem at first blush. If half of the peregrines are rendered infertile, a sample of four pairs might have a pattern of only one fertile pair as follows:

one pair with male infertile
one pair with female infertile
one pair with both sexes infertile
one pair with both sexes fertile

Not only are three pairs rendered useless for reproduction, but possibly three grade-A eyrie sites may be worthlessly preempted; thus the sublethal effects of pesticides may be swiftly cumulative. Birds which almost reproduce, but fail to, are a greater hazard than dead ones.

W. H. STICKEL: People have a tendency to blame an amorphous entity known as "pesticides" for everything that happens. This is a dangerous tendency, for pesticides—including herbicides, fungicides, miticides, insecticides, and rodenticides—are of extreme value in maintaining the health and food supply of man; we can be sure they will be used in enormous amounts far into the future despite the growing importance of biological-control methods. We must recognize that there are hundreds of pesticides and that they differ widely in their uses and dangers. Relatively few of them have any chance of reducing bird populations; the rest are too nontoxic, are too short-lived, or are used in restricted situations. It is possible to use the most toxic ones in safe ways. Even the most residual ones have certain safe and important uses, such as termite-proofing. We cannot dodge these facts. We must learn which chemicals are most likely to cause trouble and work on those. Let us not waste our efforts and lose cooperators by attacking pesticides as a group.

Even more important, let us make sure that we are not missing the real problems—the real causes—by joining a single crusade. We have outlined declines in the peregrine, Cooper's hawk, bald eagle, osprey, and perhaps other hawks. The situation is complex, with a recent sharp decline superimposed on a long-term decline. The recent decline is attributed to pesticides chiefly because it coincides in time with the advent of modern pesticides after World War II. This is awfully tricky in both logical and biological senses. Almost everything has changed or speeded up since 1945: industrial air and water pollution, development of nearly all waterfront property, suburbanization, motorboat travel in all waters, sale of telescopic sights on .22 rifles, contamination of roadsides with lead from gasoline, human travel into back country, even the disturbance that scarce hawks suffer from observers, falconers, and photographers. We will be very fortunate if we find we are faced with one or two important factors that we can isolate and deal with. This makes it extremely urgent to look for suspect factors wherever they may be and not freeze ourselves into thinking of "pesticides" as the predominant solution. Pesticides are being investigated and will be investigated. Let us look seriously at other factors, too; it is not likely that pesticides will explain everything. One could explain the observed phenomena at least as well by a theory of chronic poisoning by metals such as lead or mercury.

The long decline before 1945 suggests basic difficulties in habitat factors such as food supply, nesting sites, disturbance, disease, or pollution. Whatever the difficulties were then, they probably continue today, and very likely are more intense.

YOUNG: It seems to me that this conference has intended to downgrade the relation between raptor-population crashes and pesticides because the evidence is circumstantial. This is a very easy way to brush off valuable ecological data. In other fields of science we see circumstantial evidence being routinely used. The relation of lung cancer to the use of tobacco is one example. The use of thalidomide is another. In both these cases, scientists reached a conclusion without waiting for disinterested controlled experiments to be carried out. Nor do I feel that we need definitive experiments to show that the environment has been and is now being seriously damaged by the pesticide programs currently being carried out in the United States.

COVER: As I consider all the reports given at the conference, I reach this conclusion: That where the peregrine falcon has suffered a serious decline, the population of peregrines has either nested or wintered, or both, in an area where pesticide sprays appear to have been used commonly.

In the eastern part of the United States, where we learn from banding recoveries that the peregrines both nested and wintered in areas where pesticides were commonly used, we see a complete decline. Although the State of Massachusetts gave its peregrines extensive protection from human molestation, even to the extent of hiring full-time wardens to protect some of the most vulnerable eyries, the falcons disappeared about the same time as all the other falcons in the east.

In the Rocky Mountain area of the United States, we still find a population of peregrines in very remote parts, and on the British Columbia coast of Canada we see a healthy population of Peale's peregrine falcons. It would appear that the reason for this is that they nest in an extremely remote section, and winter in approximately the same area. I presume the amount of pesticides used in this area would be almost nil. We had a favorable report from Arctic Canada of an estimated population of 7,500 pairs; here we have a population that nests in a very remote area in which probably no pesticides are used.

In the report of Glading for California we see that the peregrines are now found in remote areas, far from agricultural sections. This seems to be also true in Britain not only of the peregrine but also of the sparrow-hawk. In the southern portion of England, the sparrow-hawk nesting near the open, agricultural sections was definitely declining. However, the farther away we get from the agricultural areas, the less decline we find in the sparrow-hawk population. This was true also of peregrines. Those nesting in the agricultural areas were the most drastically affected. The same thing was true of northern France, whereas in the remote mountain region of southern France a fairly healthy population was reported. As we travel farther south into Spain, a country which, to my knowledge, does not use pesticides extensively, we find a very healthy peregrine population.

In Finland, where a decline of approximately 90 per cent was reported, most of the winter banding recoveries came from the agricultural areas of France. The decline of the peregrine is probably accentuated in areas like France where apparently raptors are also shot annually on a large scale.

In eastern Germany, where, I believe, the average person is not allowed to carry firearms, we see a definite decline in the peregrine; I would assume that pesticide sprays are commonly used here. But if we go south into the mountains of Bavaria, away from agricultural areas, we find a more or less average population.

Because this pattern persists in so many areas of the world, I cannot conclude other than that pesticide sprays are responsible for the decline of the peregrine.

THE PEREGRINE ON THE LIST OF ENDANGERED BIRDS

CADE: With the expressed concern of our present Administration over such problems as environmental pollution and contamination, preservation of endangered species, and beautification of the landscape, etc., I hope the plight of the peregrine will not be neglected much longer by the United States Government. The Fish and Wildlife Service has wisely and justifiably undertaken the responsibility of monitoring on a long-term basis the effects of pesticidal contamination on bald eagle and osprey populations. Is it not time for the US Department of the Interior to assume the same responsibility for the peregrine falcon, which is even more seriously threatened than either of the former two species?

I do not know which species of birds are to be placed on the official list of "endangered species." Such decisions are bound to be rather arbitrary and somewhat academic. From my point of view, when a species, whose populations have shown remarkable historical constancy in numbers, as peregrine populations have until recent years in both Europe and North America, suddenly begins disappearing over very large portions of its breeding range on two continents, it is—if not an endangered species—at least one which requires immediate, intensive investigation, until the extent, cause, and remedy of its decline are known. The interests of wildlife preservation coupled with the strong implication of pesticides in the whole affair argue convincingly for federal support of research on the peregrine. I think such research will have to be a long-term enterprise.

SOME REFLECTIONS ON THE PESTICIDE CONTROVERSY

CLEMENT: The psychologists tell us that, when we reach the summing-up stage, we are past our productive stage. I find this true increasingly as an administrator. But, as I have been involved in this pesticide controversy for a number of years and of course have been active in helping the National Audubon Society plot its course regarding some of these problems, I have been increasingly impressed with the fact that the time has come for us to formulate fully and specifically, and as carefully as we can, this thesis or hypothesis that some of the chemical insecticides are responsible for the great decline of our raptorial birds. This is a necessary scientific step, because we cannot test an hypothesis that is not fully formulated.

Now concerning the background and the history of conflict in this area, I suggest also that the case which has been drawn, particularly by our British friends, but which is also developing rapidly in this country in connection with the work on the bald eagle and the osprey, is one that would be accepted except for the fact that there is a conflict of interest involving commercial considerations. The only reason there is a continuing conflict of opinion over the effect of smoking tobacco, for example, is that it has a commercial involvement. We have to recognize this as a fact of life. Our society has committed itself in certain directions without forethought, and it is difficult now to pull out.

In addition, however, there is another problem that we have a tendency to overlook because we grew up with it. As I grow older I find, in order to understand what I am trying to get at and what we are all involved in, that I have had to study philosophy more and more, more than science. We do not realize to what extent we are the victims of the positivism of the nineteenth century. We are all fascinated with facts, but we refuse to put any value judgment on these facts. And this is one of our problems, because it has been easy—in view of the commercial implications—to contend over the meaning of facts; and there have been many different definitions of fact. But as Roger Peterson has pointed out, it is a very good scientific principle to use the most economic hypothesis. Ockham's razor should still be operating in our day just as it was in Roger Bacon's day.

Now one of the problems that makes it difficult for us to get together when we contend over these things is that the first statement of a problem is always necessarily vague. And in this case it was particularly so, because the problem was discovered and developed by a group of field naturalists who are working with difficult-to-define situations. The problem seemed so completely vague and general that the laboratory scientist found it very difficult to accept as serious; and this is another problem. I agree, for example, that the use of the word "pesticide" is unfair. But in the beginning, when we are groping for an answer, we must use general terms; and it was necessary to use "pesticides" first because some of the people in opposition had a tendency to equate pesticides with agricultural chemicals. Because, as we all know, agricultural chemicals are useful and valuable, the tendency was to try to make the public assume that, if we eliminated anything, we would go back to the dark ages of agricultural production. Unfortunately, there is a tendency to feel insulted by the use of general words, because to those who are more technically sophisticated—and now I have particular reference to the chemists and the agricultural workers—this has seemed unscientific.

Finally, in view of the fact that there is always a tendency to be pessimistic about these problems, I would like to remind everyone that the constructive processes take a long time, and this is why it is difficult for us to be optimistic about results that are so far in the future. Destruction is always short-lived, and we can see a great deal of destruction when we observe on a day-to-day basis. But it takes the long view to see that we are making progress; and I think, if all of us reflect on this, we can see that we have made a great deal of progress—if only since Rachel Carson jarred all of us to take a hard look at this. So I am optimistic about this. I am pleased with the results we have brought together here. It has indicated how much more work needs to be done, but it is not necessary to let this detailed work interfere with action programs. On the other hand, the sooner we can provide our regulatory agencies with specifics, the sooner we can convince other people in government and in industry that these changes have got to be made.

Research Needs

PRAIRIE FALCONS AS SUBJECTS FOR STUDY

GLADING: The depression in prairie falcon populations in agricultural parts of Utah, mentioned by White (Chapter 30), has its parallel in the Upper Sonoran zones surrounding our great valley in California. In Nevada, I am told, this species is surviving extremely well. This suggests that the prairie falcon may well be a model species to study with regard to pesticide effects in the American west.

CADE: Individual pairs of prairie falcons in California certainly vary importantly in their feeding habits. Some will feed almost entirely on ground squirrels (*Citellus*); a few miles away will be another pair feeding almost entirely on mourning doves or something of that sort. A study of these birds might be most profitable.

SAMPLING RAPTOR POPULATIONS

SIMONYI: It would seem appropriate to collect a half dozen of each species of raptor during its migration and have a complete residue analysis run on the specimens at some central laboratory. Specimens could also, of course, be taken at the beginning and end of, say, the winter season so that the build-up of chemical residues could be studied.

GEOGRAPHIC GAPS IN ECOLOGICAL KNOWLEDGE OF THE PEREGRINE

BEEBE: In my experience, falcons are usually to be found much more abundantly in regions where humans are rare or absent than they are in areas of high densities of human population. On the other hand, studies of falcons are much more easily undertaken in areas where high or reasonably high human populations permit fairly intimate access to the countryside. Applying this thinking to this conference, I find that the reports from wilderness or near-wilderness areas are fewer in number than those from settled regions, and that further, the tremendous size of these areas tends to make these reports, of necessity, rather sketchy. There are several very large wilderness areas of the world from which reports are either entirely wanting or almost so, that appear to be very nearly ideal for peregrines in view of what we know of the preferences in habitat and diet of these falcons. The least studied and possibly the most important of these are maritime habitats.

The Greenland coast has been studied fairly recently by Salomonsen (1950, *The Birds of Greenland*), but the west side of Davis Strait—the coast of Labrador and the east coast of Baffin Island—remains a mystery insofar as peregrines are concerned. The tremendous populations of alcids known to breed on these coastlines would lead one to suspect that peregrine densities might well be comparable to those of the Queen Charlotte Islands. Reporting from Greenland, however, Salomonsen (1950) lists the peregrine as being most abundant in the low Arctic, generally south of the large breeding colonies of the dovekie, and inland rather than as a bird of the outer coast. He lists snow and Lapland buntings as the chief food, but nevertheless considers this falcon to be a common species in the low Arctic region of Greenland. No estimates of population are made. It is known that peregrines breed in coastal situations in some areas of the Canadian Arctic archipelago, but a clear relationship between the great colonies of dovekies of Davis Strait and breeding peregrines has not yet been established, and this is something that should be known.

Next, quite aside from the outer islands of the Alexander archipelago of southeastern Alaska, which, being directly north of the Queen Charlottes, would seem quite as suitable to a high density of peregrines as are these islands, much more should be known about population densities of these falcons in the Aleutians. Probably one of the most important reasons for lack of information in both of these areas is to be found in the restrictive attitudes of the Alaska fish and game authorities. Falconers are not allowed legally to take birds out of this state, a situation which results in the suppression of any information obtained by falconers; for of course some birds are taken and smuggled out. Restrictions have their price.

Farther afield, but still in the maritime situation, are the Kuriles, which, like the Aleutians, appear to be prime peregrine habitat, as also do the thousand miles or so of broken, island-dotted coastline of southern Chile. Here the little diving-petrels come ashore in millions to nest in burrows, matching, almost exactly in size and habits, the small alcids of the northern coastlines. Two other maritime regions should be mentioned where peregrines are known to occur but where little or nothing is known of population densities. One of these is the tropical Philippine–New Guinea region; the other is the south coast of Australia.

Of inland situations the largest area known to be suitable to peregrines and unreported from, at this conference, is the tremendous square mileage of Siberia; even on our own continent there is the huge area of the central Canadian barrens west of Hudson's Bay—an area that, even excluding the great wilderness lakes of Athabasca, Great Slave, and Great Bear, still covers a land area greater than half of the total range of the prairie falcon.

NEED FOR RESIDUE ANALYSES

W. H. STICKEL: Perhaps one of the most striking facts revealed by our discussions is that—at the time of this conference in 1965—none of us knows of a single American peregrine or Cooper's hawk that has been analyzed. The desirability of analyzing peregrines or other hawks from areas where trouble is suspected is evident to all of us. As representatives of the US Fish and Wildlife Service, we appeal to you to send in hawks of significance in this connection. We can have them analyzed, and we will try to interpret the results as well as existing knowledge permits, but we are dependent on people like you to supply this rare and critical material.

NELSON: Wayland Hayes in a much-quoted experiment investigated the presence of DDT and its breakdown products in the urine of prisoners at the Ohio State Penitentiary. Could one similarly check the excreta of birds for chlorinated hydrocarbons and get some indication of residue levels in the living bird?

HICKEY: This has not been attempted, as far as I know. Perhaps the simplest index available to ornithologists is to run gas chromatograph analyses of residue levels in birds' eggs. Mrs. Stickel has been experimenting with hollow needles as a means of getting subcutaneous fat from living birds.

MRS. STICKEL: This needle technique is theoretically possible, but at the Patuxent Wildlife Research Center we have run into unending difficulties with it, so that I would not say "Yes, it can be done."

RESEARCH ON ALASKAN PEREGRINES

CADE: If we are going to end up, as I believe, with only a highly migratory population of peregrines which—excluding *F. peregrinus pealei* off the coast of British Columbia and in the Aleutians—breeds in Arctic and subarctic North America and winters in some as yet vaguely defined part of tropical America, then we ought to concentrate our efforts on finding out as much as possible about these northern birds. My monograph on the peregrine and gyrfalcon populations of Alaska based on eight seasons of field work (1960; Univ. Calif. Publ. Zool., 63:151–290) was designed to be a broadly based, extensive, regional survey "to establish a background of information with which to interpret continuing observations of these species over an extended period of time." Although it has always been my intention to follow up this extensive survey with a detailed study of some local population in Alaska, at the time these investigations were being carried out in the 1950's I had no idea that my study might one day provide the basis for evaluating an unprecedented population decline of the peregrine falcon on the North American continent. Such I now believe to be the case, and intensive, long-term studies exist along the major rivers of Alaska, especially along the upper Yukon and its tributaries and along the Colville on the Arctic Slope.

I had always thought of the Alaskan peregrines as being rather safe from human molestation. In 1899 L. B. Bishop found a pair of peregrines nesting about every 10 miles (16 km) along part of the upper Yukon; and in 1951 when I made my survey, there were 10 pairs of peregrines present, giving a density very close to that which Bishop had estimated 52 years earlier. In July 1965, James D. Weaver of Rockford, Illinois, made the same trip at the height of the nestling period and found but one active eyrie at Tacoma Bluff and only three adult falcons present along the entire stretch of river. If this report is correct, then even our northern peregrines are not safe from whatever factors are causing the population decline. It may very well be that some of these northern peregrines are being subjected to contamination by pesticides on their wintering grounds. This is an hypothesis which should be pursued, but the only way to do so is by means of intensive banding to establish the winter quarters of these Alaskan falcons. By contrast with this unsettling report from the Yukon, in 1964 Clayton M. White found peregrines—and gyrfalcons—in even greater numbers along the upper Colville River than I encountered them in the years 1952–59.

The need for a careful survey of nesting peregrines along the upper Yukon is indicated. Such a survey, carried out as a preliminary reconnaissance in anticipation of a more detailed and continuing program of studies, could achieve the following objectives in a single season of about 2 months: (1) a count of breeding pairs between Dawson and Circle to establish the present population density along that stretch of river (there were 20 pairs present in 1951); (2) an estimate of the current reproductive performance of this population of peregrines; (3) the acquisition of adult peregrines, nestlings, and eggs for residue analyses of pesticides; and (4) the acquisition of specimens of the main prey species of peregrines, also for residue analyses.

If this Yukon population does prove to be a deteriorating one, then we have the chance to establish a correlation between residue levels in appropriate tissues from these peregrines and the extinction process. If the population is still maintaining its numbers at the previously known density, it would still be worthwhile to have the residue analyses to compare with the data which have been obtained from British peregrines and their eggs by Ratcliffe or with similar data from any other sick populations which may be hanging on in North America (California is one possibility).

As for the prey species, it would be most illuminating to compare the difference in residue levels of pesticides between Arctic and boreal residents such as the gray jay and ptarmigan species, which are little subjected to direct applications of pesticides, and migrants such as robins, flickers, and waterfowl, which may be coming into contact with pesticides on their wintering grounds. All of these species are important prey items of peregrines in Alaska.

Should this initial survey indicate fruitful prospects for continuing studies along these lines, then I would suggst an expansion of the project to include studies on the Arctic Slope of Alaska along the Colville River, where three species of raptors with different ecologies are available for comparison—the highly migrant peregrines, bird eaters at the end of a long food-chain, the highly migrant rough-legged hawks, rodent eaters at the end of a much shorter food-chain, and the basically resident gyrfalcons, food specialists which live mainly on ptarmigan.

GENERAL SURVEY OF NORTH AMERICAN PEREGRINES

CADE: My second proposal has to do with establishing a North American Peregrine Inquiry similar to the peregrine inquiry which Ratcliffe operates in Great Britain. This inquiry would attempt to survey as many known peregrine eyries as possible each year—active as well as presently abandoned ones—to determine whether breeding birds are present or not. Such an inquiry would require some one person to act as a coordinator of the work and some agency to serve as the coordinating center and depository for the information. The bulk of the field work would be carried out by regional cooperators enlisted from the ranks of the Audubon Societies and other interested local groups and individuals. The lists of eyrie locations previously drawn up by Hickey and Bond would serve as an excellent basis for starting this program. Such a network for gathering data, covering as much of the continent as possible, could provide valuable information over the next years on how the present continental population trend progresses. It could help quickly to identify areas where the situation is worsening, as well as reveal areas where the species may attempt to reestablish. In the latter respect, I think it is particularly important to continue checking now abandoned eyries, at least a yearly sample of them. Certainly the British inquiry proved invaluable in pinpointing the decline and in showing how the pattern of decline followed so closely the geographic distribution of pesticide usage.

STRATEGIC ASPECTS OF REESTABLISHMENT TECHNIQUES

NELSON: One of the reasons that I proposed (Chapter 35) the reestablishment technique be tried as a research project is that in so doing you can gain a great increment of public respect on your side in trying it. By this I mean that at any place in the United States you would have your television stations and you could have all these people watching the progress of your project. Now this is the same thing that a falconer does when he lectures on raptorial birds to community clubs and exhibits his falcons to the public. There are a lot of birds of prey alive today because falconers have said, "Don't shoot these birds because they may be my trained ones."

In Idaho since 1952, when we passed the law protecting all of the raptorial birds in the state, there has been a definite increase in all these species except the peregrine. The trend is definite enough that the game department recognizes it. I recognize it too in the changing public opinion with respect to raptorial birds; my proposal is that the day may come when we have solved the habitat problem now confronting us; then we should have some technique with which we might try to restore these depleted populations. We will need the television coverage and all that goes with it so that we get someplace without everybody shooting the birds.

RESEARCH AND THE PUBLIC CONSCIENCE

CADE: I would like to emphasize that doubling or tripling our present increment of information about the accumulation of pesticide residues in the environment and their progressive concentration in living organisms at the different trophic levels—playing the parts per million game indefinitely—will not double or triple the cogency of the position, which I believe a majority of the conferees agree upon, that the environment is indeed dangerously contaminated with pesticide residues and that strict government control over the use of these poisons is the only way to alleviate the situation.

I submit that the more diagrammatic lessons which we have learned from western grebes at Clear Lake during the gnat-control program with TDE, from salmon in the Miramichi River during the spruce budworm spraying in Canada, from a host of vertebrates—both wild and domestic—during the fire-ant fiasco with dieldrin and heptachlor in the southeastern United States, and now from the sorry spectacle of our peregrines, bald eagles, and ospreys being brought to extinction through reproductive malfunctions, so suspiciously and insidiously associated with high residue levels of chlorinated hydrocarbons in their tissues and eggs, constitute sufficient information to warrant putting into effect the kind of limited, "experimental" control of pesticide usage which I suggested for the Atlantic seaboard. If some kind of significant limitation on the use of pesticides cannot be initiated now, then it can never be done. I feel strongly that something should be done and can be done.

At the risk of being accused of fostering antiscientific attitudes, I will go a step further and say that in a real sense we are plagued by too much information about pesticides—by data of a low order of significance which tend to obscure and emasculate the more motivating bodies of information. Apologists for the use of pesticides can hide and dodge about in a veritable forest of facts on the pharmacological properties and LD_{50}'s of hundreds of synthetic poisons already approved for marketing, not to mention hosts of others yet to be screened. When we are shocked by the horrors of one chemical that has been put into use, they can describe the properties of another that pales the first into insignificance by comparison. An LD_{50} is a solid, scientific fact, so we are told, but the loss of a predator population at the end of a long food-chain up which pesticide residues have been progressively concentrated in the bodies of prey species is only an inference based on "circumstantial" evidence. Credibility is always relative to the individual's total experience, but I believe the time has come when this nation must decide which bits of information constitute irrelevant minutiae about pesticides and which are relevant for political action. We do not have time to wait for the last fact to be gathered; contrary to what Sir Francis Bacon thought at the dawn of the Scientific Revolution, good science does not require it; but good science, like prudence, does demand the exercise of judgment.

One further point about research. I remember having been asked a question about the moral obligations of the research scientist at the oral defense of my Ph.D. dissertation. Does the scientist have a moral obligation to translate his findings into social and political action for the benefit of man? My answer was that when functioning as a scientist—doing his research—he should not assume that responsibility; but as a concerned citizen in questions of social or political import he had every right to use scientific information in support of his arguments, as does every other citizen for that matter. My committee did not react favorably to the dualism which I imposed on the scientist, and I am afraid I did not argue very effectively in support of my position. I had an intuitive feeling that I was right. I think I know now why I felt that way.

When research is carried out with a view to the practical usefulness or humanistic relevance of the results, the activity immediately becomes—to some degree—a vested interest, which leaves the researcher vulnerable to misinterpretations of his results and otherwise susceptible to diversionary tactics which seem to strengthen his position, when in fact it may be quite weak. These faults can also bias the pure scientist, but they are far more easily detected and counteracted in the less committed atmosphere of unapplied investigation.

I see a danger that research "against" pesticides could become just as much of a vested interest as research and promotion "for" pesticides now are. With more and more federal funds pouring into the coffers of the universities and government research agencies, the cry "not enough research, not enough research" is all too easily voiced. Unless those of us who are charged with the conduct of applied research into questions dealing with pesticides exercise the highest degree of intellectual honesty, we face the specter of two rival groups researching happily away against each other, but neither really hoping for a final, unequivocal solution that might cut off their sources of support.

We do not need more information about the effects of pesticides nearly as much as we need more conscience to act on the information we already have. We need more of what Albert Schweitzer referred to as "reverence for life." In this nuclear age, human beings have become so jaded to the hazards of the world, which we have insisted on remaking—so lacking in respect for our own lives, as well as the lives of the animals with which we share this earth—that some madman must perpetrate an "overkill" before we feel compelled to express outrage. This is the reason that tobacco companies continue to thrive in the face of impressive evidence associating cigarette smoking with lung cancer. This is also the reason that chemical companies continue to do a multi-million-dollar business each year in the sale of pesticidal poisons that are proven killers of a wide variety of organisms other than those for which they are intended.

Must we have an "overkill" with pesticides before remedial action is taken? Could we not instead accept the notion that predatory birds at the end of long food-chains provide us with an extremely sensitive bioassay of environmental contamination by the chlorinated hydrocarbons and apply the necessary control measures at the point when their populations show deterioration rather than waiting for some darker eventuality?

CONCLUSION

CHAPTER 47

CONFERENCE SUMMARY AND CONCLUSIONS

Joseph J. Hickey
and James E. Roelle

A cosmopolitan distribution and a comparatively stable population have long marked the peregrine falcon as one of the world's most successful products of evolution. Restricted in numbers by a general dependency on cliffs as nesting sites, the peregrine has also used sloping banks and level ground in some regions, as well as trees and even buildings. Its mean clutch size varies with latitude, being about 3.5 in north temperate regions. Its mortality rates have not been calculated, but for adults they may approximate the 19% per year reported for European buzzards in which 1.2 young fledged per pair is thought to balance the population. In general, the peregrine has retreated only slowly before the inroads of civilization. This book brings into focus facts concerning the precipitous population crash that overtook these falcons in both Europe and North America shortly after World War II (Chapter 1).

THE PEREGRINE DECLINE IN NORTH AMERICA

In Alaska, White reports that the peregrine population does not appear to be decreasing (Chapter 2). In British Columbia, Beebe finds some 80–100 pairs concentrated on the coastal islands and no change in numbers yet evident (Chapter 3). However, in the Okanagan Valley, prairie falcons replaced a number of nesting peregrines prior to 1937. In a six-state area just to the south, Nelson concludes that rising temperatures and reduced precipitation are importantly associated with an 80% decline in the use of known peregrine eyries since 1938 and a possible shift of the population to higher altitudes or latitudes (Chapter 4). This replacement of peregrines by prairie falcons apparently started at a much earlier date. Enderson in 1964 found only 33% of the known peregrine eyries from New Mexico to Alberta to be still in use, many being inexplicably deserted since 1950 (Chapter 5). The picture for California involves a downward trend but is otherwise not clear. In western Mexico, where 66 nests have been recorded in the past, Banks reports a noteworthy lack of peregrines since 1960 (Chapter 6). It appears likely that the recent drought in the southwestern part of the United States almost certainly made for a marked change in waterbirds available to peregrines, that this was not offset by modern irrigation and reclamation projects, and that peregrines were breeding as far south as 20°N as late as 1963 (Chapter 7).

In northern Canada, Fyfe reports that the peregrine remains a common breeding bird and that the population there may well be on the order of 7,500 breeding pairs (Chapter 8). In Wisconsin and along the Upper Mississippi River, Berger and Mueller found that a decline became noticeable in 1959, with the last resident adult seen in 1964 (Chapter 9). Hagar's report on Massachusetts briefly summarizes one of the most intensive nesting studies of the peregrine ever undertaken. At 14 eyries, the mean number of young fledged per adult was 0.5 from 1935 to 1942 and at Hagar's better sites 0.61. Reproductive success dropped in 1947 when broken eggs were observed for the first time in this area; by 1951, occupation of these cliffs was spotty, and by 1955–57 only an occasional single bird was left (Chapter 10). In the Hudson River valley, Herbert and Herbert found net productivity in the 1930's quite similar to that of Hagar's better sites, about 1.25 young being annually fledged per occupied site. The population here slightly increased in the 1940's, but net productivity dropped importantly when about 40% of the young were taken by falconers. In the 1950's, highway construction and the shooting of adults seriously affected this population. The last year for young to be fledged along the Hudson was 1951, and for a pair to be present, 1957 or 1959. The last adult disappeared in 1961 (Chapter 11).

In Pennsylvania, according to Rice, the decline set in with none of these local factors present. Productivity held up in 1939–46 (at 1.25 young fledged per occupied site) and inexplicably dropped to 0.3 in 1947–52 and 0.4 in 1953–60. Here peregrines began to desert cliffs of medium height by 1940 or '41 and held on longest to the higher cliffs, which were entirely abandoned by 1960 (Chapter 12).

In 1964, an extensive survey of 133 known peregrine eyries in the eastern United States was carried out by Berger, Sindelar, and Gamble and failed to disclose a single bird present (Chapter 13). In northern New York and New England, Spofford found young being produced at least through 1957, and a precipitous population collapse setting in thereafter. It is possible that a single bird persisted in Vermont as late as 1965 (Chapter 14). In general, this decline in the eastern United States seems to have progressed from south to north. It is not yet known to have affected the Maritime Provinces, but is said by Simonyi to involve the peregrine in Ontario, especially in the southeastern and agricultural part of the province. The decline seems to have also affected wintering peregrines in New York City but not others wintering elsewhere on the eastern seaboard (Chapter 14).

The near impossibility of censusing Arctic populations on any large scale has led to a new interest in the compilation of population indices based on migrant peregrines. Weather fluctuations tend to bias the numbers recorded in any given year, but these apparently can be overcome by smoothing the data with 3- to 5-year running averages. Other corrections are also proving to be useful, but some remain to be worked out. On the eastern coast of the United States, Rice's banding operations have initially disclosed that Greenland birds pass along Maryland and Virginia on their way to Central and South America (Chapter 14). Other parts of the eastern Arctic may yet be found to contribute to this movement. Rice's trapping data show no significant change in the age ratio of these birds between 1954–59 and 1960–65 nor in the number of peregrines caught per day (Chapter 24). This independent evidence seems to corroborate Fyfe's statement that, up to 1965, the peregrine population of the Canadian Arctic was still intact (Chapter 8). The vagaries of a Texas index, based on peregrines seen per 100 miles travelled, are reported by Enderson, one of whose coastal birds was later sighted 65 miles (95 km) north of its original site of capture (Chapter 24).

The value of migration indices farther inland seems to be presently restricted by a lack of data on the birds' nesting and wintering areas. Five-year running averages of the migrating peregrines seen per day by Hofslund and his cooperators at Duluth, Minnesota, show a decline of about 70% from 1951–55 to 1959–63 (Chapter 1), but an index compiled by Berger and Mueller at Cedar Grove, Wisconsin (300 miles or 480 km to the southeast), showed no substantial difference in the mean number of peregrines seen annually between 1951–64 and 1960–65 (Chapter 24). The Wisconsin birds are almost certainly of Arctic origin. The Minnesota index appears to be biased by an increase of October (off-peak) observations in later years.

The North American evidence thus sums up to a stable and intact peregrine population in the Arctic and on the coast of British Columbia, a seriously reduced population in the western United States, and complete extirpation in the eastern one-third of the United States. Two slow long-term population trends seem evident: a deterioration of food supplies brought on by climatic change in the western mountain region and a steady deterioration of easily accessible nesting sites in the east. Neither of these seems to account for the precipitous population crash that overtook this species in so many states, as well as in western Mexico, following World War II. This population crash was marked by consistent reports of "nonbreeding" and by occasional descriptions of broken eggs which are now assumed to accompany the actual eating of the egg contents by the falcons. Broken and missing eggs were significantly recorded for Massachusetts in 1947, for Montreal in 1948, and for Pennsylvania in 1949. These may well be the basis of other reports of egg disappearance, recorded near New York City in 1940 and on the Hudson River in 1950 and 1952. How much this phenomenon is associated with reports of "nonbreeding" pairs is by no means known. The recent syndrome of eyrie desertion in North America can, however, be at least described as following a puzzling reproductive failure, averaging about 4 years in Pennsylvania and 8–9 years along the Hudson where, however, the birds were badly disturbed. The last year of good reproduction in Pennsylvania was 1946; along the Hudson River, perhaps 1949; and in Massachusetts at least as late as 1946. For the eastern United States, one can now conclude, the slowly eroding population of this species entered this terminal syndrome in 1947.

THE PEREGRINE DECLINE IN EUROPE

In Finland, where perhaps 1,000 pairs nested in former times, Linkola and Suominen report only a few percent now remaining of the former numbers; mean clutch size changed from 3.1–3.2 before 1950 to 2.6 since 1958; half of the recent nestings are successful, and the mean number reared per occupied site is about 1 (Chapter 15). The Finnish figures show a population decrease amounting to about 51% a year since 1958 in contrast to an annual mean decline of 14% in southwestern Sweden since 1954. The decline has also been noticed in Latvia (Chapter 22).

In West Germany, Mebs has found that the 320–380 pairs present in 1950 shrank to about 70–90 in 1965, a decrease of about 77%. The decline was greatest in the north (up to 90%) and less so (55% in Bavaria) in the south (Chapter 16). In East Germany, cliff-nesting pairs were found by Kleinstäuber to have dropped from 19 in 1950 to 8 in 1965, and tree-nesting birds are reported by Schröder to have decreased 25–30% by 1964. Kleinstäuber believes (1) that this decline started during the war or early postwar years, when a shortage of pigeons as prey might have affected reproduction, and (2) that this was in turn seemingly followed by peregrine superannuation (Chapter 17). Schröder finds the decline still in progress, with reproductive failure often preceding the disappearance of adults by several years. He emphasizes that the decline has continued despite a great recent increase in the number of pigeons and a decrease in persecution by man: in some fashion the health of adult peregrines seems to have been impaired (Chapter 18).

In France, Terrasse and Terrasse estimate that the peregrine population has dropped in the last 30 years from about 300–500 to 100–150. Here the birds have disappeared from agricultural regions but are resisting repeated killing elsewhere. The crash occurred simultaneously on both sides of the English Channel. As in Britain, the sparrow-hawk has also decreased in some parts of France. There has been a local increase of peregrines in Burgundy as the result of the disappearance of eagle owls. The process of extirpation appears to be directly related to agriculture, being relatively recent and extremely rapid in Normandy where it reached 100% in 1964–65 (Chapter 19).

Reproductive success among Swiss peregrines has been found by Herren to be dropping steadily at successful eyries from a mean of 2.99 young in 1935–49 to 1.66 young in 1960–65. There has been, as yet, no marked desertion of frequently used eyries, but the number of nonbreeding adults reached 57% in 1961–65, dropping the number fledged per occupied site to a mean of 0.5 (Chapter 20). This now-familiar syndrome clearly suggests that a major decline in breeding pairs of this relatively sedentary population is now taking place in Switzerland.

In Great Britain, Ratcliffe reports, a postmedieval desertion of the easily accessible eyries was completed by about 1860, as a result of persecution and casual disturbance by man. A slow decline in the western Highlands set in about 1890–1900 and terminated by 1950—the evident result of decreasing food supplies brought on by overly exploitive land use. A temporary extirpation of peregrines over much of southern England and a few other districts during World War II was followed by rapid recovery in numbers after 1945.

After 1955, Ratcliffe states, an unprecedented decline of the peregrine in Britain had a wave-like spread from south to north, with the total population reduced to about one-half its prewar level and near extinction recorded in southern England and Wales. The sequence of deterioration often involved egg-breakage and eating, death of embryos or young, failure to lay, and finally, desertion of the eyrie. Breeding success has stabilized since 1962 at a reduced and subnormal level (Chapter 21).

The Irish population is clearly affected by this decline, according to Ratcliffe, although the reliable field evidence comes only from the north. In Spain and at least at the time of this conference, a fantastically dense population is still regarded as intact (Chapter 22).

In Belgium, Kruyfhooft has found a steady decline in the numbers of peregrines caught by pigeon netters. Based on the number of falcons caught per 10,000 permits issued, there seems to be little doubt that a profound population decline set in about 1952–54 (Chapter 1) involving birds that presumably come from the Baltic region and Fennoscandia. This decline would appear to exceed 80%. The potential biases in this index remain to be evaluated; but the statistics follow quite well the population declines of breeding birds reported in Finland, Sweden, and Latvia.

The general picture of recent peregrine populations in western Europe appears to involve some disruption of the populations in Germany during the late war and postwar years, a rapidly increasing British population after 1945, and a disappearance of nesting pairs which set in in Finland about 1953, in Sweden about 1955, and in Britain about 1956. Reported failure to lay eggs in some countries may or may not be the result of egg-eating by the peregrines, a phenomenon that Ratcliffe has established as now common and widespead in Britain. The decline in Europe clearly involves reproductive failure as in North America, but an increase in adult mortality may have taken place in both Finland and Britain.

POPULATION TRENDS IN OTHER RAPTORS

Of the 10 common species of raptors in Britain, Prestt reports, the sparrow-hawk has suffered a severe decline similar to that of the peregrine and to that of the golden eagle in parts of Scotland, egg-eating being a conspicuous basis of the reproductive failure in each species. The kestrel has also suffered a marked recent decline in eastern England. Buzzard populations are still depressed by the decline of rabbits that resulted from myxomatosis; barn owl and merlin declines appear to be generalized over a longer period; and the tawny owl remains widespread and common (Chapter 25).

In general, the rich raptor populations of Africa are reported by Cade to be still intact. The thinly spread peregrines of Kenya have not changed since 1949–52. No major change in the numbers of resident falconiforms has been detected in South Africa in the past 15 years, but a widespread reduction in the number of Palaearctic migrants seems to have occurred on the highveld and may or may not be the result of a prolonged drought (Chapter 26).

In eastern North America, Spofford's analyses of Appalachian data on migrants reveal increased numbers of broad-winged hawks, ospreys, and kestrels since 1934 and much reduced numbers of sharp-shinned and Cooper's hawks, bald and golden eagles, and peregrine falcons (Chapter 27). The remarkable decline of the sharp-shinned and Cooper's hawks is a striking parallel to the population crash of the closely related sparrow-hawk in Britain. All three are relatively secretive species with forest-nesting habits. Their simultaneous decline on two continents clearly discounts human disturbance as a factor in some of the population changes that are considered here.

The osprey also appears to be a part of this raptorial decline although it is not affected to the same extent as the peregrine (Chapter 28). In the United States, it is rapidly declining from New Jersey to Maine, according to Peterson, the annual rate being 33% in Connecticut and the mechanism a pronounced failure of eggs to hatch. This species is reported by Stickel to be holding up well in Chesapeake Bay, but in Michigan Postupalsky found a decline of 27% in 1964–65. In Wisconsin, a local decline in nesting pairs was more associated with the deterioration of nesting sites, according to Berger and Mueller, and not with reproductive failures. In East Germany, Moll finds only a weakly declining tendency in the population.

Eagle population phenomena vary widely (Chapter 29). In the American southwest, where as many as 1,000 golden eagles seem to have been annually killed for the past 20 years, new birds are reported by Spofford to move in gradually and reoccupy vacant territories. Sprunt points out that a bald eagle population decline became rapid and drastic in Florida after World War II, and that this decline now involves the northern Lake States, New York, and New Jersey. These declines are associated with sharply decreased nesting success and a change in the age ratio of eagles wintering south of Canada. Where nesting success exceeds 50%, bald eagles still persist in significant numbers. In North Germany, sea eagles are reported by Oehme to be gradually diminishing in numbers, in part as the result of reproductive failures and in part due to adult mortality.

Some brief reports on other raptors (Chapter 30) include the wholesale destruction of birds of prey in France which Terrasse estimates at at least 100,000 each year up to about 1963. In western Pennsylvania, Schriver has found a declining Cooper's hawk population and declining reproductive success in this species since 1957. In Utah, White reports locally high populations of breeding raptors, but there is a general decrease that may reflect much indiscriminate shooting of these species. In Colorado, Enderson feels that prairie falcons are maintaining their numbers.

BEHAVIOR AND GENERAL ECOLOGY

Some interesting aspects of raptor behavior are given by Frances Hamerstrom among the results of a 7-year study of nesting marsh hawks (hen harriers) in Wisconsin. Pair fidelity from year to year in this species was extremely rare, polygyny sometimes occurred, subadults were less successful nesters than adults, and successfully nesting birds were more apt to return than those that failed. There was a 70% decrease in the number of migrants in 1960–65 and a similar decrease in the nesting success of residents, the abundance of nests apparently fluctuating with the numbers of local voles (Chapter 31). The migration index for this species at Hawk Mountain, which is much farther east, displays a gentle oscillation (Chapter 27).

British-nesting peregrines are shown by Mead to be essentially a self-contained population, but their wintering numbers are augmented by birds from Scandinavia. Banding recoveries tend to peak in April and October, and British peregrines surviving to their first January 1st have a further expectation of life of about 2.5 years (Chapter 32).

White raises the question of genetic continuity in the maintenance of peregrine eyries. Since migratory vs. sedentary behavior and variations in mean clutch size presumably are genetically controlled, there are important genetic aspects in the population dynamics of the peregrine which will be extraordinarily interesting to study if the species ever attempts to recapture its now-vacant breeding range in the eastern United States and the range that seems destined to be vacated in northwestern Europe (Chapter 33).

Beebe also raises the possibility that this eastern population of the North American peregrine once preyed upon the enormous passenger pigeon flocks of the past and was importantly sustained by the great biomass of this now-extinct species (Chapter 34). This hypothesis found little acceptance among the conference participants.

FACTORS AFFECTING PEREGRINE POPULATIONS

DISEASES

Trainer, in reviewing the published literature on the diseases of wild raptors, mentions fowl cholera, tularemia, plague, and botulism in the extensive list of bacterial diseases reported for these birds in the wild and in captivity. Newcastle, ornithosis, and the viral encephalitides are among the more interesting viral diseases reported in this group. Myiasis and trichomoniasis are recognized as the two more important parasitic diseases, but all the major groups of endoparasites have been documented for hawks. The significance of these agents to wild populations is, for the most part, unknown (Chapter 37).

Trichomonas gallinae, while widespread, varies importantly in virulence and in Stabler's judgment cannot be considered as a factor in the recent decline of the peregrine falcon (Chapter 38).

Hanson stresses the difference between population-dependent and population-independent diseases. He regards peregrines as potentially more susceptible than most predators are to their preys' parasites, particularly since they feed so importantly on domestic pigeons and might thus be exposed to emerging pathogens. These disease agents need not induce fatalities among adult hosts, but they could cause infertility and fetal defects (Chapter 39).

In general, it seems unlikely that any of the avian diseases thus far known could affect the reproductive success of so many raptorial species at the same time and on such a wide scale on two continents.

BIOCIDES

The virtually universal presence of the new biocidal chemicals in natural environments can now be taken as an accepted scientific fact. Regional variations in the levels of these chemicals are also evident. Die-offs of both songbirds and raptors have been traced in Sweden to mercury compounds used as fungicidal seed dressings. Dutch data include some high levels of BHC, dieldrin, and endrin in coastal birds and dead and dying hawks. DDE, a metabolite of DDT, is perhaps the most conspicuous residue found in both British and North American animals (Chapter 42). There is some suggestion that the concentrations may be greater in coastal environments (in which peregrines often feed during migration and winter).

A second emerging principle is the progressive concentration of these chemicals in successive trophic layers of many ecosystems. Average concentrations of 99 ppm of DDT-complex in the breast muscles of seemingly healthy herring gulls are reported from Lake Michigan; and up to 89 ppm of Lindane, 44 ppm of dieldrin, and 16 ppm of endrin in the tissues of Dutch hawks; and 2,800 ppm of DDE in the fat of a bald eagle.

While the identification of direct mortality due to these compounds is a relatively uncomplicated matter, the assessment of the significance of sublethal doses is much more difficult. Laboratory data on impairment of the reproductive function by chlorinated hydrocarbons in birds has in the past generally involved dosages far in excess of those found in nature. It was Peterson's argument, however, that raptors may well tend to select the most pesticide-burdened preys.

North American thinking on the role of these chemicals in the crash of peregrine populations has been restricted by the absence of residue data on Canadian and American peregrines, by the rather modest levels of DDT reported in Connecticut osprey eggs, and by the fact that, until this conference, the chronology of the peregrine population crash was poorly understood. At this meeting, the main arguments involving biocides in these raptor declines were importantly set forth by British investigators.

Ratcliffe regards the peregrine population crash in his country as unprecedented in British history and one requiring an unprecedented cause. Dwindling food supplies, wartime persecution, disturbance by rock-climbers, disease, and climatic change he rules out as insignificant in the present phenomenon. The geographic pattern and chronology of the British decline, he finds, are decidedly correlated with agricultural land use. Egg-breakage and reproductive failure became widespread south of the Highlands after 1950. The actual population decline began about 1955 and became severe by 1961, coinciding with the use of the more toxic chemicals, aldrin, dieldrin, and heptachlor, as well as with spectacular kills of wild birds. In 1963–65, 18 peregrine eggs averaged 14.8 ppm of chlorinated hydrocarbons, 12.7 ppm being DDE. These compounds are now widely distributed in nature throughout the country and in the falcons' prey. Dosage in one adult peregrine seems to have caused its death, and sublethal doses are in Ratcliffe's opinion an adequate explanation of reduced breeding success and failure to breed (Chapter 21).

Prestt stresses the coincident decline of sparrow-hawks in Britain and of golden eagles in some parts of Scotland, egg-eating characterizing the reproductive failures of both species. He also emphasizes that alleged cases of "nonbreeding" often have proven, upon careful examination, to be actual instances of egg-eating. The implication here is that egg-eating may have been far more common in some of the American raptor declines than has been thus far recognized.

HUMAN DISTURBANCE

There is no doubt that human disturbances have locally contributed to the extirpation of individual peregrine eyries and reduced populations in some regions; and that this group of factors has had local effects on bald eagles and ospreys. Rock-climbing, direct persecution by pigeon fanciers, irresponsible target-shooting, highway construction, and over-exploitation by falconers all appear to be local factors incapable of setting up a synchronous decline among so many species (especially the accipitrine hawks) on two continents.

PHYSIOLOGICAL ASPECTS OF THE DECLINE

The reproductive failures reported at this conference involved: (1) a failure to lay eggs, which often could not be dissociated from human disturbance or egg-eating by the birds themselves; (2) reduced clutch size; (3) failure to re-lay after the loss of an initial clutch of eggs; (4) embryonic mortality (especially noted in the osprey); (5) egg-breakage and eating (widespread in Britain); and (6) some nestling mortality. Sterile eggs have not been demonstrated.

The particular dilemma facing the conferees was the explanation of egg-breakage and eating. Eggshell flaking was reported by Keith to be associated with a 30–35% hatching failure of herring gull eggs in Wisconsin. It was also noted in a Michigan bald eagle nest by Postupalsky. Keith leaned toward a possibly abnormal undue trampling as an explanation for these phenomena. Ratcliffe felt that the average of 14.8 ppm of organochlorines in British peregrine eggs probably reflected adult residue levels that would cause central nervous system changes and the pathological behavior. The disadvantage of these behavior hypotheses is that they both require some additional mechanism to explain the other four aspects of reproductive failure listed above.

A simple single explanation thus requires one to regard egg-flaking, egg-breaking, and egg-eating, as manifestations of the same physiological mechanism making for the four other aspects of nesting failure. Such a hypothesis may be broadly taken as nutritional and, in this context, would require that eggshells have become thinner, birds have accidentally broken their eggs, and that conditioned behavior patterns have then developed.

POSTCONFERENCE RESEARCH

It is clear that the testing of the biocidal hypothesis initially requires each country to build up its own basic set of data on the residue levels that its surviving raptorial birds currently carry. In 1966, two important research projects gave us some perspective on the peregrine's problem in North America. Along the Yukon River in Alaska, Cade, Haugh, and White found the fat of four adult peregrines to average about 617 ppm of DDT-complex and dieldrin (range 204–849) and two eggs to average 15 ppm. Along the Mackenzie River in Canada's Northwest Territories, Enderson and Berger found adult fat to average 369 ppm of these compounds in nine birds; seven eggs averaged 28 ppm. These birds are all migratory, and the source of these residues could be anywhere south to South America.

A crucial testing of the egg-breakage phenomenon in Britain was next carried out by Ratcliffe by weighing a large series of eggshells in museum and private collections in Britain. Mean shell weight for peregrines changed from 3.81 g in 1900–46 to 3.09 in 1947–67. This was not accompanied by a change in the size of eggs, and it was paralleled by similar changes in sparrow-hawk eggs and golden eagle eggs from western Scotland. For ten other British species in which egg-breaking is unusual, no such change in shell weight was detected. The timing of this extraordinary event coincides with the general introduction of DDT, and other experimental work suggests the disturbance of hormonal regulation by this compound or one of its metabolites.

In a follow-up study, Hickey and Anderson (1968) found that an 18.8% change in peregrine shell weight took place in 31 eggs collected in 1947–52 in California, as against 18.9% that Ratcliffe (1967) found for 158 eggs collected in Britain in 1947–67. Each change reflected shell thickness, was statistically significant, and was without precedent in the previous history of each population recorded in museum collections. The peregrine eggshell change also took place in New England, and began in the same year—1947—as it did in Britain. This was one year after DDT came into general use in the United States. It was also the same year in which broken eggs in an American peregrine eyrie were observed for the first time by J. A. Hagar (at his eyrie M6; Chapter 10). At eyrie M10, about 60 miles (100 km) away, three eggs taken in 1947 by a collector were 20.8% below the mean weight of 4.38 ± 0.034 g for 56 eggs taken in this region in 1888–1932.

Comparable eggshell changes were also found by Hickey and Anderson for 6 eggs of the osprey taken in 1957 in New Jersey, where this species has been rapidly declining (Chapter 28), and for 20 eggs of the bald eagle taken in 1947–62 in Florida, where regional populations have also changed greatly (Chapter 29). They were not found for red-tailed hawks, golden eagles, and great horned owls—all of which are regarded as having still-normal reproductive success. The great raptor declines of Europe and North America in the past two decades thus have clearly had a common physiological basis, and there is now little doubt that the frequent allegations of "nonbreeding" pairs in the recent past actually referred, as Prestt suggested at the Wisconsin conference (Chapter 36), to cases where adult raptorial birds were breaking and eating their own eggs.

Elucidation of the mechanism producing these extraordinary changes in the calcium metabolism of bird- and fish-eating birds on two continents appeared in the scientific literature being first suggested by Peakall the field evidence and laboratory findings being first suggested by Peakall (1967*a*). By a curious accident (chlordane had been used to eliminate bedbugs [*Cimex lectularius*] in the animal house of a laboratory!), the organochlorine compounds (including not only DDT but its analogs as well) were found to stimulate the liver to secrete microsomal enzymes that metabolize drugs in the mammalian body (Hart, Shultice, and Fouts, 1963; Hart and Fouts, 1963, 1965). Evidence was quickly accumulated that these halogenated hydrocarbon insecticides also stimulated the hydroxylation of steroids, a phenomenon that possibly explained the decreased fertility found in experimental mammals under some conditions (Conney, 1967; Conney *et al.*, 1967). Peakall (1967*b*) then showed that this breakdown of sex hormones also took place in birds, even in those subjected to 1-week diets in which DDT was as low as 10 ppm and dieldrin was 2 ppm. It is these hormones that regulate the mobilization of calcium in the reproductive cycle of birds.

The mechanism producing the recent breeding failures in raptor populations thus turns out to be an endocrine one rather than a CNS (central nervous system) phenomenon. CNS effects of the organochlorines on reproduction are still hard to postulate, as Stickel argued at the Wisconsin conference (Chapter 42). But, with levels of DDT complex exceeding 300

ms possible that some adult
t these compounds in periods
nervous system and produce

s gradually taken on increas-
of raptorial birds in the last
is compound was reported by
and 2800 ppm respectively
ines studied by Cade *et al.*
DE averaged about 414 ppm
ada. A marked improvement
olmes, Simmons, and Tatton,
reported levels of *pp′*-DDT
apture gas chromatography,
olychlorobiphenyls—a group
ak down in the environment.
n of hepatic microsomal en-
(1965), and levels of DDE in
en found by Hickey and An-
eggshell thickness at Amer-
. The probability of this rela-
1 in 1,000.

Erratum

The first five lines of the last paragraph on page 564 should read:

Elucidation of the mechanism producing these extraordinary changes in the calcium metabolism of bird- and fish-eating birds on two continents appeared in the scientific literature in 1967, the connection between the field evidence and laboratory findings being first suggested by Peakall (1967*a*). By a curious accident (chlordane had been used to eliminate

CONCLUSIONS

The ability of birds to mobilize large amounts of calcium for the production of their eggs has long been an evolutionary triumph of the Class Aves. Their failures to do so in the last two decades have led to the new life-history phenomena reported for the peregrine in this volume: a failure to lay eggs (or eggs that would persist), decreased numbers of eggs, egg-breakage and egg-eating, inability to renest, and decreased viability of their young.

The ecological case against the chlorinated hydrocarbon insecticides as the pervasive factor in these phenomena is essentially complete. There is no doubt that these compounds have been of enormous benefit to mankind. But they are persisting chemicals, and they tend to be progressively concentrated in wild animals at the tops of certain food webs and ecosystems. Their effects on these species have been subtle and insidious. In raptorial birds like the peregrine falcon, they have led to the persisting widespread reproductive failures and extirpation over wide regions described in this volume. Perhaps combined with other environmental stresses, they may also involve increased adult mortality rates in some populations.

The peregrine falcon population crash almost certainly resulted from a complex of environmental factors, the complex differing slightly from one country to another and from one region to the next. The onset of the crash was masked in part by local population trends that in some cases counteracted and in others reinforced the effects of a major change in the environment of at least two continents. This change involved the introduction and wide use of organochlorine insecticides by 1947. The initial effect of the reproductive failures that then set in was to wipe out the extraordinary nonbreeding reserve that had previously characterized the peregrine populations of the past. This phenomenon was impossible for ornithologists to measure. What they saw was the second stage, the steady numerical decline in the 1950's of the breeding adults in many regions. This decline continues, and the end is nowhere yet in sight.

The persistence of DDE in the world's environments and its concentration at the tops of certain ecosystems have led to extracontinental phenomena that bind peregrine falcons, Scottish golden eagles, sparrowhawks, American ospreys, and bald eagles together in a new process of physiological deterioration. Many other species are almost certainly involved—and in regions far removed from the original points of environmental contamination.

Because environmental pollution varies regionally as well as internationally, it appears to be also true that the identification of synthetic chemicals causing these effects is still by no means complete. Dieldrin was important in Britain, DDE in at least some parts of the United States. Mercury certainly has caused widespread adult bird mortality in Sweden. How much industrial pollutants like the polychlorinated biphenyls have also contributed to some of these phenomena promises to be an absorbing chapter in the research of the immediate future.

LITERATURE AND REFERENCES CITED

Cade, T. J., C. M. White, and J. R. Haugh. 1968. Peregrines and pesticides in Alaska. Condor, 70(2):170–178.

Conney, A. H. 1967. Pharmacological implications of microsomal enzyme induction. Pharmacol. Rev., 19(3):317–366.

———, R. M. Welch, R. Kuntzman, and J. J. Burns. 1967. Pesticide effects on drug and steroid metabolism: A commentary. Clin. Pharmacol. Therap., 8:2–10.

Enderson, J. H., and D. D. Berger. 1968. Chlorinated hydrocarbon residues in peregrines and their prey species from northern Canada. Condor, 70(2):149–153.

Hart, L. G., and J. R. Fouts. 1963. Effects of acute and chronic DDT administration on hepatic microsomal drug metabolism in the rat. Proc. Soc. Exp. Biol. Med., 114: 388–392.

———, and J. R. Fouts. 1965. Further studies on the stimulation of hepatic microsomal drug metabolizing enzymes by DDT and its analogs. Arch. Exp. Pathol. Pharmakol., 249:486–500.

———, R. W. Shultice, and J. R. Fouts. 1963. Stimulatory effects of chlordane on hepatic microsomal drug metabolism in the rat. Toxicol. and Appl. Pharmacol., 5(3):371–386.

Hickey, J. J., and D. W. Anderson. 1968. Chlorinated hydrocarbons and eggshell changes in raptorial and fish-eating birds. Science, 162(3850):271–273.

Holmes, D. C., J. H. Simmons, and J. O'G. Tatton. 1967. Chlorinated hydrocarbons in British wildlife. Nature, 216(5112):227–229.

Peakall, D. B. 1967*a*. Progress in experiments on the relation between pesticides and fertility. Atlantic Nat., 22(2):109–111.

———. 1967*b*. Pesticide-induced enzyme breakdown of steroids in birds. Nature, 216 (5114):505–506.

Ratcliffe, D. A. 1967. Decrease in eggshell weight in certain birds of prey. Nature, 215(5097):208–210.

Widmark, G. 1967. Residue analysis of pesticides with the aid of gas chromatography. Abstracta VIth Intern. Congr. Plant Protection, p. 8–9.

APPENDIX

INDEX

APPENDIX

SCIENTIFIC NAMES OF BIRDS MENTIONED IN THE TEXT

Auklet, Cassin's *Ptychoramphus aleutica*
Avocet, American *Recurvirostra americana*
Bateleur *Terathopius ecaudatus*
Bee-eater, common *Merops apiaster*
Bittern, American *Botaurus lentiginosus*
Blackbird, Brewer's *Euphagus cyanocephalus*
  European *Turdus merula*
  red-winged *Agelaius phoeniceus*
Bluebird, eastern *Sialia sialis*
  western *S. mexicana*
Bobwhite *Colinus virginianus*
Brambling *Fringilla montifringilla*
Bufflehead *Bucephala albeola*
Bunting, Lapland *Calcarius lapponicus*
  lark *Calamospiza melanocorys*
  snow *Plectrophenax nivalis*
Buzzard, common *Buteo buteo*
  honey *Pernis apivorus*
  jackal *Buteo rufofuscus*
  lizard *Kaupifalco monogrammicus*
  rough-legged *Buteo lagopus*
Caracara, Guadalupe *Caracara lutosus*
Chaffinch, common *Fringilla coelebs*
Chicken, prairie *Tympanuchus cupido*
Chough, alpine *Pyrrhocorax graculus*
Condor, California *Gymnogyps californianus*
Coot, American *Fulica americana*
  European *F. atra*
Cowbird, brown-headed *Molothrus ater*
Crane, whooping *Grus americana*
Crossbill, red *Loxia curvirostra*
Crow, carrion *Corvus corone corone*
  common *C. brachyrhynchos*
  hooded *C. corone cornix*
Cuckoo, common *Cuculus canorus*
Curlew, common or Eurasian *Numenius arquata*
Dotterel *Eudromias morinellus*
Dove, collared *Streptopelia decaocto*
  mourning *Zenaidura macroura*
  rock *Columba livia*
  stock *C. oenas*
  talpacoti *Columbigallina talpacoti*
  turtle *Streptopelia turtur*
Dovekie or little auk *Plautus alle*
Dowitcher, short-billed *Limnodromus griseus*
Duck, fulvous tree *Dendrocygna bicolor*
Eagle, African Hawk *Hieraaetus spilogaster*
  bald *Haliaeetus leucocephalus*
  black or Verreaux's *Aquila verreauxi*
  black-breasted snake- *Circaetus pectoralis*
  Bonelli's *Hieraaetus fasciatus*
  booted *H. pennatus*
  brown snake- *Circaetus cinereus*
  crowned *Stephanoaetus coronatus*
  fish *Haliaeetus (Cuncuma) vocifer*
  golden *Aquila chrysaetos*
  gray sea or white-tailed *Haliaeetus albicilla*
  long-crested *Lophaetus occipitalis*
  martial *Polemaetus bellicosus*
  short-toed *Circaetus gallicus*

tawny *Aquila rapax*
Wahlberg's *A. wahlbergi*
Egret, cattle *Bubulcus ibis*
common *Casmerodius albus*
snowy *Leucophoyx thula*
Falcon, Barbary *Falco peregrinus*
black-cheeked *F. peregrinus*
Cassin's *F. peregrinus*
cuckoo *Aviceda cuculoides*
eastern red-footed *Falco amurensis*
Hose's *F. peregrinus*
lanner *F. biarmicus*
Peale's *F. peregrinus*
peregrine *F. peregrinus*
pygmy *Polihierax semitorquatus*
prairie *Falco mexicanus*
red-necked *F. chicquera*
shaheen *F. peregrinus*
Teita *F. fasciinucha*
western red-footed *F. vespertinus*
Flicker, yellow-shafted *Colaptes auratus*
Garganey *Anas querquedula*
Goldeneye, common *Bucephala clangula*
Goldfinch, common or American *Spinus tristis*
European *Carduelis carduelis*
Goose, Canada *Branta canadensis*
snow *Anser caerulescens*
Goshawk, African *Accipiter tachiro*
black *A. melanoleucus*
chanting *Melierax musicus*
common or northern *Accipiter gentilis*
dark chanting *Melierax metabates*
gabar *Micronisus gabar*
little-banded *Accipiter badius*
Grackle, common *Quiscalus quiscula*
Grebe, eared or black-necked *Podiceps (Colymbus) nigricollis*
western *Aechmophorus occidentalis*
Greenfinch *Carduelis chloris*
Greenshank *Tringa nebularia*
Grouse, red *Lagopus lagopus scoticus*
ruffed *Bonasa umbellus*
Gull, black-headed *Larus ridibundus*
Franklin's *L. pipixcan*
Heermann's *L. heermanni*
herring *L. argentatus*
western *L. occidentalis*
Gyrfalcon *Falco rusticolus*
Harrier, African marsh *Circus ranivorus*
black *C. maurus*
common or hen (marsh hawk) *C. cyaneus*
marsh *C. ranivorus*
Montagu's *C. pygargus*
pallid *C. macrourus*
Harrier-hawk, banded *Polyboroides typicus*
Hawfinch *Coccothraustes coccothraustes*
Hawk, bat *Machaerhamphus alcinus*
broad-winged *Buteo platypterus*
Cooper's *Accipiter cooperii*
duck *Falco peregrinus*
ferruginous *Buteo regalis*
great-footed *Falco peregrinus*
harrier- *Polyboroides typicus*
little sparrow- *Accipiter minullus*
marsh (or hen harrier) *Circus cyaneus*
Ovampo sparrow- *Accipiter ovampensis*
pigeon (or merlin) *Falco columbarius*
red-shouldered *Buteo lineatus*
red-tailed *B. jamaicensis*
rough-legged *B. lagopus*
sharp-shinned *Accipiter striatus*
short-tailed *Buteo brachyurus*
sparrow- (North American) *Falco sparverius*
sparrow- (Old World) *Accipiter nisus*
Swainson's *Buteo swainsoni*
Hawk eagle, African *Hieraaetus spilogaster*
Heron, black-crowned night *Nycticorax nycticorax*
great blue *Ardea herodias*
green *Butorides virescens*
Hobby, African *Falco cuvierii*
European *F. subbuteo*
Hoopoe *Upupa epops*
Jackdaw *Corvus monedula*
Jay, blue *Cyanocitta cristata*
common (Old World) *Garrulus glandarius*
gray *Perisoreus canadensis*
Kestrel, Dickinson's *Falco dickinsoni*
European or rock *F. tinnunculus*
greater *F. rupicoloides*
lesser *F. naumanni*
(North American) *F. sparverius*
Killdeer *Charadrius vociferus*
Kite, black *Milvus migrans*
black-shouldered *Elanus caeruleus*

Everglade *Rostrhamus sociabilis*
red *Milvus milvus*
white-tailed *Elanus leucurus*
yellow-billed *Milvus migrans parasiticus*
Lammergeier or bearded vulture *Gypaetus barbatus*
Lanner *Falco biarmicus*
Lapwing, common *Vanellus vanellus*
Longspur or bunting, Lapland *Calcarius lapponicus*
Loon *Gavia* sp.
Magpie, common or black-billed *Pica pica*
Mallard *Anas platyrhynchos*
Martin, house *Delichon urbica*
Meadowlark, eastern *Sturnella magna*
western *S. neglecta*
Merlin or pigeon hawk *Falco columbarius*
Moorhen (Florida gallinule) *Gallinula chloropus*
Murre or guillemot, common *Uria aalge*
Murrelet, ancient *Synthliboramphus antiquum*
Craveri's *Endomychura craveri*
Xantus' *E. hypoleuca*
Nighthawk, common *Chordeiles minor*
Nutcracker *Nucifraga caryocatactes*
Oldsquaw *Clangula hyemalis*
Osprey *Pandion haliaetus*
Owl, barred *Strix varia*
common barn *Tyto alba*
eagle *Bubo bubo*
great horned *B. virginianus*
little *Athene noctua*
long-eared *Asio otus*
short-eared *Asio flammeus*
tawny *Strix aluco*
Tengmalm's or boreal *Aegolius funereus*
Partridge, gray or common *Perdix perdix*
red-legged *Alectoris rufa*
Penguin, Adélie *Pygoscelis adeliae*
Petrel, Bonin *Pterodroma hypoleuca*
Bulwer's *Bulweria bulwerii*
fork-tailed *Oceanodroma furcata*
Leach's *O. leucorhoa*
least *Halocyptena microsoma*
Phalarope, red or gray *Phalaropus fulicarius*
Pheasant, ring-necked or common *Phasianus colchicus*
Pigeon, band-tailed *Columba fasciata*
common, carrier, or domestic *C. livia*
passenger *Ectopistes migratorius*
wood *Columba palumbus*
Pintail *Anas acuta*
Plover, Eurasian or lesser golden *Pluvialis dominica*
golden *P. apricaria*
mountain *Eupoda montana*
Ptarmigan, rock *Lagopus mutus*
Puffin, common *Fratercula arctica*
Quail, California *Lophortyx californicus*
common (Coturnix, or European, or Japanese) *Coturnix coturnix*
Quelea, red-billed *Quelea quelea*
Rail, clapper *Rallus longirostris*
Raven, common *Corvus corax*
Redstart, black *Phoenicurus ochruros*
Robin, American *Turdus migratorius*
Roller, lilac-breasted *Coracias caudata*
Rook *Corvus frugilegus*
Saker *Falco cherrug*
Sandpiper, spotted *Actitis macularia*
Secretary bird *Sagittarius serpentarius*
Shaheen, red-naped *Falco babylonicus*
Shearwater, Manx *Puffinus puffinus*
wedge-tailed *P. pacificus*
Shoveler *Anas (Spatula) clypeata*
Shrike, fiscal *Lanius collaris*
great grey or northern *L. excubitor*
Skua *Catharacta skua*
Skylark *Alauda arvensis*
Snake-eagle, black-breasted *Circaetus pectoralis*
brown *C. cinereus*
Snipe, common *Capella gallinago*
Sparrow, house *Passer domesticus*
Starling, common or European *Sturnus vulgaris*
Stilt, black-necked *Himantopus mexicanus*
Stork, marabou *Leptoptilos crumeniferus*
Swallow, Old World or barn *Hirundo rustica*
Swift, alpine *A. melba*
common *Apus apus*
Teal, common *Anas crecca*
Tern, elegant *Thalasseus elegans*
Thrush, mistle *Turdus viscivorus*

song *T. philomelos*
Tit, coal *Parus ater*
great *P. major*
Tree duck, fulvous *Dendrocygna bicolor*
Vulture, bearded (lammergeier) *Gypaetus barbatus*
Cape *Gyps coprotheres*
Egyptian *Neophron percnopterus*
griffon *Gyps fulvus*
hooded *Necrosyrtes monachus*
lappet-faced *Torgus tracheliotus*
palm-nut *Gypohierax angolensis*
white-backed *Gyps (Pseudogyps) africanus*
white-headed *Trigonoceps occipitalis*
Wagtail, blue-headed *Motacilla flava*
white or pied *M. alba*
yellow *M. flava*
Warbler, bay-breasted *Dendroica castanea*
yellow *D. petechia*
Weaver, sociable *Philetairus socius*
Widgeon (American) or baldpate *Anas (Mareca) americana*
Woodcock (American) *Philohela minor*
(European) *Scolopax rusticola*
Woodpecker, great spotted *Dendrocopos major*
green *Picus viridis*
pileated *Hylatomus pileatus*
Wren, house *Troglodytes aedon*
Yellowhammer *Emberiza citrinella*

INDEX

The text of this volume has been indexed by species, by geographic areas (countries, provinces, states), and by subject headings that for the most part follow those in the Aves section of the Zoological Record. The abbreviation f has been used for falcon, pf for peregrine falcon.